LETTERS ON YOGA

PART FOUR

Sri Aurobindo

Letters on Yoga

PART FOUR

Sri Aurobindo Ashram
Pondicherry

Third Edition (Facsimile) : 1971

Second Impression : 1979

Published by Sri Aurobindo Ashram, Publication Department
Printed at Sri Aurobindo Ashram Press, Pondicherry
PRINTED IN INDIA

Contents

Footnotes in this Volume on pages 1249, 1361, 1363, 1465
are by Sri Aurobindo himself. The other footnotes are
inserted by the editor.

Contents

PART FOUR

Footnotes in this Volume on pages 1249, 1361, 1363, 1465
are by Sri Aurobindo himself. The other footnotes are
inserted by the editor.

PART FOUR

SECTION ONE

THE TRIPLE TRANSFORMATION :
PSYCHIC — SPIRITUAL — SUPRAMENTAL

The Triple Transformation:
Psychic—Spiritual—Supramental

THE fundamental realisations of this yoga are:
1. The psychic change so that a complete devotion can be the main motive of the heart and the ruler of thought, life and action in constant union with the Mother and in her Presence.
2. The descent of the Peace, Power, Light, etc. of the Higher Consciousness through the head and heart into the whole being, occupying the very cells of the body.
3. The perception of the One and Divine infinitely everywhere, the Mother everywhere and living in that infinite consciousness.

*
**

You know the three things on which the realisation has to be based:
(1) on a rising to a station above the mind and on the opening out of the cosmic consciousness;
(2) on the psychic opening; and
(3) on the descent of the higher consciousness with its peace, light, force, knowledge, Ananda etc. into all the planes of the being down to the most physical.

All this has to be done by the working of the Mother's force aided by your aspiration, devotion and surrender.

That is the Path. The rest is a matter of the working out of these things for which you have to have faith in the Mother's working.

*
**

When one speaks of the divine spark, one is thinking of the soul as a portion of the Divine which has descended from above into the manifestation rather than of something which has separated itself from the cosmos. It is the nature that has formed itself out of the cosmic forces — mind out of cosmic mind, life out of cosmic life, body out of cosmic Matter.

For the soul there are three realisations: — (1) the realisation of the psychic being and consciousness as the divine element in the evolution; (2) the realisation of the cosmic Self which is one in all; (3) the realisation of the Supreme Divine from which both individual and cosmos have come and of the individual being (Jivatma) as an eternal portion of the Divine.

The physical is of course the basis — that of the overmind is in-between the two hemispheres. The lower hemisphere must contain all the mind including its higher planes, the vital, the physical. The upper hemisphere contains the Divine existence-consciousness-bliss, with the supermind as its means of self-formulation. The overmind is at the head of the lower hemisphere and is the intermediate or transitional plane between the two.

The psychic being stands behind the heart supporting the mind, life and body. In the psychic transformation there are three main elements: (1) the opening of the occult inner mind, inner vital, inner physical, so that one becomes aware of all that lies behind the surface mind, life and body — (2) the opening of the psychic being or soul by which it comes forward and governs the mind, life and body turning all to the Divine — (3) the opening of the whole lower being to the spiritual truth — this last may be called the psycho-spiritual part of the change. It is quite possible for the psychic transformation to take one beyond the individual into the cosmic. Even the occult opening establishes a connection with the cosmic mind, cosmic vital, cosmic physical. The psychic realises the contact with all-existence, the oneness of the Self, the universal love and other realisations which lead to the cosmic consciousness.

But all that is a result of the opening to the spiritual above and it comes by an infiltration or reflection of the spiritual light and truth in mind, life and body. The spiritual transformation proper begins or becomes possible when one rises above the mind and lives there governing all from above. Even in the psychic transformation one can rise above by a sort of going above of the mental, vital, physical being and a return, but one does not yet live above in the summit consciousness where overmind has its seat with the other planes that are above the human Mind.

The supramental transformation can only come when the lid between the lower and higher hemispheres or halves of existence is removed and the supermind instead of the overmind becomes the governing power of the existence — but of that nothing can be spoken now.

Between psychicisation and spiritualisation there is a difference. The spiritual is the change that descends from above, the psychic is the change that comes from within by the psychic dominating the mind, vital and physical.

Psychicisation means the change of the lower nature bringing right vision into the mind, right impulse and feeling into the vital, right movement and habit into the physical — all turned towards the Divine, all based on love, adoration, bhakti — finally, the vision and sense of the Mother everywhere in all as well as in the heart, her Force working in the being, faith, consecration, surrender.

The spiritual change is the established descent of the peace, light, knowledge, power, bliss from above, the awareness of the Self and the Divine and of a higher cosmic consciousness and the change of the whole consciousness to that.

The two feelings are both of them right — they indicate the two necessities of the sadhana. One is to go inward and open fully the connection between the psychic being and the outer nature. The other is to open upward to the Divine Peace, Force, Light, Ananda above, to rise up into it and bring it down into the nature and the body. Neither of these two movements, the psychic and the spiritual, is complete without the other. If the spiritual ascent and descent are not made, the spiritual transformation of the nature cannot happen; if the full psychic opening and connection is not made, the transformation cannot be complete.

There is no incompatibility between the two movements; some begin the psychic first, others the spiritual first, some carry on both together. The best way is to aspire for both and let the Mother's Force work it out according to the need and turn of the nature.

If the development of a higher consciousness did not bring things that were not before heard of by the mind, it would not be good for much. The unification of the psychic and the higher consciousness forces and activities is indispensable for the sadhana at one time or another.

The psychic is the first of two transformations necessary — if you have the psychic transformation it facilitates immensely the other, i.e., the transformation of the ordinary human into the higher spiritual consciousness — otherwise one is likely to have either a slow and dull or exciting but perilous journey....

I have never said anything about a "transformation of the psychic"; I have always written about a "psychic transformation" of the nature, which is a very different matter. I have sometimes written of it as a psychicisation of the nature. The psychic is in the evolution, part of the human being, its divine part — so a psychicisation will not carry one beyond the present evolution but will make the being ready to respond to all that comes from the Divine or Higher Nature and unwilling to respond to the Asura, Rakshasa, Pishacha or Animal in the being or to any resistance of the lower nature which stands in the way of the divine change.

I have read your account of your sadhana. There is nothing to say, I think, — for it is all right — except that the most important thing for you is to develop the psychic fire in the heart and the aspiration for the psychic being to come forward as the leader of the sadhana. When the psychic does so, it will show you the "undetected ego-knots" of which you speak and loosen them or burn them in the psychic fire. This psychic development and the psychic change of mind, vital and physical consciousness is of the utmost importance because it makes safe and easy the descent of the higher consciousness and the spiritual transformation without which the supramental must always remain far distant. Powers etc. have their place, but a very minor one so long as this is not done.

Everything is dangerous in the sadhana or can be, except the psychic change.

The soul, the psychic being is in direct touch with the divine Truth, but it is hidden in man by the mind, the vital being and the physical nature. One may practise yoga and get illuminations in the mind and the reason; one may conquer power and luxuriate in all kinds of experiences in the vital; one may establish even surprising physical Siddhis; but if the true soul-power behind does not manifest, if the psychic nature does not come into the front, nothing genuine has been done. In this yoga the psychic being is that which opens the rest of the nature to the true supramental light and finally to the supreme Ananda. Mind can open by itself to its own higher reaches; it can still itself and widen into the Impersonal; it may too spiritualise itself in some kind of static liberation or Nirvana; but the supramental cannot find a sufficient base in a spiritualised mind alone. If the inmost soul is awakened, if there is a new birth out of the mere mental, vital and physical into the psychic consciousness, then this yoga can be done; otherwise (by the sole power of the mind or any other part) it is impossible.... If there is a refusal of the psychic new birth, a refusal to become the child new born from the

Mother, owing to attachment to intellectual knowledge or mental ideas or to some vital desire, then there will be a failure in the sadhana.

The psychic being is always there, but is not felt because it is covered up by the mind and vital; when it is no longer covered up, it is then said to be awake. When it is awake, it begins to take hold of the rest of the being, to influence it and change it so that all may become the true expression of the inner soul. It is this change that is called the inner conversion. There can be no conversion without the awakening of the psychic being.

In using the expression "opening of the psychic" I was thinking not of an ordinary psychic opening producing some amount of psychic (as opposed to vital) love and bhakti, but of what is called the coming in front of the psychic. When that happens one is aware of the psychic being with its simple spontaneous self-giving and feels its increasing direct control (not merely a veiled or half veiled influence) over mind, vital and physical. Especially there is the psychic discernment which at once lights up the thoughts, emotional movements, vital pushes, physical habits and leaves nothing there obscure, substituting the right movements for the wrong ones. It is this that is difficult and rare, more often the discernment is mental and it is the mind that tries to put all in order. In that case, it is the descent of the higher consciousness through the mind that opens the psychic, instead of the psychic opening directly.

Nobody said it [the opening of the psychic] must be done necessarily from above. Naturally it is done direct and is most effective then. But when it is found difficult to do it direct, as it is in certain natures, then the change begins from above and the consciousness descending from there has to liberate the heart-centre. As it acts on the heart-centre, the psychic action becomes more possible.

It [the dynamic descent from above into the heart] can help the psychic to come forward, but it does not always do so automatically — it at least creates better conditions for the psychic.

The direct opening of the psychic centre is easy only when the ego-centricity is greatly diminished and also if there is a strong bhakti for the Mother. A spiritual humility and sense of submission and dependence is necessary.

What is meant by [the psychic's] coming to the front is simply this. The psychic ordinarily is deep within. Very few people are aware of their souls — when they speak of their soul, they usually mean the vital + mental being or else the (false) soul of desire. The psychic remains behind and acts only through the mind, vital and physical wherever it can. For this reason the psychic being except where it is very much developed has only a small and partial, concealed and mixed or diluted influence on the life of most men. By coming forward is meant that it comes from behind the veil, its presence is felt already in the waking daily consciousness, its influence fills, dominates, transforms the mind and vital and their movements, even the physical. One is aware of one's soul, feels the psychic to be one's true being, the mind and the rest begin to be only instruments of the inmost within us.

The inner mental, vital, physical are also veiled, but much nearer to the surface and much of their movements or inspirations get through the veil (but not in any fullness or purity) in the lives of developed human beings, something even in the lives of ordinary people. But these too in yoga throw down the veil after a time and come in front and their action predominates in the consciousness while the external is no longer felt as one's own self but only as a front or even a fringe of the being.

It seems to me that you must know by this time about the psychic being — that it is behind the veil and its consciousness also; only a little comes out in the mind and vital and physical. When that consciousness is not concealed, when you are aware of your soul (the psychic being), when its feelings and consciousness are yours, then you have got the consciousness of the psychic being. The feelings and aspirations of the psychic being are all turned towards truth and right consciousness and the Divine; it is the only part that cannot be touched by the hostile forces and their suggestions.

The psychic being emerges slowly in most men, even after taking up sadhana. There is so much in the mind and vital that has to change and readjust itself before the psychic can be entirely free. One has to wait till the necessary process has gone far enough before it can burst its agelong veil and come in front to control the nature. It is true that nothing can give so much inner happiness and joy — though peace can come by the mental and vital liberation or through the growth of a strong *samatā* in the being.

There is no process for it [getting the psychic in front]. It comes like the other things — you have to aspire for it and it can only happen when you are sufficiently advanced.

Then only can the psychic being fully open when the sadhak has got rid of the mixture of vital motives with his sadhana and is capable of a simple and sincere self-offering to the Mother. If there is any kind of egoistic turn or insincerity of motive, if the yoga is done under a pressure of vital demands, or partly or wholly to satisfy some spiritual or other ambition, pride, vanity or seeking after power, position or influence over others or with any push towards satisfying any vital desire with the help of the yogic force, then the psychic cannot open, or opens only partially or only at times and shuts again because it is veiled by the vital activities; the psychic fire fails in the strangling vital smoke. Also, if the mind takes the leading part in the yoga and puts the inner soul into the background, or if the bhakti or other movements of the sadhana take more of a vital than of a psychic form, there is the same inability. Purity, simple sincerity and the capacity of an unegoistic unmixed self-offering without pretension or demand are the condition of an entire opening of the psychic being.

Of course the ego and the vital with its claims and desires is always the main obstacle to the emergence of the psychic. For they make one live, act, do sadhana even for one's own sake and psychicisation means to live, act and do sadhana for the sake of the Divine.

If desire is rejected and no longer governs the thought, feeling or action and there is a steady aspiration of an entirely sincere self-giving, the psychic usually after a time opens of itself.

To bring the psychic forward, selfishness and demand (which is the base of the vital feelings) must be got rid of — at least never accepted.

It [the flow of love and joy from the heart-centre] can be misused on a large scale only if there is a strong and vehement vital ego not accustomed to correction or else a vital full of the *kāma-vāsanā*. On a small scale it can be misused by the small selfish-nesses, vanities, ambitions, demands of the lower vital support-ing themselves upon it. If you are on guard against these things then there is no danger of misuse. If the psychic puts forth psychic discernment along with the love, there is no danger, for the light of psychic discernment at once refuses all mixture or misuse.

Aspiration, constant and sincere, and the will to turn to the Divine alone are the best means to bring forward the psychic.

It [the psychic] comes forward of itself either through constant love and aspiration or when the mind and vital have been made ready by the descent from above and the working of the Force.

If there is the will to surrender in the central being, then the psychic can come forward.

The central being is above the Adhar — most people are not aware of their central being (Jivatma) — they are aware only of the ego.

    The psychic is the soul, it is a portion of the Divine that sup-ports the mind and body in the evolution. The psychic gets the Divine's help directly from the Divine.

    The central being is that on which all the others depend. If it makes its surrender, that is, renounces its separate fulfilment in order to be an instrument of the Divine, then it is easier for the mind, vital and physical to surrender.

It has nothing to do with suitable circumstances. If the will of the central being turns towards union with the Divine, then it renounces its separate fulfilment.

It [the psychic being] has to be surrendered consciously and with more and more knowledge. The psychic aspires to the Divine or answers to things divine, it is surrendered in principle, but it has to develop its surrender in detail carrying with it the surrender of all the being.

Nothing done in the past or present can prevent the psychic from coming forward if there is the true will to get rid of these things and live in the psychic and spiritual consciousness.

Your first experience was that of the opening of the psychic; you became aware of the psychic being and its aspirations and experiences and of the external being in front, as two separate parts of your consciousness. You were not able to keep this experience because the vital was not purified and pulled you out into the ordinary external consciousness. Afterwards, you got back into the psychic and were at the same time able to see your ordinary vital nature, to become aware of its defects and to work by the power of the psychic for its purification. I wrote to you at the beginning that this was the way; for if the psychic is awake and in front, it becomes easy to remain conscious of the things that have to be changed in the external nature and it is comparatively easy too to change them. But if the psychic gets veiled and retires in the background, the outer nature left to itself finds it difficult to remain conscious of its own wrong movements and even with great effort cannot succeed in getting rid of them. You can see yourself, as in the matter of the food, that with the psychic active and awake the right attitude comes naturally and whatever difficulty there was soon diminishes or even disappears.

I told you also at that time that there was a third part of the nature, the inner being (inner mind, inner vital, inner physical) of which you were not yet aware, but which must also open in turn. It is this that has happened in your last experience. What you felt as a part of you, yourself but not your physical self, rising to meet the higher consciousness above, was this inner being; it was your (inner) higher vital being which rose in that way to join the highest Self above — and it was able to do so, because the work of purifying the outer vital nature had begun in earnest. Each time there is a purification of the outer nature, it becomes more possible for the inner being to reveal itself, to become free and to open to the higher consciousness above.

When this happens, several other things happen at the same time. First, one becomes aware of the silent Self above — free, wide, without limits, pure, untroubled by the mental, vital and physical movements, empty of ego and limited personality, — this is what you have described in your letter. Secondly, the Divine Power descends through this silence and freedom of the Self and begins to work in the Adhara. This is what you felt as a pressure; its coming through the top of the head, the forehead and eyes and nose meant that it was working to open the mental centres — especially the two higher centres of thought and will and vision — in the inner mental being. These two centres are called the thousand-petalled lotus and the *ājñā cakra* between the eyebrows. Thirdly, by this working the inner parts of the being are opened and freed; you are liberated from the limitations of the ordinary personal mind, vital and physical and become aware of a wider consciousness in which you can be more capable of the needed transformation. But that is necessarily a matter of time and long working and you are only taking the first steps in this way.

When one goes into the inner being, the tendency is to go entirely inside and lose consciousness of the outside world — this is what people call Samadhi. But it is also necessary to be able to have the same experiences (of the Self, the workings in the inner consciousness, etc.) in the waking state. The best rule for you will be to allow the entire going inside only when you are alone and not likely to be disturbed, and at other times to accustom yourself to have these experiences with the physical consciousness awake and participating in them or at least aware of them.

When the psychic being awakens, you grow conscious of your own soul; you know your self. And you no longer commit the mistake of identifying yourself with the mental or with the vital being. You do not mistake them for the soul.

Secondly, when awakened, the psychic being gives true bhakti for God or for the Guru. That bhakti is quite different from mental or vital bhakti.

In the mind one may have admiration or appreciation for the intellectual greatness of the man — or Guru, but it is merely mental; it does not carry the matter very far. Of course there is no harm in having that also. But by itself it does not open the whole of the inner being; it only establishes a mental contact.

The vital bhakti demands and demands. It imposes its own conditions. It surrenders itself to God, but conditionally. It says to God, "You are so great, I worship you, and now satisfy my this desire or that ambition, make me great, make me a great sadhak, a great yogin, etc."

The unillumined mind also surrenders to the Truth, but makes its own conditions. It says to the Truth, "Satisfy my judgment and my opinion"; it demands the Truth to cast itself in the mind's own forms.

The vital being also insists on the Truth to throw itself into its own movement of force. The vital being pulls at the Higher Power and pulls and pulls at the vital being of the Guru.

Both of them (the mental and the vital) have got an *arrière pensée* (mental reservation) in their surrender.

But the psychic being and its bhakti are not like that. Because it is in direct communication with the Divinity behind, it is capable of true bhakti. Psychic bhakti does not make any demand, makes no reservation. It is satisfied with its own existence. The psychic being knows how to obey the Truth in the right way. It gives itself up truly to God or to Guru, and because it can give itself up truly, therefore it can also receive truly.

Thirdly, when the psychic being comes to the surface, it feels sad when the mental or the vital being is making a fool of itself. That sadness is purity offended.

When the mind is playing its own game or when the vital being is carried away by its own impulses, it is the psychic being which says, "I don't want these things; what am I here for after all? I am here for the Truth, I am not here for these things."

Psychic sadness is again different from mental dissatisfaction or vital sadness or physical depression.

If the psychic being is strong, it makes itself felt on the mental or the vital being, and forces them — compels them — to change. But if it is weak, the other parts take advantage of it and use the psychic sadness to their own advantage.

In some cases the psychic being comes up to the surface and upsets the mental or the vital being and throws everything into disorder. But if the mind or the vital being is stronger than the psychic, then it casts only an occasional influence and gradually retires behind. All its cry is in the wilderness; and the mental or the vital being goes on in its own round.

Lastly, the psychic being refuses to be deceived by appearances. It is not carried away by falsehood. It refuses to be depressed by falsehood — nor does it exaggerate the truth. For example, even if everything around says, "There is no God", the psychic being refuses to believe in it. It says, "I know, and I know because I feel."

And because it knows the thing behind, it is not deceived by appearances. It immediately feels the Force.

Also, when the psychic being is awakened, it throws out all the dross from the emotional being and makes it free from sentimentalism or the lower play of emotionalism.

But it does not carry in it the dryness of the mind or the exaggeration of the vital feelings. It gives the just touch to each emotion.

[The signs of the psychic's coming forward:] A central love, bhakti, surrender, giving everything, a sight within that sees always clearly what is spiritually right or wrong and automatically rejects the latter — a movement of entire consecration and dedication of all in one to the Mother.

That is one part of the psychic experience — the other is a complete self-giving, absence of demand, a prominence of the psychic being by which all that is false, wrong, egoistic, contrary to the Divine Truth, Divine Will, Divine Purity and Light is shown, falls away, cannot prevail in the nature. With all that the increase of the psychic qualities, gratitude, obedience, unselfishness, fidelity to the true perception, true impulse etc. that comes from the Mother or leads to the Mother. When this side grows, then the other, the Presence, Love, Joy, Beauty can develop and be permanently there.

The conversion which keeps the consciousness turned towards the light and makes the right attitude spontaneous and natural and abiding and rejection also spontaneous is the psychic conversion. That is to say, man usually lives in his vital and the body is its instrument and the mind its counsellor and minister (except for the few mental men who live mostly for the things of the mind, but even they are in subjection to the vital in their ordinary movements). The spiritual conversion begins when the soul begins to insist on a deeper life and is complete when the psychic being becomes the basis or the leader of the consciousness and mind and vital and body are led by it and obey it. Of course, if that once happens fully, doubt, depression and despair cannot come any longer, although there may be and are difficulties still. If it is not fully, still fundamentally accomplished, even then these things either do not come or are brief passing clouds on the surface — for there is a rock of support and certitude at the base, which even if partially covered cannot disappear altogether.

Mostly however, the constant recurrence of depression and

despair or of doubt and revolt is due to a mental or vital formation which takes hold of the vital mind and makes it run round
always in the same circle at the slightest provoking cause or even
without cause. It is like an illness to which the body consents
from habit and from belief in the illness even though it suffers
from it, and once started the illness runs its habitual course unless it is cut short by some strong counteracting force. If once the
body can withdraw its consent, the illness immediately or quickly
ceases, — that was the secret of the Coué system. So too, if the
vital mind withdraws its consent, refuses to be dominated by the
habitual suggestions and the habitual movements, these recurrences of depression and despair can be made soon to cease. But
it is not easy for this mind, once it has got into the habit of consent, even a quite passive and suffering and reluctant consent,
to cancel the habit and get rid of the black circle. It can be done
easily only when the mind refuses any longer to believe in the
suggestions or accept the ideas or feelings that start the circle.

Once the condition has come in which the thoughts that cross
are not believed, accepted or allowed to govern the conduct, it
must be understood that the vital mind is no longer dominant
— for the nature of the vital mind is always to cloud the true
mind's perception and drive it towards action. Neither the vital
mind nor the physical mind are things that have to be got rid of,
but they must be quietened, purified, controlled and transformed.
That will take place fully when the thinking mind becomes fully
conscious and when the psychic comes forward and leads and
governs both it and the vital and physical being. Your thinking
mind is becoming more and more conscious; that is shown by
what you write, for the perceptions there expressed are quite
clear-seeing and correct and show an increasingly right understanding. Moreover what is making you conscious is the increase
of pressure of the psychic behind to come forward. For what
you felt as trying to come out from behind was the psychic itself.
The feeling of flowers and fragrance and a coolness and peace
are always sure signs that the psychic is becoming active. It

has been developing in you for some time past, only it was covered over by rushes of the vital mind which did not want to lose its hold or its place. Now that the vital mind is quiet, it is again the psychic that is pressing to come forward and establish its influence.

The thoughts that came afterwards about the defects of your action towards others, repentance and the reasons why you could not establish proper relations with others were the result of this psychic emergence. For when the psychic comes forward or when it strongly influences mind or vital, then one begins to see clearly and rightly about one's own nature and action and about things and about others and to have the right feelings. It was under this pressure of the psychic also that while the mind got these right thoughts and perceptions, the vital felt repentance for what had been done and wished to ask forgiveness. But while this readiness to ask forgiveness was in itself a right feeling, to do so physically would not have been quite the wisest or best action. So the psychic itself at once told you what was the true thing to do, to ask forgiveness instead from the Mother. What was necessary having been done in the mind and vital, the psychic then cleared the whole consciousness and brought back its own quiet and peace. I explain all that to you so that you may begin to understand how these things work within and what is meant by the psychic and its action and influence.

The vision you had of the other luminous and peaceful and beautiful world was a sort of symbolic image of the true physical consciousness and the world in which it lives, the physical consciousness as it is when it is directly under the control of the psychic, and the character of the world which it tends to create for itself.

It is your psychic being which came in front, probably, or else it is the true vital being in you which was able to come in front because you took the psychic attitude. When the psychic being comes in front, there is an automatic perception of the true and untrue, the divine and the undivine, the spiritual right and wrong of things, and the false vital and mental movements and attacks

are immediately exposed and fall away and can do nothing;
gradually the vital and physical as well as the mind get full of this
psychic light and truth and sound feeling and purity, and such
violent attacks as you have are impossible. When the true vital
being comes forward, it is something wide and strong and calm,
an unmoved and powerful warrior for the Divine and the Truth,
repelling all enemies, bringing in a true strength and force, and
opening the vital to the greater consciousness above. It has to
be seen which of the two it is you feel within.

It is the psychic being in you that has come forward — and when
the psychic being comes forward all is happiness, the right attitude, the right vision of things. Of course in one sense it is the
same I that puts forward different parts of itself. But when these
different parts are all under the control of the psychic and
turned by it towards the reception of the higher consciousness,
then there begins the harmonisation of all the parts and their
progressive recasting into moulds of the higher consciousness
growing in peace, light, force, love, knowledge, Ananda which is
what we call the transformation.

It is the action of the psychic being, not the being itself, that
gets mixed with the mental, vital and physical disabilities because
it has to use them to express what little of the true psychic feeling
gets through the veil. It is by the heart's aspiration to the Divine
that the psychic being gets free from these disabilities.

If it is the sense of the Presence that you have, then you are
living in the consciousness of the psychic centre. Thinking with
the mind is good because it leads towards that, but it is not in
itself that living in the psychic centre.

That is good. It means that the psychic has come up again. When the psychic is in the front, the sadhana becomes natural and easy and it is only a question of time and natural development. When the mind or the vital or the physical consciousness is on the top, then the sadhana is a tapasya and a struggle.

What you feel is the true psychic opening and it is that for which you should always aspire and reject other things until it becomes your normal base of consciousness. Once that is there, it is possible to call down through it a strength from above which will make the vital strong and remove the weakness. Your sadhana is still too mental and therefore difficult and slow; it is the psychic opening that makes a more satisfying and rapid progress possible.

You are describing the action of the ordinary existence, not the yoga. Yoga is a seeking (not a mental searching), it is not experimenting in contraries and contradictories. It is the mind that does that and the mind that analyses. The soul does not search, analyse, experiment — it seeks, feels, experiences.

The only grain of truth in your statement is that the yoga is very usually a series of ups and downs till you get to a certain height. But there is a quite different reason for that — not the vagaries of the soul. On the contrary, when the psychic being gets in front and becomes master, there comes in a fundamentally smooth action and although there are difficulties and undulations of movement, these are no longer of an abrupt or dramatic character.

The soul in itself contains all possible strength, but most of it is held behind the veil and it is what comes forward in the nature that makes the difference. In some people the psychic element is strong and in others weak; in some people the mind is the strongest part and governs, in others the vital is the strongest part and leads or drives. But by sadhana the psychic being can be more and more brought forward till it is dominant and governs the rest. If it were already governing, then the struggles and difficulties of the mind and vital would not at all be severe; for each man in the light of the psychic would see and feel the truth and more and more follow it.

The experience you had of the wideness with many roads opening was an image of the higher consciousness in which all the movements of the being are open, true and happy — the ignorance and incapacity of the lower nature disappear. It is that that the light from above is bringing.

The psychic, when it acts as the main power, acts through a certain feeling and inherent psychic sense which repels the falsehood. But the ranges of mind above mind do not act in that way — there it is discrimination and will that act and their action is wider but less sure and less automatic so to speak.

When the concentration is at the top of the head, it means that the mental being is joining the higher consciousness there and there is not much resistance or none. The other place indicates the joining is of the psychic being to the higher consciousness, hence the greater silence, as the psychic is more central than the mental being; but also there is the attempt to join through the psychic the rest of the lower consciousness to the higher and there there is a resistance. The mental joining does not affect the vital and physical, so they remain quiet or can do so for the present — the psychic joining puts on them a pressure to which the first reaction is the sense of fatigue and the last might be a turmoil. But the psychic joining if effectual is much more powerful for the change of the whole being.

The soul is the witness, upholder, experiencer, but it is master only in theory, in fact it is not-master, *aniśa*, so long as it consents to the Ignorance. For that is a general consent which implies that the Prakriti gambols about with the Purusha and does pretty well what she likes with him. When he wants to get back his mastery, make the theoretical practical, he needs a lot of tapasya to do it.

The psychic has always been veiled, consenting to the play of mind, physical and vital, experiencing everything through them in the ignorant mental, vital and physical way. How then can it be that they are bound to change at once when it just takes the trouble to whisper or say, "Let there be Light"? They have a tremendous negating power and can refuse and do refuse point-blank. The mind resists with an obstinate persistency in argument and a constant confusion of ideas, the vital with a fury of bad will aided by the mind's obliging reasonings on its side, the physical resists with an obstinate inertia and crass fidelity to old habit, and when they have done, the general Nature comes in and says, "What, you are going to get free from me so easily? Not, if I know it," and it besieges and throws back the old nature on you again and again as long as it can. Yet you say it is the soul that wants all this "fun" and goes off laughing and prancing to get some more!

*
**

There is always a part of the mind, of the vital, of the body which is or can be influenced by the psychic; they can be called the psychic-mental, the psychic-vital, the psychic-physical. According to the personality or the degree of evolution of each person, this part can be small or large, weak or strong, covered up and inactive or prominent and in action. When it acts the movements of the mind, vital or physical accept the psychic motives or aims, partake of the nature of the psychic or follow its aims but with a modification in the manner which belongs to the mind, vital or physical. The psychic-vital seeks after the Divine, but it has a demand in its self-giving, desire, vital eagerness. The psychic has not, for the psychic has instead pure self-giving, aspiration, intensity of psychic fire. The psychic-vital is subject to pain and suffering, which there is not in the psychic.

Atma is not the same as psychic — Atma is the self which is one in all, calm, wide, ever at peace, always free. The psychic being is the soul within that experiences life and develops with evolving mind and life and body. The psychic does not suffer like the vital or body, it has not pain or anguish or despair; but it has a psychic sorrow which is different from these things. There is a kind of quiet sweet sadness of yearning which it feels when things go against the Divine, when the obscurity and obstacles are too heavy, when the mind, vital and physical follow after other things, when evil and falsehood and darkness seem to be too strong for the Light. It does not despair, — but feels that these things ought not to be and the psychic yearning for it to be otherwise becomes so intense that it is felt as if something akin to sadness.

As for the psychic not being in front, that cannot be brought about all at once, — the other parts of the being must be prepared for the change and the veil between must become thinner and thinner. It is for that experiences come and there is the working on the inner mind and vital and physical as well as on the outer nature.

The vision you had was of the way to the goal. Shiva on the way is the Power that pours the light but also scrutinises the sadhak to see whether he is ready for the farther advance. When he lets him pass, then is the rush of new and higher experiences, the march and progress of the divine forces, the Gods and their powers, the transformation of the nature into a higher consciousness. It was these powers that you saw passing in your vision.

The division of the being of which you speak is a necessary stage in the yogic development and experience. One feels that there is a twofold being, the inner psychic which is the true one and the other, the outer human being which is instrumental for the outward life. To live in the inner psychic being in union with the Divine while doing the outward work, as you feel, is the first stage in Karmayoga. There is nothing wrong in these experiences; they are indispensable and normal at this stage.

If you feel no bridge between the two, it is possibly because you are not yet conscious of what connects the two. There is an inner mental, an inner vital, an inner physical which connects the psychic and the external being. About this, however, you need not be anxious at present.

The important thing is to keep what you have and let it grow, to live always in the psychic being, your true being. The psychic will, in due time, awaken and turn to the Divine all the rest of the nature, so that even the outer being will feel itself in touch with the Divine and moved by the Divine in all it is and feels and does.

It was certainly an experience of great value, a psychic experience *par excellence*. "A feeling of velvety softness within — an ineffable plasticity within" is a psychic experience and can be nothing else. It means a modification of the substance of the consciousness especially in the vital-emotional part, and such a modification prolonged or repeated till it became permanent would mean a great step in what I call the psychic transformation of the being. It is just these modifications in the inner substance that make transformation possible. Further, it was a modification that made a beginning of knowledge possible — for by knowledge we mean in yoga not thought or ideas about spiritual things but psychic understanding from within and spiritual illumination from above. Therefore the first result was this feeling "that there was no ignominy in not understanding it, that the true understanding would come only when one realised that one was completely impotent". This was itself a beginning of understanding — a psychic understanding, something felt within which sheds a light or brings up a spiritual truth that mere thinking would not have given, also a truth that is effective in bringing both the enlightenment and solace you needed — for what the psychic being brings with it always is light and happiness, an inner understanding and relief and solace.

Another very promising aspect of this experience is that it came as an immediate response to an appeal to the Divine. You asked for the understanding and the way out and at once Krishna showed you both — the way out was the change of the consciousness within, the plasticity which makes the knowledge possible and also the understanding of the condition of mind and vital in which the true knowledge or power of knowledge could come. For the inner knowledge comes from within and above (whether from the Divine in the heart or from the Self above) and for it to come, the pride of the mind and vital in the surface mental ideas and their insistence on them must go. One must know that one is ignorant before one can begin to know. This shows that I am not wrong in pressing for the psychic opening as the only way out. For as the psychic opens, such responses and much more also become common and the inner change also proceeds by which they are made possible.

What was meant [by "plasticity within"] I suppose was the psychic plasticity which makes surrender possible along with a free openness to the Divine working from above. Plasticity within is opposed to the rigidity which insists on maintaining one's own ideas, feelings, habitual ways of consciousness as opposed to the higher things from above or from the psychic within.

If it was something in the heart it must be the psychic behind which is often felt as if deep down somewhere or rising out of a depth. If one goes to it, it is felt often as if one were going into a deep well.

The shock must have been the psychic force trying to open the mental and vital lid which covers the soul.

It is evidently the psychic — it is often seen as a deep well or abyss into which one plunges; but here it is evidently the psychic penetrating down into all the lower planes and also rising up to the higher planes above.

The psychic being is in the heart centre in the middle of the chest (not in the physical heart, for all the centres are in the middle of the body), but it is deep behind. When one is going away from the vital into the psychic, it is felt as if one is going deep deep down till one reaches that central place of the psychic. The surface of the heart centre is the place of the emotional being; from there one goes deep to find the psychic. The more one goes, the more intense becomes the psychic happiness which you describe.

I hope the pain will have gone. When these things come always call the Mother and let her force act on you.

The place of the psychic is deep within the heart, — but *deep within*, not on the surface where the ordinary emotions are. But it can come forward and occupy the surface as well as be within, — then the emotions themselves become no longer vital things, but psychic emotions and feelings. The psychic so standing in front can also extend its influence everywhere, to the mind for instance so as to transform its ideas or to the body so as to transform its habits and its reactions.

The person you saw above was probably some form of myself. The sadhak can see us in vision not only in our physical form but in others that we have on different planes of being.

The experience...is one of those dream experiences that one gets in the vital plane, — for there things good and bad, pleasant and unpleasant are very close to each other.

To recognise, as you have done, a fault in the nature does not indeed remove it altogether at once, but it is a great step towards it. It does not remove it at once because of the force of habit in the nature, but still to be conscious and have the will to remove it helps to weaken its force and assists the Mother's working very greatly.

The vision you had was of the mental plane and symbolic. It symbolised not so much your own position as the general difficulties which lie in the way of one's going deep inside into the psychic centre and living there. The *maidān* full of light was the inmost psychic centre; the dark place in between represents the veil of ignorance created by the gulf between this inmost psychic and the outer nature. The chakra turning round and round which prevents the approach from one side (the mental side) is the activity of the ordinary mind; when the mind becomes quiet, then it is easier. The serpent is the vital energy which covers up the psychic and prevents approach from another (the vital) side. There again if the vital becomes quiet, then the approach is easier.

The blows in the forehead were perhaps the working of a force to open the centre there — for there between the eyes is the centre of the inner mind, will and vision. All these centres are closed in the ordinary consciousness or else only very slightly open on the surface. If the inner mind centre opens, then the peace etc. from above can enter easily into the mind and afterwards into the vital and both mind and vital will become quiet.

The difficulty about the two parts of the mind is one that everybody has when the tendency to go within begins. It is solved in this sadhana by a sort of harmony being established by which even in doing one's work and keeping the necessary outer activities one can still live within in the fullness of the inner life and experience.

Rely on the Mother always. These things are the first beginnings of yogic experience and the difficulties of the mind and vital (which are not the old ones you had but simply the ordinary difficulties of the adjustment and harmonisation of the different parts of the being) will get solved of themselves.

It is very good, — all you write is a strong sign of the psychic emergence of which I spoke in yesterday's letter. There is at once the deep plunge into the psychic and the emergence of the psychic influence in mind and heart. The depth of the plunge is the reason why action has become so slow, because the consciousness is too much inside to act swiftly on outside things. This is a stage which one passes through in the process of the inner change. At the same time the ideas in the mind and the perceptions and the mental and vital attitude towards things and happenings and people are becoming more and more of a psychic character. Love and devotion to the Divine is the central feeling of the psychic nature and that is growing in you towards the Mother, pervading your being. A psychic love towards all is also emerging; this love is a thing inward and does not seek to express itself outwardly like the vital love which men usually have. The psychic and spiritual attitude is also not dependent on the good and bad in beings, but is self-existent regarding them as souls who carry the Divine in them however thickly concealed and are children of the Mother.

Let the sweetness and the happy feeling increase, for they are the strongest sign of the soul, the psychic being awake and in touch with us. Let not mistakes of thought or speech or action disturb you — put them away from you as something superficial which the Power and Light will deal with and remove. Keep to the one central thing — your soul and these higher realities it brings with it.

It is the soul, the psychic being in you, behind the heart, that is awake and wants to concentrate the mind on the Divine. It is the nature of the mind to go out to other things, but now when it does that, there is the unease in the heart, the psychic sorrow because the heart feels at once that this is wrong and the head also aches because of the resistance to the Divine Force at work.

This is a thing that often happens at an early stage, after the opening of the consciousness to the sadhana.

There is a psychic sorrow which usually comes when the soul feels how strong is the resistance in the world and how much the Forces in it rage against the Mother.

The vital took it [the psychic sorrow] up perhaps and gave it a more vehement and turbid expression — otherwise there is nothing disturbing in a psychic sorrow.

The psychic sadness is of a purifying and not a depressing kind.

The uneasiness created by the psychic is not depression — it is in the nature of a rejection of the wrong movement.

If the uneasiness causes depression or vital dissatisfaction, it is not the psychic.

The uneasiness is simply a reminder to you to be more vigilant in future.

The mind and the vital have always been dominant and developed themselves and are accustomed to act for themselves. How do you expect an influence [of the psychic] coming forward and for the first time to be stronger? The psychic is not uneasy, it makes you uneasy when you do the wrong thing.

You have been keeping the psychic in the background during a thousand lives and indulging the vital. That is why the psychic is not strong.

The weeping that comes to you comes from the psychic being — it is the tears of psychic yearning and aspiration. At a particular stage it so comes to many and is a very good sign. The other feelings and tendencies are also from the same source. They show that the psychic is exercising a strong influence and preparing, as we say, to come in front. Accept the movement and let it fulfil itself.

It is quite correct that weeping brings in the forces that should be kept outside — for weeping is a giving way of the inner control and an expression of vital reaction and ego. It is only the psychic weeping that does not open the door to these forces — but that weeping is without affliction, tears of bhakti, spiritual emotion, or Ananda.

Your experience was a very beautiful one — the inner being realises by such experiences that which must be established in the waking state as the foundation of the spiritual consciousness and spiritual life.

Obviously when there is that inability to control and over-eagerness, it must be a movement of a vital nature. The vital can take part in a movement but it must not be in control — it must be subordinated to the psychic.

These are movements of the vital under the psychic touch. If there is the fixed psychic foundation underneath, it will be felt as an underlying quietude and confidence or a fixed spirit of surrender.

The yearning of the heart may be there but it should not disturb the peace.

I think it is better to stop it [the yearning of the heart] for the present. It is very possible that the vital is taking advantage of it to create dissatisfaction with the progress of the sadhana. The psychic yearning brings no reaction of impatience, dissatisfaction or disturbance.

The demands were there already — when the psychic touches there is an intensification of love but the lower vital mixes up the love with all sorts of demands.

The psychic fire is the fire of aspiration, purification and Tapasya which comes from the psychic being. It is not the psychic being, but a power of the psychic being. The psychic being is a Purusha, not a flame — the psychic fire is not the being, it is something proper to it.

It is the Agni fire that you feel. Agni is at once a fire of aspiration, a fire of purification, a fire of Tapasya, a fire of transformation.

Agni in the form of an aspiration full of concentrated calm and surrender is certainly the first thing to be lighted in the heart.

It is the Mother's Force that works in the Agni.

That the constant fire of aspiration has to be lit is true; but this fire is the psychic fire and it is lit or burns up and increases as the psychic grows within and for the psychic to grow quietude is needful. That is why we have been working for the psychic to grow in you and for the quietude also to grow and that is why we want you to wait on the Mother's working in full patience and confidence. To be always remembering the Mother and always with the equal unwavering fire within means itself a considerable progress in sadhana and it must be prepared by various means such as the experiences you have been having. Keep steadfast in confidence therefore and all that has to be done will be done.

The central fire is in the psychic being, but it can be lit in all the parts of the being.

It is just in the physical consciousness that it is difficult to keep the fire burning — the physical can easily follow a constant routine, but not easily maintain a constant living endeavour. Nevertheless it can after a time be made ready to do so. All help will be given you.

It is egoistic if the ego thinks that it is the psychic fire. If the consciousness feels identified with the psychic fire and becomes conscious that the fire can burn out all impurities, then it is a true experience.

It is true that if the consciousness remains quiet, the psychic will manifest more and more from deep inside and a clear feeling will come of what is true and spiritually right and what is wrong

72

or untrue and with it also will come the power to throw away what is hostile, wrong or untrue.

The experience of the Fire is quite correct, — it is the great fire of purification and concentration (i.e. gathering up of the consciousness and turning it fixedly towards the Divine), the psychic fire which all must pass through so as to reach the Mother permanently and completely.

It [the feeling of warmth in the heart] comes sometimes from the approach of Agni fire, sometimes from that of love or Ananda, sometimes simply from a touch of the Force.

The fear of the fire you saw is misplaced, for it is the fire of purifying Agni that you see burning and that does no harm; it only clears away what should not be there. That is why it is followed by a lightness or an emptiness. You have only to be quiet and let the fire do its work. The heat one feels at that time is not the heat of fever or any other morbid heat. Afterwards, as you felt, all becomes cool and light.

All that is simply the burning of the Agni in various parts of the being. It prepares it for transformation. But the coming forward of the psychic is another matter and its signs are psychological.

It is some association in the mind probably coupling Agni with the psychic. Of course the individual Agni fire has its starting-point in the psychic, but the mere burning of the fire does not show that the psychic is coming forward.

When it burns in the heart it is the fire *in* the psychic. The psychic fire is individual and takes usually the form of a fire of aspiration or personal tapasya. This Fire is universal and it came from above.

The psychic fire may burn in the vital. It all depends on whether it is the fire of the general Force that comes from above or the fire of your soul's aspiration and tapasya.

All these things are signs, now often repeated, of the process that is going on. The heat is the result of the psychic fire burning away obstacles — the coolness and complete quietude come as a result. The tendency to sleep is really a tendency to go inside into the depths of the inner consciousness due to the pressure for the change.

The wideness of light you saw was the wideness of the true consciousness liberated from the narrow limits of the human mind, human vital, human body consciousness. It is true that the mind is narrow, not only yours, but all human minds even the most developed, compared with the wideness of the true consciousness which has no limits. It is precisely this wideness which will come by the sadhana and which these processes are preparing. The rain of flowers means a plenty of the psychic qualities and movements and the white flower of mental victory indicates the step towards it which is now being led up to — the victory of the mind of the inner light over the outer ignorance.

The heat in the body is due simply to the working that is going on within; it is what is called the heat of tapas — there is nothing unhealthy in it as in the heat of fever. The beautiful scent that you get is a subtle or psychic fragrance, just as the vision of the lotus is a subtle or psychic sight.

The psychic being is often seen or felt within in the form of a child, — it is perhaps that that you are feeling within you; it is calling for a complete sincerity, but sincerity is used here in the sense of opening to nothing but the divine influences and impulses. It does not mean that you have committed any fault, but only that the psychic in you wants you to be completely under its sole government, so that all in you may be for the Divine only. The feeling of sorrow is probably a response of the vital in you to this demand — thinking that it must have erred; but such a feeling of sorrow is not necessary. The vital can quietly wait for the psychic working to do all that is needed in due time.

The fire you saw was again the psychic fire of purification and tapasya and the garland was the offering it was preparing for the Mother, the psychic and divine consciousness (pearl and diamond) in the sadhak. The beautiful place was also probably a symbol of the psychic and the lotus indicated the opening of the psychic consciousness.

The twelve-petalled lotus and the twelve-rayed sun indicate the same thing, the complete Truth-Consciousness of the Divine Mother. It was rising but only half risen. The red colour was the sign of Power.

The fire you saw was the fire of the psychic being, the fire of aspiration and tapasya, burning under the earth, that is to say, in the subconscient. It opens the earth, the physical consciousness to the Divine Light. Moonlight may symbolise the spiritual consciousness and the room your own personal being or individual physical consciousness. With these clues it will be easy for you to understand the significance of your experience.

Agni is the psychic fire — it is not the Divine Presence. If the psychic is active and open, the Presence may be felt — it is not necessary for that that it should be in the front. Also it may be in the front, but the Divine Presence in the heart may not be felt as yet, there may be only the aspiration, bhakti, self-giving. There is no fixed law about these things — it develops differently in different natures.

If it is in the heart it may be psychic fire — it is possibly not the joy that created the fire, but the decision you had come to to believe in the Mother's action whether the mind understood or not. Such an attitude encourages the opening of the psychic and would therefore bring at once the psychic joy and the kindling of Agni in the psychic centre.

The difficulty in giving up habits is common to the physical mind in all people; nothing is more difficult to it. The fire you feel must be what we call Agni, the fire of purification acting on the physical mind to change it.

The bridge you saw was the symbol of transition from the ordinary to the spiritual consciousness; the wide plain was a symbol of the large peace and silence which comes with the spiritual consciousness when one rests in the Divine.

The perfumes you felt were true perfumes but not of the physical world. This body of flesh and blood is not the whole of ourselves; there is unseen by the eyes a subtle body also and one becomes aware of it when the inner consciousness opens. It was from deep within there that the perfumes came, perfumes of purity, of love and surrender (rose) etc. It is there deep within that the psychic being dwells and it is there that you are trying to go when the inward-going impulse or pressure comes; it was why you felt more and more peaceful, because you were going deeper and deeper into the psychic from which these perfumes came.

Sudhā is nectar or *amṛta*, the food or drink of the gods. It is applied in yoga to something that flows down from the Brahma-randhra into the palate when there is strong concentration. But this is psychological, so it must be the psychic sweetness flowing into the system.

II

All this is perfectly correct. The practice of this yoga is double — one side is of an ascent of the consciousness to the higher planes, the other is that of a descent of the power of the higher planes into the earth-consciousness so as to drive out the Power of darkness and ignorance and transform the nature.

All the consciousness in the human being who is the mental embodied in living Matter has to rise so as to meet the higher consciousness; the higher consciousness has also to descend into mind, into life, into Matter. In that way the barriers will be removed and the higher consciousness will be able to take up the whole lower nature and transform it by the power of the supermind.

The earth is a material field of evolution. Mind and life, supermind, Sachchidananda are in principle involved there in the earth-consciousness; but only Matter is at first organized; then life descends from the life plane and gives shape and organization and activity to the life principle in Matter, creates the plant and animal; then mind descends from the mind plane, creating man. Now supermind is to descend so as to create a supramental race.

The sadhana is based on the fact that a descent of Forces from the higher planes and an ascent of the lower consciousness to the higher planes is the means of transformation of the lower nature — although naturally it takes time and the complete transformation can only come by the supramental descent.

There is no fixed rule in such things. With many the descent comes first and the ascension afterwards, with others it is the other way; with some the two processes go on together. If one can fix oneself above so much the better. I have explained to you why it did not happen.

I am not speaking of mere rising above. The rising above has to be followed by the descent of the higher consciousness into the different parts of the being. That aided by the psychic development and aiding it changes the external nature.

Yes. To ascend is easier than to bring down; the higher consciousness gets entangled and impeded in the physical and the mind and vital.

In the physical consciousness the descent is the most important. Something of the subtle physical can always go up — but the external physical consciousness can only do it when the force from above comes down and fills it. There is then a sort of unification made when the higher consciousness and the physical are one undivided consciousness and there is an ascent of forces from below and descent from above, simultaneous and mutually interpenetrating.

The upward movement and the silence are indispensable for the Truth to manifest.

The ascent or the upward movement takes place when there is a sufficient aspiration from the being, i.e., from the various mental, vital and physical planes. Each in turn ascends above the mind to the place where it meets the supramental and can then receive the origination of all its movements from above. The higher descends when you have a receptive quietude in the various planes of your being prepared to receive it. In either case, whether in aspiring upward to rise to the higher or in remaining passive and open to receive the higher, an entire calmness in the different parts of the being is the true condition.

If you do not have the necessary force in a quiet aspiration or will and if you find that a certain amount of effort will help you to rise upward, you may go on using it as a temporary means, until there is the natural openness in which a silent call or a simple effortless will is sufficient to induce the action of the Higher Shakti.

Everything in the Adhara in the sadhana has at one time the tendency to rise and join its source above.

The Adhara is that in which the consciousness is now contained — mind-life-body.

To live in a higher plane and see the action in the physical from it as something separate is a definite stage in the movement towards transformation.

It is the aim of the sadhana that the consciousness should rise out of the body and take its station above, — spreading in the wideness everywhere, not limited to the body. Thus liberated one opens to all that is above this station, above the ordinary mind, receives there all that descends from the heights, observes from there all that is below. Thus it is possible to witness in all freedom and to control all that is below and to be a recipient or a channel for all that comes down and presses into the body, which it will prepare to be an instrument of a higher manifestation, remoulded into a higher consciousness and nature.

What is happening in you is that the consciousness is trying to fix itself in this liberation. When one is there in that higher station, one finds the freedom of the Self and the vast silence and immutable calm — but this calm has to be brought down also into the body, into all the lower planes and fix itself there as something standing behind and containing all the movements.

There is something in you that has become aware of the higher consciousness and gone up there — above the head where the ordinary consciousness and the higher planes meet. That has to be developed till the whole source of the consciousness is there and all the rest directed from there — with, at the same time, a liberation of the psychic so that it may support the action from above in the mind, the vital and the physical parts.

It is the Atman, the spiritual being above the mind — the first experience of it is a silence and calm (which one perceives afterwards to be infinite and eternal), untouched by the movements of mind and life and body. The higher consciousness lives always in touch with the Self — the lower is separated from it by the activities of the Ignorance.

If your consciousness rises above the head, that means that it goes beyond the ordinary mind to the centre above which receives the higher consciousness or else towards the ascending levels of the higher consciousness itself. The first result is the silence and peace of the Self which is the basis of the higher consciousness; this may afterwards descend into the lower levels, into the very body. Light also can descend and Force. The navel and the centres below it are those of the vital and the physical; something of the higher Force may have descended there.

And how is the outer nature to rise into the higher Prakriti before you realise the Self? The higher nature is that of the higher consciousness of which the first basis is the peace and wideness and realisation of the Self, the One that is all.

There are two movements — one an ascension of the lower consciousness to meet the higher, the other the descent of the higher consciousness into the lower. What you first experienced was an uprush of the lower consciousness from all parts so strong as to break the lid of the inner mind — that was the splitting of the skull — and to enable the going of the two consciousnesses above to be complete. The result was a descent. Usually the first thing that descends from the higher consciousness is its deep and entire peace — the second is the Light, here the white light of the Mother. When the higher consciousness descends or is intensely felt, there is usually an opening of the limited personal being into the cosmic consciousness — one feels a wide and infinite being which alone exists, the identification with the body and even the sense of the body disappears, the limited personal consciousness is lost in the Cosmic Existence. You had all this first in the impersonal way; but after the burning up of the psychic fire, you felt the Personal wideness, the cosmic consciousness of the Divine Mother and received her blessing.

It is very good. The ideas and feelings that come up from within you were those of the new-born psychic nature.

The feeling you had in the afternoon of the cessation of thought and the sensation of something within you going up above the head is part of the movement of the sadhana. There is a higher consciousness above you, not in the body, so above the head which we call the higher spiritual or divine consciousness, or the Mother's consciousness. When the being opens then all in you, the mind (head), emotional being (heart), vital, even something in the physical consciousness begin to ascend in order to join themselves to this greater higher consciousness. One has when one sits with eyes closed in meditation the sensation of going up which you describe. It is called the ascension of the lower consciousness. Afterwards things begin to descend from above, peace, joy, light, strength, knowledge etc. and a great change begins in the nature. This is what we call the descent of the higher (the Mother's) consciousness.

The unease you felt was because of the unaccustomed nature of the movement. It is of no importance and quickly goes away.

*
**

The experiences you describe are coherent with each other and very clearly explicable. The first shows that some part of your mind was open and this aided by an opening in the psychic enabled you to ascend into the regions above, the ranges of the liberated spiritual mind with the infinite path of the spirit leading to the highest realisation. But the rest of the nature was not ready. The straining to recover the experience was not the right thing to do then; what should have been done was the aspiration for the purification and preparation of the nature, the permanent psychic opening and the increase of the higher spiritual opening above till there could be a total release of the being. The vehemence of the action of the forces was due to the resistance and the breaking of the knots in the head and different parts of the nature was their working for the release. The "electricity" passing through the spinal column was the passage of the Force making its way down through the centres. Obviously, it is the dark resisting force of the vital, the desire nature, that rises up and clouds all up to the heart. On the other hand the flow from above and the release it creates is a sign of the opening above being still there; for the silence, the quietude of the nature is a touch from above and very necessary for purification and release. What is lacking is the full opening of the psychic being behind the heart — for that could liberate the heart from the dark force and make possible a cleaning of the rest by a quiet and steady rather than a vehement working attended by a chaotic action and struggle. When there is an opening in the spiritual mind but not a sufficient psychic change, there is or can be this

kind of vehement force-action and resistance; when the psychic
opens, then it acts on the whole nature, mind, vital, physical,
governing them from within, to transform themselves and become ready for the complete spiritual opening and spiritual consciousness. Devotion and a more and more complete inner consecration are the best way to open the psychic.

That is good — the awakening of the psychic consciousness and
its control over the rest is one of the most indispensable elements
of the sadhana.

It is what we call the higher or spiritual consciousness — it
contains or supports all the higher planes, the higher worlds.
When one begins to feel this always above, it is a great step forward in the sadhana; then the consciousness can go up there and
from there see, discern and control all that is in the mind, vital
and body. It is the meeting-place of the ascending and descending forces, as you see.

What you see above is of course the true or higher consciousness
— the Mother's — in which one sees all the world as one, a vast
free consciousness full of freedom, peace and light — it is that that
we speak of as the higher or divine consciousness. Even if it
comes and goes, yet its effect on the heart shows that a connection
has been established through the psychic — for the psychic is
behind the heart. It is there above the head that the consciousness has to ascend and remain; while it also descends into the
head and heart and lower vital and physical and brings there its
wideness, light, peace and freedom.

What you felt was not imagination at all, but the usual experience
one has when the consciousness is lifted out of the body and takes
its stand above the head. One is no longer bound then by the

physical consciousness or the sense of the body — the body becomes only an instrument, a small part of the consciousness which has to be perfected. One enters into a larger free spiritual consciousness in place of the present bound and limited physical consciousness. If this lifting up above the body can be repeated always until it can be maintained, it will be a great landmark in your progress. It is the confinement in the physical consciousness that makes you (and everybody) narrow and selfish and miserable. Hitherto the higher consciousness with its peace etc. has been descending into you with great difficulty and fighting out the vital and physical resistance. If this release upward into the higher consciousness can be maintained, then there will be no longer the same difficulty. Much will still remain to be done, but the foundation will have been made.

The consciousness is usually imprisoned in the body, centralised in the brain and heart and navel centres (mental, emotional, sensational); when you feel it or something of it go up and take its station above the head, that is the liberation of the imprisoned consciousness from the body-formula. It is the mental in you that goes up there, gets into touch with something higher than the ordinary mind and from there puts the higher mental will on the rest for transformation. The trembling and the heat come from a resistance, an absence of habituation in the body and the vital to this demand and to this liberation. When the mental consciousness can take its stand permanently or at will above like this, then this first liberation becomes accomplished (*siddha*). From there the mental being can open freely to the higher planes or to the cosmic existence and its forces and can also act with greater liberty and power on the lower nature.

Sometimes one feels an ascension above the head. I think he has had that, but that is the mind going up (when it is not simply a going out of the body) into the higher mental planes. To be

above the mind one must first realise the self above the mind
and live there.

Freedom from cares, lightness of mind and body are very good
results. They do not usually become permanent at once — it is
sufficient if they are frequently or ordinarily there.

Chest and head rising higher are sensations of the subtle
body — it means that the mind and heart consciousness (thinking mental and emotional) are rising to meet the spiritual consciousness plane above the head.

The sound is a sign of the opening of the consciousness and
of the working of the inner Force. Such subtle sounds are very
frequently heard by those who practise yoga.

When the consciousness is centred above, it can be said to be
located above. That does not mean that there is no consciousness left in the lower parts.

One may get influences from above, but so long as the mind is not
full of the higher calm, peace, silence, one cannot be in direct
contact. These influences get diminished, mentalised, vitalised
and are not the powers of the higher planes in their native character. Nor is this sufficient to get control of the hidden forces of all
the planes of consciousness, which is perhaps what he means by
occultism.

That is quite natural. The higher planes are not planes on which
one is naturally conscious and he is even not open to their direct
influence — only to some indirect influence from those nearest
to the human mind. He can reach them only in a deep inner condition or trance and the higher he goes the less easy is it for him
to be conscious of them even in trance. If you are not conscious

of your inner being, then it is more difficult to be conscious in trance.

Indirect connection (with the Divine) is when one lives in the ordinary consciousness without being able to go up above it and receives influences from above without knowing where they come from or feeling their source.

Do you realise the higher being in your ascent as wide and infinite? When you are there, do you feel it spread through infinity? Do you feel all the universe within you, yourself one with the self of all beings? Do you feel the one cosmic Force acting everywhere? Do you feel your mind one with the cosmic mind? your life one with the cosmic life? your matter one with the cosmic Matter? separative ego unreal? the body no longer a limitation? What is the use of merely saying that the higher being is wide and infinite? Do these realisations come when you are in the higher being and if not, why not? The inner being easily opens to all these realisations, the outer does not? So unless your inner being becomes conscious of itself, the mere ascent gives only height or some vague sense of other planes, not these concrete realisations.

I meant that it [the inner consciousness] is there established, even when it is covered over. Once it is there the descent of force etc. becomes more continuous or at least more frequent. The difficulties of the outer nature have still to be dealt with, but that can be done more securely and effectively with this inner consciousness as the basis.

There are two different things. One is the consciousness actually going out of the body — but that brings a deep sleep or trance. The other is the consciousness lifting itself out of the body and taking its stand outside it — above and spread round in

wideness. That can be a condition of the yogin in the waking state
— he does not feel himself to be in the body but he feels the body
to be in his wide free self, he is delivered from limitation in the
body-consciousness.

*
**

There are two different experiences which from your account
would seem to have happened together.

1. An exteriorisation of the consciousness out of the body.
Part of the consciousness, mental, vital or subtle physical or all
together rises out of the body, leaving it in a strongly internalised
condition, sleep or trance and can move about alone in other
planes or in the room and outside on the earth plane. In such
cases the body can be seen as lying below or in the room, seen
clearly as one sees a separate object with the physical eyes. A
fear such as you had can come in these exteriorisations and bring
the consciousness back with a rush to the body.

2. An ascension of the consciousness to a position which is
no longer in the body but above it. The consciousness can thus
ascend and rise higher and higher with the awareness of entering
regions above the ordinary mind; usually it does not go very far
at first but acquires the capacity to go always higher in repetitions of this experience. At the close of the experience it returns
to the body. But also there comes a definitive rise by which the
consciousness permanently takes its station above. It is no longer
in the body or limited by it; it feels itself not only above it but
extended in space; the body is below its high station and enve-
loped in its extended consciousness. Sometimes indeed the extension is felt only above on the higher level and the enveloping
extension below comes only afterwards as a later experience.
But the nature of it is to be definitive, it is not merely an experience but a realisation, a permanent change. This brings a liberation from identification with the body which becomes only a
circumstance in the largeness of the being, an instrumental part
of it; or it is felt as something very small or even non-existent,
nothing seems to be felt but a wide practically infinite consciousness which is oneself — or if not at once infinite, yet what is now
called a boundless finite.

This new consciousness is open to all knowledge from above, but it does not think with the brain as does the ordinary mind — it has other and larger means of awareness than thought. No methodical opening of the centres is necessary — the centres are in fact open, otherwise there could not be this ascent. In this yoga their opening comes automatically — what we call opening is not that, but an ability of the consciousness itself on the various levels to receive the descent of the Higher Consciousness above. By the ascent one can indeed bring down knowledge from above. But the larger movement is to receive it from above and let it flow through into the lower mental and other levels. I may add that on all these levels, in mind, heart and below there comes a liberation from the physical limitation, a wideness which no longer allows an identification with the body.

In this experience there is not usually the fear you had, unless it is in the body consciousness, as it were, which is alarmed by the unfamiliarity of the movement and fears to be abandoned or cast off. But this occurs rarely and does not usually repeat itself. It is therefore likely that there was an exteriorisation at the same time. You speak of being able to leave and enter the body at will; but this capacity is marked only for the phenomena of exteriorisation — in the ascension of consciousness the ascent and coming down become easy and ordinary actions and in the definitive realisation of a higher station above there is really no more coming down except with a part of the consciousness which may descend to work in the body or on the lower levels while the permanently high stationed being above presides over all that is experienced and done.

There are various states of experience in which the expression 'taken up out of the body' would be applicable. There is one in which one goes up from the centres in the body to a centre of consciousness extending above the physical head and takes up a position there in which one is liberated from subjection to the body sense and its heavy hold and this is certainly accompanied by a general sense of lightening. One can then be in direct connection with the higher consciousness and its power and action.

73

It is not altogether clear from the description whether this is what happened. Again, there are phenomena of the breathing which accompany states of release or of ascension. But the breath here perhaps stands, generally, for the life-principle.

It is a very usual experience. It means that for a moment you were no longer in your body, but somehow either above or somehow outside the body-consciousness. This sometimes happens by the vital being rising up above the head or, more rarely, by its projecting itself into its own sheath (part of the subtle body) out of the physical attachment. But it also comes by a sudden even if momentary liberation from the identification with the body-consciousness, and this liberation may become frequent and prolonged or permanent. The body is felt as something separate or some small circumstance in the consciousness or as something one carries about with one etc. etc., the exact experience varies. Many sadhaks here have had it. When one is accustomed, the strangeness of it (dreamland etc.) disappears.

It is the subtle parts of the physical that go up. The external consciousness can also go up, but then there is a complete trance. There is not much utility for the complete trance in this sadhana.

If all went up, there would be no existence in the body. There is always some consciousness and therefore some self supporting the body.

No, the body itself cannot go up — how could it? The body is meant for keeping the consciousness linked to the physical world.

Once the being or its different parts begin to ascend to the planes above, any part of the being may do it, frontal or other. The Sanskar that one cannot come back must be got rid of. One can have the experience of Nirvana at the summit of the mind or anywhere in those planes that are now superconscient to the mind; the mind spiritualised by the ascent into Self has the sense of *laya*, dissolution of itself, its thoughts, movements, Sanskaras into a superconscient Silence and Infinity which it is unable to grasp, — the Unknowable. But this would bring or lead to some form of Nirvana, only if one makes Nirvana the goal, if one is tied to the mind and accepts its dissolution into the Infinite as one's own dissolution or if one has not the capacity to reorganise experience on a higher than the mental plane. But otherwise what was superconscient becomes conscient, one begins to possess or else be the instrument of the dynamis of the higher planes and there is a movement, not of liberation into Nirvana, but of liberation and transformation. However high one goes, one can always return, unless one has the will not to do so.

These are the ordinary normal experiences of the sadhana when there is an opening from above — the contact with the peace of the Brahman, Self or Divine and the contact with the higher Power, the Power of the Mother. He does not know what they are, quite naturally, but feels very correctly and his description is quite accurate. "How beautiful, calm and still all seems — as if in water there were not even a wave. But it is not Nothingness. I feel a Presence steeped in life but absolutely silent and quiet in meditation," — there could hardly be a better description of this experience — the experience of the peace and silence of the Divine or of the Divine itself in its own essential peace and silence. Also what he feels about the Force is quite correct, "something from above the manifested creation (mind — matter), a Force behind that is distinct from that which gives rise to emotions, anger, lust which are all purified and transformed gradually", in other words, the Divine or Spiritual Force, other than the cosmic vital which supports the ordinary embodied consciousness; that is also very clear. I suppose it is only a contact yet, but a very true and vivid contact if it gives rise to so vivid and true a feeling. It looks as if he were going to make a very good beginning.

The experience described in your letter is a glimpse of the realisation of the true Self which is independent of the body. When this settles itself there is the liberation (*mukti*). Not only the body, but the vital and mind are felt to be only instruments and one's self is felt to be calm, self-existent and free and wide or infinite. It is then possible for the psychic being to effect in that freedom the full transformation of the nature. All your former experiences were preparing for this, but the physical consciousness came across. Now that you have had the glimpse of the self separate from the body, this physical difficulty may soon be overcome.

In the first realisation of silence in the higher consciousness there is no Time — there is only the sense of pure existence, consciousness, peace or a strong featureless Ananda. If anything else comes in it is a minor movement on the surface of this timeless self-existence. This and the sense of liberation that comes with it is the result of the mind's quiescence. At a higher level this peace and liberation remain, but can be united with a greater and free dynamic movement.

In the self or pure existence there is no time or space — except spiritual space or wideness.

Yes — in the silence of the self there is no time — it is *akāla*.

The experience you had of something going out from the head like an arrow probably indicates something going out of the mental consciousness towards some aim or object. Sometimes it is a part of the mind-consciousness itself that goes like that either upward to a higher plane or somewhere in the world around — and afterwards returns. Sometimes it is a thought-force or a will-force. Forces are always going out from us without our knowing it even, and often they have some effect there. If we think of a person or a place and things happening there, something can go out like that to that person or place. If we have a will or strong mental desire that something should happen, a will-force may go out and try to make that happen. But also forces can go out from the inner mind without any conscious cause on the surface.

The vision of the yogi may have been that of some being of the higher planes or it may have been a form of Shiva. The lotuses indicate fully developed consciousness in the places indicated.

What you desire about the self-giving free from demand is sure to fulfil itself when there is the full opening of the psychic.

The position you took finally about what happened today is right — to make the effort for one's own perfection and not to be disturbed by any mistake in others but reply by a silent will for their perfection also is always the right attitude.

The experience of the great expanse of golden light on a mountain-top came because I had asked her to aspire for the higher experiences of the consciousness from above. The symbolic image of the mountain with the light on its top comes to most sadhaks who have the power of vision at all. The mountain is the consciousness rising from earth (the physical) through the successive heights (vital, mental, above-mental) towards the spiritual heaven. The golden light is always the light of the higher Truth (supermind, overmind or a little lower down the pure Intuition) and it is represented as a great luminous expanse on the summits of the being. X by concentrating on the light entered into contact with the higher reaches and that always gives these results, peace, joy, strength, a consciousness secure in the power of the Divine. It is of course through the psychic that she got into this contact but in itself it is more an experience of the higher spiritual consciousness above mind than a psychic experience.

The nature of the meditation depends on the part of the being in which one is centred at the time. In the body (rather the subtle body than the physical, but connected with the corresponding parts in the gross physical body also) there are centres proper to each level of the being. There is a centre at the top of the head and above it which is that of the above-mind or higher consciousness; a centre in the forehead between the eyebrows which is that of the thinking mind, mental will, mental vision; a centre in the throat which is that of the expressive or externalising mind: these are the mental centres. Below comes the vital — the heart (emotional), the navel (the dynamic life-centre), another below the navel in the abdomen which is the lower or sensational vital centre. Finally, at the bottom of the spine is the Muladhara or physical centre. Behind the heart is the psychic centre. If one concentrates in the head, as many do, it is a mental-spiritual meditation one seeks for; if in the heart it is a psychic meditation; these are the usual places where one concentrates. But what rises up first or opens first may not be the mental or the psychic, but the emotional or the vital; that depends on the nature — for whatever is easiest to open in it, is likely to open first. If it is in the vital, then the meditation tends to project the consciousness into the vital plane and its experiences. But from that we can get to the psychic by drawing more and more inwards, not getting absorbed into the vital experiences but separating oneself and looking at them with detachment as if one were deep inside and observing things outside oneself. Similarly one can get the mental experiences by concentrating in the thought and by it bringing a corresponding experience, e.g. the thought of all being the Brahman, or one can draw back from the thought also and observe one's own thoughts as outside things until one enters into silence and the pure spiritual experience.

*
**

The illumination above the head as usually seen in this yoga is the Light of the Divine Truth. It is above the head that there is perfectly the Divine Peace, Force, Light, Knowledge, Ananda. These begin to descend into the body when the personal consciousness is prepared sufficiently. The preparation is usually full of vicissitudes such as these but one has to persist patiently, opening oneself more and more till that is ready.

If one can remain always in the higher consciousness, so much the better. But why does not one remain always there? Because the lower is still part of the nature and it pulls you down towards itself. If on the other hand the lower is transformed, it becomes of one kind with the higher and there is nothing lower to pull downward.

Transformation means that the higher consciousness or nature is brought down into the mind, vital and body and takes the place of the lower. There is a higher consciousness of the true self, which is spiritual, but it is above; if one rises above into it, then one is free as long as one remains there, but if one comes down into or uses mind, vital or body — and if one keeps any connection with life, one has to do so, either to come down and act from the ordinary consciousness or else to be in the self but use mind, life and body, then the imperfections of these instruments have to be faced and mended — they can only be mended by transformation.

You say you rise a little above into the higher consciousness, but where do you rise? Into the quiet mind and above the vital or above the mind itself into something always calm and pure and free?

No. I did not intend any sarcasm by my question. You had written that by rising a little above the ordinary consciousness one was free from difficulty and that this was what one felt. I thought you meant that this was your own experience. So I put the question, as the experience of the quiet mind is one that can easily be broken by the uneasiness of the vital or the inertia of the physical being. The experience of the deeper freedom and calm which belongs to the self remains but it can be covered up by the lower consciousness.

One can remain in the higher consciousness and yet associate oneself with the change of the lower nature. No doubt, it is the Mother's Force that will do what is necessary, but the consent of the sadhak, the association of his will with her action or at least of his witness-vision is necessary also.

Your tendency was to go up and to leave the higher consciousness to deal with the lower nature without any personal effort for that. That could have worked all right on two conditions: (1) that the peace and force would come down and occupy all down to the physical, (2) that you succeeded in keeping the inner being unmoved by the outer nature. The physical failed to absorb the peace, inertia arose instead; force could not come down; the suggestions from the outer nature proved too strong for you and between their suggestions and the inertia they interrupted the sadhana.

I have not said that you made a mistake. I have simply said what happened and the causes. If you had been able to remain above and let the Force come down and act while you were detached from the outer nature, it would have been all right. You were able to go up because the Peace descended. You were not able to remain above because the Peace could not occupy sufficiently the physical and the Force did not descend sufficiently. Meanwhile the inertia arose, you got troubled more and more because of the vital suggestions in the outer nature and rush of inertia, so you were unable to keep detached and let the Force descend more and more or call it down more and more. Hence the coming down into the physical consciousness.

*

That you should be able to keep your consciousness uplifted is already something. As for the opening, its coming and apparent closing is a normal experience — it needs several openings before the thing is settled by a permanent poise of the consciousness above and an increasing descent into the head and below. It is the pull from below that should get no indulgence — for that though most do indulge in it is a wrong crabby way of doing it. One must be stationed above before one can descend without a tumble. Not that the tumble if it comes precludes a going up again — it doesn't; but that is no reason for letting it happen.

*

I see no reason for either ripping or wandering or throat-slitting. Even if the permanent opening does not come at once, you have only to wait and it is bound to come. It is certainly a pity that the restlessness of the vital should kick so much against vacancy of the consciousness; for if you could stand it this emptiness, now neutral and therefore not interesting to the vital, would become positive and be the powerful recipient of the pouring from above. The difficulty is that the vital has always been accustomed either to doing something or to something doing and when it is doing nothing or nothing is doing (or it seems like that on the surface), it gets bored and begins to feel and talk or to do nonsense. However, even with this obstacle, the Descent can come down — it need not wait for the supramental.

*

I may say that the opening upwards, the ascent into the Light and the subsequent descent into the ordinary consciousness and normal human life is very common as the first decisive experience in the practice of yoga and may very well happen even without the practice of yoga in those who are destined for the spiritual change, especially if there is a dissatisfaction somewhere with the ordinary life and a seeking for something more, greater or better. It comes often exactly in the way that she describes and the cessation of the experience and the descent also come in the same way. This first experience may be followed by a very long time during which there is no repetition of it or any subsequent experience. If there is a constant practice of yoga, the interval need not be so long; but even so, it is often long enough. The descent is inevitable because it is not the whole being that has risen up but only something within, and all the rest of the nature is unprepared, absorbed in or attached to ordinary life and governed by movements that are not in consonance with the Light. Still, the something within is something central in the being and therefore the experience is in a way definitive and decisive. For it comes as a decisive intimation of the spiritual destiny and an indication of what must be reached some time in the life. Once it has been there, something is bound to happen which will open the way, determine the right knowledge and the right attitude enabling one to proceed on the way and bring a helping influence. After that, the work of clearing away the obstacles that prevent the return to the Light and the ascension of the whole being and, what is equally important, the descent of the Light into the whole being, can be begun and progress towards completion. It may take long or be rapid, that depends on the inner push and also on outer circumstances but the inner aspiration and endeavour count more than the circumstances which can accommodate themselves to the inner need if that is very strong. The moment has come for her and the necessary aspiration and knowledge and the influence that can help her.

The force which you felt must evidently have been a rising of the Kundalini ascending to join the Force above and bring down the energy needed to ease the depression and then again rising to enforce the connection between the Above and the lower centres. The seeming expansion of the head is due to the joining of the mind with the consciousness of the Self or Divine above. That consciousness is wide and illimitable and, when one rises into it, the individual consciousness also breaks its limits and feels wide and illimitable. At such times one often feels as if there were no head and no body but all were a wide self and its consciousness, or else the head or the body is only a circumstance in that. The body or the physical mind is sometimes startled or alarmed at these experiences because they are abnormal to it; but there is no ground for alarm, — these are usual experiences in the yoga.

The spine is the main channel of the descent and ascent of the Force, by which it connects the lower and the higher consciousness together.

The sensation in the spine and on both sides of it is a sign of the awakening of the Kundalini Power. It is felt as a descending and an ascending current. There are two main nerve-channels for the currents, one on each side of the central channel in the spine. The descending current is the energy from the above coming down to touch the sleeping Power in the lowest nerve-centre at the bottom of the spine; the ascending current is the release of the energy going up from the awakened Kundalini. This movement as it proceeds opens up the six centres of the subtle nervous system and by the opening one escapes from the limitations of the surface consciousness bound to the gross body and great ranges of experiences proper to the subliminal self, mental, vital, subtle physical are shown to the sadhak. When the Kundalini meets the higher Consciousness as it ascends through the summit of the head, there is an opening of the higher superconscient reaches above the normal mind. It is by ascending through these in our consciousness and receiving a descent of their energies that it is possible ultimately to reach the supermind. This is the method of the Tantra. In our yoga it is not necessary to go through the systematised method. It takes place spontaneously according to the need by the force of the aspiration. As soon as there is an opening the Divine Power

descends and conducts the necessary working, does what is
needed, each thing in its time, and the yogic Consciousness
begins to be born in the sadhak.

**
**

Sri Aurobindo cannot undertake to guide you as your Guru,
for the reason that he takes as disciples only those who follow
his special path of yoga; your experiences follow a different line.
In his yoga there may be an occasional current in the spine as in
other nerve channels or different parts of the body, but no awakening of the Kundalini in this particular and powerful fashion.
There is only a quiet uprising of the consciousness from the
lower centres to join the spiritual consciousness above and a
descent of the Divine Force from above which does its own
work in the mind and body — the manner and stages varying in
each sadhak. A perfect confidence in the Divine Mother and a
vigilance to repel all wrong suggestions and influences is the main
law of this yoga. Your opening having once been so powerful
on the more usual Tantric lines (even without your own will
intervening), it is hardly probable that it could now change
easily to other lines — any such effort might create a serious
disturbance. In speaking of a competent Guru Sri Aurobindo
meant one who had himself practised this opening of the centres
and become siddha in that line of yoga. It should not be impossible to find one — when one has the call for the Guru, the
Guru sooner or later comes. Meanwhile to put away fear and
have confidence in the Divine working is indispensable — but
no effort should be made to force the pace by concentrated meditation unless you have a guide whom you can trust — a clear
guidance from within or a guide from without. The inspiration
about the *iḍā nāḍi* and the subsequent working of the Shakti
show that there was an intervention at a critical moment and that
the call to it whenever needed is likely to be effective.

In the experiences proper related in your first letter there
is absolutely nothing that should have disturbed you — all was
quite normal, the usual experiences of the yogin at such a juncture, and very good and powerful, such as do not come except by

the grace of the Divine. Probably the opening came after slow invisible preparation as a result of the meditation on the lotus at the top of the head; for that is always an invitation to the Kundalini to awake or for the lower consciousness to rise and meet the higher. The disturbing factors came with the feeling of discomfort in the heart due to some resistance in the physical being which is very often felt and can be overcome by the work-ing of the Force itself and the fear that came afterwards in the seats of the vital Nature, heart, navel etc. But that was no part of the experience; it was an interference by a wrong reaction from the lower or exterior consciousness. If you had not allowed yourself to be disturbed, probably nothing untoward would have distorted the process. One must not get frightened by unusual states or movements or experiences, the yogi must be fearless, *abhī*; it is absurd to have a fear because one can control one's states; that is a power very much to be desired and welcomed in yoga.

The crises related in the second letter would hardly have come, if there had not been this reaction; but in any case there was the intervention and setting right of the trouble. However these reactions and the fact that the disturbance came show that something in the exterior consciousness is not altogether prepared; it is better to wait and seek for a guide so that igno-rant steps or reactions may not bring again a serious trouble or danger. It is all that Sri Aurobindo can say by way of enlighten-ment and advice. He does not usually intervene with anyone not his disciple, but as your case was an unusual one and your call was great he has given you what light he can on your experience.

Yoga means union with the Divine — a union either transcenden-tal (above the universe) or cosmic (universal) or individual or, as in our yoga, all three together. Or it means getting into a con-sciousness in which one is no longer limited by the small ego, personal mind, personal vital and body but is in union with the supreme Self or with the universal (cosmic) consciousness or with some deeper consciousness within in which one is aware of one's own soul, one's own inner being and of the real truth of existence. In the yogic consciousness one is not only aware of things, but of forces, not only of forces, but of the conscious being behind the forces. One is aware of all this not only in oneself but in the universe.

There is a force which accompanies the growth of the new consciousness and at once grows with it and helps it to come about and to perfect itself. This force is the Yoga-Shakti. It is here coiled up and asleep in all the centres of our inner being (Chakras) and is at the base what is called in the Tantras the Kundalini Shakti. But it is also above us, above our head as the Divine Force — not there coiled up, involved, asleep, but awake, scient, potent, extended and wide; it is there waiting for manifestation and to this Force we have to open ourselves — to the power of the Mother. In the mind it manifests itself as a divine mind-force or a universal mind-force and it can do everything that the personal mind cannot do; it is then the yogic mind-force. When it manifests and acts in the vital or the physical in the same way, it is there apparent as a yogic life-force or a yogic body-force. It can awake in all these forms, bursting outwards and upwards, extending itself into wideness from below; or it can descend and become there a definite power for things; it can pour downwards into the body, working, establishing its reign, extending into wideness from above, link the lowest in us with the highest above us, release the individual into a cosmic universality or into absoluteness and transcendence.

There is a Yoga-Shakti lying coiled or asleep in the inner body, not active. When one does yoga, this force uncoils itself and rises upward to meet the Divine Consciousness and Force that are waiting above us. When this happens, when the awakened Yoga-Shakti arises, it is often felt like a snake uncoiling and standing up straight and lifting itself more and more upwards. When it meets the Divine Consciousness above, then the force of the Divine Consciousness can more easily descend into the body and be felt working there to change the nature.

The feeling of your body and eyes being drawn upwards is part of the same movement. It is the inner consciousness in the body and the inner subtle sight in the body that are looking and moving upward and trying to meet the divine consciousness and divine seeing above.

The Energy in the Kundalini is the Mother's.

I do not see what is your difficulty. That there is a divine force asleep or veiled by Inconscience in Matter and that the Higher Force has to descend and awaken it with the Light and Truth is a thing that is well known; it is at the very base of this yoga.

I am afraid the attempt to apply scientific analogies to spiritual or yogic things leads more often to confusion than to anything else, — just as it creates confusion if thrust upon philosophy also. Kundalini coiled in the Muladhara is asleep, plunged in the inconscience, supporting the play of the Ignorance. Naturally, if she heaves up from there, there may be a disturbance or disruption of the states of the Ignorance, but that would be rather a salutary upheaval and helpful to the purpose of yoga. Kundalini becoming conscious rises up to meet the Brahman in the thousand-petalled lotus. A mere ejection from her uniting with the higher consciousness would hardly lead to a radical change. Of course she need not abandon connection with the physical centre altogether; but she is no longer coiled there: if she were, the great occult force residing there would not be liberated. The usual image of her risen and awake is, I believe, that of a serpent standing erect, the tail touching the lowest centre, the head the highest at the Brahmarandhra. Thus with all the centres open and active she unites the two poles, superior and inferior, of the being, the spirit with Matter.

That [rising above the head] is very good. Such risings help to break down the lid between the higher and lower planes in the consciousness and prepare the wideness.

What is to be done depends on where the block is. There are two movements that are necessary — one is the ascent through the increasing of peace and silence to its source above the mind, — that is indicated by the tendency of the consciousness to rise out of the body to the top of the head and above where it is easy to realise the Self in all its stillness and liberation and wideness and to open to the other powers of the Higher Consciousness. The other is the descent of the peace, silence, the spiritual freedom and wideness and the powers of the higher consciousness as they develop into the lower down to the most physical and even the subconscient. To both of these movements there can be a block — a block above due to the mind and lower nature being unhabituated (it is that really and not incapacity) and a block below due to the physical consciousness and its natural slowness to change. Everybody has these blocks but by persistent will, aspiration or *abhyāsa* they can be overcome.

Wideness is a sign of the extension of consciousness out of the ordinary limits — whiteness of the wideness means that it is the pure consciousness one is feeling, unless it is white light or luminous light which indicates the Mother's consciousness there or some influence of it. The subtle barrier you felt must have been the same thing that prevents your ascent from the heart and from it your going beyond into the regions above. There is always a sort of a lid there and it is only when that is opened or disappears that one can go freely above. One can be aware of "unseen wideness" but one is not a self there until that is done.

Wideness is necessary for the working of the higher consciousness — if the being is shut up in itself, there can be intense experiences and some opening to touches from the heights, but not
the full stable basis for the transformation.

The emptiness and wideness in the brain is a very good sign.
It is a condition for the opening horizontally into the cosmic consciousness and upward into the Self and higher spiritual Mind
above the head.

The lightness, the feeling of the disappearance of the head and
that all is open is a sign of the wideness of the mental consciousness which is no longer limited by the brain and its body sense
— no longer imprisoned but wide and free. This is felt in the
meditation only at first or with closed eyes, but at a later stage it
becomes established and one feels always oneself a wide consciousness not limited by any feeling of the body. You felt something of this wideness of your being in the second experience
when the Mother's foot pressed down your physical mind (head)
till it went below and left room for this sense of an infinite Self.
This wide consciousness not dependent on the body or limited
by it is what is called in yoga the Atman or Self. You are only
having the first glimpses of it, but later on it becomes normal and
one feels that one was always this Atman infinite and immortal.

I don't think the lack of sleep when it comes is due to want
of work; for even those who do no work at all get good sleep.
It is something else; but it must be got over.

The constant remembrance of the Mother is a difficult thing
and few have it, but it will come in time. Meanwhile her Force is
working in you and preparing your consciousness for that.

The Self is met first on the level of the Higher Mind, but it is not
limited to one station — it is usually felt as something outspread

in wideness, but one may also feel a centralising consciousness
in the Sahasrara or above it.

The Self governs the diversity of its creation by its unity on all the
planes from the Higher Mind upwards on which the realisation
of the One is the natural basis of consciousness. But as one goes
upward, the view changes, the power of consciousness changes,
the Light becomes ever more intense and potent. Although
the static realisation of Infinity and Eternity and the Timeless
One remains the same, the vision of the workings of the One
becomes ever wider and is attended with a greater instrumentality of Force and a more comprehensive grasp of what has to be
known and done. All possible forms and constructions of things
become more and more visible, put in their proper place, utilisable. Moreover, what is thought-knowledge in the Higher
Mind becomes illumination in the Illumined Mind and direct
intimate vision in the Intuition. But the Intuition sees in flashes
and combines through a constant play of light — through revelations, inspirations, intuitions, swift discriminations. The overmind sees calmly, steadily, in great masses and large extensions
of space and time and relation, globally; it creates and acts in
the same way — it is the world of the great Gods, the divine
Creators. Only, each creates in his own way; he sees all but sees
all from his own viewpoint. There is not the absolute supramental harmony and certitude. These, inadequately expressed,
are some of the differences. I speak, of course, of these planes
in themselves — when acting in the human consciousness they
are necessarily much diminished in their working by having to
depend on the human instrumentation of mind, vital and physical. Only when these are quieted, they get a fuller force and
reveal more their character.

The substance of knowledge is the same on all the overhead
planes, but the higher mind gives only the substance and form of

knowledge in thought and word — in the illumined mind there begins to be a peculiar light and energy and Ananda of knowledge which grows as one rises higher in the scale — or else as the knowledge comes from a higher and higher source. This light etc. are still rather diluted and diffused in the illumined mind; it becomes more and more intense, clearly defined and dynamic and effective on the higher planes so much so as to change always the character and power of the knowledge.

The Ignorance can act from above the head — but not as part of the higher planes — it comes from outside. The higher planes just above the head are not however the absolute Truth; that you only get in the supermind.

The planes and the body are not the same. Above the head are seen all the planes from the overmind down to the higher mind, but this is only a correlation in the consciousness — not an actual location in space.

[1]As thought rises in the scale, it ceases to be intellectual, becomes illumined, then intuitive, then overmental and finally disappears seeking the last Beyond. The poem does not express any philosophical thought, however; it is simply a perception of a certain movement, that is all.

"Pale blue" is the colour of the higher ranges of mind up to the intuition. Above it, it begins to become golden with the supramental Light.

---

[1] This and the following letter were written in reference to "Thought the Paraclete", a poem of Sri Aurobindo. See Sri Aurobindo, *Collected Poems* (Cent. Ed. Vol. 5), p. 582.

Thought is not the giver of Knowledge but the "mediator" between the Inconscient and the Superconscient. It compels the world born from the Inconscient to reach for a Knowledge other than the instinctive vital or merely empirical, for the Knowledge that itself exceeds thought; it calls for that superconscient Knowledge and prepares the consciousness here to receive it. It rises itself into the higher realms and even in disappearing into the supramental and Ananda levels is transformed into something that will bring down their powers into the silent self which its cessation leaves behind it.

Gold-red is the colour of the supramental in the physical — the poem describes Thought in the stage when it is undergoing transformation and is about to ascend into the Infinite above and disappear into it. The "flame-word rune" is the Word of the higher Inspiration, Intuition, Revelation which is the highest attainment of Thought.

By the intuitive self I meant the intuitive being, that part which belongs to the intuitive plane or is in connection with it. The intuition is one of the higher planes of consciousness between the human thinking mind and the supramental plane.

The intuitive mind does not get the touch *direct* from the supramental. Above it is the overmind in which there is a higher and greater intuition and above that are the supramental ranges.

I do not think it can be said that there are separate strata in the intuitive mind for purity, strength and beauty. These are separate powers of the Divine, not separate strata. But, of course, they can be arranged by the mind in that way for some organised purpose.

*
**

Revelation is a part of the intuitive consciousness.

There is a discrimination that is not intellectual — a direct perception.

One can get intuitions — communications from there [the Intuition plane] even while the ego exists — but to live in the wideness of the Intuition is not possible with the limitation of the ego.

To live in the Intuitive it is necessary first to have the opening into the cosmic consciousness and to live first in the higher and the illumined Mind, seeing everything from there. To receive constantly the intuition from above, that is not necessary — it is sufficient to have the sense of the One everywhere and to get into contact with things and people through the inner mind and sense more than with the outer mind and senses — for the latter meet only the surface of things and are not intuitive.

The cosmic consciousness has many levels — the cosmic physical, the cosmic vital, the cosmic Mind, and above the higher planes of cosmic Mind there is the Intuition and above that the overmind and still above that the supermind where the Transcendental begins. In order to live in the Intuition plane (not merely to receive intuitions), one has to live in the cosmic consciousness because there the cosmic and individual run into each other as it were, and the mental separation between them is already broken down, so nobody can reach there who is still in the separative ego.

A reflected static realisation of Sachchidananda is possible on any of the cosmic planes, but the full entering into it, the entire union with the Supreme Divine dynamic as well as static, comes with the transcendence.

It [the individual self] is not specially related [to Intuition] — intuition is the highest power the embodied individual can reach without universalising itself — when it universalises itself it is then possible for it to come in contact with overmind. If by the individual self is meant the Jivatman, it can be on any plane of consciousness.

It is not the psychic but the mind that gets raised and transformed and its action intensified by the intuitivising of the consciousness. The psychic is always the same in essence and adapts its action without need of transformation to any change of consciousness.

Yes, there are beings [on the Intuition plane]. Intuition is in direct contact with the higher Truth but not in an integral contact. It gets the Truth in flashes and turns these flashes of Truth-perception into intuitions — intuitive ideas. The ideas of the true Intuition are always correct so far as they go — but when intuition is diluted in the ordinary mind stuff, its truth gets mixed with error.

I do not remember in what context I wrote it. But intuitivising is not sufficient to prevent a drop; if it is complete (and it is not complete until not only the mind, but the vital and physical are intuitivised) it can make you understand and be conscious of all the processes in you and around but it does not necessarily make you entire master of the reactions. For that Knowledge is not enough — a certain Knowledge-Will (knowledge and will fused together) or Consciousness-Power is needed.

The overmind receives the Divine Truth and disperses it in various formations and diverse play of forces, building thus different worlds out of this dispersion.

In the Intuition the nature of Knowledge is Truth not global or whole, but coming out in so many points, edges, flashes of a Truth that is behind it and supplies it with its direct perceptions.

He seems to say that beyond the overmind there is a plane of "higher luminous Intelligence". This is impossible. Beyond the overmind there is the supermind — the overmind is the highest of the planes below the supramental, and he is not yet in touch with the supramental. What he calls here the overmind cannot be the true overmind. His experiences are those of the mind opening to the higher mental planes and trying to bring down something from them and their powers into the mind, life and body.

His classification of four worlds is an attempt of the mind to interpret something he had seen, but it has not got it all right. If Mahasaraswati stopped him at this moment, it must have been because his mind was making a wrong formation and it was no use carrying it any farther.

At this stage in his yoga he must observe what is going on, but not attach a definitive or final importance to any such classifications or mental arrangements. The mind at this stage sometimes gets these things correctly, sometimes makes formations of them which are not correct and have to be discarded or set right when a higher knowledge comes.

The consciousness which you call supramental is no doubt above the human mind, but it should be called, not the supramental, but simply the higher consciousness. In this higher consciousness there are many degrees, of which the supramental is the summit or the source. It is not possible to reach the summit or source all at once; first of all the lower consciousness has to be purified and made ready. That is the meaning of the Light you saw, whose inner body or substance is too dense and powerful to be penetrated at present.

Certainly, the overmind descent is necessary for those who want the supramental change. Unless the overmind opens, there can be no direct supramental opening of the consciousness. If one remains in the mind, even illumined mind or the intuition, one can have indirect messages or an influence from the supramental, but not a direct supramental control of the consciousness or the supramental change.

People talk very lightly of the overmind and the supermind as if it were quite easy to enter into them and mistake inferior movements for the overmental or supramental, thereby confusing the Truth and delaying the progress of the sadhana.

It is not very clear what is meant by this Knowledge-Will. It is usually a description of the supramental where there is no division between Knowledge and Will, each acting on each other or rather fixed together in oneness and therefore infallible. You say it has taken form in mind, vital and body; if that is so, it would mean the fixed and decisive transformation; so it cannot be the supramental. It must be some overmind Truth plane.

Knowledge and will have naturally to be one before either can act perfectly.

It is the experience of the transcendent planes as reflected on the higher planes of consciousness (overmind, etc.) in relation to them; just as one can have an experience of Sachchidananda and these planes as reflected in the mind or vital or physical consciousness, so one can have it there — but on each plane it appears in a different way.

Overmind experience comes when one rises to the overmind plane and sees things as they are on that plane or as they look to the consciousness which sees the other planes from the overmind view. When one is in the mind, life or physical plane, then it is the overmind Influence that comes down and modifies the mind, life or physical workings in greater or less degree according to the possibilities or the thing to be done at the moment. It is not the sole power as it is in its own plane but works under mental, vital or physical conditions. Its power is more subjective than objective — it is easy for it to change our view and experience of the object and our knowledge about it, but not so easy for it to change the object or its nature or circumstances or the outward state of things in that plane.

There are no overmind dangers — it is only the lower consciousness misusing overmind or higher consciousness intimations that can make a danger. There are also no overmind Falsehoods. The overmind is part of the Ignorance in this sense that it is the highest knowledge to which the Ignorance can attain, but the knowledge is still divided and so can be a knowledge of parts and aspects of the Truth, not the integral knowledge. As such it can be misused and turned into falsehood by the Mind.

The overmind experience does not necessarily deliver from the lower vital and physical movements — it changes them only to a certain extent and prepares them for a greater Truth.

It is perfectly natural. In these experiences you become aware of the consciousness proper to other planes. Thus you get the experience of being a form of the Divine Consciousness, the Mother, and while the experience lasts you feel her power — when the experience ceases, you come back to your normal state, the power withdraws. These experiences are proper to the consciousness with the overmind Knowledge and they prepare it for transformation.

It is perfectly simple, it is the attraction towards the Divine Consciousness represented in a concrete experience. It is the concreteness of the experiences that puzzles you. All experience there tends to be concrete, there are no "abstract" truths as in the mind, — even thought in the overmind is a concrete force and a palpable substance.

Yes — it is one aspect of the Truth, — for in the overmind there are many aspects of Truth, separate or combined together or arranged one above the other.

Why not? Both are true on the different levels of the overmind or in different cosmic formations that come from the overmind. All aspects are there in the overmind, even those which the intellect considers contradictory to each other; in the overmind they are not contradictions but complementary to each other.

It is only the supermind that has an absolute freedom from error. The overmind presents truth in all sorts of arrangements all of which taken together presents something like the whole truth — but these again are reflected in you in the terrestrial conscious-

ness or conveyed to your terrestrial consciousness by the descent
from the higher planes, but in receiving it the terrestrial consciousness can make mistakes in interpretation, in understanding,
in application, in arrangement.

Absolute certitude about all things can only come from the supermind. Meanwhile one has to go on with what knowledge the
other planes give.

III

The descent is that of the powers of the higher consciousness
which is above the head. It usually descends from centre to
centre till it has occupied the whole being. But at the beginning
the action is very variable. It is only when the Peace from above
has not only descended but established itself in the whole system
that there is a continuous action. The descent comes in order
to transform the consciousness but the transformation takes time.
It is not done all in a moment.

I have said that the most decisive way for the Peace or the
Silence to come is by a descent from above. In fact, in reality
though not always in appearance, that is how they always come;
— not in appearance always, because the sadhak is not always
conscious of the process; he feels the peace settling in him or
at least manifesting, but he has not been conscious how and
whence it came. Yet it is the truth that all that belongs to the
higher consciousness comes from above, not only the spiritual
peace and silence, but the Light, the Power, the Knowledge, the
higher seeing and thought, the Ananda come from above. It is
also possible that up to a certain point they may come from within, but this is because the psychic being is open to them directly
and they come first there and then reveal themselves in the

rest of the being from the psychic or by its coming into the front. A disclosure from within or a descent from above, these are the two sovereign ways of the Yoga-siddhi. An effort of the external surface mind or emotions, a Tapasya of some kind may seem to build up some of these things, but the results are usually uncertain and fragmentary, compared to the result of the two radical ways. That is why in this yoga we insist always on an "opening" — an opening inwards of the inner mind, vital, physical to the inmost part of us, the psychic, and an opening upwards to what is above the mind — as indispensable for the fruits of the sadhana.

The underlying reason for this is that this little mind, vital and body which we call ourselves is only a surface movement and not our "self" at all. It is an external bit of personality put forward for one brief life, for the play of the Ignorance. It is equipped with an ignorant mind stumbling about in search of fragments of truth, an ignorant vital rushing about in search of fragments of pleasure, an obscure and mostly subconcious physical receiving the impacts of things and suffering rather than possessing a resultant pain or pleasure. All that is accepted until the mind gets disgusted and starts looking about for the real Truth of itself and things, the vital gets disgusted and begins wondering whether there is not such a thing as real bliss and the physical gets tired and wants liberation from itself and its pains and pleasures. Then it is possible for the little ignorant bit of personality to get back to its real Self and with it to these greater things — or else to extinction of itself, Nirvana.

The real Self is not anywhere on the surface but deep within and above. Within is the soul supporting an inner mind, inner vital, inner physical in which there is a capacity for universal wideness and with it for the things now asked for — direct contact with the truth of self and things, taste of a universal bliss, liberation from the imprisoned smallness and sufferings of the gross physical body. Even in Europe the existence of something behind the surface is now very frequently admitted, but its nature is mistaken and it is called subconscient or subliminal, while really it is very conscious in its own way and not subliminal but only behind the veil. It is, according to our psychology, connected with the small outer personality by certain centres of consciousness of which we become aware by yoga. Only a little of the inner being escapes through these centres into the outer life, but that little is the best part of ourselves and responsible for our art, poetry, philosophy, ideals, religious aspirations, efforts at knowledge and perfection. But the inner centres are for the most part closed or asleep — to open them and make them awake and active is one aim of yoga. As they open, the powers and possibilities of the inner being also are aroused in us; we awake first to a larger consciousness and then to a cosmic consciousness; we are no longer little separate personalities with limited lives but centres of a universal action and in direct contact with cosmic forces. Moreover, instead of being unwillingly playthings of the latter, as is the surface person, we can become to a certain extent conscious and masters of the play of nature — how far this goes depending on the development of the inner being and its opening upward to the higher spiritual levels. At the same time the opening of the heart centre releases the psychic being which proceeds to make us aware of the Divine within us and of the higher Truth above us.

For the highest spiritual Self is not even behind our personality and bodily existence but is above it and altogether exceeds it. The highest of the inner centres is in the head, just as the deepest is the heart; but the centre which opens directly to the Self is above the head, altogether outside the physical body, in what is called the subtle body, *sūkṣma śarīra*. This Self has two aspects and the results of realising it correspond to these two aspects. One is static, a condition of wide peace, freedom, silence: the silent Self is unaffected by any action or experience; it impartially supports them but does not seem to originate them at all, rather to stand back detached or unconcerned, *udāsīna*. The other aspect is dynamic and that is experienced as a cosmic Self or Spirit which not only supports but originates and contains the whole cosmic action — not only that part of it which concerns our physical selves but also all that is beyond it — this world and all other worlds, the supraphysical as well as the physical ranges of the universe. Moreover, we feel the Self as one in all; but also we feel it as above all, transcendent, surpassing all

individual birth or cosmic existence. To get into the universal
Self — one in all — is to be liberated from ego; ego either becomes a small instrumental circumstance in the consciousness or
even disappears from our consciousness altogether. That is
the extinction or Nirvana of the ego. To get into the transcendent self above all makes us capable of transcending altogether
even cosmic consciousness and action — it can be the way to that
complete liberation from the world-existence which is called
also extinction, *laya, mokṣa, nirvāṇa.*

It must be noted however that the opening upward does
not necessarily lead to peace, silence and Nirvana only. The
sadhak becomes aware not only of a great, eventually an infinite
peace, silence, wideness above us, above the head as it were and
extending into all physical and supraphysical space, but also he
can become aware of other things — a vast Force in which is
all power, a vast Light in which is all knowledge, a vast Ananda
in which is all bliss and rapture. At first they appear as something essential, indeterminate, absolute, simple, *kevala*: a Nirvana into any of these things seems possible. But we can come
to see too that this Force contains all forces, this Light all lights,
this Ananda all joy and bliss possible. And all this can descend
into us. Any of them and all of them can come down, not peace
alone; only the safest is to bring down first an absolute calm
and peace, for that makes the descent of the rest more secure;
otherwise it may be difficult for the external nature to contain
or bear so much Force, Light, Knowledge or Ananda. All these
things together make what we call the higher spiritual or Divine
Consciousness. The psychic opening through the heart puts us
primarily into connection with the individual Divine, the Divine
in his inner relation with us; it is especially the source of love and
bhakti. This upward opening puts us into direct relation with
the whole Divine and can create in us the divine consciousness
and a new birth or births of the spirit.

When the Peace is established, this higher or Divine Force
from above can descend and work in us. It descends usually
first into the head and liberates the inner mind centres, then
into the heart centre and liberates fully the psychic and emotional
being, then into the navel and other vital centres and liberates

the inner vital, then into the Muladhara and below and liberates the inner physical being. It works at the same time for perfection as well as liberation; it takes up the whole nature part by part and deals with it, rejecting what has to be rejected, sublimating what has to be sublimated, creating what has to be created. It integrates, harmonises, establishes a new rhythm in the nature. It can bring down too a higher and yet higher force and range of the higher nature until, if that be the aim of the sadhana, it becomes possible to bring down the supramental force and existence. All this is prepared, assisted, farthered by the work of the psychic being in the heart centre; the more it is open, in front, active, the quicker, safer, easier the working of the Force can be. The more love and bhakti and surrender grow in the heart, the more rapid and perfect becomes the evolution of the sadhana. For the descent and transformation imply at the same time an increasing contact and union with the Divine.

That is the fundamental rationale of the sadhana. It will be evident that the two most important things here are the opening of the heart centre and the opening of the mind centres to all that is behind and above them. For the heart opens to the psychic being and the mind centres open to the higher consciousness and the nexus between the psychic being and the higher consciousness is the principal means of the siddhi. The first opening is effected by a concentration in the heart, a call to the Divine to manifest within us and through the psychic to take up and lead the whole nature. Aspiration, prayer, bhakti, love, surrender are the main supports of this part of the sadhana — accompanied by a rejection of all that stands in the way of what we aspire for. The second opening is effected by a concentration of the consciousness in the head (afterwards, above it) and an aspiration and call and a sustained will for the descent of the divine Peace, Power, Light, Knowledge, Ananda into the being — the Peace first or the Peace and Force together. Some indeed receive Light first or Ananda first or some sudden pouring down of knowledge. With some there is first an opening which reveals to them a vast infinite Silence, Force, Light or Bliss above them and afterwards either they ascend to that or these things begin to descend into the lower nature. With others there is either the descent, first into the head, then down to the heart level, then to the navel and below and through the whole body, or else an inexplicable opening — without any sense of descent — of peace, light, wideness or power, or else a horizontal opening into the cosmic consciousness or in a suddenly widened mind an outburst of knowledge. Whatever comes has to be welcomed — for there is no absolute rule for all — but if the peace has not come first, care must be taken not to swell oneself in exultation or lose the balance. The capital movement however is when the Divine Force or Shakti, the power of the Mother comes down and takes hold, for then the organization of the consciousness begins and the larger foundation of the yoga.

The result of the concentration is not usually immediate — though to some there comes a swift and sudden outflowering; but with most there is a time longer or shorter of adaptation or preparation, especially if the nature has not been prepared already to some extent by aspiration and Tapasya. The coming of the result can sometimes be aided by associating with the concentration one of the processes of the old yoga. There is the Adwaita process of the way of knowledge — one rejects from oneself the identification with the mind, vital, body, saying continually "I am not the mind", "I am not the vital", "I am not the body", seeing these things as separate from one's real self — and after a time one feels all the mental, vital, physical processes and the very sense of mind, vital, body becoming externalised, an outer action, while within and detached from them there grows the sense of a separate self-existent being which opens into the realisation of the cosmic and transcendent spirit. There is also the method — a very powerful method — of the Sankhyas, the separation of the Purusha and the Prakriti. One enforces on the mind the position of the Witness — all action of mind, vital, physical becomes an outer play which is not myself or mine, but belongs to Nature and has been enforced on an outer me. I am the witness Purusha; I am silent, detached, not bound by any of these things. There grows up in consequence a division in the being; the sadhak feels within him the growth of a calm silent separate consciousness which feels itself quite apart from the surface play of the mind and the vital and physical Nature. Usually when this takes place, it is possible very rapidly to bring down the peace of the higher consciousness and the action of the higher Force and the full march of the yoga. But often the Force itself comes down first in response to the concentration and call and then, if these things are necessary, it does them and uses any other means or process that is helpful or indispensable.

One thing more. In this process of the descent from above and the working it is most important not to rely entirely on oneself, but to rely on the guidance of the Guru and to refer all that happens to his judgment and arbitration and decision. For it often happens that the forces of the lower nature are stimulated and excited by the descent and want to mix with it and turn it to their profit. It often happens too that some Power or Powers undivine in their nature present themselves as the Supreme Lord or as the Divine Mother and claim the being's service and surrender. If these things are accepted, there will be an extremely disastrous consequence. If indeed there is the assent of the sadhak to the Divine working alone and the submission or surrender to that guidance, then all can go smoothly. This assent and a rejection of all egoistic forces or forces that appeal to the ego are the safeguard throughout the sadhana. But the ways of nature are full of snares, the disguises of the ego are innumerable, the illusions of the Powers of Darkness, Rakshasi Maya, are extraordinarily skilful; the reason is an insufficient guide and often turns traitor; vital desire is always with us tempting to follow any alluring call. This is the reason why in this yoga we insist so much on what we call Samarpana — rather inadequately rendered by the English word surrender. If the heart centre is fully opened and the psychic is always in control, then there is no question; all is safe. But the psychic can at any moment be veiled by a lower upsurge. It is only a few who are exempt from these dangers and it is precisely those to whom surrender is easily possible. The guidance of one who himself is by identity or represents the Divine is in this difficult endeavour imperative and indispensable.

What I have written may help you to get some clear idea of what I mean by the central process of the yoga. I have written at some length but, naturally, could cover only the fundamental things. Whatever belongs to circumstance and detail must arise as one works out the method, or rather as it works itself out — for the last is what usually happens when there is an effective beginning of the action of the sadhana.

The descent of Peace, the descent of Force or Power, the descent of Light, the descent of Ananda, these are the four things that transform the nature.

Presence, Peace, Force, Light, Ananda — these are five things that most commonly come down.

Like everything else, Peace, Light, Power, so wideness descends also.

Light, Peace, Force, Ananda constitute the spiritual consciousness; if they are not among the major experiences, what are?

It is not really the plane that descends, it is the Power and Truth of it that descends into the material and then the veil between the material and it no longer exists.

I did not say it [descent of Ananda] was vital and mental, but that it was Ananda manifesting itself in the mental and vital — a quite different thing; for the one Ananda (the true thing) can manifest in any part of the being.

It [the higher consciousness] descends on the atmosphere also, but for it to be effective the individual must receive and respond. It descends also in the individual independently of the atmosphere.

*
**

The consciousness from which these experiences come is always there pressing to bring them in. The reason why they do not come in freely or stay is the activity of the mind and vital always rushing about, thinking this, wanting that, trying to perform mountaineering feats on all the hillocks of the lower nature instead of nourishing a strong and simple aspiration and opening to the higher consciousness that it may come in and do its work. *Rasa* of poetry, painting or physical work is not the thing to go after. What gives the interest in yoga is the *rasa* of the Divine and of the divine consciousness, which means the *rasa* of Peace, of Silence, of inner Light and Bliss, of growing inner Knowledge, of increasing inner Power, of the Divine Love, of all the infinite fields of experience that open to one with the opening of the inner consciousness. The true *rasa* of poetry, painting or any other activity is truly found when these activities are part of the working of the Divine Force in you and you feel it as that and you feel in it the joy of that working.

The condition you had of the inner being and its silence, separated from the surface consciousness and its little restless workings, is the first liberation, the liberation of Purusha from Prakriti and it is the fundamental experience. The day when you can keep it, you can know that the yogic consciousness has been founded in you. This time it has increased in intensity, but it must also increase in duration.

These things do not "drop" — what you have felt is there in you all the time, but you did not feel it because you were living on the surface altogether and the surface is all crowd and clamour. But in all men there is this silent Purusha, base of the true mental being, the true vital being, the true physical being. It was by your prayer and aspiration that the thing came, to show you in what direction you must travel in order to have the true *rasa* of things, for it is only when one is liberated that one can get the real *rasa*. For after this liberation come others and among them the liberation and Ananda in action as well as in the static silence.

If the habit of the ordinary nature is not an obstacle to the descent, then what is the need of sadhana? What prevents the whole higher consciousness from coming down and changing you into a superman in one second? It is because the things of the lower nature offer an obstinate resistance that sadhana is necessary.

The general condition does not mean, in my sentence, the surface condition as known to you. It contains many things in it unknown to you. What comes from above can come when one is in a clear mind or when the vital is disturbed, when one is in meditation or when one is moving about, when one is working or when one is doing nothing. Most often it comes when one is in a clear concentrated state, but it may not, — there is no absolute rule. Moreover, the pull or call may produce no concrete effect and yet there may be an effect when one is no longer actually pulling or calling. All these mental reasons alleged for its coming or going are too rigid — sometimes they apply, very often they don't apply. One has to have faith, confidence, aspiration but one cannot bind down the Force as to when, how and why it will act.

It [the higher consciousness] may not come exactly according to the aspiration, but the aspiration is not ineffective. It keeps the consciousness open, prevents an inert state of acquiescence in all that comes and exercises a sort of pull on the sources of the higher consciousness.

Whenever there is a descent of the higher consciousness in the Adhar:

1. Part of it is stored up in the frontal consciousness and remains there.

2. Part of it goes behind and remains as a support to the active part of the being.

3. Part flows out into the universal Nature.

4. Part is absorbed by the inconscient and lost to the individual consciousness and its action.

The Force descends for two things:

1. To transform the nature.

2. To carry on the work through the instrument.

At first one is not conscious of either working, afterwards one becomes conscious of the Force working but not of how it works. Finally, one becomes conscious entirely and in detail.

One feels the Force only when one is in conscious contact with it.

All these are different actions of the Force on the *ādhāra* with the one intention of opening it up from above and below and horizontally also. The action from above opens it to the descent of forces from above the Mind and the ascent of consciousness above the lid of the ordinary human mind. The horizontal action opens it to the cosmic consciousness on all its levels. The action from below helps to connect the superconscient with the subconscient. Finally the consciousness instead of being limited in the body becomes infinite, rises infinitely above, plunges infinitely below, widens infinitely on every side. There is besides the opening of all the centres to the Light and Power and Ananda that has to descend from above. At present, only the mind centres seem to receive fully the descent of the Force, while the upper vital centres are being prepared with a minor action on other parts of the body. It is a matter of time and perseverance for the way to be entirely open.

It is the universal experience of sadhaks that force or consciousness or Ananda like this first comes from above — or around — and presses on or surrounds the head, then it pierces the skull as it were and fills first the brain and forehead and then the whole head and descends occupying each centre till the whole system is full and replete. Of course there are, or can be, preliminary rushes occupying the whole body for a time or some part of the system most open and least resistant to the influence.

The descent into the body first in the head, then down to the neck and in the chest is the ordinary rule. For many there is a big stop before it gets below the navel owing to some vital resistance. Once it passes that barricade it does not usually take long to come down farther. But there is no rule as to the time taken. In some it comes down like a flood, in others it goes through with a methodical and deliberate increase. I don't think the peace descent is in the habit of waiting for companions — more often it likes at first to be all by itself and then call down its friends with the message, "Come along, I have made the place all ready for you".

If you mean the descent of the higher consciousness, that is felt in the heart region, not only in the centre, just as it is felt in the head. The touching of the head is only a first pressure. Afterwards there is a feeling of a mass of peace, force, light, Ananda or consciousness coming down in the head directly and descending further to the chest and so to the navel through the body. For some it takes weeks or months, in others it descends speedily.

When things come in this order the head opens up first and the heart afterwards — finally all the centres. If you are satisfied only with peace, knowledge and mukti, then perhaps the heart centre may open to that only. But if you want the love, then the descending Power and Light will work for that also.

It is possible that there may have been too much haste in this attempt to open the navel and the lower centre. In this yoga the movement is downward — first the two head centres, then the heart, then the navel and then the two others. If the higher experience is first fully established with its higher consciousness, knowledge and will in the three upper centres, then it is easier to open the three lower ones without too much disturbance.

Yes, it was the same experience. You went inside under the pressure of the Force — which is often though not always the first result — went into a few seconds' samadhi according to the ordinary language. The Force when it descends tries to open the body and pass through the centres. It has to come in (ordinarily) through the crown of the head (Brahmarandhram) and pass through the inner mind centre which is in the middle of the forehead between the eyebrows. That is why it presses first on the head. The opening of the eyes brings one back to the ordinary consciousness of the outer world, that is why the intensity is relieved by opening the eyes.

The experience you had was simply the descent of the Divine Force into the body. By your attitude and aspiration you called for it to work in you, so it came. Such a descent brings naturally a deep inward condition and a silence of the mind, and it may bring much more — peace, a sense of liberation, happiness, Ananda. It is very often attended as in this experience by a light or luminosity. It was felt enveloping the upper part of the body down to the cardiac centre, because it is these centres, the head and heart centres that are first invaded and occupied by whatever descends from above, Consciousness, Force, Light or Ananda. Usually, there is at first a pressure from above on the head, then one feels something entering the higher part of the head and then the whole head is occupied, as you feel now with the "fourmillement" at the time of concentration. Once the head with its mental centres is open and occupied, the Force descends rapidly to the heart centre, unless there is some obstacle or a resistance in the higher vital parts. From there it sends its stream into the whole body and begins to occupy the vital and physical centres — from the navel to the Muladhara. The coming of this experience, occupation of the body, by the Force from above, is a great step forward in the sadhana.

The fear of a syncope was due only to the *saṁskāra* in the mind; it must be dismissed. The Force can very well come down in the full waking consciousness; if it brings a kind of samadhi, it is usually a conscious inner condition — the consciousness taken away from outward things, but in full power within. Even if a trance came, it would be a trance and not a swoon.

The more important of the experiences you enumerate are those below.

1. The feeling of calm and comparative absence of disturbing thoughts. This means the growth of quietude of mind which is necessary for a fully effective meditation.

2. The pressure on the head and the movements within it. The pressure is that of the Force of the higher consciousness above the mind pressing on the mind (the mind centres are in the head and throat) and penetrating into it. Once it enters there it prepares the mind for opening to it more fully and the

movements within the head are due to this working. Once the head centres and spaces are open one feels it descending freely as a current or otherwise. Afterwards it opens similarly the centres below in the body. The physical movement of the head must be due to the body not being accustomed to the pressure and penetration of the Force. When it is able to receive and assimilate, these movements no longer take place.

3. The effect of the meditation in the heart extending itself to the head and creating movements there is normal — in whatever centre the concentration takes place the yoga force generated extends to the others and produces concentration or workings there.

4. The sudden cessation of thought and all movements — this is very important, as it means the beginning of the capacity for the inner silence. It lasts only for a short while at the beginning of its manifestation but increases afterwards its hold and duration.

The direction of the sadhana is the right one and you have only to continue upon it.

We cannot say anything definitively about the outside affairs — I suppose in the circumstances you have to think about these things, but the sadhana has the greater importance.

We do not include Hathayoga practices in this sadhana. If you use only for health purposes, it must be as something separate from sadhana — on your own choice.

An entire silence and inactivity of the mind cannot come at first — what is possible is a quietude of the mind, that is to say, a cessation of its absorption in its restless miscellaneous activity of ill-connected or unconnected thoughts and a concentration on the object of the sadhana. The imagination which the Mother recommended to you was a means of such concentration. A mental idea of the omnipresence such as comes to you is a good help for that also, especially if it brings the strong faith and reliance. The feeling of the vibration of the Mother's Force around the head is more than a mental idea or even a mental realisation, it is an experience. This vibration is indeed the action of the Mother's Force which is first felt above the head or around it, then afterwards within the head. The pressure means that it is working to open the mind and its centres so that it may enter. The mind centres are in the head, one at the top and above it, another between the eyes, a third in the throat. That is why you feel the vibration around the head and sometimes up to the neck, but not below. It is so usually, for it is only after enveloping and entering the mind that it goes below to the emotional and vital parts (heart, navel etc.) — though sometimes it is more enveloping before it enters the body.... To see the light in the heart one has to go deep, but one can see light elsewhere without going in deep there. Light is often seen between the eyebrows first, or in front or at that level for there is the centre of inner vision and a slight opening of it is sufficient for that — so also light is often seen round the head or above it, outside.

The pressure from within upon the forehead centre begins very often after the pressure from above on the forehead — something of the Force has come in sufficiently to exercise this second pressure. That on the back must be a direct pressure on the psychic region (if it is in or near the middle of the back) meant to prepare the action in the heart. When the centres begin to open, inner experiences such as the seeing of light or images through the subtle vision in the forehead centre or psychic experiences and perceptions in the heart, become frequent — gradually one becomes aware of one's inner being as separate from the outer, and what can be called a yogic consciousness with all its deeper movements develops in the place of the ordinary superficial mental and vital movements.

It is good that you felt the peace within and the movement in the heart. That shows the force is working not only from above but inside you, and this promises a farther progress. The full opening will come in time — the important thing is that you are on the right way and advancing more quickly than you realise.

It is what we call the pressure of the Force (the Force of the higher spiritual or divine consciousness, the Mother's Force); it comes in various forms, vibrations, currents, waves, a wide flow, a shower like rain etc. It passes to each centre in turn, the crown of the head, the forehead centre, throat, heart, navel centres down to the Muladhara and spreads too throughout the body. The rotatory movement is the movement of the Force when it is working and forming something in the being.

Whatever comes from above can come like that in waves — whether it is Light or Force or Peace or Ananda. In your case it was the Force working on the mind in waves. It is true also that when it was like that, not in currents or as a rain or as a quiet flood, it is Mahakali's Force that is working. The first necessity when it is so, is not to fear.

The stream which you feel coming down on the head and pouring into you is indeed a current of the Mother's force; it is so that it is often felt; it flows into the body in currents and works there to liberate and change the consciousness. As the consciousness changes and develops, you will begin yourself to understand the meaning and working of these things.

Vibrations are either of a Force or a Presence.

Pressure, throbbing, electrical vibrations are all signs of the working of the Force. The places indicate the field of action — the top of the head is the summit of the thinking mind where it communicates with the higher consciousness; the neck or throat is the seat of the physical, externalising or expressive mind; the ear is the place of communication with the inner mind-centre by which thoughts etc. enter into the personal being from the general Nature. The sternum at the point indicated holds the psychic and emotional centre, with its apex on the spinal column behind.

It [the current like electricity] is the flowing of the force through the spine. In the Tantric system the spine is considered as the natural passage of the Force, because it is in the spine that all the six centres rest.

Electricity shock always indicates a passage of dynamic Force.

I am glad to hear that these experiences are coming — they are a sign of rapid progress coming. The descent as of a drizzling rain is a very characteristic and well-known way of descent of the higher consciousness; it brings peace but it also brings all other possibilities of the higher consciousness too and, as you felt, the seeds of transformation of the physical consciousness — by the coming in it of the seeds of the powers and qualities of the higher Nature.

I am very glad that the experience we have been working to bring to you has come with such force and is increasing. It is the concrete descent of the higher consciousness, which once it settles marks always a definite turning-point in the sadhana. Even if it does not settle with a full stability at once, yet when it has once come with so much strength, there cannot be the least doubt that it will come more and more till it has done its work and is your permanent consciousness. The shower and drizzle, the hold above the head and in the heart, the envelopment, the flaming of Agni within, the sense of firmness and solidity, the Peace and security and devotion, the sense of the Mother's hold are all signs of the descent — eventually it will penetrate everywhere and become something solid and stable occupying the whole consciousness and body.

A sound does sometimes come with a particular descent of the consciousness or force from above.

Your experience while going to the lawyers was an opening to the Force from above which, if sudden, is often attended by this kind of loud sound and the sensation of the opening of the head — it is in the subtle body that this opening of the head takes place though the sensation is felt as if physical. The Force came down and went up presided over by the Mother's forms of Mahalakshmi and Mahasaraswati and made the movement of ascent and descent (here in the spinal column which is the main channel of the yogic force passing through the centres) which helps to join the higher with the lower consciousness. As a result came the feeling of identity with myself in your body. The cough shows probably some difficulty against concentration in the physical mind. The best is not to force concentration, but to remain quiet and call and let things work out themselves through the force of the Mother.

That is some obstacle in the mind breaking under the pressure of Force, and each time there is a flash and a movement of the Force.

*
**

If it is a feeling of a covering being perforated, then that is a sensation one often has when the Force is opening a way for itself through some resistance — here it must be in some part of the physical mind.

Keep full reliance on the Mother. When one does that, the victory even if delayed, is sure.

*
**

When there is a pressure of the Force on the Adhar to work on it or enter, this [heaviness in the centre of the head] is often felt, especially if there is a working of the Force in the head. This heaviness disappears if the system receives and assimilates the Force and there is a free flow in the body — till then the pressure or some kind of heaviness is often felt at one centre or another where the Force is working.

*
**

A heaviness which gives strength is likely to be the indication of a descent. Sensations like a biting or pricking in the head often accompany it. It is usually a sign of some force from above trying to make its way through or to work in the physical stuff so as to prepare it for receiving.

The control over the thoughts and the power of seeing the image of the Mother and Sri Aurobindo in the head are a very good beginning. The heat in the head is not fever, but the result of the action of the Force in the mental centres working to overcome the mental resistance which there always is in the human mind — heaviness sometimes comes as a result of the pressure of the Force — it passes away of itself usually when the mind receives freely the Force.

It [the feeling of swelling of the head] was a very usual experience of feeling of enlargement in the head of the subtle body.

*
**

The sensations you describe in the crown of the head and the upper part of the forehead are such as one often gets when the higher consciousness or Force is trying to make an open passage through the mind for itself. So it is possibly that that is happening. As for the uneasiness or feebleness there when you talk loudly etc., that also happens at such times. It is because the concentration of energy which is necessary for the inner work is broken and the energies thrown out, exhausting the parts by two inconsistent pullings. It is better when any working is going on inside to be very quiet in speech and as sparing as possible. At other times it does not so much matter.

There are sensations that are due to descent and not troublesome or dangerous at all, there are others that are physical. But the description is necessary in order to distinguish.

What you saw was indeed a sun, — the sun of blue light which is the light of a higher mind than the ordinary human mind. The sun is the symbol of Light and Truth. This higher spiritual Mind is trying to wake in you, but at the beginning there is always a difficulty because the consciousness is not habituated to receive, so there is the sense of pressure deepening sometimes into a feeling of headache or this feeling of the head preparing to split. It is nothing but a sensation in the physical created by the inner mind (this part of the head is the seat of the inner mind) trying to open under the touch from above.

Your dream was not a sign of the worldly desire in you, but only a test or ordeal dream such as you have had before. Your absence of response in the dream shows that you have no such inclination towards these things as many have. The whole was only a formation or suggestion of outer forces on the vital plane to see what kind of response, if any, your consciousness would make.

The action of the Force does not always create pressure. When it does not need to press it acts quietly.

There is no necessity of feeling pressure. One feels force when something is being done or the force is flowing on or if it is there manifest in the body — but not when what is manifesting is peace and silence.

One can be receptive without being conscious — without knowing exactly what is given.

The quiet flow is necessary for permeating the lower parts. The big descents open the way and bring constant reinforcement and the culminating force at the end — but the quiet flow is also needed.

Some have this swaying of the body when the Peace or the Force begins to descend upon it, as it facilitates for it the reception. The swaying ceases usually when the body is accustomed to assimilate the descent.

The Peace comes fully at the meditation time because the Mother's concentration at that time brings down the power of the higher consciousness and one can receive it if one is able to do so. Once it begins to come, it usually increases its force along with the receptivity of the sadhak until it can come at all times and under all conditions and stay longer and longer till it is stable. The sadhak on his side has to keep his consciousness as quiet and still as possible to receive it. The Peace, Power, Light, Ananda of the higher spiritual consciousness are there in all veiled above. A certain opening upwards is needed for it to descend — the quietude of the mind and a certain wide concentrated passivity to the descending Influence are the best conditions for the descent.

That [shaking of the body] sometimes happens when the force is coming down. It must be allowed to pass off as the body becomes more quiet and assimilative.

If the pressure is too great, the remedy is to widen the consciousness. With the peace and silence there should come a wideness that can receive any amount of Force without any reactions, whether heaviness or compulsion to remain withdrawn or the difficulty of the eyes.

Probably the accumulated Force became more than the physical being could receive. When that happens the right thing to do is to widen oneself (one can do it by a little practice). If the consciousness is in a state of wideness then it can receive any amount of force without inconvenience.

There are always pauses of preparation and assimilation between two movements.

To remain quiet for a time after the descent of Force is the best way of assimilating it.

There may be empty silence and peace satisfied with themselves. Reception is a separate power. Of course, all quietude of the mind makes good conditions for the receptivity to act.

*
**

As regards your own sadhana and those of others... I think it necessary to make two or three observations. First, I have for some time had the impression that there is a too constant activity and pressure for rapidity of progress and a multitude of experiences. These things are all right in themselves, but there must be certain safeguards. First there should be sufficient periods of rest and silence, even of relaxation, in which there can be a quiet assimilation. Assimilation is very important and periods necessary for it should not be regarded with impatience as stoppages of the yoga. Care should be taken to make calm and quiet strength and inner silence the basic condition for all activity. There should be no excessive strain; any fatigue, disturbance, or inordinate sensitiveness of the nervous and physical parts, of which you mention certain symptoms in your letters, should be quieted and removed, as they are often signs of overstrain or too great an activity or rapidity in the yoga. It must also be remembered that experiences are only valuable as indications and openings and the main thing always is the steady harmonious and increasingly organised opening and change of the different parts of the consciousness and the being.

Physical fatigue like this in the course of the sadhana may come from various reasons:

1. It may come from receiving more than the physical is ready to assimilate. The cure is then quiet rest in conscious immobility receiving the forces but not for any other purpose than the recuperation of the strength and energy.

2. It may be due to the passivity taking the form of inertia — inertia brings the consciousness down towards the ordinary physical level which is soon fatigued and prone to *tamas*. The cure here is to get back into the true consciousness and to rest there, not in inertia.

3. It may be due to mere overstrain of the body — not giving it enough sleep or repose. The body is the support of the yoga, but its energy is not inexhaustible and needs to be husbanded; it can be kept up by drawing on the universal vital Force but that reinforcement too has its limits. A certain moderation is needed even in the eagerness for progress — moderation, not indifference or indolence.

*
**

Yes, the ordinary physical consciousness is not able to hold the contact and it does get tired — also it cannot assimilate much at a time. But it is not always the Divine who takes away the pressure; the lower consciousness itself loses it or gives it up.

*
**

Yes — the system has to take rest so as to assimilate and renew its receptive power.

*
**

When one is assimilating, one is not receiving.

*
**

It is quite usual to have such periods in the day. The consciousness needs time for rest and assimilation, it cannot be at the same pitch of intensity at all times. During the assimilation a calm quietude is the proper condition.

*
**

Passivity must not lead to inactivity — otherwise it will encourage inertia in the being. It is only an inner passivity to what comes from above that is needed — inert passivity is the wrong kind of passivity.

*
**

One can assimilate in sleep also. Remaining awake like that is not good, as in the end it strains the nerves and the system receives wrongly in an excited way or else gets too tired to receive.

There is always a gain or progress at some point after these periods of assimilation if one takes them rightly — however dull or troublesome they may be.

This sort of giddiness and weakness and disturbance ought not to take place. When it comes it shows that more Force is being pulled down than is assimilated by the body. At such times you ought to rest till this disturbance has passed and there is a proper balance.

I mean that you need not pull it [the Force] down, but you should aid its entry by your full aspiration and assent.

If one brings down more Force or Light than some part of the being is ready for and that part resists or if there is a struggle between descending and adverse forces in the body, then these things [burning sensation in the body etc.] can take place.

*
**

An uneasiness of that kind is always due to a resistance some-where — something that remains closed and does not open when it is touched by the Force. It is due probably not so much to yourself as to other conflicting influences that are acting upon you.

*
**

The feeling of resistance may be the result of the effort at response. When there is the free flow there is neither effort nor resistance.

Headaches "produced by a pressure from above", as you put it, are not due to the pressure or produced by it, but produced by a resistance.

The pressure does not "bring" a resistance. "If there were no resistance there would be no headache" is the proper knowledge, not the reverse. So long as you think that it is the pressure that brings the resistance, the very idea will create the resistance. X's case is not an example either of headache due to resistance or of headache due to pressure — it is due to ordinary physical and psychological causes.

No, to make people ill in order to improve or perfect them is not Mother's method. But sometimes things like headache come because the brain either tried too much or does not want to receive or makes difficulties. But the yogic headaches are of a special kind and after the brain has found out the way to receive or respond they don't come at all.

The first condition of progress in sadhana is not to fear, to have trust and keep quiet during an experience. What happened was simply that the Force came down and tried to quiet the mind and hold the body still so that it might work. If you had not feared, that would have happened. But your terror made the mind and body resist and get the impression that they were being tortured or in danger. The feeling of the tough body and great force like a hand upon it is quite usual in this kind of experience and does not terrify the sadhak, but brings a great joy and release. In future you must try to be quiet and not have any fear or imagination of danger. Naturally when you thought that you could not bear it, the Force withdrew as you are not ready to receive.

The periods of assimilation continue really till all that has to be done is fundamentally done. Only they have a different character in the later stages of sadhana. If they cease altogether at an early stage (you are still in a very early stage), it is because all that the nature was capable of has been done and that would mean it was not capable of much.

What I have written is perfectly clear. The periods of assimilation continue till all that has to be done is fundamentally done. If they stop early, it means that all has been done that could be done and nothing more is possible, the later and more advanced developments of the sadhana are not possible, — if they were, the assimilation periods would continue until all was developed and not cease. The only reason for such a premature end of the sadhana would be that the sadhak is not capable of going farther.

The only change in the assimilation periods afterwards is that certain things remain settled while the assimilation applies to others that are not yet settled in the system, e.g., one feels always a constant peace in the inner being, but disturbances go on on the surface, till the surface also has assimilated peace. Or perhaps peace is settled everywhere and always there but knowledge comes and goes or strength comes and goes. Or all these are there but Ananda comes and goes etc., etc.

If the peace once becomes stable, there is no farther assimilation needed for that, as that means the whole system is sufficiently prepared to receive and absorb continuously. There may be periods of assimilation necessary for other things, but these periods need not interrupt the inner status. For instance if Force or Ananda or Knowledge begin to descend from above, there might be interruptions and probably would be, the system not being able to absorb in continuous flow, but the peace would remain in the inner being. Or there might even be something like periods of struggle on the surface, but the inner being would remain calm and still watching and undisturbed and, if there is knowledge established within, understanding the action. Only for that the whole being vital, physical, material must have become open and receptive to the peace. Peace would then go on perhaps deepening and becoming wider and wider, but periods of interruption and assimilation would not be needed.

Yes. This feeling of being able to break a stone with the hand or for that matter break the world without anything at all except the force itself is one that comes especially when the mind and vital have not assimilated the Power. It is the feeling of something extraordinary to them and omnipotent; the idea of breaking or crushing is suggested by the rajas in the vital. Afterwards when quietly assimilated this sensation disappears and only the feeling of calm strength and immovable firmness remains.

Yes, when things begin to descend, they must come down on a solid basis. That is why it is necessary to have peace as the first descent and that it should become as strong and solid as possible. But in any case to contain is the first necessity — then more and more can come and settle itself. Once these two things are settled — peace and strength, one can bear any amount of everything else, Ananda, Knowledge or, whatever it may be.

The Peace, Purity and Calm of the Self must be fixed — otherwise the active Descent may find the forces it awakes swayed on by lower Powers and a confusion created. That has happened to many.

It is not a matter of any particular act or feeling, but a sort of excited vibration with which the vital and physical consciousness meets the vital disturbance — it is evident in the tone and language of what you write when there is the stress of vital suggestion — but it used also to rise when you got the experiences in excited vibration and bubbling of joy which would easily lapse into some rajasic movement or be replaced by the opposite excitement of suffering and disturbance. Quiet, quiet and more quiet, calm strength, calm gladness are what are needed in mind and nerves and body as a basis for the siddhi — precisely because the Force, the Light, the Ananda that come down are extremely intense and need a great stillness in the body to bear and support.

By enforcing the peace of the higher being in the lower parts down to the physical it becomes possible to (1) create that separateness which would prevent the inner being from being affected by the superficial disturbance and resistance, and (2) make it easier for the Force and other powers of the higher being to descend.

When one has gone so far that peace from above can descend, that is a considerable progress.

It is good — the strength is the next thing that has to come down after the peace and join with it. Eventually the two become one.

Peace and movement on the basis of peace are the first aspect of the One to establish themselves. Bliss and light do not fix so easily or so early — they have to grow.

In what may be called the first silence, it is like that — silence alone with no emotion or other inner activity. When it deepens one can feel the Nirvana of the Buddhists or the *ātmabodha* of the Vedantins. Both force and bliss or either can descend into the silence, filling it with calm Tapas or silent Ananda.

There are two conditions, one of Ananda, another of great calm and equality in which there is no joy or grief. If one attains the latter, afterwards a greater more permanent Ananda becomes possible.

Ananda comes afterwards — even if it comes at the beginning it is not usually constant. Wideness does not come because the consciousness is not yet free from the body. Probably when what is felt above the head comes down, it will be liberated into the wideness.

Who told you that whenever there was silence or genuine silence, knowledge would come down? The silence is a fit vessel for anything from above, but it does not follow that when there is silence, everything is bound to come down automatically.

There is no rule, but the most normal course is for a certain Peace and Force and Light which is above the mind to descend and as the result of its workings the cosmic consciousness opens and in it higher and higher levels above mind. Many people get an opening into the cosmic consciousness first but without the basis of the higher Peace and Light it brings only a mass of unorganised experiences.

The coming of the peace makes it easier to get the experience of the pure and free Self.

It must have been the descent of the higher silence, the silence of the Self or Atman. In this silence one perceives, but the mind is not active, — things are sensed, but without any responsive connection or vibration. The silent Self is there as a separate reality, not bound or involved in the activity of Nature, aloof, detached and self-existent. Even if thoughts come across this silence, they do not disturb it; the Self is separate from the thinking mind also. In this connection the feeling "I think" is a survival from the old consciousness; in the full silence what one feels is "thought occurs in me" — the identification with thoughts as well as with the perception of objects ceases.

The experience you have is the experience of the true Self, untouched by grief and joy, desire, anxiety or trouble; vast and calm and full of peace, it observes the agitations of the outer being as one might the play of children. It is indeed the divine element in you. The more you can remain in that, the firmer will be the foundation of the sadhana. In this Self will come all the higher experiences, oneness with the Divine, light, knowledge, strength, Ananda, the play of the Mother's higher forces. It does not always become stable from the first, though for some it does; but the experience comes more and more frequently and lasts more till it is no longer covered by the ordinary nature.

There is no distinction between the Self and the spirit. The psychic is the soul that develops in the evolution — the spirit is the Self that is not affected by the evolution, it is above it — only it is covered or concealed by the activity of mind, vital and the body. The removal of this covering is the release of the spirit — and it is removed when there is a full and wide spiritual silence.

When one becomes aware of the Self calm, silent, wide, universal, it is no longer covered over by the ignorance, when one identifies with the Self and not with the mind, life and body and their movements or with their small ego, that is the release of the Self.

The experience you feel is that of the Atman, the cosmic Self supporting the cosmic consciousness — not yet clear but in its first impression. When the consciousness goes down from that condition, it brings something of it into the vital and physical consciousness and the result is either that these parts or at least the vital open and get into touch with what has been brought down. The inert *tāmasikatā* or the unease in the legs comes because the physical is not able to receive or assimilate. This will disappear when that part opens and receives and is able to assimilate.

It was there the occasional descent of the Force to establish a connection — here the descent is taking another form intended to establish the fundamental experiences of the Realisation.

What is trying to come down in you is the silence and peace of the Self — when that comes fully, then there is no ego-perception, it is drowned in the wideness of the silence and peace of the Self. But this realisation is at first in the static condition of the Self only — in the dynamic movements the ego may still be there owing to past habits — but each time the ego-movement is abandoned, the sense of the loss of ego becomes deeper and more complete. It is perhaps some impression of what is trying to come that has touched you.

Yes, the sense of individuality can disappear altogether when all is peace and wideness. One feels that the peace and wideness are oneself, but not in an individual sense — for it is the "Atman" of everybody else also. Afterwards there can come an experience of another kind of I, but it is a universalised I which contains everybody else and is in unison with everybody else and is itself contained in the Divine. This is what yogins sometimes call the "large" as opposed to the small Aham. I have written of it as the true Person.

If the workings are really those of the higher consciousness or if these predominate the ego fades out — but there is also often a wideness of opening to the universal mental, vital, physical existence and, if the sadhak responds more to this than to the higher consciousness, then he does not get free. Sometimes even the ego gets aggrandised. But if the psychic is awake, then there is not this danger; one finds one's true being in place of the ego.

The peace that descends from above can stop the lower action if it settles in all the being. But that is not sufficient if one wants to develop the dynamic side of the being also on the lines of yoga.

That is to say, the power is still working on the physical consciousness (the mechanical mind and the subconscient) to bring stillness there. Sometimes the stillness comes but not complete, sometimes the mechanical mind reasserts itself. This oscillation usually takes place in a movement of the kind. Even if there is a sudden or rapid transforming shock or downrush, there has to be some working out of this kind afterwards — that at least has always been my experience. For most, however, there comes, first, this slow preparatory process.

*
**

If there is a strong activity of the higher parts of the consciousness, the possibility of the mechanical mind working is very much diminished. It may come up in moments of relaxation or fatigue but usually it is active only in a subordinate way that does not attract notice.

*
**

Your description of the solid cool block of peace pressing on the body and making it immobile makes it certain that it is what we call in this yoga the descent of the higher consciousness. A deep, intense or massive substance of peace and stillness is very commonly the first of its powers that descends and many experience it in that way. At first it comes and stays only during meditation or, without the sense of physical inertness or immobility, a little while longer and afterwards is lost; but if the sadhana follows its normal course, it comes more and more, lasting longer and in the end as an enduring deep peace and inner stillness and release becomes a normal character of the consciousness, the foundation indeed of a new consciousness, calm and liberated.

Your idea of psychic is certainly a mental construction which should be avoided. The psychic has indeed the quality of peace — but that is not its main character as it is of the Self or Atman. The psychic is the divine element in the individual being and its characteristic power is to turn everything towards the Divine, to bring a fire of purification, aspiration, devotion, true light of discernment, feeling, will, an action which transforms by degrees the whole nature. Quietude, peace and silence in the heart and therefore in the vital part of the being are necessary to reach the psychic, to plunge in it, for the perturbations of the vital nature, desire, emotion turned ego-wards or world-wards are the main part of the screen that hides the soul from the nature. It is better, therefore, to be free from the mental constructions when you take the plunge and to have only the sense of aspiration, of devotion, of self-giving to the Divine.

It is the silence and calm of the higher consciousness pressing down into the body. When it comes down fully then there is the "still statue" feeling at first. Afterwards the calm or silence become free and normal.

I presume that [feeling peace very concretely in the lobes of the brain] would mean that the peace had become or was becoming very material and solid and physically tangible — "peace in the cells". Everything is a "substance" — even peace, consciousness, Ananda, — only there are different orders of substance.

Yes, surely the peace can come into the outer consciousness also; it is meant to do so. It is perfectly possible for the body to bear the peace and stillness. It is more difficult for it to bear the full play of the Force; but if the peace is first established in it, then there is no difficulty of that kind.

Peace can be brought down into the physical — to its very cells. It is the active transformation of the physical that cannot be *completely* done without the supramental descent.

After the body is accustomed to the peace, the peace itself can become dynamic.

A sensation of coolness indicates usually some touch or descent of peace. It is felt as very cold by the human vital because the latter is always in a fever of restlessness.

The coolness is a very common experience, but the cool smell is unusual. Sometimes people get a fragrance but without this close connection — perhaps they do not observe closely.

If the coolness passed into dullness, it may well have been only physical. But perhaps there was an inflow, only afterwards came a reaction of the lower inertia which is the physical Nature's characteristic retort to peace and quietude. When the inertia comes up the old movements which the subconscient is prepared to supply always can mechanically come up with it. In a certain sense this inertia and the peace are the bright and dark counterparts of each other, tamas and *śama* — the higher Nature finding repose in peace, the lower seeking it in a relaxation of energy and a return towards the subconscient, tamas.

Silence need not bring lassitude; there is all possible strength in silence. But it is possible that in your trend towards silence there is a tendency to draw back the energy from the body consciousness. That would bring physical inertia.

Exactly. "The body felt fatigue" — that is what I mean by the habit of tamas. The body cannot bear the continuous experience, it feels it as a strain. That is the case with most sadhaks. But in your case the obstacle seems to develop a great intensity when it comes. I have already told you the means of getting rid of it, but it cannot be done in a day because it is a fixed habit of the nature and a fixed habit takes time to remove. But it can be done in not too long a time provided you don't get disturbed when it comes and deal with it firmly and steadily.

When the mental will acquiesces in the inertia, becomes passive to it, as we say — then one remains in the passive condition and there is no push against it until it of itself passes away. If the mental will or even the vital will or some dynamic part of the nature remains untouched and can react, then there is an effort to throw it off which may shorten the interim period.

There is no connection between the descent of Peace and depression. Inertia there may be if the physical being feels the pressure for quietude but turns it into mere inactivity — but that cannot be called exactly a descent — at least not a complete one, since the physical does not share in it.

There is very often a complaint of this kind [weakening of memory] made during the course of sadhana. I suppose that the usual action of memory is for a time suspended by the mental silence or else by the physical tamas.

By the change of consciousness there can be a more conscious and perfect functioning of the memory replacing the old mechanism.

When the inner being once thoroughly establishes its separateness, even oceans of inertia cannot prevent it from keeping it. It is the first thing to be done in order to have a secure basis in the yoga, to establish thoroughly this separateness. It comes most usually when the peace is thoroughly fixed in the inner parts, then the separateness also becomes fixed and permanent.

If the inner being is safe, then there is no longer any struggle or overpowering by inertia or depression or other fundamental difficulties. The rest can be done progressively and quietly, including the coming down of the Force. The outer being becomes merely a machinery or an instrumentation to be set right. It is not so easy to be entirely *mukta* in the inner being.

Tamas is to be transformed into *śama*, the peace and rest of the higher Prakriti, and then filled with *tapas* and *jyoti*. But this can only be done completely in the physical when the physical is finally transformed by the supramental Power.

You cannot drive out rajas and tamas, you can only convert them and give the predominance to sattwa. Tamas and rajas disappear only when the higher consciousness not only comes down but controls everything down to the cells of the body. They then change into the divine rest and peace and the divine energy or Tapas, — finally sattwa also changes into the divine Light. As for remaining quiet when tamas is there, there can also be a tamasic quiet.

The three Gunas become purified and refined and changed into their divine equivalents: *sattva* becomes *jyoti*, the authentic spiritual light; *rajas* becomes *tapas*, the tranquilly intense divine force; *tamas* becomes *śama*, the divine quiet, rest, peace.

What you say is correct. All undesirable things are a mistranslation in the Ignorance of something that on a higher plane is or might be desirable. Inertia, tamas, is the mistranslation of the divine Shama, rest, quietude, peace; pain is a mistranslation of Ananda, lust of love etc. It is only when the lower perversions are got rid of that the higher things in their truth can reign.

Each defect of the nature of the Ignorance is a deformation of something in the higher nature — a deformation which amounts to a perversion even. It is a symbolic perception of this that you got in your experience.

I don't think it is correct myself. It is supposed that when the three qualities [sattwa, rajas and tamas] are not in an equalised condition, when there is a diversity and movement of variation, then creation is active — otherwise all becomes quiescent original Prakriti. It is doubtful if it is actually so.

The experiences you relate mark a great progress — the passage from the perception of the ascending Force to that of the descending Shakti. For the spiral coils of Light you saw and whose effects you felt — the merging in silence and peace, the peace of the Atman or the Brahman consciousness — are usually a first effect, they are visual forms of the dynamic descent of the Divine Force from above; also the passage from the realisation of the static Brahman with the sense of the unreality of the world-existence to the realisation of the status of the dynamic one. This is a considerable step in the integral yoga.

The Brahman consciousness is sometimes described as a static one, but it has two aspects, static and dynamic, and it is when both are united that it becomes integral. This is the greater consciousness I speak of in the sentence quoted by you, greater than either that which perceives the Brahmic silence and immobility alone or that which perceives the cosmic existence and action alone.

By Force I mean not mental or vital energy but the Divine Force from above — as peace comes from above and wideness also, so does this Force (Shakti). Nothing, not even thinking or meditating can be done without some action of Force. The Force I speak of is a Force for illumination, transformation, purification, all that has to be done in the yoga, for removal of hostile forces and the wrong movements — it is also of course for external work, whether great or small in appearance does not matter — if that is part of the Divine Will. I do not mean any personal force egoistic or rajasic.

Power means strength and force, Shakti, which enables one to face all that can happen and to stand and overcome, also to carry out what the Divine Will proposes. It can include many things, power over men, events, circumstances, means etc. But all this not of the mental or vital kind, but by an action through unity of consciousness with the Divine and with all things and beings. It is not an individual strength depending on certain personal capacities, but the Divine Power using the individual as an instrument. It has no special relation to occult siddhis.

What is meant by one's own force? All force is cosmic and the individual is merely an instrument — a certain amount of the force may be stored in him, but that does not make it his own.

There are certain possibilities in the way of the experience. First there is the faith, or sometimes a mental realisation and this of itself is enough to make one open to the Mother's force so that it is always available at need or call. Even if one does not feel the Force coming, yet the results are there and visible. The next is when one feels oneself like an instrument and is aware of the Energy using it. A third is the contact with the Power above and its descent (spontaneous or at call) into the body — this is the more concrete way of having it, for one physically feels the Force working in one. Finally there is a state of consciousness of close contact with the Mother (inward) which brings a similar result.

Force is the essential Shakti; Energy is the working drive of the Force, its active dynamism; Power is the capacity born of the Force; Strength is energy consolidated and stored in the Adhar.

A passive Force has no meaning — Force is always dynamic. Only a Force can act on a basis of calm passivity just as in the material world the Force acts on the basis of inertia.

There is a force behind each action acting in a manner appropriate to that action. It takes all these many forms for the necessity of the working, but it is one Force.

I have never classified the different forms of Force; they can be hundreds or thousands in number. Force uses its form according to the work it has to do.

The knowledge comes from above like the light and peace and everything else.

As the consciousness progresses, it comes from a higher and higher level. First it is the higher illumined mind that predominates, then the intuitive, next the overmind, lastly the supermind; but the whole consciousness has to be sufficiently transformed before the supramental Knowledge can begin to come.

There are special forces of the Light and there is a play of them according to needs but the Light in itself can be lived in as much as one can live in Peace or Ananda.

As Peace and Ananda can pour through the whole system and finally stabilise themselves so that they are in the body, and the body and the whole being are in them — one might almost say, are that, are the Peace and Ananda — so it can be with Light. It can pour into the body, make every cell luminous, fix itself and surround on all sides in one luminous mass of Light.

It is not balls or flashes of light, but a flow or sea of Light entering into the body and surrounding it and illumining the whole field of consciousness. There can also be a vivid sense of Light and illumination without the vision. It can be seen or felt usually as an intense white or diamond or golden Light or something like sunlight or, for many, a blue or bluish white light.

Light or rays of light are always light of the higher consciousness working in the being to illumine or to purify or to awaken the consciousness or attune it to the Truth.

It depends upon the colour of the Light. In any case it is the

Light of Force from above. All lights are indications of a Force or Power. It is the work of the Lights and the Forces they represent to act in their descent on the lower nature and change it.

It is not necessary or possible to define. Light is light just like the light you see, only subtle — it clarifies the consciousness and works as a force and makes knowledge possible.

It [the Divine Light] has no function — it is just Light of Divine Consciousness. If you mean the result, it is supposed to illumine, to remove darkness and obscurity, to make the nature fit for true consciousness, Knowledge etc.

It [Light] is the power that enlightens whatever it falls upon — the result may be vision, memory, knowledge, right will, right impulse etc.

(1) The lid of the skull opening means that the mental being has opened to the Divine Light, and the flames indicate aspiration filled with the Light arising to join the mental part to what is above Mind.

(2) The Divine Light from above is of various colours. White is the divine Power of purity, blue the light of the spiritual consciousness, gold the hue of the supramental knowledge or of knowledge from the intermediate planes.

(3) OM (golden) rising to the sky means the cosmic consciousness supramentalised and rising towards the transcendent Consciousness.

(1) and (2) indicate either something that is happening at present or a potentiality that is trying to materialise. (3) symbolises

the process of the yoga which will be followed if this potentiality is realised and pursued to its natural goal.

The fire is the divine fire of aspiration and inner tapasya. When the fire descends again and again with increasing force and magnitude into the darkness of human ignorance, it at first seems swallowed up and absorbed in the darkness, but more and more of the descent changes the darkness into light, the ignorance and unconsciousness of the human mind into spiritual consciousness.

It is good. The Power above the head is of course the Mother's — it is the power of the Higher Consciousness which is preparing its way of descent. This Higher Consciousness carrying in it a sense of wide and boundless existence, light, power, peace, Ananda etc. is always there above the head and when something of the spiritual Force comes down to work upon the nature, it is from there that it comes. But nothing like the full descent of the peace, bliss etc. can come so long as the being is not ready. Very usually the first preparation is to work on the mind and vital and physical nature in such a way that the soul, the psychic being can have a chance of manifesting itself and influencing the rest of the nature; for that purpose all the main darknesses in the mind and vital have to be combated and thrown out and the physical also prepared in a material way so that the descent may be possible. This is what has been done so long in you. It has to be made stronger and more complete, — but sufficient has been done for it to be possible to prepare the descent of the higher consciousness. There are two things that take place; an ascent of one's consciousness to the higher levels in and above the head, and a descent of the higher consciousness which is above into one's mind, vital and body. How it is done or by what stages or how long it will take varies with each person. But this new consciousness is very different from the ordinary one and many things happen in its coming which would not happen to the mind and might seem strange to it — e.g. the dissolution of the ego and the opening into a wider self or spirit not limited by the body, to which the body is only a small instrument and nothing more. One must therefore dismiss all fear of new things and accept with calm and confidence each field of new experience, relying on the Divine Mother Force for guidance and support and protection throughout the change.

A word about your sadhana. It seems to me that the key to your future development is contained in the experience which you say you often attained for a few days at K. "A state which was full of knowledge, calm serenity, strength and wide consciousness — all questions automatically solved — a continuous stream of power passed into the body through the forehead centre — extremely powerful, having undisturbed *samatā*, calm conviction, keen sight and knowledge." This was the consciousness of the true Purusha in you aware of his own supramental being and it is this which must become your normal consciousness and the basis of the supramental development. In order that it may so become, the mind has to be made calm and strong, the emotional and vital being purified and the physical consciousness so opened that the body can hold and retain the consciousness and power. I notice that at the time you had it the body also expressed it. This is a sign that the capacity is already there in your physical being. The calm and strength will descend from above, what you have to do is to open yourself and receive it and at the same time reject all the movements of the lower nature which prevent it from remaining and which are ruled by desires and habits inconsistent with the true being, the true power and the true knowledge. Of course the superior power will itself reveal to you and remove all the obstacles in your nature. But the condition is that not only your mental but your vital and physical being must open and surrender to it and refuse to surrender themselves to other powers and forces. As you yourself experienced at that time, this greater consciousness will of itself bring the development of the higher will and knowledge. Psychic experiences of a proper kind are of course a great help but in your case it may be that any rich development of the psychic will only come after or in proportion as this consciousness with the calm knowledge, will and *samatā* takes possession of the different parts of the being.

All that you note in your letter is very encouraging, — it shows that the force is working in you and in the right way. There are two things that are necessary — the full connection of your mind and vital with your psychic being and the opening of the consciousness to Mother's consciousness above. Both of these are beginning. The voice that spoke was that of your soul, your psychic being, the impulse to go deep within was the movement to plunge into the depths of the psychic. The consciousness that rejected and threw away the anger and old movements was also that of the psychic.

The pressure you felt on the head comes always when there is the pressure from above of the Higher Consciousness, the Mother's consciousness, to come in and the coolness etc. you felt are also often felt at that time. The first result was the detachment from personal connections, the freedom, lightness, openness of heart, fearlessness, and also the sense of the Mother's presence. These things are signs of the true consciousness and part of the spiritual nature. They come first as experiences, afterwards they become more frequent, endure longer, settle into the nature.

Your experiences seem to be sound. The first is that of the higher (yogic or spiritual) consciousness coming down into the body from above the head. It is felt often like a current flowing through the head into the whole body and the first thing it brings is a descent of peace. One result of this descent is that one feels an inner being in oneself which is detached from the outer action, supports it from behind, but is not involved in it — that is the second experience. The third about the sleep is also felt when one has confidence in the Mother and goes to sleep under her protection, as if in her lap, surrounded by her presence. As for the dream the legs indicate the physical consciousness which is still under a double pull, one upward to the higher consciousness so that the physical consciousness may unite itself with the spiritual, the other downward towards the lower consciousness. The looking towards me indicates the choice of the being for the upward movement.

The wideness is that of the higher consciousness, golden being the colour of the light of Truth, and the Cow is the symbol of the Light of the higher consciousness descending turning all into the Truth-light.

The state of wideness and of quietude unaffected by anything that happens is the natural result of the descent which you saw in this figure. The impartial condition towards work or not work is also a result of this descent. Usually it is the vital that pushes to work and without this vital push one can do very little. When the higher consciousness descends into the mind and vital, this push becomes silent, but the faculty of work remains, — afterwards when the new consciousness is settled it takes up the work and carries it on with another force which replaces the push of the vital and is much greater.

The good condition of openness with the Force descending and the constant remembrance — or whatever other form the condition takes — is the beginning of the true consciousness and its duration is always short at the beginning because the ordinary consciousness is not accustomed to it, but to something else. But it always increases in duration and power until it is able to maintain itself even when the outer consciousness is occupied with other things. At first it remains there as something behind which emerges as soon as the outer preoccupation ends; afterwards it remains behind, but as something just felt, and in a later stage it is always there, so that there are two consciousnesses, the inner consciousness always connected with the Mother and full of her working or her presence or both and the surface consciousness occupied with outer things. Finally, even the surface consciousness begins to feel the direct connection in action itself. One need not mind if there are intervals when the true condition is not there. It does not prove that you are unfit; it is only a period in which what is not yet changed comes up to be worked upon and prepared for change. When the inner consciousness is well established, then these periods take place only in the surface consciousness and are no longer troublesome as before.

P.S. Probably the difficulty you feel is in the externalising mind the centre of which is in the throat. When there is no resistance there, the Force comes down to the heart level and below.

The action of the higher consciousness does not usually begin by changing the outer nature — it works on the inner being, prepares that and then goes outward. Before that, whatever change is done in the outer nature has to be done by the psychic.

It is somewhat like that. That is to say, there are always alternations in the intensity of the Force at its work. It comes with great power and effects something that has to be done; then it is either concealed or retires a little or is felt but from behind a screen as you say, while something comes up that has to be prepared for illumination and then it comes in front again and does what has to be done there. But formerly while the support, help, even the deeper consciousness was always there, as you now rightly feel, yet when a veil fell, then it was all forgotten and you felt as if there was nothing but darkness and confusion. This happens to most sadhaks in the earlier stages. It is a great progress, a decisive advance if, at the time the Force is acting behind the screen, you feel that it is there, that the help and support, the more enlightened consciousness is there still. This is the second stage in the sadhana. There is a third when there is no screen and the

Force and all else are always felt whether actively working or pausing during a transition.

Yes, it [the Force] is quite concrete. Usually at first it descends of itself from time to time — and also one calls it in face of a difficulty. But eventually it is always there supporting or determining all the action of the being.

The Power and Peace that come down come down from the higher consciousness above your head, from a greater self of which your mind, the human mind generally, is unaware. They are the power and peace of the Divine. When they envelop you from outside the body (therefore you feel them external,) it is as a protection and an atmosphere. But also they descend into the body, into the head (mind), heart and navel (vital) and through the whole body working in you and doing what is necessary to change the consciousness. When you do not feel it there, when you feel it only as external, it is because you are very much in the external physical consciousness — but in reality it is there in your inner being working in you. When you recover the inner consciousness, you feel it again within and it wakes in you your own true consciousness, the psychic — and it is only the psychic that gives faith and devotion. It is however a great progress if, even when in the external physical consciousness, you feel the Peace enveloping you.

Why should it be an imagination? When the higher consciousness touches it creates so long as it is there an essential purity in which all parts of the being can share. Or, even if the exterior being does not share actively in it, it may fall quiescent so that there is nothing to interfere with the whole inner being realising the truth of a certain experience. The state does not last because it is only a preparatory touch, not the full or permanent descent; but while it is there it is real. The sex-sensation is of course the thing in the external being, the perversion or false representation in nature, that is the chief obstacle to the experience becoming frequent and then normal. It usually happens that such an opposite tries to assert itself after an experience.

You are dealing in the right way with the sex feeling. As to why it rose when you were using the name there are two reasons. One is that when you use the name, it is the Mother's power that you call there and the first result often is that the difficulty rises like a snake whose head is touched to resist the pressure or — if you look at it from another point of view — it rises to be dealt with. The other is that when what is to be brought down is the Ananda — of the force, light etc., but especially of the love — then the vital-physical passion rises up to try and mix with and get hold of the Ananda hoping to turn it to a sort of sublimated vital pleasure. It is well known that this happens to Vaishnavas very often when they do the *saṁkīrtana*. In your case it is probably the first reason, because the love-Ananda or any other is not yet coming, so that explanation is improbable. As for the Force descending into the head, it has two sides to it — one is peace and when that is prominent, there is the sense of coolness; when there is a strong dynamic action instead, the feeling may be of heat, Agni-power. Most people feel these two things; they are not imagination.

You speak of a struggle (*yuddha*) beginning when the Force comes down, but such a result is not inevitable — it is not necessary that the progress should be through a struggle. That rather takes place before the Force is there in the being, while one is still making efforts to open oneself to it or when it is still pressing from above or has taken up something of the nature but not the whole. When the Force is there at work, the imperfections and weaknesses of the nature will necessarily arise for change, but one need not fight with them; one can look on them quietly as a surface instrumentation that has to be changed. It is not with "indifference" that one has to look at them, for that might mean inertia, a want of will or push or necessity to change; it is rather with detachment. Detachment means that one stands back from them, does not identify oneself with them or get upset or troubled because they are there, but rather looks on them as something foreign to one's true consciousness and true self, rejects them and calls in the Mother's Force into these movements to eliminate them and bring the true consciousness and its movements there. The firm will of rejection must be there, the pressure to get rid of them, but not any wrestling or struggle.

When you felt the Force, the concentration, the peace, it meant evidently the true consciousness coming; that could not produce the restlessness at night. If the restlessness were the result of the Force coming, it would follow that the more the Force comes down, the more the restlessness must increase. But that would be absurd and is not the case. What happened was simply that with the Force came a beginning of the inner or spiritual peace; in the nerves the old restlessness which was lying dormant rose up as a resistance, trying as all these habitual things of the nature do to prolong itself. As the peace enters the vital and the nervous being, these things naturally diminish and are eliminated. One has only to remain quiet and detached and let the Force in its working bring in the peace there also. If the difficulty persists, you will let us know so that we may see to it.

The attitude which he describes, if he keeps it correctly, is the right one. It brought him at first the beginning of a true experience, the Light (white and golden) and the Force pouring down from the Sahasradal and filling the system; but when it touched the vital parts it must have awakened the prana energies in the vital centres (navel and below) and as these were not pure, all the impurities arose (anger, sex, fear, doubt, etc.) and the mind became clouded by the uprush of impure vital forces. He says that all this is now subsiding, the mind is becoming calm and in the vital the impulses come but do not remain. Not only the mind but the vital must become calm; these impulses must lose their force of recurrence by rejection and purification. Entire purity and peace must be established in the whole Adhar; it is only then that he will have a safe and sure basis for further progress.

The reason why the force flows out of him must be because he allows himself to become too inertly passive and open to everything. One must be passive only to the Divine Force, but vigilant not to put oneself at the mercy of all forces. If he becomes passive when he tries to see God in another person, he is likely to put himself at the disposal of any force that is working through that person and his own forces may be drained away towards the other. It is better for him not to try in this way; let him aspire for the Peace and Strength that come from above and for entire purity and open himself to that Force only. Such experiences as the feeling of the Divine everywhere (not in this or that person only) will then come of themselves.

Our object is the supramental realisation and we have to do whatever is necessary for that or towards that under the conditions of each stage. At present the necessity is to prepare the physical consciousness; for that a complete equality and peace and a complete dedication free from personal demand or desire in the physical and the lower vital parts is the thing to be established. Other things can come in their proper time. What is the need now is not insistence on physical nearness, which is one of these other things, but the psychic opening in the physical consciousness and the constant presence and guidance there.

The opening of the vital mind (or any part) does not mean that the vital mind is absolutely open or wholly converted so that there shall never again be any darkness or ignorance or error or resistance or anything else but the consciousness there. It only means that the higher consciousness is able to come down there and work and establish something of itself in that part. Each plane, one after the other, has to open initially in that way down to the physical. So long as this initial opening is not made in all the parts, there can be no complete and final descent of the higher consciousness anywhere. If the nervous being and other physical parts are not open, even the thinking mind cannot be finally open, for it can be affected by resistance, darkness, etc. from below. If the vital mind is open, that does not mean that it is open so wholly that it is already divine and is not feeling pride or other wrong movements.

As for the nervous being, it is part of the physical consciousness, below the physical mind and not above it — the nerves are part of the body.

It [the coming of disturbances] is not the result of any pressure from above. If there were nothing coming from above, there would be no peace and clarity and the disturbances would still come and come more often.

The cravings once belonged to the vital physical, but when there is a sufficient force of peace in the being, then they go out and the vital physical is free and under the influence of the quietude. The forces of disturbance do not belong any longer to the personality, but although they have gone out, they wait in the atmosphere and, if they get a chance, try to come back and resume hold of the exterior being so as either to break or, if they can no longer do that, cover up the inner peace. Because the physical vital has been accustomed to respond to them for a time willingly, now unwillingly, they are still able to make it answer to their vibrations. The peace and clarity must acquire such a force that they will remain even if these forces come back — then there will be the phenomenon of the inner peace remaining undisturbed in the inner being even while the outer is superficially disturbed. This is a well-marked stage in the progress. Afterwards a force can be brought down strong enough to fill the outer being also with so strong a peace and clarity that the disturbances can no longer enter there. One may feel them still sometimes in the atmosphere but is no longer touched by them at all.

As for the vital physical readmitting the forces of disturbance, it is not always because it wants; it may happen also because in spite of itself certain impacts or suggestions revive the old vibrations and the habit of responding has been so strong in it that it responds *in spite of itself*, and for a time it is unable to recover its balance. This happens in all parts of the being, but it is especially true of the physical parts — physical mind yielding to habitual thoughts, physical vital yielding to habitual desires and impulsions, body yielding to habitual sensations, illnesses etc. etc. Often sadhaks write "But I don't want these things, even my vital and body feel uncomfortable and wish them away, then why do they come". It is because of this long established habit of response which is too strong for the yet too quiescent and passive will (if it can be called will) of rejection in the part affected. It is especially true of the physical parts because a passive quiescence, a habit of being driven by forces is their very nature, unless they are controlled from above or made to share in the idea and will of the higher parts.

It must be the vital-physical that is in action. It is under the pressure of the Force that the resistance recedes lower and lower down and manifests so as to have the pressure brought there also specifically for its expulsion.

It is the pressure of the higher consciousness (planes of blue light beyond the ordinary mind) that has come down and is pressing upon the resistances down to the body and below. At the same time the weight of the subconscient nature is being lifted up for release — that is the sense of these experiences.

That is good progress. As for the resisting part, there is for a long time a resistance from some layer of the physical — one layer opens, another beneath remains obscure. But if the pressure from

78

above is continuous, the resistance gets exhausted at last.

The stillness of which you speak in the meditation is a very good sign. It comes usually in that pervading way when there has been sufficient purification to make it possible. On the other side, it is itself the beginning of the laying of the foundation of the higher spiritual consciousness.

I think you are right about the change coming in many. Still chequered by remnants and returns of the old nature, it is proceeding.

In the first condition you are receiving through the mind and it is drawn back upon itself to receive the Presence and grow in the Light and Power from above. The body or external consciousness is probably not sharing in its outward-going parts, there is no effectuating energy for any work other than what the external consciousness is habituated to do.

In the second, the vital is receiving directly and transforming immediately into kinetic energy; for it is the direct reception by the vital or else the active participation of the vital in the Light, Power or Ananda that makes externalisation, effectuation, all kinds of work and action possible and easy.

What you have written is quite correct. The body is not connected ordinarily with the higher consciousness, it only receives what it can from the mind. It is being prepared for the direct connection by the ascent of the inner or subtle body into that plane and the descent from it of the higher Light.

It [the higher Force] can come into the physical consciousness direct in the sense that the rest can remain passive, but it must pass through the subtle to reach the material.

All experiences that penetrate the centres are recorded in the body and seem to be the body's experiences, but one has to distinguish between the reflection of the experiences there and the experiences that belong to the physical body-consciousness itself. It is a matter of consciousness and free discernment. There is no absolute law about the time.

I spoke only of the fact that what one feels recorded in the physical body may be actually taking place only in the subtle body. Whether in a particular case it is that or a direct experience in the physical body also, is a matter to be seen in each case. One must distinguish for oneself what it is.

Why "mere" record ? If you think the experiences in the subtle body are feeble vague things, you are mistaken — they can be quite as intense, swift, palpable, massive as those of the body.

Any reflection or outflowing from the subtle body into the physical would also be felt as tangible.

All experiences can be brought into the smallest constituents of the being.

It is the approach of the higher consciousness to the subconscient through the psychic and vital which are the connecting links. Without the vital the action would not be complete, without the psychic it would not be possible.

*
**

These are some of the effects of the descent of higher Consciousness into the most physical. It brings light, consciousness, force, Ananda into the cells and all the physical movements. The body becomes conscious and vigilant and performs the right movements, obeying the higher will or else automatically by the force of the consciousness that has come into it. It becomes more possible to control the functions of the body and set right anything that is wrong, to deal with illness and pain, etc. A greater control comes over the actions of the body and even over happenings to it from outside, e.g., minimising of accidents and small mishaps. The body becomes a more effective instrument for work. It becomes possible to minimise fatigue. Peace, happiness, strength, lightness come in the whole physical system. These are the more obvious and normal results which grow as the consciousness grows but there are as many others that are possible. There is also the unity with the earth-consciousness, the constant sense of the Divine in the physical, etc....

It is, of course, not easy to make the physical entirely conscious in this way — for it is the seat of unconsciousness and obscurity and inertia — but a partial and sufficiently effective introduction of the higher Consciousness can be established as a basis and the rest of the ground conquered as its force increases on the body.

Your recent experiences are of considerable importance: the triple condition of the being, the sense of the Divine everywhere, that of the Divine Child in the universe. The last two are self-evident in their significance. As to the triple condition, it indicates the proper direction of the realisation of the sadhana in three parts of the being. The mind has to emerge in the one infinite consciousness of the silent self which will then envelop the whole being; the heart has by adoration and love and surrender to live in the dynamic Divine and be its dwelling-place; the vital and physical (below the navel) have to be the instruments of the Divine Will, instruments pure, surrendered, expressing nothing but that Will.

The Blue Light coming below the level of the Muladhara means that it has entered into the physical (physical-mental, physical-vital, material) consciousness. The two main obstacles here are the mechanical mind with its memories and desires of the past and the most outward sex-movements; these have to be overcome (especially the mechanical mind, for the other may be easily overcome if not supported by the vital proper) for the Light to possess all the physical consciousness. It is probably why it rose so strongly when the Light came to these parts.

Dynamism is everywhere, because the Force (Shakti) is everywhere. The perfect dynamism is there in the supermind; no other can be unfailing.

How the body receives the higher dynamism depends on the condition of the body or rather of the physical and most material consciousness. In one condition it is tamasic, inert, unopen and cannot bear or cannot receive or cannot contain the force; in another, rajas predominates and tries to seize on the dynamism, but wastes and spills and loses it; in another, there is receptivity, harmony, balance and the result is a harmonious action without strain or effort.

A dynamic descent brings *tapas* not *śama*. It is a greater and greater descent of peace that brings *śama* — the dynamic descent helps it by dispersing the element of rajasic disturbance and changing *rajas* into *tapas*.

The inertia itself is not a dynamic principle. The nature of inertia is *apravṛtti* — the action of the mechanical mind is a *pravṛtti*, though a tamasic obscure *pravṛtti*.

By the descent the inertia changes its character. It ceases to be a resistance of the physical and becomes only a physical condition to be transformed into the true basic immobility and rest.

IV

He is using the word supermind too easily. What he describes as supermind is a highly illumined consciousness; a modified supramental light may touch it, but not the full power of supermind; and, in any case, it is not the supermind. He speaks of a supramental part which is unreceptive — that is impossible, the supramental cannot be unreceptive. The supermind is the Truth-Consciousness itself; it already possesses the Truth and does not even need to receive it. The word Vijnana is sometimes used for the higher illumined Intelligence in communication with the Truth, and this must be the part in himself which he felt — but this is not the supermind. One can enter into supermind only at the very end of the sadhana, when all difficulties have disappeared and there is no obstacle any longer in the way of the realisation.

Three planes —
   1. Karana 2. Hiranyagarbha 3. Virat
   The parallel between Vijnana or Karana Jagat of the Upanishad presided over by Prajna and equated with Sushupti, as the Hiranyagarbha world with Swapna and things subtle does not altogether equate with my account of the supermind. But it might be said that to the normal mind approaching or entering the supramental plane it becomes a state of Sushupti. If the writer had put the superconscient sleep of supermind — for so the supramental state appears to the untransformed mind when it touches or apprehends it, for it falls inevitably into such a superconscious sleep — then the difference would be cured.

You were quite right in what you wrote about the supermind — people here do indeed use the "big word" much too freely as if it were something quite within everybody's grasp. The first thing to be done is the psychic change and until that has progressed sufficiently, supermind is a far-off thing and people need not think of it at all. You have certainly progressed, but the change of the outer nature is always a slow movement, so that need not distress you.

All should understand that the true direct supramental does not come at the beginning but much later on in the sadhana. First the opening up and illumination of the mental, vital and physical beings; secondly, the making intuitive of the mind, through will etc. and the development of the hidden soul consciousness progressively replacing the surface consciousness; thirdly, the supramentalising of the changed mental, vital and physical beings and finally the descent of the true supramental and the rising into the supramental plane.

This is the natural order of the yoga. These stages may overlap and intermix, there may be many variations, but the last two can only come in an advanced state of the progress. Of course the supramental Divine guides this yoga throughout but it is first through many intermediary planes; and it cannot easily be said of anything that comes in the earlier periods that it is the direct or full supramental. To think so when it is not so may well be a hindrance to progress.

The psychic when sufficiently developed can be strong enough to make the preliminary clearance.

It is the supramental alone that can transform the material being, but the physical mind and the physical vital can be very much changed by the action of the psychic and of the overmind. The entire change however is made only when there is the supramental influence. But for the present the psychic is the force that may be relied on for the preliminary purification of the lower nature.

One has to know about overmind and supermind but there should be no ambition to reach them — it should be regarded as a natural end of the sadhana which will come of itself. The concentration should be all on the immediate step — whatever is being done at the time. So have the working of the Power and let it work all out step by step.

The action that took place was not supramental; the fact that you were aware of a centre in the brain shows that it was through the mind that it was done. The force that acted was the Divine Power which can work in this way on any plane, supramental, mental, vital or physical or on all the planes together. The supramental action can only be achieved after a long discipline of yoga directed towards that end; it cannot be an initial experience.

That there was no mental expectation was all to the good; if there had been an expectation, the mind might have been active and interfered and either prevented the experience or else stood in the way of its being pure and complete.

What you say about your sadhana is probably the right interpretation of your experiences. The two things of which you speak are really two sides of one movement. The opening and clearing of the lower strata can only be effectively done in proportion as this relative or mentalised supramental can lay hold on the consciousness and open to and bring down the higher or intermediate supramental from above, and this in its turn can only settle in the being in proportion as the psycho-vital and physical open and clear and change. The interaction must go on until a certain balance between the two movements is created which will enable the higher to hold the being without interruption and open it more and more to the true supramental activities. The action into which you have been cast was probably necessary because it is the dynamic part of your being in which the defects of the lower nature have the greatest hold and are most prominent.

The question arose and always arises because of an eagerness in the vital to take any stage of strong experience as the final stage, even to take it for the overmind, supermind, full Siddhi. The supermind or the overmind either is not so easy to reach as that, even on the side of Knowledge or inner experience only. What you are experiencing belongs to the spiritualised and liberated mind. At this stage there may be intimations from the higher mind levels, but these intimations are merely isolated experiences, not a full change of consciousness. The supermind is not part of mind or a higher level of mind — it is something entirely different. No sadhak can reach the supermind by his own efforts and the effort to do it by personal tapasya has been the source of many mishaps. One has to go quietly stage by stage until the being is ready and even then it is only the Grace that can bring the real supramental change.

The gate of the supramental cannot be smashed open like that. The Adhar has to be steadily prepared, changed, made fit for the supramental Descent. There are several powers between the ordinary mind and the supramental and these must be opened up and absorbed by the consciousness — only then is the supramental change possible.

To speak of "receiving power from the supramental when we are not conscious" is strange. When one is not conscious, one can still receive a higher force, the Divine Shakti works often from behind the veil, otherwise in the ignorant and unconscious condition of the human being she would not be able to work at all. But the nature of the force or action is modified to suit the condition of the sadhak. One must develop a very full consciousness before one can receive anything from the direct supramental Power and one must be very advanced in consciousness even to receive something of it modified through the overmind or other intermediate region.

It is very unwise for anyone to claim prematurely to have possession of the supermind or even to have a taste of it. The claim is usually accompanied by an outburst of superegoism, some radical blunder of perception or a gross fall, wrong condition and wrong movement. A certain spiritual humility, a serious unarrogant look at oneself and quiet perception of the imperfections of one's present nature and, instead of self-esteem and self-assertion, a sense of the necessity of exceeding one's present self, not from egoistic ambition, but from an urge towards the Divine would be, it seems to me, for this frail terrestrial and human composition far better conditions for proceeding towards the supramental change.

One must have already become intuitively conscious, to know about the overmind and the supermind. To give "signs" is useless, for the mind would only make mistakes in trying to judge by the "signs" — one has to become conscious within and know directly.

Who told you that it [the supermind] was descending in the physical consciousness without touching the mind and vital?

Certainly no part of the nature has been supramentalised — that is not possible until the whole being has been put under the supramental influence. The supramental influence must come first, the supramental transformation can only come afterwards.

A touch or influence of the supramental is not the same thing as the supramentalisation. To suppose that the physical can be supramentalised before the mental and vital is an absolute absurdity. What I said was that the mind and vital could not be supramentalised so long as the physical was left as it was, untouched by the supramental descent.

No. I have not said that at all. It is quite impossible for the supramental to take up the body before there has been the full supramental change in the mind and the vital. X and others seem always to expect some kind of unintelligible miracle — they do not understand that it is a concentrated evolution, swift but following the law of creation that has to take place. A miracle can be a moment's wonder. A change according to the Divine Law can alone endure.

It [the supermind] cannot be brought down to the mind and vital without being brought down into the physical — also one can feel its influence or get something of it but bringing down means much more than that.

The supermind is a luminous whole — it is not a mixture of light and ignorance. If the physical mind is not supramentalised, then there will be in mind a mixture of ignorance, but then it will not be supermind there, but something else — so also with the vital. All that can manifest in the mind separately is a partly supramentalised overmind.

If the supramental can stand in the mind and vital, then it must stand in the physical also. If it does not stand in the physical, it cannot stand in the mind and vital also; it will be something else, not the supramental.

That is hardly possible. The body consciousness is there and cannot be ignored, so that one can neither transform the higher parts completely leaving the body for later dealing nor make each stage complete in all its parts before going to the next. I tried that method but it never worked. A predominant over-mentalisation of mind and vital is the first step, for instance, when overmentalising, but the body consciousness retains all the lower movements unovermentalised and until these can be pulled up to the overmental standard, there is no overmental perfection, always the body consciousness brings in flaws and limitations. To perfect the overmind one has to call in the supramental force and it is only when the overmind has been partially supramenta-lised that the body begins to be more and more overmental. I do not see any way of avoiding this process, though it is what makes the thing so long.

When a higher force comes down into a lower plane, it is dimi-nished and modified by the inferior substance, lesser power and more mixed movements of that lower plane. Thus, if the over-mind Power works through the illumined mind, only part of its truth and freedom manifests and becomes effective — so much only as can get through this less receptive consciousness. And even what gets through is less true, mixed with other matter, less overmental, more easily modified into something that is part truth, part error. When this diminished indirect force descends further down into the mind and vital, it has still something of the creative overmind Truth in it, but gets very badly mixed with mental and vital formations that disfigure it and make it half effective only, sometimes ineffective.

There can be no conquest of the other planes by the supermind but only an influence, so long as the physical is not ready.

And how is it possible to perfect the mind and vital unless the physical is prepared — for there is such a thing as the mental and vital physical and mind and vital cannot be said to be perfectly prepared until these are ready.

V

There can be no immortality of the body without supramentalisation; the potentiality is there in the yogic force and yogis can live for 200 or 300 years or more, but there can be no real principle of it without the supramental.

Even Science believes that one day death may be conquered by physical means and its reasonings are perfectly sound. There is no reason why the supramental Force should not do it. Forms on earth do not last (they do in other planes) because these forms are too rigid to grow expressing the progress of the spirit. If they become plastic enough to do that there is no reason why they should not last.

Well, don't you know that old men sometimes get a new or third set of teeth in their old age? And if monkey-glands can renew functionings and forces and can make hair grow on a bald head, as Voronoff has proved by living examples, — well? And mark that Science is only at the beginning of these experiments. If these possibilities are opening before Science, why should one declare their absolute impossibility by other [yogic] means?

Death is there because the being in the body is not yet developed enough to go on growing in the same body without the need of change and the body itself is not sufficiently conscious. If the mind and vital and the body itself were more conscious and plastic, death would not be necessary.

The physical death is the dissolution of the physical form — but all form does not disappear by death.

Immunity from death by anything but one's own will to leave the body, immunity from illness, are things that can be achieved only by a complete change of consciousness which each man has to develop in himself, — there can be no automatic immunity without that achievement.

It [death] has no separate existence by itself, it is only a result of the principle of decay in the body and that principle is there already — it is part of the physical nature. At the same time it is not inevitable; if one could have the necessary consciousness and force, decay and death is not inevitable. But to bring that consciousness and force into the whole of the material nature is the most difficult thing of all — at any rate, in such a way as to annul the decay principle. It came because it is there in the subconscient and in Matter into which you are trying to bring down the intuition and overmind, — it wanted to get into the subjective centre so as to combat the higher power in the mind as well as in the body.

[1]There is no ambiguity that I can see. "En fait" and "attachée" do not convey any sense of inevitability. "En fait" means simply that in fact, actually, as things are at present all life (on earth) has death attached to it as its end; but it does not in the least convey the idea that it can never be otherwise or that this is the unalterable law of all existence. It is at present a fact for certain reasons which are stated, — due to certain mental and physical circumstances — if these are changed, death is not inevitable any longer. Obviously the alteration can only come "if" certain

---

[1] These observations are apropos of the Mother's statement: "En fait, la mort a été attachée à toute vie sur terre." See La Mère, *Entretiens* (1967 Edition), p. 49.

conditions are satisfied — all progress and change by evolution depends upon an "if" which gets satisfied. If the animal mind had not been pushed to develop speech and reason, mental man would never have come into existence, — but the "if" — a stupendous and formidable one, was satisfied. So with the ifs that condition a farther progress.

The change of the consciousness is the necessary thing and without it there can be no physical siddhi. But the fullness of the supramental change is not possible, if the body remains as it is, a slave of death, disease, decay, pain, unconsciousness and all the other results of the ignorance. If these are to remain the descent of the supramental is hardly necessary — for a change of consciousness which would bring mental-spiritual union with the Divine, the overmind is sufficient, even the Higher Mind is sufficient. The supramental descent is necessary for a dynamic action of the Truth in mind, vital and body. This would imply as a final result the disappearance of the unconsciousness of the body; it would no longer be subject to decay and disease. That would mean that it would not be subject to the ordinary processes by which death comes. If a change of body had to be made, it would have to be by the will of the inhabitant. This (not an obligation to live 3000 years, for that too would be a bondage) would be the essence of physical immortality. Still, if one wanted to live 1000 years or more, then supposing one had the complete siddhi, it should not be impossible.

That is the argument[1] of the Mayavadin to whom all manifestation is useless and unreal because it is temporary — even the life of the gods is of no use because it is in Time, not in the Timeless. But if manifestation is of any use, then it is worthwhile having a perfect manifestation rather than an imperfect one. "Have to

---

[1] "What is the need of transformation of the physical if, after all, willingly (if one reaches the consciousness of immortality) or unwillingly (in other cases) the body will have to be left?"

be left willingly" is a contradiction in terms. One keeps the body as long as one wills, with an illumined will, leaves it or changes it according to the same will. That is a very different thing from a body assailed constantly by desire and suffering and death brought on by decay and illness. Always assuming that the divine manifestation or any manifestation is worthwhile.

As for the second argument[1], change and progress are not excluded from the supramental life. I do not see why the change of cells, supposing it continues in the supramentalised body, takes away from the value of the transformation, if it is a change to something equally or more conscious and luminous.

To merge the consciousness in the Divine and to keep the psychic being controlling and changing all the nature and keeping it turned to the Divine till the whole being can live in the Divine is the transformation we seek. There is further the supramentalisation, but this only carries the transformation to its own highest and largest possibilities — it does not alter its essential nature.

Immortality is one of the possible results of supramentalisation, but it is not an obligatory result and it does not mean that there will be an eternal or indefinite prolongation of life as it is. That is what many think it will be, that they will remain what they are with all their human desires and the only difference will be that they will satisfy them endlessly; but such an immortality would not be worth having and it would not be long before people are tired of it. To live in the Divine and have the divine Consciousness is itself immortality and to be able to divinise the body also and make it a fit instrument for divine works and divine life would be its material expression only.

As for the conquest of death, it is only one of the sequelae of supramentalisation — and I am not aware that I have forsworn

---

[1] "Matter, especially the body cells, undergoes changes from second to second — then what value has the transformation for the body?"

my views about the supramental descent. But I never said or
thought that the supramental descent would automatically
make everybody immortal. The supramental can only make the
best conditions for anybody who can open up to it then or
thereafter attaining to the supramental consciousness and its
consequences. But it could not dispense with the necessity of
sadhana. If it did, the logical consequence would be that the
whole earth, men, dogs and worms would suddenly wake up to
find themselves supramental. There would be no need of an
Ashram or of yoga.

Why vital? What is vital is the supramental change of
consciousness — conquest of death is something minor and, as
I have always said, the last physical result of it, not the first
result of all or the most important — a thing to be added to complete the whole, not the one thing needed and essential. To put
it first is to reverse all spiritual values — it would mean that the
seeker was actuated, not by any high spiritual aim but by a vital
clinging to life or a selfish and timid seeking for the security of
the body — such a spirit could not bring the supramental change.

Certainly, everything depends on my success.... But did you
imagine that would mean the cessation of death on the planet and
that sadhana would cease to be necessary for anybody?

What you said on the subject was quite correct. There are three
stages of the sadhana, psychic change, transition to the higher
levels of consciousness — with a descent of their conscious forces
— the supramental. In the last even the control over death is a
later, not an initial stage. Each of these stages demands a great
length of time and a high and long endeavour.

It is absolutely idle to think of transforming the body when other
things that are so much easier to do — though of course none is
easy —are not done. The inner must change before the outermost can follow. So what is the use of such a concentration —

unless one thinks that everything else is perfect, which would be a rather astonishing claim. What has to be done with the body at first is to make it open to the Force, so as to receive strength against illness and fatigue — when they come, there must be the power to react and throw them off and to keep a constant flow of force into the body. If that is done, the rest of the bodily change can wait for its proper time.

It is quite true that the surrender and the consequent transformation of the whole being is the aim of the yoga — the body is not excluded, but at the same time this part of the endeavour is the most difficult and doubtful — the rest, though not facile, is comparatively less difficult to accomplish. One must start with an inner control of the consciousness over the body, a power to make it obey more and more the will or the force transmitted to it. In the end as a higher and higher Force descends and the plasticity of the body increases, the transformation becomes possible.

As for immortality, it cannot come if there is attachment to the body, — for it is only by living in the immortal part of oneself which is unidentified with the body and bringing down its consciousness and force into the cells that it can come. I speak of course of yogic means. The scientists now hold that it is (theoretically at least) possible to discover physical means by which death can be overcome, but that would mean only a prolongation of the present consciousness in the present body. Unless there is a change of consciousness and change of functionings it would be a very small gain.

It depends on the consciousness. As it is, at present, most people do not get tired of life; they die because they must, not because they want to — at least, that is true of the vital; it is only a minority that tire of life and for many of these it is due to the discomforts of old age, continued ill-health, misfortune. Supposing a consciousness descended in the body that got rid of these discomforts, would people get tired of life in the same way merely because of its length or would they have some source of perpetual interest within as well as without, that would keep them on — that is the question. Of course physical immortality would not mean that one is tied down to the body, but that one is not subject to disease and death, but can keep or leave the body at will. I don't know whether Ashwatthaman[1] lives on because he cannot die or because he won't die — whether it is for him a doom or a privilege. There are by the way animals that live for many centuries, but as they have not the philosophic mind the question for them does not arise — probably they take it as a matter of course.

What you say about being tired of life, is true. Edison's family was very long lived but his grandfather after a century found it too long and died because he wanted to. On the other hand there are men who are strongly vital and do not get tired of life, like the Turk who died recently at 150, I think, but was still eager to live.

It is fundamentally true for most people that the pleasure of life, of existence in itself, predominates over the troubles of life; otherwise most people would want to die whereas the fact is that everybody wants to live — and if you proposed to them an easy means of eternal extinction they would decline without thanks. That is what X is saying and it is undeniable. It is also true that this comes from the Ananda of existence which is behind everything and is reflected in the instinctive pleasure of existence. Naturally, this instinctive essential pleasure is not the Ananda, — it is only a pale and dim reflection of it in an inferior life-consciousness — but it is enough for its purpose. I have said

---

[1] Ashwatthaman is supposed to have been living near the river Narbada for 36,000 years.

that myself somewhere and I do not see anything absurd or
excessive in the statement.

*

Some people do get disgusted with the body for its uncleanness,
but I should say it is very few.

   The suggestion of Patanjali[1] supposes that the mind is everything, so if I get the idea that the body is an unclean thing, all
my feelings will harmonise with that idea. But it is not so — there
are other parts which do not care for the idea or knowledge in
the mind and are not affected by it but are led by their own instincts and desires. It is only those who have already the turn to
vairāgya who can make use of Patanjali's suggestion to help their
already existing *vairāgya*. The medical man for instance holds
his knowledge of the composition of the body as a matter of
fact of science, he keeps it separate there in the scientific compart-
ment of his mind and it does not in the least affect his other
ideas, feelings or activities.

*

The supramental perfection means that the body becomes conscious, is filled with consciousness and that as this is the Truth-
consciousness all its activities, functionings etc. become by the
power of the consciousness within it harmonious, luminous,
right and true — without ignorance or disorder.

   The Hathayogic method is to bring an immense vital force
into the body and by this and by certain processes keep it strong
and in good health and a capable instrument.

*

It is a luminous body spoken of in the Veda as possessed by the
beings of the higher planes. It is supposed by certain schools of
yoga in the East and the West that in the final transformation on

---

[1] *Śaucāt svāṅga-jugupsā.* "From cleanliness [arises] disgust for one's own body." *Yoga-sutras* of Patanjali, Ch. II, 40.

earth man will develop a body having these qualities. It was called the "Corps Glorieux" — "body of glory" — by the Mother's first spiritual instructor.

I read the Bible — very assiduously at one time.... When I have looked at it, it has always given me a sense of imprecision in the thought-substance, in spite of the vividness of the expression, and that makes it very difficult to be sure about these things. This passage about the body, for instance — although St. Paul had remarkable mystic experiences and, certainly, much profound spiritual knowledge (profound rather than wide, I think) — I would not swear to it that he is referring to the supramentalised body (*physical body*). Perhaps to the supramental body or to some other luminous body in its own space and substance, which he found sometimes as if enveloping him and abolishing this body of death which he felt the material envelope to be. This verse like many others is capable of several interpretations and might refer to a quite supraphysical experience. The idea of a transformation of the body occurs in different traditions, but I have never been quite sure that it meant the change in this very matter. There was a yogi sometime ago in this region who taught it, but he hoped when the change was complete, to disappear in light. The Vaishnavas speak of a divine body which will replace this one when there is the complete siddhi. But, again, is this a divine physical or supraphysical body? At the same time there is no obstacle in the way of supposing that all these ideas, intuitions, experiences point to, if they do not exactly denote, the physical transformation.

It has been the idea of many who have speculated on the subject that the body of the future race will be a luminous body (*corps glorieux*) and that might mean radio-active. But also it has to be considered (1) that a supramental body must necessarily be one in which the consciousness determines even the physical action and reaction to the most material and these therefore are not wholly dependent on material condition or laws as now known, (2) that the subtle process will be more powerful than the gross, so that a subtle action of Agni will be able to do the action which would now need a physical change such as increased temperature.

If the consciousness cannot determine the physical action and re-action in the present body, if it needs a different basis, then that means this different basis must be prepared by different means. By what means? Physical? The old yogis tried to do it by physical tapasya; others by seeking the elixir of life etc. According to this yoga, the action of the higher Force and consciousness which includes the subtle action of Agni has to open and prepare the body and make it more responsive to Consciousness-Force instead of being rigid in its present habits (called laws). But a different basis can only be created by the supramental action itself. What else but the supermind can determine its own basis?

I did not intend to evade anything, except that in so far as I do not yet know what will be the chemical constitution of the changed body, I could not answer anything to that. That was why I said it needed investigation.

I was simply putting my idea on the matter which has always been that it is the supramental which will create its own physical basis. If you mean that the supramental cannot *fulfil itself* in the present body with its present processes that is true. The processes will obviously have to be altered. How far the constitution of the body will be changed and in what direction is another question. As I said it may become as you suggest radio-active: Théon (Mother's teacher in occultism) spoke of it as luminous, *le corps glorieux*. But all that does not make it impossible for the supra-mental to act in the present body for change. It is what I am looking forward to at present.

Of course a certain preliminary transformation is necessary, just as the psychic and spiritual transformation precedes the supramental. But this is a change of the physical consciousness down to the submerged consciousness of the cells so that they may respond to higher forces and admit them and to a certain extent a change or at least a greater plasticity in the processes. The rules of food etc. are meant to help that by minimising obstacles. How far this involves a change of the chemical constitution of the body I cannot say. It seems to me still that whatever preparatory changes there may be, it is only the action of the supramental Force that can confirm and complete them.

TRANSFORMATION OF THE MIND

Transformation of the Mind

THERE is no reason why one should not receive through the thinking mind, as one receives through the vital, the emotional and the body. The thinking mind is as capable of receiving as these are, and, since it has to be transformed as well as the rest, it must be trained to receive, otherwise no transformation of it could take place.

It is the ordinary unenlightened activity of the intellect that is an obstacle to spiritual experience, just as the ordinary unregenerated activity of the vital or the obscure stupidly obstructive consciousness of the body is an obstacle. What the sadhak has to be specially warned against in the wrong processes of the intellect is, first, any mistaking of mental ideas and impressions or intellectual conclusions for realisation; secondly, the restless activity of the mere mind which disturbs the spontaneous accuracy of psychic and spiritual experience and gives no room for the descent of the true illuminating knowledge or else deforms it as soon as it touches or even before it fully touches the human mental plane. There are also of course the usual vices of the intellect, — its leaning towards sterile doubt instead of luminous reception and calm enlightened discrimination; its arrogance claiming to judge things that are beyond it, unknown to it, too deep for it by standards drawn from its own limited experience; its attempts to explain the supraphysical by the physical or its demand for the proof of higher and occult things by the criteria proper to Matter and mind in Matter; others also too many to enumerate here. Always it is substituting its own representations and constructions and opinions for the true knowledge. But if the intellect is surrendered, open, quiet, receptive, there is no reason why it should not be a means of reception of the Light or an aid to the experience of spiritual states and to the fullness of an inner change.

*
**

To have a developed intellect is always helpful if one can en-lighten it from above and turn it to a divine use.

The turmoil of mental (intellectual) activity has also to be silenced like the vital activity of desire in order that the calm and peace may be complete. Knowledge has to come but from above. In this calm the ordinary mental activities like the ordinary vital activities become surface movements with which the silent inner self is not connected. It is the liberation necessary in order that the true knowledge and the true life-activity may replace or transform the activities of the Ignorance.

Intellectual activities are not part of the inner being — the intel-lect is the outer mind.

The intellect can be as great an obstacle as the vital when it chooses to prefer its own constructions to the Truth.

Intellect is part of Mind and an instrument of half-truth like the rest of the Mind.

What you have said is perfectly right. To see the Truth does not depend on a big intellect or a small intellect. It depends on being in contact with the Truth and the mind silent and quiet to receive it. The biggest intellects can make errors of the worst kind and confuse Truth and Falsehood, if they have not the contact with the Truth or the direct experience.

Its [the intellect's] function is to reason from the perceptions of the mind and senses, to form conclusions and to put things in logical relation with each other. A well-trained intellect is a good preparation of the mind for greater knowledge, but it cannot itself give the yogic knowledge or know the Divine — it can only have ideas about the Divine, but having ideas is not knowledge. In the course of the sadhana intellect has to be transformed into the higher mind which is itself a passage towards the true knowledge.

The intellect of most men is extremely imperfect, ill-trained, half-developed — therefore in most the conclusions of the intellect are hasty, ill-founded and erroneous or, if right, right more by chance than by merit or right working. The conclusions are formed without knowing the facts or the correct or sufficient data, merely by a rapid inference and the process by which it comes from the premisses to the conclusions is usually illogical or faulty — the process being unsound by which the conclusion is arrived at, the conclusion is also likely to be fallacious. At the same time the intellect is usually arrogant and presumptuous, confidently asserting its imperfect conclusions as the truth and setting down as mistaken, stupid or foolish those who differ from them. Even when fully trained and developed, the intellect cannot arrive at absolute certitude or complete truth, but it can arrive at one aspect or side of it and make a reasonable or probable affirmation; but untrained, it is a quite insufficient instrument, at once hasty and peremptory and unsafe and unreliable.

The mind does not record things as they are, but as they appear to it. It catches parts, omits others; afterwards the memory and imagination mix together and make a quite different representation of it.

It is not any weakness of the will or the result of passivity, but an overhaste of decision upon a mental impulse. That is the usual movement of the mind — and it is sometimes the fruit of a certain kind of sattwic zeal. But owing to the haste there is not sufficient time taken to see the opposite side, the defects of the decision taken, or the possible objection that might be made. Peace is the basis, but into it must come the action of a certain Light from above which shows each thing in its right proportions as a whole — for the mind at its best is incomplete and usually one-sided in its perceptions without the guidance of such a higher Light.

Most people who have not knowledge are apt to be opinionated — they have their ideas and don't want them to be changed or their fixity disturbed.

The point is that people take no trouble to see whether their intellect is giving them right thoughts, right conclusions, right views on things and persons, right indications about their conduct or course of action. They have their idea and accept it as truth or follow it simply because it is *their* idea. Even when they recognise that they have made mistakes of the mind, they do not consider it of any importance nor do they try to be more careful mentally than before. In the vital field people know that they must not follow their desires or impulses without check or control, they know that they ought to have a conscience or a moral sense which discriminates what they can or should do and what they cannot or should not do; in the field of intellect no such care is taken. Men are supposed to follow their intellect, to have and assert their own ideas right or wrong without any control; the intellect, it is said, is man's highest instrument and he must think and act according to its ideas. But this is not true; the intellect needs an inner light to guide, check and control it quite as much as the vital. There is something above the intellect which one has to discover and the intellect should be only an intermediary for the action of that source of true Knowledge.

For the human thinking mind there are always many sides to everything and it decides according to its own bent or preference or to its habitual ideas or some reason that presents itself to the intellect as the best. It gets the real truth only when something else puts a higher light into it — when the psychic or the intuition touches it and makes it feel or see.

Many things are bad only in the way people look at them. Things which you consider all right, other people call bad; what you think to be bad, others find quite natural.

The proper thing is to see all with an unmoved calm, both the "good" and "bad" as a movement of Nature on the surface. But to do this truly without error or egoism or wrong reactions needs a consciousness and knowledge that is not personal and limited.

It is very usual for intuitive suggestions to come like that and the mind to disregard them. It is because the mind is accustomed to follow its own process and cannot recognise or have confidence in the intuition when it comes. The mind has to learn to look at these things when they come and give them value if experience confirms their truth.

In the sphere of the Spirit are only the eternal truths — all is eternally itself there, there is no development, nothing unrealised or striving to be fulfilled. There are no such things as possibilities therefore.

In life, on the other hand, all is a play of possibilities — nothing is realised, all is seeking to be realised — or if not yet seeking, then waiting behind the veil for that. Nothing is realised in its highest form, in its truth or completeness, but all is possible. All these possibilities are derived from the truths above, e.g., the possibility of knowledge, the possibility of love, the possibility of joy, etc.

Intellect, will, etc. are intermediaries which try to catch something of the hidden higher truths and bring them into life or else raise life to them so that the possibilities of life here may become the complete realities that are already there above.

The intellect is made up of imaginations, perceptions, inferences. The pure reason is quite another thing, but only a few are able to use it. As for knowledge in yoga, it comes first from the higher mind, but even that does not see the whole Truth, only sides of it.

Pure reason deals with things in themselves, ideas, concepts, the essential nature of things. It lives in the world of ideas. It is philosophic and metaphysical in its nature.

All depends on the meaning you attach to words used; it is a matter of nomenclature. Ordinarily, one says a man has intellect if he can think well; the nature and process and field of the thought do not matter. If you take intellect in that sense, then you can say that intellect has different strata, and Ford belongs to one stratum of intellect, Einstein to another — Ford has a practical and executive business intellect, Einstein a scientific discovering and theorising intellect. But Ford too in his own field theorises, invents, discovers. Yet would you call Ford an intellectual or a man of intellect? I would prefer to use for the general faculty of mind the word intelligence. Ford has a great and forceful practical intelligence, keen, quick, successful, dynamic. He has a brain that can deal with thoughts also, but even there his drive is towards practicality. He believes in rebirth (metem-

psychosis), for instance, not for any philosophic reason, but because it explains life as a school of experience in which one
gathers more and more experience and develops by it. Einstein
has, on the other hand, a great discovering scientific intellect,
not, like Marconi, a powerful practical inventive intelligence for
the application of scientific discovery. All men have, of course,
an "intellect" of a kind; all, for instance, can discuss and debate
(for which you say rightly intellect is needed); but it is only
when one rises to the realm of ideas and moves freely in it that
you say, "This man has an intellect." Address an assembly of
peasants, you will find, if you give them scope, that they can put
to you points and questions which may often leave the parlia-
mentary debater panting. But we are content to say that these
peasants have much practical intelligence.

The power to discuss and debate is, as I say, a common
human faculty — and habit. Perhaps it is here that man begins
to diverge from the animal; for animals have much intelligence,
many animals and even insects have some rudimentay power of
practical reasoning, but so far as we know, they do not meet
and put their ideas about things side by side or sling them at each
other in a debate,[1] as even the most ignorant human can do and
very animatedly does.

But this, though a general faculty of the race, is very often
specialised, so much so that a man whom it is dangerous to cross
in debate in the field of literature or of science or of philosophy
may yet make a fool of himself and wallow contentedly in a quag-
mire of blunders and fallacies if he discusses politics or economics
or, let us say, spirituality or yoga. His only salvation is the bliss-
ful depth of his ignorance which prevents him from seeing what a
mess he has made. Again, a man may be a keen legal or political
debater, the two very commonly go together, yet no intellectual.
I admit that a man must have some logical intellect to debate
well. But, after all, the object of debate is to win, to make your
point, and you may do that even if your point is false; success,
not truth, is the aim of debate. So I admit what you say with
reservations.

I agree also that labels, even when applied to less developed

[1] Perhaps the crows do in the crow-Parliament sometimes!

persons, are unsatisfactory. What we really do is to pick out something prominent and label with that as if it were all the person. But classification is impossible without that and man's intellect is driven always to classify, fix distinctions, set apart with a label. The philosophers have pointed out that Science does it too rigidly and in doing so cuts falsely across the truth of Nature. But if we do not do that, we cannot have any Science.

If the intellectual will always have a greater wideness and vastness, how can we be sure that he will have an equal fervour, depth and sweetness with the emotional man?

It may be that *homo intellectualis* will remain wider and *homo psychicus* will remain deeper in heart (even when the latter's inner mind opens up).

Do not confuse the higher knowledge and the mental knowledge. The intellectual man will be able to give a wider and more orderly expression to what higher knowledge he gets than the *homo psychicus*; but it does not follow he will have more of it. He will have that only if he rises to an equal width and plasticity and comprehensiveness of the higher knowledge planes. In that case he will replace his mental by his above-mental capacity. But for many intellectuals, so-called, their intellectuality may be a stumbling-block as they bind themselves with mental conceptions or stifle their psychic fire under the heavy weight of rational thought. On the other hand, I have seen comparatively uneducated people expressing higher knowledge with an astonishing fullness and depth and accuracy which the stumbling movements of their brain could never have allowed one to suppose possible. Therefore, why fix beforehand by the mind what will or will not be possible when the above-mind reigns? What the mind conceives as "must be" need not be the measure of the "will be". Such and such a *homo intellectualis* may turn out to be a more fervent God-lover than the effervescent emotional man; such and such an emotionalist may receive and express a wider knowledge than his intellect or even the intellect of the intellectual man could have harboured or organised. Let us not bind the phenomena of the higher consciousness by the possibilities and probabilities of a lower plane.

**

An unintellectual mind cannot bring down the Knowledge? What then about Ramakrishna? Do you mean to say that the majority of the sadhaks here who have not learned logic and are ignorant of philosophy will never get Knowledge?

**

If one has faith and openness that is enough. Besides there are two kinds of understanding — understanding by the intellect and understanding in the consciousness. It is good to have the former if it is accurate, but it is not indispensable. Understanding by the consciousness comes if there is faith and openness, though it may come only gradually and through steps of experience. But I have seen people without education or intellectuality understand in this way perfectly well the course of the yoga in themselves, while intellectual men make big mistakes, e.g. take a neutral mental quietude for the spiritual peace and refuse to come out of it in order to go farther.

**

Yes, the active mind in people with a very intellectual turn can be an obstacle to the deeper more silent spiritual movement. Afterwards when it is turned into the higher thought (intuitive, or overmental) it becomes on the contrary a great force.

**

The thinking mind has to learn how to be entirely silent. It is only then that true knowledge can come.

**

Good; cessation of thought and other vibrations is the climax of the inner silence. When once one has got that, it is easier for the true knowledge to come from above in place of the mental thought.

It is necessary to curb the mind's impatience a little. Knowledge is progressive — if it tries to leap up to the top at once, it may make a hasty construction which it will have afterwards to undo. The knowledge and experience must come by degrees and step by step.

In the mind there is always a certain haste to seize quickly at what is presented to it as the highest Truth. That is unavoidable, but the more one is stilled in mind the less it will distort things.

That is always the difficulty with the mind. It must learn to be silent and let the knowledge come without trying to catch hold of it for its own play.

The attempt of the mind and vital to seize on the experience is always one of the chief obstacles.

An experience should be allowed its full time to develop or have its full effect. It should not be interrupted except in case of necessity or, of course, if it is not a good experience.

During the experience the mind should be quiet. After the experience is over it can be active. If it is active while it is there, the experience may stop altogether.

To think and question about an experience when it is happening is the wrong thing to do; it stops it or diminishes it. Let the experience have its full play — if it is something like this "new life force" or peace or Force or anything else helpful. When it is over, you can think about it — not while it is proceeding. For these experiences are spiritual and not mental and the mind has to be quiet and not interfere.

There is something in you that does want to stick to the habit of mentalising about everything. So long as you were not having real experiences it did not matter. But once real experiences begin you have to learn to approach them in the right way.

You have to learn by experience. Mental information (badly understood, as it always is without experience) might rather hamper than help. In fact there is no fixed mental knowledge about these things, which vary infinitely. You must learn to go beyond the hankering for mental information and open to the true way of knowledge.

There are two centres or parts of the consciousness — one is a witness, *sākṣī*, and observes, the other consciousness is active and it is this active consciousness that you felt going down deep into the vital being. If your mind had not become active, you would have known where it went and what it went there to experience or do. When there is an experience, you should not begin to think about it, for that is of no use at all and it only

stops the experience — you should remain silent, observe and let
it go on to its end.

It was not an imagination, but an experience. When such an
experience occurs, the attempt to take hold of it mentally and
continue it may on the contrary interrupt it. It is best to let it
continue of itself; if it ceases, it is likely to recur.

Aspiration during the period of experience is not so necessary.
It is in the intervals that it should be there.

When the personal mind is still, whatever mental action is
needed is taken up and done by the Force itself which does all
the necessary thinking and progressively transforms it by bringing down into it a higher and higher plane of perception and
knowledge.

It is perfectly possible to do work in an entire emptiness without any interference or activity of the lower parts of the consciousness.

It is in the silence of the mind that the strongest and freest action
can come, e.g., the writing of a book, poetry, inspired speech,
etc. When the mind is active it interferes with the inspiration,
puts in its own small ideas which get mixed up with the inspiration or starts something from a lower level or simply stops the
inspiration altogether by bubbling up with all sorts of mere
mental suggestions. So also intuitions or action, etc. can come
more easily when the ordinary inferior movement of the mind is
not there. It is also in the silence of the mind that it is easiest for

knowledge to come from within or above, from the psychic or from the higher consciousness.

The absence of thought is quite the right thing — for the true inner consciousness is a silent consciousness which has not to think out things, but gets the right perception, understanding and knowledge in a spontaneous way from within and speaks or acts according to that. It is the outer consciousness which has to depend on outside things and to think about them because it has not this spontaneous guidance. When one is fixed in this inner consciousness, then one can indeed go back to the old action by an effort of will, but it is no longer a natural movement and, if long maintained, becomes fatiguing. As for the dreams, that is different. Dreams about old bygone things come up from the subconscient which retains the old impressions and the seeds of the old movements and habits long after the waking consciousness has dropped them. Abandoned by the waking consciousness, they still come up in dream; for in sleep the outer physical consciousness goes down into the subconscient or towards it and many dreams come up from there.

The silence in which all is quiet and one remains as a witness while something in the consciousness spontaneously calls down the higher things is the complete silence which comes when the full force of the higher consciousness is upon mind and vital and body.

The pure inspiration and conception is something quite different — it comes from deep within or from high above. This is the lower vital mind at work making formations. When the calmness is there, all sorts of things may rise on the surface — they have not to be accepted, but simply looked at. In time the calmness will be so developed as to quell the vital and outer mind also and in that complete quietude the true perceptions will come.

Not to allow the mind to bubble up with all sorts of ideas and feelings etc. but to remain quiet and learn to think and feel only what is true and right.

The danger of the mental forces is when the higher consciousness descends they tend (unless there is a deep silence) to become active in the consciousness for forming ideas of a mental type which can always be misapplied. First there should be a basis of entire calm, peace and silence — if there is activity, it should be that of a knowledge coming down and the mind silent receiving it accurately. This you can easily have, provided the mind is quiet.

The danger of the vital is that of taking hold of love, Ananda, the sense of Beauty and using it for its own purposes, for vital human relations or interchange or else some kind of mere enjoyment of its own.

In the West the physical mind is too dominant, so that the psychic does not so easily get a chance — except of course in exceptional people.

After all India with her mentality and method has done a hundred times more in the spiritual field than Europe with her intellectual doubts and questionings. Even when a European overcomes the doubt and questioning, he does not find it as easy to go as fast and far as an Indian with the same force of personality because the stir of mind is still greater. It is only when he can get beyond that that he arrives, but for him it is not so easy.

On the other hand however your statement is correct. It is "natural considering the times" and the occidental mentality prevalent everywhere. It is also probably necessary that this should be faced and overcome before any supramental realisation is possible in the earth-consciousness — for it is the attitude of the physical mind to spiritual things and as it is in the physical that the resistance has to be overcome before the mind can be over-passed in the way required for this yoga, the strongest possible representation of its difficulties was indispensable.

To reject doubts means control of one's thoughts — very certainly so. But the control of one's thoughts is as necessary as the control of one's vital desires and passions or the control of the movements of one's body — for the yoga, and not for the yoga only. One cannot be a fully developed mental being even, if one has not a control of the thoughts, is not their observer, judge, master, — the mental Purusha, *manomaya puruṣa, sākṣī, anumantā, īśvara*. It is no more proper for the mental being to be the tennis-ball of unruly and uncontrollable thoughts than to be a rudderless ship in the storm of the desires and passions or a slave of either the inertia or the impulses of the body. I know it is more difficult because man being primarily a creature of mental Prakriti identifies himself with the movements of his mind and cannot at once dissociate himself and stand free from the swirl and eddies of the mind whirlpool. It is comparatively easy for him to put a control on his body, at least on a certain part of its movements; it is less easy but still very possible after a struggle to put a mental control on his vital impulsions and desires; but to sit like the Tantric yogi on the river, above the whirlpool of his thoughts, is less facile. Nevertheless, it can be done; all developed mental men, those who get beyond the average, have in one way or other or at least at certain times and for certain purposes to separate the two parts of the mind, the active part which is a factory of thoughts and the quiet masterful part which is at once a Witness and a Will, observing them, judging, rejecting, eliminating, accepting, ordering corrections and changes, the Master in the House of Mind, capable of self-empire, *sāmrājya*.

The yogi goes still farther; he is not only a master there, but even while in mind in a way, he gets out of it as it were, and stands above or quite back from it and free. For him the image of the factory of thoughts is no longer quite valid; for he sees that thoughts come from outside, from the universal Mind or universal Nature, sometimes formed and distinct, sometimes unformed and then they are given shape somewhere in us. The principal business of our mind is either a response of acceptance or a refusal to these thought-waves (as also vital waves, subtle physical energy waves) or this giving a personal-mental form to thought-stuff (or vital movements) from the environing Nature-Force. It was my great debt to Lele that he showed me this. "Sit in meditation," he said, "but do not think, look only at your mind; you will see thoughts *coming into it*; before they can enter throw these away from your mind till your mind is capable of entire silence." I had never heard before of thoughts coming visibly into the mind from outside, but I did not think either of questioning the truth or the possibility, I simply sat down and did it. In a moment my mind became silent as a windless air on a high mountain summit and then I saw one thought and then another coming in a concrete way from outside; I flung them away before they could enter and take hold of the brain and in three days I was free. From that moment, in principle, the mental being in me became a free Intelligence, a universal Mind, not limited to the narrow circle of personal thought as a labourer in a thought factory, but a receiver of knowledge from all the hundred realms of being and free to choose what it willed in this vast sight-empire and thought-empire. I mention this only to emphasise that the possibilities of the mental being are not limited and that it can be the free Witness and Master in its own house. It is not to say that everybody can do it in the way I did it and with the same rapidity of the decisive movement (for, of course, the latter fullest developments of this new untrammelled mental power took time, many years) but a progressive freedom and mastery of one's mind is perfectly within the possibilities of anyone who has the faith and the will to undertake it.

The error comes from thinking that your thoughts are your own and that you are their maker and if you do not create thoughts (i.e. think), there will be none. A little observation ought to show that you are not manufacturing your own thoughts, but rather thoughts occur in you. Thoughts are born, not made — like poets, according to the proverb. Of course, there is a sort of labour and effort when you try to produce or else to think on a certain subject, but that is a concentration for making thoughts come up, come in, come down, as the case may be, and fit themselves together. The idea that you are shaping the thoughts or fitting them together is an egoistic delusion. They are doing it themselves, or Nature is doing it for you, only under a certain compulsion; you have to beat her often in order to make her do it, and the beating is not always successful. But the mind or nature or mental energy — whatever you like to call it — does this in a certain way and carries on with a certain order of thoughts, haphazard intelligentialities (excuse the barbarism) or asininities, rigidly ordered or imperfectly ordered intellectualities, logical sequences and logical inconsequences, etc., etc. How is an intuition to get in in the midst of that waltzing and colliding crowd? It does sometimes; in some minds often intuitions do come in, but immediately the ordinary thoughts surround it and eat it up alive, and then with some fragment of the murdered intuition shining through their non-intuitive stomachs they look up smiling at you and say, "I am an intuition, sir." But they are only intellect, intelligence or ordinary thought with part of a dismembered and therefore misleading intuition inside them. Now in a vacant mind, vacant but not inert (that is important) intuitions have a chance of getting in alive and whole. But don't run away with the idea that all that comes into an empty mind will be intuitive. Anything, any blessed kind of idea can come in. One has to be vigilant and examine the credentials of the visitor. In other words, the mental being must be there, silent but vigilant, impartial but discriminating. That is, however, when you are in search of truth. For poetry, so much is not necessary. There it is only the poetic quality of the visitor that has to be scrutinised and that can be done after he has left his packet — by results.

That is the way things come, only one does not notice. Thoughts, ideas, happy inventions etc., etc., are always wandering about (in thought-waves or otherwise), seeking a mind that may embody them. One mind takes, looks, rejects — another takes, looks, accepts. Two different minds catch the same thought-form or thought-wave, but the mental activities being different, make different results out of them. Or it comes to one and he does nothing, then it walks off saying, "O this unready animal!" and goes to another who promptly welcomes it and it settles into expression with a joyous bubble of inspiration, illumination or enthusiasm of original discovery or creation and the recipient cries proudly, "I, I have done this." Ego, sir! ego! You are the recipient, the conditioning medium, if you like — nothing more.

First of all, these thought-waves, thought-seeds or thought-forms or whatever they are, are of different values and come from different planes of consciousness. The same thought-substance can take higher or lower vibrations according to the plane of consciousness through which the thoughts come in (e.g., thinking mind, vital mind, physical mind, subconscient mind) or the power of consciousness which catches them and pushes them into one man or another. Moreover, there is a stuff of mind in each man and the incoming thought uses that for shaping itself or translating itself (transcribing we usually call it), but the stuff is finer or coarser, stronger or weaker, etc., etc., in one mind than in another. Also, there is a mind-energy actual or potential in each which differs and this mind-energy in its recipience of the thought can be luminous or obscure, sattwic, rajasic or tamasic with consequences that vary in each case.

They [the ideas in the universal Mind] take word-form in the mind when they enter into it — unless they come from beings, not as mere idea-forces.

This is a wrong psychology. Thought is quite possible without words. Children have thoughts, animals too — thoughts can take another form than words. Thought perceptions come first — language comes to express the perceptions and itself leads to fresh thoughts.

II

Mental knowledge is of little use except sometimes as an introduction pointing towards the real knowledge which comes from a direct consciousness of things.

Is getting knowledge from above and getting it by the mind in its own capacity the same thing? If the mind is capable then there is no need of knowledge from above, it can do the getting of knowledge by its own greatness.

It is not a mental knowledge that is necessary, but a psychic perception or a direct perception in the consciousness. A mental knowledge can always be blinded by the tricks of the vital.

It [greater perfection in knowledge] can come only by further development and the activity of another kind of knowledge communicating itself to the physical and taking up gradually the functions of the mind in all its parts.

Knowledge is always better than ignorance. It makes things

possible hereafter if not at the moment, while ignorance actively
obstructs and misleads.

There are different kinds of knowledge. One is inspiration, i.e.
something that comes out of the knowledge planes like a flash
and opens up the mind to the Truth in a moment. That is inspiration. It easily takes the form of words as when a poet writes or
a speaker speaks, as people say, from inspiration.

The idea is not enough. It gives only a half-light — you must get
to all the Truth that lies behind the idea and the object together.
Being, consciousness, force — that is the triple secret.

There is a power in the idea — a force of which the idea is a
shape. Again, behind the idea and force and word there is what
is called the spirit, — a consciousness which generates the force.

All consciousness comes from the one Consciousness — Knowledge is one aspect of the Divine Consciousness.

It [spiritual knowledge] is the conscious experience of the Truth,
seen, felt, lived within and it is also a spiritual perception (more
direct and concrete than the intellectual) of the true significance
of things which may express itself in thought and speech, but is
independent of them in itself.

I was speaking of your experiences of the higher consciousness, of your seeing the Mother in all things — these are what are called spiritual realisations, spiritual knowledge. Realisations are the essence of knowledge; thoughts about them, expression of them in words are a lesser knowledge and if the thoughts are merely mental without experience or realisation, they are not regarded as Jnana in the spiritual sense at all.

The mind in its higher part is aware of being one with the Divine, in all ways, in all things — having that supreme knowledge, it is not disturbed by its own ignorance and impotence in its lower instrumental parts; it looks on all that with a smile and remains happy and luminous with the light of the supreme knowledge.

The consciousness of union with the Divine is for the spiritual seeker the supreme knowledge.

Yes, it happens like that. A touch of realisation is enough to set the higher mind knowledge or the illumined mind knowledge flowing.

Such questions should not be allowed to stop the flow [of higher knowledge]. Afterwards one can consider them and get the answer. The knowledge that comes is not necessarily complete or perfect in expression; but it must be allowed to come freely and amplifications or corrections can be made afterwards.

Neither knowledge nor anything else is constant at first — and even when it is there one cannot expect it to be always active. That comes afterwards.

What is to be left out is the ego. Limitation of knowledge will necessarily be there so long as there is not the fullest wideness from above; that does not matter.

Your mind is too active. If it were more quiet and less questioning and argumentative and restlessly wanting to find devices it seems to me that there would be more chance of knowledge coming down and of intuitive, non-intellectual consciousness developing within you.

So long as the outer mind is not quiet, it is impossible for the intuition to develop. So if you want to go on asking intellectual questions about what is beyond the intellect until the intuition develops in spite of this activity, you will have to go on for ever.

It is the physical mind that raises all these questions and cannot understand or give the right answer. The real knowledge and understanding can only come if you stop questioning with the small physical mind and allow a deeper and wider consciousness which is there within you to come out and grow. You would then get automatically the true answer and the true guidance. Your mistake is to attach so much importance to the external mind and its ideas and perceptions instead of concentrating on the growth of the inner consciousness.

A thousand questions can be asked about anything whatsoever, but to answer would require a volume, and even then the mind would understand nothing. It is only by a growth in the consciousness itself that you can get some direct perception of these things. But for that the mind must be quiet and a direct feeling and intuition take its place.

When you get the true intuitive plane, there will be no need for instructions or questions as to how to do sadhana. The sadhana will do itself under the light of the intuition.

That is always the case. Things said of sadhana — or any kind of real truth — always give more meaning with the growth of consciousness and experience. That is why when one rises in the level of consciousness the truth seen before in the mind becomes a new and vastly deeper thing always.

The one thing always is to let the Peace and Power work and not allow the mind to seek after things and get disturbed. All the values of the mind are constructions of ignorance — it is only when your psychic being comes forward that you have the true knowledge — for your psychic being knows.

Yes, that is the point. The ordinary mind governed by the vital desires and its own mental formations cannot understand — it must fall quiet and allow the Peace and Force to work so as to bring another consciousness with the true Light in it. When that is done, these questionings and their reactions will have no place.

You have only to allow the consciousness to develop — at first there will be mistakes as well as true ideas, but when there is sufficient development and the Mother's force and knowledge directly working in you, things will become more and more right — not only so, but you will have the certitude. At present there is still too much of the old physical mind for perceptions to be always right. As the Peace and Force take direct and complete possession of the physical consciousness, this will change and the consciousness develop more surely and with a greater light.

Get back to the true *feeling* of the Force and Peace — the understanding will grow with the growth of that feeling and experience. For with the Force and Peace comes always something of the Light and it is the Light illumining the mind that brings the understanding. So long as you try to understand with the unillumined mind, mistakes and non-understanding are inevitable.

III

It is the nature of the physical mind not to believe or accept anything that is supraphysical unless it is enlightened and compelled by the light to do it. Do not identify yourself with this mind, do not consider it as yourself but only as an obscure functioning of Nature. Call down the light into it until it is compelled to believe.

Yes, it [the physical mind] reasons, but on the basis of external data mostly — on things as they appear to the outer mind and senses or the habitual ideas to which it is accustomed or to a purely external knowledge.

It [the physical mind] is the instrument of understanding and ordered action on physical things. Only instead of being obscure and ignorant and fumbling as now or else guided only by an external knowledge it has to become conscious of the Divine and to act in accordance with an inner light, will and knowledge putting itself into contact and an understanding unity with the physical world.

It means that the outer physical mind has a certain obscurity in it which impedes the knowledge from coming out. This obscurity is universal in the external physical mind — you feel it more just now because it is in the physical consciousness that the opposition is now centred. It will pass as soon as the Force can descend through the mind and vital and act directly on the physical nature.

***

What you felt was the obscurity of the external physical mind and nature (the centre in the throat is the centre of this external mind). So long as that is there the external nature and action remain as they always were and there is no correspondence between it and the inner spiritual consciousness and experience. This cannot disappear by a single experience; a steady will to change is necessary.

***

What you say is quite true. No personal effort can get these things done; that is why we tell you always to keep yourself quiet and let the peace and the force work. As for understanding, it is your physical mind that wants to understand, but the physical mind is incapable of understanding these things by itself — for it has no knowledge of them and no means of knowledge. Its standards also are quite different from the standards of the true knowledge. All the physical mind can do is to be quiet and allow the light to come into it, accepting it, not interposing its own ideas — then it will progressively get the knowledge. It can't get it in this way; it must surrender.

***

It is the function of the outward physical mind to deal with external things — that is why it wants always to be busy with them.
What it has to learn is to be quiet and to act only when the Will
wants to use it, when it is really needed — and also to act only
on what the Will wants to deal with, not run about in a random
manner. When it becomes quiet, it can then go inside and come
into contact and unity with the inner physical consciousness.
The wideness and peace as it grows can do much to quiet the
physical mind and give it an inward source of deeper action.

What you have now seen and describe in your letter is the ordinary activity of the physical mind which is full of ordinary
habitual and constantly recurrent thoughts and is always busy
with external objects and activities. What used to trouble you
before was the vital mind which is different, — for that is always
occupied with emotions, passions, desires, reactions of all kinds
to the contacts of life and the behaviour of others. The physical
mind also can be responsive with these things but in a different
way — its nature is less that of desire than of habitual activity,
small common interests, pains and pleasures. If one tries to control or suppress it, it becomes more active.

　　To deal with this mind two things are necessary, (1) not so
much to try to control or fight with or suppress it as to stand
back from it: one looks at it and sees what it is but refuses to
follow its thoughts or run about among the objects it pursues,
remaining at the back of the mind quiet and separate; (2) to practise quietude and concentration in this separateness, until the
habit of quiet takes hold of the physical mind and replaces the
habit of these small activities. This of course takes time and can
only come by practice. What you propose to do is therefore the
right thing.

Detach yourself from it [the habitual movement of thoughts] —
make your mind external to it, something that you can observe

as you observe things occurring in the street. So long as you do not do that it is difficult to be the mind's master.

Quite right. But that is a common experience — it is extraordinary how long it takes for the simple and right thing to do to dawn on the physical mind.

It [the psychic] can have a very great influence [on the physical mind] by giving it the right attitude and the right way of looking at things so that it supports the emotional being in its aspiration, love and surrender and itself gets interest, faith and insight in the inner truth of things instead of seeing only their outer aspects and following false inferences and appearances. It also helps it to get rid of the narrowness and doubt which are the chief defects of the physical mind.

The psychic if it gets hold of them [the physical mind and the vital physical] can change completely their will and outlook and orientation and open them to the true perception of things and right impulse. The mind and higher vital can help much towards that.

When the physical mind is disturbed by the vital, it is not easily convinced because its reasoning is supplied to it by the vital which thinks according to its own desires and feelings — unless a great clarity from the psychic or from the thinking mind above comes to the rescue.

It is the psychic consciousness, not perfect but still well developed, that supports some of those whom you mention and makes it easy for them to go on in faith — but it is only after much vital difficulty that it developed in them, — and there is no reason why that should not happen speedily in you also.

It [the physical mind being intuitivised] is when instead of seeing things as they appear to the external mind and senses, one begins to see things about them with a subtler physical mind and sense — e.g. seeing intuitively what is to be done, how to do it, what the object (even so-called inanimate objects) wants or needs, what is likely to happen next (or sometimes sure to happen), what forces are at play on the physical plane etc. etc. Even the body becomes intuitively conscious in this way, feels without being told by the mind what it has to do, what it has to avoid, what is near it or coming to it (though unseen) etc. etc.

Certainly. It [the changed physical mind] can press upon it [the physical vital] the true attitude and feeling, make the incoming of the wrong suggestions and impulsions more difficult and give full force to the true movements. This action of the physical mind is indispensable for the change of the whole physical consciousness even to the most material, though for that the enlightening of the subconscient is indispensable.

IV

For one who wants to practise sadhana, sadhana must come first — reading and mental development can only be subordinate things.

Mental development may or may not help sadhana — if the mind is too intellectually developed on certain rationalistic lines, it may hinder.

I don't know that it [mental work] helps the sadhana and I don't quite understand what is meant by the phrase. What is a fact is that mental work like physical work can be made a part of the sadhana, — not as a rival to the sadhana or as another activity with equal rights and less selfish and egoistic than seeking the Divine.

*
**

It is obvious that poetry cannot be a substitute for sadhana; it can be an accompaniment only. If there is a feeling (of devotion, surrender etc.), it can express and confirm it; if there is an experience, it can express and strengthen the force of experience. As reading of books like the Upanishads or Gita or singing of devotional songs can help, especially at one state or another, so this can help also. Also it opens a passage between the external consciousness and the inner mind or vital. But if one stops at that, then nothing much is gained. Sadhana must be the main thing and sadhana means the purification of the nature, the consecration of the being, the opening of the psychic and the inner mind and vital, the contact and presence of the Divine, the realisation of the Divine in all things, surrender, devotion, the widening of the consciousness into the cosmic Consciousness, the Self one in all, the psychic and the spiritual transformation of the nature. If these things are neglected and only poetry and mental development and social contact occupy all the time, then that is not sadhana. Also the poetry must be written in the true spirit, not for fame or self-satisfaction, but as a means of contact with the Divine through inspiration or of the expression of one's own inner being as it was written formerly by those who left behind them so much devotional and spiritual poetry in India; it does not help if it is written only in the spirit of the western artist or litterateur. Even works or meditation cannot succeed unless they are done in the right spirit of consecration and spiritual aspiration gathering up the whole being and dominating all else. It is lack of this gathering up of the whole life and nature and turning it towards the one aim, which is the defect in so many here that lowers the atmosphere and stands in the way of what is being done by myself and the Mother.

Study cannot take the same or a greater importance than sadhana.

If the power to meditate long is there, a sadhak will naturally do it and care little for reading — unless he has reached the stage when everything is part of the yogic consciousness because that is permanent. Sadhana is the aim of a sadhak, not mental development. But if he has spare time, those who have the mental turn will naturally spend it in reading or study of some kind.

Dhyāna and work are both helpful for this yoga to those who can do both. Reading also can be made helpful.

Half an hour's meditation in the day ought to be possible — if only to bring a concentrated habit into the consciousness which will help it, first to be less outward in work and, secondly, to develop a receptive tendency which can bear its fruits even in the work.

Yes, reading can be done for the improvement of the mental instrument as part of the sadhana.

In the beginning of the sadhana you need nothing more than just what you say, "concentration with faith, devotion and sincerity"

on a form of the Divine Being — you can add prayer or the name, if you like.

Reading good books can be of help in the early mental stage — they prepare the mind, put it in the right atmosphere, can even, if one is very sensitive, bring some glimpses of realisation on the mental plane. Afterwards the utility diminishes — you have to find every knowledge and experience in yourself.

This is quite a normal movement. In reading these books you get into touch with the Force behind them and it is this that pushes you into meditation and a corresponding experience.

Yes, if one has thought much of one kind of realisation and absorbed the idea deeply — then it is quite natural that the spiritual experience of it should be one of the first to come.

Your objection was to learning languages and specially French as inimical to peace and silence because it meant activity. The mind, when it is not in meditation or in complete silence, is always active with something or other — with its own ideas or desires or with other people or with things or with talking etc. None of these is any less an activity than learning languages. Now you shift your ground and say it is because owing to their study they have no time for meditation that you object. That is absurd, for if people want to meditate, they will arrange their time of study for that; if they don't want to meditate, the reason must be something else than study and if they don't study they will simply go on thinking about "small things". Want of time is not the cause of their non-meditation and pressure for study is not the cause.

Study and inner silence are good but develop one part of the
being only — the inner silence can also support a wider work and
life.

It [reading] does not take one inwards in any real sense — it only
takes one from the more physical to the more mental part of the
external consciousness.

A time must come when the reading as well as any other outward
occupation does not interfere with the pressure or activity of the
higher consciousness.

The reading must learn to accommodate itself to the pressure —
that is, be done by the outer mind while the inner being remains
in concentration.

That is good. Reading ought not to absorb the consciousness —
there ought to be the larger part behind detached and conscious
in a larger way.

You can remember at the beginning and offer your reading to the
Divine and at the end again. There is a state of consciousness in
which only a part of it is reading or doing the work and behind
there is the consciousness of the Divine always.

When the passion for reading or study seizes hold of the mind, it
is like that; one wants to spend all the time doing it. It is a force
that wants to satisfy itself — like other forces — and takes hold
of the consciousness for its purpose. One has to utilise these
forces without letting them take hold; for this there must be the

central being always in control of the forces of Nature that come to it, deciding for itself the choice of what it shall accept, how use, how arrange their action. Otherwise each Force catches hold of some part of the personality (the student, the social man, the erotic man, the fighter) and uses and drives the being instead of being controlled and used by it.

The movements you describe are not peculiar to you, they are the natural turn of the vital mind and take similar forms in most people. In sadhana this mind has to be quieted like the rest and its energy controlled, transformed and put to proper purpose; but that takes time and comes only with the growth of the larger consciousness. The pressure of these movements is too normal for it to be a good cause for discouragement.

I do not think you should stop reading so long as the reading itself does not, as a passion, fall away from the mind; that happens when a higher order of consciousness and experiences begin within the being. Nor is it good to force yourself too much to do only the one work of painting. Such compulsion of the mind and vital tends usually either to be unsuccessful and make them more restless or else to create some kind of dullness and inertia.

For the work simply aspire for the Force to use you, put yourself inwardly in relation with the Mother when doing it and make it your aim to be the instrument for the expression of beauty without regard to personal fame or the praise and blame of others.

Writing itself on ordinary subjects has the externalising tendency unless one has got accustomed to write (whatever be the subject) with the inner consciousness detached and free from what the outer is doing.

It is not so easy to do mental work and do sadhana at the same time, for it is with the mind that the sadhana is done. If one gets back from the mind as well as the body and lives in the inner Purusha consciousness then it is possible.

*
**

The only way is to separate the Prakriti and Purusha. When you feel something within watching all the mental activities but separate from them, just as you can watch things going on out-side in the street, then that is the separation of Purusha from mental Prakriti.

*
**

That only means that you cannot separate yourself from your mental consciousness in its activity. Naturally, if you take your mental consciousness off the reading, you can't understand what is being read, for it is with the mental consciousness that one understands. You have not to make the mental consciousness separate from the reading, but yourself separate from the mental consciousness. You have to be the Witness watching it reading or writing or talking, just as you watch the body acting or moving.

V

I see no objection to his going on with his studies, — whether they will be of any use to him for a life of sadhana will depend on the spirit in which he does them. The really important thing is to develop a stage of consciousness in which one can live in the Divine and act from it on the physical world. A mental training and discipline, knowledge of men and things, culture, capacities of a useful kind are a preparation that the sadhak would be all the better for having — even though they are not the one thing in-dispensable. Education in India gives very little of these things, but if one knows how to study without caring much for the form or for mere academic success, the life of the student can be used for the purpose.

*
**

There is no reason why X should not complete his studies or learn something which will make him useful in life. To be useless is not a qualification for yoga.

It does not help for spiritual knowledge to be ignorant of things of this world.

I can't give you a more definite answer. Study is of importance only if you study in the right way and with the turn for knowledge and mental discipline.

Reading and study are only useful to acquire information and widen one's field of data. But that comes to nothing if one does not know how to discern and discriminate, judge, see what is within and behind things.

No, not necessarily. It [study of Logic] is a theoretical training; you learn by it some rules of logical thinking. But the application depends on your own intelligence. In any sphere of knowledge or action a man may be a good theorist but a poor executist. A very good military theorist and critic if put in command of an army might very well lose all his battles, not being able to suit the theories rightly to the occasion. So a theoretical logician may bungle the problems of thought by want of insight, of quickness of mind or of plasticity in the use of his capacities. Besides, logic is not the whole of thinking; observation, intuition, sympathy, many-sidedness are more important.

I am not aware that by learning logic one gets freed from physical things. A few intellectuals lead the mental life and are indifferent to physical needs to a great extent, but these are very few.

Mental training consists of reading, learning about things, acquiring complete and accurate information, training oneself in logical thinking, considering dispassionately all sides of a question, rejecting hasty or wrong inferences and conclusions, learning to look at all things clearly and as a whole.

Common sense by the way is not logic (which is the least commonsense-like thing in the world), it is simply looking at things as they are without inflation or deflation — not imagining wild imaginations — or for that matter despairing "I know not why" despairs.

A well-trained intellect and study are two different things — there are plenty of people who have read much but have not a well-trained intellect. Inertia can come to anybody, even to the most educated people.

A man may have read much and yet be mentally undeveloped. It is by thinking, understanding, receiving mental influences from his intellectual superiors that a man's mind develops.

Intelligence does not depend on the amount one has read, it is a quality of the mind. Study only gives it material for its work as life also does. There are people who do not know how to read and write who are more intelligent than many highly educated people and understand life and things better. On the other hand, a good intelligence can improve itself by reading because it gets more material to work on and grows by exercise and by having a wider range to move in. But book-knowledge by itself is not the real thing, it has to be used as a help to the intelligence but it is often only a help to stupidity or ignorance — ignorance because knowledge of facts is a poor thing if one cannot see their true significance.

There is no such rule. It is better if the mind is strong and developed, but scholarship does not necessarily create a strong and developed mind.

His main grievance with respect to the intellectuals is that he is cut off from all discussion of mental things and mental stimuli and so his mental energies are becoming atrophied. But a man who has a mental life ought surely not to be dependent on others for it, since that life is found within — there ought to be springs within that flow of their own force.

What you can do is to read not for pastime but with the clear intention of furnishing your mind with knowledge.

To read what will help the yoga or what will be useful for the work or what will develop the capacities for the divine purpose. Not to read worthless stuff or for mere entertainment or for a dilettante intellectual curiosity which is of the nature of a mental dram-drinking. When one is established in the highest consciousness, one can read nothing or everything; it makes no difference — but that is still far off.

Writing and reading absorb the mind and fill it with images and
influences; if the images and influences are not of the right kind,
they naturally turn away from the true consciousness. It is only
if one has the true consciousness well established already that one
can read or write anything whatever without losing it or without
any other harm.

It is not necessary to be in touch with the outside world in this
way; it may be useful under certain circumstances and for some
purposes. It may act too as a hindrance. All depends upon
the consciousness from which it is done.

    The reading of books of a light character may act as a relaxa-
tion of the mental consciousness. In the early stages it is not
always possible to keep the mind to an unbroken spiritual concentration and endeavour and it takes refuge in other occupations, feeling even instinctively drawn to those of a lighter
character.

It depends upon the nature of the things read whether they are
helpful to the growth of the being or not. No general rule can be
made. It cannot be said that poetry or dramas ought or ought
not to be read — it depends on the poem and the play — so with
the rest.

It depends on the nature of the book. Philosophy makes the
mind subtle in certain directions — or ought to do so. The only
harm it can do is if the mind begins clinging to ideas instead of
going forward to direct experience.

Yes, that is the right way to read these things. These philosophies
are mostly mental intuitions mixed with much guessing (specula-

tion), but behind, if one knows, one can catch some Truth to which they correspond.

I don't know that there is anything false in your philosophical reflections. Philosophy is of course a creation of the mind but its defect is not that it is false, but that a philosophical system is only a section of the Truth which the philosopher takes as a whole. If one does not shut oneself up like that but looks at all sides, there is no harm in philosophising.

The Divine Truth is greater than any religion or creed or scripture or idea or philosophy — so you must not tie yourself to any of these things.

I do not know about this Commentary, but most commentaries on the Upanishads are written out of the reasoning and speculating intellect. They may be of use to people who are trying to find out intellectually the meaning of the Upanishads — but they can be of no help to you as a sadhak who are seeking experience, — it is likely rather to confuse the mind by taking it off the true basis and throwing it out from the road of experience and spiritual receptivity into the tangle of intellectual debate.

Metaphysics deals with the ultimate cause of things and all that lies behind the world of phenomena. As regards mind and consciousness, it asks what they are, how they came into existence, what is their relation to Matter, Life, etc. Psychology deals with mind and consciousness and tries to find out not so much their ultimate nature and relations as their actual workings and the rule and law of these workings.

I think some knowledge of science will be most useful to you — that field is quite a blank for most people here, and yet the greater part of modern thought and knowledge is influenced by it.

I don't quite know about the novel. People bring in the relations of man and woman because it has been the habit for centuries to make every novel turn around that — except in the few which deal with history or adventure or similar things. In a novel based on spiritual philosophy should not the man and woman idea go into the background or disappear, the spiritual love not having anything based at all on sex, but on the relation between soul and soul?

The only harm in reading these things is that the vital makes it an excuse for sexual excitement. Otherwise there is no harm in reading for knowledge — the facts of existence have to be known, and we should learn them with a free and dispassionate mind. But such reading has to be avoided, if there is any vital reaction.

It is not against the principle of yogic life to know what is happening in the world — what is unyogic is to be attached to these things and not able to do without them or to think of them as a matter of main importance. The all-important thing must be the sadhana, the growth into a new consciousness and a new inner life. The rest must be done with detachment and without getting absorbed in them. The feeling must be such that if the Mother were to tell you never to see a newspaper at all, it would be no deprivation to you and you would not even feel the difference.

Obviously there are many things that apply to all equally and cannot be avoided in that way. The dictum that each has his own way is not true; each has his own way of following the common way and the "own way" may often be very defective. Of course it is true that natures are different and the approach whether to the sadhana or to other things. One can say generally that newspaper reading or novel reading is not helpful to the sadhana and is at least a concession to the vital which is not yet ready to be absorbed in the sadhana — unless and until one is able to read in the right way with a higher consciousness which is not only not "disturbed" by the reading or distracted by it from the concentrated yoga-consciousness but is able to make the right use of what is read from the point of view of the inner consciousness and the inner life.

Reasons given of course prove nothing — they may be only excuses put forward by the mind for doing what the vital wants. The newspapers obviously carry with them a lowering atmosphere. It is a question of fact whether one can separate oneself sufficiently not to be pulled down by it. At the time of reading there is certainly a lower pitch of the consciousness in the frontal or outward parts. Only, if one has a consciousness behind which is not affected, then one can revert immediately after reading to the normal higher level.

Merely following external rules cannot of course be sufficient. They are only an aid to the inner effort until the inner consciousness is thoroughly established. Usually much reading of newspapers in the ordinary way keeps one attached to the ordinary view and vision of things and interested in that — when one has the inner consciousness one can see things happening in the world with another eye of knowledge and then reading can be of some use, though even then most of what is published is empty and futile. But the mere not-reading by itself is not effective. Also if one has need of a distraction, reading newspapers serves the purpose.

***

To be interested in outward things is not wrong in itself — it depends on the way in which one is interested. If it is done as part of the sadhana, looking on them from the true consciousness, then they become a means for the growth of the being. It is that that matters, to get the true consciousness — and it is this that comes in you when you have the sense of the Peace and the working of the Force in it. There is no real reason for discontent or dissatisfaction with yourself — since progress is being made in spite of the resistance of the lower forces. The pressure which is translated by the heaviness in the stomach has to be got rid of — it is there that there is the chief resistance still. Peace within and a cheerful confidence and gladness without is what is wanted — then this kind of nervous pressure and disorder would cease.

One does not learn English or French as an aid to the sadhana; it is done for the development of the mind and as part of the activity given to the being. For that purpose learning French is as good as learning English and, if it is properly done, better. Nor is there any reason, if one has the capacity, to limit oneself to one language only.

Knowing languages is part of the equipment of the mind.

It depends on what you want to do with the language. If it is only to read the literature, then to learn to read, pronounce and understand accurately is sufficient. If it is a complete mastery one wants, then conversation and writing have to be thoroughly learned in the language.

It depends; to read many books quickly gives freedom and ease and familiarity with the language. The other method is necessary for thoroughness and accuracy in detail.

It is the thinking mind that works out ideas — the externalising mental or physical mind gives them form in words. Probably you have not developed this part sufficiently. The gift of verbal expression is comparatively rare. Most people are either clumsy in expression or if they write abundantly, it is without proper arrangement and style. But this is of no essential importance in sadhana — all that is needed is to convey clearly the perceptions and experiences of the sadhana.

I never heard that learning logic was necessary for good expression. So far as I know, very few good writers ever bothered about learning that subject.

The power of expression comes by getting into touch with the inner source from which these things come. A calm and silent mind is a great help for the free flow of the power, but it is not indispensable, nor will it of itself bring it.

The Knowledge from above or whatever comes down can express itself in any language.

When the knowledge comes strongly from above, it very often brings its own language and the defects of the instrument are overcome. There are people who knew very little but when the knowledge began to flow they wrote wonderfully — when it was not flowing, their language became incorrect and ordinary.

Expression is another matter, but Ramakrishna was an uneducated, non-intellectual man, yet his expression of knowledge was so perfect that the biggest intellects bowed down before it.

Thought and expression always give one side of things; the thing is to see the whole but one can express only a part unless one writes a long essay. Most thinkers do not even see the whole, only sides and parts — that is why there is always conflict between philosophies and religions.

What is expressed is only a part of what is behind — which remains unexpressed and in the language of the manifestation inexpressible.

The voice brings a vibration of force which it is more difficult to put in writing which is a more mechanic vehicle — although the written word can have a special power of its own.

SECTION THREE

TRANSFORMATION OF THE VITAL

Transformation of the Vital

THE two movements whose apparent contradiction confuses your mind, are the two ends of a single consciousness whose motions, now separated from each other, must join if the life-power is to have its more and more perfect action and fulfilment or the transformation for which we hope.

The vital being with the life-force in it is one of these ends; the other is a latent dynamic power of the higher consciousness through which the Divine Truth can act, take hold of the vital and its life-force and use it for a greater purpose here.

The Life-Force in the vital is the indispensable instrument for all action of the Divine Power on the material world and the physical nature. It is therefore only when this vital is transformed and made a pure and strong instrument of the Divine Shakti, that there can be a divine life. Then only can there be a successful transformation of the physical nature or a free perfected divine action on the external world; for with our present means any such action is impossible. That is why you feel that the vital movement gives all the energy one can need, that all things are possible by this energy and that you can get with it any experience you like, whether good or bad, of the ordinary or of the spiritual life, — and that also is why, when this energy comes, you feel power pervading the body-consciousness and its matter. As for the contact with the Mother in the vital and your sense of the fine, the magnificent experience it was, — that too is natural and right; for the vital, no less than the psychic and every other part of the being, has to feel the Divine Mother and give itself entirely to her.

But this must always be remembered that the vital being and the life-force in man are separated from the Divine Light and, so separated, they are an instrument for any power that can take hold of them, illumined or obscure, divine or undivine. Ordinarily, the vital energy serves the common obscure or half-con-

scious movements of the human mind and human life, its normal
ideas, interests, passions and desires. But it is possible for the
vital energy to increase beyond the ordinary limits and, if so
increased, it can attain an impetus, an intensity, an excitation
or sublimation of its forces by which it can become, is almost
bound to become an instrument either of divine powers, the
powers of the gods, or of Asuric forces. Or, if there is no settled
central control in the nature, its action can be a confused mixture of these opposites, or in an inconsequent oscillation serve
now one and now the other. It is not enough then to have a
great vital energy acting in you; it must be put in contact with
the higher consciousness, it must be surrendered to the true control, it must be placed under the government of the Divine. That
is why there is sometimes felt a contempt for the action of the
vital force or a condemnation of it, because it has an insufficient light and control and is wedded to an ignorant undivine
movement. That also is why there is the necessity of opening to
inspiration and power from a higher source. The vital energy by
itself leads nowhere, runs in chequered, often painful and ruinous
circles, takes even to the precipice, because it has no right guidance; it must be connected with the dynamic power of the higher
consciousness and with the Divine Force acting through it for a
great and luminous purpose.

There are two movements necessary for this connection to
be established. One is upward; the vital rises to join with the
higher consciousness and steeps itself in the light and in the impulsion of a higher force: the other is downward; the vital
remains silent, tranquillised, pure, empty of the ordinary movements, waiting, till the dynamic power from above descends into
it, changes it to its true self and informs its movements with
knowledge as well as power. That is why the sadhak feels sometimes that he is rising up into a happier and nobler consciousness,
entering into a brighter domain and purer experience, but sometimes, on the contrary, feels the necessity of going back into the
vital, doing sadhana there and bringing down into it the true
consciousness. There is no real contradiction between these two
movements; they are complementary and necessary to each
other, the ascension enabling the divine descent, the descent

fulfilling that for which the ascension aspires and which it makes inevitable.

When you rise with the vital from its lower reaches and join it to the psychic, then your vital being fills with the pure aspiration and devotion natural to the psychic; at the same time it gives to the feelings its own abundant energy, it makes them dynamic for the change of the whole nature down to the most physical and for the bringing down of the divine consciousness into earth matter. When it not only touches the psychic but fuses with the higher mind, it is able to come into contact with and obey a greater light and knowledge. Ordinarily, the vital is either moved by the human mind and governed by its more or less ignorant dictates, or takes violent hold of this mind and uses it for the satisfaction of its own passions, impulses or desires. Or it makes a mixture of these two movements; for the ordinary human mind is too ignorant for a better action or a perfect guidance. But when the vital is in contact with the higher mind, it is possible for it to be guided by a greater light and knowledge, by a higher intuition and inspiration, a truer discrimination and some revelations of the divine truth and the divine will. This obedience of the vital to the psychic and the higher mind is the beginning of the outgoing of the yogic consciousness in its dynamic action upon life.

But this too is not sufficient for the divine life. To come into contact with the higher mind consciousness is not enough, it is only an indispensable stage. There must be a descent of the Divine Force from yet loftier and more powerful reaches. A transformation of the higher consciousness into a supramental light and power, a transformation of the vital and its life-force into a pure, wide, calm, intense and powerful instrument of the Divine Energy, a transformation of the physical itself into a form of divine light, divine action, strength, beauty and joy are impossible without this descending Force from the now invisible summits. That is why in this yoga the ascent to the Divine which it has in common with other paths of yoga is not enough; there must be too a descent of the Divine to transform all the energies of the mind, life and body.

*
**

All that is true Truth is the direct expression in one way or another of the Divine Consciousness. Life is the dynamic expression of Consciousness-Force when thrown outward to realise itself in concrete harmonies of formation; Love is an intense self-expression of the soul of Ananda, and Light is what always accompanies the supramental Consciousness and its most essential power.

Yes, that is the nature of the vital. It can make the absolute and enthusiastic surrender as well as cause all trouble possible. Without the vital there is no life-force of creation or manifestation; it is a necessary instrument of the spirit for life.

Yes. The spirit itself if it wants to manifest in matter must use the vital. It is so that things are arranged.

The vital is an indispensable instrument — no creation or strong action is possible without it. It is simply a question of mastering it and of converting it into the true vital which is at once strong and calm and capable of great intensity and free from ego.

The vital has to be controlled, and not allowed to do what it likes. It is not the vital that has to control you, it is you who have to control the vital.

It is through a change in the vital that the deliverance from the blind vital energy must come — by the emergence of the true vital which is strong, wide, at peace, a willing instrument of the Divine and of the Divine alone.

It means the life-energy which comes from within and is in consonance with the psychic being — it is the energy of the true vital being, but in the ordinary ignorant vital it is deformed into desire. You have to quiet and purify the vital and let the true vital emerge. Or you have to bring the psychic in front and the psychic will purify and psychicise the vital and then you will have the true vital energy.

What has been put into the vital receptacle by life can be got out by reversing it, turning it towards the Divine and not towards yourself. You will then find that the vital is as excellent an instrument as it is a bad master.

The human vital is almost always of that nature, but that is no reason why one should accept it as an unchangeable fact and allow a restless vital to drive one as it likes. Even apart from yoga, in ordinary life, only those are considered to have full manhood or are likely to succeed in their life, their ideals or their undertakings who take in hand this restless vital, concentrate and control it and subject it to discipline. It is by the use of the mental will that they discipline it, compelling it to do not what it wants but what the reason or the will sees to be right or desirable. In yoga one uses the inner will and compels the vital to submit itself to tapasya so that it may become calm, strong, obedient — or else one calls down the calm from above obliging the vital to renounce desire and become quiet and receptive. The vital is a good instrument but a bad master. If you allow it to follow its likes and dislikes, its fancies, its desires, its bad habits, it becomes your master and peace and happiness are no longer possible. It becomes not your instrument or the instrument of the Divine Shakti, but of any force of the Ignorance or even any hostile force that is able to seize and use it.

The resistance and the contrary suggestions come from the vital nature which is in all men obscure and attached to ordinary ideas and aims and easily listens to such ideas and suggestions as those you mention. Faith and devotion come from the soul and it is only when the vital has entirely submitted to the soul that one can truly lead the spiritual life.

It is a great progress if you can now do that. The chief difficulty in the way of living in the light as well as the peace and force is the confused and turbid restlessness of man's vital nature. If that is quieted, the major difficulty is gone. There still remains the obstacle of the physical nature's non-understanding or inertia — but that is less troublesome — it is more of the nature of a quiet though sometimes obstinate obstruction than a disturbance. If the vital inquietude has been cured then certainly the physical obscurity or non-understanding will go.

That [seeking enjoyment] is the attitude not of the whole vital but of the physical vital, the animal part of the human being. Of course it cannot be convinced by mental reasoning of any kind. In most men it is the natural and accepted attitude towards life varnished over with some conventional moralism and idealism as a concession to the mind and higher vital. In a few this part of the being is gripped and subordinated to the mental or the higher vital aim, forced to take a subordinate place so that the mind may absorb itself persistently in mental pursuits or idealisms or great political or personal ambitions (Lenin, Hitler, Stalin, Mussolini). The ascetic and the Puritan try to suppress it mostly or altogether. In our yoga the principle is that all must become an instrument of the Spirit and the parts of enjoyment taste the Ananda in things, not the animal enjoyment of the surface. But the Ananda will not come or will not stay so long as this part is not converted and insists on its own way of satisfaction.

Many men are not after happiness and do not believe it is the true aim of life. It is the physical vital that seeks after happiness, the bigger vital is ready to sacrifice it in order to satisfy its passions, search for power, ambition, fame or any other motive. If you say it is because of the happiness power, fame etc. gives, that again is not universally true. Power may give anything else, but it does not usually give happiness, it is something in its very nature arduous and full of difficulty to get, to keep or to use — I speak of course of power in the ordinary sense. A man may know he can never have fame in this life but works in the hope of posthumous fame or in the chase of it. He may know that the satisfaction of his passion will bring him everything rather than happiness — suffering, torture, destruction — yet he will follow his impulse. So also the mind as well as the bigger vital is not bound by the pursuit of happiness. It can seek Truth rather or the victory of a cause. To reduce all to a single hedonistic strain seems to me to be very poor psychology. Neither Nature nor the vast Spirit in things are so limited and one-tracked as that.

Most people do things because they have to, not out of the happiness they find in the things. It is only its hobbies and penchants that the nature finds some happiness in, not usually in work — unless of course the work itself is one's hobby or penchant and can be indulged in or dropped as one likes.

A vital life, "a little higher than the animals" because of some play of mind, with death as its answer is all that human existence is as it is ordinarily envisaged. And yet there is an aspiration for something more, — but the religions take hold of it and canalise it into something pointless for life and things remain as they are. Only a few indeed get beyond this limit.

The "after all"[1] is indeed only an excuse. Nobody can become more than human if he refuses to make a sacrifice of his

---

[1] "After all we are human—we have not become gods."

ego — for "human" means a vital animal ego mentalised by a little outward thought and knowledge. So long as one is satisfied with remaining that, one will remain human "even here" or anywhere.

Of course most men live in their physical mind and vital, except a few saints and a rather larger number of intellectuals. That is why, as it is now discovered, humanity has made little progress in the last three thousand years, except in information and material equipment. A little less cruelty and brutality perhaps, more plasticity of the intellect in the elite, a quicker habit of change in forms, that is all.

The times now are both worse and better than Wordsworth's — on one side there is a collapse into the worst parts of human nature and a riot of the vital forces, on the other there is in compensation a greater seeking for something beyond and a seeking with more light and knowledge in it.

Man is a mental being and cannot come from the vital, although part of him may live in the vital plane or rather in connection with it. Most men in fact live much in the vital and therefore when they practise sadhana it is first in the vital plane that they find themselves, in dreams, experiences etc. When the supramental opens then something will descend from the supramental in each as he becomes ready and forms a supramental Purusha in him. What he is now, cannot limit what he will become.

That [engagement in physical work or study] is not living in the vital — these are physical and mental occupations merely. Living in the vital is a psychological condition.

Most people live in the vital. That means that they live in their desires, sensations, emotional feelings, vital imaginations and see and experience and judge everything from that point of view. It is the vital that moves them, the mind being at its service, not its master. In yoga also many people do sadhana from that plane and their experience is full of vital visions, formations, experiences of all kinds, but there is no mental clarity or order, neither do they rise above the mind. It is only the minority of men who live in the mind or in the psychic or try to live in the spiritual plane.

In the ordinary life people accept the vital movements, anger, desire, greed, sex, etc. as natural, allowable and legitimate things, part of the human nature. Only so far as society discourages them or insists to keep them within fixed limits or subject to a decent restraint or measure, people try to control them so as to conform to the social standard of morality or rule of conduct. Here, on the contrary, as in all spiritual life, the conquest and complete mastery of these things is demanded. That is why the struggle is more felt, not because these things rise more strongly in sadhaks than in ordinary men, but because of the intensity of the struggle between the spiritual mind which demands control and the vital movements which rebel and want to continue in the new as they did in the old life. As for the idea that the sadhana raises up things of the kind, the only truth in that is this that, first, there are many things in the ordinary man of which he is not conscious, because the vital hides them from the mind and gratifies them without the mind realising what is the force that is moving the action — thus things that are done under the plea of altruism, philanthropy, service, etc. are largely moved by ego which hides itself behind these justifications; in yoga the secret motive has to be pulled out from behind the veil, exposed and got rid of. Secondly, some things are suppressed in the ordinary life and remain lying in the nature, suppressed but not eliminated; they may rise up any day or they may express themselves in various nervous forms or other disorders of the mind or vital or body without it being evident what is their real cause. This has been recently discovered by European psychologists and much emphasised, even exaggerated in a new science called psycho-analysis. Here again, in sadhana one has to become conscious of these suppressed impulses and eliminate them — this may be called rising up, but that does not mean that they have to be raised up into action but only raised up before the consciousness so as to be cleared out of the being.

As for some men being able to control themselves and others being swept away, that is due to difference of temperament. Some men are sattwic and control comes easy to them, up to a certain point at least; others are more rajasic and find control difficult and often impossible. Some have a strong mind and mental will and others are vital men in whom the vital passions are stronger and more on the surface. Some do not think control necessary and let themselves go. In sadhana the mental or moral control has to be replaced by the spiritual mastery — for that mental control is only partial and it controls but does not liberate; it is only the psychic and spiritual that can do that. That is the main difference in this respect between the ordinary and the spiritual life.

It [the reason for calm and self-control in people in ordinary life] is social pressure accompanied by a certain habit of mental control born of the social pressure. It is not from peace at all. Remove the social pressure even partly and as in England and America recently people let themselves go and do according to the vital impulses instead of controlling them — except of course those who stick to the religious and moral ideas of the past even when society drifts away from these ideas.

There is very commonly a gulf between the higher parts and the lower vital even in ordinary life — in yoga it is apt to get emphasised until the lower vital changes, but if we can judge from the majority of people here, that change is most extraordinarily difficult.

II

At present your experiences are on the mental plane, but that is the right movement. Many sadhaks are unable to advance because they open the vital plane before the mental and psychic are ready. After some beginning of true spiritual experiences on the mental plane there is a premature descent into the vital and great confusion and disturbance. This has to be guarded against. It is still worse if the vital desire-soul opens to experience before the mind has been touched by the things of the spirit.

Aspire always for the mind and psychic being to be filled with the true consciousness and experience and made ready. You must aspire especially for quietness, peace, a calm faith, an increasing steady wideness, for more and more knowledge, for a deep and intense but quiet devotion.

Do not be troubled by your surroundings and their opposition. These conditions are often imposed at first as a kind of ordeal. If you can remain tranquil and undisturbed and continue your sadhana without allowing yourself to be inwardly troubled under these circumstances, it will help to give you a much needed strength; for the path of yoga is always beset with inner and outer difficulties and the sadhak must develop a quiet, firm and solid strength to meet them.

Your former sadhana was mostly on the vital plane. The experiences of the vital plane are very interesting to the sadhak but they are mixed, i.e., not all linked with the higher Truth. A greater, purer and firmer basis for the sadhana has to be established — the psychic basis. For that reason all the old experiences are stopped. The heart has to be made the centre and through bhakti and aspiration you have to bring forward the psychic being and enter into close touch with the Divine Shakti. If you can do this, your sadhana will begin again with a better result.

*
* *

It is evident that your sadhana has been up till now in the mind — that is why you found it easy to concentrate at the crown of the head, because the centre there directly commands the whole mental range. The mind quieted and experiencing the effects of the sadhana quieted the vital disturbance, but did not clear and change the vital nature.

Now the sadhana seems to be descending into the vital to clear and change it. The first result is that the difficulty of the vital has shown itself — the ugly images and alarming dreams come from a hostile vital plane which is opposed to the sadhana. From there also comes the renewal of the agitation, the disinclination and resistance to the sadhana. This is not a going back to the old condition, but the result of a pressure of the yoga-Force on the vital for change to which there is a resistance.

It is this descent of the sadhana to free the vital being that made you feel the necessity of concentrating in the region of the heart; for in the region of the heart is the psychic centre and below, behind the navel, is the vital centre. If these two can be awakened and occupied by the yoga-Force, then the psychic (Soul-Power) will command the vital range and purify the vital nature and tranquillise it and turn it to the Divine. It will be best if you are able to concentrate at will in the heart region and at the crown of the head, for that gives a more complete power of sadhana.

The other experiences you have are the beginning of the change in the vital, e.g., peace with yourself and those you thought had injured you, joy and freedom from all worldly cares and desires and ambitions. These came too with a quieted mind, but they can be fixed only when the vital is liberated and tranquillised.

Whatever difficulties or troubles arise, the one thing is to go on quietly with full faith in the Divine Power and the guidance, opening steadily and progressively the whole being to the workings of the sadhana till all becomes conscious and consenting to the needed change.

III

It is an oscillation due to something in the resistant part (not the whole of it) being still dissatisfied at the call to change. When any vital element is disappointed, dissatisfied, called or compelled to change but not yet willing, it has the tendency to create non-response or non-co-operation of the vital, leaving the physical dull or insensible without the vital push. With the psychic pressure this remnant of resistance will pass.

The vital may understand, but that is not enough, it must wholeheartedly call for the peace and transformation. There must be a large part of it unable to change its position and give up its moods or its way of receiving things; otherwise these depressions could not be so acute. There is no reason why you should not get the peace, but this must change.

It seems to be some tamas or inertia coming down on the system. It is sometimes like that when the vital gets dissatisfied with the conditions or with what has been attained and initiates a sort of non-co-operation or passive resistance, saying, "As I am not satisfied, I won't take interest in anything or help you to do anything."

It may be because I asked to stop meditating and to wait. The vital does not like waiting. But I had to tell you that because of the burning of the centres, the disturbance of sleep and the rest — these must go before you can meditate in the right way and with success. If you meditate at all now, it should be only in calm and peace with a very quiet aspiration for the divine calm and peace to descend into you.

It is also perhaps due to your *penchant* for Nirvana. For the desire of Nirvana easily brings this kind of collapse of the energies. Nirvana is not the aim of my yoga — but whether for Nirvana or for this yoga, calm and peace in the whole being are the necessary foundation of all siddhi.

I have always told you that you ought not to stop your poetry and similar activities. It is a mistake to do so out of asceticism or with the idea of tapasya. One can stop these things when they drop of themselves, because one is full of experience and so interested in one's inner life that one has no energy to spare for the rest. Even then, there is no rule for giving up; for there is no reason why poetry etc. should not be part of sadhana. The love of applause, the desire for fame, the ego-reaction have to be given up, but that can be done without giving up the activity itself. Your vital needs some activity — most vitals do — and to deprive it of its outlet, an outlet that can be helpful and not harmful, makes it sulking, indifferent and desponding or else inclined to revolt at any moment and throw up the sponge. Without the assent of the vital it is difficult to do sadhana — it non-co-operates, or it watches with a grim, even if silent dissatisfaction ready to express at any moment doubt and denial; or it makes a furious effort and then falls back saying: "I have got nothing." The mind by itself cannot do much, it must have support from the vital and for that the vital must be in a cheerful and acquiescent state. It has the joy of creation and there is nothing spiritually wrong in creative action. Why deny your vital this joy of outflow?

I had already hinted to you that to be able to wait for the Divine Grace (not in a tamasic spirit but with a sattwic reliance) was the best course for you. Prayer, yes — but not prayer insisting on immediate fulfilment — but prayer that is itself a communion of the mind and heart with the Divine and can have the joy and satisfaction of itself, trusting for fulfilment by the Divine in his own time. Meditation? Yes, but your meditation has got into a wrong *āsana*, that of an eager and vehement wrestling followed by a bitter despair. It is no use getting on with it like

that: it is better to drop it till you get a new *āsana*. (I am referring to the old Rishis who established an *āsana*, a place and a
fixed position, where they would sit still till they got siddhi —
but if the *āsana* got successfully disturbed by wrong forces like
Asuras, Apsaras etc., they left it and sought for a new one.) Moreover, your meditation is lacking in quietude: you meditate with a
striving mind, but it is in the quiet mind that the experience
comes, as all yogis agree — the still water that reflects rightly the
sun, the cup made empty before the *soma-rasa* of the spirit may be
poured in it. Prepare the mind and heart till things begin to flow
into them in a spontaneous current when all is ready.

Yes, dryness comes usually when the vital — here certainly the
vital physical — dislikes a movement or condition or the refusal
of its desires and starts non-co-operation. But sometimes it is a
condition that has to be crossed through, e.g. the neutral or dry
quietude which sometimes comes when the ordinary movements
have been thrown out but nothing positive has yet come to take
their place (e.g. peace, joy, a higher knowledge or force and
action).

The ordinary freshness, energy, enthusiasm of the nature comes
either from the vital, direct when it is satisfying its own instincts
and impulses, indirect when it co-operates with or assents to the
mental, physical or spiritual activities. If the vital resents, there
is revolt and struggles. If the vital no longer insists on its own
impulses and instincts but does not co-operate there is either dryness or a neutral state. Dryness comes in when the vital is quiescent but passively unwilling, not interested, the neutral state
when it neither assents nor is unwilling, — simply quiescent,
passive. This, however, the neutral state can deepen into positive
calm and peace by a greater influx from above which keeps the
vital not only quiescent but at least passively acquiescent. With
the active interest and consent of the vital the peace becomes a

glad or joyful peace or a strong peace supporting and entering into action or active experience.

The vital can be all right when things are going on swimmingly, but when difficulties become strong, it sinks and lies supine. Also if a bait is held out to the vital ego, then it can become enthusiastic and active.

It is because the vital was very much under the grip of its desires and so, now that it is separately active, not controlled by mental will, it kicks and cries whenever its desires are not satisfied. That is an ordinary movement of the human vital when not dominated and kept in its place by the mental will.

No doubt it was the silence — the slight dryness must have been the reaction caused in the physical vital by the "uninterest" in external things — because the physical vital depends very much on this external interest. When it gets more accustomed to the silence, then the dryness disappears.

The nervous being is under the influence of the vital forces; when they are denied or pushed out, it becomes depressed and wants to call them back — for it is accustomed to get the pleasure and strength of life from the vital movements and not from the spiritual or divine Force above.

The feeling of the desert comes because of the resistance of the vital which wants life to be governed by desire. If that is not allowed, it regards existence as a desert and puts that impression on the mind.

The Shakti in the heart is the psychic Force.

Certainly it is better if the vital is brought to the true movement — renouncing its wrong movements and asking only for growth of the self-realisation, psychic love and psychicisation of the nature. But it is possible to get rid from above of the more active forms of obstruction even with a neutral vital.

IV

The cardinal defect, that which has been always standing in the way and is now isolated in an extreme prominence, is seated or at least is at present concentrated in the lower vital being. I mean that part of the vital-physical nature with its petty and obstinate egoism which actuates the external human personality, — that which supports its surface thoughts and dominates its habitual ways of feeling, character and action. I am not concerned here with the other parts of the being and I do not speak of anything in the higher mind, the psychic self or the higher and larger vital nature; for, when the lower vital rises, these are pushed into the background, if not covered over for the time, by this lower vital being and this external personality. Whatever there may be in these higher parts, aspiration to the Truth, devotion, or will to conquer the obstacles and the hostile forces, it cannot become integral, it cannot remain unmixed or unspoilt or continue to be effective so long as the lower vital and the external personality have not accepted the Light and consented to change.

It was inevitable that in the course of the sadhana these inferior parts of the nature should be brought forward in order that like the rest of the being they may make the crucial choice and either accept or refuse transformation. My whole work depends upon this movement; it is the decisive ordeal of this yoga. For the physical consciousness and the material life cannot change if this does not change. Nothing that may have been done before, no inner illumination, experience, power or Ananda is of any eventual value, if this is not done. If the little external personality is to persist in retaining its obscure and limited, its petty and ignoble, its selfish and false and stupid human consciousness, this amounts to a flat negation of the work and the sadhana. I have no intention of giving my sanction to a new edition of the old fiasco, a partial and transient spiritual opening within with no true and radical change in the law of the external nature. If, then, any sadhak refuses in practice to admit this change or if he refuses even to admit the necessity for any change of his lower vital being and his habitual external personality, I am entitled to conclude that, whatever his professions, he has not accepted either myself or my yoga.

I am well aware that this change is not easy, the dynamic will towards it does not come at once and is difficult to fix, and, even afterwards, the sadhak often feels helpless against the force of habit. Knowing this, the Mother and myself have shown and are still showing sufficient patience in giving time for the true spirit to come up and form and act effectively in the external being of those around us. But if in anyone this part not only becomes obstinate, self-assertive or aggressive, but is supported and justified by the mind and will and tries to spread itself in the atmosphere, then it is a different and very serious matter.

The difficulty in the lower vital being is that it is still wedded to its old self and in revolt against the Light; it has not only not surrendered either to a greater Truth or to myself and the Mother, but it has up to now no such will and hardly any idea even of what true surrender is. When the lower vital assumes this attitude, it takes its stand upon a constant affirmation of the old personality and the past forms of the lower nature. Every time they are discouraged, it supports and brings them back and asserts its right to freedom, — the freedom to affirm and follow its own crude and egoistic ideas, desires, fancies, impulses or convenience whenever it chooses. It claims secretly or in so many words the right to follow its nature, — its human unregenerate nature; the right to be itself, — its natural original unchanged self with all the falsehood, ignorance and incoherence proper to this part of the being. And it claims or, if it does not claim in theory, it asserts in practice the right to express all this impure and inferior stuff in speech and act and behaviour. It defends, glosses over, paints in specious colours and tries to prolong indefinitely the past habitual ways of thinking, speaking and feeling and to eternise what is distorted and misformed in the character. This it does sometimes by open self-assertion and revolt, branding all that is done or said against it as error or oppression or injustice, sometimes behind a cover of self-deception or a mask of dissimulation, professing one thing and practising another. Often it tries to persuade itself and to convince others that these things are the only right reason and right way of acting for itself or for all or even that they are part of the true movement of the yoga.

When this lower vital being is allowed to influence the action, as happens when the sadhak in any way endorses its suggestions, its attitude, whether masked to himself or coming to the surface, dictates a considerable part of his speech and action and against it he makes no serious resistance. If he is frank with himself and straightforward to the Mother, he will begin to recognise the source and nature of the obstacle and will soon be on the direct road to correct and change it. But this, when under the adverse influence, he persistently refuses to be; he prefers to hide up these movements under any kind of concealment, denial, justification or excuse or other shelter.

In the nature the resistance takes certain characteristic forms which add to the confusion and to the difficulty of transformation. It is necessary to outline some of these forms because they are sufficiently common, in some in a less, in others in a greater degree, to demand a strong and clear exposure.

1. A certain vanity and arrogance and self-assertive rajasic vehemence which in this smaller vital being are, for those who have a pronounced strength in these parts, the deformation of the vital force and habit of leading and domination that certain qualities in the higher vital gave them. This is accompanied by an excessive *amour-propre* which creates the necessity of making a figure, maintaining by any means position and prestige, even of posturing before others, influencing, controlling or "helping"

them, claiming the part of a superior sadhak, one with greater knowledge and with occult powers. The larger vital being itself has to give up its powers and capacities to the Divine Shakti from whom they come and must use them only as the Mother's instrument and according to her directions; if it intervenes with the claim of its ego and puts itself between her and the work or between her and other sadhaks, then whatever its natural power, it deviates from the true way, spoils the work, brings in adverse forces and wrong movements, and does harm to those whom it imagines it is helping. When these things are transferred to the smallness of the lower vital nature and the external personality and take lower and pettier forms, they become still more false to the truth, incongruous, grotesque, and at the same time can be viciously harmful, though in a smaller groove. There is no better way of calling in hostile forces into the general work or of vitiating and exposing to their influence one's own sadhana. On a smaller scale these defects of vanity, arrogance and rajasic violence are present in most human natures. They take other forms, but are then also a great obstacle to any true spiritual change.

2. Disobedience and indiscipline. This lower part of the being is always random, wayward, self-assertive and unwilling to accept the imposition on it of any order and discipline other than its own idea or impulse. Its defects even from the beginning stand in the way of the efforts of the higher vital to impose on the nature a truly regenerating tapasya. This habit of disobedience and disregard of discipline is so strong that it does not always need to be deliberate; the response to it seems to be immediate, irresistible and instinctive. Thus obedience to the Mother is repeatedly promised or professed, but the action done or the course followed is frequently the very opposite of the profession or promise. This constant indiscipline is a radical obstacle to the sadhana and the worst possible example to others.

3. Dissimulation and falsity of speech. This is an exceedingly injurious habit of the lower nature. Those who are not straightforward cannot profit by the Mother's help, for they themselves turn it away. Unless they change, they cannot hope for the descent of the supramental Light and Truth into the lower

vital and physical nature; they remain stuck in their own self-created mud and cannot progress. Often it is not mere exaggeration or a false use of the imagination embroidering on the actual truth that is marked in the sadhak, but also a positive denial and distortion as well as a falsifying concealment of facts. This he does sometimes to cover up his disobedience or wrong or doubtful course of action, sometimes to keep up his position, at others to get his own way or indulge his preferred habits and desires. Very often, when one has this kind of vital habit, he clouds his own consciousness and does not altogether realise the falsity of what he is saying or doing; but in much that he says and does, it is quite impossible to extend to him even this inadequate excuse.

4. A dangerous habit of constant self-justification. When this becomes strong in the sadhak, it is impossible to turn him in this part of his being to the right consciousness and action because at each step his whole preoccupation is to justify himself. His mind rushes at once to maintain his own idea, his own position or his own course of action. This he is ready to do by any kind of argument, sometimes the most clumsy and foolish or inconsistent with what he has been protesting the moment before, by any kind of mis-statement or any kind of device. This is a common misuse, but none the less a misuse of the thinking mind; but it takes in him exaggerated proportions and so long as he keeps to it, it will be impossible for him to see or live the Truth.

Whatever the difficulties of the nature, however long and painful the process of dealing with them, they cannot stand to the end against the Truth, if there is or if there comes in these parts the true spirit, attitude and endeavour. But if a sadhak continues out of self-esteem and self-will or out of tamasic inertia to shut his eyes or harden his heart against the Light, so long as he does that, no one can help him. The consent of all the being is necessary for the divine change, and it is the completeness and fulness of the consent that constitutes the integral surrender. But the consent of the lower vital must not be only a mental profession or a passing emotional adhesion; it must translate itself into an abiding attitude and a persistent and consistent action.

This yoga can only be done to the end by those who are in total earnest about it and ready to abolish their little human ego and its demands in order to find themselves in the Divine. It cannot be done in a spirit of levity or laxity; the work is too high and difficult, the adverse powers in the lower Nature too ready to take advantage of the least sanction or the smallest opening, the aspiration and tapasya needed too constant and intense. It cannot be done if there is a petulant self-assertion of the ideas of the human mind or wilful indulgence of the demands and instincts and pretensions of the lowest part of the being, commonly justified under the name of human nature. It cannot be done if you insist on identifying these lowest things of the Ignorance with the divine Truth or even the lesser truth permissible on the way. It cannot be done if you cling to your past self and its old mental, vital and physical formations and habits; one has continually to leave behind his past selves and to see, act and live from an always higher and higher conscious level. It cannot be done if you insist on "freedom" for your human mind and vital ego. All the parts of the human being are entitled to express and satisfy themselves in their own way at their own risk and peril, if he so chooses, as long as he leads the ordinary life. But to enter into a path of yoga whose whole object is to substitute for these human things the law and power of a greater Truth and the whole heart of whose method is surrender to the Divine Shakti, and yet to go on claiming this so-called freedom, which is no more than a subjection to certain ignorant cosmic Forces, is to indulge in a blind contradiction and to claim the right to lead a double life.

Least of all can this yoga be done if those who profess to be its sadhaks, continue always to make themselves centres, instruments or spokesmen of the forces of the Ignorance which oppose, deny and ridicule its very principle and object. On one side there is the supramental realisation, the overshadowing and descending power of the supramental Divine, the light and force of a far greater Truth than any yet realised on the earth, something therefore beyond what the little human mind and its logic regard as the only permanent realities, something whose nature and way and process of development here it cannot conceive or perceive by its own inadequate instruments or judge by its puerile standards; in spite of all opposition this is pressing down for manifestation in the physical consciousness and the material life. On the other side is this lower vital nature with all its pretentious arrogance, ignorance, obscurity, dullness or incompetent turbulence, standing for its own prolongation, standing against the descent, refusing to believe in any real reality or real possibility of a supramental or superhuman consciousness and creation, or, still more absurd, demanding, if it exists at all, that it should conform to its own little standards, seizing greedily upon everything that seems to disprove it, denying the presence of the Divine, — for it knows that without that presence the work is impossible, — affirming loudly its own thoughts, judgments, desires, instincts, and, if these are contradicted, avenging itself by casting abroad doubt, denial, disparaging criticism, revolt and disorder. These are the two things now in presence between which every one will have to choose.

For this opposition, this sterile obstruction and blockade against the descent of the divine Truth cannot last for ever. Every one must come down finally on one side or the other, on the side of the Truth or against it. The supramental realisation cannot coexist with the persistence of the lower Ignorance; it is incompatible with continued satisfaction in a double nature.

There can be only one "solution" for this kind of struggle, — to recognise these feelings for what they are, unregenerated movements of the old vital nature, and to reject these vital suggestions as suggestions of adverse forces that want to push you out of the straight path. If the mind of the sadhak supports these vital movements, if any part of his nature accepts and cherishes them, then, so long as he allows them to do so, he cannot get rid of the struggle.

All these suggestions are very familiar, and they are always the same both in expression and substance. The reactions too are always the same and their very nature is sufficient to show the source from which they come, — disappointment of unsatis-

fied desire, despondency, discontent, unhappiness, the sense of
grievance and injustice, revolt, a fall to tamas and inertia (because
the vital being refuses participation in the spiritual effort unless
its egoistic demands are conceded,) dryness, dullness, cessation
of the sadhana. The same phrases even are repeated, — "no life
in this existence", "suffocation", "limitation", "air-tight compartments"; and all this simply means that the lower vital nature
— or some part of it — is in revolt and wants something else
than the divine Truth and the tapasya that leads to the supramental change. It refuses to give up ego and desire and claim
and demand or to accept a true self-giving and surrender, while
yet it feels the pressure on it to transform itself into an instrument
of the divine life. It is this pressure that it calls suffocation. The
refusal to let it expand its desires and make a big place for itself
it calls limitation of the being. The calm, purity, collected silence
which are the basis of the tapasya for the supramental change,
— this is what it stigmatises as "no life". Right rule and insistence on self-denial and self-mastery and restraint from claim and
demand are what it calls "air-tight compartments." And the worst
suggestions and most dangerous deception come when this spirit
of demand and desire is dissimulated in a spiritual garb and takes
a form which makes it seem to the sadhak a part of the yoga.

There is only one way of escape from this siege of the
lower vital nature. It is the entire rejection of all egoistic vital
demand, claim and desire and the replacement of the dissatisfied
vital urge by the purity of psychic aspiration. Not the satisfaction of these vital clamours nor, either, an ascetic retirement
is the true solution, but the surrender of the vital being to the
Divine and a single-minded consecration to the supreme Truth
into which desire and demand cannot enter. For the nature of
the supreme Truth is Light and Ananda, and where desire and
demand are there can be no Ananda.

It is not the vital demand but the psychic urge that alone
can bring the nature towards the supramental transformation;
for it alone can change the mental and vital and show them their
own true movement. But constantly the vital demand is being
taken for the psychic aspiration; and yet the difference is clear.
In the psychic aspiration there are none of these reactions, there is

no revolt, no justification of revolt: for the psychic aspires through inner union with the Divine and surrender. It does not question and challenge, but seeks to understand through unity with the Divine Will. It does not ask for small personal satisfactions, but finds its satisfaction in the growth of the Truth within the being; what it seeks and finds is not any indulgence of a vital and physical claim, but the true nearness which consists in the constant presence of the Divine in the heart and the rule of the Divine in all the Nature. The cry of the psychic is always, "Let the Truth prevail, let Thy will be done and not mine". But the clamour of the vital is the very opposite: it calls to the Divine, "Let my will be Thine; obey my insistences, satisfy my desires, then only will I seek and accept Thee, for then only will I consent to see the Divine in Thee". It is hardly necessary to say which is the way to the Truth or which the right solution of any struggle in the nature.

The only creation for which there is any place here is the supramental, the bringing of the divine Truth down on the earth, not only into the mind and vital but into the body and into Matter. Our object is not to remove all "limitations" on the expansion of the ego or to give a free field and make unlimited room for the fulfilment of the ideas of the human mind or the desires of the ego-centred life-force. None of us are here to "do as we like", or to create a world in which we shall at last be able to do as we like; we are here to do what the Divine wills and to create a world in which the Divine Will can manifest its truth no longer deformed by human ignorance or perverted and mistranslated by vital desire. The work which the sadhak of the supramental yoga has to do is not his own work for which he can lay down his own conditions, but the work of the Divine which he has to do according to the conditions laid down by the Divine. Our yoga is not for our own sake but for the sake of the Divine. It is not our own personal manifestation that we are to seek, the manifestation of the individual ego freed from all bounds and from all bonds, but the manifestation of the Divine. Of that manifestation our own spiritual liberation, perfection, fullness is to be a result and a part, but not in any egoistic sense or for any ego-centred or self-seeking purpose. This liberation, perfection, fullness too must not be pursued for our own sake, but for the sake of the Divine. I emphasise this character of the creation because a constant forgetfulness of this simple and central truth, a conscious, half-conscious or wholly ignorant confusion about it has been at the root of most of the vital revolts that have spoiled many an individual sadhana here and disturbed the progress of the general inner work and the spiritual atmosphere.

The supramental creation, since it is to be a creation upon earth, must be not only an inner change but a physical and external manifestation also. And it is precisely for this part of the work, the most difficult of all, that surrender is most needful; for this reason, that it is the actual descent of the supramental Divine into Matter and the working of the Divine Presence and Power there that can alone make the physical and external change possible. Even the most powerful self-assertion of human will and endeavour is impotent to bring it about; as for egoistic insistence and vital revolt, they are, so long as they last, insuperable obstacles to the descent. Only a calm, pure and surrendered physical consciousness, full of the psychic aspiration, can be its field; this alone can make an effective opening of the material being to the Light and Power and the supramental change a thing actual and practicable. It is for this that we are here in the body, and it is for this that you and other sadhaks are in the Ashram near us. But it is not by insistence on petty demands and satisfactions in the external field or on an outer nearness pleasing to the vital nature and its pride or desire that you can get the true relation with the Divine in this province. If you want the realisation there, it is the true nearness that you must seek, the descent and presence of the Mother in your physical consciousness, her constant inner touch in the physical being and its activities, her will and knowledge behind all its work and thought and movement and the ever present Ananda of that presence expelling all vital and physical separateness, craving and desire. If you have that, then you have all the nearness you can ask for, and the rest you will gladly leave to the Mother's knowledge and will to decide. For with this in you there can be no feeling of being kept away, no sense of a gulf and distance, no complaint of a unity that is lacking or an empty dryness and denial of nearness.

A time comes when after a long preparation of the mind and vital being, it becomes necessary to open also the physical nature. But when that happens very often the vital exaltation which can be very great when the experience is on its own plane, falls away and the obscure obstructive physical and gross material consciousness appears in its unrelieved inertia. Inertia, tamas, stupidity, narrowness and limitation, an inability to progress, doubt, dullness, dryness, a constant forgetfulness of the spiritual experiences received are the characteristics of the unregenerated physical nature, when that is not pushed by the vital and is not supported either by the higher mental will and intelligence. This seems to be in part what has temporarily happened to you; but the way out is not to excite the physical by any vital revolt and outcry, or to blame for your condition either circumstances or the Mother, — for that will only make things worse and increase the tamas, dryness, dullness, inertia, — but to recognise that there is here an element of the universal Nature reflected in yours, which you must eliminate. And this can only be done by more and more surrender and aspiration and by so bringing in from beyond the vital and the mind the divine peace, light, power and presence. This is the only way towards the transformation and fulfilment of the physical nature.

I do not think after what I have written, I need add anything about the specific complaints that you make in your letter. Two things perhaps need to be made clear. First, the arrangements actually in existence about the work, about external demands, about correspondence and "seeing" people are the only feasible ones in the present circumstances, if the heavy work the Mother has to do is to be at all physically possible. Next, it is precisely by action in silence that we can best do our work much more than by speech or writing, which can only be subordinate and secondary. For in this yoga those will succeed best who know how to obey and follow the written and spoken word, but can also bear the silence and feel in it and receive (without listening to other voices or mistaking mental and vital suggestions and impulsions for the divine Truth and the divine Will) help, support and guidance.

***

In your letter ... you write that you are very tired, restlessness and tamas prevail in the physical, there is a constant struggle more or less intense between the psychic being and the physical nature. Now this was exactly your condition in the last months when you were here. Then you wanted to go because the pressure was too great, because the struggle with the restless and tamasic physical nature and the Asuric influence was too hard and continuous, because you felt very tired and needed to go away for a rest, for respite, to recover.

How then can you come back in the same condition? The pressure will be still greater than before, the struggle constant; you are likely to be still more tired and depressed than you were. And it will be harder for you to bear because the personal position will entirely be changed. You will have no special place, no authority delegated, no work entrusted to you; you will not be near the Mother but at a distance among others. The Asuric nature in you which had become an intolerable hindrance to the work and dangerous to yourself and to others will be given no kind of indulgence. It is clear that you would find the conditions unbearable unless you had undergone in the meantime a fundamental change. Therefore you must not ask to come here until you have acquired a stable quiet and peace both within you and in your external atmosphere.

Wherever you are, we shall always be near to your psychic being and ready to help it to conquer. As things are with you now, that help is likely to act better at a distance than when you were near and were at every moment repelling it by your wrong inner movements and reactions and your wrong speech and acts. But to profit by our help you will have to do what you have never yet really done, at least in your external being. You will have in your physical nature itself resolutely to turn from the Asura and his ways and refuse to indulge him on any pretext in any thought, feeling, speech or action which would help him still to possess your instruments and determine or influence your attitude and your acts. To become quiet and quietly and simply to maintain this persistent and patient rejection with our help, without rajasic struggle, sincerely and in fact and in every detail, not merely in wish and idea, is what you need to do. To be divided, to aspire in one part of your being and to indulge and justify and cherish the wrong movements with another part can lead to nothing but endless struggle and fatigue. Only by this turn and change will the struggle and fatigue pass away and purity come.

It is now one month since you wrote your letter announcing the new favourable turn in your sadhana. You will have had time to see whether the turn was decisive and how far it has moved towards completeness. The test will be whether it gets rid fundamentally of the Asuric turn in your external being. All ambition, pride and vanity must disappear from the thoughts and the feelings. There must be no seeking now or in the future for place, position or prestige, no stipulation for a high seat among the elect, no demand for a special closeness to the Mother, no claim or assertion of right, no attempt to thrust yourself between her and others, no endeavour to intercept what she is giving to them or to share in it, no imposing of yourself on her or on other sadhaks. All falsehood must be rejected from the speech, thought and action and all ostentation, arrogance and insolence. A simple, quiet and unpretending aspiration to the Truth and reception of it for its own sake and not for any profit it may bring you, a straightforward acceptance of the Mother's will whatever it may be, a complete casting away of all pretensions and pretences, a readiness to obey completely and without reserve and to accept any position and any discipline given are the only conditions on which a divine change can be effected in you. It is for this that you must strive.

On our side we await a certain conquest on the material plane, which is not yet accomplished, before we can tell you to return. As you yourself saw once, till this is done your stay here would not be helpful to you. When you are ready in your inner condition and things are ready here, then the Mother will call you.

If you want to change, you must first resolutely get rid of the defects of your vital being, persevering steadily, however difficult it may be or however long it may take, calling in always the divine help and compelling yourself always to be entirely sincere.

As for fitness and unfitness, nobody is entirely fit for this yoga; one has to become fit by aspiration, by *abhyāsa*, by sincerity and surrender. If you have always desired the spiritual life, it is the psychic part of you that desired it, but your vital has always come in the way. Establish a sincere will in the vital; do not allow personal desires and demands and selfishness and falsehood to mix in your sadhana; then alone the vital in you will become fit for the sadhana.

If you want your endeavour to succeed, it must become always purer and more steady and persistent. If you practise sincerely, you will get the help needed by you.

Evidently, the condition into which you have fallen is due to an upsurging of suppressed elements in the lower vital nature. It has been compelled by the mind and the higher vital part in you to give up the little "joys and pleasures" to which it was habituated, but it — or at any rate the subconscient part of it which is often the most powerful — did that without entire conviction and probably with "reservations" and "safeguards" and in exchange for a promise of compensations, other and greater joys and pleasures to replace all it was losing. This is evident from what you write; your description of the nature of the depression, the return of what you call impure thoughts which are merely indices of the subconscient lower vital desire-complex, the doubt thrown upon the generosity of the Divine, the demand for compensation for losses, something like striking a bargain with the Divine, a *quid pro quo* pact, are all unmistakable. Latterly, there has been a combination of circumstances which have rather suddenly increased the deprivation of its former outlets; this attack is its way of non-co-operation or protest. There is only one way to deal with it, — to cast the whole thing away, depression, demands, doubts, sex-thoughts, the whole undesirable baggage, and have in its place the one true movement, the call for the consciousness and the presence of the Divine.

It may be that behind this persistence of the lower vital demand for satisfaction there was something not quite clear in the obscure part of the physical mind in your mental attitude towards the yoga. You seem to regard this demand for the replacement of the old lower vital satisfactions by other joys and pleasures as something quite legitimate; but joys and pleasures are not the object of yoga and a bargain or demand for a replacement of this kind can be no legitimate or healthy element in the sadhana. If it is there, it will surely impede the flow of spiritual experience. Ananda, yes; but Ananda and the spiritual happiness which precedes it (*adhyātma-sukham*) are something quite different from joys and pleasures. And even Ananda one cannot demand or make it a condition for pursuing the sadhana — it comes as a crown, a natural outcome and its true condition is the growth of the true consciousness, peace, calm, light, strength, the equanimity which resists all shocks and persists through success and failure. It is these things which must be the first objects of the sadhana, not any hedonistic experience even of the highest kind; for that must come of itself as a result of the Divine Presence.

Meanwhile, the first thing you must do is to throw out this perilous stuff of despondency and its accompaniments and recover a quiet and clear balance. A quiet mind and a quiet vital are the first conditions for success in sadhana.

It is evident that you still cherish some misunderstanding about peace and joy and Ananda. (Peace, by the way, is not joy — for peace can be there even when joy is quiescent.) It is not a fact that one ought not to pray or aspire for peace or spiritual joy. Peace is the very basis of all the siddhi in the yoga, and why should not one pray or aspire for foundation in the yoga ? Spiritual joy or a deep inner happiness (not disturbed even when there come superficial storms or perturbations) is a constant concomitant of contact or union with the Divine, and why should it be forbidden to pray or aspire for contact with the Divine and the

joy that attends it? As for Ananda, I have already explained
that I mean by Ananda something greater than peace or joy,
something that, like Truth and Light, is the very nature of
the supramental Divine. It can come by frequent inrushes
or descents, partially or for a time even now, but it cannot remain in the system so long as the system has not been prepared
for it. Meanwhile, peace and joy can be there permanently, but
the condition of this permanence is that one should have the
constant contact or indwelling of the Divine, and this comes
naturally not to the outer mind or vital but to the inner soul or
psychic being. Therefore one who wants his yoga to be a path of
peace or joy must be prepared to dwell in his soul rather than in
his outer mental and emotional nature.

I objected in a former letter not to aspiration but to a demand, to making peace, joy or Ananda a condition for following
the yoga. And it is undesirable because if you do so, then the
vital, not the psychic, takes the lead. When the vital takes the
lead, then unrest, despondency, unhappiness can always come,
since these things are the very nature of the vital — the vital can
never remain constantly in joy and peace, for it needs their opposites in order to have the sense of the drama of life. And yet
when unrest and unhappiness come, the vital at once cries, "I
am not given my due, what is the use of my doing the yoga?"
Or else, it makes a gospel of its unhappiness and says that the
path to fulfilment must be a tragic road through the desert.
And yet it is precisely this predominance of the vital in us that
makes a necessity of the passage through the desert. If the psychic were always there in front, the desert would be no longer a
desert and the wilderness would blossom with the rose.

The Ananda you describe is evidently that of the inner vital
when it is full of the psychic influence and floods with it the external vital also. It is the true Ananda and there is nothing in it
of the old vital nature. When the psychic thus uses the vital to
express itself, this kind of intense ecstasy is the natural form it
takes. This intensity and the old vital excitement are two quite

different things and must not be confused together. Where there is the intensity with a pure and full satisfaction, contentment and gratitude leaving no room for claim, demand or depressing reaction, that is the true vital movement.

***

When the vital being has been touched by the psychic, mere vital pleasure has no longer any interest, and may also be felt as a disturbance and discomfort because of the lowering effect upon the consciousness.

Pain can be turned into Ananda, but I don't think that there is a special stage for that.

***

Once the vital being has come forward and shown its difficulty — there is nobody who has not one crucial difficulty or another there — it must be dealt with and conquered.

It must be dealt with not by the mind but directly by the supramental power.

Not peace and knowledge in the mind, but peace, faith, calm strength in the vital being itself (and especially in this part of it that is defective) is the thing to be established. To open yourself and allow all this to be brought down into it is the proper course.

The deficiency is not in the higher mind or mind proper; there is therefore no use in going back to establish mental peace. The difficulty is in that part of the vital being which is not sufficiently open and confident and not sufficiently strong and courageous and in the physical mind which lends its support to these things. To get the supramental light and calm and strength and intensity down there is what you need.

You may have all the mental knowledge in the world and yet be impotent to face vital difficulties. Courage, faith, sincerity towards the Light, rejection of opposite suggestions and adverse voices are there the true help. Then only can knowledge itself be at all effective.

Not mental control but some descent of a control from

above the mind is the power demanded in the realisation. This control derived eventually from the supermind is a control by the Divine Power.

If you see more clearly any deficiencies of your vital nature and the necessity of a transformation, that itself is a sign of psychic growth. They should not be a cause of discouragement, for these are common defects of the human vital, and by an increased psychic opening they will lose their hold and finally disappear.

As for the diminution of mental control over the vital movements, that often happens temporarily in the course of the yoga. Mental control has to be replaced by a greater control from above and by the calm, purity and strong peace of the vital itself opened to the Divine Force and its government of the whole nature.

Do not allow yourself to be troubled or discouraged by any difficulties, but quietly and simply open yourself to the Mother's force and allow it to change you.

It is not at all true that the Mother takes away the mental control — that is one of the many foolish misinterpretations that certain sadhaks make about the sadhana. What is true — and that is the cause of what you feel — is that when you try to control fully your habitual movements in the vital by the sadhana, instead of sometimes controlling them and sometimes indulging, then they make a violent resistance so that they seem to increase. The sadhak has to stand firm and refuse to be overborne or discouraged by this violence. In dream it is usually the case that even what one has thrown out from the waking state, comes up for a long time — that is because all these things remain still in the subconscient and it is the subconscient that creates a great part of people's dreams. Thus if one no longer has sexual desires in the waking state he can still have sex-dreams — and emissions — with a more or less frequent recurrence; he can still meet people in dreams whom he never sees or hears or thinks of in his waking hours — and so on. All the more are such dreams likely to come when the waking mind is nót free.

It depends on what is meant by a wrong or unnecessary movement. Certain things have to fall off before the establishment [of the higher consciousness] can be *complete*. Others that are unnecessary have to be put aside if they are incompatible with the full sadhana or the growth of the inner consciousness, but can be continued if the consciousness established is such that doing or not doing makes no difference to it.

The phrase ["wrong movements in sadhana"] covers pretty nearly everything that is hurtful to spiritual progress — movements of doubt, revolt, egoistic desire or ambition, sexual indulgence are the most common, but there are plenty of others.

The outward revolt is the refusal of discipline and obedience — the inward revolt is of many kinds, it may take many forms, e.g. a revolt of the vital against the Mother, a revolt of the mind against the Truth, a rejection of the spiritual life, a demand to enthrone the ego as the Divine or to serve something that flatters the vital ego and supports its demands and call that the Divine, a response to vital suggestions of distrust, despair, self-destruction or departure — and many others.

Vehemence comes from the unregenerate vital ego which is just the thing that stands most in the way of the transformation; other things are comparatively mild obstacles compared with this part of the being. It is much better that the Mother refused consideration to this part of you — consideration would have been a much more dangerous test than refusal.

["Vital consecration":] Consecration means offering and making sacred to the Mother so that the whole vital nature may belong to her and not to the lower nature.

It [vital consecration] is to offer all the vital nature and its movements to the Divine so that it may be purified and only the true movements in consonance with the Divine Will may be there and all egoistic desires and impulses disappear.

Sometimes the aspiration is felt at the navel, but that is part of the larger vital. The lower vital is below. The lower vital aspires by offering all its small movements in the fire of purification, by calling for the light and power to descend into it and rid it of its little greeds, jealousies, resistances and revolts over small matters, angers, vanities, sexualities etc. to be replaced by the right movements governed by selflessness, purity, obedience to the urge of the Divine Force in all things.

It is evident that the lower vital has received the Divine Consciousness when even in the small movements of life there is an aspiration to the Divine, a reference as it were to the Divine Light for guidance or some feeling of offering to the Divine or guidance by the Divine. The lower vital commands the little details of emotion, impulse, sensation, action — it is these that, when converted, it offers to the Divine control for transformation.

*
**

It is true that for the external vital an outer discipline is necessary for the purification, otherwise it remains restless and fanciful and at the mercy of its own impulses — so that no basis can be built there for a quiet and abiding higher consciousness to remain firmly. The attitude you have taken for the work is, of course, the best one and, applying it steadily, the progress you feel was bound to come and is sure to increase.

[Discipline:] To live and act under control or according to a standard of what is right — not to allow the vital or the physical to do whatever they like and not to let the mind run about according to its fancy without truth or order. Also to obey those who ought to be obeyed.

An overmastering impulse is not necessarily an inspiration of true guidance; in following always such impulses one is more likely to become a creature of random caprices. Inexhaustible energy is an excellent thing, but not an energy without discipline.

The will ought to have the same mastery over impulses as over the thoughts. Many people find it easier to control an impulse than to prevent a thought.

It [inability to accomplish anything in life] usually comes from a certain instability in the lower vital which does not give a consistent support to the Will, but is restless and fluctuates from one interest to another. It does not mean an incapacity for success — usually one who has that could succeed in many directions, but the fluctuation prevents sustained success in any. It is a defect that has to be got over and can be got over.

The first is vital indecision — the other is vital instability. Those who can't choose, have the vital indecision and it is usually due to a too active physical mind, seeing too many things or too many sides at a time. The other rises from a lack of control and too much impulse.

There are some who are solid and tenacious in their vital, it is they who can be steady — others are more mercurial and easily moved by impulses, it is these who are sometimes enthusiastic, sometimes drop into fatigue. It is a matter of temperament. On the other hand the mercurial people are often capable of a quicker ardour, so that they can progress fast if they want in their own way. In any case the remedy for all that is to find one's true self above mind and vital and so not bound by temperament.

The bitterness you feel is that of a restless and dissatisfied vital which did not get what it desired because it could not desire anything strongly and persistently. Otherwise it could have all the vital desires — marriage, friends, position, etc. — but it could stick to nothing owing to a kind of weak restlessness. In the yoga it has shown the same restless weakness, — otherwise it could by this time have attained something, and besides there was the sex-impulse which it would neither satisfy nor leave. You must know what you want and want it with your whole will — it is only so that there can be an end of this restlessness and failure.

If he wants to make himself some day fit for the spiritual life, the first thing to be avoided is vital restlessness. To do the work one has to do with a quiet mind, making an offering of it to the Divine and trying to get rid of egoism and vital desire, is the best way to prepare oneself.

You should not indulge this sense of grief — remain calm, confident, turned to the one Will in all circumstances; that is the way to secure that each step will be taken in the right measure and produce its best possible consequences. Regard henceforth the question of X and your relation with X as a minor and subordinate thing on the outer side of your sadhana. If you take it as a problem of the first importance, it will become that and stand in your way again. Look at it as a question from the past that has been firmly settled and put in its place and turn to the central aim of your sadhana.

For the rest, apart from this circumstance, you need change nothing in the inward aim and concentration of your will and endeavour on the one thing to be done — the entire self-giving and self-dedication of your inner and outer being to the Divine alone. If you can adopt firmly the right inward attitude, it may even be easier so than by an outward rule for your main guidance.

The one thing necessary is to arrive at a fixed and definite choice in the mind which one can always oppose to the vital disturbance. Disturbance in the vital will always come so long as the full peace has not descended there, but with a fixed resolution in the mind kept always to the front the acuteness of the disturbance can disappear and the road become shorter.

V

It is the lower (physical) vital that acts like that. This part of Nature does not act according to reason, it has no understanding of things. It acts only according to desire, impulse and habit. The mind and the heart and the higher vital have understood and put themselves on the side of the Peace and Force that are acting to transform the nature. But this still responds to the old forces when they touch it. It is a question of getting down the Peace and Force and Light into this part, so that whenever the outside forces of the lower Nature touch they will find that force there and not the old response. It is a little difficult because of the long past habit, but it will come more and more as the Force descends into the body and pervades it in its descent.

The opposition of the vital is never reasonable, even when it puts forward reasons. It acts from its nature and habit of desire not from reason.

There is perhaps something of all that — but this part of the vital has no precise reasons to support itself with — it takes hold of any mood of disappointment or strong sense of difficulty. It is a factor in all human natures, — restless, desiring, eager, despondent, unstable. Stand back from it and do not allow it to govern or move you. There is a right part of the vital which must be used — ardent, sensitive to the higher things, capable of great love and devotion. Strengthen that and support it on the psychic and on the peace and wideness that comes from above.

It is not a question of feeling sorrow or joy or any other emotion, everybody does that who has not overcome the ordinary Nature. That is not sentimental but emotional. Sentimentalism comes in when you take pleasure either in indulging or in displaying the feeling or when you have them for no reason or without sufficient reason.

The lower vital is not a part that listens to reason. There is no *why* to its action; it acts in a particular way because it has been accustomed to act in that way, and it goes on even if the doing brings a painful reaction.

The doubts of the sadhaks more often rise from the vital than from the true mental — when the vital goes wrong or is in trouble or depression, the doubts rise and repeat themselves in the same form and the same language, no matter how much the mind had been convinced by either patent proofs or intellectual answers. I have noticed that always the vital is irrational (even when it uses the reason to justify itself) and it believes or disbelieves according to its feeling, not according to reason.

The vital started in its evolution with obedience to impulse and no reason — as for strategy, the only strategy it understands is some tactics by which it can compass its desires. It does not like the voice of knowledge and wisdom — but curiously enough by the necessity which has grown up in man of justifying action by reason, the *vital mind* has developed a strategy of its own which is to get the reason to find out reasons for justifying its own feelings and impulses. When the reason is too clear to lend itself to this game, the vital falls back on its native habit of shutting its ears and going on its course. In these attacks, the plan of unfitness, "Since you are not pleased with my impulses and I can't change them, that shows I am unfit, so I had better go" is the counter strategy it adopts. But even if one counters that, the impulse itself is sufficient, coming strongly as it does from universal Nature, to restore to the vital for a short time its old blind irrational instinct to obey the push that has come.

The vital always prefers to cover its movements from the Light.

You have to develop discrimination so that it becomes impossible for the vital to deceive you.

Be careful about vital movements and formations — when you allow them, you are on the dangerous slope.

The whole significance of your sentences was that you had made all the necessary resolutions, but you could not carry them out because the Force refused to support you. That is the usual trick of the vital mind when it wants to rid itself of the blame for difficulties or want of progress in the sadhana: "I am doing all I can, but the Force is not supporting me". It is no use your quoting other sentences, because you write now one thing, now another, shifting your ground for the sake of your argument. If logic could help you to get rid of this trickiness of the vital mind, it would be worth while learning Logic.

As to what you ask about anything else being behind than what your mind was conscious of in its surface intention, there is more often than not something behind when the vital meddles in the matter — and it is a part of self-knowledge not to be misled by the mind's surface movements but to detect this something behind. For it is the habit of the vital to make a mask of the mind's arrangements about feelings and actions in order to conceal even from the self-observation of the doer the secret underlying motive or forces behind the speech, act or feelings.

Your letter of the morning came entirely from the disturbed and wounded vital; that was why I was in no hurry to answer. I do not know why you are so ready to believe that myself or the Mother act from ordinary movements of anger, vexation or displeasure; there was nothing of the kind in what I wrote. You had been repeatedly falling from your attained level of a higher consciousness and, in spite of our suggestions to you to see what was pulling you down, your only reply was that you could see nothing. We know perfectly well that it was a part of your vital which did not want to change and, not wanting to change, was hiding itself from the mind and the mind itself did not seem very willing to see, — so we thought it necessary when you gave us a chance by what you wrote — first about X and secondly about the thoughts of the past — to indicate plainly and strongly the nature of the obstacle — on one side your old sentiment persisting in the opposite form of anger, resentment and wounded feelings, on the other the vital's habit of self-esteem, censorious judgment of others, the sense of superiority in sadhana or in other respects, a wish to appear well before others and before yourself also. This especially has a blinding influence and prevents the clear examination of oneself and the perception of the obstacles that are interfering with the spiritual progress. Even if the mind aspires to know and change, a habit of that kind acting concealed in the vital is quite enough to stand in the way and prevent both the knowledge and the change. I was therefore careful to speak plainly of vanity and self-righteousness, so that this part of the vital might not try not to see. The Mother speaks or writes much more pointedly and sharply to those whom she wishes to push rapidly on the way, because they are capable of it, and they do not resent or suffer but are glad of the pressure and the plainness, because they know by experience that it helps them to see their obstacles and change. If you wish to progress rapidly you must get rid of this vital reaction of *abhimāna*, suffering, wounded feeling, seeking for argument of self-justification, outcry against the touch that is intended to liberate — for so long as you have these, it is difficult for us to deal openly and firmly with the obstacles created by the vital nature.

In regard to the difference between you and X. The Mother's warning to you against the undesirability of too much talk, loose chat and gossip, social self-dispersion was entirely meant and stands; when you indulge in these things, you throw yourself out into a very small and ignorant consciousness in which your vital defects get free play and this is likely to bring you out of what you have developed in your inner consciousness. That was why we said that if you felt a reaction against these things when you went to X's, it was a sign of your (psychic) sensitiveness coming into you — into your vital and nervous being, and we meant that it was all for the good. But in dealing with others, in withdrawing from these things you should not allow any sense of superiority to creep in or force on them by your manner or spirit a sense of disapproval or condemnation or pressure on them to change. It is for your personal inward need that you draw back from these things, that is all. As for them, what they do in these matters, right or wrong, is their affair, and ours; we will deal with them according to what we see as necessary and possible for them at the moment and for that purpose we can not only deal quite differently with different people, allowing for one what we forbid for another, but we may deal differently with the same person at different times, allowing or even encouraging today what we shall forbid tomorrow. X's case is quite different from yours, for there is no resemblance in your natures. I told you that or something like it long ago and I emphasised in my letter to X that what might be the rule for myself or Y was not to be applied or going to be applied in his case. To deal otherwise would be to create difficulties in his sadhana and not to make it easier for him or swifter. I have also told him quite clearly in my letter that the attempt at meeting and mixing with others — which in the ordinary human life is attempted by sociableness and other contacts — has to be realised in yoga on another plane of consciousness and without the lower mixture — for a higher unity with all on a spiritual and psychic basis. But the way, the time, the order of movements by which this is done, need not be the same for everybody. If he attempted to force himself it would lead to gloom, despondency and an artificial movement which would not be the true way to success. A human soul and nature cannot be dealt with by a set of mental rules applicable to everybody in the same way; if it were so, there would be no need of a Guru, each could set his chart of yogic rules before him like the rules of Sandow's exercise and follow them till he became the perfect Siddha!

I have said so much in order to let you understand why we do not deal in the same way with X as with you or another. The tendency to take what I lay down for one and apply it without discrimination to another is responsible for much misunderstanding. A general statement too, true in itself, cannot be applied to everyone alike or applied now and immediately without consideration of condition or circumstance or person or time. I may say generally that to bring down the supermind is my aim in the yoga or that to do that one has first to rise out of mind into overmind, but if on the strength of that, anybody and everybody began trying to pull down the supermind or force his way immediately out of mind into overmind, the result would be disaster.

Therefore concern yourself with your own progress and follow there the lead the Mother gives you. Leave others to do the same; the Mother is there to guide and help them according to their need and their nature. It does not in the least matter if the way she follows with him seems different or the opposite of that which she takes with you. That is the right one for him as this is the right one for you.

You have now begun to see the difficulties that are still there in your vital; keep to that clear perception, let it grow clearer and more precise. Concentrate on what you have to do and do not let yourself be disturbed this way and that by irrelevant preoccupations or any other influence.

It is certainly not the answering of questions that will remove the underlying cause of the recurrence. Even if the answers satisfy, it could only be for a time. The same questionings would rise either in a mechanical reiteration — for it is not truly the reason from which they arise, it is a certain part of the vital consciousness affected by the surrounding atmosphere — or else presented from a shifted ground or a somewhat changed angle of vision. The difficulty can only disappear if you remain resolute that it shall disappear — if you refuse to attach any value to the justifications which the mind is *made* to put forward for your "sadness" under this atmospheric influence and, as you did in certain other matters, stick fast to the resolution to make the yogic change, to awake the psychic fully, not to follow the voices of the mind but to do rather what the Mother asks of you, persisting *however difficult it may be* or seem to be. It is so that the psychic can fully awake and establish its influence, not on your higher vital where it is already awake, but on the lower vital, for it is there that your difficulties are and that this vital depression recurs.

It is indeed amazing that you should have lost yourself to an extravagant deception such as X has set on foot. It is simply the spirit of vital falsehood, dramatic and romantic, obscuring the reason and shutting out common sense and simple truth. To clear the vital, you must get out of it all compromise with falsehood — no matter how specious the reason it advances — and get the habit of simple straightforward psychic truth engraved in it so that nothing may have a chance to enter. If this lesson can be imprinted in that part of the vital which is capable of such compromises some good will come out of this wrong movement. Put the Mother's notice henceforth at the door of your vital being, "No falsehood hereafter shall ever enter here", and station a sentry there to see that it is put into execution.

As regards your defence of X, they sound like X's own ideas and very queer ideas they are. If they are right, we should have to come to the following conclusions: —

1. Sattwa is not the best passage towards realisation, Rajas is the best way to become spiritual. It is the rajasic man with his fierce ego and violent passions who is the true sadhak of the Divine.

2. The Asura is the best Bhakta. The Gita is quite wrong in holding up the Deva nature as the condition of realisation and the Asura nature as contrary to it. It is the other way round.

3. Ravana, Hiranyakashipu, Shishupala were the greatest devotees of the Divine because they were capable of hostility to the Divine and so were liberated in a few lives — compared with them the great Rishis and Bhaktas were very poor spiritual vessels. I am aware of the paradox about Ravana in the Purana, but let me point out that these Asuras and Rakshasas did not

pretend to be disciples or worshippers of Rama or Krishna or Vishnu or use their position as disciples to get Moksha by revolt — they got it by being enemies and getting killed and absorbed into the Godhead.

4. Obedience to the Guru, worship of the Divine are all tommy rot and fit only for sheep, not men. To turn round furiously on the Guru or the Divine, abuse him, express contempt, challenge his sincerity, declare his actions to be wrong, foolish or a trick — to assert oneself as right at every point and his judgment as mistaken, prejudiced, absurd, false, a support of devils etc., etc. is the best way of devotion and the true relation between Guru and Shishya. Disobedience is the highest respect to the Guru, anger and revolt are the noblest worship one can give to the Divine.

5. One who takes the blows of Mahakali with joy as a means of discovering his faults and increasing in light and strength and purity is a sheep and unworthy of disciplehood — one who responds to the quietest pressure to change by revolt and persisting in his errors is a strong man and a mighty Adhar and a noble disciple on the way to perfection.

I could go on multiplying the consequences, but I have no time. Do you really believe all these things? They are the natural consequences of X's theory or of this theory of revolt as the way to perfection. If you accept the premiss, you have to accept the logical consequences. That is what X did — only he called his errors Truth and the way prescribed by me as falsehood explicable only by the fact that I was a "Master who had forgotten his higher self". And the consequences led to his departure, not willed by us, but by his own choice — and under such circumstances that he has made it a practical impossibility for me to let him come back unless he undergoes a change which the experience of the past does not warrant me in thinking possible.

Your analysis is perfectly accurate — with this clear knowledge of the mechanism of the whole thing it should be easier to get rid of these ignorant forces. It is true that they care nothing for truth or reason and appeal only to the blind feelings of the vital, but still the light of the true consciousness turned steadily on them ought to so much enlighten your own vital that it will no longer lend itself to the things that seek to disturb it and be ready to take its stand in the calm and happiness of surrender to the Divine.

VI

The difficulty you have in your vital is not peculiar to you, but is in some degree and in some form or another a fairly general malady. Its constant return, the mechanical irrational return even when all the rest of the nature has rejected it, is due to the obstinacy of the material consciousness always repeating the old movement in the old groove at the least touch from the old habitual forces. It is a question of faith, patience and persistence. One must be more obstinate than the obstinate material nature and persevere until the light and truth can take permanent hold of the parts which are still responsive to the old movements. There can be no doubt that with this perseverance the Truth will in the end conquer.

It would make it easier if you could get rid of certain fixed ideas and of the habitual reaction of depression or despair when these recurrences come. For instance, dismiss any question about the "possibility" of conversion of your vital being; you should see rather that it is certain and not merely possible. When there are these recurrences, do not allow yourself to be depressed by them, but simply observe and stand back and call in the higher force with the full confidence that these are mechanical recurrences and in substance nothing more — however strong they may seem in appearance. The principle of mechanical repetition is very strong in the material nature, so strong that it makes one easily think that it is incurable. That, however, is only a trick of the forces of this material inconscience; it is by creating this impression that they try to endure. If, on the contrary, you remain firm, refuse to be depressed or discouraged and, even in the moment of attack, affirm the certainty of eventual victory, the victory itself will come much more easily and sooner.

When the vital takes hold of a thing, it is often like that — it fixes it continually on the mind till it is either satisfied or the hold thrown off.

You should not allow yourself to be discouraged by any persistence of the movements of the lower vital nature. There are some that tend always to persist and return until the whole physical nature is changed by the transformation of the most material consciousness; till then their pressure recurs — sometimes with a revival of their force, sometimes more dully — as a mechanical habit. Take from them all life-force by refusing any mental or vital assent; then the mechanical habit will become powerless to influence the thoughts and acts and will finally cease.

It is very often when one thinks a particular resistance is finished and is no longer in the vital that it surges up again.

The exacerbation of certain vital movements is a perfectly well-known phenomenon in yoga and does not mean that one has degenerated, but only that one has come to close grips instead of to a pleasant nodding acquaintance with the basic instincts of the earthly vital nature. I have had myself the experience of this rising to a height, during a certain stage of the spiritual development, of things that before hardly existed and seemed quite absent in the pure yogic life. These things rise up like that because they are fighting for their existence — they are not really personal to you and the vehemence of their attack is not due to any "badness" in the personal nature. I dare say seven sadhaks out of ten have a similar experience. Afterwards when they cannot effect their object which is to drive the sadhak out of his sadhana, the whole thing sinks and there is no longer any vehement trouble. I repeat that the only serious thing about it is the depression created in you and the idea of inability in the yoga that they take care to impress on the brain when they are at their work.. If you can get rid of that, the violence of the vital attacks is only the phenomenon of a stage and does not in the end matter.

All these things are there in human nature, habitual movements, which show their true nature only when the light of the higher consciousness is turned on them. Even after they have been rejected the possibility of a response to such suggestions from outside remains in the grain of the lower vital or vital-physical or the subconscient till there is the full enlightenment there.

The fact that your vital "goes out of the poise" and accepts them [ego, demand, desire] means that you keep yourself open to them. The sign that these things are no longer admitted is when the inner vital rejects them so that they become suggestions only and nothing else. There may arise a surge of suggestions or waves from the general nature, but they cannot get admission. It is only then that a will can be kept in which one is untouched by the general atmosphere.

It must be that on that occasion the consciousness got lowered and some vital wave came in from the atmosphere resuscitating the old vibrations of the restless vital which had quieted down. You must separate yourself from them and get the poise of quietude again. They have no longer any real basis in mind or heart, they rely only on the force of repetition that comes up from the subconscient and once started try to keep these old ideas and feelings repeating themselves so as to prevent the consciousness from settling down into quietude. But the poise once obtained is there and has only been covered up and has got to be uncovered again from these cloudings. You must get the habit of keeping quiet somewhere in yourself when these attacks come, of keeping something within that refuses to say ditto to these suggestions or accept them as its own proper thoughts and feelings.

Anyhow the Force will be put to help you; receive it and all that will go.

It was evidently not the action of something that is rooted still within, but an old movement returning from outside (from the universal Nature) to which something in the vital still responds by force of habit, force of accustomed recurrence. This is shown by the fact that you felt nothing at the time — only afterwards; also by the alternations of quiet and unrest after calling the Force, as if of something losing its hold and then trying to get it back and hold on still. Things thrown out always come back like that relying on the old habit of response in the stuff of the nature, — the old vibration. By throwing it out whenever it comes, in the end the part which responds begins to understand that it must not and is gradually or quickly liberated from the habit.

It is normal that when special pressure is put on a vital movement, a resistance whether in the vital itself (here vital-physical) or in the subconscient should manifest itself. It is sometimes a real resistance, sometimes it is only the *pravṛtti* presenting itself for purification.

The only way to get rid of these vital movements is to do persistently what he describes himself as doing with the invading forces — i.e. he must be always vigilant, try always at every moment to be conscious, always reject these things, refusing to take pleasure

in them, call on the Mother, bring down the descent of the
Light. If they return persistently he must not be discouraged;
it is not possible to change the nature at once, it takes a long time.
If, however, he can keep the psychic consciousness in the front,
then it will be much easier and there will be much less difficulty
and trouble in the change. That can be done by constant aspiration and *abhyāsa*.

The lower vital in most human beings is full of grave defects
and of movements that respond to hostile forces. A constant
psychic opening, a persistent rejection of these influences, a
separation of oneself from all hostile suggestions and the inflow
of the calm, light, peace, purity of the Mother's power would
eventually free the system from the siege.

What is needed is to be quiet and more and more quiet, to
look on these influences as something not yourself which has
intruded, to separate yourself from it and deny it and to abide
in a quiet confidence in the Divine Power. If your psychic being
asks for the Divine and your mind is sincere and calls for liberation from the lower nature and from all hostile forces and if you
can call the Mother's power into your heart and rely upon it
more than on your own strength, this siege will in the end be
driven away from you and strength and peace take its place.

It is always better to have peace. As for the vital, there is always
something in it that resists and tries to retard, but if the inner
being opens sufficiently and you can live in the inner being, peace
can descend and establish itself there in such a way that the vital
movements of the surface may be there but will not be able to
break the inner peace.

It is always better to have peace.
The one thing you have to avoid is losing patience; for that only
prolongs the vital trouble. If the vital is to be changed (funda-

mentally) it always gives constant trouble like this until one can seat oneself fixedly in the calm of the inner consciousness and keep the vital movements quite on the surface.

Why should you suppose it is vain? The purification of the vital takes a long time because until all the parts are free, none is quite free and because they use a multitude of movements which have to be changed or enlightened, — and moreover there is a great habit of persistence and resistance in the habitual movements of the nature. One therefore easily thinks that one has made no progress, — but all sincere and sustained effort of purification has its result and after a time the progress made will become evident.

It is because both your mind and vital have become sincere that the attack is strong and seems to you abnormal. Before as you were yielding from time to time, the part that wants was not acutely insistent and, when it pressed, it was not so acutely felt by the rest of the vital nature. It is your mental, psychic and higher vital beings that now stand completely apart from it. It is your physical-vital that still keeps the desire and is pushed from time to time by opposite forces to make the desire active. It was also this desire that created the physical disturbance from which you suffered a few days ago. You must get rid of this desire of the lower vital altogether.

It is not the mind, but the psychic being that made the suggestion through the mind. There is a part of the mind that is under the influence of the Truth and can be the channel of the psychic being's knowledge or feeling; there is another part that answers to the vital and expresses and supports the difficulties and oppositions in the nature. If the whole mind refuses to respond to the vital or accept or support its suggestions then much of the force of the vital attack disappears and one is more able to put a pressure on the vital and oblige it also to listen to the psychic and change.

What happened in your case was that the whole vital difficulty — the main one of the family — massed itself together and rose. When an attack like that is overcome, there is always a clearance of the inner atmosphere. It must not be allowed to gather force again — and for that the mind must always follow the psychic suggestion and refuse at once to harbour the opposite suggestions and at the same time keep itself open to the Mother, so that the Mother's Force may come down into it and occupy it and work there.

What happens usually is that something touches the vital, often without one's knowing it, and brings up the old ordinary or external consciousness in such a way that the inner mind gets covered up and all the old thoughts and feelings return for a time. It is the physical mind that becomes active and gives its assent. If the whole mind remains quiet and detached observing the vital movement but not giving its assent, then to reject it becomes more easy. This established quietude and detachment of the mind marks always a great step forward made in the sadhana.

But what do you want to do with all these obscure and useless vital movements that torment you, these wrong thoughts, suggestions, confusions, inabilities etc.? You seem to write as if you thought they must be kept and changed? But why kept and how changed? What would be the use? But precisely what you have got to do is to "shut them out", to reject, refuse to keep them, refuse to have them. It is precisely to see in another way, to see in the true way that the Force is pressing on you. It would indeed be a great blessing if you could forget these other wrong things altogether. Again, why do you want to keep and change the "wrong things" as you yourself call them? If you have an illness, do you want to keep and change the pains, the sickness and all the rest of it? It is to throw out the illness that you want, for the body to forget it, not keep any impression of it, to lose even the possibility of having it again, to live and feel in quite another way, the way of health. It is just the same here.

It is this idea that you are helpless because the vital consents to the wrong movement that comes in the way. You have to put your inner will and the Mother's light on the vital so that it shall change, not leave it to do what it likes. If one is to be "helpless" and moved by any part of the instrumental being, how is change possible? The Mother's force or the psychic can act, but on condition that the assent of the being is there. If the vital is left to do what it likes, it will always go after its old habits; it has to be made to feel that it must change.

If you want to get back your faith and keep it, you must first quiet your mind and make it open and obedient to the Mother's force. If you have an excited mind at the mercy of every influence and impulse, you will remain a field of conflicting and contrary forces and cannot progress. You will begin to listen to your own ignorance instead of the Mother's knowledge and your faith will naturally disappear and you will get into a wrong condition and a wrong attitude.

Your ailment is evidently in its foundation an illness of the nerves and not an ordinary physical disease. These maladies are a creation of the pressure of hostile forces; they increase if anything in you assents to them and accepts, and the more the mind gives value to them and dwells on them, the more they grow. The only way is to remain quiet, dissociate yourself and refuse to accept it or make much of it, allow the calm and strength that the Mother has been putting around you to enter your mind and permeate your nervous system. To do otherwise is to place yourself on the side of the hostile forces that are afflicting you. The cure may take long because your nervous system has been long subjected to these influences and, when they are evicted, they return with violence to re-establish their hold. But if you can acquire and keep patience and fortitude and the right consciousness and right attitude with regard to these things, the hold they have will progressively disappear.

There are defects in your vital nature which stand in the way of a settled spiritual progress, but they can be eliminated if, dropping all exaggerated ideas of "sin" and unfitness, you look quietly at them and recognise and reject them. Tranquillise in yourself all over-eager demands and desires, all excitement and exaggeration of opposite feelings and impulses, seek first intensity of devotion, but also calm, strength, purity and peace. Allow a quiet and steady will to progress to be settled in you; learn the habit of a silent, persistent and thorough assimilation of what the Mother puts into you. This is the sound way to advance.

It would not be at all right to yield to these suggestions which are obviously there of a force that wants to make use of the unease and disappointment of the vital in order to draw you to break your sadhana. These are the usual suggestions that come to all under the stress of the vital condition: "I am not fit for this sadhana. I must go, I cannot stay here. The Mother does not love me. I have given up everything and got nothing. The struggle makes me too miserable; let me go." As a matter of fact, there is no real foundation for these suggestions. Because an acute struggle has come, it would be absurd to conclude that you are unfit for the sadhana and to give it up after going so far. It is because you have asked the physical-vital to give up certain of its cherished attachments and habits that it is in this condition; unable to resist altogether, miserable at being deprived, it accepts these suggestions as an excuse for escape from the pressure you have put upon it. The acuteness of the struggle is due to the vehemence of the attack, but still more to this vital or a part of it responding to the suggestions; otherwise a less disturbing, even if a slower, movement would be quite possible. The Mother has in no way changed towards you nor is she disappointed with you — that is the suggestion drawn from your own state of mind and putting its wrong sense of disappointment and unfitness on the Mother. She has no reason to change or be disappointed, as she has always been aware of the vital obstacles in you and still expected and expects you to overcome them. The call to change certain things that seem to be in the grain of character is proving difficult even for the best sadhaks, but the difficulty is no proof of incompetence. It is precisely this impulse to go that you must refuse to admit — for so long as these forces think they can bring it about, they will press as much as they can on this point. You must also open yourself more to the Mother's Force in that part and for that it is necessary to get rid of this suggestion about the Mother's disappointment or lack of love, for it is this which creates the reaction at the time of Pranam. Our help, support, love are there always as before — keep yourself open to them and with their aid drive out these suggestions.

VII

All depression is bad as it lowers the consciousness, spends the energy, opens to adverse forces.

Do not allow yourself to admit any movement of vital depression, still less a depressed condition. As for the external being, it is always, not only in you but in everyone, a difficult animal to handle. It has to be dealt with by patience and a quiet and cheerful perseverance; never get depressed by its resistance, for that only makes it sensitive and aggrieved and difficult, or else discouraged. Give it rather the encouragement of sunlight and a quiet pressure, and one day you will find it opening entirely to the Grace.

The outer being does not care for the sadhana unless it gets something by it which is to it pleasant or gratifying or satisfying — depression therefore comes easy to it.

Naturally, if the vital is quiet and allows the mind to see things rightly, there will not be this depression.

These feelings of despair and exaggerated sense of self-depreciation and helplessness are suggestions of a hostile Force and should never be admitted. The defects of which you speak are common to all human nature and the external being of every sadhak is full of them; to become aware of them is necessary for the transformation, but it must be done with a quiet mind and with the faith and surrender to the Divine and assured aspiration to the higher consciousness, which are proper to the psychic being. The transformation of the external being is the most difficult part of the yoga and it demands faith, patience, quietude and firm determination. It is in that spirit that you have to throw these depressions aside and go steadily on with the yoga.

I did not receive any letter from you so recently as a fortnight or three weeks ago. If you feel in a pitiable condition, it is certainly not because you have incurred our displeasure. I have said that we are always with you and it is true, but to feel it you must draw back from your vital and be able to concentrate in your inner being. If you do that faithfully and sincerely, after a time you will feel the connection and the rapport.

The meaning of the phrase you speak of is this, that usually the vital tries to resist the call to change. That is what is meant by revolt or opposition. If the inner will insists and forbids revolt or opposition, the vital unwillingness may often take the form of depression and dejection, accompanied by a resistance in the physical mind which supports the repetition of old ideas, habits, movements or actions while the body consciousness suffers from an apprehension or fear of the called-for change, a drawing back from it or a dullness which does not receive the call.

It is these things you have to get rid of. But a sorrowful or despondent mood is not the proper condition for doing that. You have to stand back from the feeling of suffering, anguish and apprehension, reject it and look quietly at the resistance, applying always to yourself your will to change and insisting that it shall be done and cannot fail to be done now or later with the divine help because the divine help is there. It is then that the strength can come to you that will overcome the difficulties.

A weeping that comes with the feeling you speak of is the sign of a psychic sorrow — for it translates an aspiration of the psychic being. But depression and hopelessness ought not to come. You should rather cling to the faith that since there is a true aspiration in you, it is sure to be fulfilled, whatever the difficulties of the external nature. You must recover in that faith the inner peace and quietude while at the same time keeping the clear insight into what has to be done and the steady aspiration for the inner and outer change.

I do not know that sadness has the power to cure [the dryness in the vital]. I have myself followed the Gita's path of equanimity — but for some the psychic sadness may be necessary. But I think it is more an indication of a mistake than a cure.

The rule in yoga is not to let the depression depress you, to stand back from it, observe its cause and remove the cause; for the cause is always in oneself, perhaps a vital defect somewhere, a wrong movement indulged or a petty desire causing a

recoil, sometimes by its satisfaction, sometimes by its disappointment. In yoga a desire satisfied, a false movement given its head
produces very often a worse recoil than disappointed desire.

What is needed for you is to live more deeply within, less in
the outer vital and mental part which is exposed to these touches.
The inmost psychic being is not oppressed by them; it stands
in its own closeness to the Divine and sees the small surface
movements as surface things foreign to the true Being.

It is indeed good that the psychic intervened and prevented the
mind from taking the wrong direction. It is not possible that
there should not be stumbles, failures, etc. in the work of self-
purification and change, but to feel upset or remorseful over
them is harmful rather than helpful; it easily brings depression,
and depression brings clouding of the mind and weakness. To
observe calmly the wrong movement and its nature (here it was
the tongue that was at fault and the tongue is always an easily
erring member) and to set it right inwardly is always the best
way. Calm, especially when the true spiritual calm of the Self
is there, is the thing that must always be preserved; with that
everything else can be done in time and with the least trouble.

Tamasic indifference is one thing and the absence of sorrow is
another. One has to observe what is wrong and do all that one
can to set it right. Sadness in itself has no power to cure what is
wrong, a firm quiet persistent will has the power.

There was nothing wrong in helping with the cooking. But if
there were a wrong movement in that, it is not to be met by
getting depression — for depression itself is a wrong or mistaken
movement; and how can one mistake be corrected by another?
The proper way to deal with a wrong movement is to look quietly

at it and put the consciousness right at that point.

It is also a mistake to take quietude for callousness. If you are no longer disturbed by what people say or do, then that is a great progress. If you have no *abhimāna* against the Mother, that also is surely very desirable. *Abhimāna*, disturbance etc. may be signs of life but of a vital, not of the inner life. They must quiet down and give room for the inner life. At first the result may be a neutral quiet, but one has often to pass through that to arrive at a more positive new consciousness. When the mind thus falls quiet the thoughts of the past, all sorts of repetitive or mechanical thoughts begin to rise up — these are from the physical mind or the subconscient. One has to refuse them and let them pass away, aspiring for the complete mental quietude in which the new consciousness can reveal itself little by little. Remain firm and quiet with the right will in you and let the Force do its work. That will may not bear recognisable fruit at once, but adhere to it and the fruit will come.

Remorse, repentance, is the natural movement of the vital mind when it sees it has done a mistake. It is certainly better than indifference. Its disadvantage is that it disturbs the vital stuff and sometimes leads to depression or discouragement. For that reason what is usually recommended to the sadhak is a quiet recognition of the mistake with a sincere aspiration and will that it should not be repeated or at least that the habit of making such mistakes should soon be eliminated. At a higher stage of development when the inner calm is established, one simply observes the defects of the nature as defects of a machinery that one has to put right and calls down the Light and Force for its rectification. In the beginning however the movement of repentance even helps provided it does not bring discouragement or depression.

The outer reasons [for despondency] are created by the mind

and it is the mind that responds or does not respond to them. Nothing outward can affect unless the mind (vital mind usually) represents them to itself in a particular way and makes its own response.

If the mind does not respond to any suggested reasons for despondency, that is indeed a great liberation.

The vital mind is part of the vital. If mind (mental mind, vital mind, physical mind, subconscient mind) does not respond to outer things, depression is impossible. The self at one end, the stone at the other never get into depression and between them the true mind, true vital, true physical consciousness never get depression because they do not give responses to things that create depression.

You seem to rely very much on X and his experiences and ideas about them. X's experience proves nothing because he is quite ignorant. His depression comes from outside and has its causes, only his vital mind does not record or understand the causes, but there is a response to them all the same. Because the vital mind has in the past always associated depression with these causes and that impression remains in the vital stuff, so it responds to their touch with the usual reaction taught to it by the vital mind. An ignorant and untrained mind like X's cannot be expected to realise the secret machinery of the movements of his own consciousness.

After you went from here it seems that the vital difficulties which you were emerging from here came back with your return to the atmosphere and that was the cause of the violent depression and ill-health that fell upon you. The depression again was the cause why everything went wrong and the arrangements made fell through or took a wrong turn. For depression prevents the Force from flowing through and calls in the adverse forces and gives them a chance to destroy the helpful formations that are made. All the trouble and difficulty you have had will disappear or be minimised if you shake off this tendency to depression altogether.

*
**

However or from wheresoever it came, the only thing to do with a depression is to throw it out.

*
**

The weakness in yourself of which you speak is there, as the persistency of these movements show, but it is not in the heart — your heart is all right — but in the lower vital nature. All your weaknesses are there; the rest of your being is quite strong enough for the spiritual life. But this inadequacy of the lower vital is not peculiar to you, it is present in almost every human being. This tendency to irrational sadness and despondency and these imaginations, fears and perverse reasonings — always repeating, if you will take careful notice, the same movements, ideas and feelings and even the same language and phrases like a machine — is a characteristic working of the lower vital nature. The only way to get rid of it is to meet it with a fixed resolution of the higher vital and the mind and the psychic being to combat, reject and master it. As you were determined to master the sex-impulse and the desire of the palate, so you must determine to master this "irrational knot" of despondency and the lower vital nature. If you indulge it and regard it as a natural part of yourself with good causes for existence or if you busy yourself finding this or that justification when it comes, there is no reason why it should let go its unpleasant grip upon you. Be firm and courageous here, as you have learnt to be with other movements of your lower vital; you will then find less difficulty in your meditation and your general sadhana.

*
**

It is the weakness in the vital which enables them [the forces of dissatisfaction and desire] to keep up their attack. Instead of allowing the weakness revive your will and aspiration and let them throw out this egoistic darkness....

Also allow no demand of the human vital to rise up in clamour of egoistic revolt or if one rises see that you or no part of you identify yourself with it.

The feelings and movements of the past always return at night in sleep. It is only when the consciousness that generated them is changed and cleared in the waking state, that afterwards one can clear them out of the sleep also.

You are listening too much to the suggestions of the outer consciousness, "not being able," etc. etc. Since you did begin to open a little for a time, it shows that you are able. You have to get back to that movement; for that you must persuade this outer vital not to go on repeating "I am not able, my efforts cannot succeed, I am too crooked etc." — or if it goes on, you must not listen to it. You must affirm and concentrate on the possibility that was shown you and not on the supposed impossibility.

It is clear that the force and peace are descending and working more and more to fix themselves in you.

The other feelings, the wanting to be sad, the fear of being happy, the suggestion of incapacity or unfitness are the usual movements of the vital formation which is not yourself and they come up to try and prevent the change in you. You have only to refuse to accept these suggestions and put yourself persistently on the side of the Truth in you which will make you free and happy, and all will be well.

Who does not feel the confusion or ignorance somewhere in

himself so long as the full light and the true force have not come? Your mistake is to be always thinking about the confusion and struggling with it, dwelling on it, magnifying it by thinking about it, treating it as if it were the only thing real and true. When you feel the force, turn to the force and let it act — it is that Force and not you or your brooding and struggles that can get rid of the confusion and darkness. What is the use of examining whether your faith and confidence are of the "true" kind or not? To feel the force, be quiet, let it act is all that is needed.

It is good that you go back from this struggle towards the quiet foundation that helps the opening. All this struggling and confusion and harassing self-depreciation is the old wrong way of proceeding; it is mental and vital and cannot succeed; it is in the quiet mind that the opening must come. Then the psychic being, the soul in you begins to come forward. The soul knows and sees the Truth; the mind and vital do not — until they are enlightened by the soul's knowledge.

It is not true that you cannot or will never be put right. It is what appears to you when your lower vital is restless or else your physical mind comes uppermost. Only it is true that if you could keep yourself always in that part of you which is in contact, the thing would be done sooner and with much less difficulty and trouble.

If there is this unconsciousness, you have to learn to be conscious in all your actions, so that the vital movements will no longer be able to deceive you or take any cover. You must make a point of being perfectly sincere in looking at these vital movements and seeing them as they are.

If once you can open in the psychic being and keep it open, then from within yourself will come constantly a perception that

will show you at each step the actual truth and keep you on your
guard against any kind of deception. If you aspire constantly and
allow the peace to grow and the Force to work in you, this opening will come.

VIII

I have never said that to overcome doubt is easy; it is difficult
because it is the nature of something in the human physical mind
to cling to doubt for its own sake. It is not easy to overcome
gloom, depression, grief and suffering because something in the
human vital clings to it and almost needs it as part of the drama
of life. So also I have never said that sex, anger, jealousy, etc.
were easy to overcome. I have said it was difficult because they
were ingrained in the human vital and even if thrown out were
always being brought into it either by its own habit or by the invasion of the general Nature and the resurgence of its old response.... The external consciousness — the physical mind and
consciousness of man — hates its own suffering and if left to itself
dislikes also to see others suffer. But if you will try to fathom the
significance of your admission of liking drama or of the turn towards drama from which very few human beings escape, and if
you go deep enough, you will find that there is something in the
vital which likes suffering and clings to it for the sake of the
drama. It is something below the surface, but it is strong, almost
universal in human nature and difficult to eradicate unless one
recognises it and gets inwardly away from it. The mind and the
physical of man do not like suffering, for if they did, it would not
be suffering any longer, but this thing in the vital wants it in order
to give a spice to life. It is the reason why constant depressions
can go on returning and returning even though the mind longs to
get rid of them, because this in the vital responds, goes on repeating the same movement like a gramophone as soon as it is got
going and insists on turning the whole round of the oft-repeated
record. It does not really depend on the reasons which the vital
gives for starting off to the round, these are often of the most
trivial character and wholly insufficient to justify it. It is only by

a strong will to detach oneself, not to justify, to reject, not to welcome that one can in the end get rid of this most troublesome and dangerous streak in human nature. When therefore we speak of the vital comedy, of the vital drama, we are speaking from a psychological knowledge which does not end with the surface of things but looks at these hidden movements. It is impossible to deal with things for the purposes of yoga if we confine ourselves to the surface consciousness only: it is also quite according to the rule of these reactions that your despondency should have come immediately after a considerable progress in bhakti and the will to surrender in the inner being — for it comes from the spirit of darkness which attacks the sadhak whenever it can and that spirit resents fiercely all progress made and hates the very idea of progress and its whole policy is to convince him by its attacks and suggestions that he has made none or that what progress he has made is after all null and inconclusive....

The laws of this world as it is are the laws of the Ignorance and the Divine in the world maintains them so long as there is the Ignorance; if he did not, the universe would crumble to pieces — *utsīdeyur ime lokāḥ*, as the Gita puts it. There are also, very naturally, conditions for getting out of the Ignorance into the Light. One of them is that the mind of the sadhak should co-operate with the Truth and that his will should co-operate with the Divine Power which, however slow its action may seem to the vital or to the physical mind, is uplifting the nature towards the Light; when that co-operation is complete, the progress can be rapid enough. But the sadhak should not grudge the time and labour needed to make the co-operation fully possible to the blindness and weakness of human nature and effective.

All this call of yours for faith, sincerity, surrender is only an invitation to make that co-operation more easily possible. If the physical mind ceases to judge all things including those that it does not know or are beyond it, like the deeper things of the spirit, then it becomes easier for it to receive the Light and know by illumination and experience the things that it does not yet know. If the mental and vital will place themselves in the Divine Hand without reservation, then it is easier for the Power to work and produce tangible effects. If there is resistance, then it is na-

tural that it should take more time and the work should be done
from within or, as it might appear, underground so as to prepare
the nature and undermine the resistance.

The thing in you which enjoys the suffering and wants it is part
of the human vital — it is these things that we describe as the
insincerity and perverse twist of the vital; it cries out against
sorrow and trouble and accuses the Divine and life and everybody else of torturing it, but for the most part the sorrow and the
trouble come and remain because the perverse something in the
vital wants them! That element in the vital has to be got rid of
altogether.

Yes, it is so. Even there is something in the vital consciousness
that would not feel at home if there were no suffering in life. It
is the physical that fears and abhors suffering, but the vital takes
it as part of the play of life.

It is not the soul but the vital or rather something in it that takes
pleasure in groaning and weeping and in fact in sorrow and
suffering of all kinds.

The surface nature does not enjoy — but something within enjoys the *lilā* of "laughter and tears", joy and grief, pleasure and
pain, in a word the play of the ignorance. In some people this
comes up to a certain extent on the surface. Many, if you propose to them the removal of suffering from life, look askance at
you and feel that it would be terribly wrong to have nothing but
joy and Ananda and peace — many even have said it.

Disappointed vital desire must bring about suffering. Pain and suffering are necessary results of the Ignorance in which we live; men grow by all kinds of experience, pain and suffering as well as their opposites, joy and happiness and ecstasy. One can get strength from them if one meets them in the right way. Many take a joy in pain and suffering when associated with struggle or endeavour or adventure, but that is more because of the exhilaration and excitement of the struggle than because of suffering for its own sake. There is, however, something in the vital which takes joy in the whole of life, its dark as well as its bright sides. There is also something perverse in the vital which takes a kind of dramatic pleasure in its own misery and tragedy, even in degradation or in illness.

I don't think mere doubts can bring any gain; mental questioning can bring gains if it is in pursuit of truth, but questioning just for the sake of sceptical questioning or in a pure spirit of contradiction can only bring, when it is directed against the truths of the spirit, either error or a lasting incertitude. If I am always questioning the Light when it comes and refusing its offer of truth, the Light cannot stay in me, cannot settle; eventually, finding no welcome and no foundation in the mind, it will retire. One has to push forward into the Light, not always falling back into the darkness and hugging the darkness in the delusion that it is the real light. Whatever fulfilment one may feel in pain or in doubt belongs to the Ignorance; the real fulfilment is in the divine joy and the divine Truth and its certitude and it is that for which the yogin strives. In the struggle he may have to pass through doubt, not by his own choice or will but because there is still imperfection in his knowledge.

What you have noticed about the disturbance is true. There are now two consciousnesses in you, the new one that is growing and what is left of the old. The old has something in it which is a habit of the human vital, — the tendency to keep any touch of grief, anger, vexation etc. or any kind of emotional, vital or mental disturbance, to make much of it, to prolong it, not to wish to let it go, to return to it even when the cause of disturbance is past and could be forgotten, always to remember and bring it up when it can. This is a common trait of human nature and a quite customary movement. The new consciousness on the contrary does not want these things and when they happen throws them off as quickly as possible. When the new consciousness is fully grown and established, then the disturbances will be altogether rejected. Even if the causes of them happen, there will be no response of grief, anger, vexation etc. in the nature.

The gloom and other difficulties come from a resistance of inertia in the lower vital and physical consciousness. What you have to do is to prepare the consciousness by getting rid of the inertia. A sattwic gladness and calm and confidence is the proper temperament for this yoga; gloom, depression and weeping should not be indulged in, as they stand in the way of the opening, unless the tears are the psychic weeping of release or adoration or a moved love and bhakti. The progress made in controlling the sex and other rajasic movements of the lower vital is a good preparation, but not enough; by itself it is only the negative side, though indispensable. Aspire for a positive sattwic opening for strength, for light, for peace and do not worry or repine if the progress is slow at first, nor grudge the time and labour of preparation necessary before there can be a rapid advance in the yoga.

The change noted by X evidently indicates a great progress in the vital and physical being. There is nothing spiritually wrong in being glad and cheerful, on the contrary it is the right thing. As for struggles and aspiration, struggles are really not indispensable to progress and there are many people who get so habituated to the struggling attitude that they have all the time struggles and very little else. That is not desirable. There is a sunlit path as well as a gloomy one and it is the better of the two — a path in which one goes forward in absolute reliance on the Mother, fearing nothing, sorrowing over nothing. Aspiration is needed but there can be a sunlit aspiration full of light and faith and confidence and joy. If difficulty comes, even that can be faced with a smile.

This movement is one that always tries to come when you have a birthday or a darshan and is obviously a suggestion of forces that want to disturb you and give you a bad birthday or bad darshan. You must get rid of the idea that it is in any way helpful for sadhana, e.g. makes you remember the Divine etc. — if it does, it makes you remember the Divine in the wrong way and in addition brings up the weakness, also depression, self-distrust etc. etc. *À quoi bon* cheerfulness? It puts you in the right condition for the psychic to work and without knowing it you grow in just the right perceptions and right feelings for the spiritual attitude. This growth I have been observing in you for a fairly long time now and it is in the cheerful states that it is the most active. Japa, thinking of the Divine is all right, but it must be on this basis and in company with work and mental activity, for then the instrument is in a healthy condition. But if you become restlessly eager to do nothing but japa and think of nothing but the Divine and of the "progress" you have or have not made (X says you should never think of "progress", it is according to him a movement of the ego), then all the fat is in the fire — because the system is not yet ready for a Herculean effort and it begins to get upset and think it is unfit and will never be fit. So be a good cheerful worker and offer your bhakti to the Divine in all ways you can but rely on him to work out things in you.

What is needed is to profit by the discovery and get rid of the impediment. The Mother did not merely point out the impediment; she showed you very expressly how to get rid of it and at that time you understood her, though now (at the time of writing

cult and needs a great force of Tapasya. As for the Mother and myself, we have had to try all ways, follow all methods, to surmount mountains of difficulties, a far heavier burden to bear than you or anybody else in the Ashram or outside, far more difficult conditions, battles to fight, wounds to endure, ways to cleave through impenetrable morass and desert and forest, hostile masses to conquer — a work such as, I am certain, none else had to do before us. For the Leader of the Way in a work like ours has not only to bring down and represent or embody the Divine, but to represent too the ascending element in humanity and to bear the burden of humanity to the full and experience, not in a mere play or Lila but in grim earnest, all the obstruction, difficulty, opposition, baffled and hampered and only slowly victorious labour which are possible on the Path. But it is not necessary nor tolerable that all that should be repeated over again to the full in the experience of others. It is because we have the complete experience that we can show a straighter and easier road to others — if they will only consent to take it. It is because of our experience won at a tremendous price that we can urge upon you and others, "Take the psychic attitude; follow the straight sunlit path, with the Divine openly or secretly upbearing you — if secretly, he will yet show himself in good time, — do not insist on the hard, hampered, roundabout and difficult journey."

You say that you were never pointed out all this before. But it is what we have been saying in season and out of season to everybody for a long time past! But you were not inclined to regard it as feasible or at least not ready to apply it in the field of meditation, because your consciousness by tradition, owing to past lives and for other reasons, was clinging to former contrary conceptions. Something in you was harking back to one kind of Vaishnava sadhana, and that tended to bring in it its pain-giving feeling — elements of *abhimāna*, revolt, suffering, the Divine hiding himself ("always I seek but never does he show himself"), the rarity of the unfolding and the *milana*. Something else in you was inclined to see as the only alternative some harsh, grim, ascetic ideal, the blank featureless Brahman and imagined that the supramental was that; something in the vital looked on the conquest of wrong movements as a hard, desperate Tapasya, not as a passage into the purity and joy of the Divine — even now some element in you seems to insist on regarding the psychic attitude as something extraordinary, difficult, unhuman and impossible! There were these and other lingerings[1] of the mind and the vital; you have to clear them out and look at the simplicity of the Truth with a straight and simple gaze.

It is not that there is anything peculiar to you in these difficulties; every sadhak entering the Way has to get over similar impediments. It took me four years of inner striving to find a real Way, even though the divine help was with me all the time, and even then, it seemed to come by an accident; and it took me ten more years of intense yoga under a supreme inner guidance to trace it out and that was because I had my past and the world's past to assimilate and overpass before I could find and found the future.

But for you the remedy we propose, the key we offer to you, ought not to be so difficult to apply as you imagine. After all, it is only applying in "meditation" the way that has been so successful with you in your creative work. There is a way of creation by strain and tension, by breaking of the brain, by hard and painful labour — often the passage clogged and nothing coming or else coming only in return for a sort of intellectual Tapasya. There is the other way in which one remains quiet and opens oneself to a power that is there behind and waits for inspiration; the force pours in and with it the inspiration, the illumination, the Ananda, — all is done by an inner Power. The flood passes, but one remains quiet for the next flood and at its time surely it comes. Here too all is not perfect at once, but progress comes by ever-new waves of the same Power. It is the same method that the Mother proposed to you for your meditation — if meditation it must be called — not a strain of mental activity, but a restful opening to the Force that is there all the time

---

[1] E. g. the Russellian fear of emptiness which is the form the active mind gives to Silence. Yet it was on what you call emptiness, on the Silence, that my whole yoga was founded and it was through it that there came afterwards all the inexhaustible riches of a greater Knowledge, Will and Joy — all the experiences of greater mental, psychic and vital realms, all the ranges up to overmind and beyond. The cup has often to be emptied before it can be new-filled; the yogin, the sadhak ought not to be afraid of emptiness or silence.

above and around you, so that it may flow freely and do its work in peace and illumination and Ananda. The way has been shown to you, you yourself have had from time to time the true condition; only you must learn how to continue in it or recover it and you must allow the Force to do its work in its own way. It may take some time to take entire hold of it, get the other habit out and make this normal; but you must not start by deciding that it is impossible ! It is eminently possible and it is that which everyone will have to do sooner or later; for this is the door of the definitive entrance. The difficulty, the struggle were only for the period of preparation necessary to get rid of or to exhaust the obstruction in the consciousness which was a thorn-hedge round the faery palace.

What you write about X is quite correct. It is not necessary to be always serious of face or silent in doing the yoga, but it is necessary to take the yoga seriously and silence and inward concentration have a large place. One can't be all the time throwing oneself outward if to go inside and meet the Divine there is one's aim. But that does not mean that one has to be grave and gloomy all the time, or gloomy at most times, and I don't suppose the sadhaks here are like that. It is X's rhetorical way of putting his difficulty — the difficulty of a vital that wants to throw itself always outward in action and creation, while another part is dissatisfied with the result and feels that its own movement is frustrated. There are two people in him, one wanting a life of vital expansion, the other an inner life. The first gets restless because the inner life is not a life of outward expansion; the other becomes miserable because its aim is not realised. Neither personality has to be thrown away in this yoga; but the outer vital one must allow the inner to establish itself, give it the first place and consent to be only an instrument of the soul and to obey the law of the inner life. This is what X's mind still refuses to understand; he thinks one must be either all gloomy and cold and grave or else bring the vital bubble and effervescence into the inner life. A quiet, happy and glad control of the vital by the inner being is a thing he is not able as yet to conceive.

Whatever seriousness is necessary must come of itself from within. To be serious outwardly by rule is not needed.

Why on earth should people not be serious if they want? Life may be a joke — though all do not find it so — but one can't be laughing at it all the time. The idea seems to be that one can't be serious unless one is either (1) in a rage, (2) discontented, or (3) sad and miserable. But surely one can be serious when one is thinking or when one is looking at serious things or simply and purely when one is not laughing. And one can't be laughing 24 hours without stopping — the muscles of the stomach would not stand it and the American record makers might shy at such a test.

Cheerfulness is the salt of the sadhana. It is a thousand times better than gloominess.

It is an inner joy and cheerfulnesss that helps, but this is merely a vital bubbling on the surface. It is all right in ordinary life, but in yoga it merely expends the vital force for nothing.

The cheerfulness is vital. I do not say that it should not be there, but there is a deeper cheerfulness, an inner *sukhahāsya* which is the spiritual condition of cheerfulness.

In the way of meditating of which we spoke, aspiration, prayer, concentration, intensity are a natural part of it. Those who take it go quicker and develop their sadhana, once they get fixed in it, much more easily as well as smoothly than by a distressed, doubtful and anxious straining with revulsions of despondency and turning away from hope and endeavour. We spoke of a steady opening to the Divine with a flow of the force doing its work in the Adhar, a poised opening with a quiet mind and heart full of trust and the sunlight of confidence; where do you find that we said a helpless waiting must be your programme?

As for light-heartedness and insouciance — a light don't-care attitude is the last thing we would recommend to anybody. The Mother spoke of cheerfulness, and if she used the word light-hearted, it was not in the sense of anything lightly or frivolously gay and careless — although a deeper and finer gaiety can have its place as an element of the yogic character. What she meant was a glad equanimity even in the face of difficulties and there is nothing in that contrary to yogic teaching or to her own practice. The vital nature on the surface (the depths of the true vital are different) is attached on the one side to a superficial mirth and enjoyment, on the other to sorrow and despair and gloom and tragedy, — for these are for it the cherished lights and shades of life; but a bright or wide and free peace or an *ānandamaya* intensity or, best, a fusing of both in one is the true poise of both the soul and the mind — and of the true vital also — in yoga. It is perfectly possible for a quite human sadhak to get to such a poise, it is not necessary to be divine before one can attain it.

It is quite true that rising into a higher consciousness than the ordinary human consciousness is the right way towards transformation. Merely to remain in the ordinary lower consciousness and try to reject from there the wrong movements can produce no permanent or complete result. But there are several points here which you must note or this perception may be accompanied by an error.

1. As you have yourself subsequently seen, all the parts and personalities that constitute the being must share in the

higher consciousness, otherwise the old movements under various pretexts will continue.

2. You speak of rejecting the lower vital, but it is only the unregenerated lower vital movements that can be got rid of; you cannot get rid of the lower vital itself, for it is a necessary part of the manifested nature, like the higher vital or the mind. It has to be changed in the power of the higher consciousness, not left to itself or dropped from you.

3. If you do not so change it, if you simply remain content by living in the psychic or other higher consciousness internally, then you run the risk of doing like those who are satisfied to have experiences and some inner quietude or Ananda, but leave the external nature and surface active movements unchanged, either thinking them of no importance or justifying them under the plea that there is the psychic or spiritual consciousness behind them.

Happiness in the ordinary sense is a sunlit state of the vital with or without cause. Contentment is less than happiness — joy of peace or being free from difficulty is rather a state of joyful *śānti*. Happiness ought not to be a status of self-satisfaction or inertia, and need not be, for one can combine happiness and aspiration. Of course there can be a state of happy inertia, but most people don't remain satisfied with that long, they begin to want something else. There are yogins who are satisfied with a happy calm immobility, but that is because the happiness is a form of Ananda and in the immobility they feel the Self and its eternal calm and want nothing more.

There is no real reason why delight should necessarily be followed by sorrow — except, that it is the habit of the vital. But that habit can be overcome.

IX

There are three obstacles that one has to overcome in the vital and they are very difficult to overcome, lust (sexual desire), wrath and rajasic ego. Rajasic ego is the supporting ground of the other two.

Obviously, unless the object is Nirvana, the small ego has to be attended to — not indulged but transformed out of existence.

The form of ego has to be dissolved, it has not to be replaced by a bigger ego or another kind of ego. It has to be replaced by the true being which feels itself, even though individual, yet one with all and one with the Divine.

There is individuality in the psychic being, but not egoism. Egoism goes when the individual unites himself with the Divine or is entirely surrendered to the Divine.

On the higher spiritual planes there is no ego, because the oneness of the Divine is felt, but there may be the sense of one's true person or individuality — not ego, but a portion of the Divine.

Although there is no ego in the spiritual planes, yet by the spiritual experience the ego on the lower planes may get aggrandised through the pride and wrong reception of the experience. Also one may by entering into the larger mental and vital planes aggrandise the ego. These things are always possible so long as the higher consciousness and the lower are not harmonised in the being and the lower transformed into the nature of the higher.

Even if there is no consciousness of ego in the higher parts where oneness of all things has been realised, it does not follow that in the lower parts ego has been abolished. It can on the contrary become very strong and the action can be very egoistic even while the mind is thinking "I have no ego".

Ego is not so easy to get rid of. It remains not only in spite of work but in spite of knowledge or bhakti. The disappearance of ego means complete Mukti. Even the yogi who feels his separate being swallowed up in cosmic consciousness or some kind of Transcendent consciousness, yet when he comes to outward action and reaction finds the superficial ego still there. That is why the ascetic has a horror of action and says that without ego it can't be done. It can, but it is fully done only when these outermost things are fully taken up by the higher consciousness in their entirety.

Samatā does not mean the absence of ego, but the absence of desire and attachment. The ego-sense may disappear or it may remain in a subtilised or dense form — it depends on the person.

Pride is only one form of ego — there are ten thousand others. Every action of man is full of ego — the good ones as well as the bad, his humility as much as his pride, his virtues as much as his vices.

To get the ego out of the human nature is not so simple as that. If one is free from ego, does nothing with reference to himself or for his own sake but only for the Divine and all his thoughts and feelings are for the Divine, then he is Jivanmukta and a Siddha yogi.

But that is the case with all human beings. All the action is shot through with ego, acts, feelings, thoughts, everything, big or small, good or bad. Even humility and what is called altruism is with most people only a form of ego. It does not depend on having something to be proud of.

It is so with everybody. Human nature is shot through in all its stuff with the thread of the ego; even when one tries to get away from it, it is in front or could be behind all the thoughts and actions like a shadow. To see that is the first step, to discern the falsity and absurdity of the ego-movements is the second, to discourage and refuse it at each step is the third, — but it goes entirely only when one sees, experiences and lives the One in everything and equally everywhere.

It is so with everybody, because the human consciousness is permeated in all its past ideas with this substance of egoism. It is only by a constant quiet vigilance and increasing consciousness that it can be got out — for if it is not allowed to play, it conceals itself and takes subtle and disguised forms.

The mind and the vital are much more full of ego than the body.

The fight with the ego is part of the fight with the physical nature, for it is the superficial ego in the physical consciousness irrational and instinctive, that refuses to go.

The human being is naturally egoistic and ego-centred — all he does, thinks, feels has the stamp of the ego on it and it cannot be otherwise until he learns to make not the ego but the Divine the centre of his existence and thinks, acts, feels only for the Divine — or until he enters into the higher or divine consciousness or the divine consciousness into him — for in the divine consciousness there is no ego.

The ego-centric man feels and takes things as they affect him. Does this please me or displease, give me gladness or pain, flatter my pride, vanity, ambition or hurt it, satisfy my desires or thwart them, etc. The unegoistic man does not look at things like that. He looks to see what things are in themselves and would be if he were not there, what is their meaning, how they fit into the scheme of things — or else he feels calm and equal, refers everything to the Divine, or if he is a man of action, how they will serve the work that has to be done or the life of the world or the cause he serves, etc. etc. There can be many points of view which are not ego-centric.

Obviously all that must go — it is the old vital egoism of the human being always preoccupied with itself, so that the being cannot give itself simply and unquestioningly to the adoration of the Divine.

There is nothing to be troubled about. You ought rather to congratulate yourself that you have become conscious of your

ego-centricity. Very few people in the Ashram are. They are all
ego-centric and they do not realise their ego-centricity. Even in
their sadhana the I is always there, — *my* sadhana, *my* progress,
my everything. The remedy is to think constantly of the Divine,
not of oneself, to work, to act, do sadhana for the Divine; not
to consider how this or that affects *me* personally, not to claim
anything, but to refer all to the Divine. It will take time to do
that sincerely and thoroughly, but it is the proper way.

It is the ego that is showing itself in its true character. Formerly,
it was associating with the sadhana because it either got something of what it desired or had great expectations. Now that
these things are held back and the demand for the true attitude
is made on it, it resists or non-co-operates, saying, "No value in
such a sadhana". In all the sadhaks here, the ego (in its physical
or vital physical roots) is proving to be the stumbling-block.
No transformation is possible unless it changes.

Your nature like that of almost everybody has been largely
ego-centric and the first stages of the sadhana are with almost
everybody ego-centric. The main idea in it is always one's own
sadhana, one's own endeavour, one's own development, perfection, siddhi. It is inevitable for most, for without that personal
endeavour there would not be sufficient will or push to bring
about the first necessary changes. But none of these things —
development, perfection or siddhi — can really come in any degree of completeness or unmixed finality until this ego-centric
attitude changes into the God-centric, until it becomes the development, perfection, siddhi of the Divine Consciousness, its will
and its instrumentation in this body — and that can only be when
these things become secondary, and bhakti for the Divine, love
for the Divine, oneness with the Divine in consciousness, will,
heart and body, become the sole aim — the rest is then only the
fulfilment of the Divine Will by the Divine Power. This attitude

is never difficult for the psychic, it is its natural position and feeling, and whenever your psychic was in front, you had it in your central consciousness. But there were the outer mind, vital and physical that brought in their mixture of desire and ego and there could be no effective liberation in life and action till these were liberated. The thinking mind and higher vital can accept without too much difficulty, but the difficulty is with the lower vital and physical and especially with the most external parts of them; for these are entirely creatures of habit, recurring movement, an obstinate repetition of the same movement always. This habit is so blind and obstinate and persistent as to seem almost invincible, especially when it is used at a juncture like this by the Forces of Ignorance as their last refuge or point of attack. But the apparent invincibility is not true. The most ego-centric can change and do change by the psychic principle becoming established in the external nature. That it can be done only by the Divine Grace and Power is true (that is true of all spiritual change) — but with the full consent of the being. As it was done in the inner being, so it can be done in the outer; give the adhesion of your full will and faith and, whatever the difficulty, it will be done.

It is true about living and doing all for oneself, but that is the nature of man, he is centred in his ego, ego-centric, and does all for his ego; even his love and liking is mostly based on ego. All that has to be changed and all has to be centred in the Divine, done for the Divine Mother. It is the work of the sadhana to get that done. The silence, the growth of the psychic and all else is meant to bring about that — but it cannot be done all at once. When the consciousness is ready, then the psychic love, the impulse for self-giving begins to open out in the heart and the change is made — more and more till there is the complete self-giving.

If you think there is no ego or desire in you, only pure devotion, that shows a great unconsciousness. To be free from ego and desire is a condition which needs a high siddhi in yoga — even many yogis of a great spiritual attainment are not free from it. For a sadhak at your stage of development to think he is free from ego and desire is to blind himself and prevent the clear perception of one's own nature-movements which is necessary for progress towards spiritual perfection.

The Mother does not need to have your writings before her in order to see what is in you.

If your writings show ego and desire, and they certainly do, it is because they are there without your perceiving it and express themselves without your intending it. What the surface mind thinks and intends is one thing and what is behind the thoughts and actions is another thing. A man's surface mind shapes its own idea of oneself and one's nature in an entire self-ignorance. The first thing one has to do to get rid of this ignorance is to draw back from the surface mind and get into contact with the psychic which does not allow such delusions and shows one clearly the truth about one's movements.

But in what way do they [all things] belong to the Divine, so long as the ego appropriates and uses them for its own purposes? Self-giving in fact means a change from ego-centricity to God-centricity; also such a giving as would lead to a change of the whole base of the consciousness.

Yes — it is looking at things from the ego point of view that there comes all the confusion and trouble and ignorance. One has to think of the Divine, be still and let the divine consciousness come in and replace the egoistic human.— then all that disappears.

Yes, ego is the reason of the difficulty in everybody.

Without the play of ego clashes would not come and if there were no tendency to drama in the vital there would be no dramatic happenings in life.

Yes, that is right — to remember constantly and live in the peace and calmness so that the Force may work and the Light may come. The small things of daily life must go on in the surface consciousness, not filling too large a place in it, until the Force and Light have taken possession and can lay direct hold of these also. It is the ego that gives them too big a place — the ego must be discouraged — "Not for myself, but for the Divine" should grow to be the law of the whole consciousness and thought and action. It cannot be done thoroughly all at once, but that must become the insistent note in the mind as soon as possible.

Why is it [to be concentrated on the Divine] selfishness? Selfishness is to live for oneself and not for something greater than the self. To be concentrated on the Divine at all times is to get out of the personal self and its aims into something greater and serve the aims of that greater Existence. It is no more selfishness than to live for others always would be selfishness.

Obviously one must not get egoistic about it, but withdrawal from the outer or lower consciousness into the inner is not in itself an egoistic movement. If it were so, all sadhana would be egoism and to be always social and on the surface would be the only thing.

The selfishness of the ego is not a reason for not calling down the higher (divine) consciousness of which the peace and the force are as it were the front or the basis. How can you get rid of the selfish ego unless you call down that higher consciousness to which the ego is not a necessity?

In the evolution of the lower consciousness here ego and selfishness were a necessity. So long as the higher consciousness above ordinary mind does not descend, ego remains a necessity even in aspiring towards the Divine or towards Mukti, even if it becomes a sattwic ego. It is only in the higher consciousness that ego can dissolve, either by ascending there or by its descent into the consciousness below.

I suppose the ego came there first as a means of the outer consciousness individualising itself in the flux of Nature and, secondly, as an incentive for tamasic animal man to act and get something done. Otherwise he might merely have contented himself with food and sleep and done nothing else. With that incentive of ego (possession, vanity, ambition, eagerness for power etc. etc.) he began doing all sorts of things he might never otherwise have done. But now that he has to go higher, this ego comes badly in the way.

But what is this ego of which you speak? Everybody has the ego and it is impossible to get rid of it altogether except by two things — the opening of the psychic within and the descent of a wider ego-free consciousness from above. The psychic being opening does not get rid of the ego at once but purifies it and offers it and all the movements to the Divine, so that one becomes unegoistic through self-giving and surrender. At the same time the nature opens above and the wider ego-free consciousness comes down and ego disappears and by the power of the psychic you know your own true being which is a portion of the Mother. This is what has to happen, but it cannot happen in so short a time. Do not be always thinking of the vital movement and the ego — you have seen them and know that they are, it is enough. Concentrate rather in the heart on the opening there; con-

centrate persistently and aspire persistently and do not mind
if it takes time. Call in any way even if you cannot call yet deeply
— then the deeper call will come.

I think you still give an exaggerated importance and attention
to the ego and other elements that are interwoven in the nature
of humanity and cannot be entirely got rid of except by the
coming of a new consciousness which replaces them by higher
movements. If one rejects centrally and with all sincerity the
ego and rajas, their roots get loosened and sattwa can prevail
in the nature, but the expulsion of all ego and rajas cannot be
done by the will and its effort. After a certain stage of preparation, therefore, one must stress more on the positive side of the
sadhana than on the negative side of rejection, — though this of
course must remain to help the other. Still what is important is
to develop the psychic within and bring down the higher consciousness from above. The psychic, as it grows and manifests,
detects immediately all wrong movements or elements and at
the same time supplies almost automatically the true element or
movement which will replace them — this process is much easier
and more effective than that of a severe tapasya of purification.
The higher consciousness in descending brings peace and purity
into all the inner parts; the inner being separates itself from the
imperfect outer consciousness and at the same time the peace
that comes carries in it a power which can throw out what
contradicts the peace and purity. Ego can then slowly or swiftly
but surely disappear — rajas and tamas change into their divine
substitutes.

It is possible [to get rid of the ego by the action of the Force]
if your consciousness associates itself with the action; then at
least one can get rid of its major action and leave only minor
traces. To get rid of the ego altogether however comes usually
only by the descent of Consciousness from above and its occu-

88

pation of the whole being aided of course by the rule of the
psychic in the nature.

For the ego, however insistent it may be, one has to keep one's
eye on it and say no to all its suggestions so that each position it
takes up proves to be a fruitless move. Treated in that way, it
becomes ready for the moment when the psychic has only to give
a slight push for it to fall away in each field of its activity from
its loosened roots. Persevere steadily in the present movement
and it cannot fail to be effective.

The sense of ego can disappear into that of the Self or the Purusha
but that of itself does not bring about the disappearance of the
old ego-reactions in the Prakriti. The Purusha has to get rid of
these by a process of constant rejection and remoulding. The
remoulding consists in throwing everything into a consecration
to the Mother and doing all for her without regard to oneself,
one's desires, opinions, vital reactions as if they were the things
to be fulfilled. This is most easily done if the psychic being
becomes quite awake.

Without persistent rejection it [liberation from the ego] cannot
be done. Going up into the Self liberates the higher parts, but
the ego remains in the lower parts. The most effective force for
this liberation is the psychic control along with steady rejection.

*
**

It is not possible to get rid of the ego-movements all at once.
They have to be worked out of the nature by a constant consciousness and rejection. Even when the central ego has gone, the
habitual movements stick for a long time.

*
**

Without the liberation of the psychic and the realisation of the true Self the ego cannot go, both are necessary. If there is no consciousness of the Self, how can the ego disappear? The psychic can be liberated by love and devotion, but I was speaking of a case in which it is not so liberated, and the realisation of the Self seems more easy.

Yes. If you had gone inside, the psychic development would have been easier, and the conquest of ego — likewise, the widening of the consciousness.

It is rather a wider than a higher consciousness that is necessary for the liberation from the ego — going high is necessary of course, but by itself it is not sufficient.

If the ego is gone and the full surrender is there, then there should be no obstacles. If however the rajas of the vital is only quiescent, then its quiescence may bring up the tamas in its place, and that would be the obstacle.

Once the universality is established, there is no longer a secure fortress in the nature for the vital egoism — the walls of it having been broken down. They [the egoistic vital movements] may still attack from outside, but it now lies in the power of the sadhak to prevent their making a settled formation in him any longer.

Only calm in the vital is hardly sufficient. There must be something throwing out the ego from the vital.

It [the ego] rises because it is its nature to do so; it wants to take hold of the being which it considers its property and field of experience.

Of course, they [the ego and the vital being] always resist a pressure to get rid of them — and if one fixes a given time, they are all the more resistent in the hope of creating disappointment and discouragement by the failure to do it in the given time.

These things [small egoisms in the lower vital] either fade slowly out by constant rejection or else they drop off when the higher consciousness gets steadily down into the lower vital and, as it were, swallows it up. A sudden extinction is perhaps possible — at least there are reported cases of it — but usually they linger and go slowly, losing gradually force as if worn out.

Your ego does come up from time to time without your seeing that it is the ego. It comes up not in your higher parts but in your physical mind and consciousness and you think that because your higher parts are clear this also is clear.

Of course, such suggestions are meant to wake the ego. I suppose they persist because they still have a hope of waking the ego. Even when one is quite free, all kinds of suggestions can come. One either takes no notice of them or else gives a glance to see whether there is any fragment of ego still lurking somewhere.

These are the feelings of the tamasic ego — the reaction to a disappointment in the rajasic ego. Mingled with the true attitude

and experience or running concurrently along with it was a demand of the vital, "What I am having now, I must always have,
otherwise I can't do sadhana; if I ever lose that, I shall die" —
whereas the proper attitude is, "Even if I lose it for a time it will
be because something in me has to be changed in order that the
Mother's consciousness may be fulfilled in me not only in the self
but in every part." The lower forces attacked at the weak point,
made demands through the vital and brought about a state of
inertia in which what you had clung to seemed to be lost, went
back behind the veil. So came the tamasic reaction of the ego,
"What is the use of living, I prefer to die." Obviously it is not the
whole of you that says it, it is a part in the disappointed vital or
tamasic physical. It is not enough that the active demands should
be broken and removed; for this also is a passive way of demand,
"I can't have my demands; very well, I abdicate, don't want to
exist." That must disappear.

The tamasic ego is that which accepts and supports despondency,
weakness, inertia, self-depreciation, unwillingness to act, unwillingness to know or be open, fatigue, indolence, do-nothingness.
Contrary to the rajasic it says, "I am so weak, so obscure, so
miserable, so oppressed and ill-used — there is no hope for
me, no success, I am denied everything, am unsupported, how
can I do this, how can I do that, I have no power for it, no
capacity, I am helpless; let me die; let me lie still and moan",
etc. etc. Of course not all that at once or in every case; but I
am giving the general character of the thing.

Tamas and tamasic ego are implied in each other. When one
yields to tamas one indulges the tamasic ego.

So long as you had fully the attitude of surrender, the rajasic ego could only take the form of suggestions from outside, uprisings from the subconscient. It was suppressed in the vital. When the inertia rose and the energy of will receded, it began to try to come in again.

Do you mean to say that you never had any rajasic element in you? There is not a human being who has not got it in him so long as he is not divinised in his vital. What were all the vital suggestions coming to you so insistently always except appeals to the rajasic ego? When you threw out sex, jealousy, vanity etc. what were you throwing out but the rajasic ego? What was the demand at the pranam or the disturbance caused there but a movement of the rajasic ego? Some of these things you threw out successfully — others still kept a response.

But how is it that any part of you gives any value to the suggestions? If no part gives any value then surely they must seem to you too laughable and contemptible to have any effect or power to make you revolt.

If you attach no value to the suggestions then there may be the inertia but not this.

X's ego is small and not gigantic — not tall and vehement and aggressive like Y's but squat and inertly obstinate — not fat completely, nor thin but short and roundish and grey in colour.

Squat = short in stature but broad and substantial, so difficult to get rid of. Not tall and pre-eminent or flourishingly settled in self-fullness —

roundish = plenty of it all the same.

Grey = tamasic in tendency, therefore not aggressive, but

obstinate in persistance. But these are not symbols, they are the temperamental figure of the ego.

A true spiritual experience must be free from the claim of the ego. What the ego can do, however, is to get proud of having the experience and think: "What a great one am I !" Or it may think, "I am the Self, the Divine. So let me go and do what I will, for it is the Divine who wills in me." It is only if the experience of Self imposes silence on the other parts and frees the psychic that the ego disappears. Even if not ego itself, numerous fragments and survivals of ego-habit can remain and have to be eliminated.

The dream was a meeting with the Mother on the vital plane. In these dreams many of the details are symbolic, but it is not always easy to say what a particular symbol signifies, as here the condition of the hand. But the latter part of the dream is clear enough. The man there symbolises that ego-tendency in the human nature which makes a man, when some realisation comes, to think how great a realisation is this and how great a sadhak am I and to call others to see and admire — perhaps he thinks, like the man in the dream, "I have seen the Divine, indeed feel I am one with the Divine, — I will call everybody to see that". This is a tendency which has injured the sadhana of many and sometimes ruined the sadhana altogether. In the thoughts you describe you came to see something in yourself which is there more or less in all human beings, the desire to be thought well of by others, to occupy a high place in their esteem or their affection, to have honour, position, admiration. When anybody joins this feeling to the idea of sadhana, then the disposition to do the sadhana for that and not purely and simply for the sake of the Divine comes in and there must be disturbance or else an obstruction in the sadhana itself or if in spite of it spiritual experience comes, then there is the danger of his misusing the experience to magnify his ego like the man in the dream. All these dreams are coming to you to give you a vivid and concrete knowledge and experience of what these human defects are so that you may find it easier to throw them out, to recognise them when they come in the waking state and refuse them entrance. These things are not in yourself only but in all human nature; they are the things one has to get rid of or else to guard against so that one's consecration to the Divine may be complete, selfless, true and pure.

A certain exaltation of the being comes naturally with the stronger experiences and the sense of marvel or miracle may go with it, but there should be no egoistic feeling in the exaltation.

Yes, it is a thing which comes to many; exaggerated and made a principal part of the vital attitude, it has been the cause of failure and departure of several who consider themselves great sadhaks — they made it an excuse for indulging and magnifying the vital ego. Since you see that it is ridiculous, you should have no difficulty in getting rid of it. The only truth in it is that each one who opens himself in such a way that the Force can get through to his material so as to change it, will by that be contributing to the victory of the Force — but it applies to everybody, not to any one individual.

The egoism in yourself of which you speak belongs to the relation of one human being with another and is common to almost all men and women, — it is extremely difficult to get rid of, but if one sees it clearly and determines not to have it, then it can first be brought under control and then dismissed from the nature. But the egoism which made people go away from here through pride in their sadhana and attachment to the supposed greatness of their experiences is another kind and far more dangerous spiritually. You do not have it and I do not think you are in danger of ever having it.

The experience of being with the Mother and speaking to her is one that one can easily have when one is writing to her and is true because some part of the being does actually meet with her and open itself to her when one writes one's experiences.

Yes, if there is the solid experience, the ego-habit is much diminished, but it does not go altogether. It takes refuge in the sense of being an instrument and — if there is not the psychic turn — it may easily prefer to be the instrument of some force that feeds the satisfaction of the ego. In such cases the ego may still remain strong although it feels itself instrumental and not the primary actor.

The egoism of the instrument can be as dangerous or more dangerous to spiritual progress than the egoism of the doer. The ego-sense is contrary to spiritual realisation, so how can any kind of ego be a thing to be encouraged? As for the magnified ego, it is one of the most perilous obstacles to release and perfection. There should be no big I, not even a small one.

What is meant by the magnified ego is that when the limits of the ordinary mind and vital are broken, one feels a far vaster and more powerful consciousness and unlimited possibilities, but if one ties all that to the tail of one's own ego, then one becomes a thousand times more egoistic than the ordinary man. The greatness of the Divine becomes an excuse and a support for one's own greatness and the big I swells itself to fill not only the earth but the heavens. That magnification of the ego is a thing to be guarded against with a watchful care.

Yes — these are small signs. or little forms of the ego of the instrument — not very serious, but often rather sticky. There is a bigger kind of egoism which is not so common which can rise into a kind of megalomania, "I, I am *the* instrument — how great an instrument I am — through me all will be done," — there are three or four who have had that in a distressingly acute form, secretly or openly — often it ends by their going away to do great things outside — great things which somehow do not get done.

Impersonality in itself is not the Divine. All these mistakes can be and are made by many who claim to be in an impersonalised consciousness. A force may be universal but may be also a wrong force: many think they are impersonal and free from ego because they are obeying a force or something bigger than their own personality — but that force or that something may be quite other than the Divine and it may hold them by something in their personality and ego.

It is Prakriti or Nature that acts; the Divine does not compel people to do anything. Nothing can happen without the presence and support of the Divine, for Nature or Prakriti is the Divine Force and it is this that works out things, but it works them out according to the nature and through or with the will of each man which is full of ignorance — that goes on until men turn to the Divine and become conscious of Him and united with Him. Then only can it be said that all begins to be done in him by the direct Will of the Divine.

Ambition and vanity are things so natural to the human consciousness — they have even their use in ordinary life — that it is quite natural that at first they should enter into the sadhana also and linger even when they are rejected. But they have to be pushed out, before one is far on the path — otherwise they are very dangerous attendants and can pervert both aspiration and siddhi.

Ambition is always a force of the vital.

Suggestions of ambition, etc. are always born in the vital mind or, as it might be called, the mind of the vital and from there they rush up to the thinking mind and claim its assent and the sanction of the mental will. When the thinking mind gets clouded by the uprush, it is carried away and gives its assent. The thinking mind (reason) has always to remain unmoved above and judge what is right without being caught and carried away by the vital.

A spiritual humility within is very necessary, but I do not think an outward one is very advisable (absence of pride or arrogance or vanity is indispensable of course in one's outer dealings with others) — it often creates pride, becomes formal or becomes ineffective after a time. I have seen people doing it to cure their pride, but I have not found it producing a lasting result.

It [to do Namaskara to everyone] is a feeling which some have who either want to cultivate humility (X used to do it, but I never saw that it got rid of his innate self-esteem) or who have or are trying to have the realisation of Narayan in all with a Vaishnava turn in it. To feel the One in all is right, but to bow down to the individual who lives still in his ego is good neither for him nor for the one who does it. Especially in this yoga it tends to diffuse what should be concentrated and turned towards a higher realisation than that of the cosmic feeling which is only a step on the way.

Perhaps one could say that it [spiritual humility] is to be aware of the relativity of what has been done compared with what is still to be done — and also to be conscious of one's being nothing without the Divine Grace.

As for the sense of superiority, that is a little difficult to avoid when greater horizons open before the consciousness, unless one is already of a saintly and humble disposition. There are men like Nag Mahashaya (among Sri Ramakrishna's disciples) in whom spiritual experience creates more and more humility; there are others like Vivekananda in whom it creates a great sense of strength and superiority — European critics have taxed him with it rather severely; there are others in whom it fixes a sense of superiority to men and humility to the Divine. Each position has its value. Take Vivekananda's famous answer to the Madras Pundit who objected to one of his assertions saying : "But Shankara does not say so." To which Vivekananda replied: "No, but I, Vivekananda, say so", and the Pundit was speechless. That "I, Vivekananda," stands up to the ordinary eye like a Himalaya of self-confident egoism. But there was nothing false or unsound in Vivekananda's spiritual experience. For this was not mere egoism, but the sense of what he stood for and the attitude of the fighter who, as the representative of something very great, could not allow himself to be put down or belittled. This is not to deny the necessity of non-egoism and of spiritual humility, but to show that the question is not so easy as it appears at first sight. For if I have to express my spiritual experiences I must do that with truth — I must record them, their *bhāva*, their thoughts, feelings, extensions of consciousness which accompany them. What am I to do with the experience in which one feels the whole world in oneself or the force of the Divine flowing in one's being and nature or the certitude of one's faith against all doubts and doubters or one's oneness with the Divine or the smallness of human thought and life compared with this greater knowledge and existence? And I have to use the word I — I cannot take refuge in saying "This body" or "This appearance.", especially as I am not a Mayavadin. Shall I not, therefore, fall into expressions which will make X shake his head at my assertions as full of pride and ego? I imagine it would be difficult to avert it.

Another thing: it seems to me that you identify faith very much with the mental belief, but real faith is something spiritual, a knowledge of the soul. The assertions you quote in your letter are the hard assertions of mental belief leading to a great vehement assertion of one's mental creed and goal because they are one's own and must therefore be greater than those of others — an attitude which is universal in human nature. Even the atheist is not tolerant, but declares his credo of Nature and Matter as the only truth and on all who disbelieve it or believe in other things he pours scorn as unenlightened morons and superstitious half-wits. I bear him no grudge for thinking me that, but I note that this attitude is not confined to religious faith but is equally natural to those who are free from religious faith and do not believe in Gods or Gurus. You will not, I hope, mind my putting the other side of the question; I want to point out that there is the other side, that there is much more to be said than at first sight appears.

The right attitude is to see that as a separate being, as an ego, one has no importance whatever and the insistence on one's own desires, pride, position etc. is an ignorance, but one matters only as a spirit, as a portion of the Divine, not more than others but as all souls matter to the Soul of all.

Yes, the talk about advanced sadhaks is a thing I have always discouraged — but people go on because that appeals to the vital ego.

Ideas of superiority and inferiority are not of much use or validity. Each one is himself with his own possibilities to which there need be no limit except that of will and development and time. Each nature has its own lines and in things that are more developed or less developed, but the standard should be set by what he in himself aims to be. Comparison with others brings in a wrong standard of values.

This is a very common disease with the sadhaks — making comparisons with feelings of jealousy and envy — in some it leads to revolt and self-assertion, in others to self-depreciation and depression. Naturally, these feelings are quite out of place and the judgments created are out of focus. Each sadhak has his own movement, his own relation with the Divine, his own place in the work or the general sadhana and to compare with others immediately brings in a wrong standard. It is on the truth of his own inner movement that he has to take his base — *svadharma.*

Self-respect and a sense of superiority are two very different things. Self-respect is not necessarily a sign of egoism any more than its absence is a sign of liberation from egoism. Self-respect means observing a certain standard of conduct which is proper to the level of manhood to which I belong — e.g. I cannot make a false statement out of self-respect though it would be advantageous to do it and most people under the circumstances would make it. *Amour-propre* is different and belongs to the sattwic type of ego. When one is not free from ego, then *amour-propre* (as well as self-respect — for that can be with ego or without ego) are necessary supports for the maintenance of the personality at its proper level.

Hatred being very unspiritual is not an aid to be called in for the purpose.

For many sadhaks there is a first stage governed by the mind or higher vital in which they go on very well, because in the mind and higher vital there are elements that are strong enough to control the rest while the first experiences or first progress is made. But a time comes when the sadhak has to deal with the lower parts of the being, *then* all the vital difficulties arise. If the early progress or experiences have engendered pride or ego or if there is a serious flaw somewhere, then they are unable to deal with these so long as the ego is not removed or broken or the flaw mended. X developed a pride of self-righteousness that stood in his way altogether; he has also the flaw of a narrow obstinate mind that sticks to its own ideas as if they alone were right — the instances you give of his conduct are illustrations of this defect. That is why here he quarrels with everyone thinking that he is right and they are very bad and mischievous, cannot see his own faults and mistakes and when he is not heard by the Mother or myself feels hurt and offended because we do not support his saintliness and righteousness against the wicked who oppress him. He is a good and clever worker but he cannot progress in sadhana so long as he keeps this stiffness and ego.

You have capacities and yogic stuff, but along with them goes a very strong self-esteem and a self-righteous spirit which stand in the way of perfection and constitute a very serious obstacle. So long as a sadhak has that, the attempt of the Truth to manifest in him will always be baffled by his changing it into mental and vital constructions which distort it, turn it into ineffective half-truth or even make truth itself a source of error.

Yes — self-justification keeps the wrong movement going because it gives a mental support. Self-justification is always a sign of ego and ignorance. When one has a wider consciousness, one knows that each one has his own way of looking at things and finds in that way his own justification, so that both parties in a quarrel believe themselves to be on the right. It is only when one looks from above in a consciousness clear of ego that one sees all sides of a thing and also their real truth.

*
**

But that [not recognising one's defects] is a very common human weakness, although it ought not to exist in a sadhak whose progress depends largely on his recognising what has to be changed in him. Not that the recognition by itself is sufficient, but it is a necessary element. It is of course a kind of pride or vanity which considers this necessary for strength and standing. Not only will they not recognise it before others but they hide their defects from themselves or even if obliged to look at it with one eye look away from it with the other. Or they weave a veil of words and excuses and justifications trying to make it something other than it really is. X's saying[1] is very characteristic of him — that has been his main stumbling-block in the path of yoga.

It is only this habit of the nature — self-worrying and harping on the sense of deficiency that prevents you from being quiet. If you threw that out, it would be easy to be quiet. Humility is needful, but constant self-depreciation does not help; excessive self-esteem and self-depreciation are both wrong attitudes. To recognise any defects without exaggerating them is useful but, once recognised, it is no good dwelling on them always; you must have the confidence that the Divine Force can change everything and you must let the Force work.

It [vital sensitiveness] is neither good nor bad. It comes like that in the course of the development. Some are incapable of consciously or visibly opening to others because they are insensitive. On the other hand to be too open is troublesome.

It depends on the nature of the ego. Some egoists are hard-skinned and not sensitive at all, others are hyper-sensitive.

---

[1] "I would die if I had to admit my faults."

Most sensitiveness is the result or sign of ego.

*
**

Sensitiveness is one of the most persistent obstacles of many sadhaks. There are two remedies for it — the psychic's confidence in the Mother and the surrender that goes with it, that is, "whatever she wills is best for me", and the vastness which you feel now; — it is the wideness of the true self, of the true mental, vital, physical being also, from which such things fall off like dust, for they are of no importance to it whatever.

It is the one thing to do, to get permanently into the wideness, peace and silence and let the ego dissolve into it and the attachments fall away.

*
**

There can be no transformation of the being in an insensitive consciousness.

*
**

One has not to cure oneself of one's sensitiveness, but only acquire the power to rise to a higher consciousness taking such disenchantments as a sort of jumping-board. One way is not to expect even square dealings from others, no matter who the others are. And besides, it is good to have such experiences of the real nature of some people to which a generous nature is often blind; for that helps the growth of one's consciousness. The blow you wince at seems to you so hard because it is a blow the world of your mental formation has sustained. Such a world often becomes a part of our being. The result is that a blow dealt to it gives almost physical pain. The great compensation is that it makes you live more and more in the real world in contradistinction to the world of your imagination which is what you would like the real world to be. But the real world is not all that could be desired, you know, and that is why it has to be acted upon and transformed by the Divine Consciousness. But for that, knowledge of the reality, however unpalatable, is almost

89

the first requisite. This knowledge often enough is best brought
home to us through blows and bleedings. True, idealistic people,
sensitive people, refined natures smart under such disillusion-
ments more than do others who are somewhat thick-skinned, but
that is no reason why fine feelings should be deprecated and the
keen edge of fine susceptibilities be blunted. The thing is to learn
to detach oneself from any such experience and learn to look
at such perversions of others from a higher altitude from where
one can regard these manifestations in the proper perspective
— the impersonal one. Then our difficulties really and literally
become opportunities. For knowledge, when it goes to the root
of our troubles, has in itself a marvellous healing-power as it
were. As soon as you touch the quick of the trouble, as soon as
you, diving down and down, get at what really ails you, the pain
disappears as though by a miracle. Unflinching courage to reach
true Knowledge is therefore of the very essence of yoga. No
lasting superstructure can be erected except on a solid basis of
true Knowledge. The feet must be sure of their ground before
the head can hope to kiss the skies.

Your surprise at X's behaviour shows that you do not yet know
what kind of thing is the average human nature. Did you never
hear of the answer of Vidyasagar when he was told that a certain
man was abusing him, — "Why does he abuse me? I never did
him a good turn (*upakāra*)." The unregenerate vital is not grateful for a benefit, it resents being under an obligation. So long as
the benefit continues, it is effusive and says sweet things, as soon
as it expects nothing more it turns round and bites the hand that
fed it. Sometimes it does that even before, when it thinks it can
do it without the benefactor knowing the origin of the slander,
fault-finding or abuse. In all these dealings of yours there is
nothing unusual, nothing, as you think, peculiar to you. Most
have this kind of experience, few escape it altogether. Of course,
people with a developed psychic element are by nature grateful
and do not behave in this way.

X

Most men are, like animals, driven by the forces of Nature: whatever desires come, they fulfil them, whatever emotions come they allow them to play, whatever physical wants they have, they try to satisfy. We say then that the activities and feelings of men are controlled by their Prakriti, and mostly by the vital and physical nature. The body is the instrument of the Prakriti or Nature — it obeys its own nature or it obeys the vital forces of desire, passion, etc.

But man has also a mind and, as he develops, he learns to control his vital and physical nature by his reason and by his will. This control is very partial: for the reason is often deluded by vital desires and the ignorance of the physical and it puts itself on their side and tries to justify by its ideas, reasonings or arguments their mistakes and wrong movements. Even if the reason keeps free and tells the vital or the body, "Do not do this", yet the vital and the body often follow their own movement in spite of the prohibition — man's mental will is not strong enough to compel them.

When people do sadhana, there is a higher Nature that works within, the psychic and spiritual, and they have to put their nature under the influence of the psychic being and the higher spiritual self or of the Divine. Not only the vital and the body but the mind also has to learn the Divine Truth and obey the divine rule. But because of the lower nature and its continued hold on them, they are unable at first and for a long time to prevent their nature from following the old ways — even when they know or are told from within what to do or what not to do. It is only by persistent sadhana, by getting into the higher spiritual consciousness and spiritual nature that this difficulty can be overcome; but even for the strongest and best sadhaks it takes a long time.

*
**

The desire for the Divine or for bhakti for the Divine is the one desire which can free one from all the others — at the core it is not a desire but an aspiration; a soul need, the breath of existence of the inmost being, and as such it cannot be counted among desires.

Is there any time in the "straight path" for satisfying desires? If desire is not mastered, how can there be any straight walking on the straight path?

It is not yoga to give free play to the natural instincts and desires. Yoga demands mastery over the nature, not subjection to the nature.

Kāmanā bāsanā have no part in yoga, they cannot be its help (*sahāya*), they can only be hindrances. So long as desire and ego remain, there can be no surrender to the Divine, no fulfilment in the yoga. They are movements of the vital and cannot be anything else.

Egoless strength is strength which does not act for selfish motives or for the desires of the vital or to carry out the ideas of one's own mind, but exists only for the service of the Divine and as an instrument of the Divine.

Demand and desire are only two different aspects of the same thing — nor is it necessary that a feeling should be agitated or restless to be a desire; it can be, on the contrary, quietly fixed and persistent or persistently recurrent. Demand or desire comes from the mental or the vital, but a psychic or spiritual need is a different thing. The psychic does not demand or desire — it aspires; it does not make conditions for its surrender or withdraw if its aspiration is not immediately satisfied — for the psychic has complete trust in the Divine or in the Guru and can wait for the right time or the hour of the Divine Grace. The psychic has an insistence of its own, but it puts its pressure not on the Divine, but on the nature, placing a finger of light on all the defects there that stand in the way of the realisation, sifting out all that is mixed, ignorant or imperfect in the experience or in the movements of the yoga and never satisfied with itself or with the nature till it has got it perfectly open to the Divine, free from all forms of ego, surrendered, simple and right in the attitude and all the movements. This is what has to be established entirely in the mind and vital and in the physical consciousness before supramentalisation of the whole nature is possible. Otherwise what one gets is more or less brilliant, half-luminous, half-cloudy illuminations and experiences on the mental and vital and physical planes inspired either from some larger mind or larger vital or at the best from the mental reaches above the human that intervene between the intellect and the overmind. These can be very stimulating and satisfying up to a certain point and are good for those who want some spiritual realisation on these planes; but the supramental realisation is something much more difficult and exacting in its conditions and the most difficult of all is to bring it down to the physical level.

There are always two methods of living in the Supreme. One is to draw away the participation of the consciousness from things altogether and go so much inwards as to be separated from existence and live in contact with that which is beyond it. The other is to get to that which is the true Essence of all things, not allowing oneself to be absorbed and entangled by the external forms. Desire, attachment, slavery to the attractions of the external sense are the chief obstacle to this movement — so in either way they have to be got rid of. But it is quite possible to see the Supreme before the attraction of external sense is gone — only one cannot live securely in It if there is desire and external attachment because that is always taking one away from the inner poise.

All the ordinary vital movements are foreign to the true being and come from outside; they do not belong to the soul nor do they originate in it but are waves from the general Nature, Prakriti.

The desires come from outside, enter the subconscious vital and rise to the surface. It is only when they rise to the surface and the mind becomes aware of them, that we become conscious of the desire. It seems to us to be our own because we feel it thus rising from the vital into the mind and do not know that it came from outside. What belongs to the vital, to the being, what makes it responsible is not the desire itself, but the habit of responding to the waves or the currents of suggestion that come into it from the universal Prakriti.

The rejection of desire is essentially the rejection of the element of craving, putting that out from the consciousness itself as a foreign element not belonging to the true self and the inner nature. But refusal to indulge the suggestions of desire is also a part of the rejection; to abstain from the action suggested, if it is not the right action, must be included in the yogic discipline. It is only when this is done in the wrong way, by a mental ascetic principle or a hard moral rule, that it can be called suppression. The difference between suppression and an inward essential rejection is the difference between mental or moral control and a spiritual purification.

When one lives in the true consciousness one feels the desires outside oneself, entering from outside, from the universal lower Prakriti, into the mind and the vital parts. In the ordinary human condition this is not felt; men become aware of the desire only when it is there, when it has come inside and found a lodging or a habitual harbourage and so they think it is their own and a part of themselves. The first condition for getting rid of desire is, therefore, to become conscious with the true consciousness; for then it becomes much easier to dismiss it than when one has to struggle with it as if it were a constituent part of oneself to be thrown out from the being. It is easier to cast off an accretion than to excise what is felt as a parcel of our substance.

When the psychic being is in front, then also to get rid of desire becomes easy; for the psychic being has in itself no desires, it has only aspirations and a seeking and love for the Divine and all things that are or tend towards the Divine. The constant prominence of the psychic being tends of itself to bring out the true consciousness and set right almost automatically the movements of the nature.

Desire takes a long time to get rid of entirely. But, if you can once get it out of the nature and realise it as a force coming from outside and putting its claws into the vital and physical, it will be easier to get rid of the invader. You are too accustomed to feel it as part of yourself or planted in you — that makes it more difficult for you to deal with its movements and dismiss its ancient control over you.

You should not rely on anything else alone, however helpful it may seem, but chiefly, primarily, fundamentally on the Mother's Force. The Sun and the Light may be a help, and will be if it is the true Light and the true Sun, but cannot take the place of the Mother's Force.

It is good. No one can easily get rid of desires. What has first to be done is to exteriorize them, to push them out, on the surface and get the inner parts quiet and clear. Afterwards they can be thrown out and replaced by the true thing, a happy and luminous will one with the Divine's.

The *necessities* of a sadhak should be as few as possible; for there are only a very few things that are real necessities in life. The rest are either utilities or things decorative to life or luxuries. These a yogin has a right to possess or enjoy only on one of two conditions —

(1) If he uses them during his sadhana solely to train himself in possessing things without attachment or desire and learn to use them rightly, in harmony with the Divine Will, with a proper handling, a just organisation, arrangement and measure — or,

(2) if he has already attained a true freedom from desire and attachment and is not in the least moved or affected in any way by loss or withholding or deprival. If he has any greed, desire, demand, claim for possession or enjoyment, any anxiety, grief, anger or vexation when denied or deprived, he is not free in spirit and his use of the things he possesses is contrary to the spirit of sadhana. Even if he is free in spirit, he will not be fit for possession if he has not learned to use things not for himself, but for the Divine Will, as an instrument, with the right knowledge and action in the use, for the proper equipment of a life lived not for oneself but for and in the Divine.

*

It would certainly be very easy if all that one had to do were to follow one's desires; but to be governed by one's desires is not yoga.

Need and want are not the same thing. The fact that they could go on without it for so long shows that it was not a need.

*

Desire is a psychological movement, and it can attach itself to a "true need" as well as to things that are not true needs. One must approach even true needs without desire. If one does not get them, one must feel nothing.

*

As for the inconveniences, you should take them as a training in *samatā*. To be able to bear inconveniences is one of the most elementary necessities if one wants to enter into the true spirit of yoga.

*

Whether ascetic or non-ascetic, the yogi, the sadhak must become free from vital desire and spiritually master of the movements of his nature — and for that he must be free from ego and
desire and duality. I have always made that quite clear — that
indulgence of desire is no more part of this yoga than it is of
Sannyasa. One must be able to use and handle physical things
and physical life, but from the spiritual consciousness, not from
the level of the vital ego.

*
**

All belongs to the Divine — there must be no ego or desire —
only the Divine and its Light, Knowledge, Power, Ananda,
action. But all this must come from above, not from the mixed
lower cosmic forces.

*
**

All things are the Divine because the Divine is there, but hidden
not manifest; when the mind goes out to things, it is not with the
sense of the Divine in them, but for the appearances only which
conceal the Divine. It is necessary therefore for you as a sadhak
to turn entirely to the Mother in whom the Divine is manifest
and not run after the appearances, the desire of which or the
interest in which prevents you from meeting the Divine. Once
the being is consecrated, then it can see the Divine everywhere
— and then it can include all things in the one consciousness
without a separate interest or desire.

*
**

After realisation whatever the higher Will demands is the best
— but first, detachment is the rule. To reach the freedom without the discipline and development is given to few.

It is true that the mere suppression or holding down of desire is not enough, not by itself truly effective, but that does not mean that desires are to be indulged; it means that desires have not merely to be suppressed, but to be rejected from the nature. In place of desire there must be a single-minded aspiration towards the Divine.

As for love, the love must be turned singly towards the Divine. What men call by that name is a vital interchange for mutual satisfaction of desire, vital impulse or physical pleasure. There must be nothing of this interchange between sadhaks; for to seek for it or indulge this kind of impulse only leads away from the sadhana.

Your theory is a mistaken one. The free expression of a passion may relieve the vital for a time, but at the same time it gives it a right to return always. It is not reduced at all. Suppression with inner indulgence in subtle forms is not a cure, but expression in outer indulgence is still less a cure. It is perfectly possible to go on without manifestation if one is resolute to arrive at a complete control, the control being not a mere suppression but an inner and outer rejection.

You do not seem to have a correct idea of the nature of vital desire. Vital desire grows by being indulged, it does not become satisfied. If your desire were indulged, it would begin to grow more and more and ask for more and more. That has been our constant experience with the sadhaks and it confirms what has always been known about desire. Desire and envy have to be thrown out of the consciousness — there is no other way to deal with them.

Not necessarily suppression, if the refusal of food [to a desire] is accompanied by detachment in the major part of the being. The difference between suppression (*nigraha*) and self-control (*samyama*) is that one says "I cannot help desiring but I will not satisfy my desire", while the other says "I refuse the desire as well as the satisfaction of the desire".

Nigraha means holding down the movement, but a movement merely held down is only suspended — it is better to reject and dismiss, detaching yourself from it.

Everything which it hankers after is desirable to the vital — but the desire has to be rejected. "I won't desire" is quite the right thing to say, even if "I don't desire" cannot yet be said by the vital. Still there is something in the being that can even say "I don't desire" and refuse to recognise the vital desire as part of the true being. It is that consciousness which the peace and power bring that has to be recognised as the true "I" and made permanent in front.

It is always the habit of the vital being to find out things by which it persuades the mind and justifies its desires; and circumstances usually shape themselves to justify it still further. For what we have within us creates the circumstances outside us. What matters is that you should take inwardly a different position in the future.

Of course — the vital is insatiable. There are only two things that interfere with it — the limitations of the body and the disapprobation of the mind — but the latter is not always there. There is also of course the possibility of the psychic interfering, but to that the vital becomes pervious only at a certain stage. It is therefore the body that is the only check for most people.

It is difficult to get rid of desires *altogether* all at once — if the right ones have the upper hand, that already makes the ultimate victory sure. Therefore don't allow that to trouble you. A progressive change is the way these things work out — and if the progress has begun, then there can be a fundamental sense of certitude about the outcome of the sadhana and a quiet view upon what has to be done because it is sure to be done.

The vision simply means that when you clutch at anything and try to make it your own with an egoistic sense of possession, then however beautiful and wonderful it may be, it loses its value and becomes ordinary.

It is often the experience that when one gives up the insistence of desire for a thing, then the thing itself comes. The right attitude is to wait on the Divine Will and seek that only — desire always creates perturbation and even its fulfilment does not satisfy. Aspiration is a different thing. The oscillation between the two conditions you speak of, is the sign of a struggle in the physical consciousness — it must end by the Peace and Power fixing itself there, then the other will disappear.

It should be quite clear to you what the two opposite things are, the two things with which every sadhak is faced. One is the vehemence of earthly egoistic desire which brings only confusion and suffering and the other is the peace, force, joy, light of understanding which is the divine in you and which we are striving to establish in you. When you put yourself on the right side, things become easy; when you hesitate, and are divided, there is a double state; when something in you receives and clings to the desires then all goes wrong. You *must* learn to put always the weight of your choice on the right side. Certainly I shall do all to get the wrong will changed and the right one put in its place

— whatever is the resistance or difficulty, that I shall do always.

The fear is again that of the physical consciousness or of the vital element in it — it is afraid if it gives up desire that it will lose everything — or everything *it* wants — and gain nothing in exchange or at least nothing *it* wants. It does not realise that it will get something far greater and more powerful and happy in place of this troubled desire and its doubtful and precarious fruits — for it has been accustomed to think of desire as the only possible motive of life. It does not know that the divine Force is there waiting to descend with its light and peace and joy bringing much greater things and a happier life. When this part can be enlightened and persuaded to want whole-heartedly the change, then a great difficulty, indeed the central difficulty will have gone.

It is the old vital nature that feels its human worldly desires will not be satisfied and feels like this. All that has not to be indulged but rejected and swept aside. In its place must come the wideness in which there is a self-existent peace and satisfaction and into that peace and wideness must come the Mother's greater peace, force, light, knowledge, Ananda.

There was and is the opening before you of a new stage in your spiritual development. For it to realise itself you must progress first in two directions. The first we have already pressed on you — the surmounting of those vital desires which linked you to the lower movements and invited the pressure of a hostile Force on your lower vital and your body, and the complete surrender of life and body to the One alone. The other is the descent of a full calm and strength and equanimity into these parts so that you may conquer life and its difficulties and do your work for the Divine. This calm and strength had often descended into your mind and higher vital, but these other parts were still open to much weakness and attachment and a self-indulgent movement. That must go if one wants to become a hero and master of spiritual action. In your life at your previous place these things were too much sheltered and allowed to remain; at your present place you have a chance to be by yourself with the Divine Force and look life in the face from the soul's inner strength and become master of circumstances. Outer difficulties or inconveniences you should not allow to alarm or depress you. Inner difficulties should also be met with detachment, calm, equality, the unshakable will to conquer.

As for the rest you have rightly said, "I must preserve my equanimity and a faith in Divine Guidance when falsehood or any trouble or difficulty confronts me." The defect that opened the way to the bodily and other troubles was the faltering in your resolution to conquer the vital and follow the straight and high path and the consequent violent despair and depression it brought in its wake. Let these disappear altogether and do not allow them to rise in that way again. The path of spiritual calm and strength and the consecration of all your forces to the Divine is the one safe way for you and that you must now consistently follow.

It is again the old vain imagination prompted by an uprising of the dissatisfied desires of the vital nature. Evidently, the wrong attitude of desire must have been waiting for its opportunity and it gave the opportunity also for the old vital to rise and indulge in its accustomed movements. It is also evident that it was the pressure of the desire coming up from below that removed the Ananda. The psychic Ananda and the desire of the complaining and clamouring vital cannot go together; if desire comes up, the Ananda is obliged to draw back — unless you reject the desire in time and refuse to make any compromise with it. Especially when the Mother was giving you wideness and peace and intense Ananda, it was irrational in the extreme to give room to an external desire and sacrifice all that for its sake.

**

To yield to depression when things go wrong is the worst way of meeting the difficulty. There must be some desire or demand within you, conscious or subconscious, that gets excited and revolts against its not being satisfied. The best way is to be conscious of it, face it calmly and steadily throw it out.

If the lower vital (not the mind only) could permanently make up its mind that all desire and demand are contrary to the Truth and no longer call for them, these things would lose very soon their force of return.

Saturate your mind and vital with the Truth and remain calm and still. It is from unsatisfied desire that all suffering arises; take your stand on a calm free from desire. When that has come, all else of the Divine Truth, Love and Ananda can come and stand securely upon it.

You have done rightly about the things. These small desires obstruct greatly the change in the outer consciousness and the being must be free from them if the transformation is not to be hampered there.

It is the vital-physical that receives these suggestions and obeys these desires. What you have to do is to get the consciousness down into the whole of the vital proper so that not only the mind but the vital itself will reject these desires. In that case, the vital-physical desires will lose half their force.

If the peace and power that were acting on the head and in the chest, have come down into the stomach and below, that would indicate that they are no longer acting on the mind and emotional being only, but fully on the vital also — that is a great progress.

The desires you refer to are those of the vital-physical in the subtle physical consciousness — impulse to talk, essential hunger, thirst, etc. Peace and quietude full in the vital-physical and subtle physical and down even in the lowest levels, are necessary for the whole change to be made. The heat of which you speak is that of this subtle principle of vital-physical desire which exists for its own sake, not for the real needs of the body — that is why physical satisfaction does not diminish it.

It is the small habits of the lower vital being which gather all their strength to resist correction and try to occupy the consciousness. When they come you must learn to detach your inner consciousness from them entirely so that even when they strongly come they will not be able to occupy the consciousness or get any assent.

The vital in the physical easily slips back to its old small habits if it gets a chance. It is there that they stick. They go entirely only when that part gets equanimity and a simple natural freedom from all desires.

These habits of the physical-vital are almost automatic in their action and it takes either a very strong will or a persistent effort of self-discipline to get out this automatic, almost reflex action. You should not therefore be discouraged by the difficulty, but go on with the necessary perseverance of the will to press it out of existence.

XI

The fact that the anger comes with such force is itself enough to show that it is not in you that it is but that it comes from outside. It is a rush of force from the universal Nature that tries to take possession of the individual being and make that being act according to the will of this outside force and not according to the will of the soul within. These things come in the course of the sadhana because the sadhak is liberating himself from the lower nature and trying to turn towards the Mother and live in her divine consciousness and the higher nature. The forces of the lower nature do not want that and so they make these rushes in order to recover their rule. It is necessary when that comes, to remain quiet within remembering the Mother or calling her and reject the anger or whatever else comes, whenever it comes or however often it comes. If that is done, then these forces begin to lose their power to invade. It is easier if one clearly feels them to be outside forces and foreign to oneself; but even if you cannot feel that yet when they enter, still the mind must keep that idea and refuse to accept them as any longer a part of the nature. The idea of the Mother being severe was of course a suggestion that came with the invading force so as to help it to enter. Such suggestions come to many sadhaks (though not so many as before) at Pranam and is the cause to them of much disturbance. Such suggestions must be firmly rejected at once.

In fact all these ignorant vital movements originate from outside in the ignorant universal Nature; the human being forms in his superficial parts of being, mental, vital, physical, a habit of certain responses to these waves from outside. It is these responses that he takes as his own character (anger, desire, sex etc.) and thinks he cannot be otherwise. But that is not so; he can change. There is another consciousness deeper within him, his true inner being, which is his real self, but is covered over by the superficial nature. This the ordinary man does not know, but the yogi becomes aware of it as he progresses in his sadhana. As the consciousness of this inner being increases by sadhana, the surface nature and its responses are pushed out and can be got rid of altogether. But the ignorant universal Nature does not want to let go and throws the old movements on the sadhak and tries to get them inside again; owing to a habit the superficial nature gives the old responses. If one can get the firm knowledge that these things are from outside and not a real part of oneself, then it is easier for the sadhak to repel such returns, or if they lay hold, he can get rid of them sooner. That is why I say repeatedly that these things rise not in yourself, but from outside.

I think you have always had an idea that to give expression to an impulse or a movement is the best way or even the only way to get rid of it. But that is a mistaken idea. If you give expression to anger, you prolong or confirm the habit of the recurrence of anger; you do not diminish or get rid of the habit. The very first step towards weakening the power of anger in the nature and afterwards getting rid of it altogether is to refuse all expression to it in act or speech. Afterwards one can go on with more likelihood of success to throw it out from the thought and feeling also. And so with all other wrong movements.

All these movements come from outside, from the universal lower Nature, or are suggested or thrown upon you by adverse forces — adverse to your spiritual progress. Your method of taking them as your own is again a wrong method; for by doing that you increase their power to recur and take hold of you. If you take them as your own, that gives them a kind of right to be there. If you feel them as *not* your own, then they have no right, and the will can develop more power to send them away. What you must always have and feel as yours is this will, the power to refuse assent, to refuse admission to a wrong movement. Or if it comes in, the power to send it away, without expressing it.

Of course the best way will be if you can keep the contact more with the Mother and her Light and Force and receive and accept and follow only what comes from that higher force.

It is really simply the recurrence of an old habit of the nature. Look at it and see how trifling is the occasion of the rising of this anger and its outburst — it becomes more and more causeless

— and the absurdity of such movements itself. It would not really be difficult to get rid of it if, when it comes, you looked at it calmly — for it is perfectly possible to stand back in one part of the being, observing in a detached equanimity even while the anger rises on the surface — as if it were someone else in your being who had the anger. The difficulty is that you get alarmed and upset and that makes it easier for the thing to get hold of your mind which it should not do.

Help we are giving you — stand back so as to be able to feel it and not this obsession of these surface movements.

That is the right thing that must happen always when anger or anything else rises. The psychic reply must become habitual pointing out that anger is neither right nor helpful and then the being must draw back from these outward things and take its stand in its inner self, detach from all these things and people. It is this detachment that is the first thing that must be gained by the sadhak — he must cease to live in these outward things and live in his inner being. The more that is done the more there is a release and peacefulness. Afterwards when one is secure in this inner being, the right thing to do, the right way to deal with men and things will begin to come.

When it is the psychic that rules all the movements of the being, then it [anger] completely disappears and when the equanimity of the higher consciousness takes complete possession of the lower vital. Till then one can establish control, diminish and reduce it to a touch that has no outward effect or a wave that passes without life-expression.

Yes, certainly. Infinite peace, universal love can remove anger — if they are complete and stable.

It is true that anger and strife are in the nature of the human vital and do not go easily; but what is important is to have the will to change, and the clear perception that these things must go. If that will and perception are there, then in the end they will go. The most important help to it is, here also, for the psychic being to grow within — for that brings a certain kindliness, patience, charity towards all and one no longer regards everything from the point of view of one's own ego and its pain or pleasure, likings and dislikings. .The second help is the growth of the inner peace which outward things cannot trouble. With the peace comes a calm wideness in which one perceives all as one self, all beings as the children of the Mother and the Mother dwelling in oneself and in all. It is that towards which your sadhana will move, for these are the things which come with the growth of the psychic and spiritual consciousness. Then these troubled reactions to outward things will no longer come.

It is indeed when the quietude comes down from above or comes out from the psychic that the vital becomes full of peace or of kindliness and goodwill. It is therefore that the inner psychic quietude first and afterwards the peace from above must occupy the whole being. Otherwise such things as anger in the vital can be controlled but it is difficult to get rid of them altogether without this occupation by the inner quietude and higher peace. That you should depend on the Mother for the sadhana is the best attitude, for it is indeed her Force that does the sadhana in you.

These things, hard forms of speech, anger etc. are habits formed by the vital-physical consciousness and, as they are supported by the subconscient, very difficult to change. If one can conquer or change them by force of will or mental or spiritual control, so much the better. But if one cannot do this at once, one must not be upset or think oneself unfit. It is easier for most to realise the Divine or enter into the psychic consciousness than to change

this part of the nature; but once the psychic consciousness governs or the higher consciousness descends then it is much easier
for these to go. You must not therefore be discouraged by these
recurrences or persistences, but try always to stand back in an
inner quietude and if they come let them pass away like a cloud
across the light. In time these things will be finally dealt with by
the Force.

It is indeed a very good sign that the anger when it comes is brief
and subdued and no longer expressed in the outward — for that
is one very marked stage always of the rejection of something not
wanted by the nature. It comes still but it has no longer the old
force, duration, intensity, completeness. The externalised condition is often used to show or test the progress made in the outer
nature itself, for when one is entirely within these outward movements remain quiescent, so the extent to which they are changed
cannot be so easily measured. But of course it is the going inward
that most helps to deliver the nature.

If the anger did not come, it must be because the vital force of the
attack is diminishing and it must be more in the physical mind
and the external (physical) vital that it acts. You have a great
strength for action; as for the inner growth and action of the
sadhana you have a strength there too of the psychic and the
vital, — it is only the external being that finds these difficulties
in its way and is momentarily overcome or affected by them.
Things always come in the way when one wants to progress in
the sadhana, but in the end if one is sincere in one's aspiration
these troubles help to prepare the victory of the soul over all that
opposes.

The inner will prevails sometimes, sometimes it does not
prevail for the time being. That is quite normal. It depends on
certain conditions which the physical mind does not see. As one
grows in knowledge, one becomes aware of these unseen conditions and understands better what happens.

The fire is always the fire of purification — it is very red when it is acting on the vital; when the vital no longer covers the psychic, then the rose colour of the psychic comes out more and more.

The house you saw is the new building of the nature, especially in the vital, which is being prepared by the sadhana.

The reason why quietness is not yet fixed and anger returns is that you allow your physical mind to become active. In regard to the sadhana it begins to think there is this defect in you and that defect and therefore the sadhana does not become immediately effective and perfect. This makes the vital nervous or despondent and in the despondency a state of irritation arises. At the same time this mind becomes active as it has now with regard to X or begins to judge and criticise and this too leads to nervousness and irritation. These things belong to the old mind you are trying to leave and therefore stand in the way of concentration and quietude. They should be stopped at their root by rejecting the suggestions of the physical mind as soon as they begin. A new consciousness is coming based upon inner silence and quietude. You must wait quietly for that to develop. True knowledge, true perceptions of people and things will come in that new silent consciousness. The mind's view of people and things must necessarily be either limited and defective or erroneous — to go on judging by it is now a waste of time. Wait for the new consciousness to develop and show you all in a new and true light. Then the tendency to anger which arises from this mind and is a violent impatience directed against things the mind and vital do not like, would have no ground to rise at all — or if it rose without cause could be more easily rejected. Rely for the sadhana on the Mother's grace and her Force, yourself remembering always to keep only two things, quietude and confidence. For things and people, leave them to the Mother also; as you have difficulties in your nature, so they have too; but to deal with them needs insight, sympathy, patience.

About the attachment to things, the physical rejection of

them is not the best way to get rid of it. Accept what is given you, ask for what is needed and think no more of it — attaching no importance, using them when you have, not troubled if you have not. That is the best way of getting rid of the attachment.

If you look closely, you will see that all these things — the rudeness of one, the anger of another — are exceedingly slight things which should be received with indifference. Do not allow them to trouble you so much. The one thing of supreme importance is your sadhana and your spiritual growth. Let nothing touch or disturb that.

The *Essays on the Gita* explain the ordinary Karmayoga as developed in the Gita, in which the work done is the ordinary work of human life with only an inward change. There too the violence to be used is not a personal violence done from egoistic motives, but part of the ordered system of social life. Nothing can spiritually justify individual violence done in anger or passion or from any vital motive. In our yoga our object is to rise higher than the ordinary life of men and in it violence has to be left aside altogether.

An inner psychic or spiritual change is not brought about by violence. It is not a change of conduct that has to be done in the sadhaks, but a change of soul and spirit governing the mind and vital and body instead of the mind and vital governing. Violence is the drastic contradiction of that; it makes mental egoism and vital passion and fury or else cruelty the rulers. Violence in ordinary Nature does not justify violence in spiritual work.

In all things there must be a control over thought and speech also. But while rajasic violence is excluded, a calmly forceful severity of thought and speech where severity is needed is sometimes indispensable.

XII

If you want to do yoga, you must get rid of fear. Yoga and fear do not go together.

It is true that what one fears has the tendency to come until one is able to look it in the face and overcome one's shrinking. One must learn to take one's foundation on the Divine and overcome the fear, relying on the help to carry one through all things even unpleasant and adverse. There is a Force that works even through them for the seeker and carries him towards his goal.

Yes, fear creates imaginary terrors — even if there is real danger, fear does not help; it clouds the intelligence, takes away presence of mind and prevents one seeing the right thing to do.

Let the Force at work increase, till it clears out the mixed consciousness altogether.

It is a mistake to think that by fearing or being unhappy you can progress. Fear is always a feeling to be rejected, because what you fear is just the thing that is likely to come to you: fear attracts the object of fear. Unhappiness weakens the strength and lays one more open to the causes of unhappiness.

One can be quiet, happy, cheerful without being all that in a light or shallow way — and the happiness need not bring any vital reaction. All that you need to do is to be observant and vigilant, — watchful so that you may not give assent to wrong movements or the return of the old feelings, darkness, confusion, etc. If you remain vigilant, then with the increase of the Force upholding you, a power of self-control will come, a power to see and reject the wrong turn or the wrong reaction when it comes. Fear and unhappiness will not give you that. It is only by this vigilance accompanied by an opening to the supporting and guiding Force that it will come. What you describe as a capacity to choose the right and the feeling of strength or power that can stop the wrong movement and take the right one as soon as it recognises them is just this control and vigilance. It is by this control and vigilance supported by the Force that you can prevent the love and devotion too from being mixed with or replaced by selfish desires and impurities. The more you open, the more this power will increase in you.

You should throw away fear as well as anger and go quietly on your way putting your confidence in the Mother.

[Ways to remove fear:] By bringing down strength and calm into the lower vital (region below the navel). Also by will and imposing calm on the system when the fear arises. It can be done in either way or both together.

There is no fear in the higher Nature. Fear is a creation of the vital plane, an instinct of the ignorance, a sense of danger with a violent vital reaction that replaces and usually prevents or distorts the intelligence of things. It might almost be considered as an invention of the hostile forces.

XIII

Jealousy should not be there if there is no ground for it, for then it is absurd and meaningless — but also when there is reason for it according to common standards, it should not be there, for it is a sentiment lacking in nobility and quite un-yogic.

As for getting rid of *lobha*, certainly the Mother's full help will be with you.

It is of course the old reaction — jealousy is certainly there, or you would not feel this violent sorrow. That it subsists still in the recesses and rises with such vehemence shows how deeply rooted this movement was in your physical consciousness. You have not been able to root it out because when it comes you associate yourself entirely with it and abandon yourself to its outcries and violence. You must have the strength to stand back from it in that part of your nature which is free — only then will you be able to push it away from you; and it is only if it is pushed away from you each time it rises that it will consent to disappear and return no more. As for our support and help it is there, but you must remain conscious of it — and you must not allow any wrong ideas like those of this morning to diminish the sense of unity and contact with the Mother.

I do not see why you make such a big difference between the quarrels and jealousy over other women and quarrels and jealousy over other attractions not of a sexual character. They both spring from the same primary impulse, the possessive instinct which is at the base of ordinary vital love. In the latter case, as often sexual jealousy is not possible, the mind supports itself on other motives which seem to it quite reasonable and justifiable — it may not be conscious that it is being pushed by the vital, but the quarrels and the vivacity of the disagreement are there all the same. Whether you had or had not both forms of it, is not very material and does not make things better or worse. It is the getting rid of the instinct itself that matters, whether from the psychological point of view or from that of a spiritual change.

The one thing that is of any importance is the fact that the old personality which you were throwing out has reasserted itself for the moment, as you yourself see. It has confused your mind, otherwise you would not ask the question whether it is there still and how that agrees with my description of your aspiration and glimpse of turning entirely to the Mother as true and real. Of course, they were true and real and sincere and they are still there even if for a moment clouded over. You know well enough by this time that the whole being is not one block so that if one part changes, all changes miraculously at the same time. Something of the old things may be there submerged and rise up again if the pressure and fixed resolution to get rid of them slackens. I do not know to what you refer when you speak of the statement that — "Light and Darkness, Truth and Falsehood cannot dwell together"; but certainly it can only mean that in the spiritual endeavour one cannot allow them to dwell together, — the Light, the Truth must be kept, the Darkness, the falsehood or error pushed out altogether. It certainly did not mean that in human beings there can be either only all light or only all darkness and whoever has any weakness in him has no light and no sincere aspiration and no truth in his nature. If that were so, yoga would be impossible. All the sadhaks in this Ashram would be convicted of insincerity and of having no true sadhana — for who is there in whom there is no obscurity and no movement of ignorance?

If you have fallen down from the consciousness you had, it is because instead of dismissing the dispute with X as a moment's movement, you begin to brood on it and prolong the wrong turn it gave. It is no use persisting in the feelings that it creates in you. You have only to do what I have been trying to tell you. Draw back from them and, having seen what is there in the nature, dismiss them quietly and turn back again to the true consciousness, opening yourself to receive once more the Truth that is creating you anew and let it come down into all your nature.

SECTION FOUR

TRANSFORMATION OF THE PHYSICAL

Transformation of the Physical

No NEED to despise the physical being —
it is part of the intended manifestation.

It is because your consciousness in the course of the sadhana
has come into contact with the lower physical nature and sees
it as it is in itself when it is not kept down or controlled either
by the mind, the psychic or the spiritual force. This nature is in
itself full of low and obscure desires, it is the most animal part
of the human being. One has to come into contact with it so as
to know what is there and transform it. Most sadhaks of the old
type are satisfied with rising into the spiritual or psychic realms
and leave this part to itself — but by that it remains unchanged,
even if mostly quiescent, and no complete transformation is
possible. You have only to remain quiet and undisturbed and
let the higher Force work to change this obscure physical nature.

All that may be very well in theory, but practically it is found
that the physical impurity is strong enough to bar the inner
progress and limit rigidly the inner experience to some passive
peace.

All that may be very well in theory, but practically it is found
that the physical impurity is strong enough to bar the inner
progress and limit rigidly the inner experience to some passive
peace.

The opportunity for these contrary forces is given when the
sadhak descends in the inevitable course of the sadhana from
the mental or the higher vital plane to the physical consciousness.
Always this is accompanied by a fading of the first deep experiences and a descent to the neutral obscure inertia which is the
bed-rock of the unredeemed physical nature. It is there that the
Light, the Power, the Ananda of the Divine has to descend and

transform everything, driving away for ever all obscurity and all inertia and establishing the radiant Energy, the perfect Light and the unchanging Bliss. There and not in the mind or the higher vital is all the difficulty, but there too must be the victory and the foundation of the new world. I do not wish to disguise from you the difficulty of this great and tremendous change or the possibility that you may have a long and hard work before you, but are you really unwilling to face it and take your share in the great work? Will you reject the greatness of this endeavour to follow a mad irrational impulse towards some more exciting work of the hour or the moment for which you have no true call in any part of your nature?

There is no true reason for despondency; in nothing that has passed do I find any good ground for it. The difficulties you experience are nothing to those that others have felt and yet conquered them, others who were not stronger than you. All that has happened is that by this descent into the physical consciousness the ordinary external human nature has come to the front with its elemental imperfections and subconscient unsatisfied impulses and it is to these that the contrary force is appealing. The mind and the higher vital have put away from them the ideas and illusions which gave them a sanction, an illusion of legitimacy and even nobility in their satisfaction. But the root of them, their inherent irrational push for satisfaction, has not yet gone — this, for instance, is the reason for the sexual movements which you have recently felt in sleep or in waking. This was inevitable. All that is needed is for your psychic being to come forward and open you to the direct and real and constant inner contact of myself and the Mother. Hitherto your soul has expressed itself through the mind and its ideals and admirations or through the vital and its higher joys and aspirations; but that is not sufficient to conquer the physical difficulty and enlighten and transform Matter. It is your soul in itself, your psychic being that must come in front, awaken entirely and make the fundamental change. The psychic being will not need the support of intellectual ideas or outer signs and helps. It is that alone that can give you the direct feeling of the Divine, the constant nearness, the inner support and aid. You will not then feel the

Mother remote or have any further doubt about the realisation; for the mind thinks and the vital craves, but the soul feels and knows the Divine.

Cast away from you these movements of doubt, depression and the rest which are no part of your true and higher nature. Reject these suggestions of inability, unfitness and all these irrational movements of an alien force. Remain faithful to the Light of your soul even when it is hidden by clouds. My help and the Mother's will be there working behind even in the moments when you cannot feel it. The one need for you and for all is to be, even in the darkness of the powers of obscurity of the physical consciousness, stubbornly faithful to your soul and to the remembrance of the Divine Call. Be faithful and you will conquer.

When I spoke of being faithful to the light of the soul and the divine Call, I was not referring to anything in the past or to any lapse on your part. I was simply affirming the great need in all crises and attacks, — to refuse to listen to any suggestions, impulses, lures and to oppose to them all the call of the Truth, the imperative beckoning of the Light. In all doubt and depression, to say, "I belong to the Divine, I cannot fail"; to all suggestions of impurity and unfitness, to reply, "I am a child of Immortality chosen by the Divine; I have but to be true to myself and to Him — the victory is sure; even if I fell, I would rise again"; to all impulses to depart and serve some smaller ideal, to reply, "This is the greatest, this is the Truth that alone can satisfy the soul within me; I will endure through all tests and tribulations to the very end of the divine journey". This is what I mean by faithfulness to the Light and the Call.

These are things which come almost inevitably in one degree or another at a certain critical stage through which almost everyone has to pass and which usually lasts for an uncomfortably long time but which need not be at all conclusive or definitive.

Usually, if one persists, it is the period of darkest night before the dawn which comes to every or almost every spiritual aspirant. It is due to a plunge one has to take into the sheer physical consciousness unsupported by any true mental light or by any vital joy in life, for these usually withdraw behind the veil, though they are not, as they seem to be, permanently lost. It is a period when doubt, denial, dryness, greyness and all kindred things come up with a great force and often reign completely for a time. It is after this stage has been successfully crossed that the true light begins to come, the light which is not of the mind but of the spirit. The spiritual light, no doubt, comes to some to a certain extent and to a few to a considerable extent, in the earlier stages, though that is not the case with all — for some have to wait till they can clear out the obstructing stuff in the mind, vital and physical consciousness, and until then get only a touch now and then. But even at the best this earlier spiritual light is never complete until the darkness of the physical consciousness has been faced and overcome. It is not by one's own fault that one falls into this state, it can come when one is trying one's best to advance. It does not really indicate any radical disability in the nature but certainly it is a hard ordeal and one has to stick very firmly to pass through it. It is difficult to explain these things because the psychological necessity is difficult for the ordinary human reason to understand or to accept.

There is nothing to be discouraged about. The fact is that after having been so long in the mental and vital plane you have become aware of the physical consciousness, and the physical consciousness in everybody is like that. It is inert, conservative, does not want to move, to change — it clings to its habits (what people call their character) or its habits (habitual movements) cling to it and repeat themselves like a clock working in a persistent mechanical way. When you have cleared your vital somewhat, things go down and stick there. You see, if you have become self-conscious, you put pressure, perhaps, but the physical responds very slowly, hardly at first it seems to move at all. The remedy is aspiration steady and unchanging, patient work, the psychic in the physical, calling down the light and force into these obscure parts. The light brings the consciousness of what is there; the force has to follow and work on them till they change or disappear.

It is always the effect of the physical consciousness being upper-most (so long as it is not entirely changed) that one feels like this — like an ordinary man or worse, altogether in the outer consciousness, the inner consciousness veiled, the action of yoga power apparently suspended. This happens in the earlier stages also, but it is not quite complete usually then because something of the mind and vital is active in the physical still, or even if the interruption of sadhana is complete, it does not last long and so one does not so much notice it. But when from the mental and vital stage of the yoga one comes down into the physical, this condition which is native to the physical consciousness fully manifests and is persistent for long periods. It happens because one has to come down and deal with this part directly by entering into it, — for if that is not done, there can be no complete change of the nature. What has to be done is to under-stand that it is a stage and to persist in the faith that it will be overcome. If this is done, then it will be easier for the Force, working behind the veil at first, then in front to bring out the yoga consciousness into this outer physical shell and make it luminous and responsive. If one keeps steadily the faith and quietude, then this can be more quickly done — if the faith gets eclipsed or the quietude disturbed by the long difficulty, then it takes longer but even then it will be done; for, though not felt, the Force is there at work. It can only be prevented if one breaks away or throws up the sadhana, because one becomes too impatient of the difficulty to go through with it. That is the one thing that should never be done.

It means that there is only one sadhana for all parts, not a separate mental sadhana, vital sadhana or physical sadhana — but the action of the sadhana is applied sometimes separately to each part, sometimes on the contrary the action is the mental and vital together, or vital and physical together, or all three together. But it is the same sadhana always.

When I explained about the physical inertia, I meant that it was this which had been preventing the elimination of the old movements all along and enabled them to return when they had been pushed out — for it is in the material half-conscious or subconscient that there is the bed-rock of the resistance. When this comes up and shows itself in its separate existence, not sustained by the mind and vital, acting by the power of its own inertia and not covered by the sanction of the mind or the vital, only repeating the old movements by force of old habit — it is then possible to meet the resistance at its root instead of cutting off the flowers and fruits and branches when they appear.

It is precisely this loathness to do anything that must be got rid of — for it is simply an acquiescence in the force of the inertia. If you can do nothing else, the old methods of violence to yourself etc. will obviously be unfruitful — you should call on the Divine Peace and force to descend and deal with it and open yourself to the action. If this obstructing physical is made to admit and respond to that, then the key of the solution will be there.

I have said that your consciousness has come down into direct contact with the external physical nature which is always full of the lower movements and when that happens you see them as they are, when they are not under the control of the mind and psychic. Everybody has to come into this direct contact — otherwise there can be no transformation of this part of the being.

Yes, certainly, that is what I am insisting on — the bringing of realisation into this inert physical part which has made itself prominent. When any part of the being becomes prominent like this showing all its defects and limitations — here inertia or incapacity (*apravṛtti*), obscurity or forgetfulness (*aprakāśa*), it is in order to get set right, — it has come up for a first or preliminary transformation. Peace and light in the mind, love and sympathy in the heart, calm and power in the vital, a settled receptivity and response (*prakāśa, pravṛtti*) in the physical are the necessary change.

You feel as you do only because you are largely identified with the part that has not undergone change and so you feel the difficulty, even the impossibility of changing. But although the difficulty is there, the impossibility does not exist. Even this identification may be helpful, for so the change can be radical by a direct action in the part itself or an indirect influence upon it through the mind or higher vital. Rest and restore your physical forces, open so that the Mother's Force may freely work on you, all trouble pass away and a new and stronger movement commence.

*
**

What you describe is the material consciousness; it is mostly subconscient, but the part of it that is conscious is mechanical, inertly moved by habits or by the forces of the lower nature. Always repeating the same unintelligent and unenlightened movements, it is attached to the routine and established rule of what already exists, unwilling to change, unwilling to receive the Light or obey the higher Force. Or, if it is willing, then it is unable. Or, if it is able, then it turns the action given to it by the Light or the Force into a new mechanical routine and so takes out of it all soul and life. It is obscure, stupid, indolent, full of ignorance and inertia, darkness and slowness of *tamas*.

It is this material consciousness into which we are seeking to bring first the higher (divine or spiritual) Light and Power and

Ananda, and then the supramental Truth which is the object of our yoga.

I do not see why you doubt the fulfilment in your material consciousness. If there is faith, quietude, openness in the rest of the being, the material is bound to open also. Tamas, inertia, ignorance, stupidity, littleness, obstruction to the true movement are universal characteristics of the material consciousness, so long as it is not enlightened, regenerated and transformed from above, — they are not peculiar to yours. Therefore, there is here no sufficient reason or justification for the doubt you describe.

When the supramental comes down fully into the material consciousness, it will create the right conditions there. The oneness will be created, the constant presence and sense of contact will be felt in the material and there will be all the actual physical contact that is needed. The sadness you speak of is not psychic — for "painful longing" belongs to the vital, not to the psychic. The psychic never feels a sadness from disappointed desire, because that is not in its nature; the sorrow it sometimes feels is when it sees the Divine rejected or the mental, vital, physical in man or in nature turning away from the Truth to follow perversion, darkness or ignorance. However, with the reign of the supramental even the vital external nature is bound to change and therefore there will be no chance of any feelings of this character.

It is the most physical consciousness of which you have become aware; it is like that in almost everyone: when one gets fully or exclusively into it, one feels it to be like that of an animal, either obscure and restless or inert and stupid and in either condition not open to the Divine. It is only by bringing the Force and higher consciousness into it that it can fundamentally alter. When these things show themselves do not be upset by their emergence, but understand that they are there to be changed.

Here as elsewhere, quiet is the first thing needed, to keep the consciousness quiet, not allow it to get agitated and in turmoil.

Then in the quiet to call for the Force to clear up all this obscurity and change it.

I understand that you have arrived at a prolonged lull or period of emptiness in your sadhana. This often happens especially when one is thrown out into the physical and external consciousness. The nervous and physical parts then become prominent and seem to become the standard of the being with that disappearance of the yoga consciousness and the sensitiveness to small and outward things which you describe. A stage like this however may very well be an interval before a fresh progress. What you have to do is to insist on making time for meditation — at any time of the day when you are least likely to be disturbed — and through the meditation getting back the touch. There may be some difficulty because the physical consciousness is uppermost, but a persistent aspiration will bring it back. When once you again feel the connection re-established between the inner being and the outer, call down the peace and light and power into the latter so as to build up a basis for a constant consciousness in the most external mind and being which will accompany you in work and action as much as in meditation and solitude.

"At the mercy of the external sounds and external bodily sensations", "no control to drop the ordinary consciousness at will", "the whole tendency of the being away from yoga" — all that is unmistakably applicable to the physical mind and the physical consciousness when they isolate themselves, as it were, and take up the whole front, pushing the rest into the background. When a part of the being is brought forward to be worked upon for change, this kind of all-occupying emergence, the dominant activity of that part as if it alone existed very usually happens, and unfortunately it is always what has to be changed, the undesirable conditions, the difficulties of that part which rise first and obstinately hold the field and recur. In the physical it is inertia, obscurity, inability that come up and the obstinacy of these things. The only thing to do in this unpleasant phase is to be more obstinate than the physical inertia and to persist in a fixed endeavour — steady persistency without any restless struggle — to get a wide and permanent opening made even in this solid rock of obstruction.

It means that you are in full grips with the subconscient physical. However heavy and tedious the resistance you have to persevere till you have got the Peace, Knowledge, Force down there in place of the inertia.

The physical sadhana is to bring down the higher light and power and peace and Ananda into the body consciousness, to get rid of the inertia of the physical, the doubts, limitations, external tendency of the physical mind, the defective energies of the vital physical (nerves) and bring in instead the true consciousness there so that the physical may be a perfect instrument for the Divine Will. The food and care for the body is only to get it into good condition, afterwards it would not be necessary to attend to such things.

You need not worry about that. When there is a strong inward tendency, the body not being yet conscious enough to share the experience in a waking state tries to assimilate the descending forces through sleep. This is a common experience. When it has assimilated enough, it will be more ready.

The difference lies in the fact that those who are doing sadhana live on the physical plane in order to transform it — under the pressure of a Force created by the sadhana which urges towards that and must continue till it is achieved. Those who do not do sadhana live on the physical plane not to transform it but to continue it as it is — there is no such Force or pressure or necessity or urge. Those who are not sadhaks but have their minds turned to the higher consciousness are preparing for sadhana and will one day do it — whatever that sadhana may be.

The prevalence of the physical difficulties when one comes down into the physical is the same phenomenon as the prevalence of the vital difficulties when one is on the vital plane. Transformation implies facing the difficulties and changing or overcoming what arises in each part of the being so that that part may respond to what is higher, but the full change of the whole can only come by the ascent to the Above and the descent from Above. The first step of that (usually though not always) is the realisation of the self above and the descent of the higher peace into all the being down to the most physical.

So far as it [living in the physical consciousness] can be said to be distinguishable by outward signs, it is a state of fundamental passivity in which one is and does what the forces of the physical plane make one be and do. When one lives in the mind, there is an active mental intelligence and mental will that tries to control and shape action and experience and life and everything else. When one is in the vital one is full of energy and enthusiasm and passion and force which may be right or wrong but is very much alive. These things in the physical inertia either disappear or become weak or are forces that act upon the system occasionally but are not possessed by it. This condition may not be absolute, for one has a mind and a vital, but it is what predominates. There are two ways of getting out of this — one is to rise above in the self and see the physical from there as an instrument, not oneself, the other is to bring down the divine Force from above and make the physical the instrument of that Force.

You cannot so long as you have a body live without the physical consciousness but you can live more centrally in the psychic and other parts and by them transform the physical.

[Defects of the physical consciousness:] There are many — but mainly obscurity, inertia, tamas, a passive acceptance of the play of wrong forces, inability to change, attachment to habits, lack of plasticity, forgetfulness, loss of experiences or realisations gained, unwillingness to accept the Light or to follow it, incapacity (through tamas or through attachment or through passive re-action to accustomed forces) to do what it admits to be the Right and the Best.

This negation is the very nature of the physical resistance and the physical resistance is the whole base of the denial of the Divine in the world. All in the physical is persistent, obstinate, with a massive force of negation and inertia — if it were not so, sadhana would be extremely cursory. You have to face this character of the physical resistance and conquer it however often it may rise. It is the price of the transformation of the earth-consciousness.

Apart from the individual difficulty there is a general difficulty in the physical earth-nature. Physical nature is slow and inert and unwilling to change; its tendency is to be still and take long periods of time for a little progress. It is very difficult for even the strongest mental or vital or even psychic will to overcome this inertia. It is only by bringing down constantly the consciousness and force and light from above that it can be done. Therefore there must be a constant will and aspiration for that and for the change and it must be a steady and patient will not tired out even by the utmost resistance of the physical nature.

It is the nature of the physical mind to be obstinate. Physical nature exists by constant repetition of the same thing — only a constant presentation of different forms of itself. This obstinate recurrence is therefore part of its nature when it is in activity;

otherwise it remains in a dull inertia. When therefore we want to get rid of the old movements of physical nature, they resist by this kind of obstinate recurrence. One has to be very persistent in rejection to get rid of it.

There are two aspects of physical Nature as of all Nature — the individual and the universal. All things come into one from the universal Nature — but the individual physical keeps some of them and rejects others, and to those it keeps it gives a personal form. So these things can be said to be both inside it and coming outside from within or created by it because it gives a special form and also outside and coming in from outside. But when one wants to get rid of them, one first throws out all that is within into the surrounding Nature — from there the universal Nature tries to bring them back or bring in new and similar things of its own to replace them. One has then constantly to reject this invasion. By constant rejection, the force of recurrence finally dwindles and the individual becomes free and able to bring the higher consciousness and its movements into the physical being.

The earth-consciousness does not want to change, so it rejects what comes down to it from above — it has always done so. It is only if those who have taken this yoga open themselves and are willing to change their lower nature that this unwillingness can disappear.

What stands in the way, of course, is always the vital ego with its ignorance and the pride of its ignorance, and the physical consciousness with its inertia which resents and resists any call to change and its indolence which does not like to take the trouble — it finds it more comfortable to go on its own way repeating always the same old movements and, at best, expecting everything to be done for it in some way at some time.

The first thing is to have the right inner attitude — you have that; the rest is the will to transform oneself and the vigilance to perceive and reject all that belongs to the ego and the tamasic persistence of the lower nature. Finally, to keep oneself always open to the Mother in every part of the being so that the process of transformation may find no hindrance.

Dullness and dispersion are the two sides of the physical's resistance to the peace and concentrated power. They correspond to the inertia and the chaotic activity of physical Nature, that aspect of it which makes some scientists now say that all is brought about by chance and there is no certitude of things but only probability.

The inertia of the physical consciousness is always a difficult thing to eliminate — it is that, more even than any vital resistance, which keeps all the movements of the ignorance recurring even when the knowledge is there and the will to change. But this difficulty has to be faced and overcome by an equal perseverance in the will of the sadhak. It is a steady flame that must burn, as steady as the obstruction is obstinate. Do not therefore be discouraged by the persistence of the obstruction of the ignorance. The persistence of your own will to conquer with the Mother's force supporting it will come to the end of the resistance.

The physical's tendency to inertia is very great; even after the habit of living in the higher consciousness is there, some part may feel the pressure of the inertia — generally the outermost or most material parts. The inertia usually rises up from the subconscient. It does not abolish the higher consciousness in the physical, but dulls its action or else brings it down from a higher to a lower level, e.g. from the intuition to the higher mind or from the higher to the lower ranges of overmind. For some time it resists the *completeness* of the siddhi. It is only when the most material and the subconscient and the environmental consciousness are quite liberated that this retarding or lowering effect of the primal Inertia is entirely overcome.

*
**

Everything can be responded to — Inertia also can spread waves of itself like other things.

In dealing with the physical and subconscient the working is always slower than when it acts on the mind and vital because the resistance of physical stuff is always heavier and less intelligent and adaptable; but as a compensation the work done in the being by this slower movement is in the end more complete, solid and durable.

The physical obstruction is less boisterous [than the vital obstruction], but I have not found it less obstinate or less troublesome.

The difficulty of the physical nature comes inevitably in the course of the development of the sadhana. Its obstruction, its inertia, its absence of aspiration or movement have to show themselves before they can be got rid of — otherwise it will always remain undetected, hampering even the best sadhana and preventing its completeness. This coming up of the physical nature lasts longer or less according to the circumstances, but there is none who does not go through it. What is necessary is not to get troubled or anxious or impatient, for that only makes it last more, but to put entire confidence in the Mother and quietly persist in faith, patience and steady will for the complete change. It is so that the Mother's force can best work in the being.

The first means is not to get upset when it [inertia] comes or when it stays. The second is to detach yourself, not only yourself above but yourself below and not identify. The third is to reject everything that is raised by the inertia and not regard it as your own or accept it at all.

If you can do these things then there will be something in you that remains perfectly quiet even in the greatest inertia. Through that quiet part you can bring down peace, force, even light and knowledge into the inertia itself.

Inertia or anything else must be felt as separate, not part of one's real self which is one with the Divine.

The adverse forces feel that there is something in you that is discountenanced and restive because of the continuance of the inertia and they hope that by pressing more and more they will create a revolt. What is important for you in these circumstances is to make your faith, surrender and Samata absolute. That is as great and essential a progress as to have high experiences, etc.

It [the use of violence for the change of the physical] was done by some people, but I don't believe in its usefulness. No doubt the physical is an obstinate obstacle, but it must be enlightened, persuaded, pressed even to change, but not oppressed or violently driven. People use violence with the mind, vital, body because they are in a hurry, but my own observation has always been that it leads to more reactions and hindrances and not to a genuinely sound advance.

It [the result of the obstruction of the physical consciousness] depends on the weak points of the individual and the stage of his progress. In a general way the obstruction creates an inertia which impedes the working of the higher Powers. In the early stage it can obstruct progress altogether. Afterwards it works to slow it down or else impede it by intervals of stationary inertia. The main difficulty of the physical consciousness is that it is unable, before it is transformed, of maintaining any tension of tapasya — it wants periods of assimilation, sinking back into the ordinary consciousness to rest, — also there is a constant forgetfulness of what has been done etc.

It [the weakness of the will] is a first result of coming down into the physical consciousness or of the physical consciousnes̄s coming up prominently — formerly you were much in the mind and vital. The physical consciousness is full of inertia — it wants not to move but to be moved by whatever forces and that is its habit. This inertia has to be cured by putting it into contact with the right forces from above. That is why I asked you to aspire for the higher wideness, purity and peace, so that that may occupy the physical and the true Force work instead of these invading ideas and impulses.

The period of no-effort is usually when the physical conscious-ness is uppermost — for the nature of that is inertia, to be moved by the higher forces or to be moved by the lower forces or by any forces, but not to move itself. One must still use one's efforts if one can, but the great thing is to be able to call down the Force from above into the physical — otherwise to remain perfectly quiet and, undisturbed, expect its coming.

It is only by a more constant dynamic force descending into an unalterable equality and peace that the physical nature's normal tendency can be eradicated.

The normal tendency of the physical nature is to be inert and in its inertia to respond only to the ordinary vital forces, not to the higher forces. If one has a perfect equality and peace then one can be unaffected by the spreading of the inertia and bring down into it gradually or quickly the same peace with a force of the higher consciousness which can alter it. When that is there there can be no longer the difficulty and fluctuations with a preponderance of inertia such as now you are having.

The greater difficulty is because the sadhana is now taking place directly on the physical plane, where the force of a habit or habitual movement once formed is very great. When the sadhana is taking place on the mental or vital plane, it is more easy to control or change, because the mind and vital are more plastic than the physical. But on the other hand if something is definitely gained on the physical plane, there is a more lasting and complete fulfilment than when it is on the mental or vital alone.

Probably in '33 you were doing more tapasya and putting a strong control on yourself? At any rate that was the state at one time. Afterwards when you came down from the mental-vital level, you let yourself go for a time, removing much of the control, hence now you find a difficulty in re-establishing it, — due to the habit of automatic repetition which is a characteristic of the physical nature. You have now to get the control in a different way by the establishment of the peace and building the higher consciousness upon it, the spiritual control replacing that of mental tapasya.

No, it is not necessary to lose the mental control; it is best to replace it gradually by the psychic or spiritual. But it happens to many that they lose it before the other is ready or while it is still imperfect and then the Nature-forces act in the physical consciousness which is sometimes held by the descending Peace or Power from above, sometimes by the ordinary Nature-forces. This alternation happens at one stage at least to almost everybody until the higher state prevails.

This over-sensitive brooding on past blows to the vital is an unhealthy sensitiveness. What is past ought not to have a hold like that but be allowed to fade out.

In the physical being the power of past impressions is very great, because it is by the process of repeated impressions that consciousness was made to manifest in matter — and also by the habitual reactions of consciousness to these impressions, what the psychologists, I suppose, would call behaviour. According to one school consciousness consists only of these things — but that is the usual habit of stretching one detail of Nature to explain the whole of her.

What you describe is what the Gita means by the realisation that all action is done by the Prakriti. You feel it mechanical because you are in the physical consciousness where all is mechanism. On the mental and vital plane one can have the same experience, but of the actions as a play of forces. What is lacking at present in you is the other side of the experience viz. that of the silent Atman or else of the witness Purusha calm, tranquil, free, pure and undisturbed by the play of the Prakriti. It tries to come and you are on the point of going into it, but the tendency of externalisation is still too strong. This tendency took you when you came down into the physical — for it is the nature of the ordinary physical consciousness to precipitate itself into the action of the external personality. You have to get back the power of the internal consciousness — above as Atman, below as Purusha first witness and then master of the nature.

It is due to the influence of the physical consciousness. The physical consciousness or at least the more external parts of it are, as I have told you, in their nature inert — obeying whatever

92

force they are habituated to obey, but not acting on their own, initiative. When there is a strong influence of the physical inertia or when one is down in this part of the consciousness the mind feels like the material Nature that action of will is impossible. Mind and vital nature are on the contrary all for will and initiative and so when one is in mind or vital or acting under their influence will feels itself always ready to be active.

It is the neutrality of the physical consciousness which says, "I move only when I am moved. Move me who can."

The physical is the slave of certain forces which create a habit and drive it through the mechanical power of the habit. So long as the mind gives consent, you do not notice the slavery; but if the mind withdraws its consent, then you feel the servitude, you feel a force pushing you in spite of the mind's will. It is very obstinate and repeats itself till the habit, the inner habit revealing itself in the outward act, is broken. It is like a machine which once set in motion repeats the same movement. You need not be alarmed or distressed; a quiet persistent aspiration will bring you to the point where the habit breaks and you are free.

The habit in the physical is obstinate and seems unchangeable because it always recurs — even when one thinks it is gone. But it is not really unchangeable; if the physical mind detaches itself, stands separate, refuses to accept it, then the habit in the physical begins to lose its force of repetition. Sometimes it goes slowly, sometimes (but this is less frequent) it stops suddenly and recurs no more.

The condition is that you must bring the sadhana into your physical consciousness and live for the sadhana and the Divine only. You must give up positively the bad habits that still persist and never resume those that have ceased or been interrupted. Inner experiences are helpful to the mind and higher vital for change, but for the lower vital and the outer being a sadhana of self-discipline is indispensable. The external actions and the spirit in them must change — your external thoughts and actions must be for the Divine only. There must be self-restraint, entire truthfulness, a constant thought of the Divine in all you do. This is the way for the change of the lower vital. By your constant self-dedication and self-discipline the force will be brought down into the external and the change made.

II

The power to be separate is there in your psychic being and you have yourself experienced that condition. Naturally, it is still only at times, because the outer consciousness is being prepared to share in it, and it is only when that is ready that the inner can show itself always and come out into the outer being.

You ask whether the mind and vital do not come in the way as well as the physical. Yes, but when I speak of the physical consciousness, I mean the physical mind and the physical vital as well as the body consciousness proper. This physical mind and physical vital are concerned with the small ordinary movements of life and are governed by a very external view of things and by habitual small reactions and do not respond at once to the inner consciousness not because they are in active opposition to it, as the vital mind and vital proper can be, but because they find it difficult to change their habitual movements. It is this now that you feel and that makes you think you have a poor responsiveness to the inner experience. But that is not a fact; in your mind and in a great part of your vital there is a considerable capacity of response. As for the physical its difficulty is universal in everybody and not peculiar to you. It has come up because it always comes up in the sadhana when the physical consciousness has to be worked upon for the necessary change. As soon as that is done, the difficulty you feel will first diminish and then go.

It is this work that is going on and when you felt the white light in meditation and the result which lasted even after opening the eyes, the head and eyes cool and all vast and wide, it was this working taking place in your physical mind to change it. The rest of the physical consciousness was still undergoing another kind of working and so felt heat and not this release and wideness. But afterwards the working can go down first to the heart and then still lower and to all the body and the same release and wideness come there. Naturally, at present these results are not permanent but only for a time, they come as experiences, not lasting realisations. But it cannot be otherwise at the present stage. These experiences, however passing, are meant to prepare and do prepare the different parts of the nature.

I have told you that X has two different elements in her. It is the outer mind in her that wants to do the embroidery with the idea that others are doing it and that it will bring a special favour from the Mother (which is not true) and says that she is doing all the work etc. If we allow her to indulge it, it will be spiritually bad for her, especially just now when her inner being needs to be strengthened by submission, surrender and the sacrifice of her ego. That is why we have not looked with favour on making this change. When it was once done, she herself repented of it and felt that she had made a mistake. But the physical mind goes back constantly to its habitual movements and it takes time for it to learn by experience.

You should keep the holder and use it. It is Mother's gift to you. Write your experiences with it and take it as a sign of the Mother's love and grace that are working in you.

Formerly the mental will and the higher vital and the psychic were active, so their consent was sufficient for the lower vital to be kept down or to be ineffective. But now it is the physical mind that is active in you and the physical mind gives a value and therefore a power to the lower vital which it did not have before.

The opening of the physical and the subconscient always takes a long time as it is a thing of habits and constant repetition of the old movements, obscure and stiff and not plastic, yielding only little by little. The physical mind can be more easily opened and converted than the rest, but the vital-physical and the material-physical are obstinate. The old things are always recurring there without reason and by force of habit. Much of the vital-physical and most of the material are in the subconscience or depend on it. It needs a strong and sustained action to progress there.

Until they [the material and the subconscient] aspire or at least assent fully to the aspiration and will of the higher being, there can be no lasting change in them.

No, there is a limit to the resistance [of the physical mind and the vital physical]. At any rate a time comes when the fundamental resistance is broken for good and there is only left a dealing with details which is not troublesome.

A great part of the body-consciousness is subconscient and the body-consciousness and the subconscient are closly bound together.

The body and the physical do not coincide — the body consciousness is only part of the whole physical consciousness.

They [the physical mind and the vital physical] are very near to it [the inconscient] — except that part of the physical mind which is trained to deal with physical objects and affairs. But that is agile and active and competent only in its own limits. When it has to deal with supraphysical things it becomes incompetent, often imbecile and yet positive and arrogant and dogmatic in its ignorance. The rest of the physical consciousness is near to the inconscient. Here again in its own field it can have accurate perceptions and instincts if it is able to act spontaneously; but usually in the human being it is not allowed to do so, for the mind and vital intervene. The vital physical is entirely irrational in its action — even when it is right, it cannot explain why; for it is made more of automatic or habitual instincts, impulses, sensations and feelings than anything else. It is the mind that gives reasons and justifications to its movements and if the mind stands back and judges and questions, the vital physical can only answer "I want", "I like", "I dislike", "I feel like that".

Persevere quietly and let nothing discourage you. If the quietness and cheerfulness are not constant yet, that is to be expected; it is always like that at first when there is the working on the physical consciousness and its obstructions. If you persevere, they will become more and more frequent and last for a longer time, until you have a basis of peace and happiness and whatever disturbances come on the surface will no longer be able to penetrate or shake this basis or even cover it over except perhaps for a moment.

The constant changing of the mood is also common enough because the physical vital is being worked upon at the same time and this changeability is a character of the physical vital nature. Let not that discourage you, — as soon as the basis is more fixed, this will diminish and the vital become more settled and even.

The unsteadiness you speak of is the nature of the human physical mind — almost everybody has it, for the physical mind goes after all sorts of outward things. To fix the consciousness within, to keep it concentrated on the Divine alone is a great difficulty for all, it is what makes sadhana a thing for which long time and a slow development of the consciousness is usually necessary, at first at any rate. So that need not discourage you. In your inner vital there is plenty of strong will and deep down in your psychic there is the true aspiration and love which come up when the psychic is active and will eventually possess the whole nature.

It is quite natural that the unsteadiness of the physical mind should interfere with the settling of full and constant quietude and faith — it always does with everybody, but that does not mean that this quietude and faith will not or cannot settle in the nature. All that I meant was that you should try to get a constant will for that quietude, so that when the restlessness or unsteadiness come across, your will to quiet might meet it or soon reappear and dispel the disturbance. That would make the elimination of the restlessness or impatience easier; but in any case the Mother's force is there working behind the variations of the surface consciousness and it will bring you through them.

The experiences you had were renewed glimpses of the psychic working that is going on all the time even when there is no sign of it on the surface. The golden sword was the sword of Truth which will destroy the difficulties.

These small things of the physical mind are such as everybody has and they will fall off when the truer wider consciousness comes out. You have the understanding in your mind, but these things persist because they really belong to the smaller vital part and when that part widens, then they will no longer be able to recur. One can discourage them by keeping certain ideas in mind, such as that the things which vex you belong to the nature and can go only with the change of the nature, that one has to do the work well oneself but not be troubled by the defects of others in their work, that a quiet inner will for their doing right is more effective than getting vexed and disturbed by their lapses. But fundamentally it is by the widened consciousness in your mind and vital and physical that you will be

quite freed from these small reactions. You have only to continue with the Mother's Force working in you and these things will
smooth themselves out hereafter.

These small movements [useless talking etc.] are the most difficult
of all to change owing to their very smallness and the habit of
frequent indulgence as natural and trifling everyday movements
of life. The best thing to do is to mass the force and light and
peace in the mind and higher vital until they can occupy the
physical mind even — then through the physical mind, which
usually supports more or less these movements, they can be
worked on with more success.

III

The sense of helplessness, of impossibility of removal of the
obstacle, is like the obscurity itself a characteristic of the physical
consciousness which is inert and mechanical and accustomed to
be moved inertly by whatever forces take hold of it. But this
sense of helplessness or impossibility is unreal and not to yield
to it, not to accept it, to remove it, is quite possible and very
necessary for overcoming the physical obstacle which would
otherwise greatly delay the progress.

Yes; that also is the fault of the physical consciousness. It is
obsessed by the idea that, "what is" must be, — that the habit
of things cannot be altered. This inevitability it extends not only
to what is but to what it merely thinks of as a fact — it lays itself
open inertly to every suggestion or possibility that seems to be
justified by the habit of things. It is the main obstacle to the
material change.

⁎⁎

Your suggestion that I am telling you things that are untrue in order to encourage you is the usual stupidity of the physical mind — if it were so, it is not you who would be unfit for the yoga, but myself who would be unfit to be, in the search for Divine Truth, anybody's guide. For one can lead through lesser to greater Truth, but not through falsehood to Truth. As for your fitness or unfitness for the yoga, it is not a question on which your physical mind can be a judge — it judges by the immediate appearance of things and has no knowledge of the laws that govern consciousness or the powers that act in yoga. In fact, the question is not of fitness or unfitness but of the acceptance of Grace. There is no human being whose physical outer consciousness — the part of yourself in which you are now living — is fit for the yoga. It is by Grace and a light from above that it can become capable and for that the necessity is to be persevering and open it to the Light. Everybody when he enters the physical consciousness has the same difficulty and feels as if he were unfit, and nothing done, nothing changed in him since he began the yoga; he is apt to forget then all that has happened before or to feel as if he lost it or as if it had all been unreal or untrue.

I suppose that is why you object to my phrase about your having gone so far. I meant that you had had openings in your thinking mind and heart and higher vital and experiences also and had seen very lucidly the condition of your own being and nature and had gone so far that these parts were ready for the spiritual change — what remains is the physical and outer consciousness which has to be compelled to accept the necessity of change. That is no doubt the most difficult part of the work to be done, but it is also the part which, if once done, makes possible the total change of the being and nature. I therefore said that having gone so far, it would be absurd to turn back now and give up, because this resists. It always resists in everybody and very obstinately too. That is no reason for giving up the endeavour.

It is this consciousness that has expressed itself in your letter — or the obscure part of it which clings to its old attitude. It does not want to fulfil the sadhana unless it can get by it the things it wanted. It wants the satisfaction of the ego, "self-fulfilment", appreciation, the granting of its desires. It measures the Divine Love by the outward favours showered upon it and looks jealously to see who gets more of these favours than itself, then says that the Divine has no love for it and assigns reasons which are either derogatory to the Divine, or, as in your letters, self-depreciation and a cause for despair. It is not in you alone that this part feels and acts like that, it is in almost everybody. If that were the only thing in you or the others, then, indeed, there would be no possibility of yoga. But though it is strong, it is not the whole — there is a psychic being and a mind and heart influenced and enlightened by it which has other feelings and another vision of things and aim in sadhana. These are now covered in you by the upsurgence of this part which has to change. It is tamasic and does not want to change, does not want to believe unless it can be done by reassuring the vital ego. But there is nothing new in all that — it is part of human nature and has always been there, hampering and limiting the sadhana. Its existence is no reason for despair — everyone has it and the sadhana has to be done in spite of it, in spite of the mixture it brings till the time comes when it has to be definitely rejected. It is difficult to do it, but perfectly possible. These things I know and realise and it is therefore that I insist on your persevering and encourage you to go on; it is not my statement of the position that is untrue, it is the view of it taken by this obscure part of your being that is unsound and an error.

It is not because you cannot recover the true attitude, but because you admit in part of your mind the false suggestion of your inability that this mixed condition lasts longer than it should. It is a part of your physical consciousness that keeps the memory of the old movements and has the habit of admitting them and thinking them inevitable. You must insist with the clearer part of your consciousness on the true Truth, rejecting always these suggestions and feelings, till this obscure part also is open and admits the Light.

It is a suggestion of the tamasic forces that insist on the difficulty and create it and the physical consciousness accepts it. Aspiration is never really difficult. Rejection may not be immediately effective, but to maintain the will of rejection and refusal is always possible.

What do you mean by active means? The power to refuse and to reject is always there in the being and to go on rejecting till the rejecting is effective. Nothing can obstruct a quiet aspiration except one's own acquiescence in the inertia.

The thoughts and feelings expressed in your letter are born of the depression and have no truth in themselves apart from it. Your being here does not in the least take up space that could be occupied by better sadhaks. For a good sadhak there will always be a place in one way or another. The incapacity which you discover in yourself is simply the resistance of the habitual external and physical nature, which everyone has and which none, however good a sadhak, has yet been able to transform radically, because it is the last thing to change and its resistance is acute just now because it is against this that the power of the sadhana is now pressing so that the change may come. When this part presents itself, it always tries to appear as something unalterable, incapable of change, impervious to the sadhana. But it is not really so and one must not be deceived by this appearance. As for the fear of madness, it is only a nervous impression which you should throw away. It is not vital weakness that leads to such upsettings — it is an obscurity and weakness in the physical mind accompanied by movements of an exaggerated vital nature (e.g., exaggerated spiritual ambition) which are too strong for the mind to bear. That is not your case. You have had long experience of inner peace, wideness, Ananda, an inner life turned towards the Divine and one who has had that ought not to speak of general incapacity, whatever the difficulties of the external nature, — difficulties common in one form or another to all.

I have not the slightest doubt that you can do the sadhana if you cleave to it — not certainly by your own unaided strength, for nobody can do that, but by the will of the psychic being in you aided by the Divine Grace. There is a part in the physical and vital consciousness of every human being that has not the will for it, does not feel the capacity for it, distrusts any hope or promise of a spiritual future and is inert and indifferent to any such thing. At one period in the course of the sadhana this rises up and one feels identified with it. That has happened to you now, but along with an attack of ill-health and nervous indisposition which has turned this passage through the obscure physical into a dark and intense trouble. With enough sleep and a quieting of the nerves and return of physical energy that ought to disappear and it would be possible to bring the Light and Consciousness down into this obscure part. An intense concentration bringing struggle is not what is needed but a very quiet attitude of self-opening. Not any effort of sadhana just now, but the recovery of tranquillity and ease is what is wanted at present to restore the opening of the nature.

It was certainly not because the Mother was different to you from other days or pushed you to a distance, but because you came rather shut up in that part of your physical being which is still shrinking from the Light. It is this part which was always fundamentally responsible for all your bad passages and painful movements even when the direct difficulty was higher up. Its nature is to cling to the old habitual movements, shrink from yogic consciousness and shut up doors and windows against the help that is offered and lament in the darkness when it feels itself hurt. This is a thing that everybody must get rid of who wants to progress. Do not go on identifying yourself with this part and calling it yourself. Get back into your inner being and look at this only as a small though obstinate part of the nature that has to change. For apart from its insistence there is no reason why your way should enter into a desert. It should enter into a wideness of liberation — open to the calm and peace and power and light, a consciousness that is wider than the personal and into which the ego can happily disappear.

As to what has happened in your sadhana, it is that you have allowed yourself to fall into a groove of the physical mind and of the external vital nature and got fixed in a persistent or constantly recurrent repetition of the ideas and feelings which they present to you — feelings of settled disappointment and discouragement and pessimism about yourself and your spiritual future, and ideas — or, if you will allow me to call them so, notions — which come to the support of these feelings and sustain them. The result of this is to shut you up against the contact and spiritual influence and help you were once feeling or beginning to feel from us. It also shuts you up against your own deeper self and sterilises your personal effort. An accident of this kind is common enough in the path of spiritual effort, and the first thing to be done to get rid of its effects is to throw away resolutely the persistent ideas and feelings which keep you in the groove. I do not know whether you can return to the former condition, for it is seldom that one can go back to a point in the past; but it is always possible for you to go forward, recovering the force for propulsion of what you then gained and have certainly still within you assimilated in your inner being. If you want to carry on some part of the yoga by your active efforts and aspiration, there is no reason why you should not find back that capacity; but the first effort to be made is to reject persistently, fully and tenaciously — not for two or three days, but always, so long as they insist or return — these disabling thoughts and feelings which hamstring all hope and faith in you, not to accept them, not to justify them, not to give them by your acquiescence the right to go on harping on the same note always of discouragement, incapacity and failure. The ideas by which you justify them are, I repeat, notions only of the physical mind, not true things, e.g., the notion that you *cannot* understand a given idea (intellectually accepting or not accepting is another matter); for it is perfectly certain that your thinking intelligence is quite trained enough to understand anything that is put before it. It is only the physical mind that is limited even in the most intelligent and opens up fits of stupidity or at least larger or smaller spaces of blank non-understanding in the face of unaccustomed ideas or a new line of possible experience or anything else either alien to the mind's habits or unwelcome to something in the vital parts. I suppose we have all had experience of this incapable element in our nature, and if one fixes oneself in it, it can make even things that would ordinarily be easy for us seem difficult things and things difficult seem impossible. But why should a mind trained to think allow this poorer part of itself to dominate it? So with the other notions. There is nothing anyone else can do in the way of yoga that you cannot do if you have the fixed will to do it; some things may take a longer time because of past training, habits, mental associations but there is nothing impossible, too difficult, no inherently insuperable obstacle.

It is the instinctive (not mental) will in the outer being that is blind — the inner mind knows and understands and when it comes out it enlightens the rest so that all is clear. But the outer being readmits the darkness and confusion through a wrong movement of the vital or through an inert acceptance of the obscurity of the ignorant physical consciousness and the knowledge gets darkened over. But it is there and has only to come out again. The physical consciousness is constitutionally ignorant — it may be made to understand, but it goes on forgetting and feeling as if it had never known — till the Force and Light finally get hold of it and then it forgets no more.

IV

What you have been doing is to penetrate more into the physical consciousness where the peace and light of the higher consciousness has to be brought down. This often brings at first some relaxation of the intensity of experience, dispersion or recurrence of old movements which had been pushed out from the other levels, but one must not be discouraged by that. The remedy is to be more insistent on bringing down the higher forces (peace etc.) into this field.

The push to externalisation must be rejected always — it is a way the physical consciousness has of slipping out of the condition of concentrated sadhana. To keep in the inner consciousness and work from it on the external being till that also is ready is very necessary when the work of change is being specially directed towards the physical consciousness.

The moonlit *maidān* is the spiritual consciousness at the doors of which you are standing as it were and feeling its peace and ease.

The obstacle or wall of bondage which you feel is simply that of the habits of the ordinary physical consciousness. It is so with all, — the ordinary vital nature with its ego, desire, passions, disturbances, and the ordinary physical nature with its strong habits and outwardness are the chief obstacles that have to be overcome in the nature. When they fall quiet, then it is easier to enter into the true consciousness and unite with the Mother. But they are not accustomed to quietness and as soon as it is felt they want to come out of it and resume their ordinary movements. But this will go when the inner has sufficiently gained on the outer to dominate it. The inner things will grow and come out more and more as you feel the inner path growing until they are strong enough to rule the outer conduct.

The obstacles you feel, the surging up of old things and repetition of restlessness etc. are due to this strength of habit of the physical nature — it lives by repeating always the same things and the same movements to which it has been accustomed in the past. The inner influence as it comes out will more and more create for it new habits of thought and feeling and action and it will then dwell firmly in these and not in the things of the old nature.

The narrowness etc. of which you complain are normal to the physical nature. It is the same thing acting in a different way which makes X rebellious to advice and full of irritation and bad temper when her mistakes are shown to her. The physical nature of almost everybody is like that, intolerant, easily irritated, lacking in patience when dealing with others. But this physical nature can be replaced and changed by the psychic nature and you have had the experience of what this psychic nature is and how it acts. You know therefore what change has to come in you and you know also that this new nature is already there in you preparing to come out. Have the faith therefore that it is sure to come — and when the physical comes and covers with the old movements try to remember that and remind the physical mind that it is only by this change in yourself and all that things can change. What is needed now is all should make this psychic change their main object, each for himself. If some develop it, then it will spread more rapidly among the rest. It is so only that the present state of the physical consciousness full of ego and strife can become what it should be.

What has happened is that the psychic in you which had formerly been constantly in action in the mind and vital was for a time clouded or covered over by the ignorance of the physical consciousness. It is the psychic that connects you with the Mother and turns all the movements of your being towards her or drew them from her or made them united with and dependent on her. It had so done with all your mental and vital being and its movements and it had guarded you against all wrong mental and vital suggestions and attacks, showing you what was true and what was false. Now it is this psychic being which has manifested again in your physical consciousness also. You have only to live in that and your whole being will be turned towards the Mother, remain in union with her and be protected from doubt and error and false suggestion — and you can once more progress as you did before towards the full realisation of the sadhana.

All that is very good — it is the psychic condition that is increasing. The peace and spontaneous knowledge are in the psychic being and from there they spread to mind and vital and physical. It is in the outer physical consciousness that the difficulty still tries to persist and brings the restlessness sometimes into the physical mind, sometimes into the nerves, sometimes in the shape of bodily trouble into the body. But all these things can and must go. Even the illnesses can go entirely with the growth of peace and power in the nerves and physical cells — stomach pains, weakness of the eyes and everything else.

The habit of return of these feelings belongs to the physical consciousness and in his physical consciousness the human being is always weak and unable to get rid of or resist its habitual movements. There are three things that help him to do so (apart from his mental will which is not always strong enough to do it). There is first the psychic being; for a few days your psychic was extremely active and pushing these movements away whenever they tried to come or throwing them out soon when they got in. This activity of the psychic will return and eventually come down into the physical consciousness itself; then there will be very little difficulty. The second is the inner consciousness always awake. At present that is difficult, because to keep the inner consciousness awake at all times can only come by a deepening of yourself so that the veil between the outer and inner which lifts only in concentration may cease to exist even when one is in the ordinary unconcentrated condition. It is for this deepening that the strong tendency to go inside comes upon you. Lastly, the Mother's force always there and receiving also a response at once from the physical consciousness. These three things together can do anything. It takes time to make them all three constantly active together, but that is sure to come and with them these inner difficulties will disappear.

It is inevitable that in the course of the sadhana all sorts of conditions should come through which one is led towards the fullness of the true consciousness. You are now, as are most, in the physical consciousness and its principal difficulty is externalisation and this covering up of the active experience so that one does not know what is going on inside or feels as if nothing were going on. When that happens, it means that something has come up, some part or layer of the physical, which needs to be worked on and, when that has been done, — it may take longer or shorter, — the conscious active inner experience recommences. The muteness in the mind is not a bad thing in itself, it is a favourable condition for the working. Also what you describe as taking place in the head, must be the working of the Force there, — it sometimes gives the impression of a headache. There must be a working in the physical mind to get rid of some difficulty or else to prepare it better for the admission of what comes from above.

It is necessary to have a great patience — so as to go through these conditions and not get apprehensive or restless — and a confidence that all difficulties will be overcome.

It is not that something is always "wrong" within you but that there is still in the subconscient physical being a part that was accustomed to respond very strongly to the vibrations of these thoughts and feelings and can still respond. Usually you would not allow them to come up at all in thought or feeling form — it would only manifest as a depression of the body or fatigue — or, if it came, you would get over it at once and the vibrations would sink down and disappear. But in the atmosphere heavily surcharged with this invasion of the ordinary consciousness there is a lessened elasticity in the physical consciousness and they were able to rise. This is an exceedingly common experience. One has to detach oneself from these still weak parts and regard them as if a detail in the machinery that has to be set right. In your case also your nervous (vital physical) being is exceedingly conscious and sensitive and anything wrong in the atmosphere affects it more than it would most of the others.

What you felt in your chest was the attempt of the old Ignorance to bring back the vital restlessness, depression, confusion, through the physical attack — for it is on the obscuration of the physical that they now depend for stopping the Light and Force from coming and for obscuring their working and creating disturbance and destroying the quietude. Reject it as you did this time — whenever it tries to come.

It is very good that all should have gone like that and the true consciousness affirmed its control in the physical. These things are indeed attacks intended to prevent the control being established in the physical being as it was in the inner parts. Wherever the physical consciousness opens, the Force can sweep out all that could trouble. Sometimes it takes a little time to overcome the resistance, but finally all disappears before it.

It is indeed the body consciousness that is still offering difficulties — but when the restlessness and confusion come, you must immediately offer it up and call for the opening of the part that resists. In this way it is possible to establish a condition in which as soon as the difficulty is there, the counteracting Force also comes. Then no long continued difficulty will be possible.

For your sadhana it is necessary first to establish the entire openness of the physical being and stabilise in it the descent of calm, strength, purity and joy with the feeling of the presence and the working of the Mother's Force in you. It is only on that assured basis that one can become an entirely effective instrument for the work. Once that is done, there is still the dynamic transformation of the instrumental being to achieve and that depends on a descent of a higher and higher power of consciousness into the mind, vital and body — by "higher" being meant nearer and nearer to the supramental Light and Force. But that can only be done on the basis of which I have spoken and with the psychic being constantly in front and acting as an intermediary between the instrumental mind, vital and body and these higher planes of being. So this basic stabilisation must first be completed.

Yes, this is the time when you have to persist till you are quite settled in the inner consciousness and the persistence of the silence and peace is a sign that it is now possible. When one feels this kind of silence, peace and wideness, one may be sure that it is that of the true being, the real self, penetrating into the mind and vital and perhaps also the physical consciousness (if it is complete). The restlessness of the physical is probably due to the peace and silence having touched the physical but not yet penetrated the material or body consciousness. The old restlessness is there in the body struggling to remain, although it cannot invade either mind or vital or even in a general way the physical consciousness as a whole. If the peace descends there, the restlessness will disappear.

The sex-sensation comes from the waking subconscient.

When it is unable to manifest in the waking consciousness, it comes up from the subconscient in sleep. The mind must not allow itself to be disturbed — it will go out with the rest.

This is a form that the resistance in the physical easily and often takes — a restlessness of discomfort in the nervous system. When it is in the legs, it means that it is the most material part of the consciousness that is the seat of the trouble. Since it has come up, it ought to be thrown out for good. Probably this part has become sufficiently conscious to feel the greater pressure when Mother comes down, but not enough to be able to receive and assimilate it, hence the uneasiness and resistance. If so, it should go of itself with a little more opening there.

What you describe — dullness, uneasiness, weakness, feeling old and worn out or ill, are the reactions that come when the inertia of the physical Nature is resisting the Light — the others about sense of feeling dignity, self-respect (of the ego) are the reactions of the vital. Both must be refused acceptance. There is only one aim to be followed, the increase of the Peace, Light, Power and the growth of a new consciousness in the being. With that new consciousness the true knowledge, understanding, strength, feeling will come, creating harmony instead of revolt and struggle and union with the Divine consciousness and will.

A certain inertia, tendency to sleep, indolence, unwillingness or inability to be strong to work or spiritual effort for long at a time, is in the nature of the human physical consciousness. When one goes down into the physical for its change (that has been the general condition here for a long time), this tends to increase. Even sometimes when the pressure of the sadhana in the physical increases or when one has to go much inside, this temporarily increases — the body either needing more rest or turning the inward movement into a tendency to sleep or be at rest. You need not, however, be anxious about that. After a time this rights itself; the physical consciousness gets the true peace and calm in the cells and feels at rest even in full work or in the most concentrated condition and this tendency of inertia goes out of the nature.

There is always more chance of inertia at night because of the large part taken by the subconscient in sleep — but, apart from that there should be a reaction (internal) against the rising of inertia. A quietness in the cells of the body, even a sense of immobility (so that the body seems to be moved rather than to move) is a different thing and easily distinguishable from the inertia. The downflow of peace usually brings much of the static Brahman into the consciousness down to the physical, so that one feels the Upanishadic "unmoving it moves".

I don't know of any effective outward means of getting rid of it [inertia]. Some in hours when they cannot do sadhana, spend the time in other occupations — reading, writing or working — and do not try at all to concentrate. But I suspect what you need is more strength in the body.

It is quite true that the physical exercise is very necessary to keep off tamas. I am glad you have begun it and I trust you will keep it up.

Physical tamas in its roots can be removed only by the descent and the transformation, but physical exercise and regular activity of the body can always prevent a tamasic condition from prevailing in the body.

A strong mind and body and life-force are needed in the sadhana. Especially steps should be taken to throw out tamas and bring strength and force into the frame of the nature.

The way of yoga must be a living thing, not a mental principle or a set method to be stuck to against all necessary variations.

*
**

The weakness of the body has to be cured, not disregarded. It can only be cured by bringing in strength from above, not by merely forcing the body.

*
**

Overstraining only increases the inertia — the mental and vital will may force the body, but the body feels more and more strained and finally asserts itself. It is only if the body itself feels a will and force to work that one can do that.

*
**

The first rule is — there must be sufficient sleep and rest, not in excess but not too little.

The body must be trained to work, but not strained beyond its utmost capacity.

The outer means without the inner is not effective. Up to a certain point by a *progressive* training the body may be made more capable of work. But the important thing is to bring down the force for work and the Rasa of work in the body. The body will then do what is asked of it without grudging or feeling fatigue.

Even so, even when the force and Rasa are there, one must keep one's sense of measure.

Work is a means of self-dedication to the Divine, but it must be done with the necessary inner consciousness in which the outer vital and physical also share.

A lazy body is certainly not a proper instrument for yoga

— it must stop being lazy. But a fatigued and unwilling body also cannot receive properly or be a good instrument. The proper thing is to avoid either extreme.

If your body is aching after the work, it may be that you are doing too much for your physical strength and straining the body. When you work, the Force comes down in you, takes the form of vital energy and supports your body so that it does not *at the time* feel the strain; but when you stop, the body goes back to its normal condition and feels the effects — it has not yet been sufficiently open to keep the Force. You must see whether this effect (of pain) continues; if it passes away, it is all right; otherwise you must take care and not overstrain yourself by doing too much.

It is owing to the good psychic condition in which you are that this lightness and power of work comes into you; for then you are open to the Mother's Force and it is that that works in you, so that there is no fatigue. You felt the fatigue formerly *after* the work was over because your vital was open and the vital energy was the instrument of the work, but the body consciousness was not quite open and had some strain. This time the physical seems to have opened also.

The pain, burning, restlessness, weeping and inability to work which you feel, come when there is some difficulty or resistance in some part of the nature. When it comes call on the Mother and reject these things; turn to her for the peace and quietude to return to your mind and settle in the heart, so that there shall be no place for these other things.

V

It is the attachment to food, the greed and eagerness for it, making it an unduly important thing in the life, that is contrary to the spirit of yoga. To be aware that something is pleasant to the palate is not wrong; only one must have no desire nor hankering for it, no exultation in getting it, no displeasure or regret at not getting it. One must be calm and equal, not getting upset or dissatisfied when the food is not tasty or not in abundance — eating the fixed amount that is necessary, not less or more. There should be neither eagerness nor repugnance.

To be always thinking about food and troubling the mind is quite the wrong way of getting rid of the food-desire. Put the food element in the right place in the life, in a small corner, and don't concentrate on it but on other things.

It is certainly not very yogic to be so harassed by the importunity of the palate. I notice that these petty desires, which plenty of people who are not yogis at all nor aspirants for yoga know how to put in their proper place, seem to take an inordinate importance in the consciousness of the sadhaks here — not all, certainly, but many. In this as in many other matters they do not seem to realise that, if you want to do yoga, you must take more and more in all matters, small or great, the yogic attitude. In our path that attitude is not one of forceful suppression, but of detachment and equality with regard to the objects of desire. Forceful suppression[1] stands on the same level as free indulgence; in both cases, the desire remains; in the one it is fed by indulgence, in the other it lies latent and exasperated by suppression. It is only when one stands back, separates oneself from the lower vital, refusing to regard its desires and clamours as one's own, and cultivates an entire equality and equanimity in the consciousness with respect to them that the lower vital itself becomes gradually purified and itself also calm and equal. Each wave of

---

[1] Fasting comes under the head; it is of no use for this purpose. Abandon that idea altogether.

desire as it comes must be observed, as quietly and with as much unmoved detachment as you would observe something going on outside you, and allowed to pass, rejected from the consciousness, and the true movement, the true consciousness steadily put in its place.

What if people were to remember that they were here for yoga, make that the salt and savour of their existence and acquire *samatā* of the palate ! My experience is that if they did that, all the trouble would disappear and even the kitchen difficulties and the defects of the cooking would vanish.

Do not trouble your mind about food. Take it in the right quantity (neither too much nor too little), without greed or repulsion, as the means given you by the Mother for the maintenance of the body, in the right spirit, offering it to the Divine in you; then it need not create *tamas*.

What is necessary is to take enough food and think no more about it, taking it as a means for the maintenance of the physical instrument only. But just as one should not overeat, so one should not diminish unduly — it produces a reaction which defeats the object — for the object is not to allow either the greed for food or the heavy tamas of the physical which is the result of excessive eating to interfere with the concentration on the spiritual experience and progress. If the body is left insufficiently nourished, it will think of food more than otherwise.

These things still rise in you because they have been for so long prominent difficulties and, as far as the first is concerned, because you gave it much justification from the mind at one time. But if the inner consciousness is growing like that they are sure to go. Only if they rise, don't give them harbourage. Perhaps with regard to the greed for food, your attitude has not been quite correct. Greed for food has to be overcome, but it has not to be given too much thought. The proper attitude to food is a certain equality. Food is for the maintenance of the body and one should take enough for that — what the body needs; if one gives less the body feels the need and hankers; if you give more, then that is indulging the vital. As for particular foods the palate likes, the attitude of the mind and vital should be, "If I get, I take; if I don't get, I shall not mind." One should not think too much of food either to indulge or unduly to repress — that is the best.

Too much eating makes the body material and heavy, eating too little makes it weak and nervous — one has to find the true harmony and balance between the body's need and the food taken.

It depends on what you can digest. If you can digest, there is no harm in taking more since you feel hungry. All these things depend upon what is the true need of the body and that may differ in different cases according to the constitution of the body, the amount of work done or exercise taken. It is possible that you have reduced your food too much, so you can try taking more.

But it is quite natural. Exercise is always supposed to increase the appetite as the body needs more food to restore the extra expense of energy put out. Normally the more physical work the body has to do the more food it needs. On the other hand mental work requires no increase of food — that has been ascertained scientifically by experiment. Hunger may increase by other causes, but when it coincides with the taking up of play or physical exercise of a strenuous character that is sufficient to explain it.

It is true that as one reaches an advanced age a diminished diet may become desirable.

Neither neglect this turn of the nature (food-desire) nor make too much of it; it has to be dealt with, purified and mastered but without giving it too much importance. There are two ways of conquering it — one of detachment, learning to regard food as only a physical necessity and the vital satisfaction of the stomach and the palate as a thing of no importance; the other is to be able to take without insistence or seeking any food given and to find in it (whether pronounced good or bad by others) the equal *rasa*, not of the food for its own sake, but of the universal Ananda.

These generalisations on either side are not of much value. One does not need to get a hatred for food in order to get rid of the greed for food. On the other hand, to develop a dislike for certain things may help to reject them — but that too is not always the cure, for they may remain in spite of the dislike.

It is a mistake to neglect the body and let it waste away; the body is the means of the sadhana and should be maintained in good order. There should be no attachment to it, but no contempt or neglect either of the material part of our nature.

In this yoga the aim is not only the union with the higher consciousness but the transformation (by its power) of the lower including the physical nature.

It is not necessary to have desire or greed of food in order to eat. The yogi eats not out of desire, but to maintain the body.

The attachment to good food must be given up as also the personal attachment to position and service; but it is not indispensably necessary for that purpose to take to an ascetic diet or to give up all means of action such as money and service. The yogin has to become *niḥsva* in this sense that he feels that nothing belongs to him but all to the Divine and he must be ready at any time to give up all to the Divine. But there is no meaning in throwing away everything in order to be externally *niḥsva* without any imperative cause.

*
* *

I suppose you have become aware of the principle of hunger in the vital-physical. It is not really either by satisfying it or forcibly denying it that it will go — it is by putting a will on it to change and bringing down a higher consciousness that it can change.

*
* *

To suppress hunger like that is not good, it very often creates disorders. I doubt whether fatness or thinness of a healthy kind depends on the amount of food taken — there are people who eat well and remain thin and others who take only one meal a day and remain fat. By underfeeding (taking less than the body really needs) one may get emaciated, but that is not a healthy state. The doctors say it depends mostly on the working of certain glands. Anyhow the important thing is now to get the nervous strength back.

As for the liver also eating little does not help, very often it makes the liver sluggish so that it works less well. What is recommended for liver trouble is to avoid greasy food and much eating of sweets and that is also one way of avoiding fat. But to eat too little is not good — it may be necessary in some stomach or intestinal illness, but not for the ordinary liver trouble.

*
* *

As for Sannyasis and food, Sannyasis put a compulsion on these desires in this and other matters — they take ascetic food as a principle; but this does not necessarily kill the greed for food, it remains compressed and, if the compulsion or principle is removed, it can come up again stronger than before — for compression without removal often increases the force of these things instead of destroying them.

When there is this suppression [of the desire to eat] I have always noticed that there comes for a time a strong eagerness or necessity for eating largely as if the body were taking its compensation for the past want.

The first thing I tell people when they want not to eat or sleep is that no yoga can be done without sufficient food and sleep (see the Gita on this point). Fasting or sleeplessness make the nerves morbid and excited and weaken the brain and lead to delusions and fantasies. The Gita says, yoga is not for one who eats too much or sleeps too much, neither is it for one who does not eat or does not sleep, but if one eats and sleeps suitably — *yuktāhārī yuktanidraḥ* — then one can do it best. It is the same with everything else. How often have I said that excessive retirement was suspect to me and that to do nothing but meditate was a lop-sided and therefore unsound sadhana!

The idea of giving up food is a wrong inspiration. You can go on with a small quantity of food, but not without food altogether, except for a comparatively short time. Remember what the Gita says, "Yoga is not for one who eats in excess nor for one who abstains from eating altogether." Vital energy is one thing — of that one can draw a great amount without food and often it increases with fasting; but physical substance, without which life loses its support, is of a different order.

One can bring down the strength, but it is also necessary to see that the body has sufficient food, sleep and rest — absence of these things strain the nerves and if the nerves are strained the body feels fatigue — becomes weakened.

Not to eat as the method of getting rid of the greed of food is the ascetic way. Ours is equanimity and non-attachment.

It is a fact that by fasting, if the mind and the nerves are solid or the will-force dynamic, one can get for a time into a state of inner energy and receptivity which is alluring to the mind and the usual reactions of hunger, weakness, intestinal disturbance, etc., can be wholly avoided. But the body suffers by diminution and there can easily develop in the vital a morbid overstrained condition due to the inrush of more vital energy than the nervous system can assimilate or co-ordinate. Nervous people should avoid the temptation to fast, it is often accompanied or followed by delusions and a loss of balance. Especially if there is a motive of hunger-strike or that element comes in, fasting becomes perilous, for it is then an indulgence of a vital movement which may easily become a habit injurious and pernicious to the sadhana. Even if all these reactions are avoided, still there is no sufficient utility in fasting, since the higher energy and receptivity ought to come not by artificial or physical means but by intensity of the consciousness and strong will for the sadhana.

I never heard of it; but it [prolonged fasting] is just the way to get the wrong realisation. The nerves get into an excited tense condition (when they do not collapse) and invent realisations or open to a wrong Force. At least that often happens.

I think it is not safe to admit any suggestion of not eating —
sometimes it opens the door for the non-eating force to take
hold of the mind and there is trouble. That comes easily because
the inner being of course does not need any food and this non-
need is attempted to be thrown by some forces on the body also
which is not under the same happy law. It is better to allow the
condition [of concentration and peace] to grow in intensity until
it can last even through the meal and after. I suppose it is not
really the meal that disturbs but the coming out into the outer
consciousness which is a little difficult to avoid when one goes to
eat; but that can be overcome in time.

You must not let that movement [reduction of food] go too far.
It is one of the dangers of the sadhana, because of the ascetic
turn of yoga in the past that as experiences come the suggestion
comes that food or sleep etc. are not necessary and also there may
come an inclination in the body not to eat or not to sleep. But if
that is accepted the results are often disastrous. It is no more
to be accepted than the inertia itself.

If the pains are strong, you can abstain from work for a day or
two until they have subsided. Of course if you feel that you suffer
from anything else but liquid food, that settles the question.
You can take liquid food only and if you take the liquid food only
then you will not be strong enough to work. But usually the
thought takes a big part in determining these things. The mind
has the impression that any solid food will hurt and the body
follows — so naturally as a result any solid food does begin to
hurt.

The mental or vital vigour does not or need not depend on the
food — it is the physical that after a time begins to get strained

if there is not sufficient nourishment.

*
**

The transformation to which we aspire is too vast and complex to come at one stroke; it must be allowed to come by stages. The physical change is the last of these stages and is itself a progressive process.

The inner transformation cannot be brought about by physical means either of a positive or a negative nature. On the contrary, the physical change itself can only be brought about by a descent of the greater supramental consciousness into the cells of the body. Till then at least the body and its supporting energies have to be maintained in part by the ordinary means, food, sleep, etc. Food has to be taken in the right spirit, with the right consciousness; sleep has to be gradually transformed into the yogic repose. A premature and excessive physical austerity, Tapasya, may endanger the process of the sadhana by establishing a disturbance and abnormality of the forces in the different parts of the system. A great energy may pour into the mental and vital parts but the nerves and the body may be overstrained and lose the strength to support the play of these higher energies. This is the reason why an extreme physical austerity is not included here as a substantive part of the sadhana.

There is no harm in fasting from time to time for a day or two or in reducing the food taken to a small but sufficient modicum; but entire abstinence for a long period is not advisable.

*
**

I think the importance of sattwic food from the spiritual point of view has been exaggerated. Food is rather a question of hygiene, and many of the sanctions and prohibitions laid down in ancient religions had more a hygienic than a spiritual motive. The Gita's definitions seem to point in the same direction — tamasic food, it seems to say, is what is stale or rotten with the virtue gone out of it, rajasic food is that which is too acrid, pungent, etc., heats the blood and spoils the health, sattwic food is what is pleasing, healthy, etc. It may well be that different kinds of food nourish the action of the different gunas and so indirectly are helpful or harmful apart from their physical action. But that is as far as one can go confidently. What particular eatables are or are not sattwic is another question and more difficult to determine. Spiritually, I should say that the effect of food depends more on the occult atmosphere and influences that come with it than on anything in the food itself. Vegetarianism is another question altogether; it stands, as you say, on a will not to do harm to the more conscious forms of life for the satisfaction of the belly.

As for the question of practising to take all kinds of food with equal *rasa*, it is not necessary to practise nor does it really come by practice. One has to acquire equality within in the consciousness and as this equality grows, one can extend it or apply it to the various fields of the activity of the consciousness.

I think onions can be described as rajaso-tamasic in their character. They are heavy and material and at the same time excitant of certain strong material-vital forces. It is obvious that if one wants to conquer the physical passions and is still very much subject to the body nature and the things that affect it, free indulgence in onions is not advisable. It is only for those who have risen above the body consciousness and mastered it and are not affected by these things that it does not at all matter; for them the use of this or that food or its desire makes no difference. At the same time I must say that the abstinence from rajasic or tamasic foods does not of itself assure freedom from the things they help to stimulate. Vegetarians, for instance, can be as sensual and excitable as meat eaters; a man may abstain from onions and yet be in these respects no better than before. It is a change of consciousness that is effective and this kind of abstention helps that only in so far as it tends to create a less heavy and more refined and plastic physical consciousness for the higher will to act upon. That is something, but it is not all; the change of consciousness can come even in spite of non-abstinence.

Onions are allowed here because the palate of the sadhaks demands something to give a taste to the food. We do not insist on these details, or make an absolutely strict rule, as the stress here is more on the inward change, the outward coming as its result. Only so much is insisted on as is essential for organisation and inner and outer discipline and to point the way to an indispensable self-control. It is pressed on all that the greed of the palate has to be conquered, but it has to be done in the last resort from within, as also the other passions and desires of the lower nature.

It is no part of this yoga to suppress taste, *rasa*, altogether. What is to be got rid of is vital desire and attachment, the greed of food, being overjoyed at getting the food you like, sorry and discontented when you do not have it, giving an undue importance to it. Equality is here the test as in so many other matters.

No — it [taste] is not a bondage, if there is no attachment. Taste is natural and quite permissible so long as one is not the slave of the palate. Certainly, the enjoyment of taste can be offered up. I don't know that there is any fruit of eating in the sense of the phrase in the Gita.

Taste is no more a guilty thing than sight or hearing. It is the desire that it awakens that has to be thrown away.

It is possible to get rid of taste like Chaitanya, for it is something that depends on the consciousness and so inhibition is possible. In hypnotic experiments it is found that suggestion can make sugar taste bitter or bitter things sweet. Berkeley and physiology are both right. There is a certain usually fixed relation between the consciousness in the palate and the *guṇa* of the food, but the consciousness can alter the relation if it wants or inhibit it altogether. There are yogis who make themselves insensitive to pain also and that too can be done by hypnosis.

Another method is to find all things good to the taste without attachment to any.

*

It is better to be careful in these matters of food etc., as in the stage through which your sadhana is passing there is a considerable sensitiveness in the vital-physical part of the being and it may be easily disturbed by a wrong impact or a wrong movement like overfeeding.

*

When the physical consciousness has been sensitivised, too much or heavy food becomes offensive to it.

*

It is the habit in the subconscient material that feels an artificial need created by the past and does not care whether it is harmful or disturbing to the nerves or not. That is the nature of all intoxicants (wine, tobacco, cocaine etc.), people go on even after the deleterious effects have shown themselves and even after all real pleasure in it has ceased because of this artificial need (it is not real). The will has to get hold of this subconscient persistence and dissolve it.

*

These intoxicants [Bhang, etc.] put one in relation with a vital world in which such things [music, song etc.] exist.

VI

This is not a yoga in which physical austerities have to be done for their own sake. Sleep is necessary for the body just as food is. Sufficient sleep must be taken, but no excessive sleep. What sufficient sleep is depends on the need of the body.

*

If you do not sleep enough the body and the nervous envelope will be weakened and the body and the nervous envelope are the basis of the sadhana.

*
**

It must be the want of sleep that keeps your nervous system exposed to weakness — it is a great mistake not to take sufficient sleep. Seven hours is the minimum needed. When one has a very strong nervous system one can reduce it to six, sometimes even five — but it is rare and ought not to be attempted without necessity.

*
**

The normal allowance of sleep is said to be 7 to 8 hours except in advanced age when it is said to be less. If one takes less (5 to 6 for instance) the body accommodates itself somehow, but if the control is taken off it immediately wants to make up for its lost arrears of the normal 8 hours. So often when one has tried to live on too little food, if one relaxes, the body becomes enormously rapacious for food until it has set right the credit and loss account. At least it often happens like that.

*
**

It is not possible to do at once what you like with the body. If the body is told to sleep only 2 or 3 hours, it may follow if the will is strong enough — but afterwards it may get exceedingly strained and even break down for want of needed rest. The yogis who minimise their sleep succeed only after a long tapasya in which they learn how to control the forces of Nature governing the body.

*
**

Both for fevers and for mental trouble sleep is a great help and its absence very undesirable — it is the loss of a curative agency.

*
**

It is certain forces that work and certain parts of the personality that use them. In the ordinary consciousness, these part-personalities are veiled and the forces limited by the external mind, but when one gets behind the veil that limitation disappears, the action of the forces enlarges and works out automatically what has to be done.

But then these forces are each intent on its own work and do not care for anything else — e.g., here they disregard the need of the body for rest and sleep, which is bad. The central consciousness must interfere and say, "no, this is the time for sleep, not for these activities, keep them for their proper place and time".

It is a want of sleep itself that brings the symptoms of uneasiness. The action of sadhana cannot of itself bring this kind of reaction, it is only if the body gets strained by want of sleep, insufficient food, overwork or nervous excitement that there are these things. It is probably because the nerves are strained in the day time and you do not relax into ease that it is difficult to sleep.

It is restlessness in you which prevents you from keeping sleep inwardly or outwardly. To sleep well the vital and physical and mind also must learn how to relax themselves and be quiet.

Take care to rest enough. You must guard against fatigue as it may bring relaxation and tamas. To rest well is not tamas, as some people suppose; it can be done in the right consciousness to maintain the bodily energy — like the *śavāsana* of the strenuous Hathayogin.

Obviously — it [reading a novel before going to bed] threw you into a tamasic consciousness and consequently the sleep was heavy in a gross subconsciousness and the fatigue was the result.

Sleep, because of its subconscient basis, usually brings a falling down to a lower level, unless it is a conscious sleep; to make it more and more conscious is the one permanent remedy: but also until that is done, one should always react against this sinking tendency when one wakes and not allow the effect of dull nights to accumulate. But these things need always a settled endeavour and discipline and must take time, sometimes a long time. It will not do to refrain from the effort because immediate results do not appear.

It is not a right method to try to keep awake at night; the suppression of the needed sleep makes the body tamasic and unfit for the necessary concentration during the waking hours. The right way is to transform the sleep and not suppress it, and especially to learn how to become more and more conscious in sleep itself. If that is done, sleep changes into an inner mode of consciousness in which the sadhana can continue as much as in the waking state, and at the same time one is able to enter into other planes of consciousness than the physical and command an immense range of informative and utilisable experience.

What he is having now are the true spiritual and psychic experiences — not those of the vital plane which most have at the beginning. The experiences of the vital plane (in which there is much imagination and fantasy) are useful for opening up the consciousness; but it is when they are replaced by the spiritual and the psychic consciousness that there is the beginning of the true progress.

The difficulty of keeping the consciousness at night happens to most — it is because the night is the time of sleep and relaxation and the subconscient comes up. The true consciousness comes at first in the waking state or in meditation, it takes possession of the mental, the vital, the conscious physical, but the subconscious vital and physical remain obscure and this obscurity comes up when there is sleep or an inert relaxation. When the subconscient is enlightened and penetrated by the true consciousness this disparity disappears.

The Pishachic woman that tried to enter is the false vital impure Shakti — and the voice that spoke was that of his psychic being. If he keeps his psychic being awake and in front, it will always protect him against these dark forces as it did this time.

You must not try to avoid sleep at night — if you persist in doing that, the bad results may not appear immediately, but the body will get strained and there will be a breakdown which may destroy what you have gained in your sadhana.

If you want to remain conscious at night, train yourself to make your sleep conscious — not to eliminate sleep altogether, but to transform it.

Sleep cannot be replaced, but it can be changed; for you can become conscious in sleep. If you are thus conscious, then the night can be utilised for a higher working — provided the body gets its due rest; for the object of sleep is the body's rest and the renewal of the vital-physical force. It is a mistake to deny to the body food and sleep, as some from an ascetic idea or impulse want to do — that only wears out the physical support and although either the yogic or the vital energy can long keep at work an overstrained or declining physical system, a time comes when this drawing is no longer so easy nor perhaps possible. The body should be given what it needs for its own efficient working. Moderate but sufficient food (without greed or desire), sufficient sleep, but not of the heavy tamasic kind, this should be the rule.

There is no reason at all why intensity of sadhana should bring insufficient sleep.

Sadhana can go on in the dream or sleep state as well as in the waking.

All dream or sleep consciousness cannot be converted at once into conscious sadhana. That has to be done progressively. But your power of conscious samadhi must increase before this can be done.

The sleep consciousness can be effectively dealt with only when the waking mind has made a certain amount of progress.

It is usually only if there is much activity of sadhana in the day that it extends also into the sleep-state.

Once one is in full sadhana, sleep becomes as much a part of it as waking.

That is all right. It shows that the sadhana is becoming continuous and that you are being conscious and using a conscious will in sleep as well as in waking. This is a very important stage forward in the sadhana.

At night when one sinks into the subconscient after being in a good state of consciousness we find that state gone and we have to labour to get it back again. On the other hand, if the sleep is of the better kind one may wake up in a good condition. Of course, it is better to be conscious in sleep, if one can.

The gap made by the night and waking with the ordinary consciousness is the case with everybody almost (of course, the "ordinary" consciousness differs according to the progress); but it is no use wanting to be conscious in sleep; you have to get the habit of getting back the thread of the progress as soon as may be and for that there must be some concentration after rising.

You need not meditate at once [after waking in the morning] — but for a few moments take a concentrated attitude calling the Mother's presence for the day.

At night, you have to pass into sleep in the concentration — you must be able to concentrate with the eyes closed, lying down and the concentration must deepen into sleep — that is to say, sleep must become a concentrated going inside away from the outer waking state. If you find it necessary to sit for a time you may do so, but afterwards lie down keeping the concentration till this happens.

[To be conscious in sleep:] You have to start by concentrating before you sleep always with a specific will or aspiration. The will or aspiration may take time to reach the subconscient, but if it is sincere, strong and steady, it does reach after a time — so that an automatic consciousness and will are established in the sleep itself which will do what is necessary.

It was not half sleep or quarter sleep or even one-sixteenth sleep that you had; it was a going inside of the consciousness, which in that state remains conscious but shut to outer things and open only to inner experience. You must distinguish clearly between these two quite different conditions, one is *nidrā*, the other, the beginning at least of *samādhi* (not *nirvikalpa*, of course!). This drawing inside is necessary because the active mind of the human being is at first too much turned to outward things; it has to go inside altogether in order to live in the inner being (inner mind, inner vital, inner physical, psychic). But with training one can arrive at a point when one remains outwardly conscious and yet lives in the inner being and has at will the indrawn or the outpoured condition; you can then have the same dense immobility and the same inpouring of a greater and purer consciousness in the waking state as in that which you erroneously call sleep.

You are more conscious in your sleep than in your waking condition. This is because of the physical consciousness which is not yet sufficiently open; it is only just beginning to open. In your sleep the inner being is active and the psychic there can influence more actively the mind and vital. When the physical consciousness is spiritually awake, you will no longer feel the trouble and obstruction you now have and will be as open in the waking consciousness as in sleep.

This is the right attitude to have faith and not mind the difficulties. Difficulties — and serious ones — there cannot fail to be in the path of yoga, because it is not easy to change all at once the ignorant human consciousness and make it a spiritual consciousness open to the Divine. But with faith one need not mind the difficulties; the Divine Force is there and will overcome them.

The sleep you describe in which there is a luminous silence or else the sleep in which there is Ananda in the cells, these are obviously the best states. The other hours, those of which you are unconscious, may be spells of a deep slumber in which you have got out of the physical into the mental, vital or other planes. You say you were unconscious, but it may simply be that you do not remember what happened; for in coming back there is a sort of turning over of the consciousness, a transition or reversal, in which everything experienced in sleep except perhaps the last happening of all or else one that was very impressive, recedes from the physical consciousness and all becomes as if a blank. There is another blank state, a state of inertia, not only blank, but heavy and unremembering; but that is when one goes deeply and crassly into the subconscient; this subterranean plunge is very undesirable, obscuring, lowering, often fatiguing rather than restful, the reverse of the luminous silence.

In sleep one very commonly passes from consciousness to deeper consciousness in a long succession until one reaches the psychic and rests there or else from higher to higher consciousness until one reaches rest in some silence and peace. The few minutes one passes in this rest are the real sleep which restores, — if one does not get it, there is only a half rest. It is when you come near to either of these domains of rest that you begin to see these higher kinds of dreams.

According to a recent medical theory one passes in sleep through many phases until one arrives at a state in which there is absolute rest and silence — it lasts only for ten minutes, the rest of the time is taken up by travelling to that and travelling back again to the waking state. I suppose the ten minutes sleep can be called *suśupti* in the Brahman or Brahmaloka, the rest is *svapna* or passage through other worlds (planes or states of conscious existence). It is these ten minutes that restore the energies of the being, and without it sleep is not refreshing.

According to the Mother's experience and knowledge one passes from waking through a succession of states of sleep consciousness which are in fact an entry and passage into so many worlds and arrives at a pure Sachchidananda state of complete rest, light and silence, — afterwards one retraces one's way till one reaches the waking physical state. It is this Sachchidananda period that gives sleep all its restorative value. These two accounts, the scientific and the occult-spiritual, are practically identical with each other. But the former is only a recent discovery of what the occult-spiritual knowledge knew long ago.

People's ideas of sound sleep are absolutely erroneous. What they call sound sleep is merely a plunge of the outer consciousness into a complete subconscience. They call that a dreamless sleep; but it is only a state in which the surface sleep consciousness which is a subtle prolongation of the outer still left active in sleep itself is unable to record the dreams and transmit them to the physical mind. As a matter of fact the whole sleep is full of dreams. It is only during the brief time in which one is in the Brahmaloka that the dreams cease.

A long unbroken sleep is necessary because there are just ten minutes of the whole into which one enters into a true rest — a sort of Sachchidananda immobility of consciousness — and that it is which really restores the system. The rest of the time is spent first in travelling through various states of consciousness towards that and then coming out of it back towards the waking state. This fact of the ten minutes true rest has been noted by medical men, but of course they know nothing about Sachchidananda!

VII

All sleep is full of dreams. Why should night or day make any difference?

The consciousness in the night almost always descends below the level of what one has gained by sadhana in the waking consciousness, unless there are special experiences of an uplifting character in the time of sleep or unless the yogic consciousness acquired is so strong in the physical itself as to counteract the pull of the subconscient inertia. In ordinary sleep the consciousness in the body is that of the subconscient physical, which is a diminished consciousness, not awake and alive like the rest of the being. The rest of the being stands back and part of its consciousness goes out into other planes and regions and has experiences which are recorded in dreams such as that you have related. You say you go to very bad places and have experiences like the one you narrate; but that is not a sign, necessarily, of anything wrong in you. It merely means that you go into the vital world, as everybody does, and the vital world is full of such places and such experiences. What you have to do is not so much to avoid at all going there, for it cannot be avoided altogether, but to go with full protection until you get mastery in these regions of supraphysical Nature. That is one reason why you should remember the Mother and open to the Force before sleeping; for the more you get that habit and do it successfully, the more the protection will be with you.

It is the waking mind which thinks and wills and controls more or less the life in the waking state. In the sleep that mind is not there and there is no control. It is not the thinking mind that sees dreams etc. and is conscious in a rather incoherent way in sleep. It is usually what is called the subconscient that comes up then. If the waking mind were active in the body, one would not be able to sleep.

You are mixing up different things altogether — that is why you cannot understand. I was simply explaining the difference between the ordinary waking consciousness and the ordinary sleep consciousness, as they work in men whether sadhaks or not sadhaks — and it has nothing to do with the true self or psychic being. Sleep and waking are determined not by the true self or psychic being, but by the mind's waking condition or activity or its cessation — when it ceases for a time, then it is the subconscious that is there on the surface and there is sleep.

That is a different matter — it is in the yogic consciousness that one feels the seat of the subconscient below the feet, but the influence of the subconscious is not confined there — it is spread in the body. In the waking state it is overpowered by the conscious thinking mind and vital and conscious physical mind, but in the sleep state it comes on the surface.

It is the subconscient that is active in the ordinary dreams. But in the dreams in which one goes out into other planes of consciousness, mental, vital, subtle physical, it is part of the inner being, inner mental or vital or physical that is usually active.

These dreams are not all mere dreams, all have not a casual, incoherent or subconscious building. Many are records or transcripts of experiences on the vital plane into which one enters in sleep, some are scenes or events of the subtle physical plane. There one often undergoes happenings or carries on actions that resemble those of the physical life with the same surroundings and the same people, though usually there is in arrangement and feature some or a considerable difference. But it may also be a contact with other surroundings and with other people, not known in the physical life or not belonging at all to the physical world.

In the waking state you are conscious only of a certain limited field and action of your nature. In sleep you can become vividly aware of things beyond this field — a larger mental or vital nature behind the waking state or else a subtle physical or a subconscient nature which contains much that is there in you but not distinguishably active in the waking state. All these obscure tracts have to be cleared or else there can be no change of Prakriti. You should not allow yourself to be disturbed by the press of vital or subconscient dreams — for these two make up the larger part of dream-experience — but aspire to get rid of these things and of the activities they indicate, to be conscious and reject all but the divine Truth; the more you get that Truth and cling to it in the waking state, rejecting all else, the more all this inferior dream-stuff will get clear.

*
**

It is the condition of your consciousness I spoke of — the more conscious you become, the more you will be able to have dreams worth having.

*
**

Unless they are really significant dreams it [to study them] is a waste of time.

*
**

You seem to be attaching too much importance to dreams. Keep your waking mind and vital free — you can deal afterwards with the dreams which will then be only memories from the subconscient.

*
**

All dreams of this kind are very obviously formations such as one often meets on the vital, more rarely on the mental plane. Sometimes they are the formations of your own mind or vital; sometimes they are the formations of other minds with an exact or modified transcription in yours; sometimes formations come that are made by the non-human forces or beings of these other planes. These things are not true and need not become true in the physical world, but they may still have effects on the physical if they are framed with that purpose or that tendency and, if they are allowed, they may realise their events or their meaning — for they are most often symbolical or schematic — in the inner or the outer life. The proper course with them is simply to observe and understand and, if they are from a hostile source, reject or destroy them.

There are other dreams that have not the same character but are a representation or transcription of things that actually happen on other planes, in other worlds under other conditions than ours. There are, again, some dreams that are purely symbolic and some that indicate existing movements and propensities in us, whether familiar or undetected by the waking mind, or exploit old memories or else raise up things either passively stored or still active in the subconscient, a mass of various stuff which has to be changed or got rid of as one rises into a higher consciousness. If one learns how to interpret, one can get from dreams much knowledge of the secrets of our nature and of other-nature.

These figures and intimations in dream may be due to three different causes —

1. Beings whom you meet in the supraphysical world and who interest themselves in you.

2. Forces of Nature, mind nature or vital nature, that take these human appearances and in a symbolic dream convey to you some formation of the universal Mind or Life. These messages can take the form of intimations or warnings of what is going to happen. The woman must have been such a Force of Nature, for her child and box are evidently symbolic — the child of some creation or formation of hers which she wanted you to accept and keep in your consciousness, the box of some habitual movements which this force also wanted you to harbour. The offer to take care of you was only a way of saying that it wanted to control you. To dismiss all that was the right thing to do.

3. Constructions of your own mind in the form of dreams so as to convey to you intimations it had received or perceptions of some force of nature which, as in the last dream, it wanted the inner being to reject.

This is an instance of a dream of exact physical prevision. The power to have such dreams is comparatively rare, for ordinarily such previsions come in inner vision but not in sleep. In dreams vital or mental formations often take shape which sometimes fulfil themselves in essence, but not with this accuracy of detail.

It is only a particular class of dreams that do that [indicate the exact past and the future]. Most coherent dreams are either symbolic or indicate things that take place in the mental or vital planes rather than on the physical.

This indicates a power of conscious thought-formation. Thoughts have an effective power — usually by creating an atmosphere or tendencies — thus when one is ill, those around should not have thoughts of gloomy foreboding, grief or fear, for that works against cure. But the capacity of conscious thought-formation is a special power and uncommon. It can be acquired or come of itself by sadhana.

Dreams of this kind arise from the subconscient. It is one of the most embarrassing elements of yogic experience to find how obstinately the subconscient retains what has been settled and done with in the upper layers of the consciousness. But just for that reason these dreams are often a useful indication as they enable us to pursue things to their obscure roots in this underworld and excise them. No, it does not indicate that you are taking in any part of your consciousness your present pursuit of yoga as a stopgap, but merely that old vital tendencies and activities are still there in that mysterious and obscure subconscient limbo and that their ghosts can rise twittering to the surface when the conscious will is in abeyance. If the dream was trivial, it would seem to show that this ghost was not a strong demon like the militant Norwegian saga *revenants* but a phantom from an unsubstantial Hades.

It often happens that when something is thrown out of the waking consciousness it still occurs in dream. This recurrence is of two kinds. One is when the thing is gone, but the memory and impression of it remains in the subconscient and comes up in dream form in sleep. These subconscient dream-recurrences are of no importance; they are shadows rather than realities. The other is when dreams come in the vital to test or to show how far in some part of the inner being the old movement remains or is conquered. For in sleep the control of the waking consciousness and will is not there. If then even in spite of that one is conscious in sleep and either does not feel the old movement when the circumstances that formerly caused it are repeated in dream or else soon conquers and throws it out, then it must be understood that there too the victory is won. Your dream which seems to have corresponded with realities was a true experience of this kind; the old movement did come from habit, but at once you became conscious and rejected it. This is an encouraging sign and promises complete removal in a very short time.

Those dreams which are formed from subconscient impressions arranged at haphazard (subconscient mind, vital or physical) either have no significance or some meaning which is difficult to find and not very much worth knowing even if it is found. Other dreams are either simply happenings of the mental, vital or subtle physical worlds or else belong to the wider mental, vital or subtle physical planes and have a meaning which the figures of the dream are trying to communicate.

When one is in the physical consciousness, then the sleep is apt to be of the subconscious kind, often heavy and unrefreshing, the dreams also of the subconscient kind, incoherent and meaningless or if there is a meaning the dream symbols are so confused and obscure that it is not possible to follow it. It is by bringing the Mother's Light into the subconscient that this can be dispelled and the sleep becomes restful or luminous and conscious.

These experiences are normal when the inner consciousness is growing and becoming more and more the natural seat of the being — it is the spontaneous intuitive knowledge of this inner consciousness which is becoming prominent in place of the ordinary reliance of the external mind on sense data and external happenings. It is indeed the being as a whole that becomes conscious — the substance of consciousness that becomes aware of things, not an outer instrumental part.

In the sleep part of the consciousness goes out to other planes of being and sees and experiences things there. It is quite possible for the witness consciousness to follow these happenings which usually transmit themselves in a coherent transcription to the sleeping part of the consciousness — the latter receives them and 'they appear as clear significant dreams as opposed to the incoherent dreams of the subconscient. Or else the witness consciousness may feel itself there watching the happenings as well as here. This will probably develop after a while.

The physical mind (or else the subconscient) almost always interferes in the dream and gives its own version. It is only when there is a clear experience on the mental or vital plane that it does not try to interfere.

They are dreams of the mental and higher vital planes in which things happen with another rhythm than here and freer forces, but some of them are formative of things and events here — not that they are fulfilled exactly like prophecies but they create forces for fulfilment.

There is no solid connection [between the waking and the dream states], but there can be a subtle one. Events of the waking state often influence the dream world, provided they have a sufficient repercussion on the mind or the vital. Formations and activities of the dream planes can project something of themselves or of their influence into the waking physical state, though they seldom reproduce themselves with any exactness there. It is only if the dream consciousness is very highly developed that one can usually see things there that are afterwards confirmed by thoughts, speech or actions of people or events in the physical world.

These are dreams of the vital plane in which the vital plane takes up the spiritual experience and tries to turn it into forms of ego with a suggestion afterwards of loss of power and of consciousness and a fall. You should attach no importance to these dreams except as an indication of nature in the sleeping state.

They simply mean that when they come back, they are not conscious of having dreamed. In the sleep the consciousness goes into other planes and has experiences there and when these are translated perfectly or imperfectly by the physical mind, they are called dreams. All the time of sleep such dreams take place, but sometimes one remembers and at other times does not at all remember. Sometimes also one goes low down into the subconscient and the dreams are there, but so deep down that when one comes out there is not even the consciousness that one had dreamed.

The alternation of quiet and much speaking is natural when the physical being is being worked upon from within. When the sleep is more awake, so to say, then one has dreams of all kinds; when there is no such awareness of dreams, it is because the sleep of the body is more deep, — the dreams are there but the body consciousness does not note them or remember that it had them.

It depends on the connection between the two states of consciousness at the time of waking. Usually there is a turn over of the consciousness in which the dream-state disappears more or less abruptly, effacing the fugitive impression made by the dream events (or rather their transcription) on the physical sheath. If the waking is more composed (less abrupt) or, if the impression is very strong, then the memory remains at least of the last dream. In the last case one may remember the dream for a long time, but usually after getting up the dream memories fade away. Those who want to remember their dreams sometimes make a practice of lying quiet and tracing backwards, recovering the dreams one by one. When the dream-state is very light, one can remember more dreams than when it is heavy.

The subconscient [during sleep] remains in the body. The being really goes out into different planes of consciousness, but its experiences are not kept in the memory, because the recording consciousness is too submerged to carry the record to the waking mind.

Yes, certainly, dream experiences can have a great value in them and convey truths that are not so easy to get in the waking state.

It often happens like that. There is a change or reversal of the consciousness that takes place and the dream consciousness in disappearing takes away its scenes and experiences with it. This can sometimes be avoided by not coming out abruptly into the waking state or getting up quickly, but remaining quiet for a time to see if the memory remains or comes back. Otherwise the physical memory has to be taught to remember.

Most people move most in the vital in sleep because it is the nearest to the physical and easiest to remain. One does enter the higher planes but either the transit there is brief or one does not remember. For in returning to the waking consciousness it is again through the lower vital and subtle physical that one passes and as these are the last dreams they are more easily remembered. The other dreams are remembered only if (1) they are strongly impressed on the recording consciousness, (2) one wakes immediately after one of them, (3) one has learned to be conscious in sleep, i.e. follows consciously the passage from plane to plane. Some train themselves to remember by remaining without moving when they wake and following back the thread of the dreams.

The expression was of the psychic plane — and the music was of that domain. Very often coming out of a conscious sleep like that the inner consciousness (which heard the music) lasts for a few seconds even after waking, before it goes back and is entirely covered by the waking mind. In that case what was heard or seen in sleep would continue for those few seconds after waking.

In dreams on the vital plane there is always a deviation from the norm of the physical fact — sometimes this is because of the free play in the vital, but at others it is only a fantasy of formation either in the vital itself or in the subconscient mind which transcribes the incidents of the dream and sometimes alters them by contributions of its own.

The people of dream are very often different from the people of actuality. Sometimes it is the real man who comes on another plane — sometimes it is a thought, force etc. that put on his appearance by some trick of association or other reason.

That is unlike many others a symbol dream on the vital plane. But it is difficult to interpret these vital symbolic dreams unless they offer their own clue — they are a sort of hieroglyph in their forms. Once one gets the clue some of them can be very significant — others of course are rather trivial.

It is a very small number of dreams that can be so explained
[that they arise by external stimuli] and in many cases the
explanation is quite arbitrary or cannot be proved. A much
larger number of dreams arise from subconscient impressions
of the past without any stimulus from outside. These are the
dreams from the subconscient which are the bulk of those
remembered by people who live in the external mind mostly.
There are also the dreams that are renderings of vital movements and tendencies habitual to the nature, personal formations
of the vital plane. But when one begins to live within then the
dreams are often transcriptions of one's experiences on the vital
plane and beyond that there is a large field of symbolic and other
dreams which have nothing to do with memory. Of course it
has been proved that a very long and circumstantial dream can
happen in a second or two, so that objection to Bergson's statement does not stand. But there are also prophetic dreams and
many others. Memory holds together the experiences but it is
absurd to identify consciousness (even in the restricted European
idea of consciousness) with memory. This theory of memory is
part of Bergson's fundamental idea that Time is everything.
As for *spirituelle* in Europe mostly no distinction is made between
the spiritual and the mental or vital.

A great many people have these dreams. It is the vital being
that goes out in sleep and moves about in the vital worlds and
has this sense of floating in the air in its own (vital) body. The
waves of a sea having the colour of lightning must have been the
atmosphere of some vital province. I have known of some
sadhaks, when they go at first out of the body in a more conscious way, thinking they have actually levitated, the vividness
of the movement is so intense, but it is simply the vital body
going out.

The dreams are experiences on the vital plane, actual contacts
with myself and the Mother in your inner being, not symbolic

though they may have symbolic elements, but expressing relations, influences or mutual workings of our consciousness with yours. The second dream has symbolic elements. The ladder is of course a symbol of an ascent from one stage to another. The snake indicates an energy, sometimes a good one, more often a bad one (vital or hostile). It may be that the energy was quiescent and therefore not alarming, but by touching it to see how it was you awoke it and you found it was something not safe to handle. There is no clear indication what this energy was. These dream-experiences do not depend on the waking thoughts as do ordinary subconscient dreams which are dreams only and not experiences. They have a life, a structure, an arrangement and forms and meanings of their own; but they are often connected with the inner condition and experiences or movements of the sadhana. It is not clear whether the flower-incident was symbolic or only something that happened on the inner plane. It might have been possible to say if it had been indicated what flower it actually was that you had given.

These bad conditions are a lapse (often due to a very slight cause) from the inner poise to the outer consciousness. When they happen do not get affected, but remain quiet, call the Mother and get back inward.

The dreams you describe are very clearly symbolic dreams on the vital plane. These dreams may symbolise anything, forces at play, the underlying structure and tissue of things done or experienced, actual or potential happenings, real or suggested movements or changes in the inner or outer nature.

The timidity of which the apprehension in the dream was an indication, was probably not anything in the conscious mind or higher vital, but something subconscient in the lower vital nature. This part always feels itself small and insignificant and has very easily a fear of being submerged by the greater consciousness — a fear which in some may amount at the first contact to something like a panic, alarm or terror.

*
**

These are experiences of the vital plane; they have a meaning if one knows how to interpret them. This one indicates the possibility of strong attacks on the vital plane, but at the same time promises protection. These are formations of the vital plane, sometimes things that try to happen but not necessarily effective. One can observe and understand, but not allow them to influence the mind; for often adverse forces try to influence the mind by suggestion through these dream experiences.

I said this dream was an actual happening on the vital plane, not a formation. If somebody attacks you in the street, that is not a formation. But if somebody hypnotises you and suggests that you are ill — that suggestion is a formation put in by the hypnotiser.

These are dreams of the vital plane — they have probably some reference to something going on in your vital, but these dreams cannot be precisely interpreted unless there is either a clue that is clear on the surface or else you yourself can relate it to something in your experience of which you are aware. The images of the ascent and the coming down of water (consciousness or some other gift from above) are frequent and the general meaning is always the same — but the precise significance here is not clear.

It is a dream of the vital plane. In these dreams the figures of the physical life take another form and meaning and the consciousness that lives and acts among them is not the outer physical consciousness but some inner vital part of the being. The insurrection of the French soldiers is a figure of some disturbance on the vital plane which wants to happen and affect the inner life. The import of the dream is the readiness of the vital inner consciousness to put its reliance on the Mother and

take refuge in her against all possible disturbances or perils of
the inner life.

Yes, your feeling about the protection is perfectly true.

The dream about X and going to the Mother was an
experience of something that took place on the vital plane.
Things happen there that have some connection with the nature
and life here, but they happen differently because there it is not
the physical beings that meet, but the vital beings of people. One
can gather what is the nature of one's own inner vital being
— which is often very different from the physical personality
that acts in front in the body. By the acting of the consciousness
in these dreams the inner parts of the being begin to be more
active and have more influence on the outer nature. Your inner
vital being seems from the dream experiences that you have
related to be very strong, faithful, clear-minded, resolute,
able to deal with the hostile forces and their activities in the right
way and do the right thing.

The sensation of going somewhere means that part of the
consciousness is going into some other plane than the physical.
The men you saw and also the vision that came afterwards belonged to these supraphysical worlds. The vision seems to be
symbolic of something from above, but of what is not quite clear
from the details. Gold is the colour of the Truth that comes from
above.

The physical is not the only world; there are others that we
become aware of through dream records, through the subtle
senses, through influences and contacts, through imagination,
intuition and vision. There are worlds of a larger subtler life
than ours, vital worlds; worlds in which Mind builds its own
forms and figures, mental worlds; psychic worlds which are the
soul's home; others above with which we have little contact.
In each of us there is a mental plane of consciousness, a psychic,
a vital, a subtle physical as well as the gross physical and material plane. The same planes are repeated in the consciousness of

general Nature. It is when we enter or contact these other planes
that we come into connection with the worlds above the physical.
In sleep we leave the physical body, only a subconscient residue
remaining, and enter all planes and all sorts of worlds. In each
we see scenes, meet beings, share in happenings, come across
formations, influences, suggestions which belong to these planes.
Even when we are awake, part of us moves in these planes, but
their activity goes on behind the veil; our waking minds are not
aware of it. Dreams are often only incoherent constructions of
our subconscient, but others are records (often much mixed and
distorted) or transcripts of experiences in these supraphysical
planes. When we do sadhana, this kind of dream becomes very
common; then subconscious dreams cease to predominate.

The forces and beings of the vital world have a great influence on human beings. The vital world is on one side a world
of beauty, — the poet, artist, musician are in close contact with
it; it is also a world of powers and passions, lusts and desires,
— our own lusts and desires, and passions and ambitions can
put us into connection with the vital worlds and their forces and
beings. It is again a world of things dark, dangerous and horrible. Nightmares like X's are contacts with this side of the
vital plane. Its influences are also the source of much in men
that is demoniac, dirty, cruel and base.

This experience of X is a contact with something on the
wrong side of the vital plane. Her visions of gods, goddesses,
etc., are vital world experiences on the other side. This one is an
attempt of some vital force to get some kind of control on her
acting on her through her fear. If she were not afraid, it could
not invade her. If she suffers in her waking hours from desires
or despondencies and depressions, that also would help to make
her enter these worlds in sleep or have a connection with them.
Her experiences as you reported them showed a very great power
of entry into the vital plane on the good side — these dream
experiences are the other side. As they are dreams, they are not
so dangerous as a similar experience in meditation would be, but
all the same they are very undesirable.

If such an invasion is attempted, the one thing to do is to
fight it out as she did and at the same time to call the Mother.

The rule should be to call the Mother before sleeping, to concentrate on her and try to feel the Mother's protection around her and go with that into sleep. In the dream itself a habit of calling the Mother when in difficulty or peril should be formed; many sadhaks do it. Not to allow the invasion, any invasion of any power or being, whether in dream, meditation or otherwise — no force except the Divine Force, means to reject it, never to give assent, whether through attention or through weakness. To cut connection can be done by will within, a will of rejection, a concentration on higher things than the things of the vital plane; also by rejection of vital desires or despondencies and depressions, if she has them. Let her aspire most for the higher spiritual experiences, the psychic opening, calm, peace, purity, the opening to the higher light, strength, bliss, knowledge.

One thing, she should not lead too sequestered a life; some opening on the physical world is needed, also some normal mental activities of a healthy character.

These are dreams sent from the vital world. There are three things she must develop with regard to them:

(1) to get the habit of calling the Mother at once in the dream itself;

(2) not to fear — if one does not fear, these other world forces become helpless;

(3) to put no belief in the reality of such formations and regard them only as suggestions put into form, just as one gets a frightful imagination of this or that happening but the reason knows it to be a mere work of imagination and is not moved by it.

Your experience of the peace in the body was a very good one. As for the bad dream, it was a hostile formation from the vital world — a suggestion in a dream form intended to upset you. These things should be dismissed — you should say in yourself "It is false — no such thing can happen" and throw it away as you would a wrong suggestion in the waking state.

These things that come to frighten you are merely impressions
thrown on you by small vital forces which want to prevent you
(by making you nervous) pushing on the sadhana. They can
really do nothing to you, only you must reject all fear. Keep
always this thought when these things come "The Mother's
protection is with me, nothing bad can happen", — for when
there is the psychic opening and one puts one's faith in the
Mother, that is sufficient to ward these things off. Many sadhaks
learn, when they have alarming dreams, to call the Mother's
name in the dream itself and then the things that menace them
become helpless or cease. You must therefore refuse to be inti-
midated and reject these impressions with contempt. If there
is anything frightening, call down the Mother's protection.

The heat you felt was probably due to some difficulty in the
force coming down below the centre between the eyes where it
has been working up till now. When such sensations or the
unease you once felt or similar things come, you must not be
alarmed, but remain quiet and let the difficulty pass.

What you had before that, the moonlight in the forehead
was this working on the centre there between the eyebrows, the
centre of the inner mind, will and vision. The moonlight you saw
is the light of spirituality and it was this that was entering into
your mind through the centre, with the effect of the widening in
the heart like a sky filled with moonlight. Afterwards came some
endeavour to prepare the lower part of the mind whose centre is
in the throat and join it with the inner mind and make it open;
but there was some difficulty, as is very usually the case, which
caused the heat. It was probably the fire of tapas, Agni, trying
to open the way to this centre.

The experience of being taken up into the sky is a very
common one and it means an ascent of the consciousness into a
higher world of light and peace.

The idea that you must go more and more within and turn
wholly to the Mother is quite right. It is when there is no attach-

ment to outward things for their own sake and all is only for the Mother and the life through the inner psychic being is centred in her that the best condition is created for the spiritual realisation.

The dream was of a kind one often has in the vital plane — in which one gets into inextricable difficulties till suddenly one finds the way out. Gujerat in the dream was not Gujerat, but only a symbol of one part of the vital world which is opposed to the spiritual life and full of vital powers that come in the way either by fraud or by force. These dreams are indications of certain parts of vital nature (not one's own, but the general vital Nature) which stand in the way of spiritual fulfilment. When one goes there and masters them, then one is free from any intervention of these parts of Nature in the sadhana.

These dreams are quite symbolical of the vital forces that come and attack you. If you face them with courage they are reduced to helplessness. I don't think that it is at all your father and brother that you meet — although something of their hostile feelings may be taken advantage of by those forces to take their figures — also they may do it in order to create sympathy in you and prevent you from acting against them. But apart from that the figures of the physical mother and father and relatives are very often symbolical of the physical or the hereditary nature or generally of the ordinary nature in which we are born.

In these dreams the parents or relatives mean the ordinary forces of the physical consciousness (the old nature).

These dreams are of the vital plane. Those about going home

come from a part of the vital which still keeps the memory of the past relations and goes there during the sleep. The dreams about the Mother record meetings with her on the vital plane. For the first you should throw them away when you awake and not let your vital keep their impress. The experiences you had there (of the Mother coming in the heart and telling you) were psychic in character, not of the vital dream kind.

The difficulty you have in sadhana may come from the vital or physical mind becoming active. That often happens after the first experiences of calm and silence. One has to detach oneself from these activities in meditation as a witness and call down the original calm into these parts also. But this may take time. If one can in meditation sufficiently isolate oneself from the surroundings and go inside, the quietude comes more quickly.

When you practise yoga, the consciousness opens and you become aware — especially in sleep — of things, scenes, beings, happenings of other (not physical) worlds and yourself in sleep go there and act there. Very often these things have an importance for the sadhana. So you need not regret seeing all this when you sleep or meditate.

But in no case should you fear. The fact that you were able to destroy the beings that fought with you (these were beings of a hostile vital world) is very good, for it shows that in your vital nature somewhere there is strength and courage. Moreover, using the Mother's name and having her protection, you should fear nothing.

The running away [in dream] is a symbol of the inertia in part of the being which allows the forces to invade, drawing back from them and losing ground instead of facing and destroying them.

It is evident that X's experience was only what is called a nightmare — an attack in sleep from some force of the vital world, to which he probably opened himself in some way, it may be by answering to the man from the street who carried the worst vital atmosphere around him. The figure of the woman was only a form given by his subconscient mind to this force. These forces are around everywhere, not only in one particular room or house, and if one opens the door to them, they come in wherever you are. It would have no importance but for the nervous reaction of irrational terror indulged in by X. One who wants to do sadhana has no business to indulge in such panics; it is a weakness incompatible with the demands of the yoga and, if one cannot throw it aside, it is safer not to try the yoga.

The depression coming on you in sleep must have been due to one of two causes. It might have been the trace left by an unpleasant experience in some disagreeable quarter of the vital worlds, and there are places in plenty of that kind there. It can hardly have been an attack, for that would surely have left a more distinct impression of something having happened, even if there was no actual memory of it; but merely to enter into certain places or meet their inhabitants or enter into contact with their atmosphere can have, unless one is a born fighter and takes an aggressive pleasure in facing and conquering these ordeals, a depressing and exhausting effect. If that is the cause, then it is a question of either avoiding these places, which can be done by an effort of will, once one knows that it is this which happens, or putting around you a special protection against the touch of that atmosphere. The other possible cause is a plunge into a too obscure and subconscient sleep — that has sometimes the effect you describe. In any case, do not allow yourself to be discouraged when these things happen; they are common phenomena one cannot fail to meet with as soon as one begins to penetrate behind the veil and touch the occult causes of the psychological happenings within us. One has to learn the causes, note and face the difficulty and always react — never accept the depression thrown on one, but react as you did the first time.

If there are always forces around which are concerned to depress and discourage, there are always forces above and around us which we can draw upon, — draw into ourselves to restore, to fill up again with strength and faith and joy and the power that perseveres and conquers. It is really a habit that one has to get of opening to these helpful forces and either passively receiving them or actively drawing upon them — for one can do either. It is easier if you have the conception of them above and around you and the faith and the will to receive them — for that brings the experience and concrete sense of them and the capacity to receive at need or at will. It is a question of habituating your consciousness to get into touch and keep in touch with these helpful forces — and for that you must accustom yourself to reject the impressions forced on you by the others, depression, self-distrust, repining and all similar disturbances.

As for the actual mastery of a situation by occult powers, it can only come by use and experiment — as one develops strength by exercises or develops a process in the laboratory by finding out through the actual use of a power how it can and ought to be applied to the field in which it operates. It is of no use waiting for the strength before one tries; the strength will come with repeated trials. Neither must you fear failure or be discouraged by failure — for these things do not always succeed at once. These are things one has to learn by personal experiences, how to get into touch with the cosmic forces, how to relate or equate our individual action with theirs, how to become an instrument of the Master Consciousness which we call the Divine.

There is something a little too personal in your attitude — I mean the insistence on personal strength or weakness as the determining factor. After all, for the greatest as for the smallest of us our strength is not our own but given to us for the game that has to be played, the work that we have to do. The strength may be formed in us, but its present formation is not final, — neither formation of power nor formation of weakness. At any moment the formation may change — at any moment one sees, especially under the pressure of yoga, weakness changing into power, the incapable becoming capable, suddenly or slowly the instrumental consciousness rising to a new stature or developing its latent powers. Above us, within us, around us is the All-Strength and it is that that we have to rely on for our work, our development, our transforming change. If we proceed with the faith in the work, in our instrumentality for the work, in the Power that missions us, then in the very act of trial, of facing and surmounting difficulties and failures, the strength will come and we shall find our capacity to contain as much as we need of the All-Strength of which we grow more and more perfect vessels.

VIII

The whole principle of this yoga is to give oneself entirely to the Divine alone and to nobody and nothing else, and to bring down into ourselves by union with the Divine Mother-Power all the transcendent light, force, wideness, peace, purity, truth-consciousness and Ananda of the supramental Divine. In this yoga, therefore, there can be no place for vital relations or interchanges with others; any such relation or interchange immediately ties down the soul to the lower consciousness and its lower nature, prevents the true and full union with the Divine and hampers both the ascent to the supramental Truth-consciousness and the descent of the supramental Ishwari Shakti. Still worse would it be if this interchange took the form of a sexual relation or a sexual enjoyment, even if kept free from any outward act; therefore these things are absolutely forbidden in the sadhana. It goes without saying that any physical act of the kind is not allowed; but also any subtler form is ruled out. It is only after becoming one with the supramental Divine that we can find our true spiritual relations with others in the Divine; in that higher unity this kind of gross lower vital movement can have no place.

To master the sex-impulse, — to become so much master of the sex-centre that the sexual energy would be drawn upwards, not thrown outwards and wasted — it is so indeed that the force in the seed can be turned into a primal physical energy supporting all the others, *retas* into *ojas*. But no error can be more perilous than to accept the immixture of the sexual desire and some kind of subtle satisfaction of it and look on this as a part of the sadhana. It would be the most effective way to head straight towards spiritual downfall and throw into the atmosphere forces that would block the supramental descent, bringing instead the descent of adverse vital powers to disseminate disturbance and disaster. This deviation must be absolutely thrown away, should it try to occur and expunged from the consciousness, if the Truth is to þe brought down and the work is to be done.

It is an error too to imagine that, although the physical sexual action is to be abandoned, yet some inward reproduction of it is part of the transformation of the sex-centre. The action of the animal sex-energy in Nature is a device for a particular purpose in the economy of the material creation in the Ignorance. But the vital excitement that accompanies it makes the most favourable opportunity and vibration in the atmosphere for the inrush of those very vital forces and beings whose whole business is to prevent the descent of the supramental Light. The pleasure attached to it is a degradation and not a true form of the divine Ananda. The true divine Ananda in the physical has a different quality and movement and substance; self-existent in its essence, its manifestation is dependent only on an inner union with the Divine. You have spoken of Divine Love; but Divine Love, when it touches the physical, does not awaken the gross lower vital propensities; indulgence of them would only repel it and make it withdraw again to the heights from which it is already difficult enough to draw it down into the coarseness of the material creation which it alone can transform. Seek the Divine Love through the only gate through which it will consent to enter, the gate of the psychic being, and cast away the lower vital error.

The transformation of the sex-centre and its energy is needed for the physical siddhi; for this is the support in the body of all the mental, vital and physical forces of the nature. It has to be changed into a mass and a movement of intimate Light, creative Power, pure divine Ananda. It is only the bringing down of the supramental Light, Power and Bliss into the centre that can change it. As to the working afterwards, it is the supramental Truth and the creative vision and will of the Divine Mother that will determine it. But it will be a working of the conscious Truth, not of the Darkness and Ignorance to which sexual desire and enjoyment belong; it will be a power of preservation and free desireless radiation of the life-forces and not of their throwing out and waste. Avoid the imagination that the supramental life will be only a heightened satisfaction of the desires of the vital and the body; nothing can be a greater obstacle to the Truth in its descent than this hope of glorification of the animal in the human nature. Mind wants the supramental state to be a confirmation of its own cherished ideas and preconceptions; the vital wants it to be a glorification of its own desires; the physical wants it to be a rich prolongation of its own comforts and pleasures and habits. If it were to be that, it would be only an exaggerated and highly magnified consummation of the animal and the human nature, not a transition from the human into the Divine.

It is dangerous to think of giving up "all barrier of discrimination and defence against what is trying to descend" upon you. Have you thought what this would mean if what is descending is something not in consonance with the divine Truth, perhaps even adverse? An adverse Power would ask no better condition for getting control over the seeker. It is only the Mother's force and the divine Truth that one should admit without barriers. And even there one must keep the power of discernment in order to detect anything false that comes masquerading as the Mother's force and the divine Truth, and keep too the power of rejection that will throw away all mixture.

Keep faith in your spiritual destiny, draw back from error and open more the psychic being to the direct guidance of the Mother's light and power. If the central will is sincere, each recognition of a mistake can become a stepping-stone to a truer movement and a higher progress.

It is true that the sex-centre and its reactions can be transformed and that an Ananda from above can come down to replace the animal sex-reaction. The sex-impulse is a degradation of this Ananda. But to receive this Ananda before the physical (including the physical vital) consciousness is transformed, can be dangerous; for other and lower things can take advantage and mix in it and that would disturb the whole being and might lead into a wrong road by the impression that these lower things are part of the sadhana and sanctioned from above or simply by the lower elements overpowering the true experience. In the last case the Ananda would cease and the sex-centre be possessed by the lower reactions.

I have stated very briefly in my previous letter my position with regard to the sex-impulse and yoga. I may add here that my conclusion is not founded on any mental opinion or preconceived moral idea, but on probative facts and on observation and experience. I do not deny that so long as one allows a sort of separation between inner experience and outer consciousness, the latter being left as an inferior activity controlled but not transformed, it is quite possible to have spiritual experiences and make progress without any entire cessation of the sex-activity. The mind separates itself from the outer vital (life-parts) and the physical consciousness and lives its own inner life. But only a few can really do this with any completeness and the moment one's experiences extend to the life-plane and the physical, sex can no longer be treated in this way. It can become at any moment a disturbing, upsetting and deforming force. I have observed that to an equal extent with ego (pride, vanity, ambition) and rajasic greeds and desires it is one of the main causes of the spiritual casualties that have taken place in sadhana. The attempt to treat it by detachment without complete excision breaks down; the attempt to sublimate it, favoured by many modern mystics in Europe, is a most rash and perilous experiment. For it is when one mixes up sex and spirituality that there is the greatest havoc. Even the attempt to sublimate it by turning it towards the Divine as in the Vaishnava *madhura bhāva* carries in it a serious danger, as the results of a wrong turn or use in this method so often show.

At any rate in this yoga which seeks not only the essential experience of the Divine but a transformation of the whole being and nature, I have found it an absolute necessity of the sadhana to aim at a complete mastery over the sex-force; otherwise the vital consciousness remains a turbid mixture, the turbidity affecting the purity of the spiritualised mind and seriously hindering the upward turn of the forces of the body. This yoga demands a full ascension of the whole lower or ordinary consciousness to join the spiritual above it and a full descent of the spiritual (eventually of the supramental) into the mind, life and body to transform it. The total ascent is impossible so long as sex-desire blocks the way; the descent is dangerous so long as sex-desire is powerful in the vital. For at any moment an unexcised or latent sex-desire may be the cause of a mixture which throws back the true descent and uses the energy acquired for other purposes or turns all the action of the consciousness towards wrong experience, turbid and delusive. One must, therefore, clear this obstacle out of the way; otherwise there is either no safety or no free movement towards finality in the sadhana.

The contrary opinion of which you speak may be due to the idea that sex is a natural part of the human vital-physical whole, a necessity like food and sleep, and that its total inhibition may lead to unbalancing and to serious disorders. It is a fact that sex suppressed in outward action but indulged in other ways may lead to disorders of the system and brain troubles. That is the root of the medical theory which discourages sexual abstinence. But I have observed that these things happen only when there is either secret indulgence of a perverse kind replacing the normal sexual activity or else an indulgence of it in a kind of subtle vital way by imagination or by an invisible vital interchange of an occult kind, — I do not think harm ever occurs when there is a true spiritual effort at mastery and abstinence. It is now held by many medical men in Europe that sexual abstinence, *if it is genuine*, is beneficial; for the element in the *retas* which serves the sexual act is then changed into its other element which feeds the energies of the system, mental, vital and physical — and that justifies the Indian idea of Brahmacharya, the transformation of *retas* into *ojas* and the raising of its energies upward so that they change into a spiritual force.

As for the method of mastery, it cannot be done by physical abstinence alone — it proceeds by a process of combined detachment and rejection. The consciousness stands back from the sex-impulse, feels it as not its own, as something alien thrown on it by Nature-force to which it refuses assent or identification — each time a certain movement of rejection throws it more and more outward. The mind remains unaffected; after a time the vital being which is the chief support withdraws from it in the same way, finally the physical consciousness no longer supports it. This process continues until even the subconscient can no longer rouse it up in dream and no further movement comes from the outer Nature-force to rekindle this lower fire. This is the course when the sex-propensity sticks obstinately; but there are some who can eliminate it decisively by a swift radical dropping away from the nature. That, however, is more rare.

It has to be said that the total elimination of the sex-impulse is one of the most difficult things in sadhana and one must be prepared for it to take time. But its total disappearance has been achieved and a practical liberation crossed only by occasional dream-movements from the subconscient is fairly common.

Sex (occult) stands on a fair level of equality with ambition etc. from the point of view of danger, only its action is usually less ostensible — i.e. the Hostiles don't put it forward so openly as a thing to be followed after in the spiritual life.

I have not said that the sex-impulse has not been mastered in other yogas. I have said that it is difficult to be free from it entirely and that the attempt at sublimation as in the Vaishnava sadhana has its dangers. That is evidenced by all one knows of what has frequently and even largely happened among the Vaishnavas. Transcendence and transformation are different matters. There are three kinds or stages of transformation contemplated in this sadhana, the psychic transformation, the spiritual and the supramental. The first two have been done in their own way in other yogas; the last is a new endeavour. A transformation sufficient for spiritual realisation is attainable by the two former; a transformation sufficient for the divinisation of human life is, in my view, not possible except by a supramental change.

What has this yoga got to do with sex and sex-contact? I have told you repeatedly that sex has to be got rid of and overcome before there can be siddhi in this yoga.

Conversion is one thing and acceptance of the present forms in ordinary human nature is another. The reason given for indulging the sex-action is not at all imperative. It is only a minority that is called to the strict yogic life and there will be always plenty of people who will continue the race. Certainly, the yogi has no contempt or aversion for human nature; he understands it and the place given to each of its activities with a clear and calm regard. Also, if an action can be done with self-control without desire under the direction of a higher consciousness, that is the better way and it can sometimes be followed for the fulfilment of the divine will in things that would not otherwise be undertaken by the yogi, such as war and the destruction which accompanies war. But a too light resort to such a rule might easily be converted into a pretext for indulging the ordinary human nature.

The Mother has already told you the truth about this idea. The idea that by fully indulging the sex-hunger it will be finished and disappear for ever is a deceptive pretence held out by the vital to the mind in order to get a sanction for its desire; it has no other *raison d'être* or truth or justification. If an occasional indulgence keeps the sex-desire simmering, a full indulgence would only sink you in its mire. This hunger like other hungers does not cease by temporary satiation; it revives itself after a temporary abeyance and wants again indulgence. Neither sops nor gorgings are the right treatment for it. It can only go by a radical psychic rejection or a full spiritual opening with the increasing descent of a consciousness that does not want it and has the truer Ananda.

It is not a question of fear — it is a question of choosing between the Divine Peace and Ananda and the degraded pleasure of sex, between the Divine and the attraction of women. Food has to be taken to support the body but sex-satisfaction is not a necessity. Even for the *rasa* of food it can only be harmonised with the spiritual condition if all greed of food and desire of the palate disappears. Intellectual or aesthetic delight can also be an obstacle to the spiritual perfection if there is attachment to it, although it is much nearer to the spiritual than a gross untransformed bodily appetite; in fact in order to become part of the spiritual consciousness the intellectual and aesthetic delight has also to change and become something higher. But all things that have a *rasa* cannot be kept. There is a *rasa* in hurting and killing others, the sadistic delight, there is a *rasa* in torturing oneself, the masochistic delight — modern psychology is full of these two. Merely having a *rasa* is not a sufficient reason for keeping things as part of the spiritual life.

There is no "delight" in the sex-affair, it is necessarily and can only be a passing excitement and pleasure which finally wears itself out with the wearing out of the body.

Yes, it [the sex-atmosphere] has become rampant everywhere [in the modern world], especially as men no longer believe in the old moral restraints and nothing else has been substituted.

The idea of the new European mystics like Lawrence and Middleton Murry etc. is that the indulgence of sex is the appointed way to find the Overself or the Under Self, for that is what it really seems to be! X of course knows better. But if the personal Overself is all that is wanted and not the Divine, then sex and many other things are permissible. One has only to realise that one is not the body, not the life, not the mind, but the Overself and then do whatever the Overself tells you to do.

I spoke of the *personal* Overself — meaning the realisation of something in us (the Purusha) that is not the Prakriti, not the movements of mind, vital or physical, but something that is the Thinker, etc. This Purusha can give assent to any movement of nature or withhold it or it can direct the Prakriti what to do or not to do. It can allow it to indulge sex or withhold indulgence. It is usually the mental Purusha (Manomaya Purusha) that one thus realises, but there is also the Pranamaya or vital Purusha. By the word Overself they probably mean this Purusha — they take it as a sort of personal Atman.

Oneness with all would then mean satisfying the sex instinct with all — that would be a rather startling *siddhānta*, though there is something like it in the practice of Tantra of the left hand. But the left hand Tantriks are more logical than you — for why should oneness, if it is to justify sex-expression, support only the lighter and not the cruder forms of love-expression? But is sex really based on love or sex-love based on sex-instinct? and is sex-instinct an expression of the spiritual feeling of the One in all? Is it not really based on duality, except when it simply seeks satisfaction and pleasure where there is no question of love at all?

Is one attracted to a woman by the sense that she is oneself or by the fact that she is somebody else attracting one by some charm or beauty which one wants to enjoy or possess or simply by the fact of the difference from oneself, the fact of her being a female and not a male so that the sex-instinct can find a full field there?

The sex-impulse is certainly the greatest force in the vital plane; if it can be sublimated and turned upwards, *ojas* is created which is a great help to the attainment of higher consciousness. But mere restraint is not sufficient.

The sex-energy utilised by Nature for the purpose of reproduction is in its real nature a fundamental energy of Life. It can be used not for the heightening but for a certain intensification of the vital-emotional life; it can be controlled and diverted from the sex-purpose and used for aesthetic and artistic or other creation and productiveness or preserved for heightening of the intellectual or other energies. Entirely controlled it can be turned into a force of spiritual energy also. This was well known in ancient India and was described as the conversion of *retas* into *ojas* by Brahmacharya. Sex-energy misused turns to disorder and disintegration of the life-energy and its powers.

Of course, it [the sex-impulse] is perfectly natural and all men have it. Nature has put it as part of her functioning for the purpose of procreation, so that the race may continue. In the animals it is used for that purpose, but men have departed from Nature and use it for pleasure mainly — so it has taken hold of them and harasses them at all times.

Naturally, you have to conquer the sex-impulse, but it cannot be done entirely all at once; it needs a patient persistence and a firm resolve not to indulge it either physically or mentally.

Even when this has been done and there is no thought or desire, the mechanical emission can continue in sleep, but if the mind is kept free that will eventually disappear.

The sexual sensations do not "become" a principle of the physical consciousness — they are there in the physical nature already — wherever there is conscious life, the sex-force is there. It is physical Nature's means of reproduction and it is there for that purpose.

The terrestrial sex-movement is a utilisation by Nature of the fundamental physical energy for purposes of procreation. The thrill of which the poets speak, which is accompanied by a very gross excitement, is the lure by which she makes the vital consent to this otherwise unpleasing process; there are numbers who experience a recoil of disgust after the act and repulsion from the partner in it because of the disgust, though they return to it when the disgust has worn off for the sake of this lure.

The sex-energy itself is a great power with two components in its physical basis, one meant for procreation and the process necessary for it, the other for feeding the general energies of the body, mind and vital, — also of the spiritual energies of the body. The old yogis call these two components *retas* and *ojas*. The European scientists generally pooh-poohed the idea, but now they are beginning to discover the same fact for themselves. As for the thrill, — the poets make so much of — it is simply a very gross distortion and degradation of the physical Ananda which by the yoga can establish itself in the body, but this it cannot do so long as there is the sex-deviation.

That is correct — if the sex-fluid is prevented from being spent away, it turns into *tejas* and *ojas*. The whole theory of *brahmacarya* is based upon that by the yogis. If it were not so, there would be no need of *brahmacarya* for producing *tejas* and *ojas*.

It is not a question of vigour and energy *per se*, but of the physical support — in the physical support the *ojas* produced by *brahmacarya* counts greatly. The transformation of the *retas* into *ojas* is a transformation of physical substance into a physical (necessarily producing also a vital-physical) energy. The spiritual energy itself can only drive the body, like the vital and mental, but in driving it it would exhaust it if it has not a physical support. (I speak of course of the ordinary spiritual energy, not of the supramental to be, which has not only to transmute *retas* into *ojas* but *ojas* into something more sublimated.)

As for scientists, the product of sex-glands is considered by them (at least so I have read) as a great support and feeder of general energies. It has even been considered that sex-force has a great part to play in the production of poetry, art, etc. and in the action of genius generally. Finally, it is a doctor who has discovered that sex-fluid consists of two parts, one meant for sex-purposes, the other as a basis of general energy, and if the sex-action is not indulged, the first element tends to be turned into the second (*retas* into *ojas*, as the yogis had already discovered). Theories? So are the statements or inferences of the opposite side — one theory is as good as another. Anyhow, I don't think that the atrophy of sex-glands by abstinence can be supported by general experience. X's contention is however logical if we take not individual results but the course of evolution and suppose that this evolution will follow the line of the old one, for these useless organs are supposed to disappear or deteriorate. But will the supramental evolution follow the same course as the old one or develop new adaptations of its own making? — that is the uncertain element.

You have not understood. I was answering the statement that scientists don't attach any value to sex-gland product and think it is only of use for an external purpose. Many scientists on the contrary consider it a base of productive energy; among other things it plays a part in artistic and poetic production. Not that artists and poets are anchorites and Brahmacharis but that they have a powerful sex-gland activity, part of which goes to creative and part to (effectual or ineffectual) procreative action. On the latest theory and yoga theory, the procreative part would be *retas*, the creative part the basis of *ojas*. Now supposing the poet or artist to conserve his *retas* and turn it into *ojas*, the result would be an increased power of creative productivity.

The idea about impotence is rather irrational — impotence comes from over-indulgence or wrong indulgence (certain perverse habits); it does not come from self-control. Self-control means only a diversion to other powers, because the controlled sex-power becomes a force for the life-energies, the powers of the mind and the more and more potent workings of the spiritual consciousness.

In most men the sexual is the strongest of all the impulses of Nature.

The sexual impulse is its own reason to itself — it acts for its own satisfaction and does not ask for any reason, for it is instinctive and irrational.

[Why the illusion of sex does not disappear:] Too many roots in the human vital. Sex has a terrible tenacity. Besides, universal physical nature has such need of it that even when man pushes it away, she throws it upon him as long as possible.

All movements are in the mass movements of Nature's cosmic

forces, they are movements of universal Nature. The individual receives something of them, a wave or pressure of some cosmic force, and is driven by it; he thinks it is his own, generated in himself separately, but it is not so, it is part of a general movement which works just in the same way in others. Sex, for instance, is a movement of general Nature seeking for its play and it uses this or that one — a man vitally or physically "in love" as it is called with a woman is simply repeating and satisfying the world-movement of sex; if it had not been that woman, it would have been another; he is simply an instrument in Nature's machinery, it is not an independent movement. So it is with anger and other Nature-motives.

Naturally, the sex-movement is a force in itself, impersonal and not dependent on any particular object. It fastens on one or another only to give itself body and a field of enjoyment. When it is checked in the vital interchange, it tends to lose its vital character and attacks through its most physical and elemental movement. It is only when it is thrown out from the vital physical and most physical that it is conquered.

The sex exists for its own satisfaction and this or that person is only an excuse or occasion for its action or a channel for awakening its activity. It is from within, by the peace and purity from above coming into that part and holding it that it must disappear.

It [the desire to attract others by physical charms] is the usual vanity of the lower vital — it is very common. Any man can have an attraction for any woman, and vice versa, when the sex-forces are active, but that attraction is not his, it is the pull of the sex-force.

The sex-pull is that of a general force which uses the individual for its purpose and it takes advantage of any proximity of the other one.... The security lies in oneself, in immediate detachment (standing apart, not accepting as one's own) and rejecting it.

It is of course the universal sex-force that acts, but certain people are more full of it than others, have the sex-appeal as they now say in Europe. This sex-appeal is exercised especially by women even without any conscious intention of putting it on a particular person. Consciously they may turn it on a particular person, but it may exercise itself on many others whom they do not wish particularly to capture. All women have not the sex-appeal, but some force of sex-pull there is in most. There is of course a similar pull in men for women.

A smile or any movement, appearance or action of the woman can be the starting-point for these vibrations. I don't suppose it is anything inherent in the smile itself, but all these things have been the habitual means by which sex has been excited in men (*hāvabhāva*) and the woman uses them, often unconsciously and by mere habit when coming into contact with man — whether she has or has not any intention of pleasing or moving the man, it still comes up as an instinctive movement. X is of the type of woman who has this instinctive movement to please the male. But even when the woman smiles quite casually and without even the habitual instinctive movement, still there may be the vibration on the man's side owing to the habit of response in him to feminine attraction. These things are almost mechanical in their starting. As I wrote before it is the automatic answer of the physical or vital mind (imagination etc.) that prolongs it and makes it effective. Otherwise the vibrations would die away after a time.

She may not have the sex-feeling towards you, but there is a cer-

97

tain kind of vital push, throwing out of tentacles — I don't know exactly how to express it — the secret object of which in Nature is to attract the man, to draw his attention and fix it on the woman, hook and draw him in a less or greater degree. The intention may not be at all conscious in the woman's mind, that is to say, it may not be clear or even present to her mind, — it may be merely instinctive or subconscious. There need be no physical sexual intention, only the vital in spontaneous movement. All women of a strongly vital temperament (and X is that) have it — some more, some less. There may be no specific sex-impulse in it, but it will still raise the sex-idea in the man. X naturally has no psychological knowledge and these things are too subtle for her to perceive or realise. She may easily think she is acting in a perfectly innocent and natural way and not at all know this activity of the Nature push in her.

Dress has always been used by woman as an aid to her "sex-appeal" as it is now called and man has always been susceptible to it; women also often find dress in man a cause of attraction (e.g. soldier's uniform). There are also particular tastes in dress — that a sari of a particular colour should attract is quite normal. The attraction works on the sense and the vital, while it is the mind that dislikes the psychological defects and gets cooled down by their exposure; but this repulsion of the mind cannot last as against the stronger vital attraction.

The association [of touch] with sex is vital physical — otherwise there need be no connection between the expression of affection by touch and the sex-feeling. Except in unusual cases, when the mother and son or brother and sister embrace, they do not have the sex-feeling. It is a sort of habitual conversion operated in the passage from the emotional to the physical and, being a habit only, though a strong one, can be changed.

It [touch] is vital-physical. All sex movement has a vital element in it, but the mere vital movement is not directly interested in touching or the sex-act. It is interested more in the play of the emotions, domination and subjection, quarrels, reconciliations, the interchange of vital forces etc. It is a vital-physical consciousness that gives so much importance to the touch, embrace, sex-act etc.

Avoidance of touch is best so long as there is the sex-response to touch on either side. At a higher stage, it is indifferent to touch or not to touch. What it will be in the supramental culmination, let the supramental decide.

Touch may be neutral or it may imply interchange of forces. When the interchange is that of spiritual or spiritualised forces, then it has its meaning and it is that that will justify it in the supramental realisation. But till then, it is better to be circumspect.

In ordinary society people touch each other more or less freely according to the manners of the society. That is quite a different matter because there the sex-impulse is allowed within certain more or less wide or narrow limits and even the secret indulgence is common, although people try to avoid discovery. In Bengal when there is purdah, touching between men and women is confined to the family, in Europe there is not such restriction so long as there is no excessive familiarity or indecency; but in Europe sex is now practically free. Here all sex-indulgence inner or outer is considered undesirable as an obstacle to the sadhana — as it very evidently is. For that reason any excessive familiarity of touch between men and women has to be avoided, anything also in the nature of caressing, as it creates or tends to create sex-tendency or even the strong sex-impulse. Casual touching has to be avoided also if it actually creates the sex-impulse. These are commonsense rules if the premiss is granted that sex has not to have any indulgence.

Nature in the material world started with the physical sex-pull for her purpose of procreation and brought in the love on the basis of sex-pull, so the one has a tendency to wake the other. It is only by a strong discipline or a strong will or a change of consciousness that one can eliminate the pull.

It is not that it is not possible to keep the love pure [of sex-desire], but the two things are so near each other and have been so much twined together in the animal beginnings of the race that it is not easy to keep them altogether separate. In the pure psychic love there is no trace of the sex-desire, but usually the vital affection gets very strongly associated with the psychic which is then mixed though still not sexual; but the vital affection and the vital physical sex-emotion are extremely close to each other, so that at any moment or in any given case one may awake the other. This becomes very strong when the sex-force is strong in an individual as it is in most vitally energetic people. To increase always the force of the psychic, to control the sex-impulse and turn it into *ojas*, to turn the love towards the Divine are the true remedies for this difficulty. Seminal force not sexually spent can always be turned into *ojas*.

When the psychic puts its influence on the vital, the first thing you must be careful to avoid is any least mixture of a wrong vital movement with the psychic movement. Lust is the perversion or degradation which prevents love from establishing its reign; so when there is the movement of psychic love in the heart, lust or vital desire is the one thing that must not be allowed to come in — just as when strength comes down from above, personal ambition and pride have to be kept far away from it; for any mixture of the perversion will corrupt the psychic or spiritual action and prevent a true fulfilment.

What is this idea that this desire of the heart hungering to love women is not sex-desire ? That and the physical lust are both forms of sex-desire.

Why hanker when it is a vital desire? It is a form of sex and usually calls up a more physical desire.

The sex-push is not merely the impulse to the act, as X perhaps thinks, as the push to envelop and occupy the man and to possess and be possessed. That is so especially with women, the sex-act being very often less attractive to them than to men; but of course always, if the vital physical reaches a certain point, the physical sex-movement tends to follow.

Sex-sensation may begin anywhere. As vital love it begins in the vital centre, heart or navel — many romantic boys have this and it starts a love affair (often at the age of 10 or even 8) before they know anything about sex-connection. With others it begins with the nerves or with that and the sex-organ itself. There are others who do not have it. Many girls would not have it at all throughout life if they were not taught and excited by men. Some even then hate it and tolerate only under a sort of social compulsion or for the sake of having children.

There are a number of women who can love with the mind, the psychic, the vital (heart), but they shrink from a touch on the body and even when that goes, the physical act remains abhorrent to them. They may yield under pressure, but it does not reconcile them to the act which always seems to them animal and degrading. Women know this, but men seem to find it hard to believe; but it is perfectly true.

Abnormal is a word which you can stick on anything that is not quite cheap and ordinary. In that way genius is abnormal, so is spirituality, so is the attempt to live by high ideals. The tendency to physical chastity in women is not abnormal, it is fairly common and includes a very high feminine type.

The mind is the seat of thought and perception, the heart is the seat of love, the vital of desire — but how does that prevent the existence of mental love? As the mind can be invaded by the feelings of the emotional or the vital, so the heart too can be dominated by the mind and moved by mental forces.

There is a vital love, a physical love. It is possible for the vital to desire a woman for various vital reasons without love — in order to satisfy the instinct of domination or possession, in order to draw in the vital forces of a woman so as to feed one's own vital, for the exchange of vital forces, to satisfy vanity, the hunter's instinct of the chase, etc., etc. (This is from man's viewpoint — but the woman also has her vital motives.) This is often called love, but it is only vital desire, a kind of lust. If, however, the emotions of the heart are awakened, then it becomes vital love — a mixed affair with any or all of these vital motives, strong, but still vital love.

There may too be a physical love, the attraction of beauty, the physical sex-appeal or anything else of the kind awakening the emotions of the heart. If that does not happen, then the physical need is all and that is sheer lust, nothing more; but physical love is possible.

In the same way there can be a mental love. It arises from the attempt to find one's ideal in another or from some strong mental passion of admiration and wonder or from the mind's seeking for a comrade, a complement and fulfiller of one's nature, a *sahadharmī*, a guide and helper, a leader and master or from a hundred other mental motives. By itself that does not amount to love, though often it is so ardent as to be hardly distinguishable from it and may even push to sacrifice of life, entire self-giving, etc., etc. But when it awakes the emotions of the heart, then it may lead to a very powerful love which is yet mental in its root and dominant character. Ordinarily, however, it is the mind and vital together which combine; but this combination can exist along with a disinclination or positive dislike for the physical act and its accompaniments. No doubt, if the man presses, the woman is likely to yield, but it is *à contre-cœur*, as they say, against her feelings and their deepest instincts.

It is an ignorant psychology that reduces everything to the sex-motive and the sex-impulse.

Doctors advise marriage because they think satisfaction of the sexual instinct is necessary for the health and repression causes disturbances in the system. This is true only when there is no true giving up of the sexual indulgence, but only a change in the way of indulging it. Nowadays a new theory has come up which confirms the Indian theory of Brahmacharya, viz. that by continence *retas* can be changed into *ojas* and the vigour and the power of the being enormously increase.

As for what you say about the stimulus of the vital inter-change, it is true of the vital life. Men are constantly spending the vital energy and need to renew it; one way to do it is by pulling from others in a vital interchange. This however is not necessary if one knows how to draw from the universal Nature or from the Divine, i.e. from above. Moreover when the psychic is active — there is always more lost than gained by the vital interchange.

Celibacy means first "not marrying" — it can be extended to not having sexual (physical) relations with any women, though that is not its proper meaning. It is not equivalent to Brahma-charya. Brahmacharya is not binding in Bhaktimarga or Karma-yoga, but it is necessary for ascetic Jnanayoga as well as for Raja and Hatha yogas. It is also not demanded from *gṛhastha* yogis. In this yoga the position is that one must overcome sex, otherwise there can be no transformation of the lower vital and physical nature. All physical sexual connection should cease, otherwise one exposes oneself to serious dangers. The sex-push must also be overcome but it is not a fact that there can be no sadhana or no experience before it is entirely overcome, only without that conquest one cannot go to the end and it must be clearly recognised as one of the more serious obstacles and indulgence of it as a cause of considerable disturbance.

Celibacy is one thing and freedom from sex-pushes is another. These have to be conquered and got rid of, but if freedom from them were made a test of fitness to go on, I wonder how many could be declared fit for my yoga. The will to conquer must be there, but the elimination of the sex-impulse is one of the most difficult things for human nature, and if it takes time, that is only natural.

As to the question of marriage in general, we do not consider it advisable for one who desires to come to the spiritual life. Marriage means usually any amount of trouble, heavy burdens, a bondage to the worldly life and great difficulties in the way of single-minded spiritual endeavour. Its only natural purpose would be, if the sexual trend was impossible to conquer, to give it a restricted and controlled satisfaction. I do not see in what way it could help you to keep the mind under control and subjugation; a restless mind can only be quieted from within.

About your concentration, if you are accustomed to do it between the eyebrows and find it helpful, you can continue that ordinarily, but try from time to time the concentration in the heart centre (middle of the chest) and see if it succeeds with you.

It is not right once you have turned to the Divine, to allow despondency of any kind to take hold of you. Whatever the difficulties and troubles, you must keep this confidence that by relying on the Divine, the Divine will take you through. Now I answer the questions you put to me in your letter.

1. If to follow the spiritual path is your resolve, marriage and family life can only come across it. Marriage would be

the right thing only if the sexual push was so strong that there was no hope of overcoming it except by a controlled and rational indulgence for some time during which it could be slowly brought under subjection to the will. But you say its hold on you is diminishing, so that does not seem indispensable.

2. As for leaving all and coming away from there that must be only when there is a clear and settled decision within you. To do so on an impulse would be to feel all the pull of old things after you come here and entail severe disturbance and struggle in the sadhana. When the other things fall away or are cut away from you then it can be done. Persist in your aspiration, insist on your vital to have faith and be more quiet. It will come.

You are right in feeling that the protection and grace are always there and that all has been for the best. In your wife's condition, the best was that she should change her body and she has been able to do so in the state of mind which would give her the happiest conditions both after death and for a renewal hereafter of the spiritual development for which she had begun to aspire. It is good also that you have been able to keep your poise and the freedom of your spirit in this occurrence.

Again, you are entirely right in your resolution not to marry again; to do so would be in any case to invite serious and probably insuperable difficulties in your following the path of yoga, and, as in this path of yoga it is necessary to put away sexual desire, marriage would be not only meaningless but an absolute contradiction of your spiritual life. You can expect full support and protection from us in your resolve and, if you keep a sincere will and resolution in this matter, you may be sure that the Divine Grace will not fail you.

If she consents to marry, that would be the best. All these vital disturbances proceed from suppressed sex-instinct, suppressed but not rejected and overcome.

A mental acceptance or enthusiasm for the sadhana is not a sufficient guarantee nor sufficient ground for calling people, especially young people, to begin it. Afterwards these vital instincts rise up and there is nothing sufficient to balance or prevail against them, — only mental ideas which do not prevail against the instincts, but on the other hand, also stand in the way of the natural social means of satisfaction. If she marries now and gets experience of the human vital life, then thereafter there may be a chance of her mental aspiration for sadhana turning into the real thing.

I think not. It [inhibition] would not be permanently effective in itself, because the seed would always be there unless removed by a transformation of the sex-impulse; but the inhibition can help towards this transformation. It is now being recognised in Europe by the doctors — who used formerly to say that sex was to be inhibited at the risk of complications in the body, that on the contrary there is part of the seminal force that is used for health, strength, youth etc. (turned into *ojas*, as yogins say), another that serves for sex-purposes, — if a man is perfectly chaste, the latter turns more and more into the former. Only of course the external inhibition does not help this change, if the mind indulges in sex-thought or the vital or body in the unsatisfied sex-desire or sex-sensation. But if all these are stopped then the inhibition is useful.

As for the other point, the right attitude is neither to worry always about the sex-weakness and be obsessed by its importance so as to be in constant struggle and depression over it, nor to be too careless so as to allow it to grow. It is perhaps the most difficult of all to get rid of entirely; one has to recognise quietly its importance and its difficulty and go quietly and steadily about the control of it. If some reactions of a slight character remain, it is not a thing to get disturbed about — only it must not be permitted to increase so as to disturb the sadhana or get too strong for the restraining will of the mental and higher vital being.

To think too much of sex even for suppressing it makes it worse. You have to open more to positive experience. To spend all the time struggling with the lower vital is a very slow method.

As to sexual impulse. Regard it not as something sinful and horrible and attractive at the same time, but as a mistake and wrong movement of the lower nature. Reject it entirely, not by struggling with it, but by drawing back from it, detaching yourself and refusing your consent; look at it as something not your own, but imposed on you by a force of Nature outside you. Refuse all consent to the imposition. If anything in your vital consents, insist on that part of you withdrawing its consent. Call in the Divine Force to help you in your withdrawal and refusal. If you can do this quietly and resolutely and patiently, in the end your inner will will prevail against the habit of the outer Nature.

The small tendencies, rajasic-vital, which you enumerate are of minor importance. They have to be removed in this sense that attachment to these things has to be given up; the vital part of the being must be prepared to consent to their absence with quietude and indifference, taking them only if they are given freely by the Divine without demand or claim or clinging, but there is nothing very serious about them otherwise.

The one serious matter is the sex-tendency. That must be overcome. But it will be more easily overcome if instead of being upset by its presence you detach the inner being from it, rise up above it and view it as a weakness of the lower nature. If you can detach yourself from it with a complete indifference in the inner being, it will seem more and more something alien to yourself, put upon you by the outer forces of Nature. Then it will be easier to remove.

The trouble of the sex-impulse is bound to dwindle away if you are in earnest about getting rid of it. The difficulty is that part of your nature (especially, the lower vital and the subconscient which is active in sleep) keeps the memory and attachment to these movements, and you do not open these parts and make them accept the Mother's Light and Force to purify them. If you did that and, instead of lamenting and getting troubled and clinging to the idea that you cannot get rid of these things, insisted quietly with a calm faith and patient resolution on their disappearance, separating yourself from them, refusing to accept them or at all regard them as part of yourself, they would after a time lose their force and dwindle.

Your difficulty in getting rid of the aboriginal in your nature will remain so long as you try to change your vital part by the sole or main strength of your mind and mental will, calling in at most an indefinite and impersonal divine power to aid you. It is an old difficulty which has never been radically solved in life itself because it has never been met in the true way. In many ways of yoga it does not so supremely matter because the aim is not a transformed life but withdrawal from life. When that is the object of an endeavour, it may be sufficient to keep the vital down by a mental and moral compulsion, or else it may be stilled and kept lying in a kind of sleep and quiescence. There are some even who allow it to run and exhaust itself if it can while its possessor professes to be untouched and unconcerned by it; for it is only old Nature running on by a past impetus and will drop off with the fall of the body. When none of these solutions can be attained, the sadhak sometimes simply leads a double inner life, divided between his spiritual experiences and his vital weaknesses to the end, making the most of his better part, making as little as may be of the outer being. But none of these methods will do for our purpose. If you want a true mastery and transformation of the vital movements, it can be done only on condition you allow your psychic being, the soul in you, to awake fully, to establish its rule and opening all to the permanent touch of the Divine Shakti, impose its own way of pure devotion, whole-hearted aspiration and complete uncompromising urge to all that is divine on the mind and heart and vital nature. There is no other way and it is no use hankering after a more comfortable path. *Nānyaḥ panthā vidyate'yanāya*

It is the reason why the vital sex-difficulty is the hardest to get rid of — even those who have sincerely given up the more physical form are liable to the vital form of the impulse. But it is harmful because it allows a subtle infiltration of the forces that stand in the way of the sadhana. One must get rid of them if the vital is to become entirely pure and able to contain the divine love and Ananda.

In the vital physical the "response" lingers long after the mind and higher vital have turned from it. I have seen that in men who were mentally and emotionally quite sincere. A few get rid of it easily, but these are a small minority. But there must be no justification on the "what harm" basis — that is an attempt of the lower vital to get the mind and higher vital to adhere. There is always room for harm so long as the sex-response is not eliminated in *both*, not in you only.

The sexual urge is something that tries to take complete hold and leave no room for inhibition or control. It has a power of temporary possession which no other passion or life-impulse has to the same degree, more even than anger which comes second to it. That is why it is so difficult to get rid of it — because even when the mind or higher vital refuses, the vital physical feels this possessive force and has an ingrained tendency to be passive to its urge.

Coming inside [of sex] means taking hold of you so that there is a push for satisfaction. Pressure from outside however strongly felt is not coming inside.

The sex-trouble is serious only so long as it can get the consent of the mind and the vital will. If it is driven from the mind, that is, if the mind refuses its consent, but the vital part responds to it, it comes as a large wave of vital desire and tries to sweep the mind away by force along with it. If it is driven also from the higher vital, from the heart and the dynamic possessive life-force, it takes refuge in the lower vital and comes in the shape of smaller suggestions and urges there. Driven from the lower vital level, it goes down into the obscure inertly repetitive physical and comes as sensations in the sex-centre and a mechanical res-ponse to suggestion. Driven from there too, it goes down into the subconscient and comes up as dreams and night-emissions even without dreams. But to wherever it recedes, it tries still for a time from that base or refuge to trouble and recapture the assent of the higher parts, until the victory is complete and it is driven even out of the surrounding or environmental consciousness which is the extension of ourselves into the general or universal Nature.

Is it that the body does not accept the sex-thoughts and desires? If so, you are entitled to reject it as something external to you or at most existing only in the subconscient. For it is only what something in us accepts, supports, takes pleasure in, or still mechanically responds to, that can still be called ours. If there is nothing of that, it belongs to general Nature but not to us. Of course, it returns and tries to take possession of its lost terri-tory, but that is a foreign invasion. The rule of these things is that they have to be extruded outside the individual conscious-ness. Rejected by the mind and higher vital, they still try to hold on to the lower vital and physical. Rejected from the lower vital, they still hold the body by a physical desire. Rejected from the body, they retire into the environmental consciousness (sometimes into the subconscient also, rising in dreams) — I mean by the environmental a sort of surrounding atmosphere which we carry about with us and by which we communicate with the universal forces — and try to invade from there. Rejected from there, they become in the end too weak to be more than external suggestions till that too ends — and they are finished and non-existent.

The sex-impulse is the chief difficulty in your way. If it persists, it is because some part of your being still clings to it and your mind and will have remained divided and found some kind of half-justification for the continuance. The first thing is for the mind and also the higher vital to withdraw their consent altogether; if that is done, it becomes only a mechanical return from outside on the physical and finally only an active memory which will disappear when it is able to find no welcome in any part of the nature.

It is only if the whole consciousness is awake and aware of its concealed movements that such sex-reactions can be avoided. It does not mean that you are worse than others but that in all men the sexual element is there, active or dormant, indulged or suppressed. It can only be overcome by a spiritual awakening in *all* parts of the nature.

The sex-impulse is deeply rooted in the subconscient and it is difficult to get rid of it. Only the full transformation of the physical consciousness can do that — except for a few who are not strongly bound by it.

It is of course the physical that is at once responsive in the most material way to sex-suggestions. What you are doing is right. As you are controlling it in the waking state, it comes out at night. That too has to be got rid of.

Persist in concentrating in the heart and remaining unmoved by the obstacles. The suggestions must *never* be accepted — for acceptance gives them the right to return or continue. If there is no sex-response in the mind or vital and the sensation in the organic centre is isolated and without any support in the being, then it can be separately overcome. Therefore, there must be no mental assent or vital response — that is the first necessary step.

Sex is strongly connected with the physical centre but also with the lower vital — it is the lower vital that gives it most of its intensities and excitement. It can be disconnected from the lower vital and then it becomes a purely physical movement of the mechanical kind which has no great force except for the mechanical natures. If the physical centre is also freed then the sex-impulse ceases.

Of course, it is the vital that gives it [the play of sex] its intensity and power to hold the consciousness.

It is the physical centre — sex is only one of its movements. Naturally, if the sex is active (instead of giving place to Beauty and Ananda) and if the lower movements are active, it forms an obstacle to the establishment of the higher consciousness. But the higher can descend, if there is at all an opening, even before the lower movements have definitely gone — it has then to complete the work of displacing them.

Pranayama and other physical practices like Asana do not necessarily root out sexual desire — sometimes by increasing enormously the vital force in the body they can even exaggerate in a rather startling way the force too of the sexual tendency, which, being at the base of the physical life, is always difficult to conquer. The one thing to do is to separate oneself from these movements, to find one's inner self and live in it; these movements will not then any longer appear as belonging to oneself but as surface impositions of the outer Prakriti upon the inner self or Purusha. They can then be more easily discarded or brought to nothing.

Hurting the flesh is no remedy for the sex-impulse, though it may be a temporary diversion. It is the vital and mostly the vital-physical that takes the sense-perception as pleasure or otherwise.

Reduction of diet has not usually a permanent effect. It may give a greater sense of physical or vital-physical purity, lighten the system and reduce certain kinds of *tamas*. But the sex-impulse can very well accommodate itself to a reduced diet. It is not by physical means but by a change in the consciousness that these things can be surmounted.

What seems to be best is that the movement of rising above should be completed and if you can feel there the wideness, peace, calm, silence of the Self and that can come down into the body through all the centres and there can be the working of the Force in that condition of the physical being, then the vital-physical difficulty can be faced. The effort to do it by personal tapasya can carry one to a certain point, it can throw out sex etc., but for most it does not prevent all coming back by attack — unless the force of tapasya is so great and continuous that these forces get no chance. But the elimination of these things can only come, I think, by the descent of the higher consciousness — bringing it the self-existent calm and wideness, the higher force and the Ananda occupying all down to the cells of the body. It is quite certain that these three together in the body can leave no room for sex — even if sex came, it would at once get so transmuted that it would be sex no longer.

If it [the peace and silence] is established *all through*, then it brings purity and the purity throws off the sexual suggestions.

There is a force of purity, not the purity of the moralist, but an essential purity of spirit, in the very substance of the being. When that comes, then sex-waves either cannot approach or they pass without imparting any impulse, without touching anywhere.

Necessarily, you must give up the perverse habit which is one of the main causes of your despondency, vital weakness, etc. There is nothing that has more power to derange and weaken the system. If not only in your mind but in your vital also you had made the resolution to give it up, it would have disappeared long ago.

There is one way by which it is possible for you to get rid of the perverse habit: to establish a strong mental control and so get rid of the wrong movement. It is not true that it is unconquerable; on the contrary, the fact that you were able to interrupt it for some time shows that you can conquer it. It returned because these things are a movement of certain universal life-forces that, once allowed a habitual wrong response in the individual system, tend to continue in that form and, even if evicted, try always to recur. Your mind has rejected them, but something in your vital nature — the part that responds directly to the universal life-forces — still takes pleasure and has preserved the capacity and desire of the wrong response. A resolute and persistent

effort of will can enforce in the end the rejection of the desire
and finally even of any mechanical habit of the movement upon
this part of the nature also. Only you must not be discouraged
by relapses; your will must be more persevering than the habit
and persist till there is a complete conquest.

It is the entire inner rejection of the sex-pulls and vital pulls
that is necessary, a rejection by the whole lower vital itself —
the outer rejection can only be effective if this inner rejection
comes to reinforce it. Usually people attempt the outer rejection
because otherwise (if these things are indulged) the inner rejection is not likely to come since the vital trend is always being
confirmed by the outer action — but if the outer is rejected, then
the conflict is confined to the internal desire and fought out
there. Naturally an outer renunciation by itself does not liberate.

Of course one must be able to come in contact with women
without feeling or thinking about sex; but to seek contact and
test is not the way, it can too easily turn the other side when the
mastery is not complete. The feeling and conquering must be
an inner process — the Tantric outer method is not indicated.

All that happens because the vital is conscious of sex in the
approach and immediately assumes the "man to woman" attitude. To get rid of that, one must be able to look on the woman
and feel to her as to a human being only. That is difficult and
needs a certain training; for even if the mind is able to take the
position, the vital is unreliable and one has to be on guard that
it does not suddenly or surreptitiously get in into the relation with
its partiality for the sex-interchange.

*
**

You had better get rid of the influence. It won't do not to be able to look at a woman or a picture of a woman without getting sexual sensations — you must get rid of that.

If one admires all beautiful things, not women only, without desire — then there would be no harm. But specially applied to women, it is a relic of the "sex-appeal".

Strength and purity in the lower vital and wideness in the heart are the best condition for meeting others, especially women, and if that could always be there sex could hardly have a look in.

It usually happens that when actual indulgence of the vital [in sex] is given up (external exchange, touch or contact), imagination still goes on. But if this can be overcome, then the whole thing is overcome. External indulgence on the other hand keeps the activity alive. This is the *raison d'être* of the external avoidance. If anything can be got rid of without the necessity of avoidance, so much the better.

Care must be taken that the sexual or erotic imagination does not take hold of the consciousness representing itself as spiritual truth.

By giving up contact it [sex] can be reduced to two forms — dream and imagination. Dream is not of much importance unless it affects the waking mind which it need not at all do; it can besides be discouraged and, if not fed, fades out in the end. Imaginations can only be got rid of by a tapasya of the will not allowing them to run their course, but breaking them off as soon as they begin. They come most easily when lying in bed after waking from sleep in a tamasic condition. One has to break them off either by shaking off the tamas or by emptying the mind and going to sleep again. At other times one ought to be able to stop it by turning the mind elsewhere.

It is the most dangerous movement for sex-things when just after waking one remains lying in bed; one should either go to sleep again, if there is time, or else fix the mind on wholesome things.

That is a right change. There is no condition more dangerous for the sex-imagination to come than this lying in bed in a half-awake or else a relaxed inert condition unoccupied by any activity or any experience.

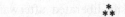

Inactivity is an atmosphere in which sex easily rises.

That is the difficulty. The imagination means a consent of the physical or else the vital mind. Otherwise the [sex] sensation is often only due to physical causes and, if not supported by this automatic assent of a part of the mind, would before long diminish in its habit of recurrence.

There is no reason for you to be depressed or discouraged. The defects of the nature of which you speak are habits of the lower vital and the external being; if you recognise them fully and frankly and detect them and reject whenever they act or try to act upon you, they will in time disappear. The sexual desires show that the subconscient still retains the old impressions, movements and impulses; make the conscious parts of the being entirely free and aspire and will for the higher consciousness to come fully into the subconscient so that even in sleep and dream something in you may be aware and on guard and reject these things when they try to take form at that time.

Naturally, if you read about these things [concerning sex] they enter the mind and pass into the subconscient where they leave their impression. If the consciousness is not free from the sexual impulse, this impression can rise up from the subconscient and work in the mind.

I have already told you not to get upset over these dreams and accidents of sleep. They come from outside yourself and something replies from the subconscient which keeps for a long time all that the conscious being rejects. It is only in the later stages of the yoga that this subconscient part can be made conscious and liberated. It is the waking consciousness that you must keep free from sexual acts and sexual suggestions. If you do that, the subconscient part can be easily liberated afterwards.

Night-dreams are involuntary upsurgings of the sex-impressions from the subconscient; most, even when they are not indulging in the sex-act, have it from time to time though it varies in period from a week, a fortnight, a month to three or four months or even less. To have it more frequently indicates either indulgence in sex-imaginations which stimulate the sex-centre or else a nervous weakness in that part due to past indulgence. Some have benefited by putting a will on the body before going to sleep at night that these dreams should not happen — though it may not succeed at the beginning, it tells in most cases after a time by fixing a certain inhibitory force on the subconscient from which these dreams arise. As to children indulging, that is not hereditary, but a thing taught by bad company and these children are sometimes spoiled in this way at a very early age.

It is a mistake to make so much of emissions — everybody has them. The subconscient has its own movement and the want of control there is a thing one can get rid of only when there is the full light down there. At most one can deal with this special factor by putting a will into the subconscient (in the sex-centre or the organ itself) for prohibition, so that even in the subconscient during sleep there may be something that reacts. Many have been able to diminish and almost get rid of the recurrence by this means, but others have succeeded less well. In one case there was a recurrence every fortnight and that stood in spite of the will.... As for the waking difficulty do not make too much of it. Press on with the positive side of the sadhana towards realisation — these things will fade and disappear when the higher consciousness is down in the sex-centre. Meanwhile it has first to be controlled and got rid of as much as possible.

There is no reason to be depressed to this extent or to have these imaginations about failure in the yoga. It is not at all a sign that you are unfit for the yoga. It simply means that the sexual impulse rejected by the conscious parts has taken refuge in the subconscient, somewhere probably in the lower vital-physical and the most physical consciousness where there are some regions not yet open to the aspiration and the light. The persistence in sleep of things rejected in the waking consciousness is a quite common occurrence in the course of the sadhana.

The remedy is:

(1) to get the higher consciousness, its light and the workings of its power down into the obscurer parts of the nature,

(2) to become progressively more conscious in sleep, with an

inner consciousness which is aware of the working of the sadhána in sleep as in waking,

(3) to bring to bear the waking will and aspiration on the body in sleep.

One way to do the last is to make a strong and conscious suggestion to the body, before sleeping, that the thing should not happen; the more concrete and physical the suggestion can be made and the more directly on the sexual centre, the better. The effect may not be quite immediate at first or invariable; but usually this kind of suggestion, if you know how to make it, prevails in the end: even when it does not prevent the dream, it very often awakes the consciousness within in time to prevent untoward consequences.

It is a mistake to allow yourself to be depressed in the sadhana even by repeated failures. One must be calm, persistent and more obstinate than the resistance.

When the waking consciousness has renounced the indulgence of the sexual desires and impulses, these take refuge in the sub-conscient as impressions, memories, suppressed desires and come up in sleep as dreams and involuntary sleep emissions. If the waking consciousness is not itself clear, if, that is to say, though there is no physical indulgence, yet there are imaginations in the mind or desires in the vital or the body, then these dreams and emissions can be frequent. Even if the waking consciousness is clear, the subconscient emergences can still come for a time, but in time they diminish. Some are able to get rid of this by putting a strong prohibiting will or force on the subconscient or on the sex-centre before going to sleep, but this does not succeed with everyone. The main thing is to get the increasing force of *brahmacarya* in the waking consciousness, complete expulsion of sex-thoughts, speech, physical craving or impulse — the subconscient remnants will either die out or be cleared out afterwards when one is able to bring the higher consciousness down here.

In order that the dream emissions may diminish or cease, it is necessary first to have complete Brahmacharya, *kāyamano-vākyena* — not only to banish sexuality from the bodily action, but also sexual impulses from the vital and body consciousness and sexual thoughts and imaginations from the mind and speech and not talk about sexual things. The dreams arise from the subconscient where all impressions and instincts are stored up and any of these things stimulates the subconscient and increases its store which can well up in dreams. If one makes the waking consciousness entirely pure, then by putting a will or force on the subconscient (especially before going to sleep) one can after a time eliminate the sex-dreams and emissions.

Apart from the total rejection of sex-thoughts and imaginations and actions, which ends by acting in the subconscient also, I don't know any remedy for sex-dreams except the putting of a force as concrete as possible on the sex-centre and organ prohibiting this urge and its result, put when about to sleep and renewed each time one wakes and goes to sleep again. But this all cannot manage to use, for they employ a mental will instead of a concrete force (the mental will can be effective, but is not always so). This method, besides, only acts for the time, it inhibits but except in rare cases does not permanently cure; it does not get rid of the sex-impressions in the subconscient, and of course it means thinking of the sex-affair though only negatively.

I have heard it said that even very advanced yogis get the dreams at least once in six months — I don't know how far it is true or what the yogis themselves say about it. But the sex-impressions in the heart can be got rid of long before the end of life, and even the seed state in the subconscient which comes up in dreams, though sticky enough, is not quite so irremovable as all that.

Anyway, the dream-kind is not so much to trouble about, unless it is frequent — it is the waking state that must be rigorously cleared out. Sometimes, if that is done, there is automatic extension of the habit of rejection to the subconscient, so that when the dream is coming there is an automatic prohibition that stops it. Under a regime like that I think the sex-pressure would become, if not non-existent, yet permanently quiescent in its seed state and so practically *non est*.

The first thing necessary in such matters is to be perfectly calm and refuse to be upset by these difficulties. If they rise, one must take it that they do so in order to be worked out. If there is nothing in the waking consciousness to encourage the sex-difficulty, then these dreams or discharges without dreams can only be a rising up of old dormant impressions in the subconscient. Such risings often take place when the Force is working in the subconscient to clear it. It is also just possible that the discharges may be due, especially where there are no dreams, to purely material causes, e.g., the pressure of undischarged urine or faecal matter near the bladder. But in any case, the thing is not to be disturbed and to put a force or will on the sex-centre or sex-organ for these things to cease. This can be done just before sleeping. Usually after a time, if done regularly, it has an effect. A calm general pressure of will or force on the physical subconscient is to be put. The subconscient may be often obstinate in its continual persistence, but it can and does accommodate itself quickly or slowly to the will of the conscious being.

Your dreams were mostly on the vital-physical plane. There if there is any physical contact of a sexual or other kind that acts strongly on the sexual centre or on a sensory contact — it may even without raising any lust produce an emission by a mechanical blind and unconscious action of the purely physical (not even vital-physical) kind. It is only when the sex-centre has become strong that this becomes impossible.

If it [the sex-emission] were normal why should it depress and weaken the system so much? People always complain of this enfeeblement and if it happens often get seriously depressed and tamasic. It is not necessary of course that it should be so, for if one reacts one can prevent the depression or weakness, but most feel it. It is of course normal in the sense that it happens when one has discontinued sex-activity without getting free of the sex-imagination or impulse or even afterwards when one is no longer troubled by sex it may continue for some time due to ineradicated impressions in the subconscient. It may sometimes relieve of an excess of secretion, but the result of weakness seems to indicate more often a loss of necessary vigour-stuff. The proper way of dealing with excess, is to turn the excess into pure energy-stuff, *retas* into *ojas*.

It is obviously an attack which falls upon your nervous system through the subconscient. It comes in sleep because in the waking consciousness you are more on your guard and able to react against attacks. Usually this kind of dream and discharge come when the physical consciousness is in a tamasic condition through fatigue or strain or any other cause, in a heavy sleep or under a stress of inertia.

The first thing to do is to reject the after consequences as you have done this time — for you say you do not feel any weakness, but rather as if nothing had happened. It is not at all inevitable that one should feel weakness after a dream of this kind and a discharge; it is only by a habitual association in the physical mind that these forces can bring these reactions of nervous weakness.

As for preventing the discharge, it can be done by becoming more conscious in sleep. You were conscious of all that happened, but you must besides develop the power of a conscious will which sees what is going to happen and interferes to prevent it, either by waking in time or by stopping the dream or prohibiting the discharge. All this is perfectly possible, it is a matter of habit and a little persistence.

It is also often found very effective to put a will or force upon the body consciousness before going to sleep that it shall not happen — especially when you feel the predisposing condition of heaviness and inertia, it should be done. This will is not always immediately successful, but after a time the subconscient gets the habit of responding to the will or force thus laid upon it and the trouble dwindles and finally disappears altogether.

This kind of sexual attack through sleep does not depend very much on food or anything else that is outward. It is a mechanical habit in the subconscient; when the sexual impulse is rejected or barred out in the waking thoughts and feelings, it comes in this form in sleep, for then there is only the subconscient at work and there is no conscious control. It is a sign of sexual desire suppressed in the waking mind and vital, but not eliminated in the stuff of the physical nature.

To eliminate it one must first be careful to harbour no sexual imagination or feeling in the waking state, next, to put a strong will on the body and especially on the sexual centre that there should be nothing of the kind in sleep. This may not succeed at once, but if persevered in for a long time, it usually has a result; the subconscient begins to obey.

The pressure from the kidneys or the intestines bringing dream of sex-tendency or imagination is the last and most physical form — it often remains when the others have gone. The body dull and the mind half awake is indeed what gives it its opportunity. But if it is only for a few minutes and leaves no after effect, then the tendency ought to disappear after a time.

Attacks [of sex-forces] can come in the daylight or in night, so they can come in electric light also. It is only the inner light that discourages attacks though it may not entirely prevent them unless there is the Force also.

Yes, of course, skin diseases have much to do with sexual desires — not of course always, but often.

I suppose it [pimples on the face] is often the result of suppressed sexuality — suppressed in act but still internally active. These things do not act in the same way with all, with some it may act on the blood, with some it may not or else not in the same form. Moreover I do not suppose that sex is the only cause of pimples on the face — there are other things also that can give that.

IX

Control of speech is very necessary for the physical change.

Mauna is seldom of much use. After it is over, the speech starts again as in the old times. It is in speech itself that the speech must change.

That is not the way. Absolute silence and looseness of talk are two extremes; neither is good. I have seen many people practising *maunavrata*, but afterwards they are just as talkative as before. It is self-mastery you must get.

On the whole you are right. Useless conversation which lowers the consciousness or brings back something of a past consciousness is better avoided. Talking about sadhana also comes under the category when it is merely mental discussion of a superficial kind.

It is something very external that takes pleasure in light talk, and it is only when the quietude and with it a certain spontaneous self-control is established in the lower vital nature that this tendency can be entirely conquered in those who have it — i.e. in most people.

All these things will be worked out in time. What is most important is to get down the quietude into all the being and with it the true force bringing the energy which you describe above.

In talking one has the tendency to come down into a lower and more external consciousness because talking comes from the external mind. But it is impossible to avoid it altogether. What you must do is to learn to get back at once to the inner consciousness — this so long as you are not able to speak always from the inner being or at least with the inner being supporting the action.

Talk is more external than writing, depends more on the physical and its condition. Therefore in most cases it is more difficult to get it out of the clutch of the external mind.

Talk — of the usual kind — does very easily disperse or bring down the inner condition because it usually comes out of the lower vital and the physical mind only and expresses that part of the consciousness — it has a tendency to externalise the being. That is of course why so many yogis take refuge in silence.

There are some who have the flow of speech by nature and those who are very vital cannot do without it. But the latter case (not being able to do without it) is obviously a disability from the spiritual point of view. There are also certain stages in the sadhana when one has to go inward and silence is at that time very necessary while unnecessary speech becomes a dispersion of the energies or externalises the consciousness. It is especially this chat for chat's sake tendency that has to be overcome.

Chat of that kind has indeed a very tiring effect when one is at all in the stream of true experience, because it dissipates the energy uselessly and makes the mind movement a thing of value-less shreds and patches instead of gathered and poised in itself so as to receive.

There is always a chance of something light and unbalancing coming in when there is levity indulged in for its own sake. The consciousness feels a little shaken in its seat, if not pulled out. Once the consciousness is well set inside, then the outward movement gets determined from within and there is no such trouble.

Yes. The speech must come from within and be controlled from within.

The difficulty you experience exists because speech is a formation which in the past has worked much more as an expression of the vital in man than of the mental will. Speech breaks out as the expression of the vital and its habits, without caring to wait for the control of the mind; the tongue has been spoken of as the unruly member. In your case the difficulty has been increased by the habit of talk about others, — gossip, to which your vital was very partial, so much that it cannot even yet give up the pleasure in it. It is therefore this tendency that must cease in the vital itself. Not to be under the control of the impulse to speech, to be able to do without it as a necessity and to speak only when one sees that it is right to do so and only what one sees to be right to say, is a very necessary part of yogic self-control.

It is only by perseverance and vigilance and a strong resolution that this can be done, but if the resolution is there, it can be done in a short time by the aid of the Force behind.

It is obvious that things which are a long habit cannot go at once. Especially, speech is a thing which in most people is largely automatic and not under their control. It is the vigilance that establishes the control, so one must be on guard against the danger of which you speak, the slacking of the vigilance. Only, the more it can be a quiet and unmixed, not an anxious vigilance, the better.

The habits of the physical or the vital-physical nature are always the most difficult to change, because their action is automatic and not governed by the mental will and it is therefore difficult for the mental will to control or transform them. You have to persevere and form the habit of control. If you can succeed in controlling the speech often, — it needs a constant vigilance, — you will finally find that the control stamps itself and can in the long run always intervene. This must be done so long as that movement is not fully opened to the Mother's Light and Force, for if that happens the thing can be done more quickly and sometimes with a great rapidity. There is also the intervention of the psychic, — if the psychic being is sufficiently awake and active to intervene each time you are going to speak at random and say "No", then the change becomes more easy.

The headache and the fatigue is always a sign that the consciousness no longer wants this outward-going thought and speech and is even physically strained by it. But it is the subconscient habit that wants to continue. Mostly human speech and thought go on mechanically in certain grooves that always repeat themselves and it is not really the mind that controls or dictates them. That is why this habit can go on for some time even after the conscious mind has withdrawn its support and consent and resolved to do otherwise. But if one perseveres, this subconscious mechanical habit runs down like all machinery that is not kept wound up to go on again. Then one can form the opposite habit in the subconscient of admitting only what the inner being consents to think or speak.

That happens very usually. Talking of an unnecessary character tires the inner being because the talk comes from the outer nature while the inner has to supply the energy which it feels squandered away.

Even those who have a strong inner life, take a long time before they can connect it with the outer speech and action. Outer speech belongs to the externalising mind — that is why it is so difficult to connect it with the inner life.

Yes, of course, complete truth of speech is very important for the sadhak and a great help for bringing Truth into the consciousness. It is at the same time difficult to bring the speech under control; for people are accustomed to speak what comes to them and not to supervise and control what they say. There is something mechanical about speech and to bring it to the level of the highest part of the consciousness is never easy. That is one reason why to be sparing in speech is helpful. It helps to a more deliberate control and prevents the tongue from running away with one and doing whatever it likes.

To stand back means to become a witness of one's own mind and speech, to see them as something separate from oneself and not identify oneself with them. Watching them as a witness, separate from them, one gets to know what they are, how they act and then put a control over them, reject what one does not approve and think and speak only what one feels to be true. This cannot, of course, be done all at once. It takes time to establish this attitude of separateness, still more time to establish the control. But it can be done by practice and persistence.

It [speech] can only be controlled if you separate yourself from the part that is speaking and are able to observe it. It is the external mind that speaks — one has to watch it from the inner witnessing mind and put a control.

It is really an inner silence that is needed — a something silent within that looks at outer talk and action but feels it as something superficial, not itself and is quite indifferent and untouched by it. It can bring forces to support speech and action or it can stop them by withdrawal or it can let them go on and observe without being involved or moved.

It is of course because the consciousness is thrown out in these things [discussions and laughter] and one comes out of the inner poise and has difficulty in going back to it — especially as there is a sort of dispersion of the vital energy. If one attains to a condition in which one can do these things only with the surface of the consciousness, keeping inside and observing what is done on the surface, but not forgetting oneself in it, then the poise is not lost. But it is a little difficult to get at this duplication of oneself — one comes to it however in time especially if the inner peace and calm become very intense and durable.

*

If the peace is very strong within, talking does not cloud it — because this peace is not mental or vital even when it pervades the mind and vital — or else it is a cloud that quickly passes without touching deeply. Usually however such talk disperses the consciousness and one can lose much. The only disadvantage of not talking is that it isolates too much, if it is absolute, but by not talking these things [news etc.] one loses nothing.

That (thinking over what was talked) is a physical mind habit which should in course of time wear out. The mind should be free to shut off immediately as soon as the talk is done.

Hastiness of speech and action — (in excess, because to a certain extent it exists in everybody) — is a matter of temperament. I do not suppose it is more in you than in many others here. Of course it has to be got rid of, but it is one of the lesser, not one of the major imperfections of nature with which the yogic Force has to deal. It is the externalising mind that has to be disciplined so that it may not leap too soon to conclusions or rush immediately from thought to speech and action.

These discussions are perfectly useless, they only deflect the mind and open the gate to falsehoods.

The psychic self-control that is desirable in these surroundings and in the midst of discussion would mean among other things:

1. Not to allow the impulse of speech to assert itself too much or say anything without reflection, but to speak always with a conscious control and only what is necessary and helpful.

2. To avoid all debate, dispute or too animated discussion

and simply say what has to be said and leave it there. There should also be no insistence that you are right and the others wrong, but what is said should only be thrown in as a contribution to the consideration of the truth of the matter.

3. To keep the tone of speech and the wording very quiet and calm and uninsistent.

4. Not to mind at all if others are heated and dispute, but remain quiet and undisturbed and yourself speak only what can help things to be smooth again.

5. If there is gossip about others and harsh criticism (especially about sadhaks), not to join — for these things are helpful in no way and only lower the consciousness from its higher level.

6. To avoid all that would hurt or wound others.

Harangues and exhortations touch only the surface of the mind. If the mind is in agreement it is pleased and stimulated, but that is all. If it is not in agreement the mind criticises or becomes impatient and turns aside. If the harangue is very forcible it may touch the vital sometimes and produce a momentary effect.

That [preaching to others what one is lacking in oneself] is not hypocrisy but a conflict between two parts of the nature. Hypocrisy comes in only when one preaches a thing one does not believe or deliberately pretends to be or aim at what one is not and has no intention of trying to become.

The depression came into you subconsciously because you had the discussion with X. When you discuss like that with people, you put something in them, but something also comes from them to you. So, as X was not in quite a good condition, though nothing like what he used to be in his depressions, you easily got a touch of it and as soon as the subconscious could find a habitual excuse it sent it up to the mind. You should always be on your guard against these automatic interchanges. A little care is sufficient — and no needless discussion.

In speaking there should be always a sort of instinctive defence — except with those who are free from the ordinary vital impulse.

It is the nervous envelope that is weak — it is this that you saw. The fact that you feel weak when talking with people shows that the origin of the whole trouble is a weakened nervous force. It is this that you have to get strong. You should avoid much talking with others — you can also take rest when you feel the symptoms very strong. But faith, quietude and openness to the higher force are the fundamental cure.

Yes, obviously, the power to say "No" is indispensable in life and still more so in sadhana. It is the power of rejection put into speech.

In all things there must be a control over thought and speech also. But while rajasic violence is excluded, a calmly forceful severity of thought and speech where severity is needed is sometimes indispensable.

The habit of criticism — mostly ignorant criticism of others — mixed with all sorts of imaginations, inferences, exaggerations, false interpretations, even gross inventions is one of the universal illnesses. It is a disease of the vital aided by the physical mind which makes itself an instrument of the pleasure taken in this barren and harmful pursuit of the vital. Control of the speech, refusal of this disease and the itch of the vital is very necessary, if inner experience has to have any true effect of transformation in the outer life.

It is also better to be more strict about not talking of others and criticising them with the ordinary mind. It is necessary in order to develop a deeper consciousness and outlook on things that understands in silence the movements of Nature in oneself and others and is not moved or disturbed or superficially interested and drawn into an external movement.

The sadhaks of this Ashram are not perfect — they have plenty of weaknesses and wrong movements. It is blindness not to be able to see that; only it should not lead to a criticising or condemnatory attitude towards persons — and it should be regarded as the play of forces which have to be overcome.

It is very evident from this inward control which you feel enlightening and guiding you and the resolution of truth-speaking that it made you take, that your psychic being is awake within you.

The fault of character of which you speak is common and almost universal in human nature. The impulse to speak what is untrue or at least to exaggerate or understate or twist the truth so as to flatter one's own vanity, preferences, wishes or to get some advantage or secure something desired is very general. But one must learn to speak the truth alone if one is to succeed truly in changing the nature.

To become conscious of what is to be changed in the nature is the first step towards changing it. But one must observe these things without being despondent or thinking "it is hopeless" or "I cannot change". You do right to be confident that the change will come. For nothing is impossible in the nature if the psychic being is awake and leading you with the Mother's consciousness and force behind it and working in you. This is now happening. Be sure that all will be done.

Useless or not, untruth should be avoided.

If you get the English original[1] from X, you will see that what is written is from the highest standpoint. If you want to be an instrument of the Truth, you must always speak the truth and not falsehood. But this does not mean that you must tell everything to everybody. To conceal the truth by silence or refusal to speak is permissible, because the truth may be misunderstood or misused by those who are not prepared for it or who are opposed to it — it may even be made a starting-point for distortion or sheer falsehood. But to speak falsehood is another matter. Even in jest it should be avoided, because it tends to lower the consciousness. As for the last point, it is again from the highest standpoint — the truth as one knows it in the mind is not enough, for the mind's idea may be erroneous or insufficient — it is necessary to have the true knowledge in the true consciousness.

Why should it be lying? One is not bound to tell everything to everybody — it might often do more harm than good. One has only to say what is necessary. Of course what is said must be true and not false and there must never be any intention to deceive.

---

[1] "If we allow a falsehood, however small, to express itself through our mouth or our pen, how can we hope to become perfect messengers of Truth? A perfect servant of Truth should abstain even from the slightest inexactitude, exaggeration or deformation."

                                                                              The Mother

"As one likes" is never a formula that leads to truth, it implies enthroning the vital and its desire as the standard or following the mind's preferences — which even in any mental discipline is regarded as contrary to the very principle of the search for Truth.

In the first place, there is a great difference between uttering as truth what one believes or knows to be false and uttering as truth what one conscientiously believes to be true, but is not in fact true. The first is obviously going against the spirit of truth, the second does homage to it. The first is deliberate falsehood, the second is only error at worst or ignorance.

This is from the practical point of view of truth-speaking. From the point of view of higher Truth, it must not be forgotten that each plane of consciousness has its own standard — what is truth to the mind, may be only partial truth to a higher consciousness, but it is through the partial truth that the mind has to go in order to reach the wider more perfect truth beyond. All that is necessary for it is to be open and plastic, to be ready to recognise the higher when it comes, not to cling to the lower because it is its own, not to allow the desires and passions of the vital to blind it to the Light or to twist and pervert things. When once the higher consciousness begins to act, the difficulty diminishes and there is a clear progress from truth to greater truth.

It is not the fact that if a man is truthful (in the sense of not lying), all he says happens. For that he must know the Truth — be in touch with the truth of things, not merely speak the truth as his mind knows it.

As for shyness, there are two kinds: one is egoistic, being ashamed of expressing the Truth or showing allegiance to it in ways which would not be understood by others, the other is a certain reserve, an unwillingness to expose one's deeper feelings to the gaze of others, the wish to keep sacred and secret the relations of love with the Divine — that is a psychic feeling.

X

I do not think X's trance has anything to do with her ill-health; I have never known the habit of trances of that kind to have any such result, only the violent breaking of a trance might have a bad result, though it would not necessarily produce a disaster. But there is the possibility that if the conscious being goes out of the body in an absolutely complete trance, the thread which connects it with the body might be broken or else cut by some adverse force and it would not be able to return into the physical frame. Apart from any such fatal possibility there might be a shock which might produce a temporary disorder or even some kind of lesion; as a rule, however, a shock would be the only consequence. The general question is a different matter. There is a sort of traditional belief in many minds that the practice of yoga is inimical to the health of the body and tends to have a bad effect of one kind or another and even finally leads to a premature or an early dropping of the body. Ramakrishna seems to have held the view, if we can judge from his remarks about the connection between Keshav Sen's progress in spirituality and the illness which undermined him, that one was the result and the desirable result of the other, a liberation and release from life in this world, *mukti*. That may or may not be; but I find it difficult to believe that illness and deterioration of the body is the natural and general result of the practice of yoga or that that practice is the cause of an inevitable breakdown of health or of the final illnesses which bring about departure from the body. On what ground are we to suppose or how can it be proved that while non-yogis suffer from ill-health and die because of the disorders of Nature, yogis die of their yoga? Unless a direct connection between their death and their practice of yoga can be proved — and this could be proved with certainty only in particular cases and even then not with an absolute certainty —

there is no sufficient reason to believe in such a difference. It is more rational to conclude that both yogis and non-yogis fall ill and die from natural causes and by the same dispensation of Nature; one might even advance the view, since they have the Yoga-Shakti at their disposal if they choose to use it, that the yogi falls ill and dies not because of but in spite of his yoga. At any rate, I don't believe that Ramakrishna (or any other yogi) fell ill because of his trances; there is nothing to show that he ever suffered in that way after a trance. I think it is said somewhere or he himself said that the cancer in his throat of which he died came by his swallowing the sins of his disciples and those who approached him: that again may or may not be, but it will be his own peculiar case. It is no doubt possible to draw the illnesses of others upon oneself and even to do it deliberately, the instance of the Greek king Antigonus and his son Demitrius is a famous historical case in point; yogis also do this sometimes; or else adverse forces may throw illnesses upon the yogi, using those round him as a door or a passage or the ill wishes of people as an instrumental force. But all these are special circumstances connected, no doubt, with his practice of yoga; but they do not establish the general proposition as an absolute rule. A tendency such as X's to desire or welcome or accept death as a release could have a force because of her advanced spiritual consciousness which it would not have in ordinary people. On the other side, there can be an opposite use and result of the yogic consciousness: illness can be repelled from one's own body or cured, even chronic or deep-seated illnesses and long-established constitutional defects remedied or expelled and even a predestined death delayed for a long period. Narayan Jyotishi, a Calcutta astrologer, who predicted, not knowing then who I was, in the days before my name was politically known, my struggle with Mlechchha enemies and afterwards the three cases against me and my three acquittals, predicted also that though death was prefixed for me in my horoscope at the age of 63, I would prolong my life by yogic power for a very long period and arrive at a full old age. In fact, I have got rid by yogic pressure of a number of chronic maladies that had got settled in my body. But none of these instances either on the favourable or unfavourable side can be made into a rule; there is no validity in the tendency of human reason to transform the relativity of these things into an absolute. Finally I may say of X's trances that they are the usual *savikalpa* kind opening to all kinds of experiences, but the large abiding realisations in yoga do not usually come in trance but by a persistent waking sadhana. The same may be said of the removal of attachments; some may be got rid of sometimes by an experience in trance, but more usually it must be done by persistent endeavour in waking sadhana.

Above all, do not harbour that idea of an unfit body — all suggestions of that kind are a subtle attack on the will to siddhi and especially dangerous in physical matters. It has been cropping up in several people who are doing the yoga and the first business is to expel it bag and baggage. Appearances and facts may be all in its favour, but the first condition of success for the yogin and indeed for anybody who wants to do anything great or unusual is to be superior to facts and disbelieve in appearances. Will to be free from disease, however formidable, many-faced or constant its attacks, and repel all contrary suggestions.

All illnesses are obviously due to the imperfect nature of the body and the physical nature. The body can be immune only when it is open to the higher consciousness and the latter can descend into it. Till then what he writes is the remedy — if he can also call in the force to throw out the illness that is the most powerful help possible.

The human body has always been in the habit of answering to whatever forces chose to lay hands on it and illness is the price it pays for its inertia and ignorance. It has to learn to answer to the one Force alone, but that is not easy for it to learn.

Attacks of illness are attacks of the lower nature or of adverse forces taking advantage of some weakness, opening or response in the nature, — like all other things that come and have got to be thrown away, they come from outside. If one can feel them so coming and get the strength and the habit to throw them away before they can enter the body, then one can remain free from illness. Even when the attack seems to rise from within, that means only that it has not been detected before it entered the subconscient; once in the subconscient, the force that brought it rouses it from there sooner or later and it invades the system. When you feel it just after it has entered, it is because though it came direct and not through the subconscient, yet you could not detect it while it was still outside. Very often it arrives like that frontally or more often tangentially from the side direct, forcing its way through the subtle vital envelope which is our main armour of defence, but it can be stopped there in the envelope itself before it penetrates the material body. Then one may feel some effect, e.g., feverishness or a tendency to cold, but there is not the full invasion of the malady. If it can be stopped earlier or if the vital envelope of itself resists and remains strong, vigorous and intact, then there is no illness; the attack produces no physical effect and leaves no traces.

All illnesses pass through the nervous or vital-physical sheath of the subtle consciousness and subtle body before they enter the physical. If one is conscious of the subtle body or with the subtle consciousness, one can stop an illness on its way and prevent it from entering the physical body. But it may have come without one's noticing, or when one is asleep or through the subconscient, or in a sudden rush when one is off one's guard; then there is nothing to do but to fight it out from a hold already gained on the body. Self-defence by these inner means may become so strong that the body becomes practically immune as many yogis are. Still this "practically" does not mean "absolutely". The absolute immunity can only come with the supramental change. For below the supramental it is the result of an action of a Force among many forces and can be disturbed by a disruption of the equilibrium established — in the supramental it is a law of the nature; in a supramentalised body immunity from illness would be automatic, inherent in its new nature.

There is a difference between yogic Force on the mental and inferior planes and the supramental Nature. What is acquired and held by the yoga-Force in the mind-and-body consciousness is in the supramental inherent and exists not by achievement but by nature — it is self-existent and absolute.

That is how illnesses try to come from one person to another — they attack, by a suggestion like this or otherwise, the nervous being and try to come in. Even if the illness is not contagious, this often happens, but it comes more easily in contagious illnesses. The suggestion or touch has to be thrown off at once.

There is a sort of protection round the body which we call the nervous envelope — if this remains strong and refuses entrance to the illness force, then one can remain well even in the midst of plague or other epidemics — if the envelope is pierced or weak, then the illness can come in.

What you felt attacked was not really the physical body, but this nervous envelope and the nervous body (*prāṇakoṣa*) of which it is an extension or cover.

They [the subtle forces of illness] first weaken or break through the nervous envelope, the aura. If that is strong and whole, a thousand million germs will not be able to do anything to you. The envelope pierced, they attack the subconscient mind in the body, sometimes also the vital mind or mind proper — prepare the illness by fear or thought of illness. The doctors themselves say that in influenza or cholera in the Far East 90 p.c. get ill through fear. Nothing to take away the resistance like fear. But still the subconscient is the main thing.

If the contrary Force is strong in the body one can move in

the midst of plague and cholera and never get contaminated.

Physical sufferings are due to attacks of the forces of the Ignorance. But if one knows how to do it, one can make them a means of purification. There are however better and less difficult means of purification.

Your theory of illness is rather a perilous creed — for illness is a thing to be eliminated, not accepted or enjoyed. There *is* something in the being that enjoys illness, it is possible even to turn the pains of illness like any other pain into a form of pleasure; for pain and pleasure are both of them degradations of an original Ananda and can be reduced into the terms of each other or else sublimated into their original principle of Ananda. It is true also that one must be able to bear illness with calm, equanimity, endurance, even recognition of it, since it has come, as something that had to be passed through in the course of experience. But to accept and enjoy it means to help it to last and that will not do; for illness is a deformation of the physical nature just as lust, anger, jealousy, etc., are deformations of the vital nature and error and prejudice and indulgence of falsehood are deformations of the mental nature. All these things have to be eliminated and rejection is the first condition of their disappearance while acceptance has a contrary effect altogether.

It was the mind that did not want it; this vital [the vital physical] when left to itself often wants illness, it finds it dramatic, thinks it makes it interesting to others, likes to indulge the tamas, etc., etc.

That [constant weakness of the body] also is tamas. If you

throw off the idea of weakness, the strength would come back. But there is always something in the vital physical which is pleased with becoming more weak and ill so that it can feel and lament its tragic case.

By will to illness I meant this that there is something in the body that accepts the illness and has certain reactions that make this acceptance effective — so there must always be a contrary will in the conscious parts of the being to get rid of this most physical acceptance.

What I meant was that the body consciousness through old habit of consciousness admits the force of illness and goes through the experiences which are associated with it — e.g., congestion of phlegm in the chest and feeling of suffocation or difficulty of breathing, etc. To get rid of that one must awaken a will and consciousness in the body itself that refuses to allow these things to impose themselves upon it. But to get that, still more to get it completely is difficult. One step towards it is to get the inner consciousness separate from the body — to feel that it is not you who are ill, but it is only something taking place in the body and affecting your consciousness. It is then possible to see this separate body consciousness, what it feels, what are its reactions to things, how it works. One can then act on it to change its consciousness and reactions.

As the body consciousness becomes more open to the Force (it is always the most difficult and the last to open up entirely), this frequent stress of illness will diminish and disappear.

All ill-health is due to some inertia or weakness or to some resistance or wrong movement there, only it has sometimes a more physical and sometimes a more psychological character. Medicines can counteract the physical results.

Illness marks some imperfection or weakness or else opening to adverse touches in the physical nature and is often connected also with some obscurity or disharmony in the lower vital or the physical mind or elsewhere.

It is very good if one can get rid of illness entirely by faith and yoga-power or the influx of the Divine Force. But very often this is not altogether possible, because the whole nature is not open or able to respond to the Force. The mind may have faith and respond, but the lower vital and the body may not follow. Or, if the mind and vital are ready, the body may not respond, or may respond only partially, because it has the habit of replying to the forces which produce a particular illness, and habit is a very obstinate force in the material part of the nature. In such cases the use of the physical means can be resorted to, — not as the main means, but as a help or material support to the action of the Force. Not strong and violent remedies, but those that are beneficial without disturbing the body.

Yes, if the faith and opening are there, medicines are not indispensable.

The Mother's advice to X was given more for his period of stay in the Ashram than as an absolute rule for the future. If a sadhak can call down the force to cure him without need of medical treatment, that is always the best, but it is not always possible so long as the whole consciousness, mental, vital, physical down to the most subconscient is not open and awake. There is no harm in a doctor who is a sadhak carrying on his profession and using his medical knowledge; but he should do it in reliance on the Divine Grace and the Divine Will; if he can get true inspiration to aid his science, so much the better. No doctor can cure all cases. You are to do your best with the best result you can.

Certainly, one can act from within on an illness and cure it. Only it is not always easy as there is much resistance in Matter, a resistance of inertia. An untiring persistence is necessary; at first one may fail altogether or the symptoms increase, but gradually the control of the body or of a particular illness becomes stronger. Again, to cure an occasional attack of illness by inner means is comparatively easy, to make the body immune from it in future is more difficult. A chronic malady is harder to deal with, more reluctant to disappear entirely than an occasional disturbance of the body. So long as the control of the body is imperfect, there are all these and other imperfections and difficulties in the use of the inner force.

If you can succeed by the inner action in preventing increase, even that is something; you have then by *abhyāsa* to strengthen the power till it becomes able to cure. Note that so long as the power is not entirely there, some aid of physical means need not be altogether rejected.

To separate yourself from the thing and call in the Mother's Force to cure it — or else to use your will force with faith in the power to heal, having the support of the Mother's Force behind you. If you cannot use either of these methods then you must rely on the action of the medicines.

Where the illness becomes pronounced and chronic in the body, it is necessary often to call in the aid of physical treatment and that is then used as a support of the Force. X in his treatment does not rely on medicines alone, but uses them as an instrumentation for the Mother's force.

Medicines are a *pis aller* that have to be used when something in the consciousness does not respond or responds superficially to the Force. Very often it is some part of the material consciousness that is unreceptive — at other times it is the subconscient which stands in the way even when the whole waking mind, life, physical consent to the liberating influence. If the subconscient also answers, then even a slight touch of the Force can not only cure the particular illness but make that form or kind of illness practically impossible hereafter.

Not necessarily, but if there is a strong force of resistance behind the illness or if there is something hiding there it may come out under the pressure. This is not however the invariable rule. Often the result of the force is immediate and without reactions or there is an oscillation, but no aggravation or increase.

The suggestions that create illness or unhealthy conditions of the physical being come usually through the subconscient — for a great part of the physical being, the most material part, is subconscient, i.e. to say, it has an obscure consciousness of its own but so obscure and shut up in itself that the mind does not know its movements or what is going on there. But all the same it is a consciousness and can receive suggestions from Forces outside, just as the mind and vital do. If it were not so, there would not be any possibility of opening it to the Force and the Force curing it; for without this consciousness in it it would not be able to respond. In Europe and America there are many people now who recognise this fact and treat their illnesses by making conscious mental suggestions to the body which counteract the obscure secret suggestions of illness in the subconscient. There was a famous Doctor in France who cured thousands of people by making them persistently put such counter-suggestions upon the body. That proves that illness has not a purely material cause, but is due to a disturbance of the secret consciousness in the body.

To bear quietly and in silence does help to release from the reaction of grief, if one makes the vital quiet; but it should be at the same time surrendered to the Mother. For the Mother to know from within is not enough; there must be this laying before her and giving up to her so that the reaction may disappear.

*
**

The morphia stuns locally or otherwise the consciousness and its reaction to the subconscient pressure and so suspends the pain or deadens it. Even that it does not always do — X took five morphia injections in succession without even diminishing his liver inflammation pains. What became of the power of the drug over the subconscient in that case? The resistance was too strong just as the resistance of Y's subconscient to the Force.

In much the same way as Coué's suggestion system cured most of his patients, only by a physical instead of a mental means. The body consciousness responds to the suggestion of the medicine and one gets cured for the time being or it doesn't respond and there is no cure. How is it that the same medicine for the same illness succeeds with one man and not with another or succeeds at one time with a man and afterwards doesn't succeed at all? Absolute cure of an illness so that it cannot return again depends on clearing the mind, the vital and body consciousness of the psychological response to the Force bringing the illness. Sometimes this is done by a sort of order from above (when the consciousness is ready, but it cannot always be done like that). The complete immunity from all illness for which our yoga tries can only come by a total and permanent enlightenment of the below from above resulting in the removal of the psychological roots of ill health — it can't be done otherwise.

Why do people make such prognostications? Suggestions of the kind ought never to be made, mentally even — they might act like suggestions and do more harm than any good medicines can do.

*
**

Prognostications of such kind should not be lightly thought of or spoken especially in the case of the Mother — in other cases even if there is a possibility or probability they should be kept confidential from the person affected, unless it is necessary to inform. This is because of the large part played by state of consciousness and suggestion in illness.

The feeling of illness is at first only a suggestion; it becomes a reality because your physical consciousness accepts it. It is like a wrong suggestion in the mind, — if the mind accepts it, it becomes clouded and confused and has to struggle back into harmony and clearness. It is so with the body consciousness and illness. You must not accept but reject it with your physical mind and so help the body consciousness to throw off the suggestion. If necessary, make a counter-suggestion "No, I shall be well; I am and shall be all right." And in any case call in the Mother's Force to throw out the suggestion and the illness it is bringing.

By suggestion I do not mean merely thoughts or words. When the hypnotist says "sleep", it is a suggestion; but when he says nothing, but only puts his silent will to convey sleep or makes movements of his hands over the face, that also is a suggestion.

When a force is thrown on you or a vibration of illness, it carries to the body this suggestion. A wave comes in the body — with a certain vibration in it, the body remembers "cold" or feels the vibrations of a cold and begins to cough or sneeze or to feel chill — the suggestion comes to the mind in the form "I am weak, I don't feel well, I am catching a cold".

Hostile here means hostile to the yoga. An illness which comes in the ordinary course as the result of physical causes — even though adverse universal forces are the first cause — is an ordinary illness. One brought by the forces hostile to yoga to upset the system and prevent or disturb progress — without any adequate physical reason — is a hostile attack. It may have the appearance of a cold or any other illness, but to the eye which sees the action of forces and not only the outward symptoms or results, the difference is clear.

The suggestion of weakness comes to the subconscient part of the body consciousness and therefore the mind is most often unaware of it. If the body itself were truly conscious, then the suggestions could be detected in time and thrown off before they took effect. Also the rejection by the central consciousness would be supported by a conscious rejection in the body and act more immediately and promptly.

A suggestion is not one's own thought or feeling, but a thought or feeling that comes from outside, from others, from the general atmosphere or from external Nature, — if it is received, it sticks and acts on the being and is taken to be one's own thought or feeling. If it is recognised as a suggestion, then it can be more easily got rid of. This feeling of doubt and self-distrust and hopelessness about oneself is a thing moving about in the atmosphere and trying to enter into people and be accepted; I want you to reject it, for its presence not only produces trouble and distress but stands in the way of restoration of health and return to the inner activity of the sadhana.

As for medical treatment it is sometimes a necessity. If one can cure by the Force as you have often done it is the best — but if for some reason the body is not able to respond to the Force (e.g. owing to doubt, lassitude or discouragement or for inability to react against the disease), then the aid of medical treatment becomes necessary. It is not that the Force ceases to act and leaves all to the medicines, — it will continue to act through the consciousness but take the support of the treatment so as to act directly on the resistance in the body, which responds more readily to physical means in its ordinary consciousness.

*
**

These are waves of the hostile force which come trying whom
they can touch. When you feel an attack of this kind, you must
realise that this comes on you from outside and touches some
weak point in you, and you have to remain as quiet as you can,
reject it and open yourself. I judge from what you have written
that it was the physical and vital-physical consciousness that it
made restless and inclined to revolt and it did not take the whole
of your consciousness. If you can keep it localised like that when
it comes and remain quiet in mind and heart and reject it, then it
will not be so difficult to throw it out. The peace and force
must be called down into this vital-physical (nervous) part and
the whole body until you feel the atmosphere and force pervading you and in you always in all the body and not only upon or
around you. If you still find a difficulty, it is because of the past
habit of reaction in the nervous being and a certain weakness
there; but persevere, do not consent to the invasion of the old
forces. The habit will lessen and disappear and the true Force
occupying the body will remove the weakness.

It is the crude vital-physical that returns upon you in this way
— and these returns must be the cause of all the feelings of illness,
weakness, tamas that you get. A purification of this part by the
descent of the higher consciousness into it is a very great necessity
for your sadhana.

There are two places into which it (the crude vital-physical)
can retire — the subconscient vital below or the environmental
consciousness around. When it returns, it surges up from below,
if it is the former, or approaches and invades from outside, if it
is the latter.

There is no mystery. These things were violent and obstinate
in you for a long time and you were indulging them — hence they
acquired a great force to return even after you began rejecting

them, first because of habit, secondly because of their belief that they have acquired a right over you, thirdly because of the habit of assent and passive response to them or endurance of them that has been stamped on the physical consciousness. This physical consciousness is not as yet liberated, it has not begun to be as responsive to the higher force as the vital, so it cannot resist their invasion. So these forces, when thrown out, retreat into the environmental consciousness and remain there concealed and at any opportunity make an attack on the centres accustomed to receive them (external mind and the external emotional) and get in. This happens with most sadhaks. Two things are necessary — (1) to open fully the physical to the higher forces, (2) to reach the stage when even if the forces attack they cannot come fully in, the inner being remaining calm and free. Then even if there is still a surface difficulty, there will not be these over-powerings.

*
**

All these suggestions that came to you were of course part of the attack on the physical consciousness, — the attack on the body is used to raise these ideas and ideas are used to make it more difficult for the body to recover. At a certain stage attacks fall heavily on the body because the opposing forces find it more difficult than before to upset the mind and vital directly, so they fall on the physical in the hope that that will do the trick, the physical being more vulnerable. But the sensibility of the body to attacks is no proof of incapacity, just as a finer sensibility of the mind or vital to attacks was no proof — it can, in due time, be overcome. As for the feelings about the Mother and that her love is only given for a return in work or to those who can do sadhana well, that is the usual senseless idea of the vital-physical mind and has no value.

There is nothing wrong in taking care of the body in regard to health and, if the liver has gone wrong, the instinct to refuse too sweet or greasy or heavy food is a right instinct. Mother has no objection to your abstaining while the illness is there nor has she insisted on your taking *dal*. Her objection is only to that which people often do, getting ideas about this food and that food and abstaining even when there is no acute illness. During an acute state of bad liver, abstaining is often necessary. Only one must not create by wrong ideas a nervous incapacity of the stomach or a chronic nervous dyspepsia. She had no other meaning.

I hope you will be all right soon. If the body does not right itself, you must keep me informed from time to time.

There seem to be two elements in the physical difficulty that is weighing on you. The first is the liver trouble which weakens and must weaken still more if it leads you to diminish your food below what the body needs for maintaining sufficient strength to react — also probably the nervous tendency to insomnia with its consequences. The second is an inertia of the lower vital and physical consciousness which prevents it from throwing off the lassitude, from reacting against the attacks and from opening steadily to the Force which would remove these things. All that is due to the breakdown of the poise that you had for so long, the vital trouble that caused it and the reaction of the lower vital to the insistence on throwing out the causes of the trouble. This reaction seems to have been a restlessness at losing the things to which it was still holding — such a reaction always brings the inertia of the physical consciousness, while the right reaction in the lower vital, on the contrary, brings a sense of peace, release, quietude which definitely opens the lowest physical parts to the higher consciousness and force. If you can get over this and get back the old poise, then all these things can be made to disappear.

Care should be taken of the body certainly, the care that is needed for its good condition, rest, sleep, proper food, sufficient exercise; what is not good is too much preoccupation with it, anxiety, despondency in the illness, etc., for these things only favour the prolongation of ill-health or weakness. For such things as the liver attacks treatment can always be taken when necessary.

But it is always the right inner poise, quietude inward and outward, faith, the opening of the body consciousness to the

Mother and her Force that are the true means of recovery —
other things can only be minor aids and devices.

What has caused all the trouble for X is his insistence on his ego,
its ideas, claims, desires, intentions and his aggressiveness in expressing them so that he quarrels with everybody. This quarrelsomeness opens him to all sorts of forces of the vital plane and
their attacks. It is also the cause of the damage done to the liver
and organs of digestion — for quarrelsomeness and anger always
lead to spoil the liver and through it the stomach and intestines.
As his quarrelsomeness is colossal, so also is the damage done to
the liver and digestion extreme. He must get rid of his egoism,
quarrelsomeness and bad feelings towards others, if he wants to
recover his health and his sadhana.

It is a great gain if you feel no depression when the attack on the
body comes.

The pain itself is, from your description, evidently nervous
and, if you develop openness in the more physical layers of the
being, then the action of the Force can always remove it or you
will yourself be able to use the Force to push it away. It is a matter of getting the habit of opening in the body consciousness.

The consciousness or unconsciousness, as you have seen in
the matter of the French studies, is dependent on the condition. It
is not that you are unconscious, but that the physical being is
prone to the tamasic condition (the condition of inertia) and then
it becomes either inactive or obscure, stupid and unconscious;
when the tamas goes away the condition becomes bright and
what was difficult before becomes natural and easy. The whole
thing is to get the physical out of its habit of falling back into
tamas or inertia, and that can be done by opening and accus-
toming it to the action of the Force. When the action of the
Force becomes constant, then there will be no more tamas.

It is not anything physical but a vital depression (or some part of the vital, not the whole) that prevents the body from recovering its elasticity. There was some part of the vital that was resisting a radical change and even unknown to your mind trying to go on as it was under cover of the change in the rest of your being. This has now, owing to this last affair, received a blow and got depressed and, when the vital is depressed like that it affects the body. You say rightly that it is part of a change or turn that is taking place. But these effects of inertia and weakness ought not to continue; as soon as the vital part acquiesces gladly in the turn or change the elasticity and energy will return.

The pains in the body come from the same source as the trouble in the vital nature; both are attacks from the same outside force that wants to mislead or, when it cannot mislead, to trouble and disturb you. When once you can get rid of the vital invasion and prevent its recurrence, it will be easier to get rid too of the physical trouble whose origin is nervous (vital-physical); although its symptoms seem to be those of a physical illness, it is usually an attack on the nervous part and weakening of it for the time that gives you the pain.

Remain always quiet and persist in opening yourself. The Force that releases you from the vital trouble can also remove the disturbance in the nervous part and the physical body.

That is what they [pains] do at first; when one drives them out of one place, they go to another. It is better than their fixing in any place.

It is neither the vital nor the body that contains these illnesses — it is a force from outside that creates these, and the nervous being (physical vital) and the body respond from habit or inability to throw it away. It is always better not to say "I will now have no

more illness"; it attracts the attention of these malevolent powers
and they immediately want to prove that they can still disturb the
body. Simply when they come, reject them.

It is by an attack on your physical consciousness that the old
forces are bringing back the wrong condition. As you got the
power before to stand back from the vital movement and localise
it, while the rest of your consciousness observed and was not
overpowered, so you must learn to stand back from the physical
pain or uneasiness and localise it. If you can do that and do it
completely, the pain or uneasiness itself will be more easily and
quietly removed and you will not be overpowered like this with
the sense of weakness. You can see that the Force has the power
to take away the pains; but you allow yourself to be nervously
overcome and therefore it is difficult for it to act with a continuous result. What was done at that time in the vital, must be
done in the physical also. It is the only way to get free from the
attacks.

You must arrive at a complete separation of your consciousness
from these feelings of the body and its acceptance of illness and
from that separated consciousness act upon the body. It is only
so that these things can be got rid of or at least neutralised.

If it [the consciousness] is separate it should not suffer from them
[the pains]. Even for the pains, the body may suffer but the consciousness should not feel itself suffering or overpowered.

Pain is caused because the physical consciousness in the Ignorance is too limited to bear the touches that come upon it.
Otherwise, to cosmic consciousness in its state of complete

knowledge and complete experience all touches come as Ananda.

To bear extreme heat and cold it is necessary to have peace in the cells first, then consolidated force. Pain and discomfort come from a physical consciousness not forceful enough to determine its own reactions to things.

The body, naturally [experiences physical pain] — but the body transmits it to the vital and mental. With the ordinary consciousness the vital gets disturbed and afflicted and its forces diminished, the mind identifies and is upset. The mind has to remain unmoved, the vital unaffected, and the body has to learn to take it with equality so that the higher Force may work.

The Self is never affected by any kind of pain. The psychic takes it quietly and offers it to the Divine for what is necessary to be done.

It is a detachment of even the physical mind from the pain that makes one able to go on as if nothing were there but this detachment of the physical mind is not so easy to acquire.

The main difficulty seems to be that you are too subject to an excitement of the nerves — it is only by bringing quietude and calm into the whole being that a steady progress in the sadhana can be assured.

The first thing to be done in order to recover is to stop yielding to the attack of the nerves — the more you yield and identify yourself with these ideas and feelings, the more they increase.

You have to draw back and find back something in you that is not affected by pains and depressions, then from there you can get rid of the pains and depressions.

If you listen to what others say and base your action on satisfying their ideas, how will you keep the right attitude which can alone support you in work? It is for the Mother that you have to work, to find her in yourself through work, — not to protect yourself from the criticism of others.

I am glad to know the disturbance was expelled last night — now the receptivity of the body consciousness has to be kept so that it may not at all return or, if it tries, may immediately be expelled. You must always try to keep the quietude, not allow depressing or disturbing thoughts or feelings to enter you or take hold of your mind or your speech — there is no true reason after one has gained the inner quietness and wideness why that should be allowed to lapse and these things enter. And if the mind keeps its quietude and receptivity to higher forces only, it can then easily pass on that quietude and receptivity to the body consciousness and even to the material cells of the body.

Whatever it may be — the power of illness to prevent the sadhana ought not to exist. The yogic consciousness and its activities must be there whether there is health or illness.

It is no use stopping work because of rheumatism (unless it is of the kind that disables one from working) — it only makes things worse.

You had opened your consciousness, so the pain disappeared. If it came back during the sleep, it must have been because you lost touch and fell back into the ordinary consciousness. That often happens.

Yes. If you don't sleep enough the physical system becomes more open to these attacks [of illness]. If it is kept in good condition, then usually it repels them automatically and one does not notice even that there has been an attack.

I said that when the body is in good condition it automatically repels any attack of illness which is in the air without the mind even having to notice that there is an attack. If the attack is automatically repelled what is the need of dealing with it?

It is a hostile pressure that is organising a habit in the body of recurrence at a fixed time or times. This habit of fixed recurrence gives a great force for any illness to persist, as the body consciousness expects the recurrence and the expectation helps it to come.

It is this expectation in the mind that helps most to maintain the rhythm of the attack. If it could be got rid of, the rhythm also could be broken.

I don't think stammering has anything to do with insufficient lung-power nor is it caused by malformation of the vocal organs — it is commonly a nervous (physico-nervous) impediment and is perfectly curable. I can't say that I know of any especial device for it — people have used various kinds of devices to get over it, but behind them all will-power and a patient discipline of the utterance are indispensable.

You have to be careful about your eyes. Reading by night (too much) is undesirable. There are two suggestions of the sun-treatment man which I have found to be not without foundation. First, one should blink freely in looking at things or reading and not fix the eyes or stare. Secondly, palming gives a very useful rest — palming means keeping the hands crossed over the closed eyes (without pressing on the eyes) so as to shut out all light.

What you describe happens very usually during a cold in the head, as ordinarily one depends upon the brain cells for the transmission of the mental thought. When the mind is not so dependent on the brain cells, then the obscuration by the cold does not interfere with clear seeing and thinking and one is not thrown back in the mechanical mind.

Fever is of course more often than not a struggle of the body to fight out impurities that have got in, but sometimes the remedy is as bad if not worse than the disease. It is the same with the difficulties — an illness sometimes results in a throwing out of some impurities but it can also do more harm than good.

[After an attack of influenza:] The first thing to do is to keep throughout a perfect equanimity and not to allow thoughts of disturbed anxiety or depression to enter you. It is quite natural after this severe attack of influenza that there should be weakness and some fluctuations in the progress to recovery. What you have to do is to remain calm and confident and not worry or be restless — be perfectly quiet and prepared to rest as long as rest is needed. There is nothing to be anxious about; rest, and the health and strength will come.

Sciatica is something more than nervous — it affects the movement of the muscles through the nerves. It can be got rid of at once, however, if you can manage to direct the Force on it.

There is no outer means. Sciatica is a thing which yields only to inner concentrated force or else it goes away of itself and comes of itself. Outer means at best can only be palliatives.

The inertia is there because there was always in your outer being a great force of tamas and it is this that is being used by the resistance. There was also a deficiency of steady will power in the outer mind which makes it more difficult for the Force to come down than for the Knowledge. When you are entirely open the Force can act on the sciatica and it lessens or disappears, but with the consciousness blocked by the inertia these difficulties come in the way.

We have always found that it [sciatica] cannot resist the force quietly and persistently applied. Other illnesses can resist, but sciatica being entirely tamasic cannot. The application of Force does not yet, probably, come natural to you, so it brings a sense of struggle not of quiet domination, hence the restlessness etc.

If you cannot get rid of the sciatica by inner means, the medical remedy (not for curing it, but for keeping free as long as possible) is not to fatigue yourself. It comes for periods which may last for weeks, then suddenly goes. If you remain quiet physically and are not too active, it may not come for a long time. But that of course means an inactive life, physically incapable. It is what I mean by eternising the sciatica — and the inertia also.

T.B. is the result of a strong psychic-vital depression. Sex cannot directly cause T.B. though it may be a factor in bringing about a fall of the vital forces and a withdrawal of the psychic supporting forces leading to T.B. The lack of vitality which easily comes as a result of modern civilisation is therefore a very strong contributing cause. Moderns have not the solid nervous system and the natural (as opposed to the artificial and morbid) zest of life that their ancestors had. But I don't know about the soldiers — the hideous trench war with all its ghastly circumstances and surroundings was, I imagine, far more difficult to bear than the open air marching and fighting of the Napoleonic times.

According to all statements the deaths in early age are much less in Europe and men live longer on the whole. But certain diseases have greatly increased in spite of the advance in hygiene — influenza, T.B. and venereals. There are also new diseases coming in that hardly existed before. That seems obviously the work of the Hostiles.

Of course it [cancer] can [be cured by yoga], but on condition of faith or openness or both. Even a mental suggestion can cure cancer — with luck of course, as is shown by the case of the woman operated on unsuccessfully for cancer, but the doctors lied and told her it had succeeded. Result, cancer symptoms all ceased and she died many years afterwards of another illness altogether.

*
**

Medicine is not exactly science. It is theory and experimental fumbling and luck.

*
**

The theory [of allopathic medicine] is imposing, but when it comes to application, there is too much fumbling and guesswork for it to rank as an exact science. There are many scientists (and others) who grunt when they hear medicine called a science. Anatomy and physiology, of course, are sciences.

Injections are all the fashion; for everything it is "inject, inject and again inject". Medicine has gone through three stages in modern times — first (at the beginning in Molière's days) it was "bleed and douche" — then "drug and diet" — now it is "serum and injection". Praise the Lord! not for the illnesses, but for the doctors. However, each of these formulas has a part truth behind it — with its advantages and disadvantages. As all religions and philosophies point to the Supreme but each in a different direction, so all medical fashions are ways to health — though they don't always reach it.

You may say what you like about the homeopathic theories, but I have seen X work them out detail by detail in cases where he had free and unhampered action and the confidence of the patients and their strict obedience and have seen the results correspond to his statements and his predictions based on them fulfilled not only to the very letter but according to the exact times fixed, not according to X's reports but according to the long detailed and precise reports of the allopathic doctor in attendance. After that I refuse to believe, even if all the allopaths shout in unison, that homeopathic theory or X's interpretation and application of it are mere rubbish and nonsense. As to mistakes all doctors make mistakes and very bad ones and kill as well as cure.... One theory is as good as another and as bad according to the application made of it in any particular case. But it is something else behind that decides the issue.

I have put down a few comments to throw cold water on all this blazing hot allopathism. But all these furious disputes seem to me now of little use. I have seen the working of both the systems [allopathy and homeopathy] and of others and I can't believe in the sole truth of any. The ones damnable in the orthodox view, entirely contradicting it, have their own truth and succeed — also both the orthodox and heterodox fail. A theory is only a constructed idea-script which represents an imperfect human observation of a line of processes that Nature follows or can follow; another theory is a different idea-script of other processes that also she follows or can follow. Allopathy, homeopathy, naturopathy, osteopathy, Kaviraji, Hakimi have all caught hold of Nature and subjected her to certain processes; each has its successes and failures. Let each do its work in its own way. I do not see any need for fights and recriminations. For me all are only outward means and what really works are unseen forces from behind; as they act, the outer means succeed or fail — if one can make the process a right channel for the right force, then the process gets its full vitality — that's all.

It is not enough for a medicine to be a specific. Certain drugs have other effects or possible effects which can be ignored by the physician who only wants to cure his case, but cannot be in a whole-view of the system and its reactions. The unfavourable reactions of quinine are admitted by medical opinion itself and doctors in Europe have been long searching for a substitute for quinine.

Tumour, syphilis etc. are specialities, but what I have found in my psycho-physical experience is that most disorders of the body are connected, though they go by families, but there is also connection between the families. If one can strike at their psycho-physical root, one can cure even without knowing the pathological whole of the. matter and working through the symptoms as a possibility. Some medicines invented by demi-mystics have this power. What I am now considering is whether homeopathy has any psycho-physical basis. Was the founder

a demi-mystic? I don't understand otherwise certain pecu-
liarities of the way in which X's medicines act.

You are very much behind the times. Do you not know that even
many doctors now admit and write it publicly that medicines
are an element but only one and that the psychological element
counts as much and even more? I have heard that from doctors
often and read it over reputable medical signatures. And
among the psychological elements, they say, one of the most
important is the doctor's optimism and self-confidence, (his
faith, what? it is only another word for the same thing) and the
confidence, hope, helpful mental atmosphere he can inspire in
or around his patient. I have seen it stated categorically that a
doctor who can do that is far more successful than one who
knows Medicine better but cannot.... I did not mean that it cannot be done without medicines. But if it is to be done with the aid
of medicines, then the right medicine is helpful, the wrong one
obviously brings in a danger.... How does his knowledge prevent intuition? Even an allopathic doctor has often to intuit
what medicine he should give or what mixture — and it is those
who intuit best that succeed best. All is not done by sole rule
or book or sole rule of thumb even in orthodox Science.

What an absurd statement! Self-confidence is an inborn thing;
it does *not* rest on knowledge and experience.... Who says that?
I never heard that Napoleon failed at Waterloo for want of self-
confidence. I have always read that he failed because he was,
owing to his recent malady, no longer so quick and self-confident
in decision and so supple in mental resource as before. Please
don't write history unless you have data for your novel version.

You have only to admit that the mind and vital can influence the body — then no difficulty is left. In this action of mind and vital on the body faith and hope have an immense importance. I do not at all mean that they are omnipotent or infallibly effective — that is not so. But they assist the action of any force that can be applied, even of an apparently purely material force, but the action may be purely material when it is a question of material objects. But in things that have life or mind or mind and life one cannot isolate the material operation like that. There is always a play of other forces mixed with it in the reception at least and for the most part in the inception and direction also.

*
**

Miracles can be done, but there is no reason why they should be all instantaneous, whether from Gods or doctors.

*
**

These things are a matter of evidence and the evidence for Coué's success is overwhelming. There have also been many great healers (*guérisseurs*) all over the world whose successes are well-attested. Faith-healing and psycho-therapy are also facts.

*
**

These auto-suggestions — it is really faith in a mental form — act both on the subliminal and the subconscient. In the subliminal they set in action the powers of the inner being, its occult power to make thought, will or simple conscious force effective on the body — in the subconscient they silence or block the suggestions of death and illness (expressed or unexpressed) that prevent the return of health. They help also to combat the same things (adverse suggestions) in the mind, vital, body consciousness. Where all this is completely done or with some completeness, the effects can be very remarkable.

TRANSFORMATION OF
THE SUBCONSCIENT AND THE INCONSCIENT

Transformation of the Subconscient and the Inconscient

So LONG as there is not the supramental change down to the subconscient, complete and full, the lower nature has always a hold on some part of the being.

The subconscient difficulty is *the* difficulty now — because the whole struggle in the general sadhana is now there. It is in the subconscient, no longer in vital or conscious physical that the resistance is all massed together.

The inner being does not depend on the subconscient, but the outer has depended on it for thousands of lives — that is why the outer being and physical consciousness's habit of response to the subconscient can be a formidable obstacle to the progress of the sadhana and is so with most. It keeps up the repetition of the old movements, is always pulling down the consciousness and opposing the continuity of the ascent and bringing the old nature or else the tamas (non-illumination and non-activity) across the descent. It is only if you live wholly and dynamically in the inner being and feel the outer as a quite superficial thing that you can get rid of the obstruction or minimise it until the transformation of the outer being can be made complete.

The subconscient is a dark and ignorant region, so that it is natural that the obscurer movements of the Nature should have more power there. It is so indeed with all the lower parts of the nature from the lower vital downwards. But it does send up good things also though more rarely. It has in the course of the sadhana to be illumined and made a support of the higher consciousness in the physical nature instead of a basis of the instinctive lower movements.

The subconscient is to be penetrated by the light and made a sort of bed-rock of truth, a store of right impressions, right physical responses to the Truth. Strictly speaking, it will not be subconscient at all, but a sort of bank of true values held ready for use.

The work [of sadhana in the subconscient] is of a general nature, not individual, but necessarily everyone here is to some extent affected by it. If consciousness and light is not brought into the subconscient, then there can be no change. For it is in the subconscient that there are the seeds of all the old lower vital instincts and movements and however much they may be cleared in the lower vital itself, they may sprout up again from below. Also the subconscient is the secret basis of the bodily consciousness. The subconscient must admit into itself the higher consciousness and the Truth light.

It is only if the mind is silent that the subconscient can be empty. What has to be done is to get all the old ignorant unyogic stuff out of the subconscient.

If the subconscient is emptied, it would mean that you have got beyond the ordinary consciousness and the subconscient itself is prepared to be an instrument of the Truth.

[First effects of the light penetrating and changing the subconscient:]

1. The subconscient begins to show more easily what is in it.

2. Things rising from there come to the awareness of the mind before they can touch or affect the consciousness.

3. The subconscient becomes less the refuge of the ignorant and obscure movements and more an automatic response of the material to the higher consciousness.

4. It gives less covert and less passage to the suggestions of the hostile forces.

5. It is more easy to be conscious in sleep and to have higher forms of dream experience. Hostile dreams — e.g. sex-suggestions can be met and stopped in the dream itself and any result like emission prevented.

6. A waking will put on the dream state before sleeping becomes more and more effective.

The conscious parts have to be prepared first — impossible to deal successfully with the subconscient till then, except in points and details. Just as the musician has first to learn the right principle and execution of his music with his mind and vital (aesthetic) perception and will — and teach his fingers to execute it — afterwards the subconscient in his fingers will learn its work and do the right thing of itself — e.g. touching the right keys without his eyes having to follow.

It is because the subconscient being just below the physical, the enlightened physical can act on it directly and completely in a way in which mind and vital cannot and by this direct action can help to liberate the mind and vital also.

It is not a fact that formless things can have no power — all that is necessary is that they should have a force in them. The subconscient influences the body because all in the body has developed out of the subconscient and all in itself still is only half conscious and much of its action can be called subconscious. It is therefore much more easily influenced by the subconscious than by the conscious mind and conscious will or even the vital mind and vital will except in those things in which a conscious mental or vital control has been established and the subconscious itself has accepted it. If it were not so, man's control of his actions and physical states would be complete, there would be no illness or if there were, it would be immediately cured by mental action. But it is not so. For that reason the higher consciousness has to be brought down, the body and the subconscient enlightened by it and accustomed to obey its control.

What you write is correct. When the physical consciousness has to be changed it is of course essential to work in the subconscient, as it has a great influence on the physical which is very dependent on it. The loss of consciousness comes naturally at first when the subconscient is being worked upon. You have to be careful that it does not become habitual. If you react with a will for the change of this tendency (no struggle is needed) it will pass in time.

It [the subconscient vital-physical] is not in touch with the psychic at all. It is full of obscurity, not conscient, entirely ignorant.

The material is for the most part subconscient — it depends upon the subtle parts for its waking consciousness.

It is good. Emptiness and silence of the consciousness prepare the being to live within with the outer consciousness only as a means of communication and action on the physical world instead of living in the external only.

As there is a superconscient (something above our present consciousness) above the head from which the higher consciousness comes down into the body, so there is also a subconscient (something below our consciousness) below the feet. Matter is under the control of this power, because it is that out of which it has been created — that is why matter seems to us to be quite unconscious. The material body is very much under the influence of this power for the same reason; it is why we are not conscious of what is going on in the body, for the most part. The outer consciousness goes down into this subconscient when we are asleep, and so it becomes unaware of what is going on in us when we are asleep except for a few dreams. Many of these dreams rise up from the subconscient and are made up of old memories, impressions etc. put together in an incoherent way. For the subconscient receives impressions of all we do or experience in our lives and keeps these impressions in it, sending up often fragments of them in sleep. It is a very important part of the being, but we can do nothing much with it by the conscious will. It is the higher Force working in us that in its natural course will open the subconscient to itself and bring down into it its control and light.

The not-speaking mind is all right. It helps usually at this stage the concentration of the being.

The dream you had was really a rising up of past formations or impressions from the subconscient. All that we do, feel or experience in life leaves an impression, a sort of essential memory of itself in the subconscient and this can come up in dreams even long after those feelings, movements or experiences have ceased in the conscious being, — still more when they have been recent and are only now or lately thrown away from the mind or vital. Thus long after one has ceased to think of old acquaintances or relatives dreams about them go on coming up from this source. So too when sex or anger no longer troubles the conscious vital, dreams of sex or dreams of anger and strife can still rise. It is only when the subconscient is cleared that they cease; meanwhile they are of not much importance (provided one understands what they are and is not affected) so long as the old movements are not allowed to recur or remain in the waking state.

It [insincerity in the subconscient vital] can only be dangerous if the waking mind accepts it. All the same, so long as it remains in the subconscient, it keeps a seed of possibility — so it must be got out altogether.

What is happening just now is that there is a great uprush of the subconscient in which are the seeds or the strong remnants of the habitual difficulties of the nature. But its character is a confusion and obscurity without order or clear mental or other arrangement — it is a confused depression, discouragement, inability to progress — a feeling of what are we doing? why are we here? how can we go on? will anything ever be attained? and along with it old difficulties recurring in a confused and random but often violent and distressing fashion.

You cannot "begin" again; it would be too difficult a thing in this confusion. You have to get back to the point at which you deviated. If you can get back to the Peace that was coming and with it aspire to the freedom and wideness of the Purusha consciousness forming a *point d'appui* of detachment and separation from all this confusion of the subconscient Prakriti, then you will have a firm ground to stand upon and proceed. But for that you must make your choice firmly and refuse to be upset at every moment and diverted from it.

There is always a great deal to do in the subconscient. But if you especially feel it [the need of clearance in the subconscient] it must be that the time for clearing it has come. If the other parts keep open and responsive this should not give too much trouble.

All that is probably things that rise from the subconscient — or perhaps the subconscient itself is being worked upon to arrive at a state of light and peace. It sometimes enters into a happy condition, sometimes into a neutral one, sometimes it raises up a causeless sorrow. The movements of the subconscient take place even without reason, of themselves, owing to the inherent habit in Nature, that is why the grief is without discoverable cause. It is only because it is in the subconscient that you cannot locate it. When the grief comes, you must dissociate yourself from it and reject it, not taking it as your own, until it ceases to come and call down the Mother's peace and Ananda in its place.

It is good; we will certainly help you in the way you ask us.

As for the mood that came on you, it comes up from the subconscient, where things of the old nature sink when they are rejected. When moods come up like that, you have to remain quiet and call the Mother till it is gone. After a time this power of mechanical repetition without reason from the subconscient gets worn out and disappears — then these moods come no more.

It is most probably something that has come from outside and covered. This happens at this stage when the working is in the physical and subconscient — for that is the nature of these parts, to live in the external with the inner being covered up by a sort of natural veil of obscurity. Therefore when one makes the opening through this veil, it has a tendency to come back. When that happens, one has to remain undisturbed and call down the Force and Light from above to remove the obstacle. This must be done till the opening is permanent and complete and no covering is possible.

It is always so with the impressions left in the subconscient physical. One day they come as pale and distant things, with no life in them, another they seem to get a certain force. It depends on whether they are caught up by a current of force from the universal or rise up of themselves with no force except what is left in them from the past.

What must have happened was that as the physical consciousness is now being worked upon, all the past impressions (which usually remain in the subconsciousness and rise up from time to time and meanwhile influence the thought and action and feelings without being noticed) rose up in a mass and threw themselves on the consciousness. This usually happens in order that the sadhak may see and reject them and get liberated entirely (in the subconscious as well as the conscious parts) from his physical past. That is why you felt afterwards the sense of release. The throat is the centre of the externalising mind (physical mind).

It is most probably from the subconscient. When these memories arise, they should be treated on the basis that they have arisen in order to be dissolved and dismissed, so that by their persistent dissolution one may not be tied by the impressions in the subconscient to the past (that is the machinery of Karma) but free for the spirit's unbound future.

The best is when you can get the true knowledge about it, why it happened and what purpose it served; then it goes easily.

This review of the past is a very good sign, for it usually comes when there is a preparation of the physical consciousness and subconscient for change. One has not to regret the stumbles of the past but look with a quiet eye and understand, for all came — the stumbles included — as part of the necessary experience by which the being learns and advances through error to the Light and through the imperfections of Nature towards the divine perfection.

What you describe seems to be in its nature an uncontrolled rushing up of the subconscient taking the form of a mechanical recurrence of old thoughts, interests or desires with which the physical mind is usually occupied. If that were all, the only thing would be to reject them, detach yourself and let them pass till they quieted down. But I gather from what you write that there is an attack, an obscure force using these recurrences to invade and harass the mind and body. It would be helpful if you could give an exact description of the main character of the thoughts that come, what things and ideas they are concerned with etc. But in any case the one thing to do is to open yourself to the Mother's force by aspiration, thought of the Mother or any other way and let it drive out the attack. We shall send Force continually till this is done. It will be better to let us know every three days or so how you go on, for that will help to make the action of the Force more precise.

These cravings and desires are old habits of the physical which came to it from the universal Nature and which it accepted and took as part of itself and its life. When these things are rejected by the waking consciousness they try to take refuge in the subconscient or else in what may be called the environmental consciousness and from there they press upon the consciousness trying to recover their hold or simply to recur for a time. If they are in the subconscient they come up most usually in dreams, but they may also surge up into the waking consciousness. If they come from the environment they take the form of thought-suggestions or impulses or a vague restless or disturbing pressure. It is probably this environmental pressure that you feel. When the body is full of the new consciousness, Peace and Power at the same time, then this outward pressure is felt but can no longer disturb and finally it recedes to a distance (no longer pressing immediately on the physical mind or body) and either gradually or rapidly disappears.

By environmental consciousness I mean something that each man carries around him, outside his body, even when he is not aware of it, — by which he is in touch with others and with the universal forces. It is through this that the thoughts, feelings etc. of others pass to enter into one — it is through this also that waves of the universal force — desire, sex, etc. come in and take possession of the mind, vital or body.

These thoughts that attack in sleep or in the state between sleep and waking do not belong to any part of your conscious being, but come either from the subconscient or from the surrounding atmosphere through the subconscient. If they are thoughts you had in the past and have thrown out from you, then what rises must be impressions left by them in the subconscient — for all things thought, felt or experienced leave such impressions which can rise from there in sleep. Or the thoughts can have gone out from you into the environmental consciousness, that is, an atmosphere of consciousness which we carry around us and through which we are connected with universal Nature and from there they may be trying to return upon you. As it is difficult for them to succeed in the waking state, they take advantage of the absence of conscious control in sleep and appear there. If it is something new and not yours, then it can be neither of these, but an attack of some outside Force.

It is to be hoped that as you have rejected them, they will not come again, but if they do, then you must put a conscious will before going to sleep that they should not come. A suggestion of that kind on the subconscient is often successful, if not at once, after a time; for the subconscient learns to obey the will put upon it in the waking state.

*
* *

What is taking place, the subsiding of the surge of subconscient thoughts and movements, and their pressure on the mind, is just what ought to take place. It is not a suppression or pulling back into the subconscient, it is an expulsion from the conscious self into which it has arisen. It is true that something more may rise from the subconscient, but it will be what is still left there. What is now rejected, if it goes anywhere and is not abolished, will go not into the subconscient but into the surrounding consciousness which one carries around him — once there it no longer belongs to oneself in any way and if it tries to return it will be as foreign matter which one has not to accept or allow any longer. These are the two last stages of rejection by which one gets rid of the old things of the nature, they go down into the subconscient and have to be got rid of from there or they go out into the environmental consciousness and are no longer ours.

The idea that one should let what rises from the subconscient go on repeating itself till it is exhausted is not the right idea. For that would needlessly prolong the troubled condition and might be harmful. When these things rise they have to be observed and then thrown out, not kept.

*
* *

Sri Aurobindo was unable up till now to answer your letter... but these answers, given below point by point, are still sent as he thinks they may be of use to you for your future sadhana:

1. "Ugly scenes" etc. —

This must be something rising up from the subconscient in which there are many strange things of the kind — or else it is formations thrown on the lower vital consciousness from the corresponding plane in universal Nature where there are forces which take delight in dirt and ugliness and all kinds of perversities. In either case a steady detached rejection is the reaction required.

2. There is no objection to using one's bed as *āsana*.

3. Sex trouble —

This is a quite usual phenomenon when one stops sexual activity and rejects it in the conscious mind and vital. It takes refuge in the subconscient where the mind has no direct control and comes up in the form of dreams causing emission. That lasts so long as the subconscient itself is not cleared. This can sometimes be done by putting a strong will or, if possible, a concrete current of Force on the sex-centre before sleeping against this thing happening. The success is not always immediate, but if effectively done it tends first to reduce frequency and finally stop it.

These things (accumulation of urine, hot stimulating food etc.) are all predisposing or auxiliary causes or can be so. There is often as described a rhythm in this subconscient urge — it happens at a particular time in the month or else after a fixed period of time (week, fortnight, month, six months).

4. Classifications of Samadhi in Vedanta —

For this yoga these divisions are not so important.

5. Experience of Samadhi —

It is not indispensable at this stage; but if it comes of itself, it can be allowed to develop. But experience in the waking state is more important for this yoga. Samadhi is a help for reaching the inner depths of the consciousness. One is able to go more easily by it inward below the surface being to get into direct contact with other supraphysical planes of experience, to pass into other worlds and return, to contact happenings distant in space and time, to see what is in the supraconscient and to enter into what is supraconscient to our mental status.

6. The cosmic Consciousness; the psychic —

These things cannot be sufficiently dealt with in a short compass. The ordinary consciousness of man is confined to his own individuality — he can enter into the consciousness of others and of the universe only by indirect means or a superficial and incomplete apprehension, by sense experience, contacts of emotional sympathy, mental concepts, analogy with his own movements, inference. In yoga at a certain point this limitation breaks down, the consciousness enlarges itself, becomes directly aware of the Cosmic Self and knows the individual self to be one with it; of the Cosmic Energy and meets directly the action of the cosmic forces; of the cosmic mind, life, matter and feels first a contact of its individual mind, life, body with them, then a unity in which one's own individual mentality, vitality, physicality is felt as only a part of the universal, a wave of the ocean, a dynamo receiving and formulating the universal forces. Finally, the individual melts into the cosmic Consciousness, the whole world is felt in oneself and oneself suffused through the world — it is the cosmic Consciousness, Mind, Life, material Energy that works through the individual function. The separate ego either does not exist or is only a convenience for the universal Spirit and its action. This is the complete consummation of the cosmic Consciousness, but in its fullness it is not common, belonging properly to what we may call the overmind realisation; but a constant partial and growing experience of it or an increasing contact with the cosmic Consciousness is a normal part of yoga.

What is meant in the terminology of the yoga by the psychic is the soul element in the nature, the pure psyche or divine nucleus which stands behind mind, life and body (it is not the ego) but of which we are only dimly aware. It is a portion of the Divine and permanent from life to life, taking the experience of life through its outer instruments. As this experience grows it manifests a developing psychic personality which insisting always on the good, true and beautiful, finally becomes ready and strong enough to turn the nature towards the Divine. It can then come entirely forward, breaking through the mental, vital and physical screen, govern the instincts and transform the nature. Nature no longer imposes itself on the soul, but the soul, the Purusha, imposes its dictates on the nature.

Your practice of psycho-analysis was a mistake. It has, for the time at least, made the work of purification more complicated, not easier. The psycho-analysis of Freud is the last thing that one should associate with yoga. It takes up a certain part, the darkest, the most perilous, the unhealthiest part of the nature, the lower vital subconscious layer, isolates some of its most morbid phenomena and attributes to it and them an action out of all proportion to its true role in the nature. Modern psychology is an infant science, at once rash, fumbling and crude. As in all infant sciences, the universal habit of the human mind — to take a partial or local truth, generalise it unduly and try to explain a whole field of Nature in its narrow terms — runs riot here. Moreover, the exaggeration of the importance of suppressed sexual complexes is a dangerous falsehood and it can have a nasty influence and tend to make the mind and vital more and not less fundamentally impure than before.

It is true that the subliminal in man is the largest part of his nature and has in it the secret of the unseen dynamisms which explain his surface activities. But the lower vital subconscious which is all that this psycho-analysis of Freud seems to know, — and even of that it knows only a few ill-lit corners, — is no more than a restricted and very inferior portion of the subliminal whole. The subliminal self stands behind and supports the whole superficial man; it has in it a larger and more efficient mind behind the surface mind, a larger and more powerful vital behind the surface vital, a subtler and freer physical consciousness behind the surface bodily existence. And above them it opens to higher superconscient as well as below them to lower subconscient ranges. If one wishes to purify and transform the nature, it is the power of these higher ranges to which one must open and raise to them and change by them both the subliminal and the surface being. Even this should be done with care, not prematurely or rashly, following a higher guidance, keeping always the right attitude; for otherwise the force that is drawn down may be too strong for an obscure and weak frame of nature. But to begin by opening up the lower subconscious, risking to raise up all that is foul or obscure in it, is to go out of one's way to invite trouble. First, one should make the higher mind and vital strong and firm and full of light and peace from above; afterwards one can open up or even dive into the subconscious with more safety and some chance of a rapid and successful change.

The system of getting rid of things by *anubhava* can also be a dangerous one; for on this way one can easily become more entangled instead of arriving at freedom. This method has behind it two well-known psychological motives. One, the motive of purposeful exhaustion, is valid only in some cases, especially when some natural tendency has too strong a hold or too strong a drive in it to be got rid of by *vicāra* or by the process of rejection and the substitution of the true movement in its place; when that happens in excess, the sadhak has sometimes even to go back to the ordinary action of the ordinary life, get the true experience of it with a new mind and will behind and then return to the spiritual life with the obstacle eliminated or else ready for elimination. But this method of purposive indulgence is always dangerous, though sometimes inevitable. It succeeds only when there is a very strong will in the being towards realisation; for then indulgence brings a strong dissatisfaction and reaction, *vairāgya*, and the will towards perfection can be carried down into the recalcitrant part of the nature.

The other motive for *anubhava* is of a more general applicability; for in order to reject anything from the being one has first to become conscious of it, to have the clear inner experience of its action and to discover its actual place in the workings of the nature. One can then work upon it to eliminate it, if it is an entirely wrong movement, or to transform it if it is only the degradation of a higher and true movement. It is this or something like it that is attempted crudely and improperly with a rudimentary and insufficient knowledge in the system of psychoanalysis. The process of raising up the lower movements into the full light of consciousness in order to know and deal with them is inevitable; for there can be no complete change without it. But it can truly succeed only when a higher light and force are sufficiently at work to overcome, sooner or later, the force of the tendency that is held up for change. Many, under the pretext of *anubhava*, not only raise up the adverse movement, but support it with their consent instead of rejecting it, find justifications for continuing or repeating it and so go on playing with it, indulging its return, eternising it; afterwards when they want to get rid of it, it has got such a hold that they find themselves helpless in its clutch and only a terrible struggle or an intervention of divine grace can liberate them. Some do this out of a vital twist or perversity, others out of sheer ignorance; but in yoga, as in life, ignorance is not accepted by Nature as a justifying excuse. This danger is there in all improper dealings with the ignorant parts of the nature; but none is more ignorant, more perilous, more unreasoning and obstinate in recurrence than the lower vital subconscious and its movements. To raise it up prematurely or improperly for *anubhava* is to risk suffusing the conscious parts also with its dark and dirty stuff and thus poisoning the whole vital and even the mental nature. Always therefore one should begin by a positive, not a negative experience, by bringing down something of the divine nature, calm, light, equanimity, purity, divine strength into the parts of the conscious being that have to be changed; only when that has been sufficiently done and there is a firm positive basis, is it safe to raise up the concealed subconscious adverse elements in order to destroy and eliminate them by the strength of the divine calm, light, force and knowledge. Even so, there will be enough of the lower stuff rising up of itself to give you as much of the *anubhava* as you will need for getting rid of the obstacles; but then they can be dealt with with much less danger and under a higher internal guidance.

I find it difficult to take these psycho-analysts at all seriously when they try to scrutinise spiritual experience by the flicker of their torch-lights, — yet perhaps one ought to, for half-knowledge is a powerful thing and can be a great obstacle to the coming in front of the true Truth. This new psychology looks to me very much like children learning some summary and not very adequate alphabet, exulting in putting their a-b-c-d of the subconscient and the mysterious underground super-ego together and imagining that their first book of obscure beginnings (c-a-t cat, t-r-e-e tree) is the very heart of the real knowledge. They look from down up and explain the higher lights by the lower obscurities; but the foundation of these things is above and not below, *upari budhna eṣām*. The superconscient, not the subconscient, is the true foundation of things. The significance of the lotus is not to be found by analysing the secrets of the mud from which it grows here; its secret is to be found in the heavenly archetype of the lotus that blooms for ever in the Light above. The self-chosen field of these psychologists is besides poor, dark and limited; you must know the whole before you can know the part and the highest before you can truly understand the lowest. That is the promise of the greater psychology awaiting its hour before which these poor gropings will disappear and come to nothing.

II

There is another cause of the general inability to change which at present afflicts the sadhak. It is because the sadhana, as a general fact, has now and for a long time past come down to the Inconscient; the pressure, the call is to change in that part of the nature which depends directly on the Inconscient, the fixed habits, the automatic movements, the mechanical repetitions of the nature, the involuntary reactions to life, all that seems to belong to the fixed character of a man. This has to be done if there is to be any chance of a total spiritual change. The Force (generally and not individually) is working to make that possible, its pressure is for that, — for, on the other levels, the change has already been made possible (not, mind you, assured to everybody). But to open the Inconscient to light is a herculean task; change on the other levels is much easier. As yet this work has only begun and it is not surprising that there seems to be no change in things or people. It will come in time, but not in a hurry.

As for experiences, they are all right but the trouble is that they do not seem to change the nature, they only enrich the consciousness — even the realisation, on the mind level, of the Brahman seems to leave the nature almost where it was, except for a few. That is why we insist on the psychic transformation as the first necessity — for that does change the nature — and its chief instrument is bhakti, surrender, etc.

*
**

The sunlit path can only be followed if the psychic is constantly or usually in front or if one has a natural spirit of faith and surrender or a face turned habitually towards the sun or psychic predisposition (e. g. a faith in one's spiritual destiny) or, if one has acquired the psychic turn. That does not mean that the sunlit man has no difficulties; he may have many, but he regards them cheerfully as "all in the day's work". If he gets a bad beating, he is capable of saying, "Well, that was a queer go but the Divine is evidently in a queer mood and if that is his way of doing things, it must be the right one; I am surely a still queerer fellow myself and that, I suppose, was the only means of putting me right." But everybody can't be of that turn, and surrender which would put everything right is, as you say, difficult. At least it is difficult to do completely. That is why we do not insist on total surrender at once, but are satisfied with a little to begin with, the rest to grow as it can.

I have explained to you why so many people (not by any means all) are in this gloomy condition, dull and despondent. It is the tamas, the inertia of the Inconscient, that has got hold of them. But also it is the small physical vital which takes only an interest in the small and trivial things of the ordinary daily and social life and nothing else. When formerly the sadhana was going on on the higher levels (mind, higher vital, etc.), there was plenty of vigour and verve and interest in the details of the Ashram work and life as well as in an inner life; the physical vital was carried in the stream. But for many this has dropped; they live in the unsatisfied vital physical and find everything desperately dull, gloomy and without interest or issue. In their inner life the tamas from the Inconscient has created a block or a bottle-neck and they do not find any way out. If one can keep the right condition and attitude, a strong interest in work or a strong interest in sadhana, then this becomes quiescent. That is the malady. Its remedy is to keep the right condition and to bring gradually or, if one can, swiftly, the light of the higher aspiration into this part of being also, so that whatever the conditions of the environment, it may keep, it also, the right poise. Then the sunlit path would seem less impossible.

*
**

The extreme acuteness of your difficulties is due to the yoga having come down against the bed-rock of Inconscience which is the fundamental basis of all resistance in the individual and in the world to the victory of the Spirit and the Divine Work that is leading toward that victory. The difficulties themselves are general in the Ashram as well as in the outside world. Doubt, discouragement, diminution or loss of faith, waning of the vital enthusiasm for the ideal, perplexity and a baffling of the hope for the future are the common features of the difficulty. In the world outside there are much worse symptoms such as the general increase of cynicism, a refusal to believe in anything at all, a decrease of honesty, an immense corruption, a preoccupation with food, money, comfort, pleasure, to the exclusion of higher things, and a general expectation of worse and worse things awaiting the world. All that, however acute, is a temporary phenomenon for which those who know anything about the workings of the world-energy and the workings of the Spirit were prepared. I myself foresaw that this worst would come, the darkness of night before the dawn; therefore I am not discouraged. I know what is preparing behind the darkness and can see and feel the first signs of its coming. Those who seek for the Divine have to stand firm persist in their seeking; after a time, the darkness will fade and begin to disappear and the Light will come.

I know that this is a time of trouble for you and everybody. It is so for the whole world. Confusion, trouble, disorder and upset everywhere is the general state of things. The better things that are to come are preparing or growing under a veil and the worse are prominent everywhere. The one thing is to hold on and hold out till the hour of light has come.

I am afraid I can hold out but cold comfort — for the present at least — to those of your correspondents who are lamenting the present state of things. Things are bad, are growing worse and may at any time grow worst or worse than worst if that is possible — and anything, however paradoxical, seems possible in the present perturbed world. The best thing for them is to realise that all this was necessary because certain possibilities had to emerge and be got rid of, if a new and better world was at all to come into being: it would not have done to postpone them for a later time. It is, as in yoga, where things active or latent in the being have to be put into action in the light so that they may be grappled with and thrown out or to emerge from latency in the depths for the same purificatory purpose. Also they can remember the adage that night is darkest before dawn and that the coming of dawn is inevitable. But they must remember too that the new world whose coming we envisage is not to be made of the same texture as the old and different only in pattern, and that it must come by other means — from within and not from without; so the best way is not to be too much preoccupied with the lamentable things that are happening outside, but themselves to grow within so that they may be ready for the new world, whatever the form it may take.

Remain firm through the darkness; the light is there and will conquer.

DIFFICULTIES OF THE PATH

Difficulties of the Path

ALL who enter the spiritual path have to face the difficulties and ordeals of the path, those which rise from their own nature and those which come in from outside. The difficulties in the nature always rise again and again till you overcome them; they must be faced with both strength and patience. But the vital part is prone to depression when ordeals and difficulties rise. This is not peculiar to you, but comes to all sadhaks — it does not imply an unfitness for the sadhana or justify a sense of helplessness. But you must train yourself to overcome this reaction of depression, calling in the Mother's Force to aid you.

All who cleave to the path steadfastly can be sure of their spiritual destiny. If anyone fails to reach it, it can only be for one of the two reasons, either because they leave the path or because for some lure of ambition, vanity, desire, etc. they go astray from the sincere dependence on the Divine.

It may be said generally that to be over-anxious to pull people, especially very young people, into the sadhana is not wise. The sadhak who comes to this yoga must have a real call, and even with the real call the way is often difficult enough. But when one pulls people in in a spirit of enthusiastic propagandism, the danger is of lighting an imitative and unreal fire, not the true Agni, or else a short-lived fire which cannot last and is submerged by the uprush of the vital waves. This is especially so with young people who are plastic and easily caught hold of by ideas and communicated feelings not their own — afterwards the vital rises with its unsatisfied demands and they are swung between two contrary forces or rapidly yield to the strong pull of the ordinary life and action and satisfaction of desire which is the natural bent of adolescence. Or else the unfit adhar tends to suffer under the stress of a call for which it was not ready, or at least not yet ready. When one has the real thing in oneself, one goes through and finally takes the full way of sadhana, but it is only a minority that does so. It is better to receive only people who come of themselves and of these only those in whom the call is genuinely their own and persistent.

There is no invariable rule of such suffering. It is not the soul that suffers; the Self is calm and equal to all things and the only sorrow of the psychic being is the sorrow of the resistance of Nature to the Divine Will or the resistance of things and people to the call of the True, the Good and the Beautiful. What is affected by suffering is the vital nature and the body. When the soul draws towards the Divine, there may be a resistance in the mind and the common form of that is denial and doubt — which may create mental and vital suffering. There may again be a resistance in the vital nature whose principal character is desire and the attachment to the objects of desire, and if in this field there is conflict between the soul and the vital nature, between the Divine Attraction and the pull of the Ignorance, then obviously there may be much suffering of the mind and vital parts. The physical consciousness also may offer a resistance which is usually that of a fundamental inertia, an obscurity in the very stuff of the physical, an incomprehension, an inability to respond to the higher consciousness, a habit of helplessly responding to the lower mechanically, even when it does not want to do so; both vital and physical suffering may be the consequence. There is, moreover, the resistance of the Universal Nature which does not want the being to escape from the Ignorance into the Light. This may take the form of a vehement insistence in the continuation of the old movements, waves of them thrown on the mind and vital and body so that old ideas, impulses, desires, feelings, responses continue even after they are thrown out and rejected, and can return like an invading army from outside, until the whole nature, given to the Divine, refuses to admit them. This is the subjective form of the universal resistance, but it may also take an objective form, — opposition, calumny, attacks, persecution, misfortunes of many kinds, adverse conditions and circumstances, pain, illness, assaults from men or forces. There too the possibility of suffering is evident. There are two ways to meet all that — first that of the Self, calm, equality, a spirit, a will, a mind, a vital, a physical consciousness that remain resolutely turned towards the Divine and unshaken by all suggestion of doubt, desire, attachment, depression, sorrow, pain, inertia. This is possible when the inner being awakens, when one becomes conscious of the Self, of the inner Mind, the inner Vital, the inner Physical, for that can more easily attune itself to the divine Will, and then there is a division in the being as if there were two beings, one within, calm, strong, equal, unperturbed, a channel of the Divine Consciousness and Force, one without still encroached on by the lower Nature; but then the disturbances of the latter become something superficial which are no more than an outer ripple, — until these under the inner pressure fade and sink away and the outer being too remains calm, concentrated, unattackable. There is also the way of the psychic, — when the psychic being comes out in its inherent power, its consecration, adoration, love of the Divine, self-giving, surrender and imposes these on the mind, vital and physical consciousness and compels them to turn all their movements Godward. If the psychic is strong and master throughout, then there is no or little subjective suffering and the objective cannot affect either the soul or the other parts of the consciousness — the way is sunlit and a great joy and sweetness are the note of the whole sadhana. As for the outer attacks and adverse circumstances, that depends on the action of the Force transforming the relations of the being with the outer Nature; as the victory of the Force proceeds, they will be eliminated; but however long they last, they cannot impede the sadhana, for then even adverse things and happenings become a means for its advance and for the growth of the spirit.

The difficulties that remain, although not identical, are similar in their cause and their fundamental nature to those you have either largely or completely overcome and they can be conquered in the same way; it is a question of time and of acquiescence within yourself in the pressure from the Divine which makes man change.

Human nature and the character of the individual are a formation that has arisen in and out of the inconscience of the material world and can never get entirely free from the pressure of that Inconscience. As consciousness grows in the being born into this material world, it takes the form of an Ignorance slowly admitting or striving with difficulty after knowledge and human nature is made of that Ignorance and the character of the individual is made from the elements of the Ignorance. It is largely mechanistic like everything else in material Nature and there is almost invariably a resistance and, more often than not, a strong and stubborn resistance to any change demanded from it. The character is made up of habits and it clings to them, is disposed to think them the very law of its being and it is a hard job to get it to change at all except under a strong pressure of circumstances. Especially in the physical parts, the body, the physical mind, the physical life movements, there is this resistance; the tamasic element in Nature is powerful there, what the Gita describes as *aprakāśa*, absence of light, and *apravṛtti*, a tendency to inertia, inactivity, unwillingness to make an effort and, as a result, even when the effort is made, a constant readiness to doubt, to despond and despair, to give up, renounce the aim and the endeavour, collapse. Fortunately, there is also in human nature a sattwic element which turns towards light and a rajasic or kinetic element which desires and needs to act and can be made to desire not only change but constant progress. But these too, owing to the limitations of human ignorance and the obstructions of the fundamental inconscience, suffer from pettiness and division and can resist as well as assist the spiritual endeavour. The spiritual change which yoga demands from human nature and individual character is, therefore, full of difficulties, one may almost say that it is the most difficult of all human aspirations and efforts. In so far as it can get the sattwic and the rajasic (kinetic) elements to assist it, its path is made easier but even the sattwic element can resist by attachment to old ideas, to preconceived notions, to mental preferences and partial judgments, to opinions and reasonings which come in the way of higher truth and to which it is attached: the kinetic element resists by its egoism, its passions, desires and strong attachments, its vanity and self-esteem, its constant habit of demand and many other obstacles. The resistance of the vital has a more violent character than the others and it brings to the aid of the others its own violence and passion and that is a source of all the acute difficulty, revolt, upheavals and disorders which mar the course of the yoga. The Divine is there, but He does not ignore the conditions, the laws, the circumstances of Nature; it is under these conditions that He does all His work, His work in the world and in man and consequently also in the sadhak, the aspirant, even in the God-knower and God-lover; even the saint and the sage continue to have difficulties and to be limited by their human nature. A complete liberation and a complete perfection or the complete possession of the Divine and possession by the Divine is possible, but it does not usually happen by an easy miracle or a series of miracles. The miracle can and does happen but only when there is the full call and complete self-giving of the soul and the entire widest opening of the nature.

Still, if the call of the soul is there, although not yet full, however great and obstinate the difficulties, there can be no final and irretrievable failure; even when the thread is broken, it is taken up again and reunited and carried to its end. There is a working in the nature itself in response to the inner need which, however slowly, brings about the result. But a certain inner consent is needed; the progress that you have marked in yourself is due to the fact that there was this consent in the soul and also in part of the nature; the change was insisted on by the mind and desired by part of the vital; the resistance in part of the mind and part of the vital made it slow and difficult but could not prevent it.

You ask what I want you to do. What I want is that you should persist and give more and more that assent in you which brought about the progress you have made so that here too the resistance may diminish and eventually disappear.

And get rid of an exaggerated insistence on the use of reason and the correctness of your individual reasoning and its right to decide in all matters. The reason has its place especially with regard to certain physical things and general worldly questions — though even there it is a very fallible judge — or in the formation of metaphysical conclusions and generalisations; but its claim to be the decisive authority in matters of yoga or in spiritual things is untenable. The activities of the outward intellect there lead only to the formation of personal opinions, not to the discovery of Truth. It has always been understood in India that the reason and its logic or its judgment cannot give you the realisation of spiritual truths but can only assist in an intellectual presentation of ideas; realisation comes by intuition and inner experience. Reason and intellectuality cannot make you see the Divine, it is the soul that sees. Mind and the other instruments can only share in the vision when it is imparted to them by the soul and welcome and rejoice in it. But also the mind may prevent it or at least stand long in the way of the realisation or the vision. For its prepossessions, preconceived opinions and mental preferences may build a wall of arguments against the spiritual truth that has to be realised and refuse to accept it if it presents itself in a form which does not conform to its own previous ideas: so also it may prevent one from recognising the Divine if the Divine presents himself in a form for which the intellect is not prepared or which in any detail runs counter to its prejudgments and prejudices. One can depend on one's reason in other matters provided the mind tries to be open and impartial and free from undue passion and is prepared to concede that it is not always right and may err; but it is not safe to depend on it alone in matters which escape its jurisdiction, especially in spiritual realisation and in matters of yoga which belong to a different order of knowledge.

There is no contradiction between my former statements about

the sunlit path and what I have said about the difficult and unpleasant passages which the yoga has to pass through in its
normal development in the way of human nature. The sunlit
path can be followed by those who are able to practise surrender, first a central surrender and afterwards a more complete
self-giving in all the parts of the being. If they can achieve
and preserve the attitude of the central surrender, if they can
rely wholly on the Divine and accept cheerfully whatever comes
to them from the Divine, then their path becomes sunlit and may
even be straightforward and easy. They will not escape all
difficulties, no seeker can, but they will be able to meet them
without pain and despondency, — as indeed the Gita recom-
mends that yoga should be practised, *anirviṇṇacetasā*, — trusting
in the inner guidance and perceiving it more and more or
else in the outer guidance of the Guru. It can also be followed
even when one feels no light and no guidance, if there is or if one
can acquire a bright settled faith and happy bhakti or has the
nature of the spiritual optimist and the firm belief or feeling
that all that is done by the Divine is done for the best even
when we cannot understand his action. But all have not this
nature, most are very far from it, and the complete or even
the central surrender is not easy to get, and to keep it always is
hard enough for our human nature. When these things are not
there, the liberty of the soul is not attained and we have instead
to undergo the law or fulfil a hard and difficult discipline.

That law is imposed on us by the Ignorance which is the
nature of all our parts; our physical being is obviously a mass
of ignorance, the vital is full of ignorant desires and passions,
the mind is also an instrument of Ignorance struggling towards
some kind of imperfect and mostly inferior and external knowledge. The path of the seeker proceeds through this ignorance;
for a long time he can find no light of solid experience or realisation, only the hopes and ideas and beliefs of the mind which
do not give the true spiritual seeing; or he gets glimpses of
light or periods of light but the light often goes out and the
luminous periods are followed by frequent or long periods of
darkness. There are constant fluctuations, persistent disappointments, innumerable falls and failures. No path of yoga is really

easy or free from these difficulties or fluctuations; the way of bhakti is supposed to be the easiest, but still we find constant complaints that one is always seeking but never finding and even at the best there is a constant ebb and tide, *milana* and *viraha*, joy and weeping, ecstasy and despair. If one has the faith or in the absence of faith the will to go through, one passes on and enters into the joy and light of the divine realisation. If one gets some habit of true surrender, then all this is not necessary; one can enter into the sunlit way. Or if one can get some touch of what is called pure bhakti, *śuddhā bhakti*, then whatever happens that is enough; the way becomes easy or, if it does not, still this is a sufficient start to support us to the end without the sufferings and falls that happen so often to the ignorant seeker.

In all yoga there are three essential objects to be attained by the seeker: union or abiding contact with the Divine, liberation of the soul or the self, the spirit, and a certain change of the consciousness, the spiritual change. It is this change, which is necessary for reaching the other two objects, necessary at least to a certain degree, that is the cause of most of the struggles and difficulties; for it is not easy to accomplish it; a change of the mind, a change of the heart, a change of the habits of the will is called for and is obstinately resisted by our ignorant nature. In this yoga a complete transformation of the nature is aimed at because that is necessary for the complete union and the complete liberation not only of the soul and the spirit but of the nature itself. It is also a yoga of works and of the integral divine life; for that the integral transformation of nature is evidently necessary; the union with the Divine has to carry with it a full entrance into the divine consciousness and the divine nature; there must be not only *sāyujya* or *sālokya* but *sādṛśya* or, as it is called in the Gita, *sādharmya*. The full yoga, Purna Yoga, means a fourfold path, a Yoga of Knowledge for the mind, a Yoga of Bhakti for the heart, a Yoga of Works for the will and a Yoga of Perfection for the whole nature. But ordinarily, if one can follow whole-heartedly any one of these lines, one arrives at the result of all the four. For instance, by bhakti one becomes close to the Divine, becomes intensely aware of him and arrives at knowledge, for the Divine is the Truth and the Reality; by knowing him, says the Upanishads, one comes to know all. By bhakti also the will is led into the road of the works of love and the service of the Divine and the government of the nature and its acts by the Divine and that is Karmayoga. By bhakti also comes spiritual change of the consciousness and the action of the nature which is the first step towards its transformation. So it is with all the other lines of the fourfold path. But it may be that there are many obstacles in the being to the domination of the mind and heart and will by bhakti and the consequent contact with the Divine. The too great activity of the intellectual mind and its attachment to its own pride of ideas, its prejudices, its fixed notions and its ignorant reason may shut the doors to the inner light and prevent the full tide of bhakti from flooding everything; it may also cling to a surface mental activity and refuse to go inside and allow the psychic vision and the feelings of the inner heart to become its guides, though it is by this vision and this feeling that bhakti grows and conquers. So too the passions and desires of the vital being and its ego may block the way and prevent the self-giving of the mind and heart to the Divine. The inertia, ignorance and inconscience of one's physical consciousness, its attachment to fixed habits of thought and feeling and action, its persistence in the old grooves may come badly in the way of the needed change. In such circumstances the Divine may have to bide his time; but if there is real hunger in the heart, all that cannot prevent the final realisation; still, it may have to wait till the obstructions are removed or at least so much cleared out as to admit an unimpeded working of the Divine Power on the surface nature. Till then, there may be periods of inner ease and some light in the mind, periods also of the feeling of bhakti or of peace, periods of the joy of self-consecration in works and service; for these will take long to stay permanently and there will be much struggle and unrest and suffering. In the end the Divine's workings will appear and one will be able to live in his presence.

I have described the difficulties of yoga at their worst, as they may hamper and afflict even those predestined to the realisation but as often there is an alternation or a mixture of the light and the darkness, initial attainment perhaps and heavy subsequent difficulties, progress and attacks and retardations, strong movements forward and a floundering in the bogs of the Ignorance. Even great realisations may come and high splendours of light and spiritual experience and yet the goal is not attained; for in the phrase of the Rig Veda, "As one climbs from peak to peak there is made clear the much that is still to be done." But there is always something that either carries us on or forces us on. This may take the shape of something conscious in front, the shape of a mastering spiritual idea, indestructible aspiration or fixed faith which may seem sometimes entirely veiled or even destroyed in periods of darkness or violent upheaval, but always they reappear when the storm has passed or the blackness of night has thinned, and reassert their influence. But also it may be something in the very essence of the being deeper than any idea or will in the mind, deeper and more permanent than the heart's aspiration but hidden from one's own observation. One who is moved to yoga by some curiosity of the mind or even by its desire for knowledge can turn aside from the path from disappointment or any other cause; still more can those who take it up from some inner ambition or vital desire turn away through revolt or frustration or the despondency of frequent check and failure. But if this deeper thing is there, then one cannot permanently leave the path of spiritual endeavour: one may decide to leave the path but is not allowed from within to do it or one may leave but is obliged to return to it by the secret spiritual need within him.

All these things are common to every path of yoga; they are the normal difficulties, fluctuations and struggles which come across the path of spiritual effort. But in this yoga there is an order or succession of the workings of the secret Force which may vary greatly in its circumstances in each sadhak, but still maintains its general line. Our evolution has brought the being up out of inconscient Matter into the Ignorance of mind, life and body tempered by an imperfect knowledge and is trying to lead us into the light of the Spirit, to lift us into that light and to bring the light down into us, into body and life as well as mind and heart and to fill with it all that we are. This and its consequences, of which the greatest is the union with the Divine and life in the divine consciousness, is the meaning of the integral trans-formation. Mind is our present topmost faculty; it is through the thinking mind and the heart with the soul, the psychic being behind them that we have to grow into the Spirit, for what the Force first tries to bring about is to fix the mind in the right central idea, faith or mental attitude and the right aspiration and poise of the heart and to make these sufficiently strong and firm to last in spite of other things in the mind and heart which are other than or in conflict with them. Along with this it brings whatever experiences, realisations or descent or growth of knowledge the mind of the individual is ready for at the time or as much of it, however small, as is necessary for its further progress: sometimes these realisations and experiences are very great and abundant, sometimes few and small or negligible; in some there seems to be in this first stage nothing much of these things or nothing decisive — the Force seems to concentrate on a preparation of the mind only. In many cases the sadhana seems to begin and proceed with experiences in the vital; but in reality this can hardly take place without some mental prepa-ration, even if it is nothing more than a turning of the mind or some kind of opening which makes the vital experiences possible. In any case, to begin with the vital is a hazardous affair; the difficulties there are more numerous and more violent than on the mental plane and the pitfalls are innumerable. The access to the soul, the psychic being is less easy because it is covered up with a thick veil of ego, passion and desire. One is apt to be swallowed up in a maze of vital experiences, not always reliable, the temptation of small siddhis, the appeal of the powers of darkness to the ego. One has to struggle through these densities to the psychic being behind and bring it forward; then only can the sadhana on the vital plane be safe.

However that be, the descent of the sadhana, of the action of the Force into the vital plane of our being becomes after some time necessary. The Force does not make a wholesale change of the mental being and nature, still less an integral transforma-tion before it takes this step: if that could be done, the rest of the sadhana would be comparatively secure and easy. But the vital is there and always pressing on the mind and heart, disturbing and endangering the sadhana and it cannot be left to itself for too long. The ego and desires of the vital, its disturbances and upheavals have to be dealt with and if not at once expelled, at least dominated and prepared for a gradual if not a rapid modification, change, illumination. This can only be done on the vital plane itself by descending to that level. The vital ego itself must become conscious of its own defects and willing to get rid of them; it must decide to throw away its vanities, ambitions, lusts and longings, its rancours and revolts and all the rest of the impure stuff and unclean movements within it. This is the time of the greatest difficulties, revolts and dangers. The vital ego hates being opposed in its desires, resents disappointment, is furious against wounds to its pride and vanity; it does not like the process of purification and it may very well declare Satyagraha against it, refuse to co-operate, justify its own demands and inclinations, offer passive resistance of many kinds, withdraw the vital support which is necessary both to the life and the sadhana and try to withdraw the being from the path of spiritual endeavour. All this has to be faced and overcome, for the temple of the being has to be swept clean if the Lord of our being is to take his place and receive our worship there.

The question you have put raises one of the most difficult and complicated of all problems and to deal with it at all adequately would need an answer as long as the longest chapter of *The Life Divine*. I can only state my own knowledge founded not on reasoning but on experience that there is such a guidance and that nothing is in vain in this universe.

    If we look only at outward facts in their surface appearance or if we regard what we see happening around us as definitive, not as processes of a moment in a developing whole, the guidance is not apparent; at most, we may see interventions occasional or sometimes frequent. The guidance can become evident only if we go behind appearances and begin to understand the forces at work and the way of their working and their secret significance.

After all, real knowledge — even scientific knowledge — comes by going behind the surface phenomena to their hidden process and causes. It is quite obvious that this world is full of suffering, and afflicted with transience to a degree that seems to justify the Gita's description of it as "this unhappy and transient world", *anityam asukham*. The question is whether it is a mere creation of Chance or governed by a mechanical inconscient Law or whether there is a meaning in it and something beyond its present appearance towards which we move. If there is a meaning and if there is something towards which things are evolving, then inevitably there must be a guidance — and that means that a supporting Consciousness and Will is there with which we can come into inner contact. If there is such a Consciousness and Will, it is not likely that it would stultify itself by annulling the world's meaning or turning it into a perpetual or eventual failure.

This world has a double aspect. It seems to be based on a material Inconscience and an ignorant mind and life full of that Inconscience: error and sorrow, death and suffering are the necessary consequence. But there is evidently too a partially successful endeavour and an imperfect growth towards Light, Knowledge, Truth, Good, Happiness, Harmony, Beauty, — at least a partial flowering of these things. The meaning of this world must evidently lie in this opposition; it must be an evolution which is leading or struggling towards higher things out of a first darker appearance. Whatever guidance there is must be given under these conditions of opposition and struggle and must be leading towards that higher state of things. It is leading the individual, certainly, and the world, presumably, towards the higher state, but through the double terms of knowledge and ignorance, light and darkness, death and life, pain and pleasure, happiness and suffering; none of the terms can be excluded until the higher status is reached and established. It is not and cannot be, ordinarily, a guidance which at once rejects the darker terms, still less a guidance which brings us solely and always nothing but happiness, success and good fortune. Its main concern is with the growth of our being and consciousness, the growth towards a higher self, towards the Divine, eventually towards a higher Light, Truth and Bliss; the rest is secondary, sometimes a means, sometimes a result, not a primary purpose.

The true sense of the guidance becomes clearer when we can go deep within and see from there more intimately the play of the forces and receive intimations of the Will behind them. The surface mind can get only an imperfect glimpse. When we are in contact with the Divine or in contact with an inner knowledge and vision, we begin to see all the circumstances of our life in a new light and can observe how they all tended, without our knowing it, towards the growth of our being and consciousness, towards the work we had to do, towards some development that had to be made, — not only what seemed good, fortunate or successful but also the struggles, failures, difficulties, upheavals. But with each person the guidance works differently according to his nature, the conditions of his life, his cast of consciousness, his stage of development, his need of further experience. We are not automata but conscious beings and our mentality, our will and its decisions, our attitude to life and demand on it, our motives and movements help to determine our course: they may lead to much suffering and evil, but through it all, the guidance makes use of them for our growth in experience and consequently the development of our being and consciousness. All advance, by however devious ways, even in spite of what seems a going backwards or going astray, gathering whatever experience is necessary for the soul's destiny. When we are in close contact with the Divine, a protection can come which helps or directly guides or moves us: it does not throw aside all difficulties, sufferings or dangers, but it carries us through them and out of them — except where for a special purpose there is need of the opposite.

It is the same thing though on a larger scale and in a more complex way with the guidance of the world-movement. That seems to move according to the conditions and laws or forces of the moment through constant vicissitudes, but still there is something in it that drives towards the evolutionary purpose, although it is more difficult to see, understand and follow than in the smaller and more intimate field of the individual consciousness and life. What happens at a particular juncture of the world-action or the life of humanity, however catastrophical, is not ultimately determinative. Here, too, one has to see not only the outward play of forces in a particular case or at a particular time but also the inner and secret play, the far-off outcome, the event that lies beyond and the Will at work behind it all. Falsehood and Darkness are strong everywhere on the earth, and have always been so and at times they seem to dominate; but there have also been not only gleams but outbursts of the Light. In the mass of things and the long course of Time, whatever may be the appearance of this or that epoch or movement, the growth of Light is there and the struggle towards better things does not cease. At the present time Falsehood and Darkness have gathered their forces and are extremely powerful; but even if we reject the assertion of the mystics and prophets since early times that such a condition of things must precede the Manifestation and is even a sign of its approach, yet it does not necessarily indicate the decisive victory — even temporary — of the Falsehood. It merely means that the struggle between the Forces is at its acme. The result may very well be the stronger emergence of the best that can be: for the world-movement often works in that way. I leave it at that and say nothing more.

This yoga is certainly difficult, but is any yoga really easy? You speak of the lure of liberation into the extra-cosmic Absolute, but how many who set out on the Path of Nirvana attain to it in this life or without a long, strenuous and difficult endeavour? Which of the paths has not to pass through the dry desert in order to reach the promised land? Even the path of Bhakti which is said to be the easiest is full of the lamentations of the bhaktas complaining that they call but the Beloved eludes their grasp, the place of meeting is prepared but even now Krishna does not come. Even if there is the joy of a brief glimpse or the passion of *milana*, it is followed by long periods of *viraha*. It is a mistake to think that any path of yoga is facile, that any is a royal road or short cut to the Divine, or that there can be, like a system of "French made easy" or "French without tears", also a system of "yoga made easy" or "yoga without tears". A few great souls prepared by past lives or otherwise lifted beyond the ordinary spiritual capacity may attain realisation more swiftly; some may have uplifting experiences at an early stage, but for most the *siddhi* of the path, whatever it is, must be the end of a long, difficult and persevering endeavour. One cannot have the crown of spiritual victory without the struggle or reach the heights without the ascent and its labour. Of all it can be said, "Difficult is that road hard to tread like the edge of a razor."

You find the path dry precisely because you have not yet touched the fringe of it. But all paths have their dry periods and for most, though not for all, it is so at the beginning. There is a long stage of preparation necessary in order to arrive at the inner psychological condition in which the doors of experience can open and one can walk from vista to vista — though even then new gates may present themselves and refuse to open until all is ready. This period can be dry and desert-like unless one has the ardour of self-introspection and self-conquest and finds every step of the effort and struggle interesting or unless one has or gets the secret of trust and self-giving which sees the hand of the Divine in every step of the path and even in the difficulty the grace or the guidance. The description of yoga as "bitter like poison in the beginning" because of the difficulty and struggle, "but in the end sweet as nectar" because of the joy of realisation, the peace of liberation or the divine Ananda and the frequent description by sadhaks and bhaktas of the periods of dryness shows sufficiently that it is no unique peculiarity of this yoga. All the old disciplines recognised this and it is why the Gita says that yoga should be practised patiently and steadily with a heart that refuses to be overcome by despondency. It is a recommendation applicable to this path, but also to the way of the Gita and to the hard "razor path" of the Vedanta, to every other. It is quite natural that the higher the Ananda to come down, the more difficult may be the beginning, the drier the deserts that have to be crossed on the way.

Certainly, the supramental manifestation does not bring peace, purity, force, power or knowledge only; these give the necessary conditions for the final realisation, are part of it, but Love, Beauty and Ananda are the essence of its fulfilment. And although the supreme Ananda comes with the supreme fulfilment, there is no real reason why there should not be the Love and Ananda and Beauty on the way also. Some have found that even at an early stage before there was any other experience. But the secret of it is in the heart, not in the mind — the heart that opens its inner door and through it the radiance of the soul looks out in a blaze of trust and self-giving. Before that inner fire the debates of the mind and its difficulties wither away and the path however long or arduous becomes a sunlit road not only towards but through love and Ananda.

Nevertheless, even if that does not come at first, one can arrive at it by a patient perseverance — the psychic change is indeed the indispensable preliminary of any approach to the supramental path and this change has for its very core the blossoming of the inner love, joy, bhakti. Some may find a mental opening first and the mental opening may bring peace, light, a beginning of knowledge first, but this opening from above is incomplete unless it is followed by an opening inward of the heart. To suppose that the yoga is dry and joyless because the struggles of your mind and vital have made your first approach to it dry is a misunderstanding and an error. The hidden springs of sweetness will reveal themselves if you persevere, even if now they are guarded by the dragons of doubt and unsatisfied longing. Grumble, if your nature compels you to it, but persevere.

The supramental is not, as you imagine, something cold, hard and rock-like. It bears within it the presence of the Divine Love as well as the Divine Truth, and its reign here means for those who accept it, the straight and thornless path in which there is no wall or obstacle, of which the ancient Rishis saw the far-off promise.

The dark path is there and there are many who make, like the Christians, a Gospel of spiritual suffering; many hold it to be the unavoidable price of victory. It may be so under certain circumstances, as it has been in so many lives at the beginning, or one may choose to make it so. But then the price has to be paid with resignation, fortitude or a tenacious resilience. I admit that, if borne in that way, the attacks of the dark forces or the ordeals they impose have a meaning. After each victory gained over them, there is then a sensible advance; often they seem to show us the difficulties in ourselves which we have to overcome and to say: "Here you must conquer"; but all the same it is a too dark and difficult way which nobody should follow on whom the necessity does not lie.

So many have done yoga relying on Tapasya or anything else, but not confident of any Divine Grace. It is not that, but the soul's demand for a higher Truth or a higher Life that is indispensable. Where that is, the Divine Grace whether believed in or not will intervene. If you believe, that hastens and facilitates things; if you cannot yet believe, still the soul's aspiration will justify itself, with whatever difficulty and struggle.

You are quite right in taking an optimistic and not a pessimistic attitude in the sadhana — progressive sadhana is enormously helped by an assured faith and confidence. Such a confidence helps to realise, for it is dynamic and tends to fulfil itself.

As for the sceptics — well, optimism even unjustified is still justifiable because it gives a chance and a force for getting things done, while pessimism even with all the grounds that appearances can give to it, is simply a clog and a "No going" affair. The right thing is to go ahead and get done all that can be, if possible all that ought to be, but at least do so much that all that ought will feel bound to come along on the heels of my doing. That is the prophets and the gospel.

If these things [wrong movements] had disappeared already, there would be the victory already. What I mean[1] is the certi-

---

[1] "You must make grow in you the peace that is born of the certitude of victory."

tude of the eventual victory which is a matter of faith and an inner reliance upon the Divine. The peace born of this certitude carries one through all persistence or return of difficulties.

I quite agree with you in not relishing the idea of another attack of this nature. I am myself, I suppose, more a hero by necessity than by choice — I do not love storms and battles, at least on the subtle plane. The sunlit way may be an illusion, — though I do not think it is, — for I have seen people treading it for years; but a way with only natural or even only moderate fits of rough weather, a way without typhoons surely is possible — there are so many examples; *durgam pathastat* may be generally true and certainly the path of Laya or Nirvana is difficult in the extreme to most (although in my case I walked into Nirvana without intending it or rather Nirvana walked casually into me not so far from the beginning of my yogic career without asking my leave). But the path need not be cut by periodical violent storms, though that it is so for a great many is an obvious fact. But even for these if they stick to it, I find that after a certain point the storms diminish in force, frequency, duration. That is why I insisted so much on your sticking — for if you stick, the turning-point is bound to come. I have seen some astonishing instances recently of this typhonic periodicity beginning to fade out after years and years of violent recurrence.

These things are not part of the normal difficulties, however acute, of the nature but special formations — tornadoes which start (usually from a particular point, sometimes varying) and go whirling round in the same circle always till it is finished ....To dissolve it ought to be possible if one sees it for what it is and is resolved to get rid of it — never allowing any mental justification of it, however logical, right and plausible the justification may seem to be — always replying to all the mind's arguments or the vital's feelings in favour of it, like Cato to the debaters, "Delenda est Carthago" — "Carthage has to be destroyed", Carthage in this case being the formation and its nefarious circle.

Anyway the closing idea in your letter is the right one. "The Divine is worth ferretting out even if oceans of gloom have to be crossed." If you could confront the formation always with that firm resolution, it should bring victory.

Thirst for the Divine is one thing and depression is quite another, nor is depression a neeessary consequence of the thirst being unsatisfied, that may lead to a more ardent thirst or to a fixed resolution and persistent effort or to a more yearning call or to a psychic sorrow which is not at all identical with depression and despair. Depression is a clouded grey state in its nature and it is more difficult for light to come through clouds and greyness than through a clear atmosphere. That depression obstructs the inner light is a matter of general experience. The Gita says expressly, "Yoga should be practised persistently with a heart free from depression" — *anirviṇṇacetasā*. Bunyan in *The Pilgrim's Progress* symbolises it as the Slough of Despond, one of the perils of the way that has to be overcome. It is, no doubt, impossible to escape from attacks of depression, almost all sadhaks go through these attacks, but the principle is that one should react against them and not allow them by any kind of mental encouragement or acceptance of their suggestions to persist or grow chronic.

It is hardly a fact that sorrow is *necessary* in order to make the soul seek the Divine. It is the call of the soul within for the Divine that makes it turn, and that may come under any circumstances — in full prosperity and enjoyment, at the height of outward conquest and victory without any sorrow or disappointment, but by a sudden or growing enlightenment, by a flash of light in the midst of sensuous passion, as in Bilwamangal, by the perception that there is something greater and truer than this outward life lived in ego and ignorance. None of these turns need be accompanied by sorrow and depression. Often one turns saying, "Life is all very well and interesting enough as a game, but it is only a game, the spiritual reality is greater than the life of mind and senses." In whatever way it comes, it is the call of the Divine or the soul's call to the Divine that matters, the attraction of it is something far greater than the things that usually hold the nature. Certainly if one is satisfied with life, entranced by it so that it shuts out the sense of the soul within or hampers the attraction to the Divine, then a period of vairagya, sorrow, depression, a painful breaking of the vital ties may be necessary and many go through that. But once the turn made, it should be to the one direction and a perpetual vairagya is not needed. Nor when we speak of cheerfulness as the best condition, do we mean a cheerful following of the vital life, but a cheerful following of the path to the Divine which is not impossible if the mind and heart take the right view and posture. At any rate, if positive cheerfulness is not possible in one's case, still one should not acquiesce in or mentally support a constant depression and sadness. That is not at all indispensable for keeping turned to the Divine.

In speaking of the Buddhist and his nine years of the wall and other instances, the Mother was only disproving the view that not having succeeded in seven or eight years meant unfitness and debarred all hope for the future. The man of the wall stands among the greatest names in Japanese Buddhism and his long sterility did not mean incapacity or spiritual unfitness; but apart from that there are many who have gone on persisting for long periods and finally prevailed. It is a common, not an uncommon experience.

I don't believe much in this Divine Darkness. It is a Christian idea. For us the Divine is Peace, Purity, Wideness, Light, Ananda.

Buddhism is the turning away from *duḥkha* and its causes to the attracting face of Nirvana. The *duḥkhavāda* did not exist in India, except in the theory of the Vaishnava *viraha*; otherwise it was not considered as a means or even a stage of the sadhana. But that does not mean that *duḥkha* does not come in the sadhana; it comes and has to be rejected and overcome, over-passed — excepting the psychic sorrow which does not disturb or depress but rather liberates the vital. To make a *vāda* or gospel of sorrow is dangerous because sorrow, if indulged, becomes a habit, sticks and few things, if once they stick, can be more sticky.

Suffering is not inflicted as a punishment for sin or for hostility — that is a wrong idea. Suffering comes like pleasure and good fortune as an inevitable part of life in the ignorance. The dualities of pleasure and pain, joy and grief, good fortune and ill-fortune are the inevitable results of the ignorance which separates us from our true consciousness and from the Divine. Only by coming back to it can we get rid of suffering. Karma from the past lives exists, much of what happens is due to it, but not all. For we can mend our karma by our own consciousness and efforts. But the suffering is simply a natural consequence of past errors, not a punishment, just as a burn is the natural consequence of playing with fire. It is part of the experience by which the soul through its instruments learns and grows until it is ready to turn to the Divine.

Sometimes pain and suffering are means by which the soul is awakened and pushed forward to the Divine. That is the experience on which X constantly dwells as he has suffered much in his life — but all do not find it like that.

The attitude you express in your letter is quite the right one — whatever sufferings come on the path, are not too high a price for the victory that has to be won and if they are taken in the right spirit, they become even a means towards the victory.

The idealists' question is why should there be pain at all even if it is outweighed by the fundamental pleasure of existence? The real crux is why should inadequacy, limit and suffering come across this natural pleasure of life? It does not mean that life is essentially miserable in its very nature.

I cannot say that I follow very well the logic of your doubts. How does the suffering of a noble and selfless friend invalidate the hope of yoga? There are many dismal spectacles in the world, but that is after all the very reason why yoga has to be done. If the world were all happy and beautiful and ideal, who would want to change it or find it necessary to bring down a higher consciousness into the earthly Mind and Matter? Your other argument is that the work of the yoga itself is difficult, not easy, not a happy canter to the goal. Of course it is, because the world and human nature are what they are. I never said it was easy or that there were not obstinate difficulties in the way of the endeavour. Again, I do not understand your point about raising up a new race by my going on writing "trivial" letters ten hours a day. Of course not — nor by writing important letters either; even if I were to spend my time writing fine poems it would not build up a new race. Each activity is important in its own place — an electron or a molecule or a grain may be small things in themselves, but in their place they are indispensable to the building up of a world; it cannot be made up only of mountains and sunsets and streamings of the aurora borealis — though these have their place there. All depends on the force behind these things and the purpose in their action — and that is known to the Cosmic Spirit which is at work; and it works, I may add, not by the mind or according to human standards but by a greater consciousness which, starting from an electron, can build up a world and, using a tangle of ganglia, can make them the base here for the works of the Mind and Spirit in Matter, produce a Ramakrishna, or a Napoleon, or a Shakespeare. Is the life of a great poet either made up only of magnificent and important things? How many trivial things had to be dealt with and done before there could be produced a "King Lear" or a "Hamlet"? Again, according to your own reasoning, would not people be justified in mocking at your pother — so they would call it, I do not — about metre and scansion and how many ways a syllable can be read? Why, they might say, is he wasting his time in trivial prosaic things like this when he might have been spending it in producing a beautiful lyric or fine music? But the worker knows and respects the material with which he must work and he knows why he is busy with "trifles" and small details and what is their place in the fullness of his labour.

As for faith, you write as if I never had a doubt or any difficulty. I have had worse than any human mind can think of. It is not because I have ignored difficulties, but because I have seen them more clearly, experienced them on a larger scale than anyone living now or before me that, having faced and measured them, I am sure of the results of my work. But even if I still saw the chance that it might come to nothing (which is impossible), I would go on unperturbed, because I would still have done to the best of my power the work that I had to do and what is so done always counts in the economy of the universe. But why should I feel that all this may come to nothing when I see each step and where it is leading and every week, every day — once it was every year and month and hereafter it will be every day and hour — brings me so much nearer to my goal? In the way that one treads with the greater Light above, even every difficulty gives its help and has its value and Night itself carries in it the burden of the Light that has to be.

As for the blows, well, are they always given by the yoga? Is it not sometimes the sadhak of the yoga who gives blows to himself? There are plenty of blows in ordinary life according to my experience. Blows are the order of existence: our own nature and the nature of things bring them upon us until we learn to present to them a back which they cannot touch.

**

It is a lesson of life that always in this world everything fails a man — only the Divine does not fail him, if he turns entirely to the Divine. It is not because there is something bad in you that blows fall on you — blows fall on all human beings because they are full of desire for things that cannot last and they lose them or, even if they get, it brings disappointment and cannot satisfy them. To turn to the Divine is the only truth in life.

All X's troubles are due partly to past Karma in another life, partly to his nature which is unable to harmonise with his surroundings or to master them by strong will and clear understanding or to face them with calm poise and balance. Life is for experience and growth and until one has learned one's lesson things go on happening that are the result of one's imperfect balance with Nature or inner imperfections. All that happens is for the best is true only if we see with the cosmic view that takes in past and future development which is aided by ill fortune, as well as good fortune, by danger, death, suffering and calamity, as well as by happiness, success and victory. It is not true if it means that only things happen which are fortunate or obviously good for the person in the human sense.

All these difficulties should be faced in a more quiet and less egoistic spirit.

This yoga is a spiritual battle; its very attempt raises all sorts of adverse forces and one must be ready to face difficulties, sufferings, reverses of all sorts in a calm unflinching spirit.

The difficulties that come are ordeals and tests and if one meets them in the right spirit, one comes out stronger and spiritually purer and greater.

No misfortune can come, the adverse forces cannot touch or be victorious unless there is some defect in oneself, some impurity, weakness or, at the very least, ignorance. One should then seek out this weakness in oneself and correct it.

When there is an attack from the human instruments of adverse forces, one should try to overcome it not in a spirit of personal hatred or anger or wounded egoism, but with a calm spirit of strength and equanimity and a call to the Divine Force to act. Success or failure lies with the Divine.

In dealing with others there is a way of speaking and doing which gives most offence and opens one most to misunderstanding and there is also a way which is quiet and firm but conciliatory to those who can be conciliated — all who are not absolutely of bad will. It is better to use the latter than the former. No weakness, no arrogance or violence, this should be the spirit.

Vital difficulties are the common lot of every human being and of every sadhak. They are to be met with a quiet determination and confidence in the Divine.

Yoga has always its difficulties, whatever yoga it be. Moreover, it acts in a different way on different seekers. Some have to overcome the difficulties of their nature first before they get any experiences to speak of, others get a splendid beginning and all the difficulties afterwards, others go on for a long time having alternate risings to the top of the wave and then a descent into the gulfs and so on till the difficulty is worked out, others have a smooth path which does not mean that they have no difficulties — they have plenty, but they do not care a straw for them, because they feel that the Divine will help them to the goal or that he is with them even when they do not feel him — their faith makes them imperturbable.

It needs either a calm resolute will governing the whole being or a very great *samatā* to have a quite smooth transformation. If they are there, then there are no revolts though there may be difficulties, no attacks, only a conscious dealing with the defects of the nature, no falls but only setting right of wrong steps or movements.

The headache if it comes is only a result of the body not being accustomed to the pressure or else to some resistance there. The difficulties of course rise up, but it is not always in the beginning. Sometimes the first effect is such that one feels as if there were no difficulties, — they rise afterwards when the exultation wanes and the normal consciousness has a chance to assert itself against the flood of power or light from above. There is a resistance that has to be fought out or worked out — fought out if the nature is unsteady or insists violently, worked out if the will is steady and the nature moderate in its reactions. On the other hand if there has been a long preparation and the resistances of the nature have been already largely dealt with by the psychic or by the enlightened mental will, then there are no primary or later aggravations but a steady and quiet pushing through of the change, the remaining difficulties falling away of themselves as the new consciousness develops, or else there may be no difficulties at all, only a necessary readjustment and change.

The rush of the experience at the beginning is often very powerful, so powerful that the resisting elements remain quiescent — afterwards they rise up. The experience has then to be brought down and settled in these parts also.

I have never said that yoga or that this yoga is a safe and easy path. What I say is that anyone who has the will to go through, can go through. For the rest, if you aim high there is always the danger of a steep fall if you misconduct your aeroplane. But the danger is for those who allow themselves to entertain a double being, aiming high but also indulging their lower outlook and hankerings. What else can you expect when people do that? You must become single-minded, then the difficulties of the mind and vital will be overcome. Otherwise, those who oscillate between their heights and their abysses will always be in danger till they have become single-minded. That applies to the "advanced" as well as to the beginner. These are facts of nature; I can't pretend for anybody's comfort that they are otherwise. But there is the fact also that nobody need keep himself in this danger. One-mindedness, surrender to the Divine, faith, true love for the Divine, complete sincerity in the will, spiritual humility (real, not formal) — there are so many things that can be a safeguard against any chance of eventual downfall. Slips, stumbles, difficulties, upsettings everyone has; one can't be assured against these things, but if one has the safeguards, they are transitory, help the nature to learn and are followed by a better progress.

Yes, but it is an absence of the one-pointed aspiration more than of strength of will — they [some sadhaks] left because some desire or other got hold of them which was incompatible with the steadfast single-minded aspiration to the Divine Realisation.

If Buddha had the will only after *tapasyā*, how was it that he left everything without hesitation in the search for Truth and never once looked back, regretted nor had any struggle. The only difficulty was how to find the Truth, his single will to find it never faltered; the intensity of his *tapasyā* itself would have been impossible without that strength of will. People less strong than Buddha may have to develop it by endeavour. Those who cannot do that have to find their strength in their reliance on the Divine Mother.

A sincere heart is worth all the extraordinary powers in the world.

If X has allowed any fall in her consciousness and action which retards her sadhana and is not yet able wholly to overcome her weakness, that is no reason why you should allow *her* difficulty to overcome *your* faith and endeavour. There is no natural connection between the two and no reason why there should be — it is only your mind that is making one. Each sadhak has his own separate sadhana, his own difficulties, his own way to follow. His sadhana is between him and the Divine; no one else has a part in it. Nor is there any reason why, even if one falls or fails, the other should torment himself for that, lose his faith and abandon his way. X's struggle, whatever its nature or limits, is her own and concerns herself and the Mother. It is not yours and ought not to touch or concern you at all; if you allow it to touch and shake you because she happens to be your sister, you bring in an unnecessary difficulty to add to your own and hamper your own progress. Keep to your own path, concentrate on your own obstacles to overcome them. As for her, you can at most pray to the Divine Power to help her and leave it there.

There is no reason to have a vague doubt about one's own future founded upon no other ground than the failure of others. That is what X and Y are always doing, and it is a great disturber of their progress. Why not instead, if one is to go by others, gather hope from the example of those who are satisfied and progressing? It is true however that these do not show their success as the others do their failure. However, that apart, failure comes by very positive errors and most by the absence of an invariable and unflagging aspiration or effort. The effort demanded of the sadhak is that of aspiration, rejection and surrender. If these three are done the rest is to come of itself by the Grace of the Mother and the working of her force in you. But of the three the most important is surrender of which the first necessary form is trust and confidence and patience in difficulty. There is no rule that trust and confidence can only remain if aspiration is there. On the contrary, when even aspiration is not there because of the pressure of inertia, trust and confidence and patience can remain. If trust and patience fail when aspiration is quiescent, that would

mean that the sadhak is relying solely on his own effort — it
would mean "Oh my aspiration has failed, so there is no hope
for me. My aspiration fails so what can Mother do?" On the
contrary, the sadhak should feel "Never mind, my aspiration
will come back again. Meanwhile I know that the Mother is
with me even when I do not feel her; she will carry me through
even the darkest period." That is the fully right attitude you
must have. To those who have it depression could do nothing;
even if it comes it has to return baffled. That is not tamasic
surrender. Tamasic surrender is when one says "I won't do
anything; let Mother do everything. Aspiration, rejection,
surrender even are not necessary. Let her do all that in me."
There is a great difference between the two attitudes. One is that
of the shirker who won't do anything, the other is that of the
sadhak who does his best but when he is reduced to quiescence
for a time and things are adverse, keeps always his trust in the
Mother's force and presence behind all and by that trust baffles
the opposition force and calls back the activity of the sadhana.

X's fall after his one year's rapid progress had obvious reasons
in *his* character which do not exist in others. It is well-known to
all yogis that a fall is possible and the Gita speaks of it more
than once. But how does the fall prove that spiritual experience is
not true and genuine? The fall of a man from a great height
does not prove that he never reached a great height.

A man who has risen high *can* fall low, especially if his experiences
are only through the spiritual mind and the vital and physical
remain as they were. But it is an absurdity to say that he is *sure*
to fall low.

II

Everyone whose psychic being calls him to the spiritual path has a capacity for that path and can arrive at the goal if or as soon as he develops a single-pointed will towards that alone. But also every sadhak is faced with two elements in him, the inner being which wants the Divine and the sadhana and the outer mainly vital and physical being which does not want them but remains attached to the things of the ordinary life. The mind is sometimes led by one, sometimes by the other. One of the most important things he has to do, therefore, is to decide fundamentally the quarrel between these two parts and to persuade or compel by psychic aspiration, by steadiness of the mind's thought and will, by the choice of the higher vital in his emotional being the opposing elements to be first quiescent and then consenting. So long as he is not able to do that his progress must be either very slow or fluctuating and chequered as the aspiration within cannot have a continuous action or a continuous result. Besides so long as this is so, there are likely to be periodical revolts of the vital, repining at the slow progress, despairing, desponding, declaring the Adhar unfit; calls from the old life will come; circumstances will be attracted which seem to justify it, suggestions will come from men and unseen powers pressing the sadhak away from the sadhana and pointing backward to the former life. And yet in that life he is not likely to get any real satisfaction.

Your circumstances are not different from those of others in the beginning and for a long time afterwards. You have come away from the family life, but something in your vital has still kept a habit of response and it is that that is being used to pull you away. This is aided by the impatience of the vital because there is no rapid spiritual progress or continuous good condition — things which even the greatest sadhaks take time to acquire. Circumstances combine to assist the pull — things like X's illness or your husband's appeals which when he soothes and flatters and prays and promises instead of being offensive succeed in mollifying you and creating a condition of less effective defence. And there is the vital Nature and its powers suggesting this and that, that you are not fit, that there is no aspiration, that the Mother and Sri Aurobindo do not help, are displeased, do not care, and it is best to go home.

All that most sadhaks have gone through and come out of

it and left the old bonds behind them. There is no reason why you should not do so too. Our help is there always, it is not given at one time and withheld at another, nor given to some and denied to others. It is there for all who make the effort and have the will to arrive. But you have to be steady in your will and not be taken in and deceived by the suggestions from outside or those that come in the shape of your own adverse thoughts and depressions — you have to fight these and surmount them. It may take a shorter or longer time according to your energy in combating and overcoming them. But everybody has to make that effort of mastery and overcome the old vital nature.

As for your going over there, you have to look at yourself and see clearly what is wanting to take you there. The plea from inability to do the sadhana has no value whatever. It is merely a plea put forward by the opposing elements in the vital and strengthened by the suggestion of adverse forces. If you say that you find your attachment to husband and son or others is so strong that your soul and your aspiration can do nothing against it and home is the real place for you, then of course your departure is inevitable — but such a statement can hardly in your case be accepted as true. Or if you say that still the pull is so great that you think it better to go for a time and test yourself and exhaust it, then that might just be true for a time, if the vital has risen up strongly; and we would not say no as we did not say no when you wanted to go and nurse X. But even in that case it would be wiser for you to examine it seriously and not make a decision on the strength of a condition which could pass otherwise. Your husband's letters have no value for us; he has always written like that whenever he saw any hope of your coming away from here; at other times he has a very different tone.

I have put the whole thing before you at length. For us the straight course is always to keep on one's way, whatever the difficulties, until one has got mastery and the way becomes smoother. But at bottom the decision must be left with the sadhak himself — one can press for the right choice but one cannot command that he should make it.

*
**

There are usually in the human being two different tendencies in two parts of the being, one psychic or mental supported by the psychic which seeks the better way and higher things, the other whose main seat is in the vital part of the being which is full of the life instincts and life desires, which is attached to or turns towards the things of the lower nature and is subject to the passions, anger, sex etc. If the higher part is dominant, then the lower is kept under control and does not give much trouble. But often the latter is supported by outer forces and powers of the lower Nature in the universe and sometimes these intrude and give the worst part of the being a separate personality and independence of its own. This may be the explanation of the dream of the ugly monster and of the resistance of this other personality. If it be so, then this must be regarded not as part of oneself but as a foreign element to the true being. It is only by a persistent choice of the dictates of the higher and a persistent rejection of the other that the latter loses ground and finally recedes. This should be met as calmly as possible without allowing the mind to be troubled by any fall or failure, with a quiet constant vigilance and resolute will.

It is not necessary to put so many questions and get their separate answers. All your ten questions resolve themselves into one. In every human being there are two parts, the psychic with so much of the thinking mind and higher (emotional, larger dynamic) vital that is open to the psychic and cleaves to the soul's aims and admits the higher experiences and on the other hand the lower vital and the physical or external being (external mind and vital included) which are attached to the ignorant personality and nature and do not want to change. It is the conflict between these two that makes all the difficulty of the sadhana. All the difficulties you enumerate arise from that and nothing else. It is only by curing the duality that one can overcome them. That happens when one is able to live within, aware of one's inner being, identified with it and to regard the rest as not oneself, as a creation of ignorant Nature from which one has separated oneself and which has to disappear and, secondly, when by opening oneself constantly to the Divine Light and Force and the Mother's presence a dynamic action of sadhana is constantly maintained which steadily pushes out the movements of the ignorance and substitutes even in the lower vital and physical being the movements of the inner and higher nature. There is then no struggle any longer, but an automatic growth of the divine elements and fading out of the undivine. The devotion of the heart and the increasing activity of the psychic being, which is best helped by devotion and self-giving, are the most powerful means for arriving at this condition.

Every man has a double nature except those who are born (not unborn) Asuras, Rakshasas, Pishachas and even they have a psychic being concealed somewhere by virtue of their latent humanity. But a double being (or a double nature in the special sense) refers to those who have two sharply contrasted parts of their being without as yet such a linking control over them. Sometimes they are all for the heights and then they are quite all right — sometimes all for the abysses and then they are nothing for the heights, and even sneer or rail at them and give full rein to the lower man. Or they substitute for the heights a smoky volcano summit in the abyss. These are extreme examples, but others while they do not go so far, yet are now one thing, now just the opposite. If they convert the lower fellow or discover the central being in themselves, then a true harmonious whole can be created.

The difficulty is that in everyone there are two people (to say the least) — one in the outer vital and physical clinging to the past self and trying to get or retain the consent of the mind and the inner being, the other which is the soul asking for a new birth. That which has spoken in you and made the prayer is the psychic being expressing itself through the aid of the mind and the higher vital, and it is this which should always arise in you through prayer and through turning to the Mother and give you the right idea and the right impulse.

It is true that if you refuse always the action suggested by the old Adam, it will be a great step forward. The struggle is then transferred to the psychological plane, where it will be much easier to fight the matter out. I do not deny that there will be difficulty for some time; but if there is the control of action, the control of thought and feeling is bound to come. If there is yielding, on the contrary, a fresh lease is given to the old self.

The reason why you have these alternating moods is because there are two different elements in you. On one side, there is trying to develop in you your psychic being which, when it awakes, gives you the sense of closeness or union with the Mother and the feeling of Ananda; on the other, there is your old vital nature, restless and full of desires and, because of this restlessness and desire, unhappy. It is this old vital nature, which you were accepting and indulging, that made you go wrong and stood in the way of your progress. It is when the desire and restlessness of the vital are rejected that the psychic in you comes forward and then the vital itself changes and feels full of the joy and the nearness. When the old unhappy and restless vital comes up again, you feel yourself unfit, without pleasure in anything. What you have to do when this returns is not to accept it, to call in the Mother's nearness again and let the psychic being grow in you. If you do that persistently, rejecting restlessness and desire, the vital part of you will change and become fit for the sadhana.

It is different parts of the being that have these different movements. It is, as you say, something in you, something in the vital that has the "insincerity" or the attraction to the wrong confused condition; but this you should not regard as yourself, but as part of the old nature which has to be transformed. So it is something in the physical that has the obscurity and the unconsciousness; but this too you should not look at as yourself, but as something formed in the exterior nature which has to be changed and will be changed. The real "you" is the inner being, the soul, the psychic being, that which calls the peace and the quiet and the working of the force.

To discuss with others, especially when they are in a bad state, is always a mistake. It is very easy for the disturbance in them to fall upon you while you speak even without your noticing it; it is afterwards that you feel it. That is why I told you to ignore X and what he says when he is in a bad state.

The being is made up of many parts. One part may know, the other may not care for the knowledge or act according to it. The whole being has to be made one in the light so that all parts may act harmoniously according to the Truth.

*
**

Everybody is an amalgamation not of two, but of many personalities. It is part of the yogic perfection in this yoga to accord and transmute them so as to "integrate" the personality.

*
**

I don't think that it can be said that you have no personality. Co-ordination and harmonisation of parts is absent in many; it is a thing that has to be attained to or built up. Moreover at a certain stage in sadhana there is almost always a disparity or opposition between the parts that are already turned towards the Truth and are capable of experience and others that are not and pull one down to a lower level. The opposition is not equally acute in all cases, but in one degree or another it is almost universal. Co-ordination and organisation can be satisfactorily done only when this is overcome. Till then oscillations are inevitable . . . . These are not difficulties that ought to prevent you from looking beyond them to the ultimate spiritual issue out of this flux of contending forces of Nature.

You must remember that your being is not one simple whole, all of one kind, of one piece, but complex, made up of many things. There are the inner parts of the being which are easily conscious of the Truth and Divine, — when these come forward, then all is well. There is the external being which is full of past ignorance and defect and weakness, but has begun to change. It is not yet sufficiently changed or changed in all its parts. When any part that is partly changed opens strongly to the peace and force, then all the rest become either quite quiet or not very active and you are aware of the peace and force and at ease or else aware only vaguely of confusion etc. somewhere. But when something ignorant comes up from below or is a little prominent (or else some old movement of consciousness that was thrown out returns and clouds you), then you feel the peace, the force as something alien to you, or non-existent or outside you or at a distance. If you keep the quiet persistently, then this instability will begin to decrease, the Mother's Force will get in everywhere and, though there will still be much to do, there will be a firm foundation for what has to be done.

I have explained to you that there is a division between your internal and external being — as it is in the case of most people. Your inner being wants and has always wanted the Truth and the Divine — when the peace and power are felt it comes forward and you feel it as yourself and understand things and grow in knowledge and happiness and true feeling. The external nature is being changed by the influence of the inner being, but what is pushed out returns constantly from old habit — and then you feel this old nature as if it were yourself. This external nature has been like that of almost all human beings, like that of most of the sadhaks here, selfish and full of desires and wanting its own desires, not the Truth and the Divine. When it returns like this and covers you up, all these old ideas and feelings which are always the same take hold of you and try to push you to despair — for it is an enemy force that pushes them back into you. The difficulty is that your physical consciousness does not yet know how to reject this when it comes. The inner being rejects it, but as the physical consciousness lets it in, the inner being is pushed back for the time being. You must absolutely learn not to allow this thing to come in, not to indulge and support it when it comes. It is a falsehood and cannot be anything else, and by falsehood I mean not only contrary to the sadhana and contrary to the Divine truth, but contrary to the truth of your own inner being and of your soul's aspiration and your heart's desire. How can such a thing be true? it exists but that does not make it the truth of your being. It is the soul, the inner being that is the true self in everyone. It is that you must know to be your self and reject this as a false thing imposed on you by the lower ignorant Nature.

There are two or three things that I think it necessary to say to you about your spiritual life and your difficulties.

First, I should like you to get rid of the idea that that which causes the difficulties is so much a part of your self that a true inner life is impossible for you. The inner life is always possible if there is present in the nature, however much covered over by other things, a divine possibility through which the soul can manifest itself and build up its own true form in the mind and life, — a portion of the Divine. In you this divine possibility exists in a marked and exceptional degree. There is in you an inner being of spontaneous light, intuitive vision, harmony and creative beauty which has shown itself unmistakably every time it has been able to throw off the clouds that gather in your vital nature. It is this that the Mother has always tried to make grow in you and bring to the front. When one has that in oneself, there is no ground for despair, no just reason for any talk of impossibility. If you could once firmly accept this as your true self, (as indeed it is, for the inner being is your true self and the external, to which the cause of the difficulties belongs, is always something acquired and impermanent and can be changed,) and if you could make its development your settled and persistent aim in life, then the path would be clear and your spiritual future not only a strong possibility but a certitude.

It very often happens that when there is an exceptional power like this in the nature, there is found in the exterior being some contrary element which opens it to a quite opposite influence. It is this that makes the endeavour after a spiritual life so often a difficult struggle: but the existence of this kind of contradiction even in an intense form does not make that life impossible. Doubt, struggle, efforts and failures, lapses, alternations of happy and unhappy or good and bad conditions, states of light and states of darkness are the common lot of human beings. They are not created by yoga or by the effort after perfection; only, in yoga one becomes conscious of their movements and their causes instead of feeling them blindly, and in the end one makes one's way out of them into a clearer and happier consciousness. The ordinary life remains to the last a series of troubles and struggles, but the sadhak of the yoga comes out of the trouble and struggle to a ground of fundamental serenity which superficial disturbances may still touch but cannot destroy, and, finally, all disturbance ceases altogether.

Even the experience which so alarms you, of states of consciousness in which you say and do things contrary to your true will, is not a reason for despair. It is a common experience in one form or another of all who try to rise above their ordinary nature. Not only those who practise yoga, but religious men and even those who seek only a moral control and self-improvement are confronted with this difficulty. And here again it is not the yoga or the effort after perfection that creates this condition, — there are contradictory elements in human nature and in every human being through which he is made to act in a way which his better mind disapproves. This happens to everybody, to the most ordinary men in the most ordinary life. It only becomes marked and obvious to our minds when we try to rise above our ordinary external selves, because then we can see that it is the lower elements which are being made to revolt consciously against the higher will. There then seems to be for a time a division in the nature, because the true being and all that supports it stand back and separate from these lower elements. At one time the true being occupies the field of the nature, at another the lower nature used by some contrary Force pushes it back and seizes the ground, — and this we now see, while formerly the thing happened but the nature of the happening was not clear to us. If there is the firm will to progress, this division is overpassed and in the unified nature, unified around that will, there may be other difficulties, but this kind of discord and struggle will disappear. I have written so much on this point because I think you have been given the wrong idea that it is the yoga which creates this struggle and also that this contradiction or division in the nature is the sign of an unfitness or impossibility to go through to the end. Both ideas are quite incorrect and things will be easier if you cast them out of your consciousness altogether.

But it is true that in your case as in others this contradiction has been given a special and very discomforting kind of intensity by a hereditary weakness of the nervous parts which has always shown itself in you by fits of despondency, gloom, unrest and self-tormenting darkness and spoiled for you the savour of life. Your mistake is to think that this is something to which you are bound and from which you cannot escape, a fate which makes a spiritual change of your nature impossible. I have seen other families afflicted by this kind of hereditary nervous weakness accompanying very often exceptional gifts of intelligence or artistic capacity or spiritual possibilities. One or two may have succumbed to it, like X, but others, sometimes after a period of acute disturbance, overcame the perturbations caused by this weakness; either it disappeared or it took some minor and innocuous form which did not interfere with the development of the life and its capacities. Why then despair of yourself or fix without any true cause the conviction that you cannot change and this thing will always be there? This despondency, this adverse conviction is the real danger for you; it prevents you from making a quiet and settled resolution and a permanent effective effort; because of it the return of this darker condition makes you quickly yield and allow the adverse external Force which uses this defect to play and do its will with you. It is this false idea that makes more than half the trouble.

There is no true reason why you should not overcome this defect of your external being as many others have done. It is only a part of your vital nature that is affected, even though it often overclouds the rest; the other parts of your being can be easily made the fit instruments of the divine possibility of which I have spoken. Especially, you have a clear and fine intelligence which, when rightly used, becomes a ready instrument of the light and can be of great use to you in overcoming this vital weakness. And this divine possibility, this truth of your inner being, if you accept it, can of itself make certain your liberation and the change of your external nature.

Accept this divine possibility in you; have faith in your inner being and its spiritual destiny. Make its development as a portion of the Divine your aim in life, — for a great and serious aim in life is a most powerful help towards getting rid of this kind of disturbing or disabling nervous weakness; it gives firmness, balance, a strong support to the whole being and a powerful reason for the will to act. Accept too the help we can give you, not shutting yourself against it by disbelief, despair or unfounded revolt. At present you cannot prevail because you have not fixed in yourself a faith, an aim, a settled confidence; the black mood has been able to cloud your whole consciousness. But if you have fixed this faith in you and can cling to it, then the cloud will not be able to fix itself for any long period, the inner being will be able to come to your help. And even the better self will be able to remain on the surface, keep you open to the light and maintain the inner ground for the soul, even if the outer is partly clouded or troubled. When that happens, the victory will have been won and the entire elimination of the vital weakness will be only a matter of a little perseverance.

*
**

I shall answer briefly the questions you put. (1) The way to set yourself right is to set your nature right and make yourself master of your vital being and its impulses. (2) Your position in human society is or can be that of many others who in their early life have committed excesses of various kinds and have afterwards achieved self-control and taken their due place in life. If you were not so ignorant of life, you would know that your case is not exceptional but on the contrary very common, and that many have done these things and afterwards become useful citizens and even leading men in various departments of human activity. (3) It is quite possible for you to recompense your parents and fulfil the past expectations you spoke of, if you make that your object. Only you must first recover from your illness and achieve the proper balance of your mind and will. (4) The object of your life depends upon your own choice and the way of attainment depends upon the nature of the object. Also your position will be whatever you make it. What you have to do is, first of all, to recover your health; then, with a quiet mind to determine your aim in life according to your capacities and preference. It is not for me to make up your mind for you. I can only indicate to you what I myself think should be the proper aims and ideals.

Apart from external things there are two possible inner ideals which a man can follow. The first is the highest ideal of ordinary human life and the other the divine ideal of yoga. (I must say in view of something you seem to have said to your father that it is not the object of the one to be a great man or the object of the other to be a great yogin.) The ideal of human life is to establish over the whole being the control of a clear, strong and rational mind and a right and rational will, to master the emotional, vital and physical being, create a harmony of the whole and develop the capacities whatever they are and fulfil them in life. In the terms of Hindu thought, it is to enthrone the rule of the purified and sattwic *buddhi*, follow the *dharma*, fulfilling one's own *svadharma* and doing the work proper to one's capacities, and satisfy *kāma* and *artha* under the control of the *buddhi* and the *dharma*. The object of the divine life, on the other hand, is to realise one's highest self or to realise God and to put the whole being into harmony with the truth of the highest self or the law of the divine nature, to find one's own divine capacities great or small and fulfil them in life as a sacrifice to the highest or as a true instrument of the divine

Shakti. About the latter ideal I may write at some later time. At present, I shall only say something about the difficulty you feel in fulfilling the ordinary ideal.

This ideal involves the building of mind and character and is always a slow and difficult process demanding patient labour of years, sometimes the better part of the life-time. The chief difficulty in the way with almost everybody is the difficulty of controlling the desires and impulses of the vital being. In many cases as in yours, certain strong impulses run persistently counter to the ideal and demand of the reason and the will. The cause is almost always a weakness of the vital being itself, for when there is this weakness it finds itself unable to obey the dictates of the higher mind and obliged to act instead under waves of impulsion that come from certain forces in nature. These forces are really external to the person but find in this part of him a sort of mechanical readiness to satisfy and obey them. The difficulty is aggravated if the *seat* of the weakness is in the nervous system. There is then what is called by European science a neurasthenia tendency and under certain circumstances it leads to nervous breakdowns and collapses. This happens when there is too great a strain on the nerves or when there is excessive indulgence of the sexual or other propensities and sometimes also when there is too acute and prolonged a struggle between the restraining mental will and these propensities. This is the illness from which you are suffering and if you consider these facts you will see the real reason why you broke down at Pondicherry. The nervous system in you was weak; it could not obey the will and resist the demand of the external, vital forces, and in the struggle there came an overstrain of the mind and the nerves and a collapse taking the form of an acute attack of neurasthenia. These difficulties do not mean that you cannot prevail and bring about a control of your nerves and vital being and build up a harmony of mind and character. Only you must understand the thing rightly, not indulging false and morbid ideas about it and you must use the right means. What is needed is a quiet mind and a quiet will, pa-tient, persistent, refusing to yield either to excitement or dis-couragement, but always insisting tranquilly on the change needed in the being. A quiet will of this kind cannot fail in the end. Its effect is inevitable. It must first reject in the waking state, not only the acts habitual to the vital being, but the impulses behind them which it must understand to be external to the person even though manifested in him and also the suggestions which are behind the impulses. When thus rejected, the once habitual thoughts and movements may still manifest in the dream-state, because it is a well-known psychological law that what is suppressed or rejected in the waking state may still recur in sleep and dream because they are still there in the subconscient being. But if the waking state is thoroughly cleared, these dream-movements must gradually disappear because they lose their food and the impressions in the subconscient are gradually effaced. This is the cause of the dreams of which you are so much afraid. You should see that they are only a subordinate symptom which need not alarm you if you can once get control of your waking condition.

But you must get rid of the ideas which have stood in the way of effecting the self-conquest.

1. Realise that these things in you do not come from any true moral depravity, for that can exist only when the mind itself is corrupted and supports the perverse vital impulses. Where the mind and the will reject them, the moral being is sound and it is a case only of a weakness or malady of the vital parts or the nervous system.

2. Do not brood on the past but turn your face with a patient hope and confidence towards the future. To brood on past failure will prevent you from recovering your health and will weaken your mind and will, hampering them in the work of self-conquest and rebuilding of the character.

3. Do not yield to discouragement if success does not come at once, but continue patiently and steadfastly until the thing is done.

4. Do not torture your mind by always dwelling on your weaknesses. Do not imagine that they unfit you for life or for the fulfilment of the human ideal. Once having recognised that they are there, seek for your sources of strength and dwell rather on them and the certainty of conquest.

Your first business is to recover your health of mind and body and that needs quietness of mind and for some time a quiet way of living. Do not rack your mind with questions which it is not yet ready to solve. Do not brood always on the one thing. Occupy your mind as much as you can with healthy and normal occupations and give it as much rest as possible. Afterwards when you have your right mental condition and balance, then you can with a clear judgment decide how you will shape your life and what you have to do in the future.

I have given you the best advice I can and told you what seems to me the most important for you at present. As for your coming to Pondicherry, it is better not to do so just now. I could say to you nothing more than what I have written. It is best for you so long as you are ill not to leave your father's care, and, above all, it is the safe rule in illnesses like yours not to return to the place and surroundings where you had the break-down until you are perfectly recovered and the memories and associations connected with it have faded in intensity, lost their hold on the mind and can no longer produce upon it a violent or disturbing impression.

Yes, the solution is certainly the Divine Grace — it comes of itself intervening suddenly or with an increasing force when all is ready. Meanwhile, it is there behind all the struggles, and "the unconquerable aspiration for the light" of which you speak is the outward sign that it will intervene. As for the two natures, it is only one form of the perpetual duality in human nature from which nobody escapes, so universal that many systems recognize it as a standing feature to be taken account of in their discipline, two Personae, one bright, one dark, in every human being. If that were not there, yoga would be an easy walk-over and there would be no struggle. But its presence is not any reason for thinking that there is unfitness; the obstinacy of the worldly element is also not a reason, for it is always obstinate in its very nature. It is like the Germans in their trenches, falling back and digging themselves in for a new mass attack, every time they are baffled. But for all that, if the

bright Person is equally determined not to be satisfied without
the crown of light, if it is strong enough to make the being
unable to rest content in lesser things, then that is the sign
that the being is called, one of the elect in spite of outward
appearances and its own doubts and despairs — who has them
not, not even a Christ or a Buddha is without them — and that
the inner spirit will surely win in the end. There is no cause
for any apprehension on that score.

What you say about the "Evil Persona" interests me greatly
as it answers to my consistent experience that a person greatly
endowed for the work has, always or almost always, — perhaps
one ought not to make a too rigid universal rule about these
things — a being attached to him, sometimes appearing like
a part of him, which is just the contradiction of the thing he
centrally represents in the work to be done. Or, if it is not there
at first, not bound to his personality, a force of this kind enters
into his environment as soon as he begins his movement to
realise. Its business seems to be to oppose, to create stumblings and wrong conditions, in a word, to set before him the
whole problem of the work he has started to do. It would seem
as if the problem could not, in the occult economy of things, be
solved otherwise than by the predestined instrument making
the difficulty his own. That would explain many things that
seem very disconcerting on the surface.

I have already let you know that I approve both the people
whose photographs you have sent me. As to A you are right
in thinking that he is a born yogin. His face shows the type of
the Sufi or Arab mystic and he must certainly have been that in
a former life and brought much of his then personality into
the present existence. There are defects and limitations in his
being. The narrowness of the physical mind of which you speak
is indicated in the photograph, though it has not come out in

the expression, and it might push him in the direction of a rather poverty-stricken asceticism instead of his expanding and opening himself richly to the opulences of the Divine. It might also lead him in other circumstances to some kind of fanaticism. But on the other hand if he gets the right direction and opens himself to the right powers these things may be turned into valuable elements, the ascetic capacity into a force useful against the physico-vital dangers and what might have been fanaticism into an intense devotion to the Truth revealed to him. There is also likely to be some trouble in the physico-vital being. But I cannot yet say of what nature. This is not a case of an entirely safe development, which can be assured only where there is a strong vital and physical basis and a certain natural balance in the different parts of the being. This balance has here to be created and its creation is quite possible. Whatever risk there is must be taken; for the nature here is born for the yoga and ought not to be denied its opportunity. He must be made to understand fully the character and demands of the Integral Yoga.

Next for B. He is no doubt what you say, a type of the rich and successful man, but the best kind of that type and cast on sound and generous lines. There is besides indicated in his face and expression a refinement and capacity of idealism which is not too common. Certainly we are not to take people into the yoga for the sake of their riches, but on the other hand we must not have the disposition to reject anyone on account of his riches. If wealth is a great obstacle, it is also a great opportunity, and part of the aim of our work is, not to reject, but to conquer for the divine self-expression the vital and material powers, including that of wealth, which are now in the possession of other influences. If then a man like this is prepared with an earnest and real will to bring himself and his power over from the other camp to ours, there is no reason to refuse him. This of course is not the case of a man born to the yoga like C, but of one who has an opening in him to a spiritual awakening and I think of a nature which might possibly fail from certain negative deficiencies but not because of any adverse element in the being. The one necessity is that he should understand and accept what the yoga demands of him, — first the seeking of a greater Truth, secondly the consecration of himself and his powers and wealth to its service and finally the transformation of all his life into the terms of the Truth, — and that he should have not merely the enthusiastic turning of his idealism but a firm and deliberate will towards it. It is especially necessary in the case of these rich men for them to realise that it is not enough in this yoga to have a spiritual endeavour on one side and on the other the rest of the energies given to the ordinary motives, but that the whole life and being must be consecrated to the yoga. It is probably from this reason of a divided life that men like D fail to progress in spite of a natural capacity. If this is understood and accepted, the consecration of which he speaks is obviously in his circumstances the first step in the path. If he enters it, it will probably be advisable for him to come after a short time and see me in Pondicherry. But this of course has to be decided afterwards....

P.S. After this letter was finished I got your last of the 12th. What you say about E there is what I could already gather about him, only made precise. I do not think that these things very much matter. All strong natures have the rajasic active outgoing force in them and if that were sufficient to unfit for the yoga, very few of us would have had a chance. As for the doubt of the physical mind as to whether the thing is possible, who has not had it? In my own case it pursued me for years and years and it is only in the last two years that the last shadow of doubt, not latterly of its theoretical feasibility, but of the practical certainty of its achievement in the present state of the world and of the human nature, entirely left me.[1] The same thing can be said of the egoistic poise, that almost all strong men have the strong egoistic poise. But I do not think judging from the photograph that it is of the same half bull and half bull-dog nature as in F. These things can only go with spiritual development and experience and then the strength behind them becomes an asset. It is also evident from what you say about his past experience of the voice and the vastness that there is, as I thought, a psychic something in him waiting for and on the verge of spiritual awakening.

[1] This was written on 16-4-1923.

I understand that he is waiting for intellectual conviction and, to bring it, some kind of assurance from an inner experience. To that also there is nothing to say. But the question is, and it seems to me the one question in his case, whether he will be ready to bring to the yoga the firm entire and absolute will and consecration that will be needed to tide him through all the struggles and crises of the sadhana. The disparity between his mental poise and his action is natural enough, precisely because it is a mental poise. It has to*become a spiritual poise before the life and the ideal can become one. Have the spoiling by luxury of which you speak and the worldly life sapped in him the possibility of developing an entire Godward will? If not, then he may be given his chance. I cannot positively say that he is or will be the *adhikārī*. I can only say that there is the capacity in the best part of his nature. I cannot also say that he is among the "best". But he seems to me to have more original capacity than some at least who have been accepted. When I wrote about the "best" I did not mean an *ādhāra* without defects and dangers; for I do not think such a one is to be found. My impression of course is founded on a general favourable effect produced by the physiognomy and the appearance, on certain definite observations upon the same and on psychic indications which were mixed but in the balance favourable. I have not seen the man as you have. Take the sum he offers, do not press him for more at present and for the rest, let him understand clearly not only what the yoga is, but the great demands it makes on the nature. See how he turns and whether he cannot be given his chance.

III

There are only three fundamental obstacles that can stand in the way:

1. Absence of faith or insufficient faith.

2. Egoism — the mind clinging to its own ideas, the vital preferring its own desires to a true surrender, the physical adhering to its own habits.

3. Some inertia or fundamental resistance in the conscious-

ness, not willing to change because it is too much of an effort or because it does not want to believe in its capacity or the power of the Divine — or for some other more subconscient reason. You have to see for yourself which of these it is.

The main difficulty in the sadhana consists in the movements of the lower nature, ideas of the mind, desires and attractions of the vital, habits of the body consciousness that stand in the way of the growth of the higher consciousness — there are other difficulties but these make the bulk of the opposition.

In one form or another the resistance of the mind and the Prana seeking to be independent and fulfil ego under the plea of spiritual realisation is a frequent obstacle in the yoga.

Each part of the nature wants to go on with its old movements and refuses, so far as it can, to admit a radical change and progress, because that would subject it to something higher than itself and deprive it of its sovereignty in its own field, its separate empire. It is this that makes transformation so long and difficult a process.

Mind gets dulled because at its lower basis is the physical mind with its principle of tamas or inertia — for in matter inertia is the fundamental principle. A constant or long continuity of higher experiences produces in this part of mind a sense of exhaustion or reaction of unease or dullness. Trance or *samādhi* is a way of escape — the body is made quiet, the physical mind is in a state of torpor, the inner consciousness is left free to go on with its experiences. The disadvantage is that trance becomes indispensable and the problem of the waking consciousness is not solved; it remains imperfect.

The rigidity was in the obstinacy with which your mind and vital clung to their own ideas and vital habits and did not want to change. But the result was rather laxity, a general looseness which did not want to tune the nature to the spiritual endeavour, but let all sorts of things wander over its strings at their pleasure. Plasticity of the consciousness is necessary, but plasticity to the true touch of the Power, not to any ordinary touch of the forces in Nature. To tune all to the Higher should be your aim — then there will be the full poetry of the spirit not in writing only but in life.

The existence of imperfections, even many and serious imperfections, cannot be a *permanent* bar to progress in the yoga. (I do not speak of a recovery of the former opening, for according to my experience, what comes after a period of obstruction or struggle is usually a new and wider opening, some larger consciousness and an advance on what had been gained before and seems — but only seems — to be lost for the moment.) The only bar that can be permanent — but need not be, for this too can change — is insincerity, and this does not exist in you. If imperfection were a bar, then no man could succeed in yoga; for all are imperfect, and I am not sure, from what I have seen, that it is not those who have the greatest power for yoga who have too, very often, or have had the greatest imperfections. You know, I suppose, the comment of Socrates on his own character; that could be said by many great yogins of their own initial human nature. In yoga the one thing that counts in the end is sincerity and with it the patience to persist in the path — many even without this patience go through, for in spite of revolt, impatience, depression, despondency, fatigue, temporary loss of faith, a force greater than one's outer self, the force of the Spirit, the drive of the soul's need, pushes them through the cloud and the mist to the goal before them. Imperfections can be stumbling-blocks and give one a bad fall for the moment, but not a permanent bar. Obscurations due to some resistance in the nature can be more serious causes of delay, but they too do not last for ever.

The length of your period of dullness is also no sufficient

reason for losing belief in your capacity or your spiritual destiny. I believe that alternations of bright and dark periods are almost a universal experience of yogis, and the exceptions are very rare. If one inquires into the reasons of this phenomenon, — very unpleasant to our impatient human nature, — it will be found, I think, that they are in the main two. The first is that the human consciousness either cannot bear a constant descent of the Light or Power or Ananda, or cannot at once receive and absorb it; it needs periods of assimilation; but this assimilation goes on behind the veil of the surface consciousness; the experience or the realisation that has descended retires behind the veil and leaves this outer or surface consciousness to lie fallow and become ready for a new descent. In the more developed stages of the yoga these dark or dull periods become shorter, less trying as well as up-lifted by the sense of the greater consciousness which, though not acting for immediate progress, yet remains and sustains the outer nature. The second cause is some resistance, something in the human nature that has not felt the former descent, is not ready, is perhaps unwilling to change, — often it is some strong habitual formation of the mind or the vital or some temporary inertia of the physical consciousness and not exactly a part of the nature, — and this, whether showing or concealing itself, thrusts up the obstacle. If one can detect the cause in oneself, acknowledge it, see its workings and call down the Power for its removal, then the periods of obscurity can be greatly shortened and their acuity becomes less. But in any case the Divine Power is working always behind and one day, perhaps when one least expects it, the obstacle breaks, the clouds vanish and there is again the light and the sunshine. The best thing in these cases is, if one can manage it, not to fret, not to despond, but to insist quietly and keep oneself open, spread to the Light and waiting in faith for it to come; that I have found shortens these ordeals. Afterwards, when the obstacle disappears, one finds that a great progress has been made and that the consciousness is far more capable of receiving and retaining than before. There is a return for all the trials and ordeals of the spiritual life.

The yogi arrives at a sort of division in his being in which the inner Purusha, fixed and calm, looks at the perturbations of the outer man as one looks at the passions of an unreasonable child; that once fixed, he can proceed afterwards to control the outer man also; but a complete control of the outer man needs a long and arduous tapasya.

But even from a siddha yogi you cannot always expect a perfect perfection: there are many who do not even care for the perfection of the outer nature which cannot be held as a disproof of their realisation and experience. If you so regard it, you have to rule out of court the greater number of yogis of the past and the Rishis of the old time also.

I own that the ideal of my yoga is different, but I cannot bind by it other spiritual men and their achievements and discipline. My own ideal is transformation of the outer nature, perfection as perfect as it can be. But you cannot say that those who have not achieved it or did not care to achieve it had no spirituality. Beautiful conduct — not politeness which is an outer thing, however valuable — but beauty founded upon a spiritual realisation of unity and harmony projected into life, is certainly part of the perfect harmony.

But when on earth were politeness and good society manners considered as a part or a test of spiritual experience or true yogic siddhi? It is no more a test than the capacity of dancing well or dressing nicely. Just as there are very good and kind men who are boorish and rude in their manners, so there may be very spiritual men (I mean here by spiritual men those who have had deep spiritual experiences) who have no grasp over physical life or action (many intellectuals too, by the way, are like that) and are not at all careful about their manners. I suppose I myself am accused of rude and arrogant behaviour because I refuse to see people, do not answer letters, and a host of other misdemeanours. I have heard of a famous recluse who threw stones at anybody coming to his retreat because he did not want disciples and found no other way of warding off the flood of candidates. I at least would hesitate to pronounce that such people had no spiritual life or experience. Certainly, I prefer that sadhaks should be reasonably considerate towards each other, but that is for the rule of collective life and harmony, not as a siddhi of the yoga or an indispensable sign of inner experience.

You write as if the moment one had any kind of spiritual experience or realisation, one must at once become a perfect person without defects or weaknesses. That is to make a demand which it is impossible to satisfy and it is to ignore the fact that spiritual life is a growth and not a sudden and inexplicable miracle. No sadhak can be judged as if he were already a siddha yogi, least of all those who have only travelled a quarter or less of a very long path. Even great yogis do not claim perfection and you cannot say that because they are not absolutely perfect, therefore their spirituality is false or of no use to the world. There are, besides, all kinds of spiritual men: some who are content with spiritual experience and do not seek after an outward perfection or progress, some who are saints, others who do not seek after sainthood, others who are content to live in the cosmic consciousness in touch or union with the All but allowing all kinds of forces to fly through them, e.g., in the typical description of the Paramhansa. The ideal I put before our yoga is one thing but it does not bind all spiritual life and endeavour. The spiritual life is not a thing that can be formulated in a rigid definition or bound by a fixed mental rule; it is a vast field of evolution, an immense kingdom potentially larger than the other kingdoms below it, with a hundred provinces, a thousand types, stages, forms, paths, variations of the spiritual ideal, degrees of spiritual advancement. It is from the basis of this truth that things regarding spirituality and its seekers must be judged, if they are to be judged with knowledge. It is only by so understanding it that one can understand it truly, either in its past or in its future or put in their place the spiritual men of the past and the present or relate the different ideals, stages, etc. thrown up in the spiritual evolution of the human being.

*
**

I reply to your letter as Mother is still too much occupied to write.

What was in her view at the time was what is called in the psychology of Indian yoga a "sattwic" perfection, perfection in the form of the qualities and actions such as would satisfy a mental idealism and be very visible and appreciable to others. This often generates a kind of pride and self-righteousness, a "sattwic" egoism, which makes the consciousness rigid and not flexible and plastic to the Divine Will. The true spiritual perfection is not so much of form; it is of the very substance of the consciousness and, as it consists at its base in an entire harmony with the Divine Consciousness and a free and plastic self-adaptation at each moment to the Divine Will, its forms and the forms of its action are not so easily visible or appreciable. The word "righteous" does not apply to its movements — they are simply right because they are in unison with the Divine.

Obviously real imperfections are not to be indulged — to take that as a principle would be dangerous; the "apparent" imperfections are those which might appear so to an outward view only. A "righteous" anger might easily be part of that self-righteousness which the Mother had in view, and to be identified with the movement of anger righteous or otherwise is spiritually undesirable. But a movement of the kind meant may seem to an outward view identical with the movements of imperfection in the nature, yet be quite the right one in the sense of rightness which I have indicated above. It is not a question of any particular action or attitude to be taken but of the consciousness within giving a free and supple expression to the Divine Will acting through it.

Çakya-Muni is a name of Buddha — "the sage of Çakyas" — the clan to which Buddha belonged by birth and of which his father was the "king".

IV

It does not matter what defects you may have in your nature. The one thing that matters is your keeping yourself open to the

Force. Nobody can transform himself by his own unaided efforts; it is only the Divine Force that can transform him. If you keep yourself open, all the rest will be done for you.

All limitations can be surmounted but if they are ingrained in the formation of the present being, it can only be done by calling in a higher power and consciousness than that of the personal mind and will. The higher consciousness can by what it brings correct or rebuild what is defective in the personal nature.

Hardly anyone is strong enough to overcome by his own un-aided aspiration and will the forces of the lower nature; even those who do it get only a certain kind of control, but not a complete mastery. Will and aspiration are needed to bring down the aid of the Divine Force and to keep the being on its side in its dealings with the lower powers. The Divine Force fulfilling the spiritual will and the heart's psychic aspiration can alone bring about the conquest.

As I have told you it is no longer useful to think of right under-standing and wrong movements and get upset when they are felt to be not there or imperfect. Nobody can change himself — even the strongest sadhaks here recognise that. Their effort is to let the Peace, Force, Light, Ananda of the Mother come in, to let that grow — for that will change them, they know. So long as it is not there, has not yet touched, is not growing, they struggle with the mind and vital, because they cannot help doing so and it is necessary for preparing the consciousness a little to admit the Peace and Force. But once these have touched, the only thing to do is to lay all the stress on that, trust to it, surrender and give oneself to it — for the straight road is found and the true power and consciousness have been experienced.

I want you to be open and in contact with the Peace and Presence and Force. All else will come if that is there and then one need not be troubled by the time it takes in the *péripéties* of the sadhana.

The only truth in your other experience, — which, you say, seems at the time so true to you, — is that it is hopeless for you or anyone to get out of the inferior consciousness by your or his un-aided effort. That is why when you sink into this inferior consciousness, everything seems hopeless to you, because you lose hold for a time of the true consciousness. But the suggestion is untrue, because you have an opening to the Divine and are not bound to remain in the inferior consciousness.

When you are in the true consciousness, then you see that everything can be done, even if at present only a slight beginning has been made; but a beginning is enough, once the Force, the Power are there. For the truth is that it can do everything and only time and the soul's aspiration are needed for the entire change and the soul's fulfilment.

To do anything by mental control is always difficult, when what is attempted runs contrary to the trend of human nature or of the personal nature. A strong will patiently and perseveringly turned towards its object can effect a change, but usually it takes a long time and the success at the beginning may be only partial and chequered by many failures.

To turn all actions automatically into worship cannot be done by thought control only; there must be a strong aspiration in the heart which will bring about some realisation or feeling of the presence of the One to whom worship is offered. The bhakta does not rely on his own effort alone, but on the grace and power of the Divine whom he adores.

These obstacles are usual in the first stages of the sadhana. They are due to the nature being not yet sufficiently receptive. You should find out where the obstacle is, in the mind or the vital, and try to widen the consciousness there, call in more purity and peace and in that purity and peace offer that part of your being sincerely and wholly to the Divine Power.

The real reason of the difficulty and the constant alternation is the struggle between the veiled true being within and the outer nature, especially the lower vital full of desires and the physical mind full of obscurity and ignorance. The struggle is inevitable in human nature and no sadhak escapes it; everyone has to deal with that obscurity and resistance and its obstinacy and constant recurrence; for the lower nature is not only persistent in its repetitions and returns, but even when it is on the point of changing, the general Powers of that plane in universal Nature try to keep up the resistance by bringing back the old movements at each step in order to prevent the progress from being confirmed for good and made final. It is true therefore that a constant sadhana persistent and unceasing is necessary if one wants to go quickly — though even otherwise one will arrive if the soul within has the call, for the soul will persist and after each obscuration or stumble will bring back the light and drive one on on the path till it feels that it is at last secure of a smooth and easy march to the goal.

A difficulty comes or an arrest in some movement which you have begun or have been carrying on for some time. How is it to be dealt with — for such arrests are inevitably frequent enough, not only for you, but for everyone who is a seeker; one might almost say that every step forward is followed by an arrest — at least, that is a very common, if not a universal experience. It is to be dealt with by becoming always more quiet, more firm in the will to go through, by opening oneself more and more so that any obstructing non-receptivity in the nature may diminish or disappear, by an affirmation of faith even in the midst of the obscurity, faith in the presence of a Power that is working behind the cloud and the veil, in the guidance of the Guru, by an observation of oneself to find any cause of the arrest, not in a spirit of depression or discouragement but with the will to find out and remove it. This is the only right attitude and, if one is persistent in taking it, the periods of arrest are not abolished, — for that cannot be at this stage, — but greatly shortened and lightened in their incidence. Sometimes these arrests are periods, long or short, of assimilation or unseen preparation, their appearance of sterile immobility is deceptive: in that case, with the right attitude, one can after a time, by opening, by observation, by accumulated experience, begin to feel, to get some inkling of what is being prepared or done. Sometimes it is a period of true obstruction in which the Power at work has to deal with the obstacles in the way, obstacles in oneself, obstacles of the opposing cosmic forces or any other or of all together, and this kind of arrest may be long or short according to the magnitude or obstinacy or complexity of the impediments that are met. But here, too, the right attitude can alleviate or shorten and, if persistently taken, h   to a more radical removal of the difficulties and greatly diminish the necessity of complete arrests hereafter.

On the contrary, an attitude of depression or unfaith in the help or the guidance or in the certitude of the victory of the guiding Power, a shutting up of yourself in the sense of the difficulties impedes the recovery, prolongs the difficulties, helps the obstructions to recur with force instead of progressively diminishing in their incidence. It is an attitude whose persistence or recurrence you must resolutely throw aside if you want to get over the obstruction which you feel so much — which the depressed attitude only makes, while it lasts, more acute.

I do not think there is any sadhak however advanced who has the full consciousness all the time. These changes come and one cannot help it because there is something of the ordinary consciousness that is still left and it comes up to be dealt with. One has to understand this and not get upset — for getting upset only delays the process. If the true consciousness were constant in its fullness, the sadhana would be finished and there would be the siddhi. That cannot come at once.

As I have constantly told you, you cannot expect all to be enlightened at once. Even the greatest yogis can only proceed by stages and it is only at the end that the whole nature shares the true consciousness which they first establish in the heart or behind it or in the head or above it. It descends or expands slowly conquering each layer of the being one after the other, but each step takes time.

You should realise that these periods of clouding are not due to any special incapacity or perversity in you — even the best sadhaks have them. It is the difficulty of the human nature in getting transformed. This difficulty sometimes takes the form of a bad will in the vital somewhere or a tendency in the physical to cling to old mistakes and old habits or to shrink from the trouble of transformation — but in these respects you have made a great progress. What is there, is the mechanical habit of the lower nature in general — mechanical, not voluntary — to repeat the old movements to which it has been or was quite recently accustomed when any strong wave of them comes in from the surrounding universal Nature. This creates a kind of recurrence of relapse into the states which the spiritual progress is pushing out and it is not easy to get rid of this recurrence altogether. The one thing when they come is not to get distressed or upset, to realise what it is and to remain very quiet calling for the Mother's Force to push it away. In this way the habit of these recurrences diminishes, the strength and intensity also, and on the other side one is able to recall the true consciousness and the true force, the bright happy peaceful open condition more and more easily and quicker. One can then proceed on an assured basis to a more and more positive progress.

These periods of difficulty inevitably come — none is without them, for the lower nature is there in all. What you have to do is to keep the firmness of which you speak and persevere till the Divine Power and your will together have dealt with what rises from below. Why do you regard what rises and shows itself as if it were peculiar to yourself? They are part of the very substance of the lower vital of the human being and there is no one who is without them. So their presence does not at all mean that you cannot reach the Mother. When the mind and soul have chosen the goal, the rest is bound to follow; only as they are more obscure, the resistance there is more blind and obstinate. But even in your vital there is now fixed the will to attain, it is only a lower part there that has had the habit of responding to these things and therefore when a wave comes, it does not know how to avoid and is swallowed up for a time. It can be for a time only, because these things are no longer really yours, since the central being and the greater part of the nature no longer desire them. You have only to go on firmly and the time will come when the waves no longer rise.

It is no doubt the pressure of the psychic in you which you express in the letter. That is how the psychic being wants it to be. But it is a mistake to accept any suggestion of self-distrust or incapacity on the ground that it is not like that yet or is not always like that. These things always take time; even after they have begun, they always take time. It is impossible to expect from the mixed and confused nature of the human being that it should be constantly in a state of ardent aspiration, perfect faith and love or full and constant openness to the Divine Force. There is the mental with its limited knowledge and its hesitations, there is the vital with its desires, unwillingnesses and its struggles;

there is the physical with its obscurity, slowness and inertia. Even to clear the field sufficiently for a beginning of experience is usually a very long labour. But afterwards if the peace begins or any other right condition, it comes and stays for a time — then what is left of the lower nature surges up on some excuse or with no excuse and veils the condition. Peace and opening may come so strongly that it seems all difficulties are gone and can never return — but that is only an indication, a promise. It shows that it will be so when the peace and opening are irrevocably settled in all the nature. For that what is needed is perseverance — to go on without discouragement, recognising that the process of the nature and the action of the Mother's force is working through the difficulty even and will do all that is needed. Our incapacity does not matter — there is no human being who is not in his parts of nature incapable — but the Divine Force also is there. If one puts one's trust in that, incapacity will be changed into capacity. Difficulty and struggle themselves then become a means towards the achievement.

The experience is correct. Everything is prepared above, then worked out through the inner being till the results are accomplished and perfected in the outer personality. Therefore the sadhak ought not to allow himself to be alarmed, upset or grieved or made despondent by any apparent difficulties of the moment. He must know that all has been prepared above and calmly and confidently watch and assist its working out here.

The action of the higher consciousness does not usually begin by changing the outer nature; it works on the inner being, prepares that and then goes outward. Before that whatever change is done in the outer nature has to be done by the psychic.

Do not allow yourself to be shaken or troubled by these things. The one thing to do always is to remain firm in your aspiration to the Divine and to face with equanimity and detachment all difficulties and all oppositions. For those who wish to lead the spiritual life, the Divine must always come first, everything else must be secondary.

Keep yourself detached and look at these things from the calm inner vision of one who is inwardly dedicated to the Divine.

One cannot say whether the conquest is near or not — one has to go on steadily with the process of the sadhana without thinking of near and far, fixed on the aim, not elated if it seems to come close, not depressed if it still seems to be far.

V

The Power does not descend with the object of raising up the lower forces, but in the way it has to work at present, that uprising comes in as a reaction to the working. What is needed is the establishment of the calm and wide consciousness at the base of the whole Nature, so that when the lower nature appears it will not be as an attack or struggle but as if a Master of forces were there seeing the defects of the present machinery and doing step by step what is necessary to remedy and change it.

The method you speak of is, I understand, that of raising up the difficulties in order to know and exhaust or destroy them. It is inevitable once one enters into yoga that the difficulties should rise up and they go on rising up so long as anything of them is left in the system at all. It may be thought then that it is better to raise them oneself in a mass so as to get the thing done once for all. But though this may succeed in some cases, it is not even in the mental and vital a safe or certain method. Exhaus-

tion, of course, is impossible; the things that create the difficulties are cosmic forces, forces of the cosmic Ignorance and
cannot be exhausted. People talk of their getting exhausted
because after a time they lose strength and dwindle, for that is
possible only by force of rejection by the Purusha and by force
of divine intervention aiding this rejection and dissolving or
destroying the difficulty each time it shows its face. Even so,
the getting rid of difficulties in a lump seldom works; something
remains and returns until suddenly there comes a divine intervention which is final or else a change of consciousness which makes
the return of the difficulty impossible. Still, in the mental and
vital it can be done.

In the physical it is much more dangerous because here it is
the physical *ādhāra* itself that is attacked and a too great mass
of physical difficulties may destroy or disable or permanently
injure. The only thing to do here is to get the physical consciousness — down to the most material parts — open to the Power,
then to make it accustomed to respond and obey and to each
physical difficulty as it arises, apply or call in the Divine Power
to throw out the attacking force. The physical nature is a thing
of habits; it is out of habit that it responds to the forces of illness; one has to get into it the contrary habit of responding to
the Divine Force only. This, of course, so long as a highest consciousness does not descend to which illness is impossible.

*
**

It is certainly possible to draw forces from below. It may be
the hidden divine forces from below that rise at your pull, and
then this motion upward completes the motion and effort of
the divine force from above, helping especially to bring it into
the body. Or it may be the obscure forces from below that respond to the summons and then this kind of drawing brings either
tamas or disturbance — sometimes great masses of inertia or a
formidable upheaval and disturbance.

The lower vital is a very obscure plane and it can be fully
opened with advantage only when the other planes above it have
been thrown wide to light and knowledge. One who concentrates

on the lower vital without that higher preparation and without knowledge is likely to fall into many confusions. This does not mean that experiences of this plane may not come earlier or even at the beginning; they do come of themselves, but they must not be given too large a place.

If you go down into your lower parts or ranges of nature, you must be always careful to keep a vigilant connection with the higher already regenerated levels of the consciousness and to bring down the Light and Purity through them into these nether still unregenerated regions. If there is not this vigilance, one gets absorbed in the unregenerated movement of the inferior layers and there is obscuration and trouble.

The safest way is to remain in the higher part of the consciousness and put a pressure from it on the lower to change. It can be done in this way, only you must get the knack and the habit of it. If you achieve the power to do that, it makes the progress much easier, smoother and less painful.

There can be no doubt that you can go through — everyone has these struggles; what is needed to pass through is sincerity and perseverance.

There is no use in inviting these struggles, as many do, or even in accepting them when they come for the sake of fighting them out, for they always repeat themselves. When they cannot be avoided, then they must be faced — one cannot be altogether without them, especially in the earlier part of the yoga; but if you can quietly evade them, that is already an advance. To become quiet and quietly to call back the true psychic state until it becomes normal and either eliminates or minimises the struggle, that is the best way to progress.

It is better to proceed by a quiet rejection and growth in consciousness — and not invite battle — though, if a struggle is
forced on you you must meet it with calm and courage.

It is the old habit of the outer consciousness from which it
refuses to be delivered. Until this will to repeat the old movements is thrown away, the Force works but under difficulties and
behind instead of taking up the frontal consciousness as it would
if the assent of the external nature were there. There is also the
old persistent habit of raising up and stressing the difficulties
instead of rejecting them — the wrong idea that accepting, ap-
proving and insisting on their presence is the only way of getting
rid of them. I have told you that that is not the way and only
prolongs the struggle.

There is no objection to doing sadhana, but it must be done
quietly without the constant struggle and disquietude — not
minding if it takes time, not getting into a constant rhythm of
"struggling against difficulties." That is my point.

No objection — it is a very good thing to keep working in the
higher consciousness. It is more effective than struggling all
the time down below with the lower forces.

There are higher forces and the lower — the latter have to be
worked out by contact with the higher and in the working out
sometimes they rise, sometimes disappear till they are done with.
It is not necessarily due to some mistake or fault that they rise.

*
**

I am not aware of any case in which the lower forces did not rise up. If such a case occurred I fancy it would be the first in human history.

All the difficulties are bound to vanish in time under the action of the Force. They rise, because if they did not rise the action would not be complete, for all has to be faced and worked out, in order that nothing may be left to rise up hereafter. The psychic being itself can throw the light by which the full consciousness will come and nothing remain in the darkness.

All comes in its time. One has to go on quietly and steadily increasing the higher consciousness till it takes possession of the vital and physical part.

VI

When some weakness comes up you should take it as an opportunity to know what is still to be done and call down the strength into that part. Despondency is not the right way to meet it.

Whatever you see, don't get disturbed or depressed. If one sees a defect one must look at it with the utmost quietude and call down more force and light to get rid of it.

Mistakes are always possible, so long as any part of the mental (even the subconscient part of it) is not thoroughly transformed. There is no need to be disturbed by that.

*
**

Of course one must not make a mistake for the purpose of bringing it out or accept the mistake once made — but if it comes, one has to take advantage of it to change.

An occurrence like that should always be taken as an opportunity of self-conquest. Put your pride and dignity in that — in not being mastered by the passions but being their master.

Do not allow yourself to be worried or upset by small things. Look at things from an inner point of view and try to get the benefit of all that happens. If you make a mistake, don't get distressed because you made a mistake — rather profit by it to see the reason so as to get the right movement in future. This you can do only if you look at it quietly from the inner being without sorrow or disturbance.

Why get excited over these small things? or let them disturb you? If you remain quiet, things will go much better and, if there is any difficulty, you are more likely to find out a way in a quiet mind open to the Peace and Power. That is the secret of going on, not to allow things and happenings, not even real mistakes, to upset you, but to remain very quiet, confiding in the Power to lead you and set things more and more right. If one does that, then things do get actually more and more right and even the difficulties and mistakes become means for learning and steps towards progress.

It is that cheerfulness that we want to be always there in you. It is the happiness of the psychic that has found its way and, whatever difficulties come, is sure that it will be led forward and reach the goal. When a sadhak has that constantly, we know that he has got over the worst difficulty and that he is now firmly on the safe path.

You ask how you can repair the wrong you seem to have done. Admitting that it is as you say, it seems to me that the reparation lies precisely in this, in making yourself a vessel for the Divine Truth and the Divine Love. And the first steps towards that are a complete self-consecration and self-purification, a complete opening of oneself to the Divine, rejecting all in oneself that can stand in the way of the fulfilment. In the spiritual life there is no other reparation for any mistake, none that is wholly effective. At the beginning one should not ask for any other fruit or results than this internal growth and change — for otherwise one lays oneself open to severe disappointments. Only when one is free, can one free others and in yoga it is out of the inner victory that there comes the outer conquest.

It would be easier to get rid of wrong movements when you bring down a settled peace and equanimity into that part of the being. There will then be more of an automatic rejection of such movements and less need of *tapasyā*.

If one part of you keeps its quietude — the inner being — then the rest can be dealt with. So not to allow the vital to be upset and the disturbance cover up the inner self, that is the most important thing. Keep up the rejection always.

It is simply a steady and quiet rejection that is needed and a quiet and steady calling down of the true Force. All this emotional excitability must be quieted down; it is that that makes the vital open itself to these forces. If it were not so, all the defects of the nature could be quietly observed and quietly mended.

Certainly, all the help possible will be given. As for the method, these are always the two ways possible — one to overcome the difficulty in its own field, the other to develop the inner realisation until it grows so strong that the roots you speak of have no longer any soil to hold by and come out easily by a spontaneous psychic change.

It is the true consciousness growing within that gives the power. As it grows, these vital forces get more and more externalised and foreign to the nature. It is only by the power of past habit that they rise.

To recognise one's weaknesses and false movements and draw back from them is the way towards liberation.

Not to judge anyone but oneself until one can see things from a calm mind and a calm vital is an excellent rule. Also, do not allow your mind to form hasty impressions on the strength of some outward appearance, nor your vital to act upon them.

There is a place in the inner being where one can always remain calm and from there look with poise and judgment on the perturbations of the surface consciousness and act upon it to change it. If you can learn to live in that calm of the inner being, you will have found your stable basis.

What you write is no doubt true and it is necessary to see it so as to be able to comprehend and grasp the true attitude necessary for the sadhana. But, as I have said, one must not be distressed or depressed by perceiving the weaknesses inherent in human nature and the difficulty of getting them out. The difficulty is natural, for they have been there for thousands of lives and are the very nature of man's vital and mental ignorance. It is not surprising that they should have a power to stick and take time to disappear. But there is a true being and a true consciousness that is there in us hidden by the surface formations of nature and which can shake them off once it emerges. By taking the right attitude of selfless devotion within and persisting in it in spite of the surface nature's troublesome self-repetitions one enables this inner being and consciousness to emerge and with the Mother's Force working in it deliver the being from all return of the movements of the old nature.

Let the peace and self-giving increase till it takes hold also of the parts in which there are imperfections and gets rid of them. As for the imperfections, it is right not to be troubled by them — only one has to be conscious of them and have the steady and quiet will that they should go.

If you remain in a fully conscious state, the cleaning of the nature ought not to be difficult — afterwards the positive work of the transformation into a perfect instrument can be undertaken.

Of course consciousness grows as the opening increases and one result of consciousness is to be able to see in oneself — but not see the weaknesses only, to see the whole play of forces. Only in the right consciousness one does not regard the weaknesses even in a too personal way so as to get discouraged. One has to see them as the play of nature, mental nature, vital nature, physical nature, common to all human beings — to see them so and remain calm and detached, calling in the Mother's Force and Light for transformation of this defective play into the true nature — not getting impatient if it is not done at once, but going on steadily and giving time for the change. The full change indeed cannot come till all is ready for the descent of a greater, calmer, larger consciousness from above and that is only possible when the ordinary consciousness has been made thoroughly ready for it.

The intense love and bhakti does not come at once. It comes as the power of the psychic grows more and more in the being. But to aspire for it is right and the sincere aspiration is sure to fulfil itself. Always seek to progress in quietude, happiness and confidence, that is the most helpful attitude. Do not listen to contrary suggestions from outside.

While the recognition of the Divine Power and the attunement of one's own nature to it cannot be done without the recognition of the imperfections in that nature, yet it is a wrong attitude to put too much stress either on them or on the difficulties they create, or to distrust the Divine working because of the difficulties one experiences, or to lay too continual an emphasis on the dark side of things. To do this increases the force of the difficulties, gives a greater right of continuance to the imperfections. I do not insist on a Couéistic optimism — although excessive optimism is more helpful than excessive pessimism; that (Coué-ism) tends to cover up difficulties and there is, besides, always a measure to be observed in things. But there is no danger of your covering them up and deluding yourself with too bright an outlook; quite the contrary, you always lay stress too much on the shadows and by so doing thicken them and obstruct your outlets of escape into the Light. Faith, more faith! Faith in your possibilities, faith in the Power that is at work behind the veil, faith in the work that is to be done and the offered guidance.

There cannot be any high endeavour, least of all in the spiritual field, which does not raise or encounter grave obstacles of a very persistent character. These are both internal and external, and, although in the large they are fundamentally the same for all, there may be a great difference in the distribution of their stress or the outward form they take. But the one real difficulty is the attunement of the nature with the working of the Divine

Light and Power. Get that solved and the others will either disappear or take a subordinate place; and even with those difficulties that are of a more general character, more lasting because
they are inherent in the work of transformation, they will not
weigh so heavily because the sense of the supporting Force and
a greater power to follow its movement will be there.

*
**

Well, that is right. The difficulty of the difficulties is self-created,
a knot of the Ignorance; when a certain inner perception loosens
the knot, the worst of the difficulty is over.

*
**

It is necessary to observe and know the wrong movements in you;
for they are the source of your trouble and have to be persistently
rejected if you are to be free.

But do not be always thinking of your defects and wrong
movements. Concentrate more upon what you are to be, on the
ideal, with the faith that, since it is the goal before you, it must
and will come.

To be always observing faults and wrong movements brings
depression and discourages the faith. Turn your eyes more to the
coming light and less to any immediate darkness. Faith, cheerfulness, confidence in the ultimate victory are the things that
help, — they make the progress easier and swifter.

Make more of the good experiences that come to you; one
experience of the kind is more important than the lapses and
failures. When it ceases, do not repine or allow yourself to be
discouraged, but be quiet within and aspire for its renewal in a
stronger form leading to a still deeper and fuller experience.

Aspire always, but with more quietude, opening yourself to
the Divine simply and wholly.

*
**

The defects should be noticed and rejected, but the concentration should be positive — on what you are to be, i.e., on the development of the new consciousness rather than on this negative side.

You have to be conscious of the wrong movements, but not preoccupied with them only.

It [getting projected from the mind into the vital] came by being preoccupied too much with the difficulties of the nature. It is always better to dwell on the good side of things within yourself. I do not mean in an egoistic way, but with faith and cheerful confidence, calling down the positive experience of which the nature is already capable so that a constant positive growth can help in the rejection of all that has to be rejected. But in fact one gets often projected into the vital difficulties at an early stage and then instead of going from the mind into the psychic (through the heart) one has to go through the disturbed vital.

It [retracing one's steps from the vital into the psychic] can be done, if you refuse to be preoccupied with the idea of your difficulties and concentrate on really helpful and positive things. Be cheerful and confident. Doubt and desire & Co. are there, no doubt, but the Divine is there also inside you. Open your eyes and look and look till the veil is rent and you see Him or Her!

Difficulties and perplexities can never be got rid of by the mind brooding on them and trying in that way to get out of them; this habit of the mind only makes them recur without a solution and keeps up by brooding the persistent tangle. It is from something above and outside the perplexities that the solution must come. The difficulty of the physical mind — not the true thinking intel-

ligence — is that it does not want to believe in this larger consciousness outside itself because it is not aware of it; and it
remains shut like a box in itself, not admitting the light that is all
round it and pressing to get in. It is a subtle law of the action of
consciousness that if you stress difficulties — you have to observe them, of course, but not stress them, they will quite sufficiently do that for themselves — the difficulties tend to stick or
even increase; on the contrary, if you put your whole stress on
faith and aspiration and concentrate steadily on what you aspire
to, that will sooner or later tend towards realisation. It is this
change of stress, a change in the poise and attitude of the mind,
that will be the more helpful process.

As for details, the method of the mind concentrating on details and trying to put them right is a slow and tardy one; it has
to be done, but as a subordinate process, not the chief one. If it
succeeds at all, it is because after some period of struggle and
stress, something is released and there is an opening and the
larger consciousness of which I speak gets through and produces
some general result. But the progress is much more rapid if one
can make the opening the main thing and keep the dealing with
details as something resultant and subordinate. When there is
this opening, some essential (therefore general) progress can be
made and, as you yourself say, "express and translate itself into
details". The mind is always trying to handle details and con-
struct out of them some general result; but what is above mind
and even the best powers of the higher ranges of mind tend rather
to bring about some *essential* change and make it or let it express
itself, translate itself in the necessary details.

I may add, however, that one can feel the essential change
without its expressing itself in details; e.g., one can feel a wide
silent peace or a state of freedom and joy and rest silent and secure in it without needing to translate it into sundry details in
order to feel the progress made.

It is not a theory but a constant experience and very tangible when it comes that there is above us, above the consciousness in the physical body, a great supporting extension as it were
of peace, light, power, joy — that we can become aware of it and
bring it down into the physical consciousness and that that, at

first for a time, afterwards more frequently and for a longer time, in the end for good, can remain and change the whole basis of our daily consciousness. Even before we are aware of it above, we can suddenly feel it coming down and entering into us. The need is to have an aspiration towards it, make the mind quiet so that what we call the opening is rendered possible. A quieted mind (not necessarily motionless or silent, though it is good if one can have that at will) and a persistent aspiration in the heart are the two main keys of the yoga. Activity of the mind is a much slower process and does not by itself lead to these decisive results. It is the difference between a straight road and an approach through constant circles, spirals or meanders.

The negative means are not evil; they are useful for their object which is to get away from life. But from the positive point of view, they are disadvantageous, because they get rid of the powers of the being instead of divinising them for the transformation of life.

By negative I mean merely repressing the desires and wrong movements and egoism, by positive I mean the bringing down of light and peace and purity in those parts from above. I do not mean that these movements are not to be rejected — but all the energy should not be used solely for rejection. It must also be directed to the positive replacement of them by the higher consciousness. The more this consciousness comes, the easier also will the rejection be.

The statement[1] is a general one and like all general statements subject to qualification according to circumstances. What I meant was to discourage what some do which is to be always dwelling on their difficulties and shortcomings only, for that makes them turn for ever like squirrels in a cage always in the

---

[1] "One should not dwell on the lower nature or its obstacles." Sri Aurobindo.

same circle of difficulties without the least breaking of light through the clouds. The sentence would be more accurate or generally applicable if it were written "dwell too much" or "dwell solely". Naturally, without rejection nothing can be done. And in hard periods or moments concentration on the difficulties is inevitable. Also in the early stages one has often to do a great amount of clearance work so that the road can be followed at all.

If the imperfection is there, one has to see it. The thing to be done is to live in the inner self and from there see the imperfection and change it.

Not to be touched or disturbed by the difficulties, to feel separate from them is the first step towards freedom.

In your dealing with your difficulties and the wrong movements that assail you, you are probably making the mistake of identifying yourself with them too much and regarding them as part of your own nature. You should rather draw back from them, detach and dissociate yourself from them, regard them as movements of the universal lower imperfect and impure nature, forces that enter into you and try to make you their instrument for their self-expression. By so detaching and dissociating yourself it will be more possible for you to discover and to live more and more in a part of yourself, your inner or your psychic being which is not attacked or troubled by these movements, finds them foreign to itself and automatically refuses assent to them and feels itself always turned to or in contact with the Divine Forces and the higher planes of consciousness. Find that part of your being and live in it; to be able to do so is the true foundation of the yoga.

By so standing back it will be easier also for you to find a quiet poise in yourself, behind the surface struggle, from which you can more effectively call in the help to deliver you. The Divine presence, calm, peace, purity, force, light, joy, wideness are above waiting to descend in you. Find this quietude behind and your mind also will become quieter and through the quiet mind you can call down the descent first of the purity and peace and then of the Divine Force. If you can feel this peace and purity descending into you, you can then call it down again and again till it begins to settle; you will feel too the Force working in you to change the movements and transform the consciousness. In this working you will be aware of the presence and power of the Mother. Once that is done, all the rest will be a question of time and of the progressive evolution in you of your true and divine nature.

He can continue his endeavour and let us know if there is any result. The difficulties that have risen in him are a quite normal and natural reaction to the effort he is making. It is usual for these resistances to rise up, for they have to manifest themselves in order that they may be dealt with and thrown out. If he perseveres, that should happen sooner or later. But it is best not to struggle with the resistances but to stand back from them, observe as a witness, reject these movements and call on the Divine Power to remove them. Surrender of the nature is not an easy thing and may take a long time; surrender of the self, if one can do it, is easier and once that is done, that of the nature will come about sooner or later. But for that it is necessary to detach oneself from the action of the Prakriti and see oneself as separate. To observe the movements as a witness without being discouraged or disturbed is the best way to effect the necessary detachment and separation. This also would help to increase the receptivity to any aid that may be given to him and to bring about the reliance.

As to the change of nature, the first step is to become conscious and separate from the old surface nature. For, this rajasic vital nature is a surface creation of Prakriti, it is not the true being;

however persistent it seems, it is only a temporary combination of vital movements. Behind is the true mental and vital being supported by the psychic. The true being is calm, wide, peaceful. By drawing back and becoming separate one creates the possibility of living in the peace of this inner Purusha and no longer identified with the surface Prakriti. Afterwards it will be much easier to change by the force of the psychic perception and the Peace and Power and Light from above the surface being.

These things rise because either they are there in the conscious part of the being as habits of the nature or they are there lying concealed and able to rise at any moment or they are suggestions from the general or universal Nature outside to which the personal being makes a response. In any case they rise in order that they may be met and cast out and finally rejected so that they may trouble the nature no longer. The amount of trouble they give depends on the way they are met. The first principle is to detach oneself from them, not to identify, not to admit them any longer as part of one's real nature but to look on them as things imposed to which one says "This is not I or mine — this is a thing I reject altogether". One begins to feel a part of the being inside which is not identified, which remains firm and says "This may give trouble on the surface, but it shall not touch me". If this separate being within can be felt, then half the trouble is over — provided there is a will there not only to separate but to get rid of the imperfection from the surface nature also.

You must remain always aware of the self and the obscure nature must not be felt as the self but as an instrument which has to be put into tune with the self.

The egoism, desires, faults of the nature are in everybody very much the same. But once one begins to be conscious of them and has the will to be free, then one has only to keep that will and there will be no real danger. For when one begins to be conscious in the way you have begun and something from within raises up all that was hidden, it means that the Mother's grace is on your nature and her force is working and your inner being is aiding the Mother's force to get rid of all these things. So you must not be sorrowful or discouraged or fear anything but look steadily at all that comes out and have the will that it should go completely and for ever. With the Mother's force working and the psychic being supporting the force, all can be done and all will surely be done. This purification is made just in order that no trouble may occur in the future such as happened to some because they were not purified — in order that the higher consciousness may come into a purified nature and the inner transformation securely take place. Go on, therefore, with faith and courage putting your reliance on the Mother.

All that you have written here is perfectly correct. It is so, by standing back from these forces, neither attracted nor disturbed by them, that one gets freedom, perceives their falsity or imperfection and is able to rise above and overcome them. The consciousness that comes forward may be either the psychic or the spiritualised mind — it is probably the former.

What the Mother spoke of was not self-analysis nor dissection; they are mental things which can deal with the inanimate or make the live dead — they are not spiritual methods. What the Mother spoke of was not analysis, but a seeing of oneself and of all the living movements of the being and the nature, a vivid observation of the personalities and forces that move on the stage of our being, their motives, their impulses, their potentialities, an observation quite as interesting as the seeing and understanding of a drama or a novel, a living vision and perception of how things are done in us, which brings also a living mastery over this inner universe. Such things become dry only when one deals with them with the analytic and ratiocinative mind, not when one deals with them thus seeingly and intuitively as a movement of life. If you had that observation (from the inner spiritual, not the outer intellectual and ethical viewpoint), then it would be comparatively easy for you to get out of your difficulties; for instance, you would find at once where this irrational impulse to flee away came from and it would not have any hold upon you. Of course, all that can be done to the best effect when you stand back from the play of your nature and become the Witness-Control or the Spectator-Actor-Manager. But that is what happens when you take this kind of self-seeing posture.

The fear that this will be dry or painful is an idea of the non-understanding intellect.

You stick to your intellectual-ethical version of the inner self-vision? Dry? policeman? criminal? Great Lord! If it were that, it would cease to be self-vision at all — for in the true self-vision there is no policemanship and no criminaldom at all. All that belongs to the intellectual-ethical virtue-and-sin dodge which is only a mental construction of practical value for the outward life but not a truth of real inner values. In the true self-vision we see only harmonies and disharmonies and set the wrong notes right and replace them by the true notes. But I say that for the sake of truth, not to persuade you to start the self-vision effort; for if you did with these ideas of it, you would inevitably start it on the policeman basis and get into trouble. Besides, evidently, you prefer in the yoga to be the piano and not the pianist, which is all right but involves total self-giving and the intervention of the supreme musician and harmonist. May it be so.

Every man is full of these contradictions because he is one person, no doubt, but made up of different personalities — the perception of multiple personality is becoming well known to psychologists now — who very commonly disagree with each other. So long as one does not aim at unity in a single dominant intention, like that of seeking and self-dedication to the Divine, they get on somehow together, alternating or quarrelling or muddling through or else one taking the lead and compelling the others to take a minor part — but once you try to unite them in one aim, then the trouble becomes evident.

VII

You should not be so dependent on outward things; it is this attitude that makes you give so excessive an importance to circumstances. I do not say that circumstances cannot help or hinder — but they are circumstances, not the fundamental thing which is in ourselves, and their help or their hindrance ought not to be of primary importance. In yoga, as in every great or serious human effort, there is always bound to be an abundance of adverse interventions and unfavourable circumstances which have to be overcome. To give them too great an importance increases their importance and their power to multiply themselves, gives them, as it were, confidence in themselves and the habit of coming. To face them with equanimity — if one cannot manage a cheerful persistence against them of confident and resolute will — diminishes, on the contrary, their importance and effect and in the end, though not at once, gets rid of their persistence and recurrence. It is therefore a principle in yoga to recognise the determining power of what is within us — for that is the deeper truth — to set that right and establish the inward strength as against the power of outward circumstances. The strength is there — even in the weakest; one has to find it, to unveil it and to keep it in front throughout the journey and the battle.

A defence organisation means the admittance that there is civil war.[1] From the point of view of a sadhak one ought not to admit the possibility of civil war. A sadhak should always remember that everything depends upon the inner attitude; if he has a per-

---

[1] Written during the disturbances in Bengal before the division of India.

fect faith in the Divine Grace, he will find that the Divine Grace will make him do the right thing at every step. He will be made to go out of the house, for example, if it is dangerous to remain in the house; and he will stay in the house if there is danger for him outside. The Grace will prompt him to do just the thing that makes him escape the danger. But for things to happen like that, you must have a deeply-rooted faith pervading your whole being, contradicted by no other movement in you. And this is naturally difficult. Also you can have the faith for yourself but there are others around you who do not share in your attitude. Being in their midst you may be obliged to admit external measures, join a defence organisation, as you say. Even so, you must bear in mind that it is only your inner attitude and faith that counts. All external means mean nothing, they may prove to be absolutely useless and come to nothing, it is only the Divine Grace that protects you.

That is the inconvenience of going away from a difficulty, — it runs after one, — or rather one carries it with oneself, for the difficulty is truly inside, not outside. Outside circumstances only give it the occasion to manifest itself and so long as the inner difficulty is not conquered, the circumstances will always crop up one way or another.

That is the real reason for all these things happening to X. When there is something in the nature that has to be got over, it is always drawing on itself incidents that put it to the test till the sadhak has overcome and is free. At least it is a thing that often happens especially if the person is making a sincere effort to overcome. One does not always know whether it is the hostiles who are trying to break the resolution or putting it to the test (for they claim the right to do it) or whether it is, let us say, the gods who are doing it so as to press and hasten the progress or insisting on the surety and thoroughness of the change aspired after. Perhaps it helps most when one can take it from the latter standpoint.

You are quite right — that is the way you must take it, that here is an opportunity given to you for overcoming this stumbling-block in the nature. When one does sadhana it is constantly seen that so long as there is an important defect somewhere, circumstances so happen that the occasion comes for the defect to rise until it is thrown out of the being. If one can take the coming of these circumstances clairvoyantly as a call and an opportunity for conquering the defect, then one can progress very quickly.

On the other point, it is very good that you have taken the right attitude and perception with regard to the criticism of others; but this must be extended to their wrong actions also, if there are any. For if their defects flow from their nature, the common human nature of all, their actions flow from the same source, and it is enough to see and understand — the same rule must apply to both these things.

Difficulty cannot be overcome by your running away from it.

All this comes from your having taken a wrong way with yourself. It is not by tormenting yourself with remorse and harassing thoughts that you can overcome. It is by looking straight at yourself, very quietly, with a quiet and firm resolution and then going on cheerfully and bravely in full confidence and reliance, trusting in the Grace, serenely and vigilantly, anchoring yourself on your psychic being, calling down more and more of the love and Ananda, turning more and more exclusively to the Mother. That is the true way — and there is no other.

It is also wise that you have reconciled yourself with the place and have the feeling of strength to deal with the situation there.

A certain power of adaptation and harmonisation of the surroundings is necessary — you had it very strongly and were therefore successful wherever you went. The recoil from your previous position made you nervous and depressed and spoiled for a time the action of this power in you. Now with your new attitude I hope it will return and bring the solution of all your difficulties.

We send you our blessings. Keep yourself always open to the Power from above and to our help from here and remain firm and strong against all difficulties that may yet remain either in the outer life or the sadhana. On these conditions victory is always sure.

*
**

Despair is absurd and talk of suicide quite out of place. However a man may stumble, the Divine Grace will be there so long as he aspires for it and in the end lead him through.

*
**

Suicide is an absurd solution; he is quite mistaken in thinking that it will give him peace. He will only carry his difficulties with him into a more miserable condition of existence beyond and bring them back to another life on earth. The only remedy is to shake off these morbid ideas and face life with a clear will for some definite work to be done as the life's aim and with a quiet and active courage.

*
**

Sadhana has to be done in the body, it cannot be done by the soul without the body. When the body drops, the soul goes wandering in other worlds — and finally it comes back to another life and another body. Then all the difficulties it had not solved meet it again in the new life. So what is the use of leaving the body?

Moreover, if one throws away the body wilfully, one suffers

much in the other worlds and when one is born again, it is in worse, not in better conditions.

The only sensible thing is to face the difficulties in this life and this body and conquer them.

Death is not a way to succeed in sadhana. If you die in that way, you will only have the same difficulties again with probably less favourable circumstances.

The way to succeed in sadhana is to refuse to be discouraged, to aspire simply and sincerely so that the Mother's force may work in you and bring down what is above. No man ever succeeded in this sadhana by his own merit. To become open and plastic to the Mother is the one thing needed.

That is not right. Throwing away the life does not improve the chances for the next time. It is in this life and body that one must get things done.

Well, that is not the right kind of quietude. The peace of Nirvana would have some meaning in it, but death into the quietness of exhausted Prakriti is no release at all.

The real rest is in the inner life founded in peace and silence and absence of desire. There is no other rest — for without that the machine goes on whether one is interested in it or not. The inner *mukti* is the only remedy.

VIII

There is no reason why you should abandon hope of success

in the yoga. The state of depression which you now feel is temporary and it comes even upon the strongest sadhaks at one time or another or even often recurs. The only thing needed is to hold firm with the awakened part of the being, to reject all contrary suggestions and to wait, opening yourself as much as you can to the true Power, till the crisis or change of which this depression is a stage is completed. The suggestions which come to your mind telling you that you are not fit and that you must go back to the ordinary life are promptings from a hostile source. Ideas of this kind must always be rejected as inventions of the lower nature; even if they are founded on appearances which seem convincing to the ignorant mind, they are false, because they exaggerate a passing movement and represent it as the decisive and definite truth. There is only one truth in you on which you have to lay constant hold, the truth of your divine possibilities and the call of the higher Light to your nature. If you hold to that always, or, even if you are momentarily shaken from your hold, return constantly to it, it will justify itself in the end in spite of all difficulties and obstacles and stumblings. All that resists will disappear in time with the progressive unfolding of your spiritual nature.

What is needed is the conversion and surrender of the vital part. It must learn to demand only the highest truth and to forego all insistence on the satisfaction of its inferior impulses and desires. It is this adhesion of the vital being that brings the full satisfaction and joy of the whole nature in the spiritual life. When that is there, it will be impossible even to think of returning to the ordinary existence. Meanwhile the mental will and the psychic aspiration must be your support; if you insist, the vital will finally yield and be converted and surrender.

Fix upon your mind and heart the resolution to live for the Divine Truth and for that alone; reject all that is contrary and incompatible with it and turn away from the lower desires; aspire to open yourself to the Divine Power and to no other. Do this in all sincerity and the present and living help you need will not fail you.

*\
**

There must be a fixed will for the spiritual life, that alone can overcome all obstacles.

There is no hopelessness except when the will chooses the worse path.

Why cannot you see that this condition is not a true consciousness, but only a clouding of the truth, a clouding which you can always get rid of if you firmly chose to do so? What you express here is not a lack of understanding, but a lack of will — and this lack of will is not your own, but is forced upon you by a lower consciousness which overpowers you and forces you to reverse all the true values of feeling and knowledge. Your being does want to be free and at peace and happy in the light — it is this Falsehood seizing hold of your external mind that makes you want to be more dark and miserable and revolted and hate yourself and not to live. Such feelings, such a perverted will is entirely opposed to the normal feelings of the nature and cannot be "true" and right. There is nobody who asks you to pretend — what we ask you is to reject false perversions and wrong feelings and ignorance and not to go on supporting them as they want you to do. It is not courage and nobility to accept these things as the law of your nature, nor is it meanness and cowardice to aspire to a higher Truth and try to act according to it and make that the law of your nature.

As for his difficulties and troubles, there is little hope of his overcoming them if he does not realise that they come from within him and not from outside. It is the weakness of his vital nature, the inefficient helplessness of his nervous being always weeping and complaining and lamenting instead of facing life and overcoming its difficulties, it is the sentimental lachrymose attitude it takes that keeps his troubles unsolved and alive.

This is a temperament which the gods will not help because they know that help is useless, for it will either not be received or will be spilled and wasted; and all that is rajasic and Asuric in the world despises and tramples upon this kind of nature.

If he had learned a calm strength and quiet courage without weakness and without fuss and violence, founded on confidence in the help he could always have received from here and on openness to the Mother's force, things would have been favourably settled by this time. But he cannot take advantage of any help given him because his vital nature cherishes its weakness and is always indulging and rhetorically expressing it instead of throwing it away with contempt as a thing unworthy of manhood and unfit for a sadhak. It is only if he so rejects it that he can receive strength and stand in life or progress in the sadhana.

It is because you yourself are so fidgety, nervous, divided and undecided that we are unable to make a final decision.

If you accept your weakness which means accepting the thing itself — some part of your nature accepts it and to that you yield — then what is the use of our telling you what to do? That part of your vital will always be able to say — "I was too weak to carry it out." The only way out of it is for you to cease to be weak, to dismiss this sentimental part of you, to call down strength to replace its weakness and to do it with a settled and serious purpose. If we cannot get you who have had some foundation in the sadhana to overcome this element in you, how do you expect us to get X to do it who says he has no foundation but is still floating?

The Mother's help and mine are always there for you. You have only to turn fully towards it and it will act on you.

What has come across is these wrong ideas about your unfitness, about bad things in you that prevent you from receiving the Mother's grace, about the lack of aspiration which prevents you from having realisation and experience. These thoughts are quite wrong and untrue — they are not even your own thoughts, they are suggestions thrown on you just as they are thrown on the other sadhaks and intended to produce depression. There is no unfitness, no bad thing inside that comes across, no lack of aspiration causing the cessation of experience. It is the depression, the self-distrust, the readiness to despair which are the only cause; there is no other. To all sadhaks, as I wrote to you, even to the best and strongest there come interruptions in the flow of the sadhana; that is not a cause for thinking oneself unfit and wanting to go away with the idea that there is no hope. A little quietude would bring back the flow. You were having the necessary experiences, the necessary progress and it was only a coming forward of some difficulties of the physical consciousness that stopped them for a time. That happens to all and is not particular to you, as I explained to you. These difficulties always come and have to be overcome. Once overcome by the working of the Force, the sadhana goes on as before. But you begin to entertain this wrong idea of unfitness and lack of aspiration as the cause and get entirely depressed. You must shake all that off and refuse to believe in the thought-suggestions that come to you. No sadhak ought ever to indulge thoughts of unfitness and hopelessness — they are quite irrelevant because it is not one's personal fitness and worthiness that makes one succeed, but the Mother's grace and power and the consent of the soul to her grace and the workings of her Force.

Turn from these dark thoughts and look to the Mother only, not with impatience for the result and desire, but with trust and confidence and let her workings bring you quietude and the renewal of the progress towards the psychic opening and realisation. That will bring surely and without doubt the fuller faith and the love which you seek.

What I meant by the change was the great improvement in your mental and vital attitude and reactions to outward things and to life which was very evident in your letters and account of happenings and gave them quite a new atmosphere warm and clear and psychic. Naturally the change is not yet absolute and integral, but it does seem to be fundamental. Moreover, it is certainly due to a growing bhakti within, especially an acceptance of bhakti as your path and the implications of that acceptance. The mind has taken a new poise less intellectual and more psychic. What prevents you from seeing the growth of bhakti (sometimes you have seen it and written about it) is a continuance of the physical mind which sets going with a constant repetitionary whirl of its fixed ideas whenever there is any touch of depression. One of these ideas is that you don't progress, will not progress and can never progress, the old thing that used to say "Yoga is not for the likes of me" etc. The activity of the physical mind (next to the wrong activity of the vital) is what most keeps one's consciousness on the surface and prevents it from being conscious within and of what goes on within; it can see something of what happens on the surface of the nature, the results of the inner movement but not the cause of the happenings, which is the inner movement itself. That is one reason why I like to see the physical mind occupied in poetry and music etc. and other salubrious activities which help the inner growth and in which the inner bhakti can express itself, for that keeps the physical mind busy, unoccupied with the mechanical rotatory movement and allows and helps the inner growth. The rotatory movement is less than it was before and I expect it one of these days to get tired of itself and give up altogether.

These ideas are only suggestions that always come up when you allow this sadness to grow up in you; instead of indulging them, they should be immediately thrown from you. There is no "why" to your feeling of our far-away-ness and indifference, for these do not exist, and the feeling comes up automatically without any true reason along with this wave of the wrong kind of

consciousness. Whenever this comes up, you should be at once
sure that it is a wrong turn and stop it and reject all its characteristic suggestions. It is when you have been able to do so for
a long time that you have made great progress and developed
a right consciousness and right ideas and the true psychic attitude. You are not hampering our work nor standing in the way
of others coming here; in cleaving to the sadhana in spite of all
difficulties you are not deceiving yourself but, on the contrary,
doing the right thing and you are certainly not deceiving the
Divine, who knows very well both your aspiration and your
difficulties. So there is not a shred of a reason for your going
away. If you "sincerely want to do yoga", and there can be no
doubt about that, that is quite a sufficient reason for your being
here. It does not matter about not having as yet any occult experiences, like the rising of the Kundalini etc.: these come to some
early, to some late; and there are besides different lines of such
experiences for different natures. You should not hanker after
these or get disappointed and despondent because they do not
yet come. These things can be left to come of themselves when
the consciousness is ready. What you have to aspire to is bhakti,
purification of the nature, right psychic consciousness and surrender. Aspire for bhakti and it will grow in you. It is already there
within and it is that which expresses itself in your poetry and
music and the feelings that rise up as in the temple of the Mother
at the Cape. As the bhakti and purity in the nature grow, the
right psychic consciousness will also increase and lead to the
full surrender. But keep steady and don't indulge these ideas
of incapacity and frustration and going away; they are stuff of
tamas and good only to be flung aside.

You are not asked to do anything that you are incapable of; it
is something that you have done already and of which therefore
you are capable. You are not asked to change your nature by
your own effort, but only to stand back from these ideas and
thoughts, refuse to indulge them and remain quiet within and
allow the Force you have repeatedly felt to change you. To

repeat constantly "I am weak, I am unfit, I am bad" will lead you nowhere.

Remind yourself always that the Divine Force is there, that you have felt it and that, even if you seem to lose consciousness of it for a time or it seems something distant, still it is there and is sure to prevail. For those whom the Force has touched and taken up, belong thenceforth to the Divine.

It is good. The more you keep that dominant sense of the force and the calmness and increase it, the more the other feeling will diminish and fade. It always happens that at first the Power and Peace only press, touch, invade at places, until a time comes when a part of the being always feels in that condition however much disturbance may assail the surface. Afterwards the disturbance is more and more pushed out till it is felt only outside the being, not in it. When that too goes, there is the complete peace and the full foundation.

The thing is that it is unavoidable in the course of the sadhana that some parts of the being should be less open, less advanced, as yet less aware of the Peace and Force, less intimate to them than others. These parts have to be worked upon, and changed, but this can be done smoothly only if you are detached from them, able to regard them as not your very self, even though a part of the nature you have to change. Then when they appear with their defects, you will not be upset, not carried away by their movements, lost to the sense of the Peace and Force; you will be able to work on them (or rather let the Force work) as one would on a machine that has to be repaired or a work that has defects and has to be done better this time. If you identify yourself with these parts, then it is very troublesome. The work will still be done, the change made, but with delay, with bad upsettings, in a painful and not in a smooth way. That is why we always tell people to be calm and detached and look upon these things not as their true selves but as an outer part that has to be worked upon quietly until it is what it should be.

It is of course a fluctuation of the mental will that often prevents a knowledge gained from being put into steady practice. If the will is not strong enough, then the greater Will behind which is the will of the Mother, her conscious Force in which knowledge and will are united, must be called in to strengthen and support it. Very often, however, even if the will as well as the knowledge are there, the habit of the vital nature brings in the old reactions. This can only be overcome by a steady undiscouraged aspiration which will bring out more and more of the psychic and its true movements to push out and displace the wrong ones. The gradual and steady replacement of the old ignorant consciousness and its movements by the true psychic and spiritual consciousness is the nature of the transformation that is to be accomplished in the yoga. But that takes time, it cannot be done easily or at once. Therefore one should not mind or be discouraged if meanwhile one finds the old movements recurring in spite of one's knowledge. Only one should try to keep more and more separate from them, so that even if they recur the consent of the being to them shall no longer be there.

The difficulties of the character persist so long as one yields to them in action when they rise. One has to make a strict rule not to act according to the impulses of anger, ego or whatever the weakness may be that one wants to get rid of, or if one does act in the heat of the moment, not to justify or persist in the action. If one does that, after a time the difficulty abates or is confined purely to a subjective movement which one can observe, detach oneself from and combat.

One is always open [to ignorant forces of Nature] so long as there is not the final change. If things do not come in it is because the consciousness is vigilant or the psychic in front; but the least want of vigilance or relaxation can allow something to enter.

One ought not to worry, but also one ought not to be negligent, that is, one ought not to give the assent of the will or of the reason to these movements. For all assent prolongs their actions or their recurrence. If they do not go when rejected by the mind and will, it is because of the habitual response in the less conscious parts of the nature. These have to become conscious by receiving the Light and Force until finally they refuse response to the calls of the lower nature.

This is quite right. If you keep this condition, not allowing it to be entirely obscured or long clouded, you can move rapidly towards a new birth of your nature and the foundation of your life and all your thoughts and acts and movements in your true being, the psychic being. Never consent to the ideas, suggestions, feelings that bring back the cloud, the confusion and the revolt. It is the consent that makes them strong to recur. Refuse the consent and they will be obliged to retire either immediately or after a time.

Remain fixed in the sunlight of the true consciousness — for only there is happiness and peace. They do not depend upon outside happenings, but on this alone.

IX

It is the usual course of the process by which the change of consciousness is effected. The lower forces seldom yield the ground without a protracted and often repeated struggle. What is gained can be covered over, but it is never lost.

Why do you indulge in these exaggerated feelings of remorse and despair when these things come up from the subconscient? They do not help and make it more, not less, difficult to eliminate what comes. Such returns of an old nature that is long expelled from the conscious parts of the being always happen in sadhana. It does not at all mean that the nature is unchangeable. Try to recover the inner quietude, draw back from these movements and look at them calmly, reducing them to their true proportions. Your true nature is that in which you have peace and Ananda and love of the Divine. This other is only a fringe of the outer personality which in spite of these returns is destined to drop away as the true being extends and increases.

There is no reason to be so much cut down or despair of your progress. Evidently, you have had a surging up of the old movements, but that can always happen so long as there is not an entire change of the old nature both in the consciousness and subconscient parts. Something came up that made you get out of poise and stray into a past round of feelings. The one thing to do is to quiet yourself and get back into the true consciousness and poise.

The liberation you feel is likely to be fundamental and definite. But in these matters, even after the liberation, one has to remain vigilant — for often these things go out and remain at a far distance, waiting to see if under any circumstances in any condition they can make a rush and recover their kingdom. If there has been an entire purification down to the depths and nothing is there to open the gate, then they cannot do it. But it is only after one has been a long time free that one can say, "Over, it is all right for ever."

As for your inner attitude, it must remain the same. Not to be excited or drawn outwards by these "incidents" of the outward life or by the coming in of new elements is the rule; they must come in like waves into an untroubled sea and mix in it and become themselves untroubled and serene.

Your present condition is all that it should be, — only you must remain vigilant always. For when the condition is good, the lower movements have a habit of subsiding and become quiescent, hiding as it were, — or they go out of the nature and remain at a distance. But if they see that the sadhak is losing vigilance, then they slowly begin to rise or draw near, most often unseen, and when he is quite off his guard, surge up suddenly or make a sudden irruption. This continues until the whole nature, mental, vital, physical down to the very subconscient is enlightened, conscious, full of the Divine. Till that happens, one must always remain watchful in a sleepless vigilance.

It is perhaps that the attitude you took of going on with the calm within and slowly changing what had to be changed, postponing certain things for the future, — though not a wrong attitude in itself, — made you somewhat lax, allowing things to play on the surface (desires, etc.) which should have been kept in check. This resolution may have opened the way for the old movements to rise through this part which was not yet ready to change at all and the hostile forces finding you off your guard took the opportunity to push the attack home. They are always vigilant for an opportunity and there must be a sufficient vigilance on the sadhak's side to refuse it to them. It is also possible that as the Force descending in the general atmosphere has carried in it some pressure on the consciousness of the sadhaks to be more ready, more awake, less engrossed in the movements of the ordinary nature than they are now, it fell upon this part and the resistance in it, which was mostly passive for a long time, became suddenly active under the pressure.

All these movements simply mean that a certain part of the

nature, full of habitual emotional movements, had been lying suppressed but not definitely dealt with and has now come up with as much force as possible, taking advantage of the descent of the consciousness from the peace and Ananda. It is an old habitual movement of the egoistic vital that is repeating itself. You had pushed it down into the subconscient and away to the outskirts of your nature, but not cleared the nature of it entirely. It is not surprising that it has pushed back the inner self and its experiences for the time being; if it had not done that, it could not last for a moment. But that is no reason why you should talk as if it were a hopeless downfall; it is not that, though it is a serious stumble. You have to recognise it for what it is and get out of the wave and throw it away from you. Steady yourself and look straight at what has happened without overstressing its importance, it will then pass away sooner.

But in reality these things are not sufficient reasons for getting sad and depressed. It is quite normal for difficulties to come back like that and it is not a proof that no progress has been made. The recurrence (after one has thought one has conquered) is not unaccountable. I have explained in my writings what happens. When a habitual movement long embedded in the nature is cast out, it takes refuge in some less enlightened part of the nature, and when cast out of the rest of the nature, it takes refuge in the subconscient and from there surges up when you least expect it or comes up in dreams or sudden inconscient movements or it goes out and remains in wait in the environmental being through which the universal Nature works and attacks from there as a force from outside trying to recover its kingdom by a suggestion or repetition of old movements. One has to stand fast till the power of return fades away. These returns or attacks must be regarded not as parts of oneself, but as invasions — and rejected without allowing any depression or discouragement. If the mind does not sanction them, if the vital refuses to welcome them, if the physical remains steady and refuses to obey the physical urge, then the recurrence of the thought, the vital impulse, the physical feeling will begin to lose its last holds and finally they will be too feeble to cause any trouble.

There is no reason for despondency. When one has progressed as far as you did, that is, so far as to feel and maintain the calm and have so much of the psychic discrimination and the psychic feeling, one has no right to despair of one's spiritual future. You could not yet carry out the discrimination into an entire psychic change, because a large part of the outer physical consciousness still took some pleasure in old movements and therefore these roots remained alive in the subconscient. When you were off your guard, the whole thing rose up and there was a temporary and violent lapse. But this does not mean that the nature is not changeable. Only the calm inner conscious poise, the psychic discrimination and above all a will to change, stronger and steadier than before, must be so established that no upsurging or invasion will be able to cloud even partly the discrimination or suspend the will. You saw the truth but this part of the old nature which rose up did not want to acknowledge — it wanted its play and imposed that on you. This time you must insist on a complete truthfulness in the whole being which will refuse to accept any denial of what the psychic discrimination sees or any affirmation or any consent anywhere to what it disapproves, spiritual humility and the removal of self-righteousness, self-justification and the wish to impose yourself, the tendency to judge others, etc. All these defects you know are in you; to cast that out may take time, but if the will to be true to the inner self in all ways is strong and persistent and vigilant and always calls in the Mother's Force, it can be done sooner than now seems possible.

So long as you have not learned the lesson the past had to teach you, it comes back on you. Notice carefully what kind of remembrances come, you will see that they are connected with some psychological movements in you that have to be got rid of. So you must be prepared to recognise all that was not right in you and is still not corrected, not allow any vanity or self-righteousness to cloud your vision.

X

Our help will be there. It can be effective in spite of your physical mind, but it will be more effective if the steady working will is there as its instrument. There are always two elements in spiritual success — one's own steady will and endeavour and the Power that in one way or another helps and gives the result of endeavour.

Your tendency was to go up and leave the higher consciousness to deal with the lower nature without any personal effort for that. That could have worked all right on two conditions: (1) that the peace and force would come down and occupy all down to the physical; (2) that you succeeded in keeping the inner being uncovered by the outer nature. The physical failed to absorb the peace, inertia rose instead; force could not come down; the suggestions from the outer nature proved too strong for you and between these suggestions and the inertia they interrupted the sadhana.

I have not said that you made a mistake. I have simply stated what happened and the causes. If you had been able to remain above and let the Force come down and act while you were detached from the outer nature, it would have been all right. You were able to go up because the Peace descended. You were not able to remain above because the Peace could not occupy sufficiently the physical and the Force did not descend sufficiently. Meanwhile the inertia rose, you got troubled more and more because of the vital suggestions in the outer nature and the rush of inertia, so you were unable to keep detached and let the Force descend more and more or call it down more and more. Hence the coming down into the physical consciousness. In saying all that I am not giving any blame, or saying you made a mistake or acted against the Mother's Will. These notions of mistake or not doing the Will are your own, not mine.

When the mind and the vital take hold of the physical and make it an instrument, then there is no inertia. But here the physical consciousness has been dealt with. If it could have received the peace of the self into itself — without covering it over with inertia, then it would have been all right. But the vital has intervened somehow with its demand and dissatisfaction, so there has been this obstruction and inability to progress. This thing often happens in the sadhana and one must have the power either to reject it dynamically or else to remain detached until it has exhausted itself. Then the true movement begins again.

You are always expecting the Mother to do it — and here again the laziness and tamas come in — it is the spirit of tamasic surrender. If the Mother puts you back into a good condition, your vital pulls you down again. How is that to stop so long as you say Yes to the vital and accept its discouragement and violences and the rest of it as your own? Detachment is absolutely necessary.

I wanted to stress two things, that is why I have written so much about them.

1. There must be no tamasic (inert, passive) surrender to the Mother — for that will bring as its reaction a passive inert helplessness before the lower or hostile forces or suggestions, an unresisting or helplessly resisting acquiescence or sufferance of these inroads. A passive condition can bring much peace, quietude, joy even, but it disperses the being instead of concentrating it in wideness and the will becomes atrophied. Surrender

must be luminous, active, a willed offering to the Mother and reception of her force and support to its workings, at the same time
a strong vigilant will to reject all that is not hers. Too many
sadhaks cry before the attacks of their lower nature "I am helpless, I cannot react, it comes and makes me do what it wants."
This is a wrong passivity.

2. One must not get into the habit of a state in which one is
always in a struggle with suggestions and forces. People very
easily fall into this and make it a habit — the vital part takes a
sort of glowing satisfaction in crying out "I am attacked, overborne, suffering, miserable! How tragic is my fate! Why do you
not help, O Divine? There is no help, nor Divine Grace? I am
left to my misery and downfall etc. etc. etc." I do not want one
more sadhak to fall into this condition — that is why I am calling
Halt! before you get entangled into this kind of habit of constant
struggle. It is what these forces want — to make you feel helpless, defeated, overcome. You must not allow it.

All that is the physical mind refusing to take the trouble of the
labour and struggle necessary for the spiritual achievement. It
wants to get the highest, but desires a smooth course all the way,
"who the devil is going to face so much trouble for getting the
Divine?" — that is the underlying feeling. The difficulty with the
thoughts is a difficulty every yogi has gone through — so the
phenomenon of a little result after some days of effort. It is only
when one has cleared the field and ploughed and sown and
watched over it that big harvests can be hoped for.

One must either use effort and then one must be patient and
persevering, or one can rely on the Divine with a constant call
and aspiration. But then the reliance has to be a true one not
insisting on immediate fruit.

The Power can do everything, change everything and will do that
but it can do it perfectly and easily and permanently only when

your own will mental, vital and physical has been put on the side of the Truth. If you side with the vital ignorance and want to fight against your own spiritual change, it means a painful and difficult struggle before the work is done. That is why I insist on quietude at the very least and patient confidence with it, as far as you can — so that there may be a quiet and steady progress, not a painful and tormented movement full of relapse and struggle.

The Force also produces no definite and lasting fruit unless there is the will and resolution to achieve within the sadhak.

You had written: "I need not bother about it — if peace is needed it will bring itself." Certainly, the main stress should be on the Force but the active assent of the sadhak is needed; in certain things his will also may be needed as an instrument of the Force.

The higher action does not preclude a use of the will — will is an element of the higher action.

These things cannot be done in that way. For transformation to be genuine, the difficulty has to be rejected by all the parts. The Force can only help or enable them to do it, but it cannot replace this necessary action by a summary process. Your mind and inner being must impart their will to the whole.

So long as there is not a constant action of the Force from above or else of a deeper will from within, the mental will is necessary.

The Force can bring forward and use the will.

There is a will in the mind and not merely the power of thought.

To be conscious is the first step towards overcoming — but for the overcoming strength is necessary and also detachment and the will to overcome.

The energy which dictates the action or prevents a wrong action is the will.

There can be no persistence or insistence without will.

The will can make itself work — it is in its nature a force or energy.

There is no such thing as an inert passive will. Will is dynamic in its nature. Even if it does not struggle or endeavour its very presence is dynamic and acts dynamically on the resistance. What you are speaking of is a passive wish — I would like it to be like that, I want it to be like that. That is not will.

It is not the right kind of will-power then, probably they use some fighting or effortful will-power instead of the quiet but strong will that calls down the higher consciousness and force.

Peace is not a necessary precondition for the action of the will. When the being is troubled, it is often the business of the will to impose quiet on it.

Will is will whether it is calm or restless, whether it acts in a yogic or unyogic way, for a yogic or an unyogic object. Do you think Napoleon and Caesar had no will or that they were yogis? You have strange ideas about things. You might just as well say that memory is memory only when it remembers the Divine and it is not memory when it remembers other things.

There is no process. The will acts of itself when the mind and vital agree as in the case of a desire. If the desire is not satisfied, it goes on hammering, trying to get it, insisting on it, repeating the demand, making use of this person or that person, this device or that device, getting the mind to support it with reasons, representing it as a need that must be satisfied etc. etc. till the desire is satisfied. All that is the evidence of a will in action. When you have to use the will for the sadhana, you have not the same persistence, the mind finds reasons for not getting on with the effort, as soon as the difficulty becomes strong it is dropped, there is no continuity, no keeping of the will fixed on its object.

By development it [the will] becomes fit to merge into the Mother's will. A will that is not strong is a great hindrance to sadhana.

If there is a constant use of the will the rest of the being learns however slowly to obey the will and then the actions become in conformity with the will and not with the vital impulses and desires. As for the rest (the feelings and desires etc. themselves)

if they are not indulged in action or imagination and not supported by the will, if they are merely looked at and rejected when they come, then after some struggle they begin to lose their force and dwindle away.

I suppose it must be because you have not been in the habit of using the will to compel the other parts of the nature — so when you want it done, they refuse to obey a control to which they are not accustomed and it also has not any habitual hold upon them.

The will is a part of the consciousness and ought to be in human beings the chief agent in controlling the activities of the nature.

That [lack of will] is the suggestion that has been impressed on you by the physical inertia. It has covered up your will and persuaded you that there is no will left and no possibility of any will.

You cannot expect a persistent inertia like that to disappear in three days because you made some kind of a beginning of effort to resist it.

[Source of inability to stand up against the opposing forces:] In the indolence of the will which does not want to make a sustained effort for a long period. It is like a person who moves slightly half a leg for a second and then wonders why he is not already a hundred miles away at the goal after making such a gigantic effort.

It simply means that your will is weak and not a true will. Queer kind of will! Perhaps it is like a motor car that won't go and you have to push from behind.

*
**

When you feel the better condition, the peace and force at work, it is better to allow the force to work, keeping yourself still and quiet, and not try to do things by the mind.

When there is the confusion or wrong condition, then you have to call down the quiet, to try to get back to the true position, not listening to the wrong thoughts but rejecting them. If you cannot do that at once, still remain as quiet as possible and aspire and offer yourself. The Divine Force can always do more than the personal effort; so the one thing is to get quiet and call it down or back to the front — for it is always there behind or above you.

*
**

X has always been like that. It is the activity of his mind which is very restless; sometimes he gets a psychic opening and is all right, then the mind comes across and he becomes confused and miserable. Going away will not cure him; "thinking over things" will only make him more confused and lost. He is a man who can be rescued from all that only by a complete and permanent psychic opening, through the heart not the mind.

*
**

Whatever resistance there is in the outer being will go, only it takes time. It is always best to take one's foundation on that certitude and remain quiet and steadfast with it in mind even when one cannot react actively against the difficulty. For the quiet passive resistance will make it pass sooner, — even if one is disturbed and anxious.

Even when one cannot call in actively the Mother's Force one must keep the reliance that it will come.

*
**

The way in which the pains went shows you how to deal with the whole nature, — for it is the same with the mental and vital as with the physical causes of ill-ease and disturbance. To remain quiet within, to hold on to the faith and experience that to be quiet and open and let the Force work is the one way. Naturally, to be wholly conscious is not possible yet, but to feel it, to open, to let it work, to observe its result, that is the first thing. It is the beginning of consciousness and the way to complete consciousness.

Cling to the help always, — when you cannot feel, call for it and remain quiet till you feel it again. It is only the covering you spoke of that comes between you and the sense of its presence — for it is always there.

If you cannot do anything else, you must at least remain detached — there is always a part of the being that can remain detached and go on persisting, calling down the force from above.

Whatever is difficult can indeed be made easy by truth in the heart and sincerity and faith in the endeavour, even what is impossible can become possible. It is often found too that often after some amount of practice and faithful endeavour, there comes an intervention from within and what might have taken long is decisively and quickly done.

Your prayer will surely be answered, for it is to that you are moving.

Help is given in whatever way is necessary or possible. It is not limited to Force, Light, Knowledge. Of course, if by Force etc. you mean anything or everything then the formula holds.

It depends. If the consciousness is developed on the side of knowledge it will warn only. If on the side of will or power it will help
to effectuate.

The need for calling help diminishes as one gets higher and higher
or rather fuller and fuller, being replaced more and more by the
automatic action of the Force.

*
**

There is no reason why you should stop writing letters — it is
only one kind of letter that is in question and that is not a very
good means of contact; you yourself felt the reaction was not
favourable. I asked you to write because your need of unburden-
ing the perilous matter in you was very great at the time and,
although it did not relieve you at once, it kept me exactly informed
of the turns of the fight and helped me to put a certain pressure
on the attacking forces at a critical moment. But I do not believe
any of these necessities now exists. It is rather a discouragement
from within yourself of the source of these movements that is now
the need; but putting them into words would tend, as I have
said, to give them more body and substance.

It is an undoubted fact proved by hundreds of instances
that for many the exact statement of their difficulties to us is the
best and often, though not always, an immediate, even an instantaneous means of release. This has often been seen by sadhaks
not only here, but far away, and not only for inner difficulties,
but for illness and outer pressure of unfavourable circumstances.
But for that a certain attitude is necessary — either a strong faith
in the mind and vital or a habit of reception and response in the
inner being. Where this habit has been established, I have seen
it to be almost unfailingly effective, even when the faith was uncertain or the outer expression in the mind vague, ignorant or
in its form mistaken or inaccurate. Moreover, this method
succeeds most when the writer can write as a witness of his own
movements and state them with an exact and almost impartial
precision, as a phenomenon of his nature or the movement of a

force affecting him from which he seeks release. On the other hand, if in writing his vital gets seized by the thing he is writing of and takes up the pen for him, — expressing and often supporting doubt, revolt, depression, despair, it becomes a very different matter. Even here sometimes the expression acts as a purge; but also the statement of the condition may lend energy to the attack, at least for the moment, and may seem to enhance and prolong it, exhausting it by its own violence perhaps for the time and so bringing in the end a relief, but at a heavy cost of upheaval and turmoil — and the risk of the recurring decimal movement, because the release has come by temporary exhaustion of the attacking force, not by rejection and purification through the intervention of the Divine Force with the unquestioning assent and support of the sadhak. There has been a confused fight, an intervention in a hurly-burly, not a clear alignment of forces — and the intervention of the helping force is not felt in the confusion and the whirl. This is what used to happen in your crises; the vital in you was deeply affected and began supporting and expressing the reasonings of the attacking force, — in place of a clear observation and expression of the difficulty by the vigilant mind laying the state of things in the light for the higher Light and Force to act upon it, there was a vehement statement of the case for the Opposition. Many sadhaks (even "advanced") had made a habit of this kind of expression of their difficulties and some still do it; they cannot even yet understand that it is not the way. At one time it was a sort of gospel in the Ashram that this was the thing to be done, — I don't know on what ground, for it was never part of my teaching about the yoga, — but experience has shown that it does not work; it lands one in the recurring decimal notation, an unending round of struggle. It is quite different from the movement of self-opening that succeeds, (here too not necessarily in a moment, but still sensibly and progressively) and of which those are thinking who insist on everything being opened to the Guru so that the help may be more effectively there.

It is inevitable that doubts and difficulties should arise in so arduous an undertaking as the transformation of the normal nature of man into the spiritual nature, the replacement of his system of externalised values and surface experience into profounder inner values and experience. But the doubts and difficulties cannot be overcome by giving them their full force; it can be rather done by learning to stand back from them and to refuse to be carried away; then there is a chance of the still small voice from within getting itself heard and pushing out these louder clamorous voices and movements from outside. It is the light from within that you have to make room for; the light of the outer mind is quite insufficient for the discovery of the inner values or to judge the truth of spiritual experience.

One should not expect too much from the Divine Protection, for constituted as we are and the world is, the Divine Protection has to act within limits. Of course, miracles happen, but we have no claim to it.

The attitude you have taken is the right one. It is this feeling and attitude which help you to overcome so rapidly the attacks that sometimes fall upon you and throw you out of the right consciousness. As you say, difficulties so taken become opportunities; the difficulty faced in the right spirit and conquered, one finds that an obstacle has disappeared, a first step forward has been taken. To question, to resist in some part of the being increases trouble and difficulties — that is why an unquestioning acceptance, an unfailing obedience to the directions of the Guru was laid down as indispensable in the old Indian yogas — it was demanded not for the sake of the Guru, but for the sake of the Shishya.

This kind of acute struggle comes very often to a sadhak when he wants to make a complete and decisive progress instead of the slow elimination which is the usual course of nature; the strong urge upward is resisted by a vehement pull back from below. But the advantage is that when one persists and conquers, much has been gained by the struggle and in that part of the being that resists the decisive advantage. Persevere therefore and do not grieve for occasional waverings or stumbles which can easily happen in so arduous a combat. It should always be the rule for the sadhak not to linger over such things but to pick oneself up again and go resolutely forward.

Our help, our force, our blessings will be with you always aiding each step till the final victory.

The grace and protection are always with you. When in any inner or outer difficulty or trouble do not allow it to oppress you; take refuge with the Divine Force that protects.

If you do that always with faith and sincerity, you will find something opening in you which will always remain calm and peaceful in spite of all superficial disturbances.

Yes, that is so. Each victory gained over oneself means new strength to gain more victories.

It is indeed true that when one conquers a difficulty or goes forward, it creates a right current in the atmosphere. Moreover each time one gets an opening, it becomes more possible to make it more permanent.

Yes, a great progress should only spur one to a greater progress beside which the first will appear as nothing.

Yes — one should always have one's look turned forwards to the future — retrospection is seldom healthy as it turns one towards a past consciousness.

*
**

Take with you the peace and quietude and joy and keep it by remembering always the Divine.

If the thoughts about the past and the future come merely as memories and imaginations, they are of no use and you should quietly turn away your mind from them back to the Divine and to the yoga. If they are anything to the purpose, then refer them to the Divine, put them in the light of the Truth, so that you may have the truth about them or the right decision or formation for the future, if any decision is needed.

There is no harm in the tears of which you speak, they come from the soul, the psychic being, and are a help and not a hindrance.

*
**

One cannot go back to the past, one has always to go in the future.

*
**

It is always preferable to have one's face turned towards the future than towards the past.

*
**

The past has not to be kept, — one has to go into the future realisation. All that is necessary in the past for the future will be taken up and given a new form.

OPPOSITION OF THE HOSTILE FORCES

Opposition of the Hostile Forces

IT IS a fact always known to all yogis and occultists since the beginning of time, in Europe and Africa as in India, that wherever yoga or Yajna is done, there the hostile Forces gather together to stop it by any means. It is known that there is a lower nature and a higher spiritual nature — it is known that they pull different ways and the lower is strongest at first and the higher afterwards. It is known that the hostile Forces take advantage of the movements of the lower nature and try to spoil through them, smash or retard the siddhi. It has been said as long ago as the Upanishads (hard is the path to tread, sharp like a razor's edge); it was said later by Christ "hard is the way and narrow the gate by which one enters into the kingdom of heaven" and also "many are called, few chosen" — because of these difficulties. But it has also always been known that those who are sincere and faithful in heart and remain so and those who rely on the Divine will arrive in spite of all difficulties, stumbles or falls.

Normal human defects are one thing — they are the working of the lower nature of the Ignorance. The action of the hostile forces is a special intervention creating violent inner conflicts, abnormal depressions, thoughts and impulses of a kind which can be easily recognised as suggestions e.g. leaving the Ashram, abandoning the yoga, revolt against the Divine, suggestions of calamity and catastrophe apparently irresistible, irrational impulses and so on. It is a different order from the usual human weaknesses.

The normal resistance of the lower Nature in human beings and the action of the Hostiles are two quite different things. The former is natural and occurs in everybody; the latter is an intervention from the non-human world. But this intervention can come in two forms. (1) They use and press on the lower Nature forces making them resist where they would otherwise be quiescent, making the resistance strong or violent where it would be otherwise slight or moderate, exaggerating its violence when it is violent. There is besides a malignant cleverness, a conscious plan and combination when the Hostiles act on these forces which is not evident in the normal resistance of the forces. (2) They sometimes invade with their own forces. When this happens there is often a temporary possession or at least an irresistible influence which makes the thoughts, feelings, actions of the person abnormal — a black clouding of the brain, a whirl in the vital, all acts as if the person could not help himself and were drawn by an overmastering force. On the other hand instead of a possession there may be only a strong Influence; then the symptoms are less marked, but it is easy for any one acquainted with the ways of these forces to see what has happened. Finally it may be only an attack, not possession or influence; the person then is separate, is not overcome, resists.

There are some who are never touched by the hostile forces.

There is a natural movement of the ordinary human nature in the material consciousness which takes time to get rid of. Of course we call them forces of the lower nature but one must not regard them as hostile, only ordinary. They have to be changed but it usually takes time and it can be done quietly. One must be more occupied with the positive side of the sadhana than with them. If one is always thinking of them as hostile things, getting disturbed when they come, considering them as hostile possessions, then it is not good.

The things that are really hostile are few and must be distinguished from the ordinary movements of the nature. The first must be repelled, the second dealt with quietly and without getting troubled or discouraged by their appearance.

The defects of the nature are nothing, they can be dealt with progressively. It is these outward attacks, these suggestions and throwing in of wrong forces to which the sadhak must shut himself altogether.

*
**

The lower nature is ignorant and undivine, not in itself hostile but shut to the Light and Truth. The hostile forces are anti-divine, not merely undivine; they make use of the lower nature, pervert it, fill it with distorted movements and by that means influence man and even try to enter and possess or at least entirely control him.

Free yourself from all exaggerated self-depreciation and the habit of getting depressed by the sense of sin, difficulty or failure. These feelings do not really help, on the contrary, they are an immense obstacle and hamper the progress. They belong to the religious, not to the yogic mentality. The yogin should look on all the defects of the nature as movements of the lower Prakriti common to all and reject them calmly, firmly and persistently with full confidence in the Divine Power — without weakness or depression or negligence and without excitement, impatience or violence.

*
**

It [the vital ego] is part of the ordinary human nature, everybody has it. It has to be purified and transformed, the ego being replaced by the true vital being of which it is a distorted shadow. The forces of the lower nature are often rebellious and resist transformation out of attachment to the familiar movements of the Ignorance, desire, vanity, pride, lust, self-will etc., but they are not in their nature hostile. The hostile forces are those whose very *raison d'être* is revolt against the Divine, against the Light and Truth and enmity to the Divine Work.

*
**

The forces of the Ignorance are a perversion of the earth-nature and the adverse Powers make use of them. They do not give up their control of men without a struggle.

The hostile forces have a certain self-chosen function: it is to test the condition of the individual, of the work, of the earth itself and their readiness for the spiritual descent and fulfilment. At every step of the journey, they are there attacking furiously, criticising, suggesting, imposing despondency or inciting to revolt, raising unbelief, amassing difficulties. No doubt, they put a very exaggerated interpretation on the rights given them by their function, making mountains even out of what seems to us a mole-hill. A little trifling false step or mistake and they appear on the road and clap a whole Himalaya as a barrier across it. But this opposition has been permitted from of old not merely as a test or ordeal, but as a compulsion on us to seek a greater strength, a more perfect self-knowledge, an intenser purity and force of aspiration, a faith that nothing can crush, a more powerful descent of the Divine Grace.

About the contact with the world and the hostile forces, that is of course always one of the sadhak's chief difficulties, but to transform the world and the hostile forces is too big a task and the personal transformation cannot wait for it. What has to be done is to come to live in the Power that these things, these disturbing elements cannot penetrate, or, if they penetrate, cannot disturb, and to be so purified and strengthened by it that there is in oneself no response to anything hostile. If there is a protecting envelopment, an inner purifying descent and, as a result, a settling of the higher consciousness in the inner being and finally, its substitution even in the most external outwardly active parts in place of the old ignorant consciousness, then the world and the hostile forces will no longer matter — for one's own soul at least; for there is a larger work not personal in which of course they will have to be dealt with; but that need not be a main preoccupation at the present stage.

There is always a pressure on the forces of the lower nature to change — through that the pressure is felt by the hostiles; but whether they change or are destroyed seems to be left very much for them to choose.

That is true. As things are the vital falsehood seems to take a temporary advantage over the superior sattwic nature.

It is quite true that falsehood reigns in this world, that is the reason why these difficulties manifest. But you have not to allow yourself to be shaken. You must remain calm and strong and go straight, using the power of Truth and the Divine Force supporting you to overcome the difficulties and set straight what has been made crooked by the falsehood.

I suppose so. Whenever anything has to be done, there are always forces that want to interfere. I suppose they want to show that smooth walking and the "wide unbarred and thornless path" belong only to the Vedic *ṛtam satyam bṛhat* and we must get up there — if we can.

Whatever point the adverse forces choose for attack, however small it may seem to the external human mind, becomes a crucial point and to yield it up may be to yield to them one of the keys of the fortress. Even if it is a small postern door, it is enough for them if they can enter.

Nothing is really small and unimportant in the Great Path.

Especially, when the struggle has come down to the physical level, these distinctions cease to have any value; for there "small" things have a not easily calculable index value and are of great importance. On that level to lose a small post may be to make certain the loss of the big battle.

All have had to pass through the ordeal and test through which you are passing. We would have avoided it for you if it had been possible, but since it has come we look to you to persist and conquer. Patience, quiet endurance, calm resolution to go through to the end and triumph, these are the qualities now required of you — the less spectacular but more substantial of the warrior virtues.

Also, perspicacity and vigilance. Do not shut your eyes to the difficulty in you or turn away from it, but also let it not discourage you. Victory is certain if we persevere, and what price of difficulty and endeavour can be too great for such a conquest?

Yes, certainly. Men are being constantly invaded by the hostiles and there are great numbers of men who are partly or entirely under their influence. Some are possessed by them, others (a few) are incarnations of hostile beings. At the present moment they are very active all over the earth. Of course in the outside world there is no consciousness, such as is developed in yoga, by which they can either become aware of or consciously repel the attacks — the struggle in them between the psychic and the hostile force goes on mostly behind the veil or so far as it is on the surface is not understood by the mind.

The first attempt of the possessing entity is to separate the person from his psychic, and it is that that creates the struggle. All depends on the extent and persistence of the possession — how much of the being it occupies and whether it is constant or not.

*
**

Do you not know the story of the Elephant Brahman? All is Brahman, but in action you have to treat the elephant as the Elephant Brahman and the Asura as the Asura Brahman and neither as merely Brahman pure and simple. One has either to avoid the Rakshasa or overcome him; otherwise the Rakshasa may eat up the man, all Brahman though both be. The Brahman realisation is an inner static realisation, until one has become the dynamic instrument of the Divine Consciousness and Force — then the problem of the elephant and the Rakshasa won't arise, for the Divine Consciousness will know and the Divine Force will execute what is to be done in each case. There is no need to have *vaira* inside, but to be friendly with the Rakshasa is not prudent, as the Rakshasa is impervious to that kind of thing — he will take advantage of it to farther his own purpose.

It is one thing to see things and quite another to let them enter into you. One has to experience many things, to see and observe, to bring them into the field of the consciousness and know what they are. But there is no reason why you should allow them to enter into you and possess you. It is only the Divine or what comes from the Divine that can be admitted to enter you.

To say that all light is good is as if you said that all water is good — or even that all clear or transparent water is good: it would not be true. One must see what is the nature of the light or where it comes from or what is in it, before one can say that it is the true Light. False lights exist and misleading lustres, lower lights too that belong to the being's inferior reaches. One must therefore be on one's guard and distinguish; the true discrimination has to come by growth of the psychic feeling and a purified mind and experience.

The mere intensity of the force does not show that it is a bad power; the Divine Force often works with a great intensity. Everything depends on the nature of the force and its working:

what does it do, what seems to be its purpose? If it works to purify or open the system, or brings with it light or peace, or prepares the change of the thought, ideas, feelings, character in the sense of a turning towards a higher consciousness, then it is the right force. If it is dark or obscure or perturbs the being with rajasic or egoistic suggestions or excites the lower nature, then it is an adverse force.

II

I do not see how I could say that you were not for this yoga when you had and still get the experiences that are characteristic of the yoga. The obstacles in the consciousness and the attacks are no proof that a man is not fit for yoga. There is no one practising yoga who does not get them. Even those who have become great siddha yogis had them during their time of sadhana.

It is not a fact that the Rajayogin or others are not attacked by environmental forces. Whether Moksha or transformation be the aim, all are attacked — because the vital forces want neither liberation nor transformation. Only the yogins speak of it in general terms as Rakshasi Maya or the attacks of *kāma, krodha, lobha,* — they don't care to trace these things to their sources or watch how they come in, — but the thing itself is known to all.

Hostile forces attack every sadhak; some are conscious of it, others are not. Their object is either to influence the person or to use him or to spoil his sadhana or the work or any other motive of the kind. Their object is not to test, but their attack may be used by the guiding power as a test.

There is always this critical hostile voice in everybody's nature, questioning, reasoning, denying the experience itself, suggesting doubt of oneself and doubt of the Divine. One has to recognise it as the voice of the Adversary trying to prevent the progress and refuse credence to it altogether.

There are no sadhaks who are never attacked by wrong forces — but if one has a complete faith and self-consecration, one can throw off the attack without too much difficulty.

If the faith and surrender are complete in all parts of the being then there can be no attack. If there is a strong central faith and surrender at all times, there can be attacks but the attacks will have no chance of success.

There are two things that make it impossible for them [the hostile forces] to succeed even temporarily in any attack on the mind or the vital — first, an entire love, devotion and confidence that nothing can shake, secondly, a calm and equality in the vital as well as in the mind which has become the fundamental character of the inner nature. Suggestions then may still come, things go wrong outside, but the being remains invulnerable. Either of these two things is sufficient in itself — and in proportion as they grow, even the existence of the hostile forces becomes less and less of a phenomenon of the inner life — though they may still be there in the outer atmosphere.

It is those who are of a highly sattwic nature, especially if strongly surrendered to the Mother, who escape the invasion or attacks of the hostile Forces in the mind and vital. That does not mean that they escape the difficulties of the lower human nature or of the sadhana, but these are not complicated by the effective support given to them by the hostiles. It is not that there is no point in them that might be pressed upon by the hostiles but in actual fact they cannot get at these points because of the build of the nature which is fortified against them owing to the large proportion of *prakāśa* and *sukha* (see Gita) which the sattwic brings with it. But otherwise there is an internal clarity, a balance, a happy composition in the being reflecting sunlight easily, less amenable to the touch of cloud and tempest, which gives no handle to the hostile forces. The nature refuses to be violently agitated or disturbed or upset. At most it is the body that the hostiles can attack and there too because the nervous being is calm and, it is only through the most material that it can be done.

Vital purity is very necessary, but it is not easy to make it immune from attack unless the wideness is there along with a solid *spiritual* purity and peace descending in the wideness. Of course, wideness *by itself* is not sufficient.

They [the hostile forces] come because they were freely permitted in the past — so they want to renew and continue their action. An entire rejection and a complete turning to the Divine are the way to meet them.

Evil forces can always attack in moments of unconsciousness or half-consciousness or through the subconscient or external physical — so long as all is not supramentally transformed. Only if the force is there, they can at once be pushed back.

The hostile forces do not need a cause for attacking — they

attack whenever and whoever they can. What one has to see is that nothing responds or admits them.

*
* *

You ask whether the adverse Force is stronger than the Divine Force. The implication is that man has no responsibility for his action and whatever he does or however he errs and falls in consequence, the Divine Force is to blame. It may be so, but in that case there is no need or utility in doing sadhana. One has only to sit still and let the adverse Force or the Divine Force do what they like! According to that theory the Devil was quite right in telling Christ, "Cast thyself down from this mountain and let His angels come and upbear thee," and Christ was quite wrong in rejecting the suggestion and saying, "It is written 'Thou shalt not tempt (put to a test) the Lord thy God!'" He ought to have jumped and if he got smashed, it would only have proved that the adverse forces were greater than the Divine Force!

If an adverse Force comes, one has not to accept and welcome its suggestions, but to turn to the Mother and refuse to turn away from her. Whether one can open or not, one has to be loyal and faithful. Loyalty and fidelity are not qualities for which one has to do yoga. They are very simple things which any man or woman who aspires to the Truth ought to be able to accomplish.

It is what everybody should realise. It is the psychic fidelity that brings the power to stand against the Asuras and enables the Protection to work.

III

About the attacks and the action of the cosmic forces — these attacks very ordinarily become violent when the progress is becoming rapid and on the way to be definite — especially if they find they cannot carry out an effective aggression into the inner being, they try to shake by outside assaults. One must take it as a trial of strength, a call for gathering all one's capacities of calm and openness to the Light and Power, so as to make oneself an

instrument for the victory of the Divine over the undivine, of the
Light over the darkness in the world-tangle. It is in this spirit
that you must face these difficulties till the higher things are so
confirmed in you that these forces can attack no longer.

He is quite right in saying that the heaviness of these attacks was
due to the fact that you had taken up the sadhana in earnest and
were approaching, as one might say, the gates of the Kingdom of
Light. That always makes these forces rage and they strain every
nerve and use or create every opportunity to turn the sadhak back
or, if possible, drive him out of the path altogether by their suggestions, their violent influences and their exploitation of all
kinds of incidents that always crop up more and more when these
conditions prevail, so that he may not reach the gates. I have
written to you more than once alluding to these forces, but I did
not press the point because I saw that like most people whose
minds have been rationalised by a modern European education
you were not inclined to believe in or at least to attach any
importance to this knowledge. People nowadays seek the
explanation for everything in their ignorant reason, their
surface experience and in outside happenings. They do not
see the hidden forces and inner causes which were well-known
and visualised in the traditional Indian and yogic knowledge.
Of course, these forces find their *point d'appui* in the sadhak
himself, in the ignorant parts of his consciousness and its
assent to their suggestions and influences; otherwise they could
not act or at least could not act with any success. In your
case the chief *points d'appui* have been the extreme sensitiveness
of the lower vital ego and now also the physical consciousness
with all its fixed or standing opinions, prejudices, prejudgments,
habitual reactions, personal preferences, clinging to old ideas
and associations, its obstinate doubts and its maintaining these
things as a wall of obstruction and opposition to the larger light.
This activity of the physical mind is what people call intellect and
reason, although it is only the turning of a machine in a circle of
mental habits and is very different from the true and free reason,

the higher Buddhi, which is capable of enlightenment and still more from the higher spiritual light or that insight and tact of the psychic consciousness which sees at once what is true and right and distinguishes it from what is wrong and false. This insight you had very constantly whenever you were in a good condition and especially whenever Bhakti became strong in you. When the sadhak comes down into the physical consciousness, leaving the mental and higher vital ranges on which he had first turned towards the Divine, these opposite things become very strong and sticky and, as one's more helpful states and experiences draw back behind the veil and one can hardly realise that one ever had them, it becomes difficult to get out of this condition. The only thing then, as X has told you and I also have insisted, is to stick it out. If once one can get and keep the resolution to refuse to accept the suggestions of these forces, however plausible they may seem, then either quickly or gradually this condition can diminish and will be overpassed and cease. To give up yoga is no solution.

You are right. The hostile forces, their attacks, their suggestions ought now to be superannuated, out of date, out of place here in this sadhana. If somebody would realise that and fulfil it in his sadhana, the others might perhaps get strength to follow. At present these things are still here because the sadhaks open themselves to them out of habit, out of desire, out of attraction for the drama of the vital, out of fear, out of passive response and unresisting inertia. But there is no real necessity for them any longer or true justification for their presence here, — the outer world is a different matter. The sadhana could very well go on and should go on as an unfolding, a natural falling away of defects and difficulties, a coming of greater and greater light and power and transformation.

When I said "no more necessary", I did not mean that their action could not go on — I think I expressly said that if the sadhaks persisted in opening themselves to it, it would continue. There is a difference between the action of the hostile powers and the ordinary action of the lower nature. The latter of course goes on until it is changed but there is no necessity for it to take the form of hostile attacks and upsettings; it can be treated as a machinery that has to be set right and with the aid of the higher Light and Power can be set right. There are several who were once taken by hostile attacks who have now reached the point where they can follow this method, others are approaching it — some of course have always followed and never were attacked, at least in their mind and vital. But there are still many who are very far from it and so the action of the Hostiles continues.

I wrote because now there is a sufficient descent of Light and Power, for one not to be subject to the ordeals and tests which the Hostile Powers are permitted to put when one has only the mental, or ordinary spiritual forces on the plane of mind to support one's progress. If you look closely, you will see that when these Forces work now it is in a perfectly irrational instinctive way, repeating always the same movements without any intellectual or higher vital power behind them. Theirs is now an irrational mechanical method which obscures more in the lowest physical and subconscient than anything else. That means that their true justification for being there is gone.

The things enumerated are not causes of the attacks, but they are the occasion, the weakness in the sadhaks that allows them when they could very well be dismissed. The hostile forces are there in the world to maintain the Ignorance — they were there in the sadhana, because they had the right to test the sincerity of the sadhaks in their power and will to cleave to the Divine and overcome all difficulties. But this is only so long as the higher Light has not descended into the physical; now it is descending, it is sufficiently there for anyone to receive it more and more fully, so that the way becomes smooth and open, a progressive development and not a struggle.

It is not the pressure from above that creates difficulties. There is a strong resistance to change in the lower planes and certain Forces take advantage of it to throw in vortices of disturbance and try to upset as many people as possible. The only action of the Pressure from above on these is to push them out from the atmosphere of the person touched or from the atmosphere generally. After a time they are pushed out of the atmosphere of the person and can no longer work on him except from a distance with very slight effect. When that can be done generally — so as to push them to a distance from the atmosphere of the Ashram, then all this trouble will cease.

That [going away from the Ashram] is not due to the pressure of yoga but to the pressure of something in them that negates the yoga. If one follows one's psychic being and higher mental call, no amount of pressure of yoga can produce such results. People talk as if the yoga had some maleficent force in it which produces these results. It is on the contrary the resistance to yoga that does it.

IV

A progress made often stirs the adverse forces to activity, they want to diminish its effect as much as possible. When you get a decisive experience of this kind, you should remain concentrated and assimilate it — avoiding self-dispersion and all externalising of the consciousness.

It is very often after a good experience or a decisive progress that the beings of the vital world try to attack and threaten.... They have always the hope that they can turn back the sadhak from his path by attacks and menaces.

It often happens like that. When a progress has been made (here it is the opening of the inner vision) the hostiles attack in a fury. You must be especially on your guard when you are making a progress — so as to check the attack before it can get in.

That is right. The rest is the remnant of the attack — such an attack, sudden and violent, as sometimes indeed often comes when one is making full progress to the straight and open way. It cannot permanently deflect the progress and, when it disappears, there is usually a chance of going on more firmly and swiftly towards the goal. That is what we must do now.

Naturally, the hostile forces are always on the watch to rob what they can of the things received by the sadhak, — not that they profit by them but they prevent them from being used to build up the Divine in life.

There is always a struggle going on between the forces of Light and the opposing forces — when there is a true movement and progress the latter try to throw a wrong movement across to stop or delay the progress. Sometimes they do this by raising up old movements in yourself that have still the power to recur; sometimes they use movements or thoughts in the atmosphere, things said by others to disturb the consciousness. When a settled peace and working of the Power and self-giving of the being can be fixed in the physical, then there comes a secure basis — there are no more fluctuations of this kind, though superficial difficulties may continue.

*
**

Either the higher consciousness has to descend into the vital and physical or else by the psychic consciousness coming forward one has to detect whatever imperfection is in the vital and reject it.

There are always hostile forces that try to stop or break the experience. If they come in, it is a sign that there is something in the being — vital or physical — that either responds or is too inert to oppose.

*
**

Your description is too vague. From what you write it may just as well be the reaction that frequently follows an experience; the adverse force coming in with a contrary movement. Tests come sometimes from the hostile forces, sometimes in the course of Nature. I suppose they must be necessary, since they always come in sadhana.

*
**

There is no use of testing at all — whatever test is needed, comes of itself in the ordinary way in the very use of the capacity and in the very steps of the progress — no other is needed. Beyond that the tests that come are from the hostile forces — but their way of testing is to take advantage of any point of weakness and push with all their force at that point to break down the sadhana or else to hurl all the adverse forces on the consciousness while it is still in process of transition and not yet mature so as to shatter all that has been done. It is not a true test but mere destruction replacing the constructive method. By unnecessary "testing" one dangerously invites this hostile pressure and raises up things which one has to banish. To be conscious is necessary, but quiet self-examination is sufficient for that — raising up difficulties under plan of testing is quite the wrong method.

*
**

The method of the Divine Manifestation is through calm and harmony, not through a catastrophic upheaval. The latter is the sign of a struggle, generally of conflicting vital forces, but at any rate a struggle on the inferior plane.

You think too much of the adverse forces. That kind of pre-occupation causes much unnecessary struggle. Fix your mind on the positive side. Open to the Mother's power, concentrate on her protection, call for light, calm and peace and purity and growth into the divine consciousness and knowledge.

The idea of tests also is not a healthy idea and ought not to be pushed too far. Tests are applied not by the Divine but by the forces of the lower planes — mental, vital, physical — and allowed by the Divine because that is part of the soul's training and helps it to know itself, its powers and the limitations it has to outgrow. The Mother is not testing you at every moment, but rather helping you at every moment to rise beyond the necessity of tests and difficulties which belong to the inferior consciousness. To be always conscious of that help will be your best safeguard against all attacks whether of adverse powers or of your own lower nature.

*
**

If one knows how to profit by experience, even the Hostile Forces and their attacks can be useful; — although of course that does not mean that the attacks should be invited. What they do is to press with all their force upon some weak point of our nature and if we are vigilant, we can see and throw away that weakness. Only the attack method of these Forces is too violent and up-heaving and endangers the good things in one also, faith and peace etc. — so one has to be careful to keep these against all attacks.

*
**

The hostiles when they cannot break the yoga by positive means, by positive temptations or vital outbreaks, are quite willing to do it negatively; first by depression, then by refusal at once of ordinary life and of sadhana.

Indirect attacks are not of this kind, a violent rush and covering by hostile forces — they are done through covert suggestions, half-truth, half-falsehood, attempts to represent the falsehood in the garb of the Divine Truth or to mix the lower conscious-ness cleverly with the higher. Their attempt is to mislead by guile rather than to conquer by force.

When the vital forces or beings throw an influence, they give it certain forms of thought, action and put them in the minds and vital of people so that they feel, think, act and speak in a particular way. Whoever opens to their influence acts according to this formation, perhaps with variations due to his own vital temperament.

There is no particular number — but sometimes there are parti-cular vital beings that attach themselves to a man if he accepts them.

V

Attacks are always going about and it is a period when they have fallen on many. But with a strong faith founded in the Mother and a whole-hearted aspiration, no attack can leave any lasting result.

Either to reject by dynamic means or to remain unaffected and let it pass are the two usual ways of dealing with the attacks.

This state which tries to come upon you and seize is not part of your true self, but a foreign influence. To yield to it and to ex-press it would therefore be not sincerity, but the expression of something false to your true being, something that will grow more and more foreign to you as you progress. Always reject it, when it comes, even if you feel strongly its touch; open in your mind and soul to the Mother, keep your will and faith and you will find it receding. Even if it returns obstinately, be equally and more obstinate against it, firm in rejection — that will discourage and wear it out and finally it will grow weak, a shadow of itself and disappear.

Be true to your true self always — that is the real sincerity. Persist and conquer.

They [the lower forces] hope by persistence to tire you out or to get in by sheer obstinacy — or at least to delay the realisation by their attacks. That is always their method. If they can shake the faith, the peace and *samatā*, they think themselves richly recompensed.

The one thing wrong would be to allow yourself to be overcome by them [the adverse forces]. If you remain steady in yourself, you can repel the attack or else it will exhaust itself and pass. In such circumstances you have to be like a cliff attacked by a stormy sea but never submerged by it.

It is not sincerity to express only what the adverse forces suggest or what you feel when you are in a bad condition, full of obscurity and a wrong outlook. When you are in the Truth, you feel quite the opposite and it is not insincerity to cling to that and recall it. It is only by bringing it back that the Truth can grow in you.

The trouble in your chest comes only from a vital resistance and it continues because you identify yourself with that resistance. It is only by quietude and opening to the Mother that these things can disappear. There is no other way to progress.

If you have not got quietude, you can always aspire first and a sincere aspiration will bring it back.

I do not see what reasons can be so subtle as to justify or even appear to justify something that opposes and tries to destroy the sadhana. Whatever stands in the way of spiritual progress, must be a falsehood whatever reasons it gives in its own favour. The best thing is not to listen to its reasons.

From your last letter it is clear that it is not your own will that pushes you to go but something that has taken hold of your mind, a clutch of some Force which is using an old movement of the outward mind and vital to drive the action. All the more reason to reject this action as contrary to the soul's and heart's true feeling. The pride that says: "I am one of those who can break but will not bend", is a poor thing and conceals the fact that one is bending before forces and impulses that are ignorant and obscure. Its result is, as you yourself have seen at the end of your letter, that one bends to the lower forces of nature but refuses to bend to the Divine.

If sadhana is a struggle between the higher Will and the old forces of nature bringing suffering and inner torment, we do not want you to do that kind of sadhana. That is not the spirit of our yoga. What we want you to do is to recover your quietude and go on in that. To have the basis of quietude and allow the Divine Force to work in you firmly and quietly is always the best method — it is not necessary to proceed through a big personal effort, disturbance and struggle. Come back to this — open yourself once more as you did before — then you got back sleep or health in a day or two and were growing inwardly without excessive trouble — and let the Mother's Power and Grace lead you.

I shall do all to help you and pull you out, but that which has closed itself in you must open for the help to work quickly

as it did before. Otherwise too it can pull you out, but if there
is this strong obstruction that has to be undone, time is needed.
A central change of attitude in your mind would, I believe, make
all the difference — it has done before.

You ought to realise that these things are attacks which come
on you from an adverse Force to which your nature was responsive because of vital desire and the vital ego — what you call selfishness. When it comes, you have to realise that it is an attack
and refuse instead of accepting it — and in order to be able to
do that you must always discourage desire and selfishness in you
and all that comes from them such as jealousy, claim, anger etc.
It is no use alleging that there are good reasons for their rising
— even if all the alleged reasons were true, they would not justify
your indulging them, for in a sadhak nothing can justify that.
There is no need to understand — for there is only one thing that
is necessary to understand — that, reason or no reason, desire,
selfishness, jealousy, demand, anger have no place in the spiritual
life.

     If you keep to what you have resolved, then all will be right
— and the right knowledge will come not from the mind and its
reasonings but from the soul and its true vision of things.

Yes, the difficulty is always that something in the nature gives a
hold to the attack. It either still indulges it or likes it or even,
if wanting to be free, is too accustomed to receive and respond
to the old feelings, thoughts, suggestions and does not yet know
how *not* to respond. The first thing is for the mental being to
stand back, refuse to accept, say "This is no longer mine." Then,
even if the vital being responds to the attack, one part of the
nature can be free and observe and discourage it. The next thing
is for this free part to impose the same will of detachment on the
vital so that after a time this also when the attack comes feels
that it is something foreign, not its own, — as if a stranger had

come into the room and was trying to impose his ideas or his will on the inmates. After that it becomes more easy to get rid of it altogether. Of course, there is the Mother's Force working, but this kind of assent from the mind and vital makes the result quick and easy — otherwise it takes time and more labour and struggle.

When there is an attack or obstruction, the call or the thinking of the Mother may not succeed at once, even the will to get rid of the attack or obstruction may not succeed at once, but one must persevere till the result comes, and if one perseveres the result is bound to come.

One sees the negative side only during the attacks, because the first thing the attack or obstruction does is to try to cloud the mind's intelligence. If it cannot do that it is difficult for it to prevail altogether for the time being. For if the mind remains alert and clings to the truth, then the attack can only upheave the vital and, though this may be painful enough, yet the right attitude of the mind acts as a corrective and makes it easier to recover the balance and the true condition of the vital comes back more quickly. If the vital keeps its balance, then the attack touches the physical consciousness only with its suggestions and is much more superficial or even it can do no more than create a temporary restlessness, uneasiness or ill-health in the body — the rest of the consciousness remaining unaffected. It is therefore very important to accustom oneself to keep the right mental attitude even in the midst of an attack, however strong it is. To keep faith is the best help for that — the faith that the Divine is always there and I shall pass to him through whatever trials. That helps to look at other things also in the true light.

By tamasic ego is meant the ego of weakness, self-depreciation, despondency, unbelief. The rajasic ego is puffed up with pride and self-esteem or stubbornly asserts itself at every step or else wherever it can; the tamasic ego, on the contrary, is always feeling "I am weak, I am miserable, I have no capacity, I am not loved or chosen by the Divine, I am so bad and incapable — what can the Divine do for me?" Or else "I am especially chosen out for misfortune and suffering, all are preferred to me, all are progressing, I only am left behind, all abandons me, I have nothing before me but flight, death or disaster," etc., etc., or something or all of these things mixed together. Sometimes the rajasic and tamasic Ahankar mix together and subtly support each other. In both cases it is the "I" that is making a row about itself and clouding the true vision. The true spiritual or psychic vision is this: "Whatever I may be, my soul is a child of the Divine and must reach the Divine sooner or later. I am imperfect, but seek after the perfection of the Divine in me and that not I but the Divine Grace will bring about; if I keep to that, the Divine Grace itself will do all." The "I" has to take its proper place here as a small portion and instrument of the Divine, something that is nothing without the Divine but with the Grace can be everything that the Divine wishes it to be.

The Mother's help is always there but you are not conscious of it except when the psychic is active and the consciousness not clouded. The coming of suggestions is not a proof that the help is not there. Suggestions come to all, even to the greatest sadhaks or to the Avatars — as they came to Buddha or Christ. Obstacles are there — they are part of Nature and they have to be overcome. What has to be attained is not to accept the suggestions, not to admit them as the truth or as one's own thoughts, to see them for what they are and keep oneself separate. Obstacles have to be looked at as something wrong in the machinery of human nature which has to be changed — they should not be regarded as sins or wrong-doings which make one despair of oneself and of the sadhana.

But when the suggestions come, surely it is possible to know from their very character what they are and that itself shows that they must come from wrong vital Forces. The only thing is that they must be at once rejected and the entry into your own mind and vital refused to them — i.e. they must not be accepted or allowed to influence. Very few have the direct occult perception of the Forces behind the suggestion — at least until the cosmic consciousness fully opens, for then direct perception becomes more easily possible, — but the mental understanding can be used with good effect.

Do not allow these suggestions to prevail. Each time these powers attack, if you hold them at bay, you gain an added force for progress. They attack and suggest to you a wrong understanding in the hope that, if you accept, their power to return on you will last a little longer. Do not allow them to prevail for however short a time.

It is sufficient if you can keep in touch with the Force and reject any strong attack of the confusion. The rest will be done by the Force itself — for none is really strong enough to change himself, it is the Divine Force called down that does it.

Yes, the Power with its help and inner working is always there with you and always will be. In the strongest attacks and darkest hours it was covered up and hidden, but it was never absent or withdrawn and never will be.

All naturally in these difficulties has its original roots in the vital and its expectations of all kinds. When one wants to get rid of them, the vital resists and is unwilling to part with them, but this by itself would not be anything more than a work of change, adjustment, re-arrangement which might take time but not cause serious conflicts and upheavals. For once the mind and inner will are settled to be rid of these movements, the will of the higher vital would also come into line and the rest which is more obstinate against change because it is a thing of habitual movements, supported on the subconscient and not governed by reason or knowledge, would yet be unable to resist permanently or vehemently the pressure from the higher will of the being. Its force of resistance would diminish and the habitual reactions wear out or fall away. But the prolongation of the difficulty and its acuteness come from the fact that there are Forces in Nature, not personal or individual but universal, which live upon these movements and through them have long controlled the individual nature. These do not want to lose their rule and so when these movements are thrown out, they throw them back on the sadhak in strong waves or with great violence. Or they create in the vital a great depression, discouragement, despair — that is their favourite weapon — because it is losing its former field of desires and has not yet in any certainty something that would replace it, the assured continuous psychic or spiritual condition or experience. To prevent that is the whole effort of these Forces. So they create these upheavals and the vital admits them because of its own habit of response to the lower Forces. At the same time they put in suggestions to the mind so as to make it also accept the disturbance, discouragement and depression. That is what I meant by saying that these are attacks from outside and must be rejected. If they cannot be rejected altogether, yet one must try to keep a part of the mind conscious which will refuse to admit the suggestions or share in the depression and the trouble, — which will say firmly "I know what this is and I know that it will pass and I can resume my way to the goal which nothing can prevent me from reaching, since my soul's will is and will always be for that." You have to reach the point where you can do that always; then the power of the Forces to disturb will begin to diminish and fall away. Our Force is there with you and will not fail to support and strengthen you. The suggestion that we are indifferent is obviously nothing but a suggestion intended to help and fortify the depression. As such you should regard it and not accept it as true or as your own thought; for it could not possibly be true. Your success in reaching peace and light is as much our concern as yours and even more so.

There are almost always some parts of the being that are either unwilling or feel an incapacity for the effort demanded of them. It is the psychic and the mind and the higher vital usually that join together for the yoga — for if these three do not join, it is difficult to do any yoga at all beyond getting a few experiences from time to time. But in the lower vital there is almost always something recalcitrant and there is much of the physical that is too obscure. If the sadhak were left to himself this could be remedied without much difficulty, but it is here that the hostility in the universal (lower) forces comes in — they want to keep their reign over the being. The result is an exacerbation of the resistance of the lower vital and an exaggeration of the obstruction (inertia, passive resistance) in the physical which then admit these suggestions of self-destruction, depression or despair.

VI

They [the hostile attacks on the outer being] are felt as suggestions, or a touch on the surface mind, vital, physical or as movements in the atmosphere (the personal or the general environmental consciousness) — but for the inner being it is like gusts or storms outside. If they penetrate by chance into the house, they are immediately ejected and the doors and windows banged on them — there is nothing that accepts them or tolerates them inside.

It must have been an indication of the source and location of the suggestion or influence. Either thoughts or vibrations or some pressure of wrong force can be felt being thrown or sent in a very concrete way when the consciousness is open. When it is not, they come in without being noticed, only the result is felt.

From the higher mind upwards, all is free from the action of the hostile forces. For they all belong to the spiritual consciousness though with varying degrees of light and power and completeness.

Vital forces can attack the mind and do. Many receive suggestions from them through the brain, so it is quite possible that it may be felt as coming in through the head from above. That does not mean that it came from regions above the mind (higher Mind, intuition or overmind). Correct reasoning means no more than coherent argument from a certain standpoint and does not validate a fit of anger or indicate for it a non-adverse source.

You were getting the true consciousness down into the vital but as the old difficulty rose again in the physical, there is again the vital attack. The sign of complete liberation will be when your vital can face this attack always without being upset or crying out, repelling its force by a calm rejecting force from within.

There has been progress in all these parts, but they seem to be subject still to a response to the suggestions of the hostile forces. Everybody gets these suggestions, but they ought not to be allowed to enter inside, especially in the heart, or to be accepted by the vital. Evidently, they enter through the physical mind (from the throat upwards meant that) and affect the surface vital and emotional being. You must get the power to reject them from there by a constant and steady denial and refusal of their suggestions. So long as anything in you says "yes" or accepts, there is always the possibility of a return.

As I have said, the response of the physical mind or vital to these forces is a habit. You get upset as soon as they touch either and lose control over yourself. The concentration in the heart is the way to get rid of them, but there must also be a detachment of the consciousness so that it can stand back from the attack and feel separate from it.

If the attacks of the hostile forces have been made less strong by concentrating in the heart (or if they have become less frequent) you must continue that concentration until you are able to join the head and the heart, the psychic and the higher consciousness. It all depends on that. The psychic must be strong enough to compel the vital and physical to give themselves to the Divine — or the higher consciousness must so descend and occupy everything that the old movements can only at most move on the surface without being able to enter in or touch the inner calm — or the two together, psychic and higher consciousness must occupy the whole being. These are the three ways in which the yoga moves. If the concentration in the heart which means the awakening of the psychic is most effective against the attacks, then it is that you must follow.

If you can feel even in these attacks that part in you in which there is constant Peace even amidst the pains and darkness, and if you can keep it always, that is an immense gain. The something in you which does not always feel it, which remains half way, undecided, must also now take the step of complete surrender. It is only a part of your physical mind that does not understand, that receives back the old ideas — that must be converted. It does not matter about the weakness and incapacities — when the full peace and Power is there in the physical, they will be removed. The new birth in you is certain to come — the first touch of it is already there in the awakened psychic — the rest cannot fail to come.

*
**

It is more the lack of sleep that is responsible, I think; also the excess of struggle which the constant pressure of the vital disturbances and the physical tamas bring in and by that weaken the nerves.

Like the vital disturbance the physical inertia with all its symptoms is an attack of the hostile forces intended to cut short and prevent the higher opening. The ideas that arise to justify it are of no value — it is not true that physical work is of an inferior value to mental culture, it is the arrogance of the intellect that makes the claim. All work done for the Divine is equally divine, manual labour done for the Divine is more divine than mental culture done for one's own development, fame or mental satisfaction.

This inertia, numbness, pain should be thrown off with the same resolution as the vital disturbances. The only peculiarity of it in your case is the persistent violence of the attack as in the case of the vital — otherwise, it is what others get also; but each time they reject, call on the Mother and get free, after a little time if the attack is violent, at once if it is of a lesser character.

If there is temporary physical inability, one can take rest, but solely for the purpose of recovering the physical energy. The idea of giving up physical work for mental self-development is a creation of the mental ego.

The inertia gives room and power for the hostile forces to act.

*
**

The attacks you speak of can come anywhere. It is an attack of the nervous centres and on the nervous being by contrary vital forces. The fact that it was not allowing you to come here and that it began to go when you steeped yourself in the atmosphere and ideas of *The Yoga and its Objects* is significant of its origin. As for the other symptoms they were amassing to a height of the restlessness of the nervous being and are quite familiar in such cases. The desire to run away somewhere is a very usual symptom. Hysteria is also an attack by similar forces, but it is only one form; the attack need not take the appearance of any illness. The Doctors usually consider it as a type of what they call neurasthenia, nerve-weakness; but that simply locates the thing without explaining its real nature and cause. In both cases, here and there, it was an attempt to come across your spiritual life by creating a disability and state of disturbance in the vital-physical part of the being. Anyhow the fact that you could not go from here and that the whole thing could be removed by us at once as soon as you opened somewhere by this feeling of sorrow at going shows that the spiritual life is stronger and deeper within you, even when covered over, than the opposite forces at their height. That is the main thing.

What is there in you is the capacity for response to these suggestions that still remains owing to the stamp of the past habit on the physical, especially the subconscient physical. I have explained to you what happens — that these things when rejected by the mind and vital descend into the subconscient or else go out into the environmental consciousness and from there they can return when pushed by the hostile forces. It is in these two ways that the hostiles try to recover their hold. But the rising from the subconscient is not so important except for its long persistence — it comes up in dream or it is, in the waking consciousness, fragmentary. But when it comes from the environmental consciousness then it can be a strong attack and it is evidently that which is taking place now.

I think what lends force to these attacks and tends to upset you, is a feeling of impatience somewhere that things are not going forward, progress of a definite kind is not being made and that these things are not done with already forever. A period of apparent halt is not necessarily an adverse thing, it can be a preparation for a fresh progress of a more decisive character — that often happens in the sadhana — but you have to keep vigilantly the advance gained in spite of attacks. The next progress ought to be the descent of the full spiritual calm and peace from above — an opening of the consciousness into wideness. Till it comes,

112

keep yourself firm and do not allow these attacks to shake your basis.

*
**

The exterior consciousness can be invaded by what rises up from the subconscient or comes in from outside and owing to a renewed vibration of the past habit can respond — but that does not mean that the will of the vital or of the physical mind is for these things. If there was anything in them normally on the side of sex or violence, then you could say the impurities were there. But if it were so, there would be more than these attacks, there would be a daily struggle with anger and desire.

If one had to wait for an absolute purity free from all possibility of these attacks before beginning to realise the Divine, nobody would ever be able to realise. It is as the realisation progresses, that the fundamental transformation takes place.

*
**

These attacks should not discourage you. There are always moments — so long as there is not the complete basis in the physical when old movements seem to revive. But so long as it is only a rush of an outside force churning up the subconscient and it does not last, it does not at all mean that the progress is not there. We have to deal with all the complexity of the human consciousness in its hidden parts as well as on its surface — and there are layers and layers of the consciousness in which something may lurk of the old reactions, but each conquest makes the control stronger and brings the full purification nearer.

*
**

You need not be upset about the matter; it is sufficient if you note movements like these and are vigilant that they should find no ground in you again. The cause is probably to be found in the contact with the outside world renewing some possibilities of the old Adam in you. When there is some lowering or diminution of the consciousness or some impairing of it at one place or another, the Adversary — or the Censor — who is always on the watch presses with all his might wherever there is a weak point lying covered from your own view, and suddenly a wrong movement leaps up with unexpected force. Become conscious and cast out the possibility of its renewal, that is all that is to be done.

These [forces of dullness, depression, etc.] are things that wander about in the atmosphere and jump upon one without notice. It is often difficult to see where precisely they come from and often there is no reason at all or any inviting cause in oneself. They have simply to be thrown off as when something falls on the body.

It happens so with everybody so long as there is not the positive siddhi of transformation by which it becomes contrary to the very nature of the instrument to respond to these vibrations — because they have become foreign to it. Till then all depends on the vigilance of the consciousness and its will. The repetition of the response does not increase the difficulty — it only retards the clearing out of the invading forces.

The response-giving mechanism is like that in everybody. It is not by something shocking but by something enlarging and uplifting that it can get out of its rut of habit.

It is better not to trouble about the hostile forces. Keep your aspiration strong and sincere and call in the Divine in each thing and at each moment for support and in all that you feel keep yourself open to us. That is the easiest way to the Divine.

If you begin to concern yourself about the hostile forces, you will only make the path more difficult.

It is so that they [the hostile suggestions] must be regarded — without interest, with indifference. That removes the necessity for constant struggle which is itself a form of interest, and it is as discouraging and more to these suggestions.

It is quite true. To talk of one's experiences to others tends to diminish the power of the experience. Also to think too much of the hostile Powers is to bring in their atmosphere. One has to recognise them when they come and repel them, but to think much about them, to fear, to be expecting or looking out for them is a mistake.

The worst thing for sadhana is to get into a morbid condition, always thinking of "lower forces, attacks." If the sadhana has stopped for a time, then let it stop, remain quiet, do ordinary things, rest when rest is needed — wait till the physical consciousness is ready. My own sadhana when it was far more advanced than yours used to stop for half a year together. I did not make a fuss about it, but remained quiet till the empty or dull period was over.

Yes, the adverse forces take advantage of any perturbation of that kind, for it opens, as it were, a passage to their action. Fear is the one thing that one must never feel in face of them, for it makes them bold and aggressive.

Moreover, fear, as you justly say, calls the thing feared — it must therefore be thrown out altogether.

That is very interesting — for it agrees with the Mother's constant insistence that to feel sympathy or any emotion of the weak philanthropic kind with those possessed by vital forces is most dangerous as it may bring an attack upon oneself which may take any form. One must do what is to be done but abstain from all such weakness.

VII

There is no such thing as a mere accident. There is some — perhaps a very slight unconsciousness in the physical and it is taken advantage of by these small beings of the vital physical plane — who are more mischievous than consciously hostile.

It is not a bad shakti that gets inside you and from there does these things; it is small forces from outside that amuse themselves by creating small accidents of that kind, taking advantage of some inattention or forgetfulness etc.

You are right about the accidents. It is chiefly the physical mind's unconsciousness that makes these accidents or interventions of mischievous forces easy.

That is right. These accidents happen only to disturb you. You must not allow yourself to be disturbed.

Yes — it is because they [the hostile forces] know that Peace is the basis and if that is there in full, all the rest will come. So they want anyhow to prevent it.

Yes, it was an attack — the hostile forces often take the form of this or that person to get through the physical association a more concrete grip on the physical consciousness.

It sometimes happens that by a carefully formed formation like this and through the instrumentality of a third person whose movements they control, the hostile forces get through the conscious guard and bring about an accident like this. It is through the subconscient that they manage to do this, for the subconscient has not yet either the mass of force descended from above which could have repelled the arriving cycle and turned its movement away or the instinctive sureness which would have felt beforehand what the cyclist was going to do and done just the thing to avoid it. However when the protection is there such accidents even when grave in character are usually reduced to something minor in their results.

It has often been seen that when an accident takes place at a particular spot, there is a tendency for some time for other accidents to happen there. It was so with a place near Villianur some years ago. There is the same tendency with suicides at a particular place. It is a sort of powerful formation that remains there with or without a vital being (spirit) in charge of the formation.

VIII

I must say however that it is not the push for union with the Divine nor is it the Divine Force that leads to madness — it is the way in which people themselves act with regard to their claim for these things. To be more precise, I have never known a case of collapse in yoga as opposed to mere difficulty or negative failure, — a case of dramatic disaster in which there was not

one of three causes — or more than one of the three at work.
First, some sexual aberration — I am not speaking of mere
sexuality which can be very strong in the nature without leading
to collapse — or an attempt to sexualise spiritual experience
on an animal or gross material basis; second, an exaggerated
ambition, pride or vanity trying to seize on spiritual force
or experience and turn it to one's own glorification ending in
megalomania; third, an unbalanced vital and a weak nervous
system apt to follow its own imaginations and unruly impulses
without any true mental will or strong mental will to steady or
restrain it, and so at the mercy of the imaginations and suggestions of the adverse vital world when carried over the border
into the intermediate zone of which I spoke in a recent message.[1]
All the causes of collapse have been due to these three causes
— to the first two mostly. Only three or four of them have
ended in madness — and in these the sexual aberration was
invariably present; usually a violent fall from the way is the
consequence. X is no exception to the rule. It is not because
X pushed for union with the Divine that X went mad, but because X misused what came down for a mystic sexuality and the
satisfaction of megalomaniac pride, in spite of my repeated
and insistent warnings.

Usually there is some predisposition behind, hereditary, natal
(due to some circumstances of birth) or founded in insufficient
nervous balance. Often there is in the vital excessive ambition,
lust or some other violent Ripu. But these though they might
distort or break the sadhana by opening it to undesirable Forces
could not bring madness (megalomania, erotic mania, or what
is called religious mania) — only if there is some taint or want
of nervous balance. Anxiety or excessive stress of meditation
would not bring it either except by acting upon some such
predisposing weakness. In some cases possession by beings of
the vital worlds without any such predisposing cause may be
possible, but that will be more easily curable. There are however

[1] See Part Three, pp. 1039-1046.

cases of people who break down their nervous balance by wrong practices — there the madness has nothing really to do with the sadhana.

As to gratitude, it is a psychic feeling and all that is psychic helps the soul to flower. There is nothing wrong from the spiritual point of view in emotion. The only thing is that it should not become a tie of bondage in the path.

It is quite impossible for the descent of the Divine Grace to produce nausea and nervousness — to think so is self-contradictory. Sometimes when one has pulled or strained, there is a headache or a sensation as if of headache, or if one pulls down too much Force then there may be a giddiness, but one has only to remain quiet and that sets itself right by an assimilation of what has come down or otherwise. There is never any adverse or troublesome after-consequence.

The idea that X was sent mad by a Divine Force is an absurdity and an irrational superstition. People go mad because they have a physical predisposition due either to heredity or to some kind of organic cause or secret illness like syphilis, the action being often brought up by some psychological factor (ambition turning to megalomania, hypochondria, melancholia, etc.). All that happens in everyday life and not only in yoga: the same causes work here. The one thing is that there may be an invasion of an alien Force bringing about the upsetting, but it is not the Divine Force, it is a vital Force that invades. The Divine Force cannot by its descent be the cause of madness any more than it can be of apoplexy or any other physical illness. If there is no predisposition, one may have all kinds of attacks from vital or other forces or from one's own movements of the lower nature, as violent as possible, but there will be no madness.

A descent cannot possibly produce nausea and vomiting etc. There can, if one pulls down too much force, be produced a headache or giddiness; both of these go if one keeps quiet a little, ceases pulling and assimilates. A descent cannot possibly produce blood pressure, madness or apoplexy or heart failure or any other illness.

Illness does not rise up by the descent of the Force; nor hereditary taint nor madness. They come up of themselves, as in X's case who never had even the smallest grain of a descent or a Force anywhere. It is only after he went off his centre that we are putting Force (not as a descent, but as an agent) to keep him as straight and as sound as possible.

It is quite possible that if a too intense Ananda is allowed before the purity and peace are in the nature, it may disturb the system — though I don't know whether there is any instance of madness as a consequence. At any rate, it is a fact that normally Ananda comes (in the natural course, I mean, if not pulled down) only occasionally so long as the peace and purity are not there as a base. It is probably right that it should be so.

Those who fall into insanity have lost the true touch and got into the wrong contact. It is due either to some impurity and unspiritual desire with which the seeker enters into the way or some insincerity, egoism and false attitude or to some weakness in the brain or nervous system which cannot bear the Power it has called down into it.

The safest way is to follow the guidance of someone who has himself attained to mastery in the path. Only that guidance should be implicitly and sincerely followed; one's own mind and its ideas and fancies must not be allowed to interfere. It goes without saying that it must be a true guidance, not the leading of a tyro or an impostor.

Epilepsy is not possession — it is an attack or at most a temporary seizure. Insanity always indicates possession. The hereditary
conditions create a predisposition. It is not possible for a vital
Force or Being to invade or take possession unless there are doors
open for it to enter. The door may be a vital consent or affinity
or a physical defect in the being.

Epilepsy is itself a sign of vital attack, even if there is a physical
cause for it — the attacking force not being able to disturb the
mental and vital (proper) falls on the body and uses some physical cause (latent or growing) for the base of its action. For
everything manifested in the physical must have a physical
support or means for its expression.

Insanity is always due to a vital attack, or rather possession
although there is often a physical reason as well. Hysteria is due
to a pressure from the vital world and there may be momentary
possessions also. The same thing cannot be said of ordinary
delirium the cause of which is physical only — except in so far
as all illness is an attack of lower forces of Nature, but these
lower forces are not vital beings or what we call specifically hostile forces — they are simply performing their role in nature and
of course there may be and probably is a being of some kind pre-
siding over each kind of illness — in Bengal they give a special
name to some of them and worship them as goddesses to avert
the visitation. But as I say these are really Forces, not vital
hostiles.

As for the interest of vital beings in possessing men — beings
of the vital world are not constituted like men — they take a
delight in struggle and suffering and disorder — it is their natural
atmosphere. They want besides to get the taste of the physical
world without being under the obligation of taking on birth and
developing the psychic being and evolving towards the Divine.
They wish to remain what they are and yet amuse themselves

with the physical world and physical body.

In these cases of hysteria usually nothing is gained by humouring or indulgence — firmness generally pays better, because most often there is something there that wants to be interesting and get sympathy and have a fuss made over the person. As for cure, that is a different matter, the subjective cause has to be got rid of and it is not easy.

Loss of balance produces disorder in the consciousness and the adverse forces use that loss of balance for attacking and wholly upsetting the system and doing their work. That is why people become hysterical or mad or filled with the desire to die or go away.

[Occurrence of loss of balance:] More easily in the women than in the men but in some of the latter also. What produces the loss of balance is an inability to control the vital movements by the reason and an instability of the vital itself so that it sways from one feeling to another, one impulse to another without harmony or order.

I may observe that X does not seem to me to be mad — there is no sign of a dislocation of the thinking mind due to lesion or accident or illness. What there is is a fixed idea and what is called *folie de persécution*, but that is not due to insanity — people have it who have otherwise an acute and perfectly well-ordered intelligence. X from his photograph appears to have had a mediumistic element in him and to have by some ill-chance entered into contact with powers of the vital plane which were able to put their suggestions in him — in that part of the consciousness which we call the vital mind so that he is unable to ascertain things in their proper light and is tormented by the suggestions that have driven their furrows there in the form of habitual ideas that tyrannise over him and which he is unable to embrace or refuse. Unfortunately this is a malady of the consciousness, which it is very difficult to cure because the patient himself gives no assistance, as he clings to his fixed idea and even when the influence is taken away, calls it back upon him. Certainly he could be told from here that he is not mad and is not cursed of God — but that of itself might not be sufficient to cure him.

I am writing today about your son X and his illness if it can be called by that name. I shall state first in general terms the nature of the malady and its usual developments, that is to say, the normal course it takes when no psychic or spiritual force is brought in to remove it. Afterwards I shall indicate the two possible means of cure.

I think it is best for me to state the case in its worst and not only in its best possible terms because it is necessary that you should know the full truth and have the courage to face it. These cases are not those of a truly physical malady, but of an attempt at possession from the vital world; and the fits and other physical symptoms are signs, not of the malady itself, but of the struggle of the natural being against the pressure of the hostile influence. Such a case in a child of this age indicates some kind of accumulation in the physical heredity creating an opportunity or a predisposition of which the vital invasion takes advantage. It is especially the physical consciousness and physico-vital which contain the germs or materials of this predisposition. The physical being is always changing its constituents and in each period of seven years a complete change is effected. If the symptoms of this predisposition in the nature are detected and a wise influence and training used by the parents to eradicate them and this is done so effectively that in the first seven years no seeds of malady appear, then usually there is no further danger. If on the contrary they manifest by the seventh year, then the next period of seven years is the critical period and, ordinarily, the case would be decided one way or the other by or before the fourteenth year.

There are normally three possible eventualities. The difficulty in dealing with the case of so young a child is that the mind is not developed and can give no help towards the cure. But as the mind develops in the second seven years it will, if it is not abnormally weak which I think is not the case here, react more and more against the influence. Aided by a good control and influence it may very well succeed in casting out the hostile intrusion and its pressure altogether. In that case the fits and other signs of the physical struggle pass away, the strange moral and vital tendencies fade out of the habits and the child becomes mentally, morally and physically a healthy normal being.

The second possibility is that the struggle between the natural being and the intruding being may not be decisive in the psychic sense, that is to say, the intruder cannot take full possession but also he cannot be thrown out entirely. In that case anything may happen, a shattered mind and health, the death of the body or a disturbed, divided and permanently abnormal nature.

The third and the worst possibility is that the intruding being may succeed and take entire possession. In that case the fits and other violent symptoms will disappear, the child may seem to be physically cured and healthy, but he will be an abnormal and most dangerous being incarnating an evil vital force with all its terrible propensities and gifted with abnormal powers to satisfy them.

In X's case there is not as yet possession in the full sense of the word, but a strong pressure and influence indicated by the strange habits of which you have written. These are suggested and dictated by the intruding being and not proper to the boy himself. The fearlessness and security with which he does these things is inspired from the same source. But the fits prove that there is as yet no possession. There is a struggle indicated by them and a temporary hold which passes out again. He is evidently in the earlier part of the critical period. I have indicated the course normally taken by the illness, but it is not necessary to pass through it and take its risks. There are other means which can come to his help and effect a complete cure.

The first and easiest is to cure by hypnotic suggestion. This if properly applied is an absolutely sure remedy. But in the first place it must be applied by someone who is not himself under the influence of evil powers, as some hypnotists are. For that obviously will make matters worse. Moreover, it must be done by someone who has the proper training and knows thoroughly what he is about; for a mistake might be disastrous. The best conditions would be if someone like yourself who has a natural relation and already an influence over the child could do it with the necessary training and knowledge.

The other means of cure is the use of spiritual power and influence. If certain psycho-spiritual means could be used, this would be as sure and effective as the other. But this is not possible because there is no one there who has the right knowledge. The spiritual influence by itself can do it but the working is likely to be slow. It must ordinarily be conveyed through someone on the spot and you yourself are obviously the right instrument. What you have to do is to keep the idea that I am sending to you power for this object, to make yourself receptive to it and at the same time make your own will and natural influence on the child a direct channel for it. The will must be a quiet will, calm and confident and intent on its object, but without attachment and unshaken by any amount of resistance and unalarmed and undiscouraged by the manifestations of the illness. Your attitude to the child must be that of a calm and firm protecting affection free from emotional weakness and disturbance. The first thing is to acquire such an influence as to be able to repel the attack when it comes and if it takes any hold to diminish steadily its force and the violence of its manifestation. I understand from your letter that you have already been able to establish the beginning of such an influence. But it must be able to work at a distance as well as in his presence. Further you must acquire the power of leaving a protection around him when you are absent. Secondly, you must be able to convey to him a constant suggestion which will gradually inhibit the strange undesirable habits of which you speak in your letter. This, I may say, cannot be effectively done by any kind of external coercion. For that is likely to make these impulses more violent. It must be a will and suggestion and silent influence. If you find the control increasing and these habits diminishing, you can understand that the work of cure has begun. Its completion may take some time because these vital beings are very sticky and persistent and are always returning to the attack. The one thing which will make the cure rapid is if the boy himself develops a will in his mind to change for that will take away the ground of the hostile influence. It is because something in him is amused and takes pleasure in the force which comes with the influence that these things are able to recur and continue. This element in him calls the invading presence back even when it has been centrally rejected. I shall of course try to act directly on him as well as through you, but the instrumentality of one on the spot greatly enforces and is sometimes indispensable to the action.

END OF PART FOUR

INDEX

seen or felt as deep well,
1114-15
and self, 1078
and Self and Spirit, 1195
and soul, 267-68, 268-69,
284, 290-95 *passim*, 301,
1100
and soul-spark and Jivatman,
280-81, 282-83
spiritual personality put
forward by the soul in
its evolution, 281, 283
support of individual
evolution 1078
and surrender, 588-89
surrender of, 1101
and transformation, 1010
true psychic and psychic
opening to mental, vital
and other worlds, 1047
and universal forces, 1088
and the vital, 299, 1647,1649
voice of, 548
way of in doing yoga, 594
See also Antaratman;
Chaitya Purusha; Soul
Psychic change
(transformation), 725,
784, 1091-1125 *passim*,1631
and experience, 902-03
first necessity, 1609
and spiritual change,1093-94
and supermind, 1223
three main elements of,1092
See also Psychicisation
Psychic experience, 339, 1113
Psychic feeling, 289
Psychic fire, 1120-25 *passim*
Psychicisation,
and spiritualisation, 1093
See also Psychic change
Psychic love, 755-56, 759, 764,
820
and Divine Love, 764, 765
and love of the spiritual
planes, 765
and universal or cosmic
love, 766
and vital love, 817-18, 820,
1117
Psychic-mental, 1111
See also Mental psychic;
Psychic mind
Psychic mind, 324, 325
See also Mental psychic;
Psychic-mental

Psychic opening, 636, 1091,
1092, 1094, 1096, 1101,
1109, 1114, 1131-32,
1166, 1360
from above and direct,
1096, 1097
condition for, 1098-99
and descent of the
supramental, 1051
and experience, 887
and getting rid of ego, 1376
and self-giving, 1141
Psychic personality, 1605
See also Psychic being
Psychic sadness (sorrow),
1104, 1112, 1117-18,
1347, 1616
and vital longing, 1430
Psychic-vital, 1111-12
Psychic world, 439-40, 1499
guardians of, 440, 442-43
immediate transition to by
soul, 438
no communication with
earth, 458
rest of soul in after death,
433-37 *passim*
Psychoanalysis, 1298, 1605-06,
1608-09
Psychology, 321-22, 1281,
1606, 1608
Pulling the Force, *see* Force,
the, pulling
Puṇya and *pāpa*,
and rebirth, 441, 444
Puranas,
and historicity of Krishna
and the Brindavan story,
425-26
and the ten avatars, 402-04
Purification, 130, 574-75
of Adhara, and
manifestation of higher
truth, overmental,
supramental, 890
and experience, 886, 887-88,
889, 902-03, 906
of the heart, 902-04
by personal effort and by
intervention of the
Grace, 591
and realisation, 905
by work, 533
Purity, 644-45
divine, 645
essential, of spirit, 1538

from touch of higher
consciousness, 1212
vital, and spiritual, 1740
Purna Yoga,
as fourfold path, 1622
two main elements of, 504
See also Integral Yoga
Purusha,
on all planes, 276
Chaitya, 289; *see also*
Psychic being
and determinism, 473-74
as giver of sanction, 1009
and godhead, 390
in the heart, 289
impersonal, makes a
surface of personality,1006
individual, 1079
Kshara and Akshara, 291
manomaya puruṣa, 302,
1005; *see also* Mental
being
mental, 1257
observing, 693; *see also*
below witness; *see also*
Witness Purusha
prāṇamaya Purusha, 1005;
see also Vital being
Purusha consciousness, 287
witness, 1006, 1008-09,
1010, 1168; *see also*
above Purusha, observing;
see also Witness
Purusha and Prakriti, 284,
286-87, 301, 1008-09,
1079, 1080, 1111
and liberation in action,
683-85 *passim*
separation of, 525, 535,
673, 1005, 1168
for getting rid of thought,
731, 732
in mental activity, 1276
Purushottama,
and Parashakti, 39-40
Purushottama consciousness,
72-73

Q

Qualities,
idea of creation by
inequality of, 1202
See also Gunas
Quarrels, 824-25

BIBLIOGRAPHICAL NOTE

The greater part of the vast body of Sri Aurobindo's letters, mostly to his disciples, was written during the years 1930 to 1938, reaching its maximum at the middle of this period. His letters, before and after these years, were on a very restricted scale and confined to a few persons for special reasons.

Small selections from these letters were published in *The Riddle of this World* (1933), *Lights on Yoga* (1935), *Bases of Yoga* (1936) and *More Lights on Yoga* (1948). A few letters were also published periodically in the Ashram journals: *Sri Aurobindo Circle, Sri Aurobindo Mandir Annual, The Advent* and *Mother India*. All these letters were seen and revised by Sri Aurobindo before publication.

In 1945 the compilation of a complete edition of letters was started with Sri Aurobindo's approval and four series were successively brought out during 1947 to 1951 under the title *Letters of Sri Aurobindo* by Sri Aurobindo Circle, Bombay. The first, second and fourth series contained letters on yoga and the third on poetry and literature. All the work of compiling and editing these series was done under the direct guidance of Sri Aurobindo, and the letters included in them were seen and revised by him before publication.

The first and second series of *Letters of Sri Aurobindo* were reissued in 1950 and 1954 respectively.

In 1958 all the above letters, excepting those on poetry and literature, were published again with additional material as Volumes VI and VII of the Sri Aurobindo International Centre of Education Collection under the title *On Yoga II*, in two Tomes. Tome One was reissued in 1969 with further additions.

A new edition, under a new title, *Letters on Yoga*, was issued in three Volumes, Nos. 22, 23 and 24 of the Sri Aurobindo Birth Centenary Library, in 1970 and contained a very large number of additional letters besides those included in the two Tomes of the earlier edition. These three Volumes in the Sri Aurobindo Birth Centenary Library were issued in de luxe and popular editions and were also reproduced in a reduced format in 1971.

This second impression of *Letters on Yoga* is a facsimile reproduction of the Sri Aurobindo Birth Centenary Library edition in reduced format; only a few typographical errors have been rectified and an index added.

Letters of Sri Aurobindo on poetry and literature (which comprised the third series of *Letters of Sri Aurobindo* published in 1949) was considerably enlarged by the inclusion of a large number of additional letters and was published again in 1971 along with *The Future Poetry* as Volume 9 of the Sri Aurobindo Birth Centenary Library.

BIBLIOGRAPHICAL NOTE

The greater part of the vast body of Sri Aurobindo's letters, mostly to his disciples, was written during the years 1930 to 1938, reaching its maximum at the middle of this period. His letters, before and after these years, were on a very restricted scale and confined to a few persons for special reasons.

Small selections from these letters were published in *The Riddle of this World* (1933), *Lights on Yoga* (1935), *Bases of Yoga* (1936) and *More Lights on Yoga* (1948). A few letters were also published periodically in the Ashram journals: *Sri Aurobindo Circle, Sri Aurobindo Mandir Annual, The Advent* and *Mother India*. All these letters were seen and revised by Sri Aurobindo before publication.

In 1945 the compilation of a complete edition of letters was started with Sri Aurobindo's approval and four series were successively brought out during 1947 to 1951 under the title *Letters of Sri Aurobindo* by Sri Aurobindo Circle, Bombay. The first, second and fourth series contained letters on yoga and the third on poetry and literature. All the work of compiling and editing these series was done under the direct guidance of Sri Aurobindo, and the letters included in them were seen and revised by him before publication.

The first and second series of *Letters of Sri Aurobindo* were reissued in 1950 and 1954 respectively.

In 1958 all the above letters, excepting those on poetry and literature, were published again with additional material as Volumes VI and VII of the Sri Aurobindo International Centre of Education Collection under the title *On Yoga II*, in two Tomes. Tome One was reissued in 1969 with further additions.

A new edition, under a new title, *Letters on Yoga*, was issued in three Volumes, Nos. 22, 23 and 24 of the Sri Aurobindo Birth Centenary Library, in 1970 and contained a very large number of additional letters besides those included in the two Tomes of the earlier edition. These three Volumes in the Sri Aurobindo Birth Centenary Library were issued in de luxe and popular editions and were also reproduced in a reduced format in 1971.

This second impression of *Letters on Yoga* is a facsimile reproduction of the Sri Aurobindo Birth Centenary Library edition in reduced format; only a few typographical errors have been rectified and an index added.

Letters of Sri Aurobindo on poetry and literature (which comprised the third series of *Letters of Sri Aurobindo* published in 1949) was considerably enlarged by the inclusion of a large number of additional letters and was published again in 1971 along with *The Future Poetry* as Volume 9 of the Sri Aurobindo Birth Centenary Library.